Handbook of Environmental Law

The Oxford India Handbooks are an important initiative in academic publishing. Each volume offers a comprehensive survey of research in a critical subject area and provides facts, figures, and analyses for a well-grounded perspective. The series provides scholars, students, and policy planners with a balanced understanding of a wide range of issues in the social sciences.

Other Titles in the Series

HANDBOOK OF HUMAN DEVELOPMENT
Sakiko Fukuda-Parr and A.K. Shiva Kumar (Editors)

HANDBOOK OF LAW, WOMEN, AND EMPLOYMENT
Policies, Issues, Legislation, and Case Law
Surinder Mediratta

HANDBOOK OF ENVIRONMENTAL DECISION MAKING IN INDIA
An EIA Model
O.V. Nandimath

GLOBALIZATION AND DEVELOPMENT
A Handbook of New Perspectives
Ashwini Deshpande (Editor)

HANDBOOK OF URBANIZATION IN INDIA (Second Edition) (OIP)
K.C. Sivaramakrishnan, Amitabh Kundu, and B.N. Singh

HANDBOOK OF HUMAN RIGHTS AND CRIMINAL JUSTICE IN INDIA
The System and Procedure (Second Edition)
South Asia Human Rights Documentation Centre

HANDBOOK OF WATER RESOURCES IN INDIA
Development, Management, and Strategies
The World Bank

HANDBOOK OF AGRICULTURE IN INDIA
Shovan Ray (Editor)

HANDBOOK OF INTERNATIONAL HUMANITARIAN LAW IN SOUTH ASIA
V.S. Mani (Editor)

HANDBOOK OF INDIAN SOCIOLOGY (OIP)
Veena Das (Editor)

MAKING NEWS (OIP)
Handbook of the Media in Contemporary India
Uday Sahay (Editor)

HANDBOOK OF POVERTY IN INDIA
Perspectives, Policies, and Programmes
R. Radhakrishna and Shovan Ray (Editors)

Handbook of Environmental Law

Second Edition

P.B. SAHASRANAMAN

OXFORD
UNIVERSITY PRESS

OXFORD
UNIVERSITY PRESS

Oxford University Press is a department of the University of Oxford.
It furthers the University's objective of excellence in research, scholarship,
and education by publishing worldwide. Oxford is a registered trademark of
Oxford University Press in the UK and in certain other countries

Published in India by
Oxford University Press
YMCA Library Building, 1 Jai Singh Road, New Delhi 110001, India

© Oxford University Press 2009

The moral rights of the author have been asserted

First published 2009
Second Edition 2012

ISBN 13: 978-0-19-808734-2
ISBN 10: 0-19-808734-9

Typeset in Adobe Jenson Pro 11/13 by Jojy Philip

Contents

Preface

Environment is a science based on principles of common sense. Such principles can be found in all ancient literatures and in all religions. In the present situation, the need for protection of the environment is being felt across the world. Several international conferences and treaties have been entered into. Most of the laws made for the protection of environment are enacted on the basis of international commitments.

Three decades ago, there was no legislation to protect the environment. The need to protect the environment was felt by the Supreme Court of India. The apex court interpreted Article 21 of the Constitution of India declaring that 'right to life' also includes the right to environment. Several judgements are rendered by various courts based on this principle.

Environmental law has advanced in India, much more than in any other country. Besides legislation, several judgements rendered by the courts in India have been internationally recognized. This book covers not only the environmental laws but it also includes the ancient literature, statutes, the case laws, and a brief outline of foreign cases and laws. The international treaties, legal principles, and the necessary matters which a person should know while filing a Public Interest Litigation for environment protection has been explained. Some common laws like law against nuisance, and land-use laws have also been included which are also used for the creation of good conditions of living.

The legislative and judicial treatises have been reworded or synthesized in some parts, for easy understanding. A study on environment cannot be complete, unless it is accompanied by the scientific and historical bases from which the need for protection arose in the first place. I have tried to be comprehensive in this respect. In addition to law journals, certain online and other reports were relied on while compiling this book. These have proven to be a reliable source of information. The subject of environment is very wide and therefore I have only concentrated on the aspects where important legal questions have arisen.

I hope this book will be helpful to all those who want to understand environmental law.

Acknowledgements

I take this opportunity to thank all the people, without whom this book would not have seen the light of day.

Ms Bridget Cormack, graduated with a Bachelor of Law with honours from the University of Adelaide, Australia in 2007, and Bachelor of Media. In her final year of law school she attended the University of Oregon, School of Law in the United States in order to specialize in International Environmental Law. During this time, she developed a great fascination for the ability of the law to tackle global environmental dilemmas and the varying responses given by different nations. She has helped me by providing a lot of material on international law, and has assisted me in editing this book while doing her internship with me. Her enthusiasm and knowledge of international environmental law is reflected in many of the pages of this book.

Mr Aravind Menon is a student of the National University of Advanced Legal Studies, Cochin, Kerala. He has provided his intellectual assistance in compiling this book, especially on Constitutional Laws, Environmental Impact Assessment (EIA), e-waste, slap, and the like. His articles on various fields of law have already appeared in law journals and he has authored the sixth edition of *Intepretation of Statutes*, a popular book on the subject.

There are experts in each branch of environmental law. Mr Peter Rodrick, director of the Climate Justice Programme and international expert on the subject, has provided me with information and guidance. Professor M.K. Prasad, Former Vice Chancellor of Calicut University, has also assisted me in the compilation of the material. The assistance rendered by Advocates Sanjay, T.S. Harikumar, and K. Jagadeesh cannot be forgotten.

The OUP editorial team for going through each line of this book while editing deserve special accolades. Finally, I take this opportunity to thank Oxford University Press for publishing my work.

Abbreviations

ABC	Animal Birth Control
ACF	Australian Conservation Foundation
AIA	Advance Informed Agreement
AIBTMF	All India Brick and Tile Manufacturer's Federation
AIR	All India Reporter
AIRSCW	All India Supreme Court Weekly
All ER	All England Reporter
AQUA	Aquaculture
B&H	Bandhs and Hartals
BGHZ	Bundesgerichtshof (Federal Court of Justice, Germany)
BGS	British Geological Society
BJP	Bharatiya Janata Party
BMW	Bio-Medical Waste
BOD	Biological Oxygen Demand
CAIT	Climate Analysis Indicators Tool
CAFMPA	Compensatory Afforestation Fund Management and Planning Authority
CBD	Convention on Biological Diversity
CBI	Central Bureau of Investigation
CCOL	Coordinating Committee of the Ozone Layer
CEC	Centrally Powered Committee
CEE	Council for Environment Education or (Central Europe and Russia Fund)
CER	Certified Emission Reduction
CERCLA	Comprehensive Environmental Response, Compensation and Liability Act
CETP	Common Effluent Treatment Plant
CFC	Chloro Fluoro Carbons
CHR	Cardamom Hill Reserve
CITES	Convention on International Trade in Endangered Species
CIWMB	California Integrated Waste Management Board

CLRTAP	Convention on Long-Range Transboundary Air Pollution
CZMA	Coastal Zone Management Authority
CMS	Convention on Migratory Species
CMZ	Coastal Management Zone
CNG	Compressed Natural Gas
CPCB	Central Pollution Control Board
CPCSEA	Committee for the Purpose of Control and Supervision of Experiments on Animals
CrPC	Criminal Procedure Code
CRT	Cathode Ray Tubes
CRZ	Coastal Regulations Zone
CSE	Centre for Science and Earth
CSIR	Council for Scientific and Industrial Research
CUSAT	Cochin University of Science and Technology
CWW	Chief Wildlife Warden
CZA	Central Zoo Authority
CZMP	Coastal Zone Management Plan
DC	District Court
DDA	Delhi Development Authority
DDT	Dichloro Diphenyl Trichloroethane
DEFRA	Department for Environment Food and Rural Affairs
DFO	Divisional Forest Officer
DO	Dissolved Oxygen
EC	Environmental Clearance
ECA	Environment Conservation Act
ECJ	European Court of Justice
EEC	European Economic Community
EIA	Environmental Impact Assessment
EIS	Environmental Impact Statement
EMP	Electromagnetic Pulse
EPA	Environment (Protection) Act
EPR	Environment (Protection) Rules
EP&A	Environmental Planning and Assessment
ESA	Endangered Species Act
ESIA	Environmental and Social Impact Assessment
ETP	Effluent Treatment Plant
ETS	Environmental Tobacco Smoke
EU	European Union
EXIM	Export and Import

FAC	Forest Advisory Committee
FCA	Forest Conservation Act
GAIA	Global Alliance for Incinerator Alternatives
GHG	Green House Gas
GIS	Geographical Information Centre
GNP	Gross National Product
HC	High Court
HQ	Headquarters
HTL	High Tide Line
IAS	Indian Administrative Officer
IBP	International Biological Programme
ICAM	Integrated Coastal Area Management
ICF	Indian Circus Federation
ICJ	International Court of Justice
ICSM	Integrated Inter-Sectoral Management
ICZM	Integrated Coastal Zone Management
IDRL	International Disaster Response Law
INGO	International Non-Governmental Organizations
IPC	Indian Penal Code
IPCC	Intergovernmental Panel on Climatic Change
IQ	Inuit Quajimajatugangit
IRY	International Relief Union
IST	Indian Standard Time
IT	Information Technology
IUCN	International Union for Conservation of Nature
IWC	International Whaling Commission
IWRB	International Waterfowl and Wetland Research Bureau
KHC	Kerala High Court
KSEB	Kerala State Electricity Board
LIC	Life Insurance Corporation of India
LTL	Low Tide Line
MCD	Municipal Corporation of Delhi
MIC	Methyl Isocyanate
MIC	Monitoring and Information Centre
MLA	Member of the Legislative Assembly
MoEF	Ministry of Environment and Forests
MVA	Motor Vehicles Act
MVR	Motor Vehicles Rules
NBA	National Biodiversity Authority

NCT   National Capital Territory
NDMC   New Delhi Municipal Council
NEERI   National Environmental Engineering Research Institute
NEMA   National Environmental Management Act
NEPA   National Environmental Policy Acts
NHRC   National Human Rights Commission
NIC   National Informatic Centre
NIS   Network Information Service/National Identification Service
NPDES   National Pollution Discharge and Elimination System
NPV   Net Present Value
NRC   National Research Council/Nuclear Regulatory Commission
NRCA   National River Conservation Authority
NSC   National Steering Committee
NSW   New South Wales
ODA   Overseas Development Agency
ODS   Ozone Depleting Substances
OECD   Organization for Economic Cooperation and Development
OPIC   Overseas Private Investment Corporation
PAN   Proxy Aisle Nitrite
PC   Personal Computers
PCB   Pollution Control Board
PIC   Prior Informed Consent
PIL   Public Interest Litigation
POP   Persistent Organic Pollutant
RCRA   Resource Conservation and Recovery Act
R&R   Relief and Rehabilitation
SARA   Superfund Amendments and Reauthorization Act
SBA   State Biodiversity Board
SCMC   Supreme Court Monitoring Committee
SEA/SEIA   Strategic Environment Assessment
SEAC   State Expert Appraisal Committee
SEIAA   State Environment Impact Assessment Authority
SLAPP   Strategic Lawsuits Against Public Participation
SMA   Special Management Area
SO$_2$ Sulphur Dioxide
SPCB   State Pollution Control Board
SPM   Suspended Particulate Matter
TBGRI   Tropical Botanical Garden and Research Institute
TEIA   Trans-boundary Environmental Impact Assessment

TERI	Tata Energy Research Institute
ToR	Terms of Reference
TTZ	Taj Trapezium Zone
UCC	Union Carbide Corporation
UCIL	Union Carbide of India Limited
UKELA	United Kingdom Environmental Law Association
UN	United Nations
UNCCD	United Nations Convention to Combat Desertification
UNCED	United Nations Conference on Environment and Development
UNCLOS	United Nations Convention on the Law of Seas
UNECE	United Nations Economic Commission for Europe
UNEP	United Nations Environment Programme
UNFCCC	United Nations Framework Convention on Climatic Change
UNICEF	United Nations Children's Fund (originally United Nations International Children's Emergency Fund)
UTPCC	Union Territory Pollution Control Committee
WEEE	Waste Electrical and Electronic Equipments
WG	Working Group
WHO	World Health Organization
WIPO	World Intellectual Property Organization
WMO	World Meteorological Organization
WPA	Wildlife Protection Act

Introduction
The Environment and the Constitution

Man's paradise is on earth. This living world is a beloved place of all. It has blessings of nature's bounties, love in lovely spirit.

—Atharva Veda

Man's association with nature is primeval. In ancient India, nature in all its splendour and forms was revered. Thus, Nature (*Prakriti*), is manifested in the form of:

1. Earth or *Prithvi*.
2. Fire or *Agni*.
3. Water or *Jal*.
4. Sky or *Akash*.
5. Wind or *Vayu*.

The elements of nature were known as *Panchmahabhut*, and were worshipped throughout India. It is believed that the universe comprising the Earth was the creation of Brahma. Likewise, all major religions have references to the environment and its intricate link to God.

India has a rich heritage which shows deep reverence towards the environment. Ancient Indians worshipped the forces of nature, including animals and plants. A peep into environmental jurisprudence will show that preservation of environment emanated from spiritual teachings and sacred texts. Gautama Buddha, Mahavira, and Prophet Mohammad, had all echoed the same thought of love and harmony between man and environment.

The first efforts to codify the aspect of environmental protection came from Kautilya, Prime Minister of Chandragupta Maurya. As early as 300 BC, he realized the significance of the environment and formulated rules which mandated the rulers to protect forests and animals.[1] Penalties were also prescribed. This is the first documented case of legislation on environmental protection anywhere in the world. Similar writings were also found in the fifth Rock Edict of Asoka.[2]

ENVIRONMENTAL PROTECTION— THE BEGINNING AT STOCKHOLM

It was at the First UN Conference on the Human Environment in 1972 in Stockholm that concern for environmental protection

[1] In laws concerning forests, there were specific rules on the State to maintain forests; selling of trees; damaging trees; forest produce; forest reserves for wild animals; protection of wild life; fee for hunting etc.; see V. Gupta 'Kautilyan Jurisprudence' (1987) 155 in Divan Shyam and Rosencranz Armin, *Environment Law and Policy in India*, 2nd edn, 7th impression 2005, New Delhi: Oxford University Press, p. 24.

[2] Romila Thapar, *Asoka and the Decline of the Mauryas*, 2nd edn,1973, New Delhi: Oxford University Press, p. 264.

was raised. The Conference had the effect of initiating worldwide participation[3]—by urging governments all over the world to consider that the environment must be protected in order to operationalize the right to life.[4]

The Stockholm Conference was attended by Indira Gandhi, the then prime minister of India. She criticized the attitude and the apparent 'double-standards' adopted by developed countries towards environmental pollution. She said that to the Third World, development and environment were complementary to each other, 'while the rich countries may look upon development as the cause of environmental destruction, for the Third World—it is one of the primary means of improving the environment.'

Gandhi firmly asserted that neither could the environment be improved in poverty nor could poverty be eradicated without science and technology. She declared that modern man must establish an unbroken link between himself and nature. Finally, she reminded the world of an ancient Indian saying that, 'one can take from earth and atmosphere only so much as one puts back to them.'[5]

The manifesto, 'Protect environment to save mankind' saw a worldwide evolution as a result of this conference.[6] It had a profound impact on the way in which environment and environmental protection would be addressed by member countries in the future. The first few to recognize the connection between environment and life were regional conventions like the African Charter,[7] Protocol of San Salvador,[8] American Convention on Human Rights,[9] and the Convention on the Rights of the Child (1989). Thus, the Stockholm Declaration can be rightly hailed as the 'Magna Carta on Human Environment'. 'Man is both the creature and moulder of his environment and [that he] has [got] the fundamental right to freedom, equality and adequate conditions of life, in an environment of quality that permits a life of dignity and well being.'[10]

ENVIRONMENT AND THE CONSTITUTION IN INDIA

During the time of the British, there were several laws.[11] But these early legislative efforts were 'piecemeal and grossly inadequate'.[12] It took about another twenty years after the enactment of the Constitution for comprehensive environmental legislation to be formulated.

The UN Declaration has resulted in the 42nd Amendment to the Constitution and the enactment of various laws. By amending the Indian Constitution for the forty-secondth time in 1972, the government had imposed an obligation to protect the natural environment upon both the State as well as the citizens of India.

---

[3] G.S. Karkara, 'Environment—Development as Human Rights Imperative', in Satish C. Shastri (ed.), *Human Rights, Development and Environmental Law—An Anthology*, 2006, Delhi: Bharat Law Publications, p. 49.
[4] See Sarath Chandran, *Human Rights and Environment Protection*, 2002, Cochin University Law Review, pp. 175–6.
[5] *Atharva Veda.*
[6] Supra note 4, p. 59.

[7] Article 24 of the African Charter on Human and People's Right (1981).
[8] Article 11 of Ibid.
[9] Article 24 of Ibid.
[10] See Principle 1 of the Stockholm Declaration, 1972.
[11] Shore Nuisance (Bombay and Kolaba) Act, 1853; Indian Fisheries Act, 1897; Bengal Smoke Nuisance Act, 1905; Bombay Nuisance Act, 1912; Elephant Preservation Act, 1879; Wild Birds Protection Act, 1887; Indian Forest Act, 1927; Wild Birds and Animals Protection Act, 1912; Hailey National Park Act, 1936, and other Acts were some of them. Supra note 3, pp. 30–1.
[12] Supra note 4, p. 31.

Article 48A, inserted in Part IV of the Constitution, reads, 'The state shall endeavour to protect and improve the environment and to safeguard the forests and wildlife of the country.'

Article 51A (g), inserted in the newly christened 'Fundamental Duties' (Part IV A), reads, 'It shall be the duty of every citizen to protect and improve the natural environment including forests, lakes, rivers and wildlife, and to have compassion for living creatures.'

The amendment makes twofold provisions on environmental protection, the duty of the State and the citizen. Together, these provisions highlight the national consensus on the importance of environmental protection and improvement and also lay the foundation for jurisprudence of this important area of law.[13]

The above two Articles of the Indian Constitution are inserted under the heads 'Directive Principles of State Policy' and 'Fundamental Duties' which are distinct from fundamental rights. There is no fundamental right for the people to clean and unpolluted environment under the Indian Constitution. Instead, the same has been included as 'fundamental duties', which does not have a mandatory tinge as things stand today.

Directive Principles are not enforceable by Constitutional courts by issuing a writ to enforce them. In case of a conflict between Fundamental Rights and Directive Principles, the former always prevail. In short, Directive Principles were always subservient to Fundamental Rights.[14]

Likewise, courts cannot issue writ directions for the enforcement of fundamental duties. They can be used for interpreting ambiguous statutes.[15]

It is because of the said limitations that courts were issuing directions to protect the environment by invoking the power conferred on them for the enforcement of the right to life, which is a fundamental right.

Whenever a problem of ecology is brought before a court, the court is bound to bear in mind Article 48A and Article 51A (g) of the Constitution. When the court is called upon to give effect to the Directive Principles and Fundamental Duties it cannot shrug its shoulders and say that priority is a matter of policy, and so it is a matter for the policy-making authority to comment on. The least the court should do is to examine whether appropriate considerations are borne in mind and irrelevancies excluded in such matters.[16]

DUTY OF THE STATE TO IMPROVE PUBLIC HEALTH

Traces of environmental protection can be seen in Article 49 of the Constitution of India. Human health is intrinsically linked with holistic well-being. Right to healthy living is a basic human right. In a 'welfare country' like India, the State is duty-bound to raise the level of nutrition and standard of living, and to improve public health. Article 47 of the Constitution imposes the duty of raising the level of nutrition and standard of living and improving public health on the State. The Supreme Court of India explained the provision when it directed the Madhya Pradesh State Government to make available

[13] *M.C. Mehta v. Union of India*, AIR 1992 SC 225, 'The Indian Constitution, in the 42nd Amendment, has laid the foundation in Articles 48A and 51A for a jurisprudence of environmental protection', p. 227.

[14] *State of Madras v. Champakam Dorairajan*, AIR 1951 SC 226: *Mohd Hanif Qureshi v. State of Bihar*, AIR 1958 SC 731; *In re Kerala Education Bill*, AIR 1958 SC 956.

[15] *Mumbai Kamgar Sabha v. Abdullabhai*, AIR 1976 SC 1455.

[16] *Sachdanand Pandey v. State of West Bengal*, AIR 1987 SC 1109.

financial assistance to the Ratlam Municipality to enable it to fulfil its obligation to construct public latrines, drains, provide water supply and scavenging service so as to ensure sanitation. The court has held that 'State has got a duty under Article 47 to ensure that steps are taken for the improvement of public health as amongst its primary duties'.[17]

By directing the Central Government to destroy the rice which was unfit for human consumption in public interest, the Supreme Court has declared that 'Environmental Protection is dealt with in Article 47 of the Constitution of India, and that life, public health, and ecology should have priority over unemployment and loss of revenue'.[18]

JUDICIAL ACTIVISM FOR ENVIRONMENTAL PROTECTION

The development of environmental law is mainly based on the principles developed in international conventions and treaties and by giving a broader interpretation to Article 21 of the Constitution of India. Environmental protection has become a part of life and is accepted as a human right and also a fundamental constitutional right.

Judicial recognition of environmental rights was achieved in India through the device of Public Interest Litigation (PIL). Although the chief sources of environmental protection were Article 48A and 51A (g), the judiciary elevated environmental protection to the rank of a fundamental right by bringing it within the ambit of Article 21, that is, 'Right to Life and Personal Liberty'.

The Supreme Court of India in *Rural Litigation and Entitlement Kendra v. State of Uttar Pradesh*,[19] declared that the right of the people to live in a healthy environment (with minimal disturbance to ecological balance) should be safeguarded. The Supreme Court ordered the closure of mining operations in certain areas. While ordering the closure it 'weighed in balance' the need for limestone quarrying for industrial purpose and the environmental disturbance it creates. The Court also gave directions for the shifting of mining to other states and rehabilitation of mining workers to other areas like reclamation, afforestation, soil conservation programmes, and other such programmes.

By referring to the Stockholm Declaration, 1972 and Rio Declaration, 1992, the Supreme Court has stated the importance of the Polluter Pays principle,[20] the Precautionary principle, the Intergenerational Equity principle,[21] the Absolute Liability principle,[22] the Public Trust doctrine,[23] and the Reversal of Burden of Proof.[24]

Though various laws were enacted for the protection of environment in India, the same were not always implemented effectively. The Supreme Court of India has issued several directions to implement the laws and has held that non-enforcement of the law is equivalent to not enacting the law at all.[25]

[17] *Ratlam Municipality v. Vardhichand*, AIR 1980 SC 1622.

[18] *M.C. Mehta v. Union of India*, (1987) 4 SCC 463 reiterated in *M.C. Mehta v. Union of India*, (2004) 12 SCC 118; see generally *Thapan Kumar Sadhu Khan v. Food Corporation of India*, (1996) 6 SCC 101.

[19] *Rural Litigation and Entitlement Kendra v. State of Uttar Pradesh*, AIR 1985 SC 652.

[20] *Vellore Citizens Welfare Forum v. Union of India and Others*, AIR 1996 SC 2715.

[21] *T.N. Godavaraman v. Union of India*, 2006 (1) SCC 1.

[22] *M.C. Mehta v. Union of India*, 1987 (1) SCC 95.

[23] *M.C. Mehta v. Kamal Nath and Others*, (1997)1 SCC 388.

[24] *AP Pollution Control Board v. Prof. M.V. Nayudu*, AIR 1999 SC 812.

[25] *Indian Council for Enviro-legal Action v. Union of India*, 1996 (4) JT 263.

Under common law, the Municipal Corporation can be restrained by an injunction in an action brought by a riparian owner who has suffered on account of the pollution of the water in a river being caused by the discharging of untreated waste. When M.C. Mehta, a noted environmentalist who had filed a PIL before the Supreme Court of India, challenged the pollution in River Ganga, the Court had explained the rule that nuisance caused by the pollution of the River Ganga was a public nuisance, which was widespread in range and indiscriminate in its effect and it would not be reasonable to expect a particular person, to take proceedings to stop it, as distinct from the community at large. On the facts and in the circumstances the court held that in order to enforce statutory provisions which impose duties on the authorities[26] the common law limitations on persons moving the court has been expanded for the prevention of water pollution. It signalled the opening of the era of public interest environmental litigations in India.

The Supreme Court had occasion to expand the scope of Article 19(1)(d), that is, the right to move freely throughout the territory of India, when the people of Himachal Pradesh approached the court on being denied proper roads. The Court held that every person is entitled to life as enjoined in Article 21 read in conjunction with Article 19(1)(d) of the Constitution in the background of Article 38(2),[27] and is entitled to move freely throughout the territory of India. That right embraces not only physical existence of life but also the quality of life. For residents of hilly areas, access to roads is access to life itself. Therefore, the denial of roads is equivalent to denial of life. To the residents of the hilly areas, as far as feasible and possible, society has a constitutional obligation to provide roads for communication.[28]

The Supreme Court declared that the right to environment is contemplated in Article 21 of the Constitution of India.[29] The Court has shown remarkable leadership in implementing the global environment concerns in several environment cases.[30]

Article 32[31] does not merely confer power on the Supreme Court to issue directions for the enforcement of fundamental rights, but also lays down a constitutional obligation to protecting the Fundamental Rights of the people. For that purpose, the Court has all incidental and ancillary powers, including the power to forge new remedies and fashion new strategies designed to enforce the fundamental rights.[32]

An interesting question was raised on the powers of the Supreme Court in a case where petitions were filed before it, claiming compensation from a company which had discharged oleum gas, causing danger to the

---

[26] M.C. Mehta v. Union of India, AIR 1988 SC 1115.
[27] State to secure a social order for the promotion of welfare of the people.

[28] State of Himachal Pradesh v. Umeed Ram, AIR 1986 SC 847.
[29] Chhetriya Pardushan Mukti Sangarsh Samiti v. State of Uttar Pradesh, AIR 1990 SC 2060.
[30] M.C. Mehta v. Union of India, AIR 1988 SC 1037, p. 1038; Rural Litigation and Entitlement Kendra, Dehradun v. State of Uttar Pradesh, AIR 1988 SC 2187, p. 2199; Kinkeri Devi v. State of Himachal Pradesh, AIR 1988 HP 8; Virender Gaur v. State of Haryana and others, 1995 (2) SCC 577, 1997 (10) JT 600, 1994 (5) SCALE 211; M.C. Mehta v. Union of India, (1998) 8 SCC 589; T.N. Godavarman Thirumulpad (87) v. Union of India, (2006) 1 SCC 1; Intellectuals Forum v. State of Andhra Pradesh, AIR 2006 SC 1350, (2006) 3 SCC 549; Susetha v. State of Tamil Nadu, AIR 2006 SC 2893, (2006) 6 SCC 543.
[31] Remedies for the enforcement of fundamental rights.
[32] Bandhua Mukti Morcha v. Union of India, (1984)3 SCC 161.

health and safety of the people. The Court held that in appropriate cases of breach of fundamental rights, compensation can be granted. However, it cautioned that it is not in every case of breach of fundamental rights that need compensation be granted based on the 'principle of Absolute Liability'.[33]

It is not only the eco-friendly NGOs who must actively persuade courts in delivering eco-friendly judgments. Courts have time and again reminded the decision-making authority of their solemn responsibility of giving due weightage and regard to ecological factors in granting permission to projects.[34] The Supreme Court also declared that if a government decision fails to take into account relevant considerations affecting the environment, that decision is invalid.[35]

JUDICIAL ACTIVISM BY STATE HIGH COURTS

The State High Courts have also issued various directions declaring the 'right to clean and healthy environment' under Article 21. In fact, high courts in the country have enthusiastically declared that right to environment was included in the right to life concept in Article 21 of the Constitution.

When the degree of pollution generated by the factory exceeded the tolerance limits, the Kerala High Court (KHC) held that it invaded the rights under Article 21 and it cannot pass the mustering might of the Constitution. The Court directed the closure of the industry in the event of non-compliance with regulatory measures.[36]

To curb smoking in public places, which adversely affects others, the KHC has sought the help of Article 21. Maintenance of health and environment falls within the purview of Article 21 and a healthy body is the foundation of all human activities.[37]

The calling of *bandh* (total strike paralysing the all activities by force) by political parties infringes the fundamental rights of others. In the absence of law to prevent such nuisance, the KHC has declared that calling for bandh and the enforcement of that call is illegal and unconstitutional.[38]

Restrictions imposed on mining as a precautionary measure were upheld by the KHC, upholding the rights of the people of the locality to have a decent environment flowing from Article 21 of the Constitution of India. The court held that conditions imposed on quarrying regarding prohibited distance of mining and prohibition of pumps for mining are necessary for the protection of environment. 'If every landowner, driven by profit motive, is to dig his land to win sand as he likes up to any depth, no land except pits will be left for future generations,' the Court added.[39]

The KHC has held that no person can claim absolute right to indulge in activities resulting in environmental degradation of even his own land. While exploiting natural resources, the capacity of the environment to repair and replenish should be taken note of, otherwise nature's backlash could be catastrophic.[40]

The Rajasthan High Court, while considering a petition challenging the attempt to convert an open space in their vicinity into another residential

---

[33] *M.C. Mehta v. Union of India*, (1987) 1 SCC 395.
[34] *State of Himachal Pradesh v. Ganesh Wood Products*, AIR 1996 SC 149, at 159 and 163.
[35] Ibid, see also *Pleasant Stay Hotel v. Palani Hills Conservation Council*, (1995) 6 SCC 127, p. 136, 139–40.
[36] *Mathew Lukose v. Kerala State Pollution Control Board*, 1990 (2) KLT 686.

[37] *K. Ramakrishnan v. State of Kerala*, AIR 1999 Ker 385.
[38] *Bharat Kumar v. State*, AIR 1998 SC 184.
[39] *Soman v. Geologist*, 2004 (3) KLT 577.
[40] *Tilakan v. Circle Inspector of Police*, 2008 (1) KLT 141.

complex for the Life Insurance Corporation of India (LIC), made the following observation.[41]

Examining the matter from the above constitutional point of view, it would be reasonable to hold that the enjoyment of life and its attainments and fulfilment guaranteed by Article 21 of the Constitution embraces the protection and reservation of nature's gift without which life cannot be enjoyed. The slow poisoning by the polluted atmosphere caused by environmental pollution and spoliation should be regarded as amounting to violation of Article 21 of the Constitution.

The Rajasthan High Court held that citizens had the fundamental right to seek affirmative action under Article 21 in matters relating to maintenance of health, sanitation, and environment.[42]

In another case challenging the establishment of industries in residential areas contrary to the zoning of land use in a development plan,[43] the Karnataka High Court 'recognized entitlement to clean environment as a basic human right'.[44] The right to life is inherent in Article 21 and it requires the aspect of quality of life, which is possible only in a quality environment.

However, the benchmark for this decision and later decisions of the Supreme Court seems to have been set in the judgement of Sankaran Nair in the *Mathew Lukhose* case.[45] Among these were the express articulations of the right to a wholesome environment as a facet of the right to life under Article 21, by way of securing assistance from *amicus curiae* and by reference to the emergent norm of 'Intergenerational Equity'.[46]

CONSTITUTIONAL DIRECTIONS FOR WATER REQUIREMENT

'Water is a basic human need for health, indeed, for survival and therefore it is not an exaggeration to call it one of the basic human rights.'[47] It is the basic need for the survival of human beings, and right to water is the right to life,[48] enshrined in Article 21 of the Constitution.[49] Many a times, courts in India have reminded both the states and local authorities that 'failure of state to provide safe drinking water to citizens in adequate quantities would amount to violation of fundamental right to life enshrined in Article 21 and would be violation of human rights.'[50]

The KHC has held that the right to drinking water and free air are attributes of the right to life, for these are the basic elements which sustain life itself. In this case, there was apprehension that the scheme for pumping ground water for supplying potable water to Lakshadweep Islands would lead more to environmental harm than benefits. This case also recognized, 'the right to enjoy life as a serene experience, unlike a mere animal experience.'[51]

[41] *T. Damodhar Rao v. Special Officer, Municipal Corporation of Hyderabad*, AIR 1987 AP 171.
[42] *L.K. Koolwal v. State of Rajasthan*, AIR 1988 Raj 2.
[43] For more on town planning, see p. 213.
[44] *V. Lakshmipathy v. State of Karnataka*, AIR 1992 Kant 57, p. 67.
[45] *Mathew Lukhose v. Kerala Pollution Control Board*, 1990 (2) KLT 686.

[46] Supra note 60, p. 255.
[47] P. Leelakrishnan, *Environmental Law in India*, 2nd edn, 2005, New Delhi: LexisNexis Butterworths, p. 195.
[48] *State of Karnataka v. State of Andhra Pradesh*, (2000) 9 SCC 572.
[49] *Narmada Bachao Andolan v. Union of India*, AIR 2000 SC 3751; *Tehri Bandh Virodhi Sangarsh Samiti v. State of Uttar Pradesh*, (1992) Supp 1 SCC 44.
[50] *Vishala Kochi Kudivella Samrakshana Samiti v. State of Kerala*, 2006 (1) KLT 919; also see *Shajimon Joseph v. State of Kerala*, 2007 (1) KLT 368.
[51] *Attakoya Thangal v. Union of India*, 1990 KLT 580; *F.K. Hussain v. Union of India*, AIR 1990 Ker 321.

The menace of water pollution has been tackled to a considerable extent thanks to the interference of courts. In a plethora of cases, courts have upheld the aspect of the right to clean water as a facet of the right to life, like in the case of rejecting the proposal to construct a castor oil derivative factory within a 10-km radius of Himayat Sagar and Osman Sagar;[52] tanneries discharging effluents in Ganga;[53] pollution to ground water sources caused by the leather industries;[54] by distillery effluents;[55] other industrial effluents,[56] and other such polluting industries.

The Rajasthan High Court has explained the six basic principles enunciated in Article 21, 48A, and 51A (g),[57] as follows:

1. All human beings have a fundamental right to unpolluted environment, pollution-free water, and air;
2. The State is obliged to preserve and protect the environment;
3. It is mandatory for the State and its agencies to conceive, anticipate, prevent, and attack causes of environmental degradations;
4. Industry cannot be permitted to continue as a matter of right, in case it creates pollution;
5. Polluter must meet cost of repairing environment and ecology and pay reparation to those who have suffered

because of pollution caused by them (Polluter Pays Principle);
6. Considerations of economy cannot prevail over concerns for environment and ecology.

By elucidating six principles from a battery of decisions in its armoury, the judiciary has asserted its position as the 'guardian and custodian of Indian environment'.

Article 48A reflects an increasing awareness of people of the need to preserve the environment from pollution, especially in urban areas. It rightly emphasizes the fact that the state should try not only to protect, but also to improve the environment.[58]

ENVIRONMENT AND EDUCATION

Education is essential for the development of human personality. It strengthens respect for human rights and fundamental rights. The Stockholm Conference on Human Environment in 1972 heralded the efforts, both national and international, to establish programmes of environmental education, interdisciplinary in approach, in school and out of school encompassing all levels of education, and directed towards the general public in particular the ordinary citizens living in rural and urban areas, youth and adult alike, with a view to educating him as to simple steps he might take, within his means to manage and control his environment.[59] Educational institutions are considered to be the 'seed beds of culture', in which the future will be schooled and trained.[60] Article 41 of the Constitution

---

[52] *Andhra Pradesh Pollution Control Board v. M.V. Nayadu*, (1999) 2 SCC 718.

[53] *M.C. Mehta v. Union of India*, AIR 1988 SC 1037; (1987) 2 SCC 463.

[54] *Vellore Citizens Welfare Forum v. Union of India*, AIR 1996 SC 2715.

[55] *Rajiv Ranjan Singh v. State of Bihar*, AIR 1992 Pat 86; also *President of India v. Bhavni River*, AIR 1998 SC 2578; (1998) 6 SCC 335.

[56] *M/s Narula Dyeing & Printing Works v. Union of India*, AIR 1995 Guj 185.

[57] *Singh Punia v. Rajasthan State Board of Pollution Control of Water Pollution*, AIR 2003 Raj 286.

[58] H.M. Seervai, *Constitutional Law of India*, 4th edition, 1991, Mumbai: N.M. Tripathi Private Limited, vol. II, p. 2019.

[59] Article 26 (1) and (2) of Universal Declaration of Human Rights, 1948.

[60] *Unnikrishnan v. State of Andhra Pradesh*, (1993) 1 SCC 645.

provides for the right to education. Article 21A, which was inserted into the Constitution by the 86th Amendment Act, 2001,[61] made free and compulsory education for all children up to the age of fourteen years, a fundamental right. The apex court in a catena of cases, much before this right being made fundamental, reiterated that right to education is a fundamental right.[62] The right to education flows directly from 'right to life'.[63]

The Supreme Court of India accepted in principle that through the medium of education, awareness of the environment and problems related to pollution should be taught as a compulsory subject in the school syllabus, the non-compliance of which would attract penal action.[64]

ENVIRONMENTAL PROTECTION AND LOCAL BODIES

'Democratic De-centralization' is seen as the ultimate manifestation of democracy. It has multifarious advantages in that it enhances efficiency by streamlining the administration miles away from entangling red-tapism; ensuring citizen participation at the grass-root level; initiating and implementing developmental activities. It was Mahatma Gandhi's dream of a 'self-sufficient village Panchayat'. In one sense, it is the pinnacle of federalism, as these local bodies can be termed as 'Micro-Federating Units'.

In India, the institution of Panchayati Raj, was created as a 'constitutional Third Tier structure of Sub-National Administration'

in the Federal system of India, through the adoption of the 73rd and 74th Constitutional Amendment Acts 1993.[65] These Acts gave Panchayati Raj institutions and urban local bodies a 'constitutional status' and made it obligatory for all states to establish this three-tier system.[66] Under that, a new Part IX was introduced titled 'The Panchayats'.[67] Part IX-A was inserted by the 74th Amendment Act 1994, titled 'The Municipalities'. Under these two Amendment Acts, state governments can 'delegate' certain functions to these entities. The legislature of a state can make laws endowing the panchayats with such powers and authority for the preparation of plans for economic development and social justice and its implementation in relation to the matters listed in the Eleventh Schedule.[68] From the point of environmental conservation, the panchayats would be responsible for activities like land improvement, soil conservation, water and wasteshed management, social and farm forestry, non-conventional energy sources, and similar activities. Under the Twelfth Schedule,[69] urban planning, public health, solid waste management, urban forestry, and the like, fall under the domain of municipalities. These Amendments and constitutional provisions truly empower the local bodies in taking concrete steps towards environmental conservation. These bodies are expected to play a dominant role in environment management at the district

---

[61] 86th Amendment was primarily based on 165th Law Commission report.

[62] *In re Kerala Education Bill*, AIR 1958 SC 956.

[63] *Unnikrishnan v. State of Andhra Pradesh*, (1993) 1 SCC 645.

[64] *M.C. Mehta v. Union of India*, (1992) 1 SCC 358, AIR 1992 SC 382.

[65] Subhash Kashyap C., *Constitution of India—Review and Reassessment*, 2006 edn, Universal Law Publishing, pp. 166–7.

[66] Municipal corporations, municipalities, and panchayats.

[67] Inserted by the 73rd Amendment Act, 1993.

[68] Eleventh Schedule, inserted by the 73rd Amendment Act, 1993 (Article 243-G).

[69] Twelfth Schedule inserted by the 74th Amendment Act, 1993 (Article 243-W).

level.[70] Thus, we can rightly conclude that the aspect of environmental conservation has permeated to the grass-root level.

THE REPORT OF THE NATIONAL COMMISSION TO REVIEW THE WORKING OF THE CONSTITUTION AND ENVIRONMENTAL PROTECTION

The National Commission to Review the Working of the Constitution was constituted by the Government of India in 2001 to review the working of the Indian Constitution, under the chairmanship of M.N. Venkatachalliah. The Commission was constituted to:

examine, in the light of the experience of the past fifty years, as to how best the Constitution can respond to the changing needs of efficient, smooth and effective system of governance and socio-economic development of modern India within the frame work of Parliamentary democracy and to recommend changes, if any, that are required in the provisions of the Constitution without interfering with its basic structure or features.[71]

The Commission in its final report recommends the incorporation of 'right to safe drinking water, prevention of pollution, conservation of ecology and sustainable development' in a new Article 30-D. Every person shall have the right:

1. To safe drinking water;
2. To an environment that is not harmful to one's health or well-being; and
3. To have the environment protected, for the benefit of present and future generations so as to:
   a) Prevent pollution and ecological degradation;
   b) Promote conservation; and
   c) Secure ecologically sustainable development and use of natural resources while promoting justifiable economic and social development.

This provision is a progressive provision giving due importance to safe drinking water, pollution control, conservation of ecology, and sustainable development. Vital provisions regarding climate change are, however, missing. The Ministry of Environment and Forests (MoEF) has not, so far, shown any interest in incorporating these provisions.

THE ENVIRONMENT IN THE CONSTITUTIONS OF THE WORLD

Almost every country in the world has a constitution, unique and dexterously engineered to be the supreme law of that country. Many of the countries have incorporated 'environmental provisions' in their constitutions and concepts of international environmental law. This becomes all the more necessary in the light of threats raised by global warming and other environmental hazards. One way or another, it is a 'ground norm', as Hans Kelson puts it.[72]

Constitutions in the world are unique, but also starkly diverse. Some are written, some are un-written, mostly based on ancient customs, like Great Britain; some long and complex, like erstwhile Yugoslavia or Indian. There are also simple constitutions like that of the USA.[73]

Countries like China, Cambodia, the Phillipines, Thailand, and Sri Lanka have provisions for the protection of natural resources, which protect the environment.

---

[70] Article 243ZD, Indian Constitution; see sub-section (3).
[71] Res. 1/21/2000-NCRWC dated 22 January 2001, National Commission to Review the Working of the Constitution, New Delhi.

[72] Hans Kelson, *General Theory of Law and State*, NJ: The Lawbook Exchange Ltd, 1999.
[73] 'Brevity, Restraint and Simplicity' are the hallmarks of original US Constitution, Ibid., xi.

The Constitution of Pakistan empowers it to compulsorily acquire or take possession of any property for preventing danger to life, property, or public health.[74]

Islamic countries like Iran, Saudi Arabia, and Kuwait have provisions for the preservation of the environment, in which present as well as future generations have been provided with a right to flourishing social existence. Certain neo-liberal Islamic countries like Jordan and Egypt have shown a willingness to imbibe western concepts of Human Rights, Fundamental Freedoms, Women's Rights, and other such rights.

Most of these countries have recognized the right to life and healthy environment as a fundamental human right. Many aspects of environmental law like sustainable development, conservation of wild life and natural heritage, enjoyment of property without causing harm to environment, and other such aspects have made their way into these constitutions. India certainly has a lot of useful provisions to imbibe from these constitutions.

The Supreme Court of India has held that principles based on the provisions of the American Constitution cannot always be applied to Indian conditions and while some of the principles adumbrated by the American decisions may provide a useful guide, close adherence to those principles while applying them to the provisions of our Constitution is not to be favoured because social conditions in our country are different.[75]

A Constitution is the basic law of the country, upon which all activities are based. In the absence of constitutional provisions providing for fundamental rights to have a clean and an unpolluted environment, courts have an onerous responsibility to safeguard and protect the environmental interests of the country. Most of the valuable principles of environmental law, like Sustainable Development, Public Trust Doctrine, Absolute Liability, Intergenerational equity, and Reversal of Burden of Proof have become the law of the land in view of judicial intervention. Environmental problems mainly affect developing countries. Unregulated wasteful consumption of natural resources affects the people. Unless there is a strong constitutional will, a popular mandate, political will, and clear constitutional safeguards, it will not be possible to protect the natural resources of the country that will be the life-sustaining force for the future generations. Man's future on earth should not be dictated by industrial development but by ecological factors. Kevin Costner's magnum opus 'Waterworld' has subtly reminded us about the stark reality that beholds us. Global warming and rapid climatic changes are already wrecking havoc all over the world.

---

[74] Article 24 (3) of the Pakistan Constitution.

[75] *M.C. Mehta v. Union of India*, (1987)1 SCC 395.

I

Development of
Environmental Jurisprudence

1 Basic Environmental Protection Laws

The *Rig Veda* praises the beauty of dawn (*usha* in Sanskrit) and worships nature in all its glory. 'Nature never did betray'.

The Bible recognizes and grapples with environmental issues, but starts with appreciating God's gift to mankind. It is explained thus:

And the Lord God took the man and put him in the Garden of Eden to tend and guard and keep it.[1]

Quranic injunctions also emphasize on the need to protect the environment. There are repeated warnings in the Quran that man should not corrupt the Earth, since it has has implications for man's social and physical environment. The intent is that man should also develop a communal relationship with the flora and fauna as these are also communities like mankind:

Although there is no beast that walks on earth and no bird that flies on its two wings which is not (Allah's) creature like yourselves: no single thing have. We neglected to our Decree. And once again Unto their Sustainer shall they (all) be gathered.[2]

And Allah has caused you to grow out of the earth in (gradual) growth: (like vegetation).[3]

The following traditions from the Holy Prophet bear testimony to the special importance and spiritual nature of the environment:

—Who plants even a single sapling deserves gardens in the Hereafter.
—Any Muslim who plants a tree or raises a crop whereof eats a human being or a bird or an animal it will be a Sadaqa from the planter and even if the produce is stolen by a thief the planter will surely get recompense in the Hereafter (for this virtuous deed).[4]

In another tradition reported by Hazrat Aisha in *Kanz-ul-Amal*,[5] the Holy Prophet said, 'If you are sure that doomsday has arrived and you have a sapling in your hand that can be planted, do plant it.'

INDIAN LAW

Man is Nature's best promise and worst enemy. If industry is a necessity, pollution is inevitable. Since progress and pollution go together, there can be no end to progress, and consequently, no escape from pollution. If industry is a necessary evil, pollution is the surest sufferance.

Several enactments have been made to combat pollution. 'Pollution' is a noun derived

---

[1] Genesis 2:15. Bible.
[2] Al-Anam: 38.
[3] Nuh: 17, verse 17 of 28 in chapter 71.

[4] al-Munami, Fayd al-Qadir, iii, 30. Extracted from the Doctoral Research Paper titled *An Islamic Approach to the Environment* by Ibrahim Ozdemir, 2002.
[5] Vol. 6, p. 81.

from the transitive verb 'pollute' which means to make foul, unclean, or dirty; to make impure or morally unclean. In Halsbury's *Laws of England*,[6] 'pollution' means the direct or indirect discharge by man of substances or energy into the aquatic environment resulting in hazard to human health, harm to living resources and aquatic ecosystems, and damage to amenities on interference with other legitimate use of water.[7]

The anxiety to save the environment manifested itself in the Constitution (Forty-Second Amendment Act 1976) by the introduction of a specific provision for the first time to 'protect and improve' the environment. Since then, several enactments have been made for the protection of the environment of the country.

The Environment (Protection) Act, 1986 (EPA) was enacted as a measure to implement the decisions made at the United Nations Conference on the Human Environment held in Stockholm in June 1972 to which India was a party. The conference passed a resolution, known as the Stockholm Declaration, which is dilated upon later by us. At this stage, it is sufficient to note that the EPA reflects, in large measure, the Stockholm Declaration. According to the Statement of Objects and Reasons of the enactment, the multiplicity of regulatory agencies engenders a need for an authority that can assume the lead role for the study, planning, and implementation of long-term requirements of environmental safety, give directions, and co-ordinate a system of speedy and adequate responses to emergency situations threatening the environment. The EPA has been enacted by invoking the powers conferred on the Central Government under Entry 13 of List I, Schedule VII of the Constitution of India, which reads,

'Participation in international conferences, assessment and other bodies and implementing of decisions made thereat.'

The EPA is an umbrella legislation, under which most of the pollution control regulations were framed. Section 3 of the Act grants the Central Government power to take all such measures as it deems necessary and expedient for the purpose of protecting and improving the quality of the environment and land, and controlling and abating environmental pollution.

Duties of Industries

Section 25 has empowered the Central Government to make rules fixing the standards of pollution. Thereafter, such rules must be placed before the Parliament. By virtue of these powers, the Central Government has enacted the Environment (Protection) Rules, 1986 (EPR) which prescribes standards for controlling noise pollution, management of bio-medical wastes, management of hazardous wastes, coastal area protection, environment impact assessment, and other such measures. Persons carrying on industrial operations or processing have been restrained from discharging any polluting substances in excess of the standards prescribed by law.[8] Different standards have been prescribed for different industries as per Rule 3 of the EPR.

If no values are prescribed as in the above, then the industry must satisfy the general parameters and standards specified in Schedule VI. The combined effect of emission or discharge of environmental pollutants in an area, from industries, operations, processes, automobiles, and domestic sources shall not be permitted to exceed the relevant concentration in ambient air quality as specified in Schedule VII of the EPR.

---

[6] Fourth edn, vol. 38, para 66.

[7] Ibid.

[8] Section 7, EPA.

Persons handling hazardous substances are bound by the prescribed procedural safeguards. The industries have to furnish information required by the authorities and allow entry into the industrial unit so as to carry out inspection. Section 11 of the EPA empowers officers of the Pollution Control Board to take samples and test them in approved laboratories. Every person carrying on an industry, operation, or process requiring consent under the Water (Prevention and Control of Pollution) Act, 1974, and/or Air (Prevention and Control of Pollution) Act, 1984, or an authorization under the Hazardous Wastes (Management and Handling) Rules, 1989, had to submit an environmental statement in the prescribed Form V to the concerned State Pollution Control Board before 13 September 1993.[9]

The Central Government has been empowered to prohibit and restrict the location of industries and the carrying on of processes and operations in different areas.[10] Areas that have reached or are likely to reach the critical level, and which have been identified as such, can be categorized as 'sensitive' or 'critically polluted'. Rule 13 of the EPR grants powers to the Central Government to prohibit or make restrictions on the handling of hazardous substances in different areas.

Act to Override Other Laws

Under Section 24, the provisions of the EPA and the Rules or Orders made thereunder have been given overriding effect over any other enactment. The Patna High Court had made it clear that the provisions of the EPA have not been superceded by the Air (Prevention and Control of Pollution) Act, 1981, and Water (Prevention and Control of Pollution) Act, 1974.[11]

Offences Under the EPA

Anyone who fails to comply with or contravenes any of the provisions of EPA or EPR, or any of the notifications issued, is punishable with imprisonment for a term of upto five years with a fine that may extend to one lakh rupees. If the offence is being continued, the industrialist has to pay an additional fine that may extend to five thousand rupees for each day.[12] If the offence is being committed by a company, the officer responsible for it is liable for punishment. In the case of government departments, the head of the department shall be deemed guilty of the offences under the EPA.[13]

On the basis of a written complaint from authorized officers of the Pollution Control Board, any magistrates' court can take cognizance of the offences. Section 19 (b) also empowers any private persons to initiate prosecution proceedings, provided the person serves notice of ninety days upon the defendant in the prescribed manner.

In one instance, an officer of the Pollution Control Board noticed the dumping of hazardous waste. He filed an application seeking directions from the high court to take action against such erring industries in order to compel them to abate such activities. The Gujarat High Court held that it is entirely for the Board to identify the culprits and take determined and speedy action as demanded by law. The court clarified that no provision mandates that a direction by the high court be made before taking action.[14]

---

[9] Schedule I, EPR.

[10] Section 14, EPR.

[11] Rule 5, EPR.

[12] *Bihar State Pollution Control Board v. Hiranand Stone Works*, AIR 2005 Patna 62.

[13] Section 15, EPA.

[14] Sections 16 and 17, EPA.

Directions for Closure of Industries

Section 5 of the EPA empowers the Central Government to issue directions for the closure, prohibition, or regulation of any industry, operation, or process. The said power also includes the power to issue directions for the stoppage or regulation of the supply of electricity, water, or any other service.

The Karnataka High Court has held that the order for the closure of an industrial establishment should state the reasons. The opportunity of a hearing should be given to the operator of the industrial unit.[15]

Accountability of Pollution Control Boards

Members, officers, and employees of the authorities constituted, including the Pollution Control Board, are public servants within the meaning of Section 21 of the Indian Penal Code, 1860. No suit, prosecution, or other legal proceeding shall lie against the said officers in respect to any act done or intended to be done in good faith in pursuance of the EPA or EPR or any other directions issued.[16] Civil courts are barred from entertaining any suit or proceeding in respect of anything done, action taken, or order or direction issued by the said officers or government. As the Act itself is a self-contained code, if other authorities start interfering with their working, it will make the law unworkable.

In the USA, the Environmental Protection Agency is responsible for the implementation of most of the pollution control enactments. It is headed by an administrator appointed by the President. The regional offices are responsible for the issuance of permits to individual sources and for initiating enforcement action. There are also a number of other federal administrative agencies with environmental responsibilities, like the Department of Energy, the Occupational Safety and Health Administration, Food and Drug Administration, and Department of Interior.

FOREIGN LAWS

United States of America

According to *US* v. *Amadio*, environment means

the totality of physical, economic, cultural, aesthetic, and social circumstances and factors which surround and affect the desirability and value of property and which also affect the quality of people's lives.[17]

The National Environmental Policy Act, 1970 (NEPA)[18] is the basic national chapter for the protection of environment in the USA. It is not a regulatory statute imposing pollution control requirements on anyone. Rather, the NEPA is largely an information statute. Its purpose is to enforce quick action, not to generate paperwork. The Act is intended to help public officials make decisions that are based on an understanding of environmental consequences, and to take actions that protect, restore, and enhance the environment.

Section 101 of NEPA establishes certain broad national policies relating to the protection of the environment. Section 102 (2)(c) requires the federal agency to prepare an Environment Impact Statement (EIS) when it is proposing to take certain major actions. The Act also establishes the Council

---

[15] *Suo Motu v. Vatva Industries*, AIR 2000 Guj 33.

[16] *M/s Brindavan Phosphates Pvt Ltd v. Karnataka State Pollution Control Board*, AIR 2003 Kant 476, Sec.18, EPA; *M/s Jadar Soap Works v. Union of India*, AIR 2000 Guj 43.

[17] *US v. Amadio*, CA. Ind, 215 F. 2d 605.611.

[18] Code of Federal Regulations, Title 40. Protection of Environment. Chapter V: Council on Environmental Quality.

on Environmental Quality (CEQ) to advise the President on environmental issues. This is responsible for overseeing the implementation of NEPA, co-ordination among federal agencies, and publishing an annual report that summarizes the state of environmental conditions in the USA.

The President, the federal agencies, and the courts share responsibility for enforcing this legislation.

The US Supreme Court has described NEPA as essentially procedural. The decision taken by the Federal Department of Housing and Urban Development to construct low-income housing in Manhattan was challenged on the ground that the assessment was procedurally inadequate and the decision arbitrary and capricious. The decision of the Court of Appeal was reversed by the Supreme Court, which held that NEPA requires no more than an adequate consideration of environmental factors. The ruling strongly implied that a court could not reject an agency decision under NEPA, based on the court's assessment of the agency's weighing of information contained in an otherwise adequate EIS.[19]

A majority of states have adopted legislation based on NEPA; these are often termed the 'little NEPA[s]' or State Environmental Policy Acts (SEPAs). State laws are interpreted based on NEPA.

Georgia

Even countries like Georgia established legal bases for public participation and access to information in the course of the issuance of an environmental permit for performance of an activity in their territory, during a state ecological examination or Environmental

Impact Assessment (EIA), or during the decision-making process on such matters.

Malaysia

Section 21 of the Environmental Quality Act, 1974, empowers the minister, after consultation with the Council, to specify acceptable conditions for the emission, discharge, or deposit of environmentally hazardous substances, pollutants, or wastes, or the emission of noise into any area, segment, or element of the environment. The minister may then set aside any area, segment, or element of the environment within which the emission, discharge, or deposit is prohibited or restricted. Section 22 mandates that no person shall, unless licensed, emit or discharge environmentally hazardous substances, pollutants, or wastes into the atmosphere in contravention of the acceptable conditions specified under Section 21. Noise pollution is regulated by Section 23 of the Act. Section 25 restrains water pollution in inland waters, and Section 27 restrains the discharge of oil into Malaysian waters. The throwing of hazardous wastes without permission is prohibited by Section 29 of the Act. In 2000, the Act was amended to restrain and ban open burning in any premises.[20] The enactment is a comprehensive legislation to prevent most forms of pollution.

Sri Lanka

Sri Lanka has the National Environmental Act, 1980, which mandates that certain projects require clearance from the Government.

Pakistan

The Pakistan EPA, 1997, is intended to provide for the protection, conservation, rehabilitation,

---

[19] *Strycker's Bay Neighbourhood Council Inc. v. Karien*, 444 US 223; 62 L.Ed.2d 433 (1980).

[20] Section 29A of the Act.

and improvement of the environment; for the prevention and control of pollution; and for the promotion of sustainable development. The prime minister is the chairman of the Pakistan Environment Protection Council, constituted under Section 3 of the Act. The Act also provides for the establishment of an Environment Protection Agency.[21] The law further restrains the discharge or emission of any effluent or waste or air pollutant or noise in an amount, concentration, or level that is in excess of the National Environmental Quality Standards.[22]

Bangladesh

Bangladesh has enacted the Environment Conservation Act, 1995 (Act 1 of 1995). The Environment Conservation Rules, 1997, framed under the Act, empower the Government to declare any area as an Environmentally Critical Area.[23] Vehicles emitting smoke, and thus injurious to health, must obtain a fitness certificate.

It can be observed that a legislative framework is common in most jurisdictions, where power over the environment is often vested in the state and its agencies. Such legislation is fundamental to any legal system that intends to take the environment into consideration, as rights and duties are articulated and mechanisms provided for dealing with matters that may arise in this context. Underpinning the very foundations of environmental law are moral, social, economic, political, and even spiritual beliefs and obligations. These will differ according to the society in which the laws operate. What remains constant, however, is that the protection of the environment is necessary for the good of mankind. Political or economic considerations should not put the human race itself at peril. Sustainable development should be the new slogan for progressive growth.

---

[21] Section 8 of the Pakistan EPA.
[22] Section 11 of the Pakistan EPA.
[23] Section 3 of the ECA.

2 The Concept of Sustainable Development

Human beings and nature are inextricably connected and this fact has led to the view that protection of nature is a prerequisite for the survival of mankind. For over a century, industrial society has viewed nature not only as a rich reserve of resources but also as a dump for refuse, reflecting Lavoisier's Law.[1] This false notion on which the economic superstructure has been built has led to the adoption of an economic growth model founded on indiscriminate exploitation of natural resources. Another misconception is the equation of economic growth with development, which has lured mankind into adopting a 'developmental model' based on material prospects because this offered immediate and attractive benefits.[2] The global ramifications of the adversity of environmental degradation, triggered by this growth model,

awakened the worldwide community to seriously consider ecological realities.[3] The overwhelming reality blanketing our planet is a grim picture of impoverished masses getting sick and dying, due to the lack of basic needs.

THE RIGHT TO DEVELOPMENT

These ecological realities hastened the need to reconcile the 'Right to Development', which was a corollary of human rights, and the duty to maintain and improve the environment.[4] The 'development' is not only the growth of GNP (Gross National Product). 'The issue of development, however, cannot be separated from the conceptual frame work of human right[s].'[5]

Development, however, does not mean that of only the elite and urban rich, but also of the people who live in so-called developing and under-developed countries.[6] It must be 'a comprehensive, economic, social, and

[1] Nicholas de Sadeleer, *Environmental Principles: From Political Slogans to Legal Rules*, Oxford: Oxford University Press, 2005, p. 14.

[2] V. Rajya Lakshmi, 'Sustainable Development—What it Means? A Few Reflections', *The Academy Law Review*, 23 (1 and 2), 1999, pp. 107–8.

[3] Ibid., p. 107; also see Ramsay Muir, 'The Interdependent World and its Problems', cited in David W. Orr and Marvin S. Soroos (eds), *The Global Predicament: Ecological Perspectives on World Order*, Chapel Hill: University of North Caroline Press, 1979, p. 284.

[4] Infra note 6, p. 238, 240. 'Right to development is an inalienable human right', Article 1, Declaration on the Right to Development, 1986.

[5] Amartya Sen, *Development as Freedom*, Oxford: Oxford University Press, 1999.

[6] Kamala Priya P.T., 'Environment and Sustainable Development', [2002 III], *Madras Law Journal*, vol. 8, p. 9.

cultural process which aims at the constant improvement and well-being of the entire population and of all individuals on the basis of their active, free, and meaningful participation in development and in the fair distribution of the benefits resulting there from.'[7]

Some of the earlier measures to address these problems proceeded on the basis of a pre-determined notion of considering 'economic growth and ecological viability' as mutually contradictory. The 'Zero Growth Model' formulated by the 'Club of Rome' in 1972 is an example. Increasing environmental stresses began to expose the fragility of the ecosphere, which had a direct bearing on limiting economic pursuits, signalling an impending catastrophe at our door-step. From this understanding emerged the mantra 'Sustainable Development', connoting a notion of enduring development or one that lasts.

THE PRINCIPLE OF SUSTAINABLE DEVELOPMENT

Poverty is an anathema to development. The phantom of poverty looming large over vast landscapes of underdeveloped and developing countries, including India, poses a unique challenge to economic development. One mantra to escape from this quagmire seems to be a positive approach towards industrialization. Hence, the biggest challenge before the underdeveloped and developing nations today is to peddle an acceleration in industrialization, viewed as instrumental in reducing poverty and ignorance. However, industrialization, if is pursued without any consideration, can lead to indiscriminate exploitation of nature. Hence, the middle ground: the revolutionary concept of Sustainable Development.

The traditional concept that development and ecology are opposed to each other is no longer an acceptable argument. Sustainable Development is the new buzzword, used to counter traditional notions of development and ecology as incongruous concepts. It places human beings at the centre of its concern.[8] Although the ideas underlying the concept of Sustainable Development have permeated several international documents, both in letter and in spirit,[9] the concept came to be known for the first time in the Stockholm Declaration of 1972.[10] Thereafter, in 1987, it was given further definition by the World Commission on Environment and Development in its report titled 'Our Common Future'. Here, the concept was defined as: 'development that meets the needs of the present without compromising the ability of the future generations to meet their own needs'.[11] The Commission was chaired by the then prime minister of Norway, G.H. Brundtland; hence the report is commonly known as the 'Brundtland Report'. In 1991, the World Conservation Union, United Nations Environment Programme and Worldwide Fund for Nature, jointly produced a document called 'Caring for the Earth' which is a strategy for sustainable living. Finally, the Earth Summit held in June 1992 at Rio saw the largest gathering of world leaders in history.[12] After much deliberation

---

[7] See Preamble to the Declaration on the Right to Development, (1986); also quoted in separate opinion of Vice-President Weeramantry in *Gabcikovo-Nagymaros (Hungary/Slovakia)*.

[8] See Principle 1 of Rio Declaration, 1992.

[9] Founex Meeting of Experts, Switzerland, 1971; The Conference on Environment and Development, 1971; United Nations General Assembly No. 2849 (XXVI) etc.

[10] Principle 11.

[11] Philippe Sands, 'Principles of International Environmental Law', *Frameworks, Standards & Implementation*, vol. 1, Manchester: Manchester University Press: 1995, p. 198.

[12] UN Conference on Environment and Development, Rio De Janeiro (Brazil), 3–14 June 1992.

they managed to chalk out a blueprint for the survival of planet Earth, known as the Rio Declaration. Among the tangible achievements of the Rio Conference was the signing of two conventions, one on biological diversity[13] and another on climate change.[14] These were signed by 153 nations. The delegates also approved, by consensus, three non-binding documents: a Statement on Forestry principles, a declaration of principles on environmental policy and development initiatives,[15] and Agenda 21,[16] a programme for action over the next century in relation to issues such as poverty, population, and pollution.

Sustainable Development, as defined by the Brundtland Commission, is built upon two foundations. The first is the objective concept of 'human needs like food, clothing, shelter, clean water, and all other essentials which contribute to the quality of life', while the other is a normative concept that 'emphasizes a balance of equity, environment, and growth, by contemplating [the] fully apparent non-renewal capacity of our environment.'[17]

Four recurring principles appear to comprise the legal elements of the concept of Sustainable Development as reflected in these international agreements. They are:

1. Intergenerational equity.
2. Sustainable use, vis-à-vis use and conservation of natural resources.

3. Intragenerational equity.
4. Integration.[18]

There is an incumbent duty on the part of the present generation to preserve the environment from deterioration, ensuring a fair measure of resources provided by the environment for future generations. The logic behind this doctrine of Intergenerational Equity is to ensure that, for the benefit of the present generation, the survival of future generations is not jeopardized. All that the ethics of 'Intergenerational Equity' demand is a care for the future.[19] This has been given more impetus by holding environmental degradation as a violation of the enjoyment of private and family life.

Sustainable Development as a balancing concept between ecology and development has been accepted as a part of customary international law, though its salient features have yet to be finalized by international legal jurists. These salient features can be described as: The Precautionary Principle; The Polluter

---

[13] Convention on Biological Diversity, held at Rio De Janeiro, 1760 UNTS 79.

[14] United Nations Framework Convention on Climate Change 1771 UNTS 107.

[15] Rio Declaration on Environment and Development, UN Doc. A/CONF.151/26 (vol. I).

[16] UN GAOR, 46th Sess., Agenda Item 21, UN Doc A/Conf.151/26 (1992).

[17] See R.N. Batta and J.P. Bhatti, 'Environmental Policy Challenges of the New Millennium', in S. Radha and Amar Singh Sankhyan (eds), *Environmental Challenges of the 21st Century*, Delhi: Deep & Deep Publications, 2004, p. 4.

[18] Ibid.; Principle 11, Stockholm Declaration, 1972, 'The environmental policies of all States should enhance and not adversely affect the present or future development potential of developing countries, nor should they hamper the attainment of better living conditions for all, and appropriate steps should be taken by States and international organizations with a view to reaching an agreement on meeting the possible national and international economic consequences resulting from the application of environmental measures'; Principle 1, Rio Declaration, 1992, 'Human beings are at the centre of concerns for sustainable development. They are entitled to a healthy and productive life in harmony with nature'; Agenda 21, 14 June 1992; General Assembly Resolution 42/187. Report of the World Commission on Environment and Development, 96th plenary meeting, 11 December 1987; see also Brundtland Commission Report.

[19] a .v. Secretary, DENR, 22, Philippine Supreme Court Report Annotated, 33 ILM 173 (1994).

Pays Principle; Eradication of Poverty and Financial Assistance to the Developing Countries Principle; and the Principle of Prevention.[20]

There is no universally accepted standard definition of the Precautionary Principle. A variety of common-sense elements can be recognized as part of the definition.

1. It acknowledges that the vulnerability of the environment and scarcity of resources necessitate their protection and conservation.

2. Science has a limited ability to accurately predict threats to the environment. This element is important in fisheries management, where it is especially difficult to determine the relationship between an observed effect in the marine environment and a particular fishing activity suspected of causing the effect. It has been argued that experience in fisheries has indicated that delaying regulation in order to accumulate data may lead to undesirable changes in stocks, such as stock collapse. There indeed may be cases where perfect or better information will not greatly enhance the management process.[21]

3. There is a need to set conservative evidentiary thresholds for taking action. Two terms have been used most often to define the threshold, that is, 'threats of serious or irreversible harm' (in the Rio Declaration) and 'unacceptable impacts' (in UN General Assembly Resolution 44/225).[22] These set the levels of risk or harm which trigger a determination that the proposed fishing or whaling activities are not compatible with precautionary management.

4. There is no requirement to remove the burden of proof from those opposing a potentially destructive activity and to place it on those seeking to promote such an activity. In this context, it is interesting to note that John Gummer, who made the UK's opening statement at the IWC's 44th Meeting in Glasgow (1992), said that the 'burden of proof for lifting the moratorium...must rest with those who say they want to continue to exploit [whale stocks].'[23]

5. Impact assessments should be conducted prior to undertaking a proposed activity. It has been suggested that in the context of fisheries, this would involve an evaluation of the environmental and the socio-economic effects of any proposed fishing activity.[24]

The other features of Sustainable Development are best understood by an analysis of Indian case laws.

INDIAN CASE LAWS

After the Rio Declaration (1992), which saw the formal incorporation of the 'Sustainable

---

[20] See T.S. Doabia J., *Environmental and Pollution Laws in India*, vol. 1, Nagpur: Wadhwa Publications, p. 460; also refer de Sadeleer, *Environmental Principles*, pp. 61–89.

[21] A. Constable, 'The Role of Science in Environment Protection', *Australian Journal of Marine and Freshwater Research* (1991), cited in G.J. Hewison, 'The Precautionary Principle and Application to the Management of Straddling Stocks and Highly Migratory Fish', paper presented at the Greenpeace symposium on high seas fishing (Wellington, New Zealand), 2 July 1993.

[22] UN General Assembly Resolution, 'Large Scale Drifnet Fishing and its Impacts on the Living Resources of the World's Oceans and Seas', reprinted in 29 ILM 1556 (1990). http://www.un.org/documents/ga/res/50/ares50-25.htm/

[23] IWC/44/OS UK para 7.

[24] Simon Marr, *The Precautionary Principle in the Law of the Sea: Modern Decision Making in International Law*, Leiden: Martinus Nijhoff Publishers, 2003.

Development Principle', courts in India incorporated it in their judgements. Thus, in the *Vellore Citizens Welfare Forums* case,[25] and the *M.C. Mehta* case,[26] the balance between environmental protection and developmental activities could only be maintained by the strict compliance of the Principle of Sustainable Development.[27] The symbiotic balance between the right to environment and development can be maintained by Sustainable Development. In fact, the principle of Sustainable Development is *sine qua non* for nurturing the weighty concepts of intergenerational equity,[28] the Public Trust doctrine,[29] the Polluter Pays principle,[30] and the Precautionary principle.[31] The testimony of judicial acumen that is mirrored in the plethora of decisions indicates that the Indian judiciary has been successful to a considerable extent in striking a harmonious balance between development and ecological concerns.

There are two conflicting, yet complementary, aspects involved. These are the 'Right to Development'[32] and the 'Right to Clean and Healthy Environment'. Both had been declared an integral part of the 'Right to Life' under Article 21. A swift glance through contemporary judgements delivered by the apex court shows a clear tilt towards 'Pro-Developmental Approach' away from the erstwhile 'Pro-Ecological Approach'. However, it would be incorrect to say that the apex court altogether forgot its environmental concerns, or tilted towards an entirely pro-developmental approach. In fact, in *Doon Valley's* case,[33] which was the first case involving issues relating to environment and development, even while ordering the closure of lime stone quarries, the court was concerned about developmental issues. It could be that the concept of 'Sustainable Development' which was in its infancy at the time, failed to catch the attention of the court.

The Indian judiciary has accepted the principle of Sustainable Development as law in a case of pollution being created by the tanneries in Tamil Nadu.[34] The leather industry in India has become a major source of foreign revenue, while also providing employment. At the same time, tanneries cause much damage and degradation towards ecology and environment, and also pose a hazard to public health. It is in these circumstances that the Supreme Court has held that the Precautionary Principle and the Polluter Pays Principle are essential features of Sustainable Development and part of the law of the land. The Precautionary Principle was elucidated by the Supreme Court, inter alia, as follows:

1. The State Government and statutory authorities must anticipate, prevent, and attack the causes of environmental degradation.
2. Where there is a threat of serious and irreversible damage, lack of scientific certainty should not be used as a reason

---

[25] *Vellore Citizens Welfare Forum v. Union of India*, (1996) 5 SCC 647.

[26] *M.C. Mehta v. Union of India*, (2002) 4 SCC 353.

[27] *N.D. Jayal v. Union of India*, 2004 KHC 898, para 22; also see *Narmada Bachao Andolan v. Union of India*, (2002) 10 SCC 664.

[28] *State of Himachal Pradesh v. Ganesh Wood Products*, (1995) 6 SCC 363.

[29] *M.C. Mehta v. Kamal Nath*, (1997) 1 SCC 388.

[30] *Indian Council for Enviro-Legal Action v. Union of India*, (1996) 3 SCC 212; *M.C. Mehta v. Union of India*, AIR 1987 SC 1086.

[31] *Vellore Citizens Welfare Forum v. Union of India*, (1996) 5 SCC 647 (Tanneries Case).

[32] *Samatha v. State of Andhra Pradesh*, (1997) 8 SCC 191; *Madhu Kishore v. State of Bihar*, (1996) 5 SCC 125.

[33] *Rural Litigation and Entitlement Kendra v. State of UP*, AIR 1985 SC 652.

[34] *Vellore Citizens Welfare Forum v. Union of India*, AIR 1996 SC 2715, (1996) 5 SCC 647.

for postponing measures to prevent environmental degradation.

3. The 'onus of proof' to show that the action is environmentally benign is on the actor or the developer.

Hence, actors or developers must err on the side of caution in the face of scientific uncertainty. The Precautionary Principle has been followed in a number of cases. To control emissions from motor vehicles, various directives have been issued by the Supreme Court.[35] Applications made by the Government of India for allowing variation from emission directives were dismissed by the Supreme Court. The Court held that the directives issued by the committee appointed by it were statutory. These continue to be in force. Standards have been prescribed to check air pollution created by motor vehicles. The emission norms stipulated by the Government have failed to monitor air pollution, which has reached dangerous levels across the country. Therefore, the Supreme Court observed that to recommend that the role of the Government be limited to specifying norms is a clear abdication of the constitutional and statutory duty cast upon the Government to protect and preserve the environment, and contradicts the Precautionary Principle.

Development and protection of the environment need not be antagonistic. It is possible to avoid degradation of the environment or to minimize adverse effects by applying stringent safeguards and the Principles of Sustainable Development when undertaking developmental activities. One cannot lose sight of the eventuality that development must go on: there will always be a need for developing industries, irrigation

resources, and power projects, and the like, as well as a need to improve employment opportunities and generate revenue. Thus, a balance needs to be struck. Principle 15 of the Rio Conference of 1992, relating to the applicability of the Precautionary Principle, stated that:

…[w]here there are threats of serious or irreversible damages, lack of full scientific certainty shall not be used as a reason for postponing cost-effective measures to prevent environmental degradation.

In such matters, many a time, the preferable option is not clear. If an activity is allowed to go ahead, there could be irreparable damage to the environment; if it is stopped, there could be irreparable damage to economic interests. In case of doubt, however, protection of environment should take precedence over economic interest. The Precautionary Principle requires anticipatory action to be taken to prevent harm. This harm can be prevented even on a reasonable suspicion. It is not always necessary that there should be direct evidence of harm to the environment.[36]

Acquisition and development of land for industrial purposes is always a problem in India. The Supreme Court has made it mandatory to obtain clearance from the State Pollution Control Board and Department of Ecology before setting up an industry. Based on the principle of Sustainable Development, the Supreme Court has held that before the acquisition of land for development, the consequent impact of the proposed development on the environment must be properly comprehended in order to ensure that the ecology and the environment are not gravely impaired in the process.[37]

---

[35] M.C. Mehta v. Union of India, AIR 2001 SC 1862, 2001 (4) JT 396 , 2001 (4) SCC 729.

[36] M.C. Mehta v. Union of India, AIR 2004 SC 4033.
[37] Karnataka Industrial Areas Development Board v. C. Kenchappa, AIR 2006 SC 2038, 2006 AIR SCW 2547.

TAJ MAHAL—PROTECTION OF ANCIENT MONUMENTS

To protect the world famous monument, the Taj Mahal, the Supreme Court has issued various directions for the relocation of certain industries. The employees working in these industries were given protection when passing the closure orders. This was done with the application of the Precautionary Principle,[38] as such directions were made to prevent further environmental degradation.

Depleting ground-water levels is a threat to ecology. The National Environmental Engineering Research Institute (NEERI) has opined in its report filed before the Supreme Court that management of water resources in a manner that achieves the goal of Sustainable Development warrants legal intervention, based on the principle of Intergenerational and Intragenerational Equity, the Precautionary Principle, conservation of natural resources, and environmental protection.[39] To protect ground water, the Supreme Court has issued orders invoking the Precautionary Principle. The ground water authority was constituted as a result of this judgement.

POLLUTER PAYS PRINCIPLE

Industrialization was seen as a means for mankind to attain the Promised Land, the *paradise* of economic prosperity. In pursuit of his goals, man yielded to his basic instincts of greed and selfishness, and began to exploit nature. Little did he heed the prophecy of Gandhi that: 'The earth provides enough for everyone's need but not for some people's greed'.[40] Economists argued that the use of natural resources for industrialization has had both positive and negative externalities. Economic progress and a general rise in standards of living, etc., contributed to positive externalities. In that case it is axiomatic that industrial pollution came to be regarded as a negative externality. Ultimately, it all came down to economics—when negative externalities began to outpace positive outcomes, the question arose as to who should be made liable for this effect. The simple answer was to make the polluter pay for the pollution generated. Thus emerged the Polluter Pays Principle'.[41] Industrial units polluting the river were directed to bear the expenses of cleaning polluted river and dams and pay compensation to affected farmers. The Supreme Court held that the principles of 'polluter-pay' and 'precautionary principle' have to be read with the doctrine of 'sustainable development'. It becomes the duty of the industries to carry out their industrial activities without polluting the water.[42]

The Polluter Pays Principle is an economic as well as an administrative measure to curb and control the menace of pollution. It is an economic rule of cost allocation because it requires polluters to take responsibility for external costs arising from pollution by internalizing them.[43] It is an administrative measure in that it involves intervention by public authorities, by prescribing taxation corresponding to the economic costs of

[38] *M.C. Mehta v. Union of India*, (1997) 1 SCC 353, AIR 1997 SC 734.

[39] *M.C. Mehta v. Union of India*, (1997) 11 SCC 312.

[40] Speech titled 'Environment—Problems and Solutions', delivered by D.M. Dharmadhikari, AIR 2003, Journal 161.

[41] Ibid.

[42] *Tirupur Dyeing Factory Owners Association v. Noyyal River Ayacutdara Protection Association*, 2009 (9) SCC 737: AIR 2010 SC 3645.

[43] A.C. Pigou, *The Economics of Welfare*, 2nd edn, London: Macmillan, 1924, argued that 'external costs should be internalized: that is, integrated into the price of the goods or services in question, by charging those responsible for them.

environmental damage;[44] and by prescribing regulatory standards to prohibit or limit the damage associated with an economic activity.[45] Judicial activism in India saw the application of this principle, implicitly, in the *Oleum Gas Leakage* case,[46] and, explicitly, in *Indian Council for Enviro-Legal Action v. Union of India*.[47] As we have seen, the Polluter Pays Principle is an offshoot of the principle of Sustainable Development. Since Sustainable Development is an integral part of Article 21, and the Polluter Pays Principle an essential part of Sustainable Development, the former naturally comes under the umbrella of right to life under Article 21.[48] The adage 'Prevention is better than cure' forms the bedrock on which the Precautionary Principle is based. There are several laws in India based on the principle of prevention, like the Prevention of Damage to Public Property Act, 1984; Prevention of Corruption Act, 1988; Prevention of Cruelty to Animals Act, 1960; Conservation of Foreign Exchange and Prevention of Smuggling Activities Act, 1974; Prevention of Dangerous Activities of Bootleggers, Drug-offenders, Gamblers, Goondas, Immoral Traffic Offenders, and Slum Grabbers Act, 1985; and many other

Acts. Likewise, before carrying out any activity that affects the ecology, prior sanction from the authorities concerned is required.

Case Law

The Polluter Pays Principle basically provides that producers of goods or other items should bear the financial and practical responsibility of preventing or remedying any pollution caused by their activities. This includes all environmental costs, as well as direct costs to people or property. It also extends to costs incurred in avoiding pollution, and not just to those related to remedying damage. The responsibility encompasses all environmental costs and not just those that are immediately tangible. Having said this, the principle cannot be used to allow a person to pollute on the basis that they will pay for it. The nature and extent of the costs and the circumstances in which the principle will apply differ depending on the case. It has been established by the Supreme Court, however, that the principle is to be given a broad interpretation.[49]

The KHC had the occasion to consider the above rule when considering an assignment of forest land. The Court held that each occupier/encroacher of forest land who pays for regularization and consequent issue of title deeds in his favour shall pay a reasonable amount of compensation to the State for the injury caused by him to the general public.[50]

An officer empowered to grant licences for mining in the state of Kerala has imposed a condition that no quarrying shall be done within 75 metres of a railway line and 50 metres of public road, water course, residential building, boundary wall of place of worship,

---

[44] An example that can be cited in this respect is the direction of Supreme Court to collect pollution fines from tanneries (in *Vellore Citizens Welfare Forum v. Union of India*, [1996] 5 SCC 647) and from shrimp culture ponds violating CRZ Regulations (in *S. Jagannath v. Union of India*, AIR 1997 SC 811, [1997] 2 SCC 87), under a separate head called 'Environment Protection Fund' for compensating affected persons and also for restoring damaged environment.

[45] Ibid; also Public Liability Insurance Act, 1991; National Environment Tribunal Act, 1995.

[46] *M.C. Mehta v. Union of India*, AIR 1987 SC 1086.

[47] (1996) 3 SCC 212.

[48] *Vellore Citizens Welfare Forum v. Union of India*, (1996) 5 SCC 647; *M.C. Mehta v. Union of India*, AIR 1997 SC 734; *S. Jagannath v. Union of India*, 1997 SC 811; (1997) 2 SCC 87; *M.C. Mehta v. Kamalnath*, (1997) 1 SCC 388.

[49] *Research Foundation v. Union of India*, 2003 (8) SCALE 258.

[50] *Nature Lovers Movement v. State of Kerala*, AIR 2000 Ker 131 ILR 2000 (1) Ker 677.

burial grounds or burning *ghats*. This rule can be accepted under and in accordance with the previous permission of the state government or the competent authority. However, no removal of water from the mine pit using a pump is permissible. Once this becomes necessary, mining must cease—manual mining is then required. This was challenged before the KHC where it was contended that mining legislation does not empower a geologist to impose conditions not found in statute. However, the geologist explained that the prohibition against the use of pumps was imposed taking into consideration geological parameters and other scientific components so as to avoid the danger of lateral collapse in the sand mining pit. In view of the principle of Sustainable Development, and the Polluter Pays and Precautionary principles, it has been held that the conditions imposed are necessary to protect the environment.[51]

The KHC, in extending the principle of Sustainable Development, has held that no person can claim an absolute right, even on his own land, to indulge in activities resulting in environmental degradation.[52]

In Rajasthan, certain factories carrying on the business of dyeing and printing cloth were discharging toxic substances in canals from which water was being used for agriculture and drinking. The Rajasthan High Court, while dealing with the issue, directed industries and the State and its agencies to set up a common effluent treatment plant so that effluents were not discharged into the said water body.[53]

The Supreme Court, accepting the principle of Sustainable Development, has held that in future, the project proponent must carry out a necessary exercise regarding the impact of development on ecology and the environment before acquisition of land for industrial development. Necessary sanction must be obtained from the State Pollution Control Board concerned before the land is allotted for development.[54]

There are several state laws in India that impose a duty on the authorities to impose mandatory duties that are necessary for the protection of the health of the public.[55] These laws also contain provisions based on the Precautionary Principle. Besides, local self-government institutions like municipalities *grama panchayats*, and *mahapalikas* have also been entrusted with the duty to protect public health.

AWARDING OF DAMAGES

A question arose as to whether the Supreme Court can award damages in a PIL invoking the Polluter Pays Principle. The powers of the Supreme Court under Article 32 are not restricted and it can award damages in a PIL or a writ petition.[56] The Polluter Pays Principle has been also used as a basis for awarding damages. In addition to assessed damages, the person guilty of causing pollution can be held liable for exemplary damages, thus acting as a deterrent.

DEVELOPMENTS ABROAD

The first cases to utilize the Precautionary Principle in the USA involved public health. Major Precautionary Principle cases arise under specific statutes that refer to pollution that 'endangers' public health, rather than in common law litigation. The term 'endanger' has

---

[51] *Soman v. Geologist*, 2004 (3) KLT 577.

[52] *Thilakan v. Circle Inspector of Police*, 2007 (4) KLT 536.

[53] *Singh Punia v. Rajasthan State Board of Pollution Control of Water Pollution*, AIR 2003 Raj 286.

[54] *Karnataka Industrial Areas Development Board v. C. Kenchappa*, (2006) 6 SCC 371.

[55] Madras Public Health Act, 1939.

[56] *M.C. Mehta v. Union of India*, AIR 2000 SC 1997, 2000 (5) SCALE 69.

been interpreted as mandating a precautionary approach.

For example, in *Reserve Mining Co. v. U.S. Environmental Protection Agency*[57] a case involving an appeal by Reserve Mining Co. after losing in the District Court in *U.S. EPA v. Reserve Mining Co.* the Court said:

In assessing probabilities in this case, it cannot be said that the probability of harm is more likely than not. Moreover, the level of probability does not readily convert into a prediction of consequences. On this record it cannot be forecast that the rates of cancer will increase from drinking Lake Superior water or breathing Silver Bay air. The best that can be said is that the existence of this asbestos contaminant in air and water gives rise to a reasonable medical concern for the public health. The public's exposure to asbestos fibers in air and water creates some health risk. Such a contaminant should be removed.

The US Court of Appeals for the Eighth Circuit (covering the midwestern states of the USA) quoted, with approval, J. Skelly Wright's dissent in *Ethyl Corp. v. EPA* (US Court of Appeals for the DC Circuit). Wright's dissent (in a 2:1 decision) became the majority a year later, when the DC Circuit re-heard the case *en banc*. The judges voted 5:4 in favour of his precautionary interpretation of the term 'endanger' in the *Clean Air Act* case. In that case, the DC Circuit (J. Skelly Wright for the majority) wrote:

Where a statute is precautionary in nature, the evidence difficult to come by, uncertain, or conflicting because it is on the frontiers of scientific knowledge, the regulations designed to protect the public health, and the decision that of an expert administrator, we will not demand rigorous step-by-step proof of cause and effect. Such proof may be impossible to obtain if the precautionary purpose of the statute is to be served.[58]

Meanwhile, in *Reserve Mining*,[59] the Eighth Circuit applied federal statutory law, as the DC Circuit had done in the *Ethyl* case. It held that the 'federal common law of nuisance' did not apply because there was no evidence of effects outside the single state of Minnesota. The Eighth Circuit also interpreted and applied state law, finding specific statutory violations of state law:

In light of this statute, we deem it unnecessary to discuss whether Reserve's air emissions could constitute a public nuisance independently of violations of the state's air pollution control regulations.[60]

Hence, *Reserve Mining* is not a legal precedent involving either federal or state common law (nuisance law), but is a clear holding that the Precautionary Principle must be used to interpret federal and state statutory law.

After the landmark 1975 decision by the Eighth Circuit, the case was remitted to the US District Court for further proceedings. The District Court ordered 'that Reserve and its parent corporations cease discharge of taconite tailings into Lake Superior one year from today, at midnight on 7 July 1977'. The company appealed again to the Court of Appeals, which then ruled that: 'The district judge properly construed our mandate and his ruling must be affirmed.'[61]

The importance of *Reserve Mining* in the development of US legal doctrine has been commented on. John S. Applegate writes:

Reserve Mining remains the archetype for the regulation of chemical threats to human health, because the central problem for the court was the management of scientific uncertainty, the salient characteristic of this area of environmental law

---

[57] 514 F.2d 492 (US Court of Appeals for the 8th Circuit, 14 March 1975).

[58] *Ethyl Corp. v. EPA*, 541 F.2d 1 (DC Cir. 1976) (en banc).

[59] Ibid.

[60] *Reserve Mining Co. v. U.S. Environmental Protection Agency*, 514 F.2d 492 (8th Cir. 1975).

[61] *United States v. Reserve Mining Co.*, 543 F.2d 1210 (8th Cir., 28 October 1976).

and policy. The facts of *Reserve Mining* posed the problem of uncertainty in a particularly stark way: the inhalation hazards of asbestos were well known, but what was the danger from ingestion of asbestos fibers in drinking water? To decide the case, the court had to analyse the parties' scientific disagreement in detail, and it had to determine whether the applicable law was remedial and based on proven harm, or precautionary and seeking to avoid harms before they are realized or even fully understood. The Eighth Circuit took up this challenge in *Reserve Mining*, and the result was a landmark of environmental law whose science-based, precautionary approach continues to influence the regulation of toxic threats to human health and the environment.[62]

The story of the *Reserve Mining* litigation is a fascinating one. The litigation was catalysed by a community activist who attended a conference, where she was handed a published study about a Japanese study of stomach cancer resulting from drinking water with asbestos fibres (whereas previously the only public health threat had been thought to be via air pollution). She mentioned it to the participants in the conference and was mostly ignored. However, a scientist sitting in the audience took note, informed his boss, and they started testing the water for the asbestos fibres. The scientist saw a dream that people were dying from the water, which propelled him to go to the office and do more research, resulting in him finding a scientist in New York who concluded that there was indeed such a threat. However, when the District Judge was considering the matter, the EPA refused to ask for an injunction, while scientists were troubled by uncertainties.

They were not willing to state flatly that there was a problem.

The judge then asked the chief EPA scientist, the Director of the National Water Quality Laboratory, if he was still drinking public water (which came from the lake). He replied that he had stopped drinking it. At this point, proceedings progressed rapidly.

Applegate writes, further, that:

The government's case in *Reserve Mining* was indeed scientifically tenuous, but rather than accept inaction in the face of danger, the court found in federal environmental law a precautionary approach to scientific uncertainty. This is the great legacy of the case and the outstanding principle for which it stands today. Substantively, precaution meant sharply distinguishing preventive regulation from tort law. The court accepted *risk*, instead of actually demonstrated or more-likely-than-not harm, as the basis for environmental regulation. Procedurally, the Eighth Circuit sitting en banc concluded (as did the DC Circuit in *Ethyl*, also sitting en banc) that the burden of uncertainty must lie with the risk-creator. Otherwise, uncertainty would be a virtually insurmountable barrier to the environmentally protective action that Congress clearly intended.

The foregoing are also the central tenets of the Precautionary Principle, a concept that has gained broad acceptance in international environmental law. Its most common formulation echoes *Reserve Mining*, and it, too, identifies scientific uncertainty as the central problem in environmental regulation. Like *Reserve*, the Precautionary Principle requires a firm scientific basis for concern and a serious harm in prospect, and it permits regulatory action before the uncertainty has been resolved. That is clearly the gist of Brown's statement, quoted by the court, 'As a medical person, sir, I think that I have to err, if err I do, on the side of what is best for the greatest number'.

The facts of *Reserve Mining* posed the problem of uncertainty in a particularly stark way: despite the fact that the inhalation hazards of asbestos are well known, what is

[62] John S. Applegate, 'The Story of Reserve Mining: Managing Scientific Uncertain in Environmental Regulation', Richard Lazarus and Oliver Houck (eds), in *Environmental Law Stories*, US: Thomson & West, 2005.

the danger from ingestion of asbestos fibres in drinking water?

The Eighth Circuit faced this challenge in *Reserve Mining*, and the result was a landmark in environmental law whose rational and pragmatic, precautionary approach continues to influence the regulation of toxic threats to human health and the environment.

EXTENDED POLLUTER PAYS

The Swedish government introduced the system of Extended Polluter Pays (EPR) in 1975. EPR seeks to shift the responsibility of dealing with waste from governments to the entities producing it. In effect, it internalizes the cost of waste disposal into the cost of the product, theoretically meaning that the producers will improve the waste profile of their products, thus decreasing waste and increasing possibilities for reuse and recycling.

The Organization for Economic Co-operation and Development (OECD), France, defines EPR as follows:

a concept where manufacturers and importers of products should bear a significant degree of responsibility for the environmental impacts of their products throughout the product life-cycle, including upstream impacts inherent in the selection of materials for the products, impacts from manufacturers' production process itself, and downstream impacts from the use and disposal of the products. Producers accept their responsibility when designing their products to minimize life-cycle environmental impacts, and when accepting legal, physical or socio-economic responsibility for environmental impacts that cannot be eliminated by design.

An industry which is earning millions may be prepared to pay lakhs as pollution fine, which is only a pittance to them. But if EPR principle is applied such industries will be able to go scot free, unless it pays a heavy fine as a reformative fine.

ECOLOGICALLY SUSTAINABLE DEVELOPMENT

Ecologically Sustainable Development (ESD) represents one of the greatest challenges facing Australia's governments, industry, business, and community. There is no universally accepted definition of ESD. However, Commonwealth Government suggested the following definition for ESD in Australia:

using, conserving and enhancing the community's resources so that ecological processes, on which life depends, are maintained, and the total quality of life, now and in the future, can be increased.[63]

Australia has the Department of the Environment, Water, Heritage and the Arts for the transition of ESD.

A litigation was launched by a local resident challenging the approval of a Concept Plan of a development at Sandon Point. The Plan was for the development of 285 homes and care facility for the aged to be built on flood-prone coastal land. It was contended that the minister failed to take into consideration the recommendations and findings of a Commission of Inquiry report, and that the minister failed to apply the principles of ESD when deciding to approve the proposal.

The Land Environmental Court of New South Wales by a detailed judgement reviewed the principles of ESD as well as US and Australian case law on climate change. The court found that the Minister for Planning had failed to consider ESD by failing to consider whether the impacts of the proposed development would be compounded by climate change; in particular, by failing to consider whether changed weather patterns would lead to an increased flood risk in connection with the proposed development in circumstances

---

[63] http://www.environment.gov.au/esd/national/nsesd/strategy/intro.html#WIESD.

where flooding was identified as a major constraint on development of the site.[64]

Proceedings were initiated in the Land and Environment Court challenging the validity of the approval granted for re-development of the Carlton United Brewery site for 1600 residential apartments, commercial offices, and retail premises. It was argued that the Minister for Planning had failed to properly consider the principles of ESD when approving the site. It is contended that the application of ESD required a detailed consideration of the climate change impacts of the development. Rejecting the arguments that consideration of ecologically sustainable development as mere 'lip service', 'cursory', 'derisory', and 'cosmetic', and thus no consideration at all, the court accepted the decision of the minister. The project involved a very large residential and commercial development on former industrial site. Specific greenhouse gas emissions ratings were also required for the commercial component. The court felt that the applicant has not established either that the minister could only consider ecologically sustainable development by considering a quantitative assessment of greenhouse gas emissions or that the minister in fact failed to consider ecologically sustainable development, apply the precautionary principle, or consider inter-generational equity as relevant to the project, the court held.[65]

The decision of the Federal Minister for the Environment and Water Resources, a proposal to open cut a coal mine (Anvil Hill project) was challenged on the ground that it was not a controlled action under the *Environment Protection and Biodiversity Conservation Act 1999*. As a result it would not have to undergo any sort of environmental assessment at the national level because it is not, in the Commonwealth's (central government) view, likely to have a significant impact on a matter of national environmental significance. The Federal Court accepted the Minister's argument and dismissed the application[66] which was confirmed in appeal.[67]

The law related to Sustainable Development is still evolving. Much remains to be done or achieved because there are many factors involved. As we are increasingly challenged by environmental problems, which one would not have comprehended a decade ago and which threaten human health and survival, the principle of Sustainable Development will require to more clearly understood by litigants and judges alike.

---

[64] *Walker v. Minister for Planning,* [2007] NSWLEC 741 (27 November 2007).

[65] *Drake-Brockman v. Minister for Planning and Another,* [2007] NSWLEC 490.

[66] *Anvil Hill Project Watch Association Inc v. Minister for Environment and Water Resources and Another,* (2008) FCAFC 3.

[67] *Anvil Hill Project Watch Association Inc v. Minister for Environment and Water Resources and Centennial Hunter Pty Ltd,* (2007) FCA 1480.

3 The Public Trust Doctrine

By the law of nature these things are common to mankind—the air, running water, the sea and consequently the shores of the sea.[1]
—Institutes of Justinian 2.1.1

THE PUBLIC TRUST DOCTRINE EXPLAINED

The Public Trust Doctrine was originally espoused by the Emperor Justinian, during the Roman Empire. It provided that 'certain common properties such as rivers, seashore, forests, and the air were held by government in trusteeship for the free and unimpeded use of the general public.'[2] This formed the basis for the English common law Public Trust Doctrine.

This doctrine of ancient prodigy is the most comprehensive and prudent among all environmental doctrines. The Public Trust Doctrine is based on the fact that natural resources are a legacy of mankind, their conservation a common concern of all mankind; states are the sole trustees of these natural resources and it is their duty to protect common heritage for the benefit of present and future generations. It is the ostensible affirmation of the fact that management of natural resources, being the administrative responsibility of the state, cannot be delegated to anyone. The doctrine thus serves a twofold function. On the one hand, it preserves the integrated system of the sovereign power of the state in protecting this public trust; on the other hand it discharges an environmental mandate, a societal contract, and a generational duty of preserving the property as a trust for future generations.[3]

The Public Trust Doctrine is an example of ancient dexterity. This theory is supposed to have been developed by the Ancient Roman Empire, which considered rivers, forests, and other natural resources, as common to everyone (*res communious*) and owned by no particular individual (*res nullious*). Historically, India, for a long time, had recognized the public duty of rulers to protect natural resources and to maintain those that were of common good and use.[4] Ancient Indian legal texts like the *Manusmriti* and *Arthashastra* extolled this prudent doctrine.[5] Even Buddhist sermons

---

[1] *M.C. Mehta v. Kamal Nath and Others*, reported in (1997)1 SCC 388, 1996 (9) SCALE 141, JT 1996 (II) SC 467, 32.

[2] Ibid., 24.

[3] See *National Audubon Society v. The Superior Court of Alpine Country*, 658 P. 2d 709 (1983); also *W.I.F Reality Corp and Reed Rubin v. State of New York*, (1998).

[4] *Madras Railway Co. v. Zamindar of Carvetnagar*, (1874) LR IA 364, ibid p. 195, FN. 1.

[5] *Manusmriti*, VII: 14; Kautilya's *Arthashastra*:

A king shall augment his power by promoting the welfare of his people; for power comes from the country side which

contained the first principles of trusteeship of the Earth's resources.[6]

However, the evolution of the modern doctrine of public trust can be traced to Emperor Justinian (AD 530) and its integration into English common law.[7] From this common law, the doctrine spread to the USA where it deeply imbedded itself in the law and culture.[8]

By a catena of cases since 1892, the Federal Supreme Court of America began to accommodate the Public Trust Doctrine,[9] playing an important role in making this doctrine a part of the law of land.[10] In addition, several state constitutions of the USA have explicitly or implicitly recognized this doctrine.[11]

Likewise, the Indian legal system, derived from English common law, includes the Public Trust Doctrine. This doctrine forms the crux on which Article 47 of the Constitution is based.[12] In fact, the objectives enshrined in the Preamble and Directive Principles of State Policy impose an obligation on the state as well as its citizens to preserve the environment and its use for the maximum benefit of people. Certain statutes reflect the Public Trust Doctrine in certain sections.[13]

However, the Indian judiciary, which thrives on the prophetic words of V.R. Krishna Iyer, 'judges are the trustees of the human estate, the world's great heritage' enunciated the Public Trust Doctrine implicitly through a plethora of cases.[14]

---

is the source of all economic activity. He shall build forts, because they provide a haven to the people & the king himself; waterworks since reservoirs make water continuously available for agriculture; trade routes since they are useful available for agriculture; trade routes since they are useful for sending and receiving clandestine agents and war materials and mines for they are sources of war materials; productive forests, elephant forests and animal herds provide various useful products and animals...' {7.12.2–28}.

Translated by L.N. Ranga Rajan (Delhi: Penguin Books, 1997), pp. 180–1. See also Kautilya's *Arthashastra*: 47 (4th edition) translated by R. Shamasastry (Mysore: Sri Raghuveer Press, 1951): 'the earth does not belong to man; man belongs to the earth...for some special purpose gave you (man) dominion over his land...'; also see supra note 283. p. 195.

[6] 'O great King, the birds of the air and the beasts have as equal a right to live and move about in any part of the land as thou. The land belongs to the people and all living beings; thou art only the guardian of it'. Quoted by Weeramantry, in *Gabcikovo-Nagymaros Project* case (*Republic of Hungary v. Slovak Federal Republic*) (1997) ICJ Reports 7.

[7] Magna Carta 1215, Colonial Ordinance 1647 etc.

[8] ...our dead never forget this beautiful earth, for it is the mother of Red man. We are part of the earth and it is part of us. The perfumed flowers are our sister. The horse, the great eagle, these are our brothers...the earth does not belong to man: man belongs to the earth. This we know; All things are connected like the blood which unites one family...man did not weave the web of life: he is merely a strand in it: whatever he does to the web he does to himself.

Quoted by Indian Seattle Chief to the White Chief of Washington, Mother Earth (aboriginals of USA-Tribal People, Red Indians), quoted in *Shri Sachindanand Pandey v. State of West Bengal*, AIR 1987 SC 1109, at 1112–13.

[9] *Illinois Ventral Railroad v. Illinois*, 146 US 387 (1892); *Gverr v. Connecticut*, 161 US 519, (1896).

[10] *National Audubon Society v. Superior Court of Alphine County*, 22 Cal 3d 419 cf; *Missouri v. Holland*, 252 US 416 (1920); *Kleppe v. New Mexico*, 426 US 529, (1976).

[11] States like Alabama, Alaska, California, Hawaii, Louisiana, Colorado, Florida, Illinois, Michigan, Massachusetts, Missouri, New Mexico, New York, Washington, and others, have strengthened their constitution to accommodate the Public Trust Doctrine.

[12] *Municipal Council v. Ratlam Vardhichand*, AIR 1980 SC 1622.

[13] Section 2, Forest (Conservation) Act, 1980.

[14] *M.C. Mehta v. Union of India*, AIR 1988 SC 1115; *Shri Sachidananda Pandey v. State of West Bengal*, AIR 1987 SC 1109; *T. Damodar Rao v. S.O. Municipal Corporation, Hyderabad*, AIR 1987 AP 171; *People United for Better Living in Calcutta v. State of West Bengal*, AIR 1993 Cal. 215; *Banwasi Sewa Ashram v. State of Uttar Pradesh*, AIR 1987 SC 374.

The English common law Public Trust Doctrine only applies to navigable waters. In the Indian case of *M.C. Mehta* v. *Kamal Nath and Others*,[15] the court provides an analysis of English and American law that has applied the Public Trust Doctrine, and comes to the conclusion that the English version of the doctrine is somewhat narrower than the American version. It notes that the English doctrine is restricted to 'traditional uses such as navigation, commerce, and fishing'.[16]

The Preamble envisages India to be a 'socialist' state, whose main aim should be to distribute the common richness and wealth of the country in a way that serves the needs and requirements of the common man.[17] This will only suffice the mandate for social and economic retransformation as envisaged by the Directive Principles of State Policy.[18] This doctrine finds its contemporary relevance as a 'legal and planning tool for the fulfilment of the sovereign's role as trustee of the environment for future generations.'[19]

Although the doctrine is labelled a 'trust', the categorization of the doctrine as a particular area of law is difficult. As the doctrine is often used to protect public spaces, it is often categorized as a feature of property law.[20] However, it has also been categorized as an aspect of constitutional law, trust law, and administrative law.[21]

Indian courts, and the legislature for that matter, have expressed their preference for the American version of the doctrine that 'encompasses the entire spectrum of the environment'[22] and contemplates Indian values relating to the environment as defined in international and domestic legal instruments.

The landmark case of *M.C. Mehta* v. *Kamal Nath*[23] held that the Public Trust Doctrine is 'the law of the land in India.'[24] A wide interpretation of the doctrine was adopted in protecting a valuable river and forest area from a private tourist enterprise.

In the case, a private company constructed a club resort adjacent to the river Beas. In 1995, the river swelled up and engulfed the club, destroying it. For the purposes of reconstructing the club, the developers decided to divert the river Beas to a minimum of one kilometre downstream. This was a particularly difficult task and even the

---

[15] Reported in (1997)1 SCC 388, 1996 (9) SCALE 141, JT 1996(II) SC 467.

[16] *M.C. Mehta* v. *Kamal Nath and Others*, reported in (1997)1 SCC 388, 1996 (9) SCALE 141, JT 1996 (II) SC 467, 33.

[17] *Haryana State Electricity Board* v. *Suresh*, (1999) 2 SCC 601, 2000 KHC 540. 'Article 39 is a pointer in this direction'; also see *T.N. Godavarman Thirumulkpad* v. *Union of India*, (2002) 7 SCC 620, 'This aesthetic use and the pristine glory cannot be permitted to be eroded for public, commercial or any other purpose' (p. 635).

[18] *Samatha* v. *State of Andhra Pradesh*, (1997) 8 SCC 191.

[19] S. Shantha Kumar, *Environmental Law: An Introduction*, Bharathiyar University Materials, 1st edn, Tamil Nadu, 2001, p. 122.

[20] Huffman poses that the doctrine is part of property law; see James L. Huffman, 'Fish Out of Water: The Public Trust Doctrine in a Constitutional Democracy', 19 *Envtl. L. Rev.* 527 (1989) reprinted in 'Joseph Sax and the Idea of the Public Trust'. Published in Issues in Legal Scholarship—on 8 October 2003 (Joseph Sax and The Public Trust), *Issues in Legal Scholarship* 1 (2003), article 6, see also http://goliath.ecnext.com/coms2/gi0199-84001/Joseph-Sax-and-the-idea.html.

[21] Ibid.

[22] *Intellectuals Forum* v. *State of AP*, 2006 AIR SCW 1309; *M.C. Mehta* v. *Kamal Nath and Others*, (1997)1 SCC 388, 1996 (9) SCALE 141, JT 1996(II) SC 467, Section 33.

[23] (1997)1 SCC 388, 1996 (9) SCALE 141, JT 1996 (II) SC 467.

[24] *M.C. Mehta* v. *Kamal Nath and Others*, (1997) 1 SCC 388, 1996 (9) SCALE 141, JT 1996 (II) SC 467, Section 39 (1).

developers were sceptical about the successful diversion of the river, fearing that it would engulf the resort again.

The Minister for Environment and Forests, Kamal Nath, approved the project during his tenure but when the project commenced, he ceased to hold this position. It was claimed that he had a strong interest in the development of the club. The minister acknowledged that his family held a business interest in the developing company but denied any management responsibility of the said company and any 'right, title, or interest in the property known as Span Resorts owned by Span Motels Pvt Ltd, or in the lands leased out to the said company by the State of Himachal Pradesh.'[25]

The minister had approved the company's application for a lease of forest land which existed up until the banks of the River Beas.[26] The resort existed on the flood plain of the river, between the relief channel and the main channel of the river. Before the flood occurred in 1995, the motel had constructed concrete blocks at the spill channel of the river and along its banks. After the flood, the river was dredged to increase its capacity and wire crates were built along the banks to prevent erosion and landslides.[27] Finally, without expert advice, Span Motels divided the river into two streams, using a clause in the lease agreement that permitted the motel to protect the land from the river.

The Pollution Control Board stated that the clause in the agreement did not permit the motel to block the natural flood spill/relief channel of the river.[28] In a landmark ruling, the court's reasoning reflected the Public Trust Doctrine, stating that the 'Beas is a young and

dynamic river...The area being ecologically fragile and full of scenic beauty should not have been permitted to be converted into private ownership and for commercial gains.'[29]

The protection of natural resources from damage by private enterprise is an element of the doctrine. The court then goes on to explain the relevance of the Public Trust Doctrine, noting that the court's concern for the environment 'bear[s] a very close conceptual relationship to this legal doctrine.'[30] It recounted the evolution of the doctrine in English common law and pointed out that gifts of nature should be preserved for the benefit of the whole public and should remain free from private ownership.[31]

There are certain restrictions on such properties that the court identifies: 'first, the property subject to the trust must not only be used for a public purpose, but it must be available for use by the general public; second, the property may not be sold, even for a fair cash equivalent; and third, the property must be maintained for particular types of uses.'[32]

The court adopts the American interpretation of the doctrine, to the exclusion of the English version, as it incorporates ecological values and so may apply to places of great beauty or aesthetic value. Parliament is charged with balancing the interests of those who want places preserved in their natural state and those who wish to develop the land to respond to the changing needs of society.[33]

---

[25] Ibid.
[26] Ibid.
[27] Ibid.
[28] Ibid.

[29] Ibid.
[30] Ibid.
[31] Ibid.
[32] Joseph L. Sax, Professor of Law, University of Michigan—proponent of the Modern Public Trust Doctrine—in an erudite article 'Public Trust Doctrine in Natural Resource Law: Effective Judicial Intervention', *Michigan Law Review* 68(3), part 1, January 1970, p. 473. Cited in Ibid.
[33] Supra note 24, Section 35.

In applying the law to the facts of the case, the court had 'no hesitation in holding that the Himachal Pradesh Government had committed a patent breach of public trust by leasing the ecologically fragile land to the motel management',[34] as the forest was protected by the Public Trust Doctrine, which vested title in the state for the benefit of the people. The Polluter Pays Principle was then used in devising an appropriate remedy. The motel was to pay the costs of remedying the pollution caused by their interference with the river. Span Motels was also charged with the burden of proving that it should not be subjected to additional fines. The area within the motel's original lease was to be clearly demarcated so as to prevent it from encroaching or disturbing the river basin, and an injunction was imposed on it to refrain from causing any more pollution in the future.

In *M.I. Builders Pvt Ltd* v. *Radhey Shyam Sahu and Others*, the court reiterated the above ruling in holding that the proposed construction of an underground shopping centre below a park was in violation of the Public Trust Doctrine. The court held that the municipality of Mahapalika held the park on trust for the citizens of Lucknow and it 'could only manage the park and could not alienate it or convert it into something different from the park'.[35] The park was of historical importance, and was a sanctuary in the midst of the bustling city of Lucknow. The court noted that the construction of the shopping centre had deprived the place of its essential quality as a park[36] and 'irreversible changes have been made'. The court stated that one of its main concerns was in preserving the ecology of the park, thus adopting the wider version of the

Public Trust Doctrine as posed by the court in *M.C. Mehta* v. *Kamal Nath and Others*. Construction of the complex would not only destroy the character of the park, but also cause additional congestion and pollution in the area.

Interestingly, the court also observed that the Public Trust Doctrine is a tenet of Article 21 of the Constitution. Consequently,

When a state holds a resource which is available for the free use of the general public, a court will look with considerable scepticism upon any governmental conduct which is calculated either to reallocate the resource to more restricted uses or to subject public uses to the self-interest of private parties.[37]

Considering the court's predisposition, it may be onerous on the government to show that it has not infringed on the doctrine.

It was also argued that the Public Parks Act can be used to uphold the Public Trust doctrine.[38] Under this act, the Mahapalika was bound 'to maintain public places, parks, and to plant trees'.[39] Since the shopping centre now occupied the ground underneath the park, the opportunity to plant trees had been thwarted and the park now existed more as 'a terrace park'.[40] In conclusion, the court held that the Mahapalika had infringed both on the doctrine and Section 144 of the Parks Act.[41] The remedy awarded by the court reflected its disgust with the Mahapalika in ignoring the public's interest in the area when it decided to allow the construction. As the builders were conscious of a pending appeal against the project's approval and continued to build at their own risk, the court did not hesitate in

---

[34] Ibid.

[35] *M.I. Builders Pvt Ltd* v. *Radhey Shyam Sahu and Others*, AIR 1999 SC 2468, (1999) 6 SCC 464, Section 47(5).

[36] Ibid.

[37] Ibid.

[38] Ibid.

[39] Public Parks Act.

[40] Supra note 39.

[41] Ibid.

ordering the project to be dismantled and the park restored to its original state.[42]

Apart from land, the doctrine, in India, has been extended to apply to tanks. In *Intellectuals Forum v. State of A.P.*,[43] the Supreme Court of India considered the application of the Public Trust Doctrine to two tanks located in the Tirupathi area, which were 'historical in nature being in existence since the time of Sri Krishnadevaraya, the Great (AD 1500).'[44] The government decided to authorize alienation of the land on which the tanks stood, to respond to growing housing pressures arising from the increasing population of the area. When the high court approved this decision, there was a wave of public opposition against the action. The Intellectuals Forum was the principal appellant, while a number of other groups supported their appeal. A number of 'socially spirited citizens' wrote a letter pleading that the area of the tank beds not be used for any purpose other than the purpose for which they were originally meant. The Indian Medical Association also beseeched that the government restore the tanks to their original nature as percolation tanks, in order to improve the groundwater quality, which had recently become inundated with toxins such as fluorides and salts.[45]

The counsel for the appellant argued that the High Court had erred on a number of grounds. Its main contention was that the high court had committed an error in holding the tanks, which were of such importance, to be non-existent.[46] In particular, it had failed to take into account the principle of Sustainable Development[47] and had erred 'in coming to the conclusion that urban development could be given primacy over and above the need to protect the environment and valuable fresh water resources.'[48] The Forum alleged that the respondents had failed to take the necessary practical measures to ensure water quality and quantity of the tanks and as a result both were becoming drastically impaired.[49]

The court considered the capacity of the tanks to be used for their designated purpose as it was argued on the part of the respondent that the capacity of the tanks to serve their purpose was defunct in any case. An Expert Committee was constituted to examine the state of the tanks, and the court used its findings to answer the questions: Does a natural resource exist, and if it has deteriorated, can it be revived?[50]

M.C. Mehta v. Kamal Nath was applied by the court because of the 'competing interests of protecting the environment and social development.'[51] The court decided:

The issues presented in this case illustrate the classic struggle between those members of the public who would preserve our rivers, forests, parks, and open lands in their pristine purity and those charged with administrative responsibility, who under the pressures of the changing needs of an increasingly complex society find it necessary to encroach to some extent upon open lands heretofore considered inviolate to change.[52]

Ordinarily, the power to resolve this issue is vested in Parliament and not in courts, but where Parliament fails to legislate, the common

[42] Ibid., Section 83.

[43] 2006 AIR SCW 1309.

[44] *Intellectuals Forum v. State of A.P.*, AIR 2006 SC 1350, 2006 AIR SCW 1309, Section 45.

[45] *Intellectuals Forum v. State of A.P.*, AIR 2006 SC 1350, 2006 AIR SCW 1309.

[46] *Intellectuals Forum v. State of A.P.*, 2006 AIR SCW 1309, Section 8(1).

[47] Ibid.

[48] Ibid.

[49] Ibid.

[50] Ibid.

[51] Ibid.

[52] *M.C. Mehta v. Kamal Nath and Others*, (1997) 1 SCC 388, 1996 (9) SCALE 141, JT 1996 (II) SC 467, Section 35.

law doctrine of Public Trust restricts the actions which may be taken by the executive in relation to natural resources.[53]

In a principled fashion, the Supreme Court of India made the connection between the Public Trust Doctrine and international and domestic environmental obligations. This can be done easily by the adoption of a wider interpretation of the doctrine as espoused by the USA, which also aims at protecting the ecology. The Stockholm Convention, to which India is a party, imposes an obligation on the state to preserve and protect natural resources for future generations.[54] This led to the conclusion that the state is undoubtedly obligated to protect and preserve the tanks. In resolving the conflict between environment and development, the court applied the principle of Sustainable Development which is found in both domestic and international legal instruments.[55] Furthermore, the principle of Intergenerational Equity holds a symbiotic relationship with the Public Trust Doctrine, complementing each other. Finally, the court noted Articles 48A and 51A of the Indian Constitution as guiding principles to be used in adjudicating upon the matter.

In applying the above principles to the facts of the case, the court balanced the appellant's arguments against the competing need to provide housing and shelter to citizens. It concluded that the division bench of the High Court of Andhra Pradesh did not properly consider the wishes of the citizens in relation to the tanks that served their needs in providing both irrigation and benefitting the

groundwater table.[56] It had failed to strike an adequate balance between the valuable fresh water resource and development, especially since the right to shelter as advocated by the respondent would not be violated if the housing construction did not proceed. The housing was directed at medium to high level-income families, which would find shelter regardless. Unfortunately, development had already depleted much of the natural resources in relation to the tanks, but despite this, the court issued a number of orders directing the tanks to be restored to as close to their original state as possible.[57]

INDIAN CASE LAW

The application of the doctrine in suits against private development is common in areas that are rich in resources or environmentally valuable. In *Karnataka Industrial Areas Development Board v. C. Kenchappa and Others,*[58] a group of agriculturalists filed a writ petition against the development of lands that they claimed to use for grazing cattle. They brought the petition under Articles 14, 21, and 226 of the Constitution, claiming that the villagers would lose their *gomal* lands to the said development, which would also cause environmental degradation. The Karnataka Industrial Areas Development Board and the state government disputed the character of the lands, asserting that they were not in fact gomal. The land was to be allotted to Gee India Technology Centre Pvt Ltd for the purposes of conducting research in human psychology. The administrative process prescribed was that under the Karnataka Industrial Areas Development Board Act, 1966, Section 28:

---

[53] Ibid.

[54] United Nations Conference on the Human Environment, Stockholm 1972 (Stockholm Convention), cited in supra note 47, Section 29.

[55] Ibid.; Principle 4, Rio Declaration on Environment and Development, 1992.

[56] Ibid.

[57] Ibid.

[58] 2006 AIRSCW 2546.

Acquisition of Land - (1) If at any time, in the opinion of the State Government, any land is required, for the purpose of development by the Board, or for any other purpose in furtherance of the objects of this Act, the State Government may by notification, give notice of its intention to acquire such land.

The high court decided against the development, declaring that a one kilometre area was to be left around a village as a green belt in order to protect the environment and ecology.[59] On appeal, the court noted the extreme importance of the environment and ecology, emphasizing its relationship with Article 21 of the Constitution. Reference was also made to the Directive Principles of State Policy, which provide under Article 48A:

Protection and improvement of environment and safeguarding of forests and wild life—The State shall endeavour to protect and improve the environment and to safeguard the forests and wild life of the country.

The court also noted the reference in Article 51A (g) that requires all persons 'to protect and improve the natural environment including forests, lakes, rivers, and wildlife, and to have compassion for living creatures.'[60] Principle 4 of the Stockholm Convention was discussed and the issue at hand was again identified as the striking of 'a golden balance between development and ecology'[61] where the resolution of such a case is done under the principle of Sustainable Development. Development need not be irreconcilable with ecology,[62] and reference to guiding principles

may be made to satisfy both elements. The court identified three principles that can be used to protect ecology: the Precautionary Principle,[63] the Polluter Pays Principle,[64] and the Public Trust Doctrine.[65]

A wide interpretation of the doctrine was taken and it was pointed out that the principle of Sustainable Development is maintained by the Public Trust Doctrine.[66] The court remains consistent with the approach taken in *M.C. Mehta v. Kamal Nath*[67] but is perhaps more insistent that the principle be upheld as an ingredient of Sustainable Development.[68] Consequently, the court directed that:

in future, before acquisition of lands for development, the consequence and adverse impact of development on environment must be properly comprehended and the lands be acquired for development that they do not gravely impair the ecology and environment.

An EIA would be an obvious way of implementing this direction, although the court did not require an EIA in explicit terms. In relation to the facts at hand, the court ordered the appellant developers to gain permission from the Karnataka State Pollution Control Board before the land was allotted for development.[69]

In *Perumatty Grama Panchayat v. State of Kerala*,[70] the actions of the Coca-Cola Company, when they extracted large quantities of ground water at Moolathara in Perumatty Grama Panchayat, ignited a wave of public scrutiny. Alarmingly, in evidence adduced before the court, it became apparent that the

---

[59] *Karnataka Industrial Areas Development Board v. C. Kenchappa and Others*, 2006 AIRSCW 2546, Section 14.

[60] Ibid.

[61] Ibid.

[62] *Vellore Citizens' Welfare Forum v. Union of India*, (1996) 5 SCC 647) cited in ibid., Section 70; *M.C. Mehta v. Union of India* (1997) 2 SCC 353 cited in ibid., Section 98.

[63] Ibid., For more, see p. 25.

[64] Ibid., For more, see p. 26.

[65] Ibid., For more, see p. 34.

[66] Ibid.

[67] Ibid.

[68] Ibid.

[69] Ibid.

[70] 2004 (1) KLT 731.

company used 3.75 litres of water for every 1 litre of beverage it produced.[71] The people complained to the Panchayat that the company was exploiting ground water, causing a shortage of drinking water, and environmental degradation. Consequently, on 15 May 2003, the Panchayat issued an order to the effect that it would not renew the company's licence on the grounds of public interest. One particular group of indigenous people, the Adivasis, were resilient in their opposition to the company, protesting outside its gates for one year. Coca-Cola appealed to the government, which directed a team of experts to conduct an investigation into the allegations against the company which would then form the basis for a final opinion by the Panchayat. In response to this order, the Panchayat filed a petition in the KHC, alleging that the government's action was essentially ultra vires and 'the protection and preservation of water sources is the exclusive domain of the Panchayat.'[72]

The question before the court was whether the Panchayat had the authority to revoke the licence and order the closing of the unit, and whether the government's intervention was legal.[73]

The court first noted that the Panchayat had perhaps gone too far in ordering the units to be closed down, and in this sense the government's intervention was justified. However, it may be within the power of the Panchayat to direct that no more groundwater be extracted on grounds of public policy. The court analysed the nature of the water, stating that 'Ground water is a national wealth and belongs to the entire society. It is a nectar, sustaining life on earth.'[74] The respondent pointed out the lack

of legal constraints on its ability to extract ground water and contended that there was an unfettered right to do so. Despite an absence of rigid legal regulation, the court did not hesitate to rebut this presumption with reference to Principle 2 of the Stockholm Declaration and Article 21 of the Indian Constitution, both instruments that hold the environment in great stead.

The court recounted the decision of the Apex Court in *State of Tamil Nadu v. Hind Stone*:[75]

Rivers, forests, minerals, and such other resources constitute a nation's natural wealth. These resources are not to be frittered away and exhausted by any one generation. Every generation owes a duty to all succeeding generations to develop and conserve the natural resources of the nation in the best possible way. It is in the interest of mankind. It is in the interest of the nation.

Recognition of this decision is an obvious precursor to the application of the Public Trust Doctrine, which reflects the concern that India has for the environment.[76] The Court emphasized previous decisions that make the Public Trust Doctrine a part of the law of India, and concluded that water is a common public resource to be protected by the state as trustee for the benefit of the people. Notably, the Court stressed that an abdication of this duty will necessarily result in an infringement of the rights under Article 21. This case is of interest because of the way in which the Public Trust Doctrine is applied to the preservation of groundwater, despite any clear laws shaped to deal with groundwater. Extraction creates an ecological imbalance, posing the risk of converting ecologically fragile lands of the Panchayat into deserts.

---

[71] *Perumatty Grama Panchayat v. State of Kerala*, 2004 (1) KLT 731, Section 9.
[72] Ibid.
[73] Ibid.
[74] Ibid.

[75] *State of Tamil Nadu v. Hind Stone* (1981) 2 SCC 205, Section 6 cited in ibid.
[76] Ibid.

In conclusion, the court upheld the order of the Panchayat that directed the company to refrain from extracting ground water on the grounds that, (1) The underground water belongs to the general public and the second respondent[77] has right to claim a huge share of it and the Government have no power to allow a private party to extract such a huge quantity of ground water, which is a property, held in trust. (2) If the second respondent is permitted to draw such huge quantities of water, then similar claims of other landowners will also have to be allowed. It will also result in the drying up of underground aqua-reservoirs.

As the government had failed to uphold the Public Trust Doctrine and the rights of the public, the court's ability to review the merits of the decision was activated. The second respondent company was directed not to extract any more groundwater in excess.[78]

Other natural resources in India have been protected using the Public Trust Doctrine. Sand mining of river beds has been prohibited wherever it causes environmental degradation to the river.[79] The government cannot permit such illegal activities for commercial gain. In Andhra Pradesh it was also held that groundwater is subject to the doctrine. Consequently, the rights of agricultural landowners are restricted in the sense that they may not deprive other users of this groundwater or contaminate it in any way.[80] The state has ultimate authority over the trust and may restrict use where necessary by executive instructions issued under statutory powers.

Some states have incorporated the principles of the Public Trust Doctrine in order to protect natural resources. The Kerala Forest (Vesting and Management of Ecologically Fragile Lands) Act, 2001 is one such example, and vests in the state, the management of ecologically fragile lands in order to preserve ecological balance and promote biodiversity.[81] The Preamble recognizes that the

Earth's biological resources, with their intrinsic ecological, genetic, economic, social, cultural, scientific, educational, recreational, and aesthetic values are global assets and public trust vital to the sustained economic and social development, maintenance of ecological balance and the very existence of humanity.

The Act gives the government wide powers and vests ownership and possession in the state of any ecologically fragile lands, even to the extent that other title holders' rights may be extinguished[82] subject to reasonable compensation.[83]

The doctrine has since been adopted by numerous other common law countries in varying degrees.

ENGLAND

In England, the traditional position in relation to the foreshore still stands. The Crown is vested with the management of the foreshore and may permit easements over the foreshore to be created, as long as public rights are not impaired.[84] At common law, the public still enjoys a right to fish 'in the tidal reaches of all rivers and estuaries and in the sea and arms of the sea within the limits of the territorial waters

[77] Hindustan Coca Cola Co.

[78] *Perumatty Grama Panchayat v. State of Kerala*, 2004 (1) KLT 731.

[79] *L.V. Varadarajulu Naidu v. The Collector of Tiruvalluvar District*, (2000)1 MLJ 41.

[80] *M.P. Rambabu v. D.F.O.*, AIR 2002 AP 256.

[81] Preamble, Kerala Forest (Vesting and Management of Ecologically Fragile Lands) Act, 2001.

[82] Ibid.

[83] Ibid.

[84] *Mercer v. Denne*, [1904] 2 Ch 534 (affd [1905] 2 Ch 538, CA) in *Halsbury's Laws of England: Water*, 49 (2), (2004 re-issue), para. 1399; 49 (3) (2004 re-issue), para. 400806/2.

of the kingdom';[85] this right can only be modified by the legislature. The right is still somewhat restrictive, however, as it does not apply to non-tidal waters, even if they are navigable.[86] The Public Trust Doctrine still operates narrowly in this respect and is very much based on the historical origins of the doctrine.

The treatment of 'common land' reflects some elements of the Public Trust Doctrine. Common rights must be registered under the Commons Registration Act, 1965[87] and land that is not subject to these common rights may not be deemed common land.[88] Common land is difficult to define. However, it can be generally stated that, 'common land is land owned by one person over which another person is entitled to exercise rights of common (such as grazing animals or cutting bracken for livestock bedding), and these rights are generally exercisable in common with others'.[89]

Thus, common land may be more accurately defined by the rights that attach to it and its definition becomes rather circular. A major feature of commons is that others, in particular the public, are entitled to exercise some rights over it. It may be privately owned, publicly owned, or have no owner and still attract public rights provided it is registered as common land. In England today, statutes grant authorities significant powers over commons to ensure that they are available for public access.[90]

Various executive bodies are charged with authority over commons. Legislation provides that the Secretary of the State and the Assembly are to ensure public access over common land,[91] protect common land, and regulate various activities on common land.[92] The National Trust also has some powers in relation to commons but must keep all commons land that it acquires 'unenclosed and unbuilt on as an open space for the recreation and enjoyment of the public and to resist encroachments'.[93] Although not all commons are exclusively owned by the state, the functions given to the state are devised to ensure the protection of commons so that current and future generations may enjoy use of them.

The Countryside and Rights of Way Act[94] provides for the designation of access land, or common land, which the public may enjoy access to. Various administrative authorities such as National Parks Authorities and Boards Authorities are charged with the power to ensure public access, and may even supersede the will of owners of the land who obstruct reasonable access by the public.[95] In some circumstances, landowners may restrict such access, but may not do so for more than twenty-eight days in a calendar year.[96]

---

[85] Halsbury's Laws of England: Fisheries (18)/1.

[86] Halsbury's Laws of England: Fisheries (18)/1.

[87] United Kingdom.

[88] Halsbury's Laws of England: Commons, vol. 6 (2003 re-issue), 1.

[89] Department for Environment, Food and Rural Affairs (UK), 'What is Common Land: Definition. http://www.defra.gov.uk/wildlife-countryside/issues/common/definitions.htm (last updated 26 May 2006).

[90] Ibid.

[91] Countryside and Rights of Way Act, 2000 Pt I (Sections 1–46); the Law of Property Act, 1925, Section 193 (as amended); and paras 565 et seq, 573 ante cited in Halsbury's Laws of England: Commons (vol. 6, 2003 re-issue).

[92] Halsbury's Laws of England: Commons, vol. 6 (2003 re-issue).

[93] National Trust Act, 1907, Section 29 (A), (E) cited in Halsbury's Laws of England: Commons vol. 6 (2003 re-issue).

[94] 2000 (England).

[95] Countryside and Rights of Way Act, 2000, Sections 37, 38(1), (3)-(7), 39 in Halsbury's Laws of England: Commons vol. 6 (2003 re-issue).

[96] Countryside and Rights of Way Act, 2000, Section 22.

The Law of Property Act[97] also provides the public with rights of access 'for air and exercise to any land (except as mentioned below) that is a metropolitan common, a manorial waste, or a common'.[98] The Lord Manor or the holder of the land is subject to common rights and may grant rights of access with rights of commons.

It can be seen that the designation of common land and the rights of public access codify and reflect some elements of the Public Trust Doctrine. In this sense, elements of the Public Trust Doctrine are reflected in the laws of England that protect land and natural resources, although the full scope of the doctrine applicable to navigable waters may not apply. The authorities are to ensure that public rights of use are not impeded and thus act for the benefit of the public, even though the Crown may not have absolute title over common land. To the extent that private rights conflict with public access, authorities may intervene in many cases. The Public Trust Doctrine is very much a part of the law of England today.

UNITED STATES OF AMERICA

The case of *Illinois Central Railroad Co. v. People of the State of Illinois*[99] is often cited by Indian courts as a representative of the application of the Public Trust Doctrine in the USA.[100] In this case, the English Public Trust Doctrine was adopted by the American court and adapted to reflect the fact that lakes are not affected by tides. Such an application is based on the intent or purpose of the doctrine.

Illinois Central Railroad Co. took action against the State of Illinois and others when it attempted to repeal a grant of land along the shoreline of Lake Michigan. In 1852, Congress granted to Illinois a right of way through public land to create a railway. The right was essentially a right of way and carried with it all of the rights necessary and incidental to construction of the railway. After Illinois Central Railroad became incorporated, Illinois charged it with the rights and powers to construct and operate the railroad.

In 1869, the legislature granted to the railway company the rights to 'appropriation, occupancy, use, and control in and to the land submerged' extending one mile along the shoreline of Lake Michigan and one mile from the shoreline into the lake. The company was granted the right in perpetuity and was not permitted to sell or convey the land.[101] It was also restricted from impairing public navigation of the waters.

The scope of this right was gradually extended by a number of ordinances by which the common council of Chicago permitted to lay the railroad through the city[102] and extend its works to a specified degree into the lake.[103] When the present litigation commenced, the railroad company claimed a tract that was 200 feet wide of the lake, and constructed its railway.

The issue in the case was whether the railway company could assert rights over the lands adjacent to the lake and build piers and other structures that would inevitably extend into the lake, involving the exercise of riparian

---

[97] 1925.

[98] *Halsbury's Laws of England: Commons* vol. 6 (2003 re-issue).

[99] 146 US 387, 36 Ed 1018 (1892).

[100] See *M.C. Mehta v. Kamal Nath and Others*, (1997)1 SCC 388, 1996 (9) SCALE 141, JT 1996(II) SC 467, Section 26; *Intellectuals Forum v. State of AP*, 2006 AIR SCW 1309, Section 31.

[101] *Illinois Central Railroad Co. v. People of the State of Illinois*, 146 US 387, 449.

[102] Ibid., 387, 441.

[103] Ibid., 387, 442.

rights. Acting under the Act of 1869, the railroad company claimed that it had absolute title to submerged lands, being the bed of Lake Michigan, to erect whatever structures it wishes, while the State of Illinois claimed that it has exclusive rights to the area and that the railroad company acted unlawfully in erecting various structures.

The court looked at whether Congress did in fact have the power to make such a grant. It asked the question: could Congress divest the state of the power to manage and control the harbour of Chicago, and transfer these powers to a corporation railway company? It was explained by the court that the great lakes are subject to the dominion and sovereignty of the Crown, which holds the lakes for the benefit of the public. This title is not open for pre-emption and sale:

It is a title held on trust for the people of the state, that they may enjoy the navigation of the waters, carry on commerce over them, and have liberty of fishing therein, freed from the obstruction or interference of private parties.[104]

Congress may grant portions of submerged lands under navigable waters where these rights do not interfere with public interest. Private rights may only be carved out around the Public Trust Doctrine and cannot detract from it, although they may act to further the interests of the people under the trust. The doctrine gives absolute title to the state and entertains the interests of the people as a whole.

Consequently, Congress may not deprive the state of its control over a substantial portion of the lake or harbour.[105] On the facts,

A corporation created for one purpose, the construction and operation of a railroad between designated points, is by the act converted into a corporation to manage and practically control the harbour of Chicago, not simply for its own purpose as a railroad corporation, but for its own profit generally.[106]

After analysing the doctrine, the above proposition takes on the character of an absurdity and is 'a gross perversion of the trust over the property under which it is held'.[107] Thus, the original grant was invalid to the extent that it attempted to divest the state of its sovereignty of control of the land and the repealing Act was valid in the sense that it restored the state to its correct position before the original Act.

The USA has also extended the doctrine to land. In *Mildred L. Gould et. al v. Greylock Reservation Commission et. al*,[108] a group of citizens sought to prevent a ski resort and supporting structures from being built in an area of natural forest. In particular, they asked the court to invalidate a lease granted to Mount Greylock Tramway Authority and prevent the authority from developing a ski resort in the area.

The plaintiffs were an associated group of citizens formed to preserve the area as an 'unspoiled natural forest'.[109] The court explained the nature of the forest as follows:

The Greylock range has a varied forest. In 1,450 acres which lie above the 2,800 foot contour may be found interesting trees, plants, birds, and animals generally found in Canada. The area contains unusual geological formations. It is frequently visited by students, ornithologists, scientists, and naturalists, as well as by tourists, motorists, and persons walking on the trails.[110]

[104] Ibid., 387, 452.
[105] Ibid., 387, 453.
[106] Ibid., 387, 451.
[107] Ibid., 387, 455.
[108] *Mildred L. Gould and Others v. Greylock Reservation Commission and Others*, 350 Mass. 410.
[109] Ibid., 410, 411.
[110] Ibid., 410, 412.

The citizens formed the Greylock Park Association that eventually resulted in the creation of the Greylock State Reservation. The Greylock Reservation Commission was the body appointed to oversee the management of the reservation for public benefit.

In 1960, a lease was granted to the Greylock Tramway Authority of over 4,000 acres of the Greylock State Reservation, under an enabling statute. The Authority was originally formed for the purposes of operating an aerial tramway. It subsequently formed an agreement with the Commission whereby both authorities proposed to build an aerial tramway, ski resort, and ski lifts in the reservation. By partaking in the agreement, the Commission essentially divested itself of the powers to maintain access roads and public rights of way on the land.[111] The Authority further entered into joint ventures with other corporations that were willing to finance the project and engage in profit-sharing schemes. The proposed development required the clearing of significant areas of forest, creating ski routes and pathways, and constructing ski lifts.

While considering the case, the court noted that:

The Greylock Reservation, as rural park land, is not to be diverted to another inconsistent public use without plain and explicit legislation to that end. The policy of the [C]ommonwealth has been to add to the common-law inviolability of parks express prohibition against encroachment.[112]

Despite the fact that the Authority was given the power 'to construct and operate' an aerial tramway and all appurtenances thereto 'together with certain related facilities',[113] the court felt that the damage caused to the ecology by the extensive clearing required for the delineation of ski slopes and trails was not contemplated by the statute. Legislation that permits a lease to be granted over the land must be interpreted on the basis of the intent of the statute. In light of the functions of the Commission, the statute only permitted the lease of a section of the reservation 'which may prove to be reasonably necessary to a project of permitted scope'.[114] Hence, the lease exceeded the scope intended by the statute as it granted such a significant portion of the land.

The court was particularly wary of other joint ventures that the Authority had created in constructing the resort. Due to the limited financial capacity of the Authority, it was likely that joint parties would exert considerable control over the area and thus encroach upon the resort's supervisory powers. The court found that the Authority was not entitled by the statute to delegate the majority of its statutory powers to third parties, as this was not contemplated by the narrow power to make contracts. In conclusion, the court was firm in condemning the commercial character of the agreement, which was evident from its profit-sharing features and delegation of powers to corporate entities. The statute simply did not foresee the land being dealt with in such a manner. Authorities are hence prohibited from dealing with public lands to generate private profit, unless expressly authorized by statute.

On the face of the judgement, the court did not explicitly state that it was applying the Public Trust Doctrine. Rather, elements of the doctrine were discussed in conjunction with statutory interpretation. Clearly, the authority was entrusted with protecting the public park in the name of public interest, signifying essential ingredients of the doctrine. The court's failure to explicitly discuss the

[111] Ibid., 410, 416.
[112] Ibid., 410, 418.
[113] Ibid., 410, 420.

[114] Ibid., 410, 422.

Public Trust Doctrine perhaps acts a reminder that the doctrine is a creature of common law and although it is often persuasive, legal scholars must remember to look at statutes also. However, the reasoning in the *Gould* case can be used to reinforce the doctrine in situations where public authorities attempt to divest themselves of statutory powers and engage in profit sharing with private entities. For example, in Madras, it was held that the government cannot permit commercial use of certain natural resources that are subject to the Public Trust Doctrine.[115] Consequently, government officials who permitted the illegal sand mining of a river bed were directed to take action to remedy the wrong. In many ways, the ruling is an authority for certain facets of the doctrine.

New Zealand

The application of the Public Trust Doctrine can be observed along water margins. The 'Queen's Chain' is popularly identified as the origin of the Public Trust Doctrine as Queen Victoria intervened in governmental action in the 1840s to preserve a definitive strip of land along the coasts.[116] The public is to enjoy access to a twenty-metre strip of land along most water bodies, and although the term 'Queen's Chain' is not a legal doctrine in itself, it does signify general custom. This provided the foundations for the Public Trust Doctrine, by which the public now enjoys access to the sea and most rivers.

There is also a history of legislation in New Zealand that is reflective of the elements of the Public Trust Doctrine. In 1892, the Land Act provided that:

There shall be reserved from sale or other disposition a strip of land not less than sixty-six feet in width along all high-water lines of the sea, and of its bays, inlets, or creeks, and along the margins of all lakes exceeding fifty acres in area, and along the banks of all rivers and streams of an average width exceeding thirty-three feet, and, in the discretion of the Commissioner, along the bank of any river or stream of less width than thirty-three feet.[117]

Section 15 of the Act also empowered the Governor to preclude sale of 'any road-lines which may be required through or over any such lands and to reserve any of the said lands which are situated on the seashore, the margin of lakes, or on river-banks'.[118] Such provisions clarify the fact that the public is to enjoy the specified area of land along the seashore and water bodies, while also ensuring that they actually have access to these areas via roads. The elements of crown ownership, limitations on private sale, and public benefit can be observed in this early Act and clearly indicate the operation of the Public Trust Doctrine.[119]

The Resource Management (Foreshore and Seabed) Act, 2004 aims to 'preserve the public foreshore and seabed in perpetuity as the common heritage of all New Zealanders in a way that enables the protection by the Crown of the public foreshore and seabed on behalf of all the people of New Zealand'.[120] Absolute legal and beneficial title over the

---

[115] *L.V. Varadarajulu Naidu v. The Collector of Tiruvalluvar District*, (2000)1 MLJ 41.

[116] Ministry of Agriculture and Forestry (New Zealand), 'The Law on Public Access along Water Margins,' available at http://www.maf.govt.nz/mafnet/rural-nz/people-and-their-issues/access/access-along-water-margins/access-along-water-margins-01.htm#P67_1467 (last visited 4 May 2007).

[117] Land Act, 1892 (New Zealand), Section 110.

[118] Ibid., Section 15.

[119] Webpage 1 (provincial government). Thanks to Michael McDonnell and Candy Gonzalez for their assistance in New Zealand Law.

[120] Resource Management (Foreshore and Seabed) Act 2004, Section 3.

[121] Ibid., Section 4(a).

public foreshore and seabed is vested in the Crown,[121] and the Crown may not dispose of the land or allow it to be alienated unless enabled by the legislature.[122] It should be noted that the Crown does not enjoy such extensive rights as the government in Kerala, as it may not extinguish private title that existed prior to the Act coming into force.[123] The Act further meets its objects by 'providing for the general rights of public access and recreation in, on, over, and across the public foreshore and seabed and general rights of navigation within the foreshore and seabed'. 'Access' has a broad meaning and encompasses the right to physically be in or on the foreshore and seabed area[124] and 'engage in recreational activities in or on the public foreshore and seabed'.[125] The public is also granted rights of navigation[126] and the Act does not affect any rights of fishing granted by other enactments.[127] As alluded to in the title of the Act, the statutory scheme only applies to marine areas[128] and thus, is not applicable to non-navigable waters such as lakes. In this sense, the Act reflects the English position on the Public Trust Doctrine.

Sri Lanka

The Sri Lankan Supreme Court has been less enthusiastic about the application of the doctrine. In the *Eppawela* case,[129] residents of Eppawela sought to prevent the government, in conjunction with Freeport Mac Moran of the USA and IMCO Agrico, from mining

phosphate in Eppawela, in the Anuradhapura district. Land in the designated area was of significance to the petitioners who occupied, owned, and cultivated it, with the proposed development posing a significant economic and environmental hazard. They claimed that the development would infringe Articles 12(1), 14(1)(g), and 14(1)(h) of the Sri Lankan Constitution, and that it was contrary to the Public Trust Doctrine.

The Court identified the existence of the doctrine in other jurisdictions, citing *M.C. Mehta v. Kamal Nath*[130] and *Illinois Central R. Co v. Illinois*.[131] The respondents attempted to use the doctrine to prevent the Court from interfering with the government's actions. They argued that the Court could not interfere with governmental action in relation to the said project as the government was the trustee of the resources. This argument was rejected by the Court, which stated that 'The organs of state are guardians to whom the people have committed the care and preservation of the resources of the people'[132] and as one of these organs, courts may have a role to play in scrutinizing government action where it concerns resources.

The respondents also cited the doctrine in support of the proposition, that as the guardian of natural resources, the state is propelled to make use of the phosphorous deposit. They argued that a failure to utilize the resources would amount to neglect of its duties as trustee.[133] The court acknowledged that the resources should be put to use, but instead of acknowledging the Public Trust Doctrine as support for this, it looked to the principle of Sustainable Development as a means of

[122] Ibid., Section 13(1).

[123] Ibid., Section 13.

[124] Ibid., Section 7(1)(a)(c).

[125] Ibid., Section 7(1)(d).

[126] Ibid., Section 8(1).

[127] Ibid., Section 9.

[128] Ibid., section 5: definition of foreshore and seabed.

[129] *Bulankulama and Others v. Secretary, Ministry of Industrial Development and Others* (Eppawela Case) (2000) LKSC 20; (2000) 3 Sri LR 243 (7 April 2000).

[130] (1977) 1 SCC 388.

[131] 146 US 387 at 452, 135 S Ct 110 at 118 (1892).

[132] Ibid.

[133] Ibid.

resolving the friction between environment and development.

Contrary to many academic writings, the Court appears to characterize the Public Trust Doctrine as a creature of trust law.[134] It construes its operation narrowly, stating that it 'should prefer to continue to look at our resources and the environment as our ancestors did, and our contemporaries do, recognizing a shared responsibility'.[135] Although it recognizes that the Executive has some responsibility in resource management, the Court also notes that this is subject to scrutiny by the courts in judicial review and to acts of Parliament while legislating. Consequently, the case was resolved on the basis of constitutional compliance, and not compliance with the doctrine.

CANADA

In *British Columbia v. Canadian Forest Products Ltd*,[136] the court applied elements of the Public Trust Doctrine while considering whether the Crown could sue for compensation on behalf of the public for environmental damage. The claim was instigated after Canadian Forest Products (Canfor), a licensee of an area of forest land, caused a fire to occur in an area of British Columbia that burnt and damaged 1,491 hectares of forest. The Crown brought a suit against the licensee for '(1) expenditures for suppression of the fire and restoration of the burned-over areas; (2) loss of stumpage revenue from the trees that would have been harvested in the ordinary course (harvestable trees); and (3) loss of trees set aside for various

environmental reasons (non-harvestable or protected trees).'[137] The trial judge awarded damages for the suppression of the fire and restoration of the affected areas but not for the other two categories. The court of appeal awarded damages for the third head, but not for the second.

Canfor appealed the award of damages for the non-harvestable or protected trees, while the Crown cross-appealed the award, claiming it to be inadequate. The Crown asserted its appeal for environmental damages as a landowner and on behalf of the public.[138] Canfor contested the Crown's action on behalf of the public and proposed that it should only be able to commence suit as a landowner. In resolving this question, the court utilized elements of the Public Trust Doctrine, detailing the relationship between the Crown and public rights. It notes that, '[t]he notion that there are public rights in the environment that reside in the Crown has deep roots in the common law'.[139] The Institutes of Justinian and the common law of England were cited as the origin of public rights in common resources. American law was also persuasive—*Illinois Central Railroad Co. v. Illinois*[140] was cited as authority for the Public Trust Doctrine, where the state's title over the land differs from ordinary land that may be subject to sale and is held on trust for the benefit of the public.[141] The court even cited Article 538 of the French Civil Code, which recognizes the 'common property in navigable rivers and streams, beaches, ports, and harbors'.[142] In conclusion, it had no difficulty in holding that,

---

[134] Huffman poses that the doctrine is part of property law, see James L. Huffman, 'Fish Out of Water: The Public Trust Doctrine in a Constitutional Democracy', 19 *Envtl. L. Rev.* 527 (1989) reprinted in 'Joseph Sax and The Public Trust', *Issues in Legal Scholarship*, Article 6 (2003) 1.

[135] Supra note 130, 9.

[136] [2004] 2 SCR 74, 2004 SCC 38.

[137] *British Columbia v. Canadian Forest Products Ltd*, (2004) 2 SCR 74, 2004 SCC 38, Section 3.

[138] Ibid.

[139] Ibid.

[140] 146 US 387 (1892).

[141] *Illinois Central Railroad Co. v. Illinois*, 146 US 387 (1892) 452 cited in ibid., Section 79.

[142] French Civil Code, Section 75.

'there is no legal barrier to the Crown suing for compensation as well as injunctive relief in a proper case on account of public nuisance, or negligence causing environmental damage to public lands'.[143]

As *parens patriae*, the Crown was entitled to seek compensation for the destruction of the protected trees on behalf of the public, and to protect the public interest.

Canadian academic and attorney Andrew Gage proposed that statutes should be interpreted in a manner by which they do not interfere with public rights:

Legislation will only authorize interference with public rights where the legislator's intention to do so is clear and unambiguous on the face of the legislation or where an intention to negatively affect public rights is the unavoidable consequence of the operation of the Act.[144]

He arrived at this conclusion by examining statutory interpretation regarding such rights in numerous Canadian decisions. For example, in interpreting the Navigable Waters Protection Act, the Supreme Court of Canada held that there was no clear statutory intention 'to allow the Governor-General in Council to authorize the city of Vancouver to interfere with the public right of navigation by building a sea-wall'.[145] Notably, the Court has held that although Aboriginal rights to commercial fishing may have constitutional supremacy over public rights to fishing as 'Section 35 of the Constitution Act, 1982 did not indicate a sufficient intention to extinguish public rights'.[146] Gage concludes that unless

there is a clear evidence of statutory intention to the contrary, there is a strong statutory presumption in favour of public rights in Canada.

Although Gage insists that the Public Trust Doctrine should be viewed separately from these principles of statutory interpretation, it can be observed that in many instances these principles of statutory interpretation are conductive to the doctrine. Especially since Canadian courts have not expressly adopted the doctrine, statutory interpretation 'may well be a first step towards the development of a made-in-Canada version of the Public Trust Doctrine'.[147]

Italy

In Italy, at first glance, the Public Trust Doctrine appears to be significantly wide. Bianchi, in his article[148] 'Harm to the Environment in Italian Practice: The Interaction of International Law and Domestic Law' discusses the evolution of liability for environmental damage. He points out that the scheme was initiated by 'judicial activism' and that the state auditor's court began bringing suits for environmental damage 'on the assumption that harm to the environment should be equated with financial damage to the state's accounts'.[149] The state was considered the trustee and brought its action on behalf of, and for the benefit of, the public.[150] Subsequent legislation incorporated

---

[143] Ibid., Section 81.

[144] Andrew Gage, 'Public Rights and the Lost Principle of Statutory Interpretation', *Journal of Environmental Law and Practice* vol. 15 (April 2005), p. 107.

[145] *Champion and White v. Vancouver*, (1917), 1 SCR 216, cited in ibid.

[146] *R. v. Gladstone*, (1996) 2 S.C.R. 723 at 770.

[147] Supra note 141.

[148] Andrea Bianchi, 'Harm to the Environment in Italian Practice: The Interaction of International Law and Domestic Law', in Peter Wetterstein (ed.), *Harm to the Environment: The Right to Compensation and the Assessment of Damages* (Clarendon Press: Oxford, 1997), ch. 7.

[149] See for example judgement No. 39 of 15 May 1973 (Sezione I), in (1973) 49 Foro Amministrativo I, 247 cited in Bianchi, supra note 150, n. 133, 104.

[150] Supra note 148.

these common law principles, vesting the state and its agencies with the exclusive power to bring actions for ecological damage.[151] These principles obviously provide a very narrow basis for standing. Bianchi identifies the limitation of standing to government and its instrumentalities, as a shortcoming of the legislative framework. He notes that 'the state has hardly ever acted to seek compensation for environmental damage' where '[r]egions, provinces and municipalities have shown no greater initiative in this respect'.[152] Bianchi's analysis is telling. For the Public Trust Doctrine to be effective, the state must exercise its function as trustee and actively protect the environment. If citizens are refused standing in such matters, a proper safeguard against the neglect of state duties is lost. It is the right of citizens and environmental NGOs to seek judicial review of administrative acts that can ultimately propel the state to act.

The Public Trust Doctrine can be extremely useful in protecting the environment and common heritage for the benefit of present and future generations. In many circumstances, the Crown or public authorities are in the best position to guard public rights in relation to land and water and the activities to be conducted on them. It can be observed that although the doctrine exists independently as a creature of common law, it does not operate in a vacuum. The doctrine is often incorporated into statutes and used to re-enforce environmental values that are entrenched in other sources. Perhaps the confusion in classifying the doctrine also represents its versatility.

---

[151] Act No. 349 of 8 July 1986 Article 18, 'Instituzione del Ministero dell' ambiente e norme in material di danno ambientale', in (1986) 162 Gazetta Ufficiale, Suppl. Ord. No. 59, 5 ff cited in Bianchi, supra note 149, n. 133, 104.

[152] Ibid.

4 Absolute Liability of the Polluter

THE SUPREME COURT OF INDIA

The Supreme Court of India evolved the theory of absolute liability of the polluter in the case of *M.C. Mehta v. Union of India*, popularly known as the *Oleum Gas Leak* case.[1]

In this case, the main question regarding compensation to victims was centred on the interpretation of Articles 21 and 32 of the Constitution of India. The Court permitted Shriram Foods and Fertilisers Industries to restart its power plant and units for the manufacture of caustic soda, glycerine, and technical hard oil subject to conditions laid down in the judgement dated 17 February 1986. While the writ petition was pending, there was leakage of gas on the 4th and 6th of December 1986, and applications were filed claiming compensation.

These applications raised a number of legal questions on the interpretation of Articles 21 and 32 of the Constitution such as:

1. Does the Constitutional Court have the jurisdiction to grant compensation? and;
2. Is Article 21 available against the said company engaged in an industry vital to public interest with the capacity to affect the life and health of the people?

Very broadly interpreting its power under Article 32, the Supreme Court held that it is free to devise any procedure appropriate for the particular purpose of the proceedings, namely, enforcement of a fundamental right. It further held that the Court has power to issue necessary directions in a given case, including all incidental or ancillary powers necessary to enforce a fundamental right. Article 32 is not powerless to assist a person when the court finds that his fundamental rights have been violated. The infringement must be gross and patent, that is, incontrovertible and ex facie glaring where such infringement should be on a large scale affecting the fundamental rights of a larger number of persons, or it should appear unjust or unduly harsh or oppressive on account of their poverty, disability, or socially or economically disadvantaged position to require a person or persons affected by such infringement to initiate and pursue action in the civil courts.[2]

The Supreme Court evolved the 'Principle of Absolute Liability' of compensation through interpretation of constitutional provisions relating to the right to life. This new position represented a fundamental shift from the earlier position. In matters of tortuous liability and determination of compensation, the earlier rule was the rule of 'strict liability', introduced in Britain by Blackburn in the

[1] *M.C. Mehta v. Union of India*, (1987) 1 SCC 395.

[2] See para 7 of the above judgement.

celebrated case of *Rylands* v. *Fletcher*.[3] In that case, Blackburn held:

The person who for his own purposes brings on his lands and collects and keeps there anything likely to do mischief; if it escapes, must keep it in at his peril, and, if he does not do so, is prima facie answerable for all the damage which is the natural consequence of its escape. He can excuse himself by showing that the escape was owing to the plaintiff's default; or perhaps that the escape was the consequence of vis major, or the act of God; but as nothing of this sort exists here, it is unnecessary to inquire what excuse would be sufficient.

Speaking for the Constitution Bench, Bhagwati expressed in no uncertain terms, the Court's unwillingness in following 'British-Indian vintage':

We cannot allow our judicial thinking to be constricted by reference to the law as it prevails in England or for the matter of that in any other foreign country. We no longer need the crutches of a foreign legal order.[4]

The Court further stated:

We are of the view that an enterprise which is engaged in a hazardous or inherently dangerous industry which poses a potential threat to the health and safety of the persons working in the factory and residing in the surrounding areas owes an *absolute and non-delegable duty to the community* to ensure that no harm results to anyone on account of hazardous or inherently dangerous nature of the activity which has undertaken. The enterprise must be held to be under an obligation to provide that the hazardous or inherently dangerous activity in which it is engaged must be conducted with the highest standards of safety and if any harm results on account of such activity, the enterprise must be *absolutely liable to compensate for such harm* and it should be no answer to the enterprise to say that it had taken all reasonable

care and that the harm occurred without any negligence on the part.

Thus, the Constitutional Bench established the Principle of Absolute Liability, approving the decision in *Burnie Port Authority's* case,[5] where the High Court of Australia held that: '[t]he rule in *Rylands* v. *Fletcher*, with all its difficulties, uncertainties, qualifications, and exceptions, should now be seen, for the purposes of the common law of this country, as absorbed by the principles of ordinary negligence.'[6]

The Supreme Court of India evolved the doctrine of absolute liability, refining the principle of strict liability that was developed in *Rylands* v. *Fletcher*. It also identified the principle that compensation can be claimed under writ jurisdiction by evolving the public law remedy, although victims must still approach ordinary civil courts to file a suit for damages.

The absolute liability theory laid down by the Supreme Court in the *Oleum Gas Leak* case was first applied by the Madhya Pradesh High Court to support its award of interim compensation to the victims of the Bhopal gas tragedy.[7] Environmental law has succeeded in unshackling man's right to life and personal liberty from the clutches of the common law theory.[8] The Supreme Court has since gone further in stating that:

the powers of the Supreme Court under Article 32 are not restricted and it can award damages in a Public Interest Litigation, or a writ petition... In

---

[3] (1868) (19) LT 220.

[4] *M.C. Mehta* v. *Union of India*, (1987) 1 SCC 395.

[5] *Burnie Port Authority* v. *General Jones Pty Ltd* (1994) 68 ALJ 331; also see P.S.A. Pillai, *Law of Tort*, 9th edition 2004, Delhi: Eastern Book Company, p. 281.

[6] *Burnie Port Authority* v. *General Jones Pty Ltd*, (1994) HCA 13 at [43].

[7] *Union Carbide Corporation* v. *Union of India*, Civil Revision No. 26 of 1988, 4 April 1988.

[8] *T. Damadhar Rao* v. *Special Officer, Municipal Corporation of Hyderabad*, AIR 1981 AP 171, p. 181.

addition to damages, the person guilty of causing pollution can also be held liable to pay exemplary damages so that it may act as a deterrent for others not to cause pollution.[9]

In a case on contamination of groundwater, the Supreme Court found that compensation can be recovered under the Environment (Protection) Act, 1986.[10] Likewise, when the Supreme Court found that illegal shrimp farms caused damage to the ecology, the Court directed the closure and demolition of shrimp farms and payment of compensation on the basis of the Polluter Pays Principle as well as cost of remedial measures to be borne by the industries.[11] Thereafter, the Government has framed the Coastal Aquaculture Authority Act, 2005 to overrule the judgement. Though the Supreme Court rendered the judgement, the damage to the environment has not been remedied.

When the ecology of the river Beas was damaged by the construction of a hotel, the Supreme Court applied the Public Trust Doctrine and imposed a fine.[12] The doctrine of 'absolute liability' is compatible and even complementary to the Public Trust Doctrine and Polluter Pays Principle because its general deterrence and mandatory penalty encourages those engaged in construction to respect the benefit of the public.

PUBLIC INTEREST LITIGATION SEEKING COMPENSATION FOR VICTIMS

A claim in public law for compensation for contravention of human rights and fundamental freedoms of human rights will lie as a constitutional remedy in addition to the private remedy in tort for damages resulting from the contravention of a fundamental right. The Court can evolve new tools and mould a remedy to provide redressal in cases where fundamental rights have been disrespected, particularly of have-nots under Article 21. Adverting to the grant of relief to the heirs of a victim of custodial death, for the infraction of the victim's rights guaranteed under Article 21 of the Constitution of India, it was not enough to relegate him to the ordinary remedy of a civil suit to claim damages for torturous acts of the State, as that remedy in private law is available to the aggrieved party.[13]

An advocate filed a PIL seeking damages for an aggrieved woman who was raped by the employees of the Railway. Rejecting the argument that a PIL by a private person is not maintainable, the Supreme Court held that the petition for damages or compensation for the victim was maintainable. The running of a railway is a commercial activity. Establishing Yatri Niwas at various railway stations to provide lodging and boarding facilities to passengers on payment of charges is part of the commercial activity of the Union of India and cannot be equated with the exercise of sovereign power. Employees of the Union of India, who are deputed to run the Railways and manage the establishment, including the railway stations and Yatri Niwas, are essential components of the government machinery that carries on commercial activity. If any of these employees commit a tort, the Union Government, of which they are the employees, can be, subject to other legal requirements being satisfied, held vicariously liable in damages to the person wronged by those

---

[9] *M.C. Mehta v. Kamal Nath and Others*, AIR 2000 SC 1997, (2000) 6 SCC 213.

[10] *Indian Council for Enviro-Legal Action v Union of India* (Bichuri Case), 1996 (5) SCC 212.

[11] *S. Jagannath v. Union of India*, 1997 (2) SCC 87.

[12] *M.C. Mehta v. Union of India* (Kamal Nath case), 1997 (1) SCC 388.

[13] *Nilabati Behra v. State of Orissa*, AIR 1993 SC 1960, (1993)2 SCC 746.

employees. Where public functionaries are involved and the matter relates to the violation of Fundamental Rights or the enforcement of public duties, the remedy would still be available under public law, notwithstanding that a suit can be filed for damages under private law.[14]

A PIL was filed before the Madras High Court for redressal of public injury suffered by a section of the community on account of arson and looting in the wake of the assassination of the then Prime Minister Rajiv Gandhi. The High Court held that wherever there is a public wrong or public injury caused by an act or omission of the State or a public authority that is contrary to the Constitution or the law, any member of the public acting bona fide and having sufficient interest can maintain an action for redressal of such public wrong or injury. Public-minded persons or organizations must be allowed to move court and act generally or in group interest.[15]

FOREIGN LAW

Australia[16]

As earlier discussed, the doctrine of *Rylands v. Fletcher* is largely obsolete in Australia. However, the concepts of 'strict liability' and 'absolute liability' can be readily observed in statutory offences. The High Court of Australia has discussed the different types of liability in the case of *He Kaw Teh v. R.*;[17] accordingly there are three categories of statutory offences:

1. mens rea applies in full;
2. the offence might be one of strict liability so that the prosecution does not have to rebut mens rea in proving the actus reus but, if the evidence raises a likelihood of honest and reasonable mistake, the prosecution must rebut that beyond reasonable doubt; and
3. that the offence creates absolute liability.

Strict liability and absolute liability both lack the element of mens rea, that is, the offence consists of the act. However, these two concepts can be distinguished on the basis that the defence of an honest and reasonable mistake may be available for strict liability offences. There are a wide range of statutory environmental offences in Australia that are included under strict liability, for example, Section 143 of the Protection of Environment and Operations Act, 1997 (NSW).[18] Some jurisdictions even go as far as deeming certain environmental offences to be absolute liability offences. For example, in the case of *Allen v. United Carpet Mills Pty Ltd*,[19] it was held that Section 39(1) of the Environment Protection Act 1970 (Vic) is an absolute liability offence.[20] This section provides that 'A person shall not pollute any waters…' and it can be observed that the language suggests that the offence is absolute, as nothing in the section suggests that knowledge is an element of the offence. The *Allen* case was considered in the case of *Wilson v. Gahan*,[21] which upheld the finding that Section 40(1)(b) of the Agricultural and Veterinary Chemicals (Control of Use) Act, 1992 (Vic) was an absolute liability offence. It was also held that Section 13(1) of the Ozone Protection Act, 1989 (Cth), which applies to

---

[14] *Chairman , Railway Board v. Chandrimadas*, AIR 2000 SC 988, 2000 (2) SCC 465.

[15] *R. Gandhi v. Union of India*, AIR 1989 Madras 205.

[16] Butterworths', *Commentary of Local Government Planning and Environment: New South Wales* (2004), [pp. 552, 530] (last updated 27 June 2006) was of general assistance in preparing this section.

[17] *He Kaw Teh v. R.*, (1985) 157 CLR 523, 533–4.

[18] Ibid.

[19] [1989] VR 323.

[20] Ibid.

[21] (1999) VSC 72.

the unlicensed manufacture, import, or export of chlorofluorocarbons (CFCs), is likely to be an absolute liability offence in the case of *Selectrix Pty Ltd v. Humphrys*.[22]

There is a general readiness in Australia to classify offences under strict liability, but the reluctance to deem them as absolute is properly expressed by Hedigan, in *Selectrix Pty Ltd v. Humphrys*: 'The categorization of the offence as one requiring strict liability, that is, allowing a defence of honest and reasonable mistake, has the virtue of protecting the so-called luckless victim.'[23]

By removing the availability of the defence for some offences, there arises the risk that the result may be inequitable. It is apparent that the principle of absolute liability can be used as a strong deterrent against environmental offences in both India and Australia.

UNITED STATES OF AMERICA[24]

The doctrine of *Rylands v. Fletcher* is utilized in some American states,[25] although in the beginning its acceptance was not easy.[26] The principle of 'strict liability', which appears to be used interchangeably with the term 'absolute liability' in the USA, commonly crops up in relation to ultra hazardous, abnormally dangerous, and inherently dangerous activities. Where such dangerous activities are carried out and an injury to a person or property is sustained as a result, it is immaterial whether the person carrying out the activity exercised reasonable care. The principle can be used to address harm done to the environment in two ways:

1. to protect land;
2. to protect environmental human rights, for example, air and water quality.

The decision of the District Court in *Sterling v. Velsicol Chemical Corp.*[27] reveals a dictum that is remarkably similar to that enunciated by Bhagwati in the case of *M.C. Mehta v. Union of India*. The court spells out the factors outlined in the American Restatement of Torts that guide the application of the principle of strict liability:

1. One who carries on an abnormally dangerous activity is subject to liability for harm to the person, land, or chattels of another resulting from the activity, although he has exercised the utmost care to prevent the harm.
2. This strict liability is limited to the kind of harm, the possibility of which makes the activity abnormally dangerous.

Section 520 lists factors to be considered in determining what constitutes an abnormally dangerous activity:

(a) existence of a high degree of risk of some harm to the person, land, or chattels of others;
(b) likelihood that the harm that results from it will be great;
(c) inability to eliminate the risk by the exercise of reasonable care;

---

[22] *Selectrix Pty Ltd v Humphrys*, (2001) VSC 45, (17).

[23] Ibid.

[24] American Jurisprudence (2nd edition) was of general assistance in preparing this part. See in particular: Dangerous Agencies, Instrumentalities, and Activities, Strict Liability in Cases of Abnormally Dangerous or Ultrahazardous Activities, 57A Am. Jur. 2d Negligence, Section 392 (last updated March 2008).

[25] Dangerous Agencies, Instrumentalities, and Activities, Strict Liability in Cases of Abnormally Dangerous or Ultrahazardous Activities, 57A Am. Jur. 2nd edition Negligence, Section 377 (updated March 2008).

[26] Danielle Keats Citron, *Reservoirs of Danger: The Evolution of Public and Private Law at Dawn of the Information Age*, 80 S. Cal. L. Rev. 241.

[27] 647 F. Supp. 303, 313.

(d) extent to which the activity is not a matter of common usage;

(e) inappropriateness of the activity to the place where it is carried on; and

(f) the extent to which its value to the community is outweighed by its dangerous attributes.[28]

It can be seen that the Indian position is more akin to the USA position than that of England. Although the principle is to be construed narrowly, American courts have applied the principle to situations involving contamination of human drinking water due to the carrying out of such activities.[29] Perhaps the guiding principles of the American Restatement of Torts could be used to further define what a hazardous or inherently dangerous activity is for the purposes of absolute liability in India.

Some statutes also provide for strict liability offences. The Comprehensive Environmental Response, Compensation, and Liability Act[30] section 107 deems the discharge of hazardous waste and various actions connected thereto,

strict liability offences. It does, however, provide that a defence may be available where the defendant can establish that the release or threat of release of the hazardous substance and resultant damages was caused by an act of God, an act of war, or an act or omission of a third party (other than an employee or agent of the defendant). There are, hence, varying degrees of liability that come under the definition of 'strict liability' or 'absolute liability' in the USA.

Law must grow and change to meet the requirements of a fast-changing society and keep abreast with economic developments taking place in the country. Courts cannot allow judicial thinking to be constricted by reference to the law as it prevails in other countries. They must evolve new principles and lay down new norms that adequately deal with new problems that arise in a highly industrialized economy. New principles to meet situations should be the rule of law and courts should not hesitate to evolve such principles of liability.

---

[28] Restatement (Second) of Torts, Section 519 (United States).

[29] See for example: *Sterling v. Velsicol Chemical Corp.*, 647 F. Supp. 303; *Yommer v. McKenzie* 255 Md. 220, 257 A.2d 138 as identified in Strict Liability, Abnormally Dangerous Activities, Restatement (Second) of Torts, section 520 (1977) (last updated June 2007).

[30] 42 USCA, Section 9607.

5 Reversal of the Burden of Proof

The normal rule is that the burden of proof lies on the person who wants to prove his or her case. In other words, if a person wants a judgement that punishes another person for committing a crime, the person wanting the judgement has to prove that the other person has committed the offence, unless it is provided by any law that the proof of that fact shall lie on any particular person.[1]

The inadequacies of science have led to the 'precautionary principle', which in turn, has led to the special principle of burden of proof in environmental cases where burden as to the absence of any injurious effect of the actions proposed is placed on those who want to change the status quo.[2]

The 1998 Wingspread Conference on the Precautionary Principle gathered health experts, who summarized four components that should guide its implementation:

1. Action to prevent harm despite uncertainty.
2. Shifting the burden of proof to proponents of a potentially harmful activity.
3. Examination of a full range of alternatives to potentially harmful activities, including no action.

4. Democratic decision making to ensure inclusion of those affected.

Simply stated, the precautionary principle means that proponents of activities that might lead to serious or irreversible damage are obliged to take, or permit, measures to be taken to prevent this damage (including halting proposed activities), in spite of lack of full scientific certainty as to the existence of the risk, its nature, or the potential damage. An essential element of this technique is reversal of the burden of proof.[3]

In view of Articles 47, 48A, and 51A(g) of the Constitution of India and various environmental statutes, the Supreme Court has held that that the Precautionary Principle and the Polluter Pays Principle are part of the environmental law of the country. The Court also affirmed to be a part of environmental law, the procedural rule that shifts the onus of proof to the actor or the developer/industrialist[4] to show that their action is environmentally benign. The basis of this principle of 'reversal of burden of proof' is that the party attempting to preserve the status quo by maintaining a less-polluted state should not

---

[1] Section103, Indian Evidence Act, 1872.
[2] Wynne, *Uncertainty and Environmental Learning*. 2 *Global Envtl Change*, 111 (1992) at p. 123.

[3] Precaution in International Principle on Sustainable Development Law. http://www.cisdl.org/pdf/brief_precaution.pdf - <last accessed on 16 April 2008>
[4] *Vellore Citizens' Welfare Forum v. Union of India and Others*, 1995(5) SCC 647.

carry the burden of proof and the burden is thus shifted to the person who is attempting to alter the status quo.[5]

INDIAN CASE LAW

Where there is an identifiable risk of serious or irreversible harm including, for example, extinction of species or widespread toxic pollution, posing major threats to essential ecological processes, it may be appropriate to place the burden of proof on the person or entity proposing the activity that is potentially harmful to the environment.[6] The principle of shifting of burden of proof has been accepted by the Supreme Court of India in the case of *A.P. Pollution Control Board* v. *M.V. Nayudu*.[7]

If the environmental risks run by regulatory action are in some way 'uncertain but non-negligible', then regulatory action is unjustified. This leads to the question as to what is a 'non-negligible risk.' In such a situation, the burden of proof is to be placed on those attempting to alter the status quo. They are to meet the standard of proof by showing the absence of a 'reasonable ecological or medical concern.' If insufficient evidence is presented by them to alleviate concern about the level of uncertainty, then the presumption should operate in favour of environmental protection. Such a presumption has been applied in *Ashburton Acclimatisation Society* v. *Federated Farmers of New Zealand*.[8] The 'reasonable person' test is now the appropriate standard for examining the harm to the environment and human health in public interest cases.[9] This test is also applicable in environmental PILs in India.[10]

In following the above mentioned dictum, the KHC held that when considering a petition for abating nuisance under Section 133 of the Criminal Procedure Code,[11] it is for the respondent party to show that the nuisance has been abated.[12]

The above principle is applicable only to environmental PILs and not to all types. In one such case, an application was filed in regard to the non-appointment of judges and there was an averment that all formalities for their appointment had been completed. The counsel was asked how he came to know of such a statement. As it is not a burden to counter such a statement, he replied that whenever such matters had been heard by the Court in the past, the Attorney General would appear and make this contention. He submitted that the petitioner was in the dark, and knew nothing because he had no access to the relevant files. He submitted that the Court should not look at technicalities but at the files instead in view of the principle of reversal of burden of proof. The Supreme Court held that it is not open for the petitioner to make averments and ask the court to look into records to see if they are correct in all cases, while deprecating the practice.[13]

It may be noted that the principal of reversal of burden of proof is an exception to the general rule of evidence and it cannot be applied to all cases.

---

[5] See James M. Olson, 'Shifting the Burden of Proof', 20 *Envtl. Law*, p. 891 at 898 (1990). (Quoted in vol. 22 (1998) *Harv. Env. Law Review*, p. 509 at 519, 550).

[6] Report of Sreenivasa Rao Pemmaraju, Special Rapporteur, *International Law Commission*, dated 3 April 1998, para 61.

[7] AIR 1999 SC 812.

[8] 1988(1) NZLR 78.

[9] Charmian Barton, 'The Status of the Precautionary Principle in Australia', vol. 22 (1998) *Harv. Env. Law Review*, p. 509 at 549.

[10] *A.P. Pollution Control Board* v. *M.V. Nayudu* (Retd), AIR 1999 SC 812.

[11] See the separate chapter under the Nuisance for more.

[12] *Sujatha* v. *A. Prema*, 2005 (3) KLT 458.

[13] *R. Singh* v. *Union of India*, 1999(5) SCC 187, 1999 (8) JT 450.

Foreign Laws

China

In China, Article 4, Section 3 of the Supreme People's Court Various Regulations Regarding Evidence for Civil Suits, states that:

in compensation lawsuits concerning environmental pollution, the polluter carries the burden of proof with respect to...demonstrating the lack of causal link between the polluter's actions and the harmful result.[14] Given the difficulty of proving causation in environmental pollution cases, this reversal of burden of proof is often the critical determinant of the outcome in environmental litigation.

Germany

The reversal of burden of proof has been suggested by the German Advisory Council on Global Change for all cases of environmental damage and risk. Instead of the full proof of standard, which reverses the burden of proof of Section 6 of the Environmental Liability Act, the balance of profitability was proposed where in a given circumstance, the balance of evidence suggested that damage had been caused by an action relevant to the case.[15] Relaxation of the burden of proof was suggested in many cases in the German High Court. In a case of water pollution, the High Court has stated that as long as a particular substance was generally capable of causing the relevant damage in conjunction with other substances, causation would be presumed.[16]

People affected by the tampering of the environment are disorganized, and in most cases, poor. Proceedings initiated against the interferors of natural resources are generally in public interest. As the judiciary is also intended for the benefit of the public, courts always take up the cause of such a disorganized public and try to find the persons who alter natural situations. Courts act as the watch-dog of the environment, and have every right to question the rights of the so-called violator of the said natural rights.

---

[14] Supreme People's Court Various Regulations Regarding Evidence for Civil Suits (promulgated by the Sup. People's Ct. 6 December 2001, effective 1 April 2002) LawInfoChina (last visited 19 March 2007) (P.R.C.) (author's translation).

[15] WBGU Report 1988, *World in Transition: Strategies for Managing Global Environmental Risks.*
[16] BGHZ 57, 257 at 262. Huhnergugulle-Fall.

6 The Significance of Public Interest Litigation

Litigation is generally filed by a person aggrieved by an action or inaction. But activities causing pollution differ in the sense that they adversely affect the entire public. Is it necessary that each individual files a separate petition before the court to stop the offending activity? The Constitution of India confers power on all citizens to approach the State High Courts[1] and the Supreme Court of India[2] in cases of violation of fundamental rights. Such writs can be invoked by individual citizens aggrieved by the pollution.

The Supreme Court has taken a broader view of the above powers and invented the tool of PIL. The expression 'public interest litigation' is used to denote

[A] legal action initiated in a court of law for the enforcement of public interest or general interest in which the public or class of community have pecuniary interest or some interest by which their legal rights or liabilities are affected.[3]

DEFINING PUBLIC INTEREST LITIGATION

PIL is a strategic arm of the legal aid movement, intended to bring justice within the reach of the poor masses, who form the low-visibility area of humanity. It is a totally different kind of litigation from the ordinary traditional litigation. The Council for Public Interest Law, set up by the Ford Foundation in the USA, defined 'public interest litigation' in its report on Public Interest Law, USA, 1976:

'Public Interest Law' is the name that has been recently been given to efforts [to] provide legal representation to previously unrepresented groups and interests. Such efforts have been undertaken in the recognition that [the] ordinary market place for legal services fails to provide such services significant segments of the population and to significant interests. Such groups and interests include the proper environmentalists, consumers, racial and ethnic minorities, and others.[4]

This view is consistent with that of the Supreme Court of India ruling that the purpose of a PIL is not to enforce the right of one individual against another, but to promote and vindicate public interest. This demands that violation of constitutional or legal rights of a large number of people who are poor,

---

[1] Article 226 of the Constitution empowers the High Court to issue writs for the enforcement of fundamental rights and for any other purpose.

[2] Article 32 empowers the Supreme Court to issue a writ for the enforcement of fundamental rights.

[3] *Janatha Dal* v. *H.S. Chowdhary*, AIR 1993 SC 892, (1992) 4 SCC 305.

[4] *B. Singh* v. *Union of India*, (2004) 3 SCC 363.

ignorant, or in a socially or economically disadvantageous position should not go unnoticed. Such neglect would be destructive to the Rule of Law, which is an essential feature of any democracy. The Court made these observations when justifying interference in public interest, in a case when a PIL was brought against the denial of minimum wages, which amounted to forced labour. This was the first time the Court ruled that a writ petition could be filed against the government or local authority to ensure that private contractors pay minimum wages to their employees.[5]

PIL is a weapon that must be used with great care and circumspection; the judiciary should be extremely careful, and should be able to detect malice behind the veil of public interest in some cases. The court should be satisfied with the credentials of the applicant; the prima facie correctness or nature of information given by him; the information being not vague and indefinite. The information provided should also show the gravity and seriousness of the matter involved. The court must strike a balance between two principles: (i) nobody should be allowed to make wild and reckless allegations besmirching the character of others; and the aim of (ii) avoidance of public mischief and mischievous petitions seeking to assail, for oblique motives, justifiable actions. In such cases, the court cannot afford to be liberal. It has to be extremely careful to see that under the guise of redressing a public grievance, it does not encroach on the sphere reserved by the Constitution for the Executive and the Legislature. It must act ruthlessly while dealing with imposters and busybodies or meddlesome interlopers impersonating as holy men. The Supreme Court expressed its caution in dealing with those who pretend to act in the name of Pro Bono Publico, despite having no public or personal interest to protect.[6]

PROCEDURE FOR FILING A PIL

There are prescribed procedures and rules for filing a PIL. The Supreme Court of India has relaxed some of the technical hurdles in matters involving public interest, particularly when it has entertained the petition. In matters where public interest is involved, the Court shall not adopt a technical or narrow manner.[7]

There is no written law on how a PIL is to be filed and how it should be dealt with. On several occasions, the Supreme Court has treated letters, telegrams, postcards, and news reports as writ petitions. The lack of procedural law for entertaining a PIL has allowed certain persons to misuse this type of litigation. The full court of the Supreme Court of India on 1 December 1988 issued certain guidelines to be followed for entertaining letters and petitions received in the Court as a PIL. Petitions falling under the following categories alone would ordinarily be entertained as a PIL:

1. Bonded labour matters.
2. Neglected children.
3. Non-payment of minimum wages to workers and exploitation of casual workers and complaints of violation of labour laws (except in individual cases).
4. Petitions from jails complaining of harassment, for premature release and seeking release after having completed fourteen years of jail, death in jail, transfer, release on personal bond, speedy trial as fundamental right.
5. Petitions against police for refusing to

---

[5] *People's Union for Democratic Rights v. Union of India,* AIR 1982 SC 1473, (1982) 2 SCC 235.

[6] Supra note 3.

[7] *Mohamed Aslam v. Union of India,* (2002) 4 SCC 1.

register a case, harassment by police, and death in police custody.

6. Petitions against atrocities on women, in particular harassment of bride, bride-burning, rape, murder, kidnapping, and other such deeds.

7. Petitions complaining of harassment or torture of villagers by co-villagers or by police of persons belonging to Schedule Castes and Schedule Tribes and economically backward classes.

8. Petitions pertaining to environmental pollution, disturbance of ecological balance, drugs, food adulteration, maintenance of heritage and culture, antiques, forest and wildlife, and other matters of public importance.

9. Petitions from riot victims.

10. Family pension.

All letter-petitions are received in the PIL Cell of the Supreme Court and are first screened in the Cell. Only petitions that fall within the above-mentioned categories are placed before a judge to be nominated by the Honourable Chief Justice of India. Directions are then issued, and the case is listed for a particular bench, which usually consists of one judge, but may be increased to two or three depending on the workload.

It was also decided that cases falling under the following categories would not be entertained as a PIL, and such matters may be returned to the petitioners:

1. Landlord-tenant matters.

2. Service matters and those pertaining to pension and gratuity.

3. Complaint against Central/State Government Departments and local bodies except those relating to item numbers (1) to (10).

4. Admission to medical and other educational institutions.

5. Petitions for early hearing of case pending in High Courts and Subordinates Courts.

With regard to petitions concerning maintenance of wife, children, and parents, the petitioner might be asked to file a petition under Section 125 of the Criminal Procedure Code, 1973 or a suit in a court of competent jurisdiction, and for that purpose to approach the nearest Legal Act Committee for legal advice.[8] The above guidelines are followed while entertaining writ petitions in the Supreme Court of India.

The Supreme Court of India even entertains letters and newspaper reports, which are converted into writ petitions.[9] The Court has also approved the practice of entertaining PILs where there is a threat to public interest by arbitrary and perverse executive action; in such a case, it was held to be the duty of the high court to issue a writ. The concerned high court, before issuing the process or exercising the powers in public interest, should be prima facie satisfied that the information provided to the Court was of such a nature that it required examination. Prima facie satisfaction can be derived by ascertaining the credentials of the person approaching the Court, or the nature of the information given, or the gravity and seriousness of the complaint set out in the petition, or other circumstances brought to the notice of the Court that require interference for the purpose of instilling confidence in the common man in the democratic setup of the country in general, and the judiciary in particular. Such a litigant shall not be permitted to make wild and reckless allegations besmirching the character of others. To ensure avoidance of

[8] Published in 'Parivesh', newsletter of Central Pollution Control Board, December 2002.

[9] *Sheela v. State of Maharashtra*, AIR 1983 SC 378; *Veera v. State of Bihar*, AIR 1983 SC 339.

public mischief, the Court is required to act promptly by giving appropriate directions.[10]

A decision of the Vice Chancellor allowing certain students to take certain examinations in accordance with the relevant Act was challenged by the Students Council. The affidavit did not disclose whether the Council had funds to pay for the litigation, or whether it was authorized to file the PIL, or who the PIL was to be filed by. The Supreme Court held that such litigation should not be allowed to proceed lightly in the name of a PIL.[11]

A PIL was filed against the operator of some stone crushing units established near a village, which were causing pollution. The crushers were not shifted to a safe location despite directions from Supreme Court. The Court held that a PIL filed to safeguard the health of the citizens should not be dismissed by the high court for want of approaching[12] the State Government prior to filing the petition.[13] Individuals in all walks of life, as well as organizations in many fields, by their values and the sum of their actions, shape the environment of the future. Whenever it is found that the atmosphere and environment was being polluted, the Court would not hesitate to issue appropriate directions for the preservation of a pollution-free atmosphere.

It has been observed by the high courts and Supreme Court that the noble concept of the PIL has been abused by filing frivolous petitions. To curb this abuse and in order to preserve the purity and sanctity of the PIL the Supreme Court of India[14] has issued several directions, which read thus:

1. The courts must encourage genuine and *bona fide* PIL and effectively discourage and curb the PIL filed for extraneous considerations.

2. Instead of every individual judge devising his own procedure for dealing with the public interest litigation, it would be appropriate for each high court to properly formulate rules for encouraging the genuine PIL and discouraging the PIL filed with oblique motives. Consequently, we request that the high courts who have not yet framed the rules, should frame the rules within three months. The registrar general of each high court is directed to ensure that a copy of the rules prepared by the high court is sent to the secretary general of this court immediately thereafter.

3. The courts should *prima facie* verify the credentials of the petitioner before entertaining a PIL.

4. The court should be *prima facie* satisfied regarding the correctness of the contents of the petition before entertaining a PIL.

5. The court should be fully satisfied that substantial public interest is involved before entertaining the petition.

6. The court should ensure that the petition which involves larger public interest, gravity, and urgency must be given priority over other petitions.

7. The courts before entertaining the PIL should ensure that it is aimed at redressal of genuine public harm or public injury. The court should also ensure that there is no personal gain, private motive, or oblique motive behind filing the PIL.

[10] *Chaitanya v. State of Karnataka*, AIR 1986 SC 825.
[11] *Barathiya Homeopathy College v. Students Council, H.M. College, Jaipur*, AIR 1998 SC 1110, (1998) 1 JT 359, (1998) 2 SCC 449.
[12] The normal rule for the issuance of a writ of mandamus is that the person should approach the concerned authority before approaching the High Court. Only on inaction or refusal to act, the writ will lie.
[13] *Iswar Singh v. State of Haryana*, AIR 1996 P & H. 30.

[14] *State of Uttaranchal v. Balwant Singh Chaufal*, AIR 2010 SC 2550: 2010 (3) SCC 402: 2010 AIR SCW 1029.

8. The court should also ensure that the petitions filed by busybodies for extraneous and ulterior motives must be discouraged by imposing exemplary costs or by adopting similar novel methods to curb frivolous petitions and the petitions filed for extraneous considerations.

LOCUS STANDI

The question of locus standi in a PIL is an interesting one. Traditionally, a person must suffer a legal injury by reason of violation of his legal right in order to be granted locus standi. This theory underwent a radical change when, for the first time, the Supreme Court of India held[15] that the law was a social auditor and this audit function could be put into action only when someone with real public interest ignites the jurisdiction. The Court held that activism was essential for participative public justice, for which certain risks were considered to be taken by affording more opportunities for public-minded citizens to rely on the legal process and not be repelled from it by narrow pedantry that existed. The Court held:

If a citizen is no more than a way-farer or officious intervener without any interest or concern beyond what belongs to any one of the 660 million people of the country, the door of the court will not be ajar for him. But he belongs to an organization which has special interest in the subject matter, if he has some concern deeper than that of a busybody, he cannot be told off at the gates, although whether the issues raised by him is justiciable may still remain to be considered. I therefore, take the view that present petition would clearly have been permissible under Article 226.

When the Government of India decided to transfer the judges of the high court from one state to another, it was challenged by an advocate named S.P. Gupta, who successfully established standing despite having no concrete legal interest in the matter. The old rule was diluted, and for the first time the Supreme Court of India held that any member of the public having sufficient interest could maintain an action for judicial redress, arising from a breach of public duty, the Constitution, or the law, and seek enforcement of such public duty or observance of the constitutional or legal provision. This is absolutely essential for maintaining the Rule of Law, the Court held. This historical judgement opened a Pandora's box for many litigants.[16]

An interesting question arose before the Supreme Court of India when M.C. Mehta[17] filed a PIL to protect the river Ganga from pollution. At common law, the Municipal Corporation can be restrained by an injunction, brought by the riparian owner who has suffered from the discharge of insufficiently treated sewerage into the river. The Court held that the pollution creates a public nuisance that is widespread in range and indiscriminate in effect, it being unreasonable to expect any particular person to take proceedings to stop it as distinct from the community at large.[18] Hence, Mehta was able to proceed with the application.

The KHC held maintainable a PIL by an non-government organization (NGO) seeking judicial review of administrative action, to avoid devastation of a major portion of forest land and ecological imbalance that could amount to an environmental disaster. The Rule of Law constitutes the core of our Constitution and demands that the exercise of State power be within constitutional limitations. If any

---

[15] *Fertilizer Corporation of India v. Union of India*, AIR 1981 SC 344.

[16] *S.P. Gupta v. Union of India*, AIR 1982 SC 149.

[17] Environmentalist lawyer, Magsaysay Award Winner.

[18] *M.C. Mehta v. Union of India*, AIR 1988 SC 1115, (1988) 1 SCC 471, 1988 (1) JT 69.

practice is adopted by the Executive that is in flagrant and systematic violation of its constitutional limitations, the petitioner as a member of the public has sufficient interest to challenge such practice by filing a writ petition, the Court observed.[19]

Challenging illegal construction in violation of the Coastal Regulation Zone notification, a PIL was filed before the Bombay High Court. On the question of locus standi, the Court held that a petition by a public-spirited body working in the field of environment with the object of maintaining ecological balance is maintainable.[20]

Upon the discovery of clandestine felling and smuggling of timber from forests, any citizen can file a writ petition. Such a petitioner performs a laudable public duty and no technicalities should prevent him/her from approaching the court for implementation of the promises that form the basis of Articles 48A and 51A of the Constitution of India, the KHC held.[21]

A students' union filed a PIL questioning the teaching standards of universities. The norms and standards for imparting technical education to students provide that they must receive proper teaching by competent teachers. A PIL by a students' union challenging such recruitment is maintainable, the Gauhati High Court held.[22]

The assignment of land belonging to a college in favour of an association was challenged in a PIL. The petitioners felt that the activities of the association would adversely affect the academic atmosphere of the college campus. The writ petition by PIL was maintainable, despite the fact that the petitioners could not be described as aggrieved or affected parties, the KHC ruled.[23]

Other types of litigants have been granted standing. A worshipper can challenge the actions of the temple authorities if they amount to an intrusion upon any matter of the particular religion.[24] The right of a taxpayer to challenge the appointment of the Tourism Development Corporation on the ground of disqualification has also been upheld by the KHC.[25] People have a right to object, within the law, to the setting up of liquor shops, according to several High Court decisions.[26]

GOVERNMENT BODIES AND AUTHORITIES

The West Bengal Government filed a PIL before the Calcutta High Court to protect the interests of millions of small depositors in residuary non-banking companies that were not conducting their business in accordance with the directives of the Reserve Bank of India. The Court held that a PIL can be brought for the purpose of upholding the rights of the people who are poor and under the veil of ignorance of their rights and obligations. The PIL was maintainable and the Reserve Bank was directed to take suitable steps to protect the interests of small depositors so that they could obtain their deposits with interest within a specified time limit.[27]

[19] *Nature Lovers Movement v. State of Kerala*, ILR 2000 (1) Kerala 677.
[20] *The Goa Foundation v. The Conservator of Forests*, AIR 1999 Bom 177.
[21] *V.M. Abraham v. State of Kerala*, 1987(I) KLT SN 79; p. 57.
[22] *Biswajit Sinha v. Dilburgh University*, AIR 1991 Gau 27.

[23] *Parent Teacher Association, Maharaja's College v. State*, AIR 1995 Ker 209.
[24] *Ram Mohandas v. Travancore Devaswom Board*, 1975 KLT 55.
[25] *Parameswaran v. State of Kerala*, 2002 (2) KLT 863.
[26] Supra note 18, p.109.
[27] Angela Z. Cassar and Carl E.Bruch, 'Transboundary Environmental Impact Assessment in International Watercourse Management', *NYU Environmental Law Journal*, 12 (2003), 169 at p. 175.

Political parties have also approached the Supreme Court to invoke PIL jurisdiction. While hearing a challenge of the rejection of a petition by the Karnataka High Court, the Supreme Court held that in defining the rule of locus standi, no 'rigid litmus test' can be applied. The broad contours of PIL are still developing apace with divergent views on several aspects of the concept of this newly developed law and jurisdiction of judicial activism, with far reaching change, both in the nature and in the form of the judicial process. The Supreme Court held that the determination of locus standi depends on the circumstances.[28]

Can a member of the legislative assembly (MLA) file a PIL? In one case, an MLA challenged an enactment that had the disastrous effect of giving shelter and protection to foreign nationals who had illegally transgressed international borders to reside in India. The Supreme Court of India held that the PIL could not be rejected on the grounds that the MLA was trying to achieve a purpose that his party could not achieve politically.[29]

A Municipal Councillor can file a PIL against the decision of the Municipality. In Gujarat, a PIL was filed challenging the allotment of land by municipal authorities for a newspaper press. A resolution to that effect was passed by the Corporation. The petitioner was a councillor voting for the allotment, and felt that the publishing of the newspaper in the city would help stimulate public opinion on various issues and possibly contribute to public education. No construction was carried out on the plot and upon notice of this non-compliance, a PIL was filed. The Gujarat High Court held that the action was maintainable.[30]

Pleadings

Rules have been framed by the Supreme Court and high courts prescribing the form and formalities to be observed while filing a writ petition. Generally, all writ petitions should be drafted stating separately, the full name and address of the parties, statement of facts, grounds, and reliefs. If any interim relief is sought, that should also be shown separately as prescribed by the rules. The documents relied on must be produced along with the said writ petition and if the court prima facie finds that there is a genuine case to answer, it will invite the opposite parties to make their objections. There is no separate format for filing a PIL, which is filed in the same manner as a writ petition.

Courts have always been liberal in their interpretation of pleadings in a PIL. Objections raised on technical matters are always overruled so as to protect public interest. The plea to dismiss a writ petition for vagueness and want of necessary details, especially after admitting the case, will usually be rejected.

In matters involving public interest, a technical manner is not adopted by the court, particularly when it has entertained the petition, issued notices to parties, impleaded new parties, and issued interim orders. On several occasions, the Supreme Court has treated letters, telegrams, postcards, and news reports as writ petitions. On the basis of pleadings that emerge after notice to the parties, relief has been given or refused.[31]

A PIL activates the jurisdiction of the Constitutional Court which acts to redress public injury, enforce public duty, protect social rights, and uphold constitutional and democratic values. Technicalities do not deter the Court in wielding the power to do justice, enforce the law, or balance equities. No objection can be upheld for want of

---

[28] Paragraph 7, III, Stage (3), EIA Notification, 2006, wef 14 September 2006.

[29] *Sarbananda Sonowal v. Union of India*, AIR 2005 SC 2918, 2005 (2) SCC 689.

[30] *Kanchanbhai Kanbhai Tadvi v. Municipal Corporation*, AIR 2002 Guj 31.

[31] *Mohamed Aslam v. Union of India*, (2002) 4 SCC 1.

pleadings, the Supreme Court clarified while dealing with an objection pointing to lack of jurisdiction.[32]

In a particular case, a writ petition with a request for direction to whoever it may concern was made. The request was very vague and sought a direction to cease the clandestine business and smuggling in a certain area, and also to direct the Union of India to make arrangements for the export of items like brown sugar from the specified premises. The court held that the petitioner should have clearly stated the facts and allegations and indicated how public interest was involved.[33]

A petition drafted in a careless manner with meaningless and self-contradictory pleadings, clumsy allegations, and irrelevant facts should be rejected.[34] The basis of the knowledge on which the writ petition is filed should be stated. The Supreme Court deprecated this practice and held that it is not open for the petitioner to make vague averments and ask the court to look into records to ascertain their correctness.[35]

A dispute arose in respect of a contract entered into with the Delhi Vidyut Board for providing electrical connections. The petitioner made a prayer for relief for appointing him as an authorized contractor, filed the writ petition, and incorporated a prayer for investigation by the Central Bureau of Investigation (CBI) to transform it into a PIL. The court held that merely by making such an additional prayer, the writ petition would not become a PIL.[36]

Whenever the court comes to the conclusion that the process of the court is being abused, the court would be justified in refusing to proceed further with the case. But, if the concealed fact is material one in the sense that had it not been suppressed, it would have an effect on the merit of the case or order, no false statement shall be made in the pleadings, intentionally to mislead the court and obtain favourable orders. The making of such statements tends to impede the administration of justice and will amount to criminal contempt. The court can appoint an *Amicus Curiae*, to strike a balance between the interests of the parties.[37]

The Supreme Court has held that mere pendency of a civil suit by others for similar relief will not affect the maintainability of writ petition in public interest.[38]

Procedural Rules—Res Judicata

One of the main defences mounted in cases is the general rule of res judicata, which means that an issue that has already been decided once cannot be the subject of further litigation.[39] The grounds which might and ought to have been made grounds of defence or attack in a former suit shall be deemed to have been a matter directly and substantially in issue in such suit the principle of constructive res judicata.[40]

A PIL is not an adversarial style of adjudication, as the petitioner merely brings to the court, notice of how the public has been jeopardized by arbitrary and capricious action on the part of the authorities. Therefore, the principles of constructive res judicata cannot be made applicable to each and every PIL,

[32] *Padma v. Hiralal Motilal Desarda*, 2002 (7) SCC 564: AIR 2002 SC 3252.

[33] *Giani Devender Singh Sant Sepoy Sikh v. Union of India*, AIR 1995 SC 1847, (1995)1 SCC 391.

[34] *Charan Lal Sahu v. Union of India*, (1988) 3 SCC 255, AIR 1988 SC 107.

[35] *R. Singh v. Union of India*, 1999 (5) SCC 187, 1999 8 JT 450.

[36] *Ambedkar Basti Vikas Sabha v. Delhi Vidyut Board*, AIR 2001 Delhi 223.

[37] *Narmada Bacaho Andolan v. State of MP*, 2011 AIRSCW 2337.

[38] *Meghwal Samaj Shiksha Samithi v. Lakh Singh*, 2011 AIRSCW 3759.

[39] Section 11, Code of Civil Procedure (CPC), 1908.

[40] Explanation IV, Section11, CPC.

irrespective of the nature of litigation itself, its impact on society, and the larger public interest being served. There cannot be any dispute that in competing rights of public interest against individual interests, public interest would take precedence.[41]

Of course, if the earlier litigation is bona fide, a judgement in the PIL would be a judgement in rem. It binds the public at large and bars any member of the public from coming forward before the court and raising any specific or ancillary issue connected therewith which has or should have been raised on an earlier occasion.[42]

PIL ON MATTERS OF JUDICIAL OFFICE

A PIL was filed to compel a judge to vacate office on the basis of a resolution passed by the Bar Association. The Supreme Court explained the procedure for making a complaint against a judge. It held that if the complaint relates to a judge of the high court or the Chief Justice of that high court, verification and a confidential inquiry by an independent source may be necessary to establish the truth of the imputation made by the Bar Association through its office bearers. Subsequent to this, the Chief Justice of India may be consulted and all the information should be placed before him.[43]

When a PIL was filed challenging the transfer of judges from the high court, the Supreme Court made it clear that no one other than the transferred judge himself can question the validity of the transfer.[44] Hence, only the particular judge has locus standi in such cases.

A writ petition by a representative body like the Sub-Committee on Judicial Accountability and Supreme Court Bar Association, for directions to the Union of India to take immediate steps to enable an Inquiry Committee to be constituted under the Judges (Enquiry) Act, 1968 to discharge its functions under the Act and to restrain the concerned judge from performing judicial functions during the pendency of proceedings before the Committee, is maintainable. Constitutional protection afforded to judges is not for their personal benefit, but is a means of protecting the independence of the judiciary and is, therefore, in the larger public interest. The Supreme Court held that the law on standing to sue in a public interest action has undergone a vast change over the years and now recognizes liberal standards for locus standi, expanding the said principle.[45]

A PIL was filed for the removal from office of a sitting judge of the Supreme Court, initiated by the notice of motion given to the Speaker by some members in the Lok Sabha. The judge concerned was not made a party. Since the petitioner persisted in not impleading the concerned judge, the Court dismissed the proceedings. Cases may arise where public injury is undoubtedly caused by an act or omission of the state or a public authority, but such act or omission also causes a specific legal injury to an individual or to a specific class or group of individuals. In such cases, a member of the public having sufficient interest can maintain an action challenging the legality of such act or omission. But if the person or specific class or group of persons who are primarily injured as a result of such act or omission do not protest and do not wish to claim any relief or accept such act or omission,

---

[41] V. Purushotham Rao v. Union of India, 2001 (9) JT 187.
[42] State of Karnataka v. All India Manufacturers Organisation, AIR 2006 SC 1926, 2006 (5) SCC 192.
[43] C. Ravichandra Iyer v. Justice A.M. Bhattacharjee, (1995) 5 SCC 457, (1995) (6) JT 339.
[44] K. Ashok Reddy v. Union of India, AIR 1994 SC 1685, (1994) 2 SCC 303.

[45] Sub-Committee on Judicial Accountability v. Union of India, (1992) 4 SCC 97, AIR 1992 SC 63.

the member of the public who complains of secondary public injury cannot maintain the action. This is because the effect of entertaining the action at the instance of such member of the public would be to foist a relief on the person or specific class or group of person primarily injured, which they do not want.[46]

PIL BY RIVALS IN TRADE

If there is an allegation of violation of statutory rules that have been brought to the notice of the authorities and the authorities fail to act, any aggrieved citizen has the right to bring notice to the High Court of such inaction. In such an event, the Court is always open to pass the orders it deems fit and proper in the circumstances and depending on the facts of the case. The fact that the PIL was filed by a business rival is irrelevant, the Supreme Court held.[47]

The test for maintaining a PIL has come under consideration. The Supreme Court of India has held that it is wrong for the Court to judge the petitioner's interest without looking into the subject matter of his complaint. If the petitioner proves a failure of public duty, the Court would be in error in dismissing the PIL.[48]

In Sikkim, the State Government failed to take steps to demolish hotel buildings which were in a deplorable condition. A writ petition filed by some hotel owners in the city in the form of a PIL was not liable to be dismissed on the ground that the applicants, being hotel owners, were business rivals of the owners of the buildings in question. The High Court held that the action was maintainable as the applicants were residents of the state and were concerned for the safety of their residents.

Challenging the allotment of industrial plots, a PIL was filed by persons actively engaged in social work, on behalf of small entrepreneurs proposing to start new industries. A bulk allotment was made at a very low price without inviting applications or notifying the public. The Karnataka High Court held that this was a deplorable exercise of power by the board and a petitioner who files in public interest cannot be said to have no locus standi.[49]

A PIL was filed challenging the grant of licences by the Railways to run food stalls at railway platforms. People who can be considered have a legitimate expectation to put in an application and compete to qualify to obtain a licence. A writ petition by public-spirited persons challenging the action of railway authorities in awarding catering licences is maintainable, the Madhya Pradesh High Court held.[50]

PROTECTION OF GOVERNMENT LAND

On several occasions the courts have to protect the public interest, wherein the authorities used to sell the government property for a pittance for extraneous reasons. While upholding such a view of the Gujarat High Court, the Supreme Court has held that where the public interest has been given a complete go-by in an action of haste at the behest of others, a PIL is maintainable.[51]

The question of whether an assignment of government land to private persons can be questioned by any person in the public

---

[46] *M. Krishna Swami v. Union of India*, (1992) 2 SCC 341, AIR 1993 SC 1407.

[47] *Mehsana District Central Co-operative Bank Ltd v. State of Gujarat*, AIR 2004 SC 1576 .

[48] *Vishwanath Chaturvedi v. Union of India*, 2007 AIRSCW 2045.

[49] *P. Gururaja v. Executive Member*, AIR 1998 Kant 223.

[50] *Mahendra Kumar Tiwari v. Union of India*, AIR 1998 MP 178.

[51] *Bahadurishn Lakhubhai Gohil v. Jagdishbhai M. Kamalia*, AIR 2004 SC 1159, 2004 (2) SCC 67.

interest was considered by the KHC, which held that where authorities are taking steps to assign government property to private persons discarding and by-passing statutory inhibitions and mandatory provisions, a writ petition to interdict the perpetuation of the illegality and resultant injury to the public cannot be thrown overboard by conducting an investigation into the juristic existence of the petitioner. In such cases, the petitioner's role gets transformed into that of a mere informant enabling the court to take cognizance of the issue.[52]

PIL BY KNOWLEDGEABLE PERSONS

The authority of bankers to round up the interest rate to 0.25 per cent has been questioned by a firm of chartered accountants in a PIL before the Karnataka High Court. The Court allowed the writ petition and held that the rounding up of interest rates to the next 0.25 per cent is illegal, arbitrary, and untenable. The same was questioned in appeal before the Supreme Court. In the Supreme Court's exercise of its jurisdiction under Article 32 of the Constitution of India, and the High Court under Article 226, a petition moved by a person having knowledge on the subject matter and an interest therein can be maintained. Such an action is contra distinguished from a busybody because the welfare of the people is concerned. The rule of locus standi is relaxed by the Court to vindicate legal injury or legal wrong caused to a section of people by way of violation of any statutory or constitutional right. The petitioner, a chartered accountant firm, is granted locus to maintain the PIL or writ petition filed by him *pro bon publico* before the High Court, the Supreme Court held.[53]

Can any person challenge the creation of a district? Any citizen of the state is allowed to question any illegal or ultra vires action by the government. Before intervening in any such manner, the court will exercise the discretion vested in it by the law and the Constitution. It will only take into account relevant factors like the nature of harm that might be a consequence of the impugned action, the difficulties that might crop up consequent to the court's decision in the matter, and the extent and nature of the complainant's interest in the matter.[54]

INVOLVEMENT OF PUBLIC FUNCTIONARIES

The allotment of petrol outlets by the Minister of State for Petroleum in the Union Cabinet was questioned in a PIL on the basis that it potentially abused the discretionary quota available. The Supreme Court held that when public functionaries are involved, and the matter relates to a violation of fundamental rights or the enforcement of public duties, the remedy in PIL lies under public law, notwithstanding that damages are also claimed in the petition. In spite of the fact that the Council of Ministers is collectively responsible to the Lok Sabha, there may be an occasion where the conduct of a minister may be censured if he or his subordinates have blundered and have acted contrary to law. It was open to the Lok Sabha to consider the issue in the capacity of the concerned person as minister, by initiating debate on the floor of the house, but his failure to do so did not make the allotments of petroleum outlets by him immune from judicial scrutiny by the Court under Article 32 of the Constitution. Therefore, even if the matter was not raised on the floor, it would be amenable to the jurisdiction of the writ court, the Supreme Court held.[55]

---

[52] *Youth Voice Arts Social and Cultural Organisation v. State of Kerala and Others*, 2001 (3) KLT 909.

[53] *Indian Banks Association v. Devkala Consultancy Service*, 2004 AIRSCW 2491, (2004) 4 JT 587.

[54] *Madhusoodhanan Nair v. Governor*, 1983 KLT 43.

[55] *Common Cause v. Union of India*, (1999) 6 SCC 669, AIR 1999 SC 2979.

Before making allegations against ministers and other public persons, it is essential that they be personally heard. Where an authority in discharge of the duties fastened upon it by law, raises a question that has the potential to adversely affect the personal reputation of a minister, they must give the minister an opportunity to comment on the issue.[56]

WITHDRAWAL OF A PUBLIC INTEREST LITIGATION

Ordinarily, a person who files a case can withdraw the same if they like. But this principle is not applicable to a PIL because there is no determination or adjudication of individual rights. The Supreme Court had the occasion to deal with the issue when a request was made to withdraw a PIL. In declining the request, the Court explained that the technique of PIL serves to provide an effective remedy to enforce rights and interests of a group, where the relief granted looks to the future and is generally corrective rather than compensatory, although it can be both. The pattern of relief need not necessarily be derived logically from the rights asserted or found. The Court is not merely a passive or disinterested umpire or onlooker, but has a more dynamic and positive role with the responsibility of organizing the proceedings and tailoring and implementation of relief.[57]

The Supreme Court has made it clear that a PIL cannot be withdrawn without prior permission of the Court. Permission cannot be granted where a petitioner seeks to raise the same question in different courts. Permission to withdraw the suit is based on a consideration of public interest, and whether

there is an abuse of process of court, the Supreme Court clarified.[58]

In a PIL challenging the validity of an amendment to the Civil Procedure Code, 1908, the applicant sought to withdraw the case. The court found that the case raised an important issue that adversely affects the law and hence declined the prayer and appointed an *amicus curiae* to proceed with the matter.[59]

Permission granted by the Sessions Judge for withdrawal of a criminal case against the chief minister was challenged in public interest. It is well settled that once criminal proceedings are pending, they cannot be interfered with. The question of withdrawal of any criminal complaint depends upon the complainant and no direction can be issued under the guise of a PIL. In this particular case, the government withdrew all ten cases pertaining to an alleged incident dated 15 August 1994. While disposing off the case without discussing the merits, the court directed the Magistrate's Court to consider the material facts and the substance of the earlier application after obtaining comments on the withdrawal in public interest. This was thought to be in the interests of justice.[60]

PUBLIC INTEREST IN PRIVATE LITIGATION

On certain occasions, courts adjudicating private litigation have issued directions in public interest. In a writ petition before the Allahabad High Court, the Court was dealing with the issue of an allotment of two shops by the local body. While dealing with the same, the Court

---

[56] *Public Concern for Governance Trust & Others v. Vinay Mohan Lal,* 2007 AIR SCW 474.

[57] *Sheela Barse v. Union of India,* AIR 1988 SC 2211, (1988) 4 SCC 226.

[58] *S.P. Anand v. H.D. Deve Gowda,* AIR 1997 SC 272, 1996 (1) 6 SCC 734.

[59] *Salem Bar Association v. Union of India,* AIR 2003 SC 189, 2003 (1) SCC 49.

[60] *Raghunathgowda v. The Director of D.G.P. Karnataka State and Others,* CDJ 2005 Kar HC 145. Karnataka High Court.

proceeded to nullify several government orders in public interest. The effect of the directions so issued was to nullify as unconstitutional several government decisions, despite the fact that their validity was not specifically in issue before the Court. The Supreme Court was of the view that the High Court should have adopted a different approach and outlined the issues affecting public interest before giving the state specific notice, inviting its pleadings and documents. Parties who were interested or likely to be adversely affected should have been given the opportunity to be heard. Such a large issue that involves public interest and has far-reaching implications should not have been dealt with so lightly, casually, and hurriedly, the Supreme Court observed.[61] The over enthusiastic judges had issued certain directions to the authorities under the guise of judicial activism and had failed to adopt the correct procedure, according to the Supreme Court.

Courts are concerned only with the legality of the decision in question and cannot possibly provide an answer to all of the various political, social, and economic problems that confront society in modern times. In his famous polemic *Truth versus Ashurst*, written in 1792 and published in 1823, Jeremy Bentham made a searing criticism of judge-made criminal law, which he called 'dog-law'.

It is the judges (as we have seen) that make the common law? Do you know how they make it? Just as a man makes laws for his dog. When your dog does anything you want to break him of, you wait till he does it, and then beat him for it. This is the way you make laws for your dog: and this is the way the judges make law for you and me. They won't tell a man beforehand what it is he should not do—they won't so much as allow of his being told: they lie by till he has done something which they say he should not have done, and then they hang him for it.

Courts, while pronouncing their judgement, are not engaged in an exercise on law reform, but are only supposed to interpret the existing law. The court's duty is to affirm what the law is and not what the law should be.

THIRD PARTIES AND CRIMINAL COURT ACTIONS

Can a third party, who is a stranger to a criminal prosecution in which the accused is convicted, challenge the conviction and sentence imposed upon the accused? The Supreme Court answered the question in the negative on the basis that no fundamental right of the petitioner was violated. In attempting to assert locus standi, the stranger would essentially be arguing that their rights were infringed by the conviction. If locus was granted in such a case, then every person could challenge convictions even if the persons convicted do not welcome this and are inclined to acquiesce in the decision. A third party may be allowed to represent the convict only if they are under some disability recognized by law,[62] the Court clarified.[63]

If the State fails to appeal against the acquittal of a criminal, a citizen can prefer an appeal in the Supreme Court. That Court can take action through its extraordinary jurisdiction under Article 136 of the Constitution as it has a broader appellate jurisdiction.[64]

Neither a public interest litigant nor the accused have a right to question the mode of collection of evidence by the investigating

---

[61] *State of U.P. v. Satya Narain Kapoor*, (2004) 8 SCC 630.

[62] Habeas Corpus petition can be filed by third parties against conviction.

[63] *Simranjit Singh Mann v. Union of India*, (1992) 4 SCC 653.

[64] *P.S.R. Sadhanantham v. Arunachalam*, (1980) 3 SCC 141, AIR 1980 SC 856.

agency, or to interfere in the progress of the investigation, the Supreme Court held.[65]

SERVICE MATTERS—NO PIL

The appointment of the President of a Tribunal[66] was questioned in the Supreme Court. In service jurisprudence only an aggrieved person can challenge the offending action. A third party, has no locus standi to challenge the appointment. Only public law declaration would be made at the behest of the public-spirited person, the Supreme Court added.[67]

FOREIGN LAWS

Some jurisdictions have been very receptive of the PIL movement and others have not. Strict standing requirements still exist in countries such as Australia; these requirements make it considerably more difficult to bring a PIL than in a country like India, for example. In their article titled 'Securing Environmental Rights Through Public Interest Litigation in South Asia', Hassan and Azfar note that South Asia has been revolutionary in relaxing standing and procedural requirements, to allow litigants better access to justice.[68] Part of this can be attributed to the fact that many countries of the region have sophisticated environmental legislation that has not been properly implemented. The authors point out that neglect on the part of administrative authorities has often led citizens to turn to

the courts.[69] This can be contrasted to the developed world, where standing regimes are much stricter, largely because citizens are more equipped, economically and educationally, to access the courts using traditional routes.[70]

United States of America

PIL has increased individual participation in the enforcement of environmental standards in the USA where locus standi has been granted, for example, in *Japanese Whaling Association* v. *American Cetacean Society*.[71] The court has held that the political question doctrine does not bar judicial resolution of the court. Courts have the authority to construe international treaties and executive agreements and to interpret congressional legislation. The challenge to the Secretary's decision not to certify Japan presents a purely legal question of statutory interpretation. The judiciary's constitutional responsibility to interpret statutes cannot be shirked simply because a decision may have significant political overtones.

Bangladesh

The Appellate Division of the Supreme Court of Bangladesh broadened the principle of locus standi in a case filed by Mohiuddin Farooque. Allowing his appeal, the Supreme Court held that the expression 'any person aggrieved' in Article 102 of the Constitution is not confined to individually affected persons only, but extends to the people in general, as a collective and consolidated personality. The Court considered the submissions made by the Bangladesh Environmental Lawyers Association in the writ, and concluded that the Association should be given locus standi

---

[65] *Janatha Dal* v. *H.S. Chowdhary*, AIR 1993 SC 892, (1992) 5 JT 231.

[66] Customs, Excise and Gold (Control) Appellate Tribunal.

[67] *R.K. Jain* v. *Union of India*, (1993) 4 SCC 119, AIR 1993 SC 1769.

[68] Parvez Hassan and Azim Azfar, 'Securing Environmental Rights Through Public Interest Litigation in South Asia', 22 *Va. Envtl LJ* 2003–4, 215 at p. 217.

[69] Ibid., n. 73, at p. 223.

[70] Ibid., n. 73, at p. 226.

[71] 478 US 221 (1986).

to maintain the writ petition. It further held that the Association was a 'person aggrieved' within the meaning of Article 102 of the Constitution

because the cause it bona fide espouses, both in respect of fundamental rights and constitutional remedies, is a cause of an indeterminate number of people in respect of a subject matter of great public concern.[72]

Pakistan

While PIL in Pakistan can be traced back to cases such as *Darshan Masih* v. *State*,[73] the case of *Shela Zia*[74] gave environmental rights constitutional legitimacy[75] as the court specified that Article 9 of the Pakistani Constitution, which refers to the right to life, includes the right to a healthy environment. This had a similar effect on rulings in India, where this right is now actionable by citizens. In this case, the resident petitioners opposed the construction of a grid station in their area on the basis that it had the capacity to emit electromagnetic radiation and thus adversely affect their health. The court found influential, Indian decisions that had treated the right to life as necessitating the right to a healthy environment, while also taking account of the Rio Declaration. Consequently, the petition was entertained and the citizens were permitted locus standi. The court directed that further research into the effects of the grid station on human health be carried out before its construction could continue.[76]

United Kingdom

In the High Court of Justice, the Queen's Bench had the opportunity to widen the scope of locus standi in the case of *R. (David Edwards)* v. *(1) The Environment Agency (2) First Secretary of State & Rugby Ltd*.[77] An action was brought challenging the sanction granted to a cement company that was established in Rugby. It was contended that the claimant was no longer residing in Rubgy and had no locus standi. The Environment Agency also contended that the claimant did not have sufficient standing and was only brought into the matter for the purposes of obtaining funding on the basis that he was homeless. It was also alleged that he had not taken part in the consultation process. Justice Keith, after considering the issue elaborately, held that the claimant had a sufficient interest in the outcome. Even though he was temporarily homeless, he had always been a resident of Rugby, and therefore had an interest in the environment of Rugby which was being polluted by the cement plant. The Court held that it would not be an abuse of process to grant standing to the applicant.[78]

Australia

The question of standing is answered very differently in Australia. According to the traditional English common law position, it has been the role of the Attorney General to vindicate the rights of the public in the courts.[79] Unless a person or body has a 'special interest in the subject matter of the action',[80] it is unlikely that they will be granted locus standi.

---

[72] Ibid.

[73] *Shela Zia* v. *WAPDA*, 715.

[74] *Shela Zia and Others* v. *WAPDA PLD*, 1994 SC 693.

[75] Supra note 73, at 216.

[76] *Shela Zia* v. *WAPDA* 715 in supra note 65, 73, p. 239.

[77] (2004) EWHC 736 (ADMIN).

[78] (2004) 3 All ER 21.

[79] *Bateman's Bay Local Aboriginal Land Council* v. *The Aboriginal Community Benefit Fund Pty Ltd*, (1998) HCA 49 (6 August 1998), Section 35.

[80] *Australian Conservation Foundation* v. *The Commonwealth*, (1980) 146 CLR 493 (Gibbs J, at Section 14).

Busybodies or those with a mere 'intellectual or emotional concern'[81] will be denied standing. In the hallmark case of *Australian Conservation Foundation v. The Commonwealth*,[82] the Australian Conservation Foundation (ACF) brought a suit against the Commonwealth, some ministers, and the Reserve Bank of Australia. ACF challenged the respondent's approval of the development and operation of a tourist area and the sufficiency of an EIA prepared in relation to it. The proposed development was to take place in an area to which some members of the foundation had access and it would adversely affect their rights. The court held that the Act outlining the administrative procedure in relation to the EIA and approval process did not create actionable private rights. The question therefore was, did the ACF have standing to action a public wrong? Despite being an incorporated body with written objectives to conserve 'the distinctive vegetation and fauna and important natural and archaeological features of Australia' the Foundation was denied standing in the matter. Even if some members could claim a private right in the matter, this could not be imputed to the Foundation as a whole. The objectives of the Foundation were equated to mere 'beliefs' and were not sufficient to prove the 'special interest in the subject matter of the action' necessary to obtain standing. Although this case appears to construe standing fairly narrowly, it must be remembered that standing depends on the subject matter of the action. The rule will thus operate on a case-by-case basis.

STRATEGIC LAWSUITS AGAINST PUBLIC PARTICIPATION (SLAPPs)

Another hurdle faced by public interest litigants is the Strategic Lawsuit Against Public Participation, commonly termed as 'SLAPP'. A SLAPP is different from ordinary litigation in the sense that it is brought with an ulterior motive. Such suits commonly arise in environmental matters, where a person or body is criticized for their environmentally destructive activities and in an effort to avoid scrutiny, they file a lawsuit against the critic. The instigator of a SLAPP is likely to be more concerned with the effect that the act of litigating will have on the defendant than the actual subject matter of the SLAPP. Such suits are a reaction to citizen participation in the political process, and aim at reducing participation in the future.[83] If effective, the SLAPP removes the dispute from the public arena and transforms it into a private lawsuit.[84] Governments, individuals, or corporations may bring a SLAPP with the aim of silencing the activists.[85] Some SLAPP suits may even aim to discredit the activist's claim entirely and counteract the effects of the activism.

SLAPPs can be quite effective as their success lies in the very nature of litigation. Time, expense, and inconvenience are common features of litigation and many recipients of SLAPPs will abandon their environmental activism if it means avoiding this trouble. Those who continue the fight are also defeated in some way as their attention must be focused

---

[81] Ibid., (Gibbs J, at Section 20).

[82] (1980) 146 CLR 493.

[83] Andrew T. Kenyon, 'Defamation and Critique: Political Speech and New York, *Times v. Sullivan*', in Australia and England, 25 *Melb. U.L. Rev.* pp. 522, 530 (2001) citing George W. Pring and Penelope Canan, *SLAPPs: Getting Sued For Speaking Out*, vol. 8 (Philadelphia: Temple University. Press, 1996).

[84] Pring and Canan, supra note 80.

[85] Sharon Beder, 'SLAPPs—Strategic Lawsuits Against Public Participation: Coming to a Controversy Near You', *Current Affairs Bulletin* 72(3), 22 (October/November1995), http://www.uow.edu.au/arts/sts/sbeder/SLAPPS.html.

on the SLAPP, thus leaving them little time and resources to pursue environmental advocacy.

Identification of SLAPPs in the public sphere needs to happen in order to encourage public participation in environmental matters and debate of matters fundamental to public interest. Now, approximately twenty-five states in the USA[86] have some form of anti-SLAPP legislation that aims to identify the SLAPP at an early stage of litigation and give the defendant the opportunity to file for a summary judgement and shift the burden of proof on the claimant. Once a SLAPP loses its mystery and the motives of the claimant

are exposed, negative attention is drawn to the claimant. This results in the SLAPP losing many of its functional qualities.

When considering PILs, it is important to remember that the cause is more important than the cause-maker. Indian courts have adopted a broad and liberal stance towards PILs, where this new species of litigation manages to shine a light upon the judicial system as the third pillar of justice, renewing the confidence of the people. It is fortunate for environmental justice that PIL exists, for it enables a greater number of activists to vindicate such a valuable cause.

[86] California Anti-SLAPP Project, http://www.casp.net/menstate.html (last updated 19 July 2007).

7 Environment Impact Assessment
An Early Warning System

Development is sine qua non for human progress. However, in the rush for progress and economic development man should not compromise the ability of the present and future generations to fulfil their needs from natural resources. This does not mean 'shutting the door' to all developmental activities. There has to be a 'common ground'. Herein lies the relevance of EIA, an important legal instrument to reconcile environmental considerations into socio-economic development. It is the process of identifying, predicting, evaluating, and mitigating the bio-physical, social, and other relevant effects of developmental proposals prior to major decisions being taken and commitments made.[1] It aims at predicting environmental impacts at an early stage in project planning and design, finding ways and means to reduce adverse impacts, so as to shape the project to suit the local environment in addition to presenting predictions and options to decision-makers.[2] The EIA duly accommodates environmental concerns

into the decision-making process. This concept has its foundations in the principle of sustainable development. Basically, an EIA is an administrative tool used by agencies to foresee and reduce the impact on the environment from a developmental activity, vis-à-vis, balancing socio-economic concerns pari passu with environmental concerns. EIA is thus a beacon for the formation of a viable environmental policy.

EIA—What Does it Mean?

EIA is an assemblage of three words. If we analyse them, the meaning would be clearer.

1. Environment: In case of an EIA, the environment constitutes three main sub-systems, vis-à-vis: the physical environment (air, water, atmosphere, geology, and other physical features); the biological environment (flora and fauna, their habitats, endangered species, and other biological creations); the socio-cultural environment (demography, customs, culture, development, public health, and other social issues).

2. Impact: The Oxford Dictionary defines 'impact' as 'the powerful effect that something has on somebody/something'. Impact literally means effect (adverse

[1] 'Principles of Environmental Impact Assessment Best Practice', published in the website of International Association for Impact Assessment http://www.iaia.org/modx/assets/files/Principles%20of%201A_web.pdf
[2] United National Environment Programme—Division of Technology, Industry, and Economics.

effect). EIA, as a planning tool, anticipates the likely changes or consequences that a project may cause and suggests likely alternatives if any. Thus, impact as far as EIA is concerned means the positive and negative consequences that a proposed project may have on the environment.

3. Assessment: To assess means to judge or calculate. Assessment is the act of judging or forming an opinion about something. Assessment is assembling, summarizing, organizing, and interpreting pieces of existing knowledge, and communicating them so that an intelligent but inexpert policy maker will find them relevant and helpful in their deliberations.[3]

An EIA provides decision-makers with information on the environmental consequences of proposed activities, requiring decisions to be influenced by that information.[4]

EIA is a planning tool, which anticipates, minimizes, and even avoids the adverse effect of a development proposal, thereby protecting the environment and promoting sustainable development. It ensures that environmental concerns are fully and properly incorporated and addressed in the developmental decision-making process. It is guided by three core values:

1. Integrity: The EIA process should be fair, objective, unbiased, and balanced.
2. Utility: The EIA process should provide balanced and credible information for decision-making.

3. Sustainability: The EIA process should result in environmental safeguards.[5]

COMMON PROCESS OF EIA

The EIA consists of certain steps that are equally important in determining the overall performance of the project. They are considered as 'operating principles', which describe how the basic principles are to be applied to the main steps and specific activities of the EIA process.[6] These processes are:[7]

1. Screening: The first stage that determines whether the proposed project requires an EIA or not, and if it requires EIA, then the level of assessment required.
2. Scoping: If during the screening stage it is ascertained that a proposed project has potential to cause an impact on the environment and that it requires an EIA, then scoping follows. This stage identifies the key issues and impacts that are

[3] Munn, 1979. Available in the book titled 'Green Development' Environment and Sustainability in the Third World, by William Mark Adams, (New York, USA: Routledge) 1992, p. 146.

[4] Phillippe Sands, Principles of International Environmental Law, vol. 1, 1995, UK: Manchester University Press, p. 579.

[5] 'The Manual in Perspective' (Section A), EIA Training Resource Manual, UNEP, 2002, p. 110.

[6] International Association for Impact Assessment (IAIA), in 'Principles of Environment Impact Assessment Best Practice', has formulated two-tier EIA principles. They are: Basic Principles and Operating Principles. Basic principles apply to all stages of EIA, including Strategic Environmental Assessment (SEA). They are: Environment Impact Assessment should be: i) purposive ii) rigorous iii) practical iv) relevant v) cost-effective vi) efficient vii) focused viii) adaptive ix) participative x) interdisciplinary xi) credible xii) integrated xii) transparent xiv) systematic, p. 3. Supra note 1.

[7] Supra note 5, pp. 113–114; also see 'Principles of Environment Impact Assessment Best Practice' of IAIA, see Supra note 3 p. 4 <>http://www.iaia. org/Members/Publications/Guidelines_Principles/Principles%20of%20IA.PDF -6-12-07; also see Centre for Science and Earth (CSE India) 'Introduction to Environment Impact Assessment'<> http://www.cseindia.org/programme/industry/eia/introduction_eia.htm <> 3-12-07.

likely to be important and needs further investigation. Scoping also establishes the terms of references (ToR) for the EIA.

3. Impact analysis: After scoping, the EIA reaches a preliminary conclusion as to likely environmental and social impact of the proposed project and evaluates the significance.

4. Mitigation: This stage recommends the actions to reduce, avoid, or even minimize the potential adverse environmental consequences of developmental activity. EIA can also suggest alternative methods, which are benign to the environment, to achieve the proposed objective.

5. Reporting: The result of the EIA is presented in the form of a report (Environmental Impact Statement or EIS) to the decision-making body and other interested parties.

6. Review of EIS: It examines and determines whether the report meets its ToR and provides a satisfactory assessment of the proposal. It must provide information necessary for the decision-making authority. This stage ascertains the adequacy and effectiveness of an EIA report.

7. Public participation: This is one of the most important stages in an EIA process. Usually, public participation may occur at any time during processes 2 to 6. But it may also occur at any other stage of the EIA process.

8. Decision-making: It decides whether the project is rejected, approved, conditionally approved, or needs further changes.

9. Follow-up/Post-monitoring and Environmental auditing: This stage comes into play once the project is commissioned. It checks whether the impacts of the project exceed the legal standards or not and the implementation of the mitigation measures are in the manner described in the EIA report. An environmental

audit is helpful to verify compliance with the EIS. It can also be helpful in identifying unprecedented impacts or failed mitigation strategies and ensure that they are addressed in a timely manner.

The above is a common structure of the EIA process. The stages required for an EIA process depends upon requirements of the respective countries.

FACETS OF ENVIRONMENT IMPACT ASSESSMENT

Strategic Environment Assessment (SEA/SEIA)

A Strategic Environment Assessment (SEA) is an impact assessment tool and a facet of the EIA. An SEA can be defined as 'the formalized systematic and comprehensive process of evaluating the environmental impacts of a policy, plan, or programme to ensure that they are fully included and appropriately addressed at the earliest possible stage of decision making on a par with social and economic considerations.'[8] The purpose of an SEA is to ensure that significant environmental consequences of certain policies, plans, or programmes are identified and assessed during their preparatory stage, which are communicated to the decision-makers and are mitigated before their adoption. The SEA process was envisaged to facilitate public involvement, and giving relevant stakeholders an opportunity to get involved in decision-making, thereby enhancing the

[8] B. Sadler and R. Verheem, *Strategic Environment Assessment: Status, Challenges and Future Directions*, Ministry of Housing, Spatial Planning and the Environment, The Netherlands, 1996, p. 188; also see *Bio Diversity in EIA and SEA, Background Document to CBD Decision VIII/28: Voluntary Guidelines on Bio-Diversity Inclusive Impact Assessment*, April 2006, Commission for Environment Assessment, The Netherlands, p. 47.

transparency in the decision-making process. SEA involves a holistic approach, covers a wider area of projected environmental impacts, and involves a longer life span than an EIA. SEA, in contrast to EIA, provides decision-makers with the information, strategies, and actual and projected information on environmental effects on a large scale. SEA does not in effect reduce or replace an EIA, but complements and streamlines the EIA process of individual development. By integrating environmental consideration, SEA supports sustainable development. In India, the SEA is not developed, although developed countries like the European Union have incorporated the SEA in their environmental law.[9]

Rapid Environment Impact Assessment (Rapid EIA)

An EIA is an elaborate process of assessing the future effects of a current project. However, a criticism often levelled against it is that it is a cumbersome and time-consuming process. Normally, an EIA report will take one year or more to complete. This is said to create impediments for project proponents and to adversely affect the blossoming of a proposed project. Rapid EIA is a 'shortcut' to pacify the concerns of the project proponents and to advance the impact assessment regime. Here, the project proponents are allowed to furnish an EIA report known as a Rapid EIA report to the nodal agency (Impact Assessment Agency, EIA Notification 1992) based on one season date, other than the monsoon season. The project proponents are required to submit a detailed report when asked to by the nodal agency.

A Rapid EIA is feasible from a developmental point-of-view. However, it is prone to abuse. Firstly, an EIA report based on a single

season is meagre and inadequate. For large development projects, giving an Environment Clearance (EC) on the basis of a Rapid EIA is a perfect recipe for disaster. Secondly, project proponents may tend to conceal and evade significant impacts to ecology in a Rapid EIA. There have been instances where the project proponent has given a Rapid EIA prepared during the monsoon season.[10] It was because of this that a comprehensive EIA report was made compulsory for obtaining an EC, by an amendment in 2002.

EIAs are sometimes tailor-made, without actually conducting any studies. For example, a Rapid EIA was prepared to mine bauxite in the Ratnagiri District of Maharashtra. The Rapid EIA prepared by the project proponent in April 2005 was actually a cut-and-copy version of the Environmental and Social Impact Assessment (ESIA) for a proposal by a Russian aluminium company, the SUAL Group, to mine bauxite in the Komi Republic of Russia, prepared by CSIR Environmentek (a South African consultant) in April 2004 and submitted to the European Bank for Reconstruction and Development.[11]

Trans-boundary Environmental Impact Assessment (TEIA)

A Trans-boundary Environmental Impact Assessment (TEIA) is another facet of the EIA, where the potential impact assessed has the potential to affect two or more

---

[9] European Union Directive 2001/42/EC.

[10] It was alleged by the petitioners in the writ petition that the Tropical Botanical Garden and Research Institute (TBGRI), which was entrusted by KSEB to prepare a Rapid EIA for Athirappilly Hydro Electric Project, had conducted the assessments during monsoon months, in *Athrirappilly Grama Panchayat v Union of India*, WP C Nos 9542, 11254 and 260763 of 2005). See supra.

[11] http://www.ebrd.com/projects/eias/s20318e.pdf accessed on 20 July 2007.

states. Normally, an EIA is envisaged as a 'national instrument'. However, when there is a risk of significant environmental impact to states other than the 'source state' (it is where the environmental harm originates), a TEIA becomes relevant. It is very similar to the domestic EIA, but since it deals with multiple states, the process is multilayered and cumbersome. It is thus the 'internationalized version of EIA'.

Initially, the EIA process at the international level didn't have many takers, barring few implicit references in the 'no-harm principle'.[12] However, later international instruments like the United Nations Convention on the Law of Seas, 1982 (UNCLOS);[13] Antarctic Environment Protocol, 1991;[14] The Espoo Convention, 1991; The Convention on Biological Diversity, 1992 (CBD, Article 14); United Nations Convention on the Law of the Non-Navigational Uses of International Watercourses, 1997 (Watercourses Convention) have given an explicit mandate to Environmental Impact at the international level. Besides these, certain customary cases decided by the International Court of Justice and other tribunals have also helped to evolve this concept.[15]

INDIAN LAW

An EIA is basically envisaged as a 'national instrument', and the onus to initiate an EIA

on any proposed activity that is likely to pose a 'significant adverse impact' on the environment and to take a decision vests with a 'competent national authority'.[16]

Till 1994, the EIA in India was a purely administrative decision. It began in 1976-7 when the Department of Science and Technology was entrusted by the Planning Commission to examine the environment impact of river-valley projects. The inherent flaws in the Discretionary Model of the EIA, which heavily banked on 'administrative machinery', were blamed for lack of transparency in project clearance and ignoring environmental and human concerns. The Bhopal Gas Tragedy was an inevitable outcome of this fiasco. It was only in 1994 that the MoEF promulgated the Environment Impact Assessment Notification making EC mandatory for expansion or modernization of any activity or for projects listed in Schedule 1 of the notification.[17] The notification made it mandatory to obtain EC from the Central Government for all listed projects. This notification, for the first time, sought to develop an integrated and coordinated approach to consider the environmental and social impacts on development planning.[18] However, this notification was amended more than thirteen times, diluting its impact. Even during its operative days, the former notification was considered cumbersome and time-consuming. This was opposed on the ground that it would adversely affect India's development. Therefore, a committee was set up to examine

[12] Principle 21, Stockholm Declaration; Principle 21(d), World Charter of Nature, 1982.

[13] Article 206.

[14] Article 8.

[15] Trial Smelter Arbitration (US v. Canada), 3 R.I.A.A (1941); Corfu Channel Case (UK v. Albania) 1949 ICJ Reports.4; Lake Lanoux Arbitration (France v. Spain) 12 RIAA 281 (1957); Gabchikovo-Nagymaros case (Hungary/Slovakia) 1997 I.C.J. Reports 7; Nuclear Test Case (New Zealand v. France) 1995 ICJ Reports 288.

[16] See Principle 17 of Rio Declaration.

[17] http://www.cseindia.org/programme/industry/eia/introduction_eia.htm, accessed on 3 December 2007.

[18] Leo F. Saldanha, Abhayraj Naik, Arpita Joshi, and Subramanya Sastry, Green Tapism:A Review of the Environmental Impact Assessment Notification 2006, Bangalore, India: ESG, 2007), p. 105.

existing procedures for investment approvals and project implementation, and also to suggest measures to simplify and expedite the process of public and private projects. On the basis of the said recommendations, a new notification with a proposed objective to create a transparent, decentralized, and efficient regulatory mechanism was issued,[19]

in order to incorporate necessary environmental safeguards at the planning stage, involve stakeholders in the public participation process, and identify developmental projects based on impact potential instead of the investment criteria.[20]

This notification mandates to obtain prior site clearance before commencement of any construction work or preparation of land by project management from the MoEF, which is the concerned 'regulatory authority' in all matters falling under Category A[21] and the State Environment Impact Assessment Authority (SEIAA) in all matters falling under Category B. Unlike the former notification, the current notification has put the onus of clearing the project on state governments depending upon the size or capacity of the project.

Applicants are also required to furnish a copy of the 'pre-feasibility project report' along with the application for any project except building or construction projects, area development projects, and townships In case of building and construction projects, mentioned as Item 8, applicants are required to submit a copy of the 'conceptual plan.'

Projects that Require Clearance

Projects and activities are classified on the basis of the spatial extent of potential impact on human health and the environment.

Projects like offshore and onshore oil and gas exploration, nuclear power projects; petroleum refining industries, asbestos and milling and asbestos-based products; man-made fibres manufacturing; petrochemical industries and other such projects require clearance from the MoEF.

Projects like mining in less than 50 ha, river valley projects of less than 50 MW, thermal power plants of less than 500 MW, coal washeries that process less than one million tonnes per annum, mineral beneficiation that process less than 0.1 million tonnes per annum, cement plants that produce less than one million tonnes per annum require clearance from the SEIAA. Common effluent treatment plants, common municipal solid waste management facility, and aerial ropeways also require clearance from the SEIAA. Building or construction projects require clearance from the SEIAA—if the built-up area is above 20,000 square metres and below 1,50,000 square metres and if the area development projects and township projects cover more than 50 ha or the built-up area is above 1,50,000 square metres.[22]

The notification envisages a maximum of four stages in the process of EC for new projects.

Screening

The process of the EIA begins when a proponent of a project approaches the authority entrusted with making a decision regarding environmental impacts. Screening will involve scrutinizing of the application seeking prior EC. The aim of 'screening' is to determine

---

[19] EIA Notification, 2006, published in *the Gazette of India*, SO 1533, dated 14 September 2006.

[20] www.ciionline.org/services/70/dr.pdf, on 14 March 2007.

[21] Projects likely to have more impact are listed as Category A and other projects under Category B. For more, see the next sub-heading.

[22] Annexure 5.

whether or not any project or activity requires any further studying in order to prepare an EIA for its appraisal prior to its granting of EC. When deciding whether to grant EC or not, the nature and location of project is considered.

Screening applies only to projects and activities entailed in 'Category B'. The screening process is conducted by the State Expert Appraisal Committee (SEAC) and is based on a defined list. After screening, the SEAC categorizes the projects under two heads. Projects requiring an EIA report are categorized as 'B1', and those that don't are categorized as 'B2'. This categorization is based on the guidelines issued by the MoEF. However, exemption of projects from undergoing the public consultation requirement is unjustifiable and puts the effectiveness of this notification under intense scrutiny.[23] If it is found, at the screening stage, that a proposed project is likely to have potential environmental impact, scoping follows.

Scoping

In the second stage, that is, Scoping, the party preparing the EIA determines which impact should be considered, that is, it is a process in which the committee determines the 'ToR', in respect of the project or activity for which prior EC is sought. This ToR addresses, in a detailed and comprehensive manner, all environmental concerns for the preparation of an EIA

report. If the EIA report is not favourable, the application can be rejected by the regulatory authority, after stating reasons.

No scoping is required for buildings projects and construction of a built-up area above 20,000 square metres and below 1,50,000 square metres. Likewise, for townships and area development projects covering an area of 50 ha or built-up area above 1,50,000 square metres.[24]

Scoping is globally understood as a component stage that integrates public involvement with the charting out of vital issues regarding the potential environmental and social impacts of a project.[25] During scoping, public participation is ideal as it helps to identify impact, come up with alternatives, and data sources. But in India, the current notification has completely backtracked from the international standards. Firstly, the onus of scoping is put on the expert committee on the basis of the information provided by the proponent. This means that the final ToR is prepared on the basis of this above received information. Moreover, the notification provides that in case the EAC does not decide on the ToR within a stipulated time period, the proponent ToR will be final. This completely undermines the credibility of the scoping process and the expertise of EACs.

Secondly, consultation with the public is made optional and depends upon the discretion of the expert committee. This is a shortcoming in the current notification, as it puts the EIA regime on the back foot compared to other developed countries. Scoping in developed countries is comprehensive and involves public consultation, even with the NGOs. In addition to environmental impacts, the parties

---

[23] Projects like modernization of irrigation projects; all projects or activities located within industrial estates or parks; expansion of roads and highways which do not involve any further acquisition of land; all building and construction projects, area development projects and townships; all Category 'B2' projects and activities'; all projects or activities concerning national defence and security or involving other strategic considerations as determined by the Central Government, are all exempted.

[24] Item 8(b) Schedule EIA Notification 2006, wef 14 September 2006.
[25] Supra note 18, p. 109.

preparing an EIA may consider social, cultural, and economic impacts.[26]

Public Participation

This is one of the most significant stages in any EIA, without which an EIA will not be complete. 'Public Consultation refers to the process by which the concerns of local affected persons and others who have a plausible stake in the environmental impacts of the project or activities are ascertained with a view to taking into account all the material concerns in the project or activity design as appropriate.'[27] This involves two facets.[28] The first one is the 'public hearing' at the site or in its close proximity in order to ascertain concerns of local affected persons. The second one, 'public consultation', is the stage where responses of persons having a 'plausible stake' in the environmental aspects of the project are invited in writing. Public participation is built-in as far as the EIA is concerned. Public participation provides the local people and unrepresented interests with an opportunity to be heard and to participate in the decision-making of a project that affects their environment and livelihood. An EIA is an important practical mechanism for advancing the transparency, participation, and accountability advocated by Principle 10 of the Rio Declaration.[29]

The process of public participation contemplated in the EIA Notification, 2006 has two components. Instead of having a single and comprehensive public hearing involving all the stakeholders and interested parties, including NGOs, the current notification divides it into two processes. The first round of public participation is known as a 'public hearing', which is conducted at the site or in its close proximity of the project in order to ascertain and address the concerns of local affected persons. By limiting the hearing to the 'local affected', the concerns of environmentalists, researchers, NGOs and concerned citizens are excluded. The local people would find it hard to comprehend the technical jargons and intricacies associated with the EIA process. But, Paragraph 7 (i) (III) (v) even provides for the regulatory authority doing away with the public hearing if 'owing to the local situation' it is not possible to conduct a hearing. This has every potential to be abused and used as an excuse. However, holding of or doing away with public hearing is just an escapism. On the contrary, the respective authorities must be duty bound to facilitate a congenial and safe environment to conduct a public hearing. It reassures both project managers and the public. Every possible effort must be made to make public hearing meaningful.[30] Otherwise, the public hearing will be inconclusive.[31]

---

[26] Angela Z. Cassar and Carl E. Bruch, 'Transboundary Environmental Impact Assessment in International Watercourse Management', *NYU Environmental Law Journal*, 12 (2003), 169 at p. 175.

[27] Paragraph 7, III, Stage (3), EIA Notification, 2006, wef 14 September 2006.

[28] Paragraph 7 (i) (III) (ii) divides the public consultation process in two components.

[29] Principle 10 of Rio Declaration, 'Environmental issues are best handled with participation of all concerned citizens, at the relevant level. At the national level, each individual shall have appropriate access to information concerning the environment that is held by public authorities, including information on hazardous materials and activities in their communities, and the opportunity to participate in decision-making processes. States shall facilitate and encourage public awareness and participation by making information widely available. Effective access to judicial and administrative proceedings, including redress and remedy, shall be provided'. Also refer to supra note 19, p. 177.

[30] *Centre for Social Justice v. Union of India*, AIR 2001 Guj. 71.

[31] See 'Public hearing for POSCO Project inconclusive', *Down to Earth*, 15 March 2007.

The second round of public participation is known as 'public consultation' involving collecting concerns in writing from other 'concerned persons having a plausible stake'. This virtually slams the door for any NGO or any environmental support group to have any meaningful discussions in the proposed project. There seems to be purposeful agenda to exclude them from EIA process. A written response doesn't deserve that much attention and would seldom address those concerns which an open public hearing could effectively address. The shroud of the bureaucratic veil is omnipresent throughout the provision. The former notification is certainly generous as far as public participation is concerned.[32]

Public hearing is to be conducted by the State Pollution Control Board (SPCB) in states and by the Union Territory Pollution Control Committee (UTPCC) in Union Territories. The current notification states that, 'The District Magistrate or his or her representative not below the ranks of an Additional District Magistrate assisted by a representative of the SPCB or UTPCC shall preside over the entire public hearing process'.[33] Even though the notification provides for the constitution of the public hearing panel,[34] no quorum requirement

has been stipulated. Obviously, this change will drastically alter the composition of the public hearing panel, which can now be stuffed with officials, giving little representation to local interests. While the previous notification envisioned the need for local viewpoints to be directly represented in the public hearing panel, the EIA Notification, 2006 completely and unwarrantedly removes such representation for the decision-making process.[35]

The current notification is time-bound. Starting from the date of receipt of the request letter from the applicant, the process of public hearing must be completed within a period of forty-five days. In case of a failure to conduct the hearing within the stipulated time period, the respective authorities shall engage other agencies to complete the process. This fixed timeframe puts strain on the entire EIA process, thereby reducing its effectiveness. In short, the scope of public participation envisioned under the current notification is very limited and vulnerable to abuse.

After 'public consultation', the applicant shall address all material environmental concerns expressed and make appropriate changes in the draft EIA and EMP or produce a supplementary report to the draft EIA and EMP. Public consultation shall be undertaken in all 'Category A and Category B1' projects with certain exceptions.[36]

Appraisal

The fourth stage, Appraisal, is a process whereby the EAC or SEAC scrutinizes in detail, all documents submitted by the applicant, including the application, the

---

[32] Paragraph (2)(ii), Schedule IV of the EIA Notification, 1994 mentions that 'all persons including bona fide residents, environmental groups, and others located at the project site or sites of displacement or sites likely to be affected can participate in the public hearing. They can also make oral or written suggestions to the SPCB.'

[33] Paragraph 4.1 of Appendix IV.

[34] Paragraph 3, Schedule IV 'The composition of Public Hearing Panel may consist of the following, namely: (i) Representative of SPCB; (ii) District Collector or his nominee; (iii) Representative of State Government dealing with the subject; (iv) Representative of Department of the State Government dealing with Environment; (v) Not more than three representatives of the local bodies such as Municipalities or panchayats;

(vi) Not more than three senior citizens of the area nominated by the District Collector'.

[35] EIA Notification 2006.

[36] Modernization of irrigation projects (item 1(c) (ii) of the Schedule) to the EIA Notification 2006.

final EIA report, the public consultation report, and the like to make categorical recommendations to the concerned regulatory authority either for the granting of a prior EC on stipulated terms and conditions or to reject the application. Transparency is paramount in the appraisal process. The recommendations of the EAC or SEAC are placed before the regulatory authority, which normally accept the recommendations. In case of disagreement, it is further sent to the EAC or SEAC for reconsideration, the intimation of which is simultaneously conveyed to the applicant. The regulatory authority is expected to convey its decision to the applicant within forty-five days from the receipt of the recommendations from the EAC or SEAC, or 105 days from the receipt of a final EIA. In case of non-communication or expiry of the said period, the final recommendations of the EAC or SEAC become public documents and the applicant may proceed on the basis of terms of final recommendation of the EAC or SEAC. Clearance from other regulatory authorities is not required, unless required by the law or due to technical necessities.

Environmental Clearance (EC)

The validity of an Environmental Clearance is the period from which a prior EC is granted by the regulatory authority or may be presumed by the applicant [paragraph 7(iv)] to start the project to which the application for a prior EC refers. The validity of EC is determined on the basis of the project life estimated by the EAC or SEAC. Thus, a river valley project has valid EC of ten years; a mining project has thirty years; regarding area development projects and townships, and other such projects the validity shall be limited only to such activities as may be the responsibility of the applicant as developer, whose validity shall be extended by the regulatory authority to a maximum of five years.

Deliberate concealment or submission of false or misleading information, data or material prior to EC shall make the prior EC liable to be rejected or cancelled. However, such a step shall be taken only after giving the applicant a personal hearing in consonance with the principles of natural justice. A prior EC is transferable during its validity to another legal person entitled to undertake the project or on application by the transferor. The notification also mandates for the submission of a 'half-yearly compliance report' by the project management, which shall be a public document. This constitutes 'post-EC monitoring'.

EIA—Expert Agency

The Indian law contemplates the preparation of an EIA by the project proponent itself. Along with the application for clearance, an EIA conducted by an agency and selected by the project proponent, is also attached. The same has been subjected to severe criticism for the reason that such EIAs are tailor made.

The EIAs prepared for five different mining projects in five different villages of Rajasthan have been found to be fake. The EIA reports, individually prepared, stated that each project was surrounded by exactly the same ambient air quality with identical data for some stations. The consultant clarified that it was a mistake which had crept in during the cut and paste. The Government of India refused to accept the same and has banned the said EIA consultant for three years.[37]

The Supreme Court of India had the occasion to consider the issue in a public interest litigation. The Court found that the environmental impact studies in that particular case were not conducted either by

[37] *The Hindu* daily dated 7 April 2011.

the Ministry of Environment and Forests or any organization under it or even by any agencies appointed by it. All the three studies that were finally placed before the Expert Appraisal Committee and which the Court had also taken into consideration, were made at the behest of the project proponents and by agencies of their choice. The Court observed that 'it would have been more comfortable if the environment impact studies were made by the MoEF or by any organization under it or at least by agencies appointed and recommended by it.'[38]

However, the practice followed in United States is different. In the US, the National Environmental Policy Act (NEPA), 42 U.S.C. Sec. 4321 et seq., requires federal agencies to prepare an environmental impact statement (EIS) for all major federal actions significantly affecting the environment. The EIS is prepared by the consultants. Under the US federal law, agencies may use consultants to prepare an EIS. If the agency hires an outside consultant to prepare the EIS, the responsible federal official shall furnish guidance and participate in the preparation and shall independently evaluate the statement prior to its approval and take responsibility for its scope and contents. In the US, there are regulations designed to ensure that a consultant does not have a conflict of interest in the project.

In 1981, the US Supreme Court considered the application of NEPA to some military activities when plaintiffs challenged the Navy's plans to build a facility, known as West Loch, for the purpose of storing nuclear weapons. The plaintiffs complained that the Navy had incorrectly determined that the facility was not likely to pose a significant impact on the environment (thus foregoing preparation of an (EIS) because the Navy

had failed to consider 'the enhanced risk of a nuclear accident resulting from West Loch's proximity to three nearby air facilities, the effects of such an accident on the population and environment of Hawaii, and the effects of radiation from the storage of nuclear weapons in a populated area.'[39]

The Supreme Court noted that although the facility would be capable of storing nuclear weapons, the Navy had not actually confirmed whether nuclear weapons would be stored at the site. The Court explained that the Navy's regulations actually forbade it from admitting or denying whether such weapons would be stored there. The Navy had prepared a generic EIS that generally explained 'the environmental hazards associated with the storage, handling, and transportation of nuclear weapons', but did not conduct any analysis for the specific West Loch site and its surrounding environment. The generic EIS concluded that no significant hazards to the environment were present. The Court concluded:

[I]f the Navy proposes to store nuclear weapons at West Loch, the Department of Defense's regulations can fairly be read to require that an EIS be prepared solely for internal purposes, even though such a document cannot be disclosed to the public. The Navy must consider environmental consequences in its decision making process, even if it is unable to meet NEPA's public disclosure goals by virtue of FOIA Exemption 1.[40]

The concurring opinion was careful to point out that to the extent the Navy could segregate classified and non-classified material pertaining to the EIS, it would be obligated to disclose the non-classified material to the public.

Expert bodies have their own recognition

---

[38] *Anand Arya v. T.N. Godavarama Thirumulpad*, 2011 (1) SCC 744.

[39] *Weinberger v. Catholic Action of Hawaii/ Peace Education Project*, 454 U.S. 139 (1981). Id. at 142.
[40] Ibid.

before the court of law. In a petition for the protection of Victoria Memorial, a historical monument in Kolkata, the expert committee appointed by the Calcutta High Court made certain suggestions. The high court though did not approve of the same. However, when the case came before the Supreme Court of India, the Court held that in the absence of *mala fide* allegations or disqualification raised against any member of the said committee, the rejection of the said report without assigning any valid and good reason was illegal.[41]

Therefore, the present practice of preparing the EIA on the needs of the project proponents should change for making its purpose more transparent.

INDIAN CASE LAW

One of the oldest cases is against the setting up of a hydroelectric project in 1973 in the State of Kerala, when environmental laws were not developed in the country. It was contended that the project would destroy the ecology of the fragile forest, 'Silent Valley'. The KHC held that consideration of the scientific, technical, and ecological concerns was the job of the government, and not for the court to evaluate. Since this had been done, the court refused to interfere, and dismissed the petition.[42] The people's fight against the setting up of the dam continued, and finally the area was declared as the National Park by the Government of India, invoking the provisions of Section 35(4) of the Wildlife (Protection) Act, 1972.[43] The ten-year fight by the people

against the proposal to establish the dam was succeeded when the area was declared the National Park, wherein the establishment of the dam could not be permitted. Finally, nature secured justice for the people that the court had denied. Justice that was delayed by the courts was thus finally delivered by the sustained efforts of the people, and the dam could not be constructed.

Another important case where the environmental impact of a developmental project came under the judicial anvil was the *Konkan Railways* case.[44] In this case, a proposal for the laying of a railway line was challenged on the basis that the alignment of the track, which was passing through parts of Goa, would disturb the biological eco-system, destroying the *kazan* paddy fields, thus causing damage to the environment. Further, it was alleged that the proposed alignment was planned and undertaken without an adequate EIA. However, the court found that the proposed project was a matter of national importance. It held that the extent of damage is negligible compared to the magnitude of the project. Further, this project was the manifestation of the aspirations of the people of the west coast. The court opined

No development is possible without some adverse effect on the ecology and environment, but the projects of public utility cannot be abandoned and it is necessary to balance the interests of the people as well as the necessity to maintain the environment.[45]

No discussion regarding the EIA can be complete without mentioning the *Tehri Dam*[46]

---

[41] *Secretary and Curator, Victoria Memorial Hall v. Howrah Ganathanthrik Nagarik Samithy,* 2010 (3) SCC 735: AIR 2010 1285.

[42] *Society for Protection of Silent Valley v. Union of India,* OP No. 2949 & 3025 of 1975. Kerala High Court (unreported).

[43] *Kerala Gazette* No. XXIX, dated 23 November 1984.

[44] *Goa Foundation v. Konkan Railways Corporation,* AIR 1992 Bom. 471.

[45] Ibid, at p. 474.

[46] *Tehri Bandh Virodhi Sangarsh Samiti v. State of Uttar Pradesh,* (1992) Supp. SCC 44.

and *Narmada Bachao Andolan* cases.[47] The path-breaking decisions rendered by the court in these cases determined the course of the EIA regime in India. A PIL was filed challenging the establishment of the Tehri Hydro Electric project. It was alleged that the plan for the construction of the dam had not considered the safety aspect of the dam, and serious threat existed due to its construction as the area was prone to earthquakes. Rejecting the contention, the court held that the government had considered the question of safety of the project in various details more than once and that it had taken into account the reports of experts. In such circumstances, the court held that it was not possible to hold that the Union of India had not applied its mind or had not considered the relevant aspects of safety of the dam.[48] The court lacked the expertise in deciding such technical and scientific details, but would always judge whether or not the Government had taken all relevant considerations into account while clearing the project or not within the parameters of judicial review. The court only scanned the decision-making process and not the decision.

An NGO challenged the EC given by the State Government to the Gujarat Electricity Board, Dhuvaran, for the establishment of a thermal power project, on the grounds that the public hearing proceedings were not properly conducted. After considering all the aspects, the Gujarat High Court felt that the process of public hearing should be meaningful and transparent.[49]

The EC granted to a mini blast furnace was challenged before the Gujarat High Court. The court found that the company was under a genuine and bona fide belief that for mere construction work, without starting of any manufacturing process, no clearance was required. Since the Government of India had taken a conscious decision after considering all aspects, and since there was no allegation of emission or discharge of pollutants by mere construction, the Court did not interfere and made it clear that the clearance granted by authorities in respect of the blast furnace cannot be treated as *ex post facto* clearance'.[50] In regards to the contention that a public hearing is contemplated by law, the Court took a view that public hearing does not mean personal hearing:

A fair 'hearing' does not necessarily mean that there must be an opportunity to be heard orally. In some situations it is sufficient if written representations are considered. Where word 'hearing' or 'opportunity to be heard' is used in legislation, it usually requires a hearing at which oral submissions and evidence can be tendered. However, in a many statutory contexts, a duty of 'consultation' is placed upon the decision-maker. This is almost always interpreted by the courts to require merely an opportunity to make written representations, or comments upon announced proposals.[51]

If a law prescribes a public hearing, there is no substitute for it, the KHC held while considering the issue of granting of clearance to the Athirampally Hydro Electric Project.[52] It is contended that no public hearing was conducted by the project proponent as contemplated by the law at that time. It is also contended that the

---

[47] *Narmada v. Union of India*, 2000 (10) SCC 664, AIR 2000 SC 3151.

[48] *Tehri Bandh Virodh Sangarsh Samiti v. State of UP* (1992), Supp. SCC 44.

[49] Ibid.

[50] *B.K. Sharma v. Union of India*, AIR 2005 Guj 203, p. 216.

[51] Ibid.

[52] *Chalakudy Puzha Samrakshana Samithi v. Union of India*, Judgement of the Kerala High Court in O.P. No. 3581 of 2001, dated 17 October 1991 (unreported judgement).

original application for the project was rejected in the 1989. Thereafter, additional information sought for in 1990 was received in 1994 and was approved on 20 January 1998, taking into consideration all relevant information including the environmental impact. Therefore, according to the project proponent, public hearing was made mandatory only from 1997 and so is not essential to conduct a public hearing. Rejecting the contention, the court held that the amendment made public hearing and publication of the executive summary of the project mandatory before clearance was granted. Since it was not complied with by the government, the court directed the authorities to conduct the public hearing afresh. One of the main reasons for interference was that a lot of material had been produced to support the argument that there had been no proper investigation or assessment at the stage of planning or at the stage of taking a final decision to go ahead.

The project proponent thereafter conducted a public hearing on 6 February 2002. The majority of the people objected to the project. The hearing panel unanimously found that the Rapid EIA report was incomplete and recommended the conduct of a comprehensive and participatory EIA, its publication, and a further public hearing before a decision is taken on the application for EC. A new comprehensive EIA was prepared by another expert agency and the project was again cleared.

The clearance granted was challenged again on the ground that no public hearing was conducted again after the preparation of the new EIA. The KHC again interfered with the matter and directed the project proponent to publish the new EIA and conduct a fresh hearing.[53]

The project proponent again obtained clearance from the Government of India. In the third round of litigation, the said clearance granted was challenged and the matter is pending consideration of the court.

Mining is always a problem that adversely affects the environment and requires clearance from the MoEF. A PIL was filed challenging the renewing of clearance to many mining projects in the Kudremukh area, without conducting any EIA. The Supreme Court of India refused to accept the contention that the notification that requires EC would not apply to leases that came up for consideration for renewal after the issue of notification. The notification mandates that the mining operation shall not be undertaken in any part of India unless EC has been accorded by the Central Government. No mining operation can commence without obtaining an EIA on the terms of the notification.[54]

The Court stated that environmental degradation has taken place due to mining activities. It reiterated that, 'it is imperative on the part of mining operators to carry out the mine operations in such a fashion that it has least impact on the ecology of the area'. In view of this, the Court directed the constitution of a Monitoring Committee to individually examine and inspect mines from an environmental angle and submit a report to the Court on an individual mine-to-mine basis, and consider lifting the ban imposed on them by an order dated 6 May 2002.[55]

The challenge against the Sardar Sarovar Dam project was launched by the Narmada Bachao Andolan, an NGO. The court apprised the EIA and the clearance procedure and held that the government was aware of the fact that a number of studies and data had to be collected

[53] *Athirappally Grama Panchayat v. Union of India and Others* [WP (C) Nos 9542, 11254 & 260763 of 2005], High Court of Kerala, judgment, dated 23 March 2006.

[54] *M.C. Mehta v. Union of India*, AIR 2004 SC 4016, 2004 (4) JT 181, 2004 AIRSCW 4033, 2004 (3) Scale 221.
[55] *M.C. Mehta v. Union of India*, 2006 AIRSCW 2214.

relating to the environment. Keeping this in mind, a conscious decision was taken to grant EC and in order to ensure that Environmental Management Plans are implemented *pari passu* with engineering and other works, the Narmada Management Authority was directed to be constituted.[56]

Meeting the contention that no EIA was conducted as contemplated under the 1994 notification, the court held that the EC was granted to the project in 1987. It was essentially an administrative decision, having no obligation to obtain any statutory clearance, the court held.

But in a dissenting judgement, Bharucha has held that clearance was contrary to the policy of the government at that time and it cannot be considered a clearance. According to him, a project of this magnitude given EC without proper studies would have an adverse impact on the environment, having disastrous consequences for present and future generations. The court cannot place its seal of approval on a project of this magnitude unless and until a detailed EC is accorded on the basis of an elaborate EIA report and grievance redressing authorities in the states certify that all evictees have been satisfactorily rehabilitated. Till then, the construction of the dam should cease.

The *Narmada* case was subjected to severe criticism. The World Commission on Dams in its report says that, 'large dams generally have a range of extensive impacts on rivers, watersheds, and aquatic eco-systems—these impacts are more negative than positive and in many cases, have led to irreversible loss of species and eco-systems.'[57]

According to the Apex Court, when it comes to large dams, an ecological change brought about as a result of their construction cannot be equated with environmental degradation. Moreover, the precautionary principle is required only in cases involving pollution and other projects where the extent of damage is not known. The Court seems to have been more concerned about the fallout on investment and the economic consequences that succeed any adverse ruling regarding the construction of these projects. Both projects were started with significant foreign assistance. The government raised the plea of fait accompli. The Court accepted that the stopping of construction of the project upon which crores had been spent would be against national interest. The Court was also confronted with the question as to whether the EIA Notification, 1994 can be applied retrospectively in bringing the river valley project to obtain prior EC. It refused to follow four American case laws wherein the NEPA was made applicable to projects commenced before the Act.[58] But the Court categorically stated that the EIA Notification operation was prospective in nature.

Another aspect to be considered is the relief and rehabilitation (R&R) associated with the project. While the Court's insistence that R&R should be carried *out pari passu* with the construction project is certainly a welcome decision, it is estimated that some forty to eighty million people are displaced by dams.[59] In addition to this persuasive and systematic failure to assess the range of potential negative impacts and implement adequate mitigation,

[56] *Narmada Bachao Andolan v. Union of India*, AIR 2000 SC 3751, 2000 KHC 1685.

[57] *Dams and Development—A New Framework for Decision Making, The Report of the World Commission on Dams* (London and Sterling, VA: Earthscan Publications, November 2000), p. xxxi.

[58] *Tennessee Valley Authority v. Hiram G. Hill*, 437 US 153, 57 L Ed 2d 117, 98 S Ct 2279; *Sierra Club et. al v. Robert F. Froehlke*, 350 b F Supp 1280 (1973); *Arlington Coalition on Transportation v. John A. Volpe*, 458 F 2d 1323 (1972); and *Environmental Defence Fund, Inc. v. Corps of Engineers of United States Army*, 325 F Supp 749 (1971).

[59] Supra note 18.

resettlement, and development programmes for the displaced, and the failure to account for the consequences of large dams for downstream livelihood have led to the impoverishment and suffering of millions.[60] The majority judgement seems to be quite convinced that the evictees enjoy a much better lifestyle than before. However, environmental and social costs of large dams are difficult to account for in economic terms. Nor are the social impacts caused by these projects assessed. A displacement is a logistical nightmare. How displaced people cope with a displaced lifestyle, completely different from the one they followed for generations, has to be considered. This is best illustrated by the subsequent dissenting judgement of Dharmadhikari, in *N.D. Jayal v. Union of India*:

Man living in the hills and valleys is dependent on natural resources for survival. To remove him and rehabilitate him in the plains is taking a fish from the river and putting it into an artificial reservoir or an aquarium where it might survive but can never be [is] happy.[61]

What is needed is a comprehensive rehabilitation policy. Displacement should be minimized to the maximum, that is, it should be pursued only if there is no alternative. It should be based on prior informed consent. The replacement value should be the norm for compensation, instead of the current market value. Replacement value encompasses the real cost of changing the lifestyle pursued earlier. The foremost aspect that the authorities have to keep in mind is that the evictees are giving up their property for the sake of national development. The right to live with human dignity guaranteed under Article 21 should be respected. The displaced persons should

be the first beneficiaries of the project and be provided with alternative land. In the case of tribals and indigenous populations, the compensation should encompass common property resources and forest lands that are acquired from them. The rehabilitation work should be done simultaneously with development work. Thus, a comprehensive rehabilitation policy can mitigate the plight of evictees to a considerable extent and reduce public opposition to a project.

If a person sells his residence, he will get the price at the time of sale. He can therefore decide as to whether he will buy a new property for his residence or make alternative plans as he is has cash in his hands. But if he acquires land by invoking the provisions of the Land Acquisition Act, 1894, he will get the fair price only after a long legal battle. Landowners who do not have any other lands or funds will be put into jeopardy if their lands are acquired.

River valley projects are considered viable alternatives to cleaner energy and various other purposes. The mega dams are engineering marvels; however, in constructing big dams, a comprehensive EIA must be conducted. Big dams are overshadowed to a considerable extent due to the irreversible environmental harm they cause. Lack of a proper EIA study or overlooking certain vital aspects for the sake of development seems to be the cause. The Aswan Dam of Egypt and the Three Gorges Dam of China were construed as good projects, but they ended up in causing environmental harm. No one says that river valley projects should cease to exist. However, in construing the entire project certain core ideals have to be incorporated: equity, efficiency, participatory decision-making, sustainability, and accountability.[62]

Can a court assess the environmental impact of any development project? The Supreme

---

[60] Ibid.

[61] AIR 2004 SC (Supp) (1) 867, p. 897, 2004 KHC 898 (para 112).

[62] Supra note 51.

Court of India had the occasion to consider such a question in a case where sanction had been granted for the drawing of oil pipelines through a wildlife sanctuary. The Supreme Court in its judgement said that the

Court cannot be asked to assess the environmental impact of the pipelines on the wildlife but can at least oversee that those with established credentials and who have the requisite expertise have been consulted and that their recommendations have been abided by, by the State Government.[63]

INTERNATIONAL LAW

The EIA first appeared as a 'non-binding instrument' in the Stockholm Declaration, 1972.[64] From then onwards, the EIA has steadily made its way into all international legal instruments.[65] However, an EIA is basically envisaged as a 'national instrument', and the onus to initiate an EIA on any proposed activity that is likely to pose 'significant adverse impact' on the environment and to take a decision vests with a 'competent national authority'.

The Organization for Economic Cooperation and Development (OECD) 'Declaration on Environmental Policy, 1974' was the first international document to incorporate the EIA. Article 9 of the Declaration states that it is critical that the environmental impact of significant public or private activities be assessed prior to implementation. This declaration,

which precedes the Stockholm Declaration, 1972, set the trend for environmental policy in OECD member countries.

The United Nations Environmental Programme (UNEP) is the mouthpiece of the UN as far as environmental matters are concerned. Under its auspice, the World Charter of Nature, 1982 was passed. In 1987, UNEP came up with the 'Goals and Principles of Environmental Impact Assessment', which aimed at facilitating the introduction and promotion of EIA systems in its member countries. The UNEP has also come up with a EIA Training Resource Manual.

In 1984, the World Bank came out with its 'Environmental Policy and Procedures', with the objective of integration of environmental consideration at the initial stages of defining and preparation of a project. The World Operation Directive outlines, to World Bank staff, the methods and procedures for EIA implementation to proposed projects.

The *Gabcíkovo-Nagymaros Project* case (Hungary/Slovakia)[66] involved a dispute between Hungary and Slovakia concerning the Gabcíkovo-Nagymaros Project. The initial 1977 treaty contemplated construction and operation of dams on the river Danube for the production of electricity, flood control, and improvement of navigation. A Joint Conceptual Plan was provided to guide the technical specifications. Each party would have equal footing with respect to financing, construction, and operation of the system. Hungary would be responsible for the project in their part and Slovakia on their side of border.

The problem started in early 1989, when Hungary suspended its part of work at Nagymaros, citing uncertainty with respect to environmental impact studies. Talks between the sides broke down, which led to the total

---

[63] *Essar Oil Ltd v. H.U. Samithi and Others*, AIR 2004 SC 1834.

[64] Principles 12, 13, 14, 15, 17, 18.

[65] Principle 20, UNEP Draft Principles, 1978; World Charter for Nature, 1982, paras 11(b) & (c); Agenda 21; Principle 17, Rio Declaration, 1992,; Article 14, Convention on Biological Diversity; EC Directive on EIA, Council Directive 85/337/EEC, OJL 175, 5 July 1985; UNEEC Convention on Environmental Impact Assessment in a Transboundary Context (1991); Espoo Convention, etc.

[66] 1997 ICJ Reports, 7.

abandonment of work by Hungary. Meanwhile, Slovakia had built their dam spending billions. Aggrieved by this, Slovakia unilaterally constructed 'Variant C' as a 'Provisional Solution', to divert the river Danube into a reservoir, and Hungary purported to terminate the treaty.

By an agreement of parties the matter was referred to the International Court of Justice (ICJ). The Court was asked to decide: (1) Whether Hungary was entitled to suspend and subsequently abandon, in 1989, work on the Nagymaros Project and on the part of the Gabcíkovo Project for which the treaty attributed responsibility to the Republic of Hungary; (2) Whether the Czech and Slovak Federal Republic was entitled to proceed in November 1991 to the provisional solution; (3) What the legal effects of the 19 May 1992 notification of Hungary's termination of the treaty were. The Court found that Hungary was not entitled to suspend the work of its project in Nagymaros on the doctrine of treaty law and the environmental necessity raised by Hungary was not a sufficient excuse to do so. Consequently, Hungary's termination of the treaty was not effective. With respect to the second question, the Court found that Slovakia was not entitled to take unilateral action to construct and implement Variant C. Both parties were still bound by the treaty obligations and were ordered to reach an agreement on the proper disposition of the proposed project.

Vice-President Weeramantry gave a concurring yet separate opinion, stating 'had the possibility of environmental harm been the only consideration to be taken into account in this regard, the contention of Hungary could well have proved conclusive'. He endorsed the principle of Sustainable Development as 'an integral part of modern international law' and protection of the environment is a vital part of the contemporary human rights doctrine. He concurred with the opinion of the Court in that the EIA was built into the treaty by Articles 15 and 19:

Environmental law in its current state of development would read into treaties which may reasonably be considered to have a significant impact upon the environment, a duty of environmental impact assessment and this means also, whether the treaty expressly so provides or not, a duty of monitoring the environmental impacts of any substantial project during the operation of the scheme.[67]

According to him, the EIA should not be confined to the pre-project assessment of the possible environmental impacts, but should be a continuing assessment and evaluation as long as the project is in operation. Modern doctrines of international environmental law should apply equally to all projects regardless of the date on which the agreement has been made.[68] With regard to the dispute, he stated that 'a joint operation regime must be established in accordance with the 1977 Treaty in order to carry out continuous monitoring of environmental impact of the project'. Although he concurred with the majority in holding that treaty law governed this case, his opinion was much more direct in citing the scientific and environmental matters.

The case of Gabcíkovo-Nagymaros presented the ICJ with a golden opportunity to establish an international obligation to conduct an EIA before implementing projects having the potential to impact the environment. Instead, the Court found that, 'unless EIA

---

[67] http://www.icj-cij.org/docket/files/92/7383.pdf, p. 112.
[68] Erika L. Preiss, 'The International Obligation to Conduct Environmental Impact Assessment: The ICJ Case Concerning Gabcikovo-Nagymaros Project', *NYU Environmental Law Journal*, 7 NYUELJ 1999 307, p. 348–9.

is specifically required by a treaty or is the customary international practice at the time the treaty is formed, parties do not have an obligation to undertake environmental impact assessment when implementing that treaty.'[69]

Despite this, the opinion of Weeramantry finds favour with many scholars and leads them to believe that the EIA should be firmly established as a principle of customary international law.[70]

European Law

The EIA procedure was introduced in Europe to implement the Council Directive on the assessment of the effects of certain public and private projects on the environment. The Directive recites that

the best environmental policy consists in preventing the creation of pollution or nuisances at source, rather than subsequently trying to counteract their effects [and] affirm[s] the need to take effects on the environment into account at the earliest possible stage in all technical planning and decision-making processes...

The general principle is said to be that:

Whereas development consent for public and private projects which are likely to have significant effects on the environment should be granted only after prior assessment of the likely significant environmental effects of these projects has been carried out; whereas this assessment must be conducted on the basis of the appropriate information supplied by the developer, which may be supplemented by the authorities and by the people who may be concerned by the project in question...

The primary obligation is to 'adopt all measures necessary to ensure that before consent is given,

projects likely to have significant effects on the environment by virtue, inter alia, of their nature, size, or location are made subject to an assessment with regard to their effects'.[71]

The United Kingdom implemented the Directive by the Town and Country Planning (Assessment of Environmental Effects) Regulations 1988.[72] An application for planning permission for a development that is likely to have significant effects on the environment by virtue of its nature, size, or location must accompany an environmental statement in accordance with the regulation.

Beliz

In Beliz, Chapter 328 of the Environment Protection Act requires an EIA for certain activities. As per Section 20 of the Act, any person intending to undertake any project, programme, or activity which may significantly affect the environment shall cause an EIA to be carried out by a suitably qualified person, and shall submit the same to the Department of Environment for evaluation and recommendations. The EIA shall identify and evaluate the effects of specified developments on human beings, flora and fauna, soil, water, air and climatic factors, material assets, including the cultural heritage and the landscape, natural resources, the ecological balance, and the like. The EIA shall include measures that a proposed developer intends to take to mitigate any adverse environmental effects and a statement of reasonable alternative sites (if any), and reasons for their rejection. When making an EIA, a proposed developer shall consult with the public and other interested bodies or organizations. The department may make its own EIA and synthesize the views of the

---

[69] Ibid., p. 309.

[70] Ibid, p. 310; also see generally, Adriana Koe, 'Damming the Danube: The International Court of Justice and the Gabcikovo-Nagymaros Project (*Hungary v. Slovakia*)', *Sydney Law Review* (1998), vol. 27.

[71] Article 2(1).

[72] Section 2(2), European Communities Act, 1972.

public and interested bodies. A decision by the department to approve an EIA may be subject to conditions which are reasonably required for environmental purposes. Section 21 empowers the minister charged with the responsibility for environment to make regulations prescribing the types of projects, programmes, or activities for which an EIA is required and prescribe the procedures, contents, guidelines, and other matters relevant to such an assessment.

Georgia

The law of Georgia State also requires an EIA as a necessary environmental measure, carried out in the course of decision-making on the issue of environmental licences for the bodies performing activities. These activities include business, industries, or any other types of activity, drafting and development of plans, infrastructure projects, construction and sector development plans, projects for exploitation and use of waters, forests, mineral wealth, land, and other natural resources in the territory of Georgia; also activities required for major reconstruction and technical and technological renovation of the existing enterprises.

South Africa

The Constitutional Court in South Africa has considered the need to apply principles of sustainable development to the EIA process, and has held that fulfilling zoning law requirements is not sufficient in fulfilling EIA requirements.[73] Section 22(1) of the Environment Conservation Act, 1989 (ECA) forbids any person from undertaking an activity that has been identified in Section 21(1) as one that may have a substantially detrimental

impact on the environment without written authorization by the competent authority.[74] The decision to grant or refuse authorization in terms of Section 22(1) of the ECA must be made in the light of the provisions of the National Environmental Management Act, 1998 (NEMA).[75] One of the declared purposes of NEMA is to establish principles that will guide organs of the state in making decisions that may affect the environment. One of these principles requires environmental authorities to consider the social, economic, and environmental impacts of a proposed activity including its 'disadvantages and benefits'.[76]

[74] Section 22, Environment Conservation Act provides:

'(1) No person shall undertake an activity identified in terms of section 21(1) or cause such an activity to be undertaken except by virtue of a written authorization issued by the minister or by a competent authority or local authority or an officer, which competent authority, authority or officer shall be designated by the minister by notice in the *Gazette*.

(2) The authorization referred to in subsection (1) shall only be issued after consideration of reports concerning the impact of the proposed activity and of alternative proposed activities on the environment, which shall be compiled and submitted by such persons and in such manner as may be prescribed.

(3) The minister or the competent authority, or a local authority or officer referred to in subsection (1), may at his or its discretion refuse or grant the authorization for the proposed activity or an alternative proposed activity on such conditions, if any, as he or it may deem necessary.

(4) If a condition imposed in terms of subsection (3) is not being complied with, the Minister, any competent authority or any local authority or officer may withdraw the authorization in respect of which such condition was imposed, after at least 30 days' written notice was given to the person concerned.' (is the entire section necessary?)

[73] *Fuel Retailers Association of Southern Africa v. DACEMP* (Case CCT 67/06), 7 June 2007.

[75] Act 107 of 1998.
[76] Section 2(4)(i).

The Fuel Retailers Association of Southern Africa challenged the decision to grant authorization for constructing a proposed filling station in the Pretoria High Court, primarily on the ground that the environmental authorities in Mpumalanga had not considered the socio-economic impact of constructing the proposed filling station, as they should have. In rejecting the application, the Department of Environment contended that need and desirability were considered by the local authority when it decided the re-zoning application of the property for the purposes of constructing the proposed filling station. Therefore, it did not have to reassess these considerations.

Allowing the appeal, the Constitutional Court held that the environmental authorities were bound to consider the impact of the proliferation of filling stations on the environment and the impact of the proposed filling station on existing ones. The Court held that the obligation to consider the socio-economic impact of a proposed development is wider than the requirement to assess its need and desirability. NEMA makes it clear that the obligation of the environmental authorities includes the consideration of socio-economic factors as an integral part of its environmental responsibility,[77] while also considering the cumulative impact on the environment. A consideration of socio-economic conditions therefore includes consideration of the impact of the proposed development not only in combination with the existing developments, but also its impact on existing ones.[78]

Pakistan

In Pakistan, no proponent of a project shall commence construction or operation unless it has filed an initial environmental examination with the Federal Agency or, where the project is likely to cause an adverse environmental effect, an EIA, and has obtained from the Federal Agency approval in respect thereof.[79]

Malaysia

The Natural Resources And Environment Management Order, 1997 requires that any person who intends to undertake any of the prescribed activities, having an impact on environment and natural resources shall submit to the Natural Resources and Environment Board a report in the form of an EIA, which is to be prepared by such expert or authority approved by the Board.

United States of America

The EIA was first established in the domestic jurisdiction of the USA with the National Environmental Protection Act, 1969 (NEPA). This phrase comes from Section 102(2) of the Act. NEPA is a typical example of a mandatory system of EIA, making it mandatory for federal agencies to include environmental protection in all their plans and activities.

Australia

The environmental impacts of the proposals for diverting a river and effects on various animals lead to an assessment process which includes

---

[77] This principle was considered in the following cases: *BP Southern Africa (Pty) Ltd v. MEC for Agriculture, Conservation, Environment and Land Affairs* 2004 (5) SA 124 (W) at 140E-151H; *Turnstone Trading CC v. Director General Environmental Management, Department of Agriculture, Conservation & Development*, case no. 3104/04 (T), 11 March 2005, unreported, at paras 17–19; *MEC for Agriculture, Conservation, Environment and Land Affairs v. Sasol Oil (Pty) Ltd and Another* 2006 (5) SA 483 (SCA) at para 15.

[78] Supra note 64.

[79] Section 12, Pakistan Environment Protection Act, 1997.

a public comment. Though the Government approved the mining company's proposal, it imposed certain conditions. The decision was challenged by various indigenous group. The main challenge was the decision of the Minister for Environment and Heritage didn't properly consider environmental impacts and did not properly account for ecologically sustainable development and precautionary principle. It is argued that the extent of impacts which should be considered under this environmental assessment and approval process is not just any direct effect that the mine's operation may have on threatened or migratory species' but also 'secondary effects that can be said to be consequences of the action on those species. The Federal Court dismissed the claim and held that although the Minister didn't consider all the relevant matters, that didn't significantly change his decision and so the decision cannot be invalidated on that ground. The requirements of law for applying 'the principal of ecologically sustainable development [and] the precautionary principle' were properly met in the Minister's decision, evidenced by an ongoing monitoring and management plan and potential for stricter environmental controls in the future.[80]

AARHUS CONVENTION, 1998

The Convention on Access to Information, Public Participation in Decision-Making and Access to Justice regarding Environmental Matters was adopted by the United Nations Economic Commission for Europe (UNECE) 4th Ministerial Conference in Aarhus, Denmark on 25 June 1998. It is popularly known as the 'Aarhus Convention' and is an international environmental treaty that aims to involve citizens in the environmental decision-

making process.[81] The Convention derives its inspiration mainly from Principle 1 of the Stockholm Declaration and Principle 10 of the Rio Declaration and recognizes the fact that, 'adequate protection of the environment is essential to human well-being and the enjoyment of basic human rights including the right to life itself'.

The Aarhus Convention recognizes the manifold advantages of involving public participation in environmental matters. Firstly, improved access to information and public participation in decision-making would enhance the quality and implementation of decisions. Secondly, it contributes to public awareness in environmental issues. Thirdly, it gives the public an opportunity to express their concerns, which will enable public authorities to comprehend it and take due account of such concerns. This will go a long way in furthering accountability and transparency in decision-making, thereby strengthening public support for decisions on the environment.

The Convention is based on three pillars. Article 1 lays down the objective of the Convention,

In order to contribute to the protection of the right of every person of present and future generations to live in an environment adequate to his or her health and well-being, each Party shall guarantee *the rights of access to information, public participation in decision making, and access to justice in environmental matters* in accordance with the provisions of this Convention.

The first pillar of the Convention deals with access to environmental information. The Convention imposes clear obligations on public authorities to provide and facilitate access to environmental information to the general public. Article 4 (Access to Environmental

---

[80] *Lansen v. Minister for Environment and Heritage*, [2008] FCA 903 (13 June 2008).

[81] Jens Hamer, 'The Arhus Convention', p. 1, < > http://www.eel.nl/documents/aarhus.pdf < > on 16-12-07.

Information) and Article 5 (Collection and Dissemination of Environmental Information) constitutes this first pillar. The information sought to be accessed can include: information on the state of the environment, state of human health and safety that can be affected by the state of government, policies and measures taken by government, and other such information. Citizens are entitled to obtain the information sought within one month of the request. Public authorities are obliged to disseminate the information in their possession, unless they can claim grounds of refusal or unless they do not have such information.

Public participation means giving the public an opportunity to participate in the environmental decision-making process, thereby giving them a key role. Articles 6 to 8 deal with the second pillar. Public authorities are duty bound to make arrangements to enable citizens and environmental organizations to participate. It also provides an opportunity for interaction between policy-makers, project proponents, the general public, independent experts, and the like. Citizens who are most likely to be affected by the decision or project can express their concerns. Independent experts and environmental groups can raise technical questions at the end and even suggest viable alternatives. The policy-makers can take into consideration these comments and suggestions, reassure the general public, and take them into confidence in the decision-making, which makes it a win-win situation for all.

Courts are the last refuge for an aggrieved citizen who has been denied justice. The third pillar of the Convention (Article 9) gives the citizen an access to justice, a right to challenge before a court of law, a public decision taken without adhering to the above two pillars and violating environmental rights generally:

In the circumstances where a party provides for such a review by a court of law, it shall ensure that such a person has access to an expeditious procedure established by law, which is free/ inexpensive for reconsideration by a public authority or reviewed by an independent and impartial body other than a court of law.

The final decision of court shall be considered binding.

Man is both the creator and moulder of his environment. He must be given a constructive role in making decisions that concern him. Surely, environmental issues are best handled with the participation of all concerned citizens, and only then is an environmental decision complete and meaningful. In that respect, the Aarhus Convention is a watershed, as it provides an ideal framework for involving citizens in the environmental decision-making process. The Convention is based on the core doctrine of 'sustainable development' and provides a clear link between environmental rights and human rights in a democratic context. As Kofi Annan, the UN Secretary General at that time remarked, it is 'the most ambitious venture in environmental democracy undertaken under the auspices of the United Nations'.[82]

Development is the need of the hour for a developing country like India. However, it is also incumbent on such countries to ensure that development takes place on a sustainable basis. Man should not undermine nature for his temporary gains. Under the guise of development, mankind has interfered with nature, which was sometimes considered acceptable in earlier times. The development

---

[82] See generally, Jens Hamer, 'The Arhus Convention', < > http://www.eel.nl/documents/aarhus.pdf; Czeslaw Walek, 'The Aarhus Convention and its practical impact on NGOs. Examples of CEE and NIS Countries', < > http://www.icnl.org/journal/vol3iss1/ar_walek1.htm (I found the article at a different website - http://www. icnl.org/knowledge/ijnl/vol3iss1/art_5.htm)

of science has produced new norms and standards for development that have to be given proper weight, not only when the state contemplates new activities, but also when activities are continued. The need to reconcile economic development with protection of the environment is aptly expressed in the concept of sustainable development.

The EIA acts as a vector for introducing environmental considerations into developmental projects. The EIA has now become a mandatory rule for getting EC and is an accepted environmental management tool across the world. However, disparities are evident in terms of implementation. While developed countries have been strict in implementing EIA norms, developing countries have a tendency to dilute their EIA norms to facilitate smoother and faster development. This is a detrimental tendency that must be discouraged. The EIA is certainly not a panacea for all problems, but an 'early warning system', alerting the proponent about the potential fallout of a project with the environment. It is another facet of sustainable development. Certainly, preventing the adverse fallout on the environment is better than curing it after the disaster. The EIA is a positive answer to this perennial problem.

8 Commitments under International Law

International law is primarily a creation of almost every facet of inter-state activity. During the last fifty-seven years, the United Nations system has pronounced new hope for millions of people over the world. International law is expressed in the form of conventions, covenants, protocols, declarations, agreements, treaties, and resolutions. India has been a member of the United Nations since 1945, and has accepted many such documents.

Mere attendance at an international convention will not make it a law. A treaty entered into by India cannot become law of the land unless Parliament passes a law as required under Article 253 of the Constitution of India. A commitment to a convention will become law only after signature, ratification, and implementation. The executive in India can enter into any Treaty, be it bilateral or multilateral with other countries.[1]

THE CONSTITUTION OF INDIA

The Indian Parliament has been empowered to make any law for the whole or any part of the territory of India for implementing any treaty, agreement, or convention with any other country or countries or any decision made at any international conference, association, or body.[2]

Entry 13 of List I, Schedule VII of the Constitution of India, reads, 'Participation in international conferences, assessment, and other bodies and implementing of decisions made there at.'

In view of the Directive Principles, Supreme Court has held that the court must interpret the language of the Constitution, if not traceable, which is after all a Municipal Law, in the light of the United Nations Charter and solemn declarations subscribed to by India.[3] It is the duty of the courts to construe the legislation so as to be in conformity with International Law and not in conflict with it.[4]

The cessation of National Territory involves a foreign state which can be done by the Central Government in exercise of its treaty making power.[5]

---

[1] *State of West Bengal v. Kesoram Industries*, 2004 AIRSCW 5998, at p. 6161.

[2] Art. 253 of the Constitution of India.

[3] *Kesavananda Bharti v. State of Kerala*, 1973 (4) SCC 255.

[4] *Corocraft v. Ram American Airways*, 1969 A11 ER82.

[5] In Reference by the Reference by President of India, AIR 1960 SC 845, also in *Union of India v. Azadi Bachao Andolan*, 2003 (8) SCALE 287.

In the *Visakha* case,[6] the Supreme Court of India declared that in the absence of domestic law occupying the field, international conventions and norms are significant for the purpose of interpretation of the guarantee of gender equality and right to work with human dignity as specified in Articles 14, 15, 19 (1)(g), and 21 of the Constitution. Any international convention consistent with the fundamental rights and in harmony with its spirit must be read into these provisions to enlarge the meaning and content thereof, promoting the object of the constitutional guarantee. This is implicit from Article 51(c) and the enabling power of Parliament to enact laws for the implementation of international conventions and norms by virtue of Article 253 read with Entry 14 of the Union List in the Seventh Schedule of the Constitution.

Article 73 of the Indian Constitution is also relevant. It provides that the executive power of the Union shall extend over matters with respect to which Parliament has the power to make laws. The executive power of the Union is, therefore, available till the Parliament enacts to expressly provide measures needed to curb the evil. The Supreme Court was considering the issue of sexual harassment of working women in the *Visakha* case and laid down certain guidelines consistent with international law on the subject.

Independence of the judiciary is an integral part of the Indian Constitution. The court has clarified that where there is no inconsistency between them, international conventions and norms can be read into the provisions, in the absence of domestic law occupying the field. It is now an accepted rule of judicial construction that regard must be given to international conventions and norms when construing domestic law, when there is no inconsistency between them and there is a void in the domestic law. The High Court of Australia in the case of *Minister for Immigration and Ethnic Affairs* v. *Teoh*,[7] has recognized the concept of legitimate expectation, that is, that international law will be observed in the absence of contrary legislative provision, even in the absence of a Bill of Rights in the Constitution of Australia.

INTERNATIONAL COURT OF JUSTICE

The ICJ, also known as the World Court or the Hague Court, is the principal organ of the UN. Jurisdiction of the Court over a particular dispute depends on whether the court has been invoked in a contentious case between two or more states, or to give advisory opinions on questions of law at the request of states or certain international organizations.[8] In July 1993 the Court established a seven-member Chamber for Environmental Matters.

THE PRINCIPLE OF *SIC UTERE TUO ALIENUM NON LAEDAS*

This customary principle of international law mandates that states shall not use, or allow the use of, their territory for acts contrary to the rights of other states and hence it underlies many bilateral and multilateral treaties relating to the environment. The liability of the state for environmental damage due to transboundary pollution is based on the principle of non-interference established by customary international law, based on the principle, *sic utere tuo alienum non laedas*

---

[6] *Vishaka et. al v. State of Rajasthan et. al*, AIR 1997 SC 3011, 1997 (6) SCC 241.
[7] 128 ALR 535.

[8] International Court of Justice, Communique 93/20, 19 July 1993. The Chamber was established under Article 26 (1) of its Statute.

(enjoy your own property in such a manner as not to injure that of another person). The principle can be seen in the Helsinki Rules on the Uses of International Rivers, adopted by the International Law Association in 1966. The state cannot damage the watercourse of another sate or prevent its use, as by doing so it would incur liability under other rules of international law, for instance, those pertaining to large-scale pollution of the environment. It is also evident in a number of the conventions discussed below.

In a landmark judgement in the *Trail Smelter* case,[9] the above principle was considered in detail. The case is on account of operations of a Canadian Company smelting lead and zinc at Trail on the river Columbia. The river Columbia rises in Canada and flows past a lead and zinc smelter at Trail, British Columbia. The smoke, containing sulphur dioxide discharged by the company, was carried through the river across into the USA. It is said that from 1925 to 1931, the International Joint Commission recommended payment of $350,000 in respect of damage. The USA informed Canada that the conditions were still unsatisfactory and an Arbitral Tribunal was set up to 'finally decide' whether further damage had been caused in Washington and the indemnity due, whether the smelter should be required to cease operation; the measures to be adopted to this end; and compensation due. The Tribunal, applying the principles of law and practice in the USA as well as international law and practice, came to the conclusion that 'no state has the right to use or permit the use of its territory in such a manner so as to cause injury by fumes in or to the territory of another or the properties or persons there in, which the case is of serious consequence and the injury is established by clear and convincing evidence.'

[9] Trail Smelter Case, 3 RIAA 1905, 35 AJIL, 684 (1941).

The above principle has been judicially pronounced in the *Corfu Channel* case (United Kingdom of Great Britain and Northern Ireland-Albania)[10] by the ICJ. The case arose from incidents that occurred on 22 October 1946 in the Corfu Strait. Two British destroyers struck mines in Albanian waters and suffered damage, including serious loss of life. Two questions were considered: (1) Is Albania responsible for the explosions, and is there a duty to pay compensation? (2) Has the UK violated international law by the acts of its navy in Albanian waters, firstly on the day on which the explosions occurred and, secondly, on 12 and 13 November 1946, when it undertook a sweep of the Strait? The Court held that Albania was responsible for the explosion in Albanian waters, and for the damage and loss of human life that resulted. This liability flowed from well-recognized principles of humanity that are even more exacting in times of peace than in war, from the principle of freedom of maritime communication, and from the obligation of all states not to knowingly allow their territory to be used contrary to the rights of other states.

In a case filed by Australia and New Zealand against France, an argument was raised that nuclear tests were carried out on French territory, the Pacific Ocean and it is an infringement on the sovereignty of another state by the deposit of nuclear fall over its territory.[11]

Moreover, international project funding organizations, such as the World Bank, have indicated that they will not provide

[10] *United Kingdom of Great Britain v. Northern Ireland-Albania*, International Court of Justice, I.C.J. Reports 1949, p. 4 Per Curiam. Geneva Convention on the Territorial Sea. 1958. Art. 14. 516 UNTS 205.
[11] Nuclear Tests Case (*Australia v. France* and *New Zealand v. France*), 1973 ICJ Rep 253 and 457.

financial support for projects that are likely to cause appreciable harm to the territory of other states.

The concept of sustainable development has received approval in a judgement of the ICJ. This is apparent from the judgement of the ICJ in the *Gabčíkovo-Nagymaros Project (Hungary/Slovakia)* case, where the Court held:

Throughout the ages, mankind has, for economic and other reasons, constantly interfered with nature. In the past, this was often done without consideration of the effects upon the environment. Owing to new scientific insights and to a growing awareness of the risks for mankind—for present and future generations—of pursuit of such interventions at an unconsidered and unabated pace, new norms and standards have been developed, set forth in a great number of instruments during the last two decades. Such new norms have to be taken into consideration, and such new standards given proper weight, not only when states contemplate new activities but also when continuing with activities begun in the past. This need to reconcile economic development with protection of the environment is aptly expressed in the concept of sustainable development.[12]

THE MARINE ENVIRONMENT

International Convention for the Prevention of Pollution of the Sea by Oil, 1954

The Convention was held at London on 12 May 1954. It was intended to take action by common agreement to prevent pollution of the sea by oil discharged from ships. Standards were prescribed for discharging oil in the sea. The principles were later on amended at the meet held on 11 April 1962, fixing zones of the Arabian Sea, Bay of Bengal, and Indian Ocean. In 1981, the conditions of the Convention were made applicable to India.

The Convention on Fishing and Conservation of the Living Resources of the High Seas, 1958[13]

The Convention, held at Geneva on 29 April 1958, was intended for the development of modern techniques to counter the exploitation of the living resources of the sea, increasing man's ability to meet the need of the world's expanding population for food, which exposed some of these resources to the danger of being over-exploited.

London Convention on the Dumping of Wastes at Sea[14]

The Intergovernmental Conference on the Convention on the Dumping of Wastes at Sea met in London in November 1972, with the intention of preventing marine pollution, which resulted in the adoption of an instrument, generally known as the London Convention. The Convention has a global character, and contributes to the international control and prevention of marine pollution. It prohibits the dumping of certain hazardous materials including mercury, DDT, PCBs, oil, and persistent plastics. It mandates a prior special permit for the dumping of a number of other identified materials and a prior general permit for other wastes or matter. This convention made a number of decisions aimed at protecting the marine environment.

---

[12] Gabčíkovo-Nagymaros Project (Hungary/Slovakia) 37 ILM 162 (1998) 200 at para 140. In a Separate Opinion, Vice-President Weeramantry held that the concept of sustainable development is part of international customary law. See Separate Opinion at 207.

[13] Convention on Fishing and Conservation of the Living Resources of the High Seas, 29 April 1958, 559 UNTS 285.

[14] Convention on the Prevention of Marine Pollution by Dumping of Wastes and Other Matter, entered into force 30 August 1975, 1046 UNTS 120.

It recognizes that the sea's ability to sustain living organisms, which support mankind, assimilate wastes and render them harmless, and regenerate natural resources, is not unlimited.

The Oslo Convention for the Prevention of Marine Pollution by Dumping from Ships and Aircraft[15]

The Convention held at Oslo on 15 February 1972 recognized that the marine environment and the living resources that it supports are of vital importance to all nations. The ecological equilibrium and legitimate uses of the sea are increasingly threatened by pollution. The Convention recognized that concerted action by governments at national, regional, and global levels is essential to prevent and combat marine pollution. The Convention acknowledged that immediate international action can and should be taken without delay to control the pollution of the sea by the dumping of harmful substances from ships and aircrafts.

AIR POLLUTION

The Geneva Convention on Long-Range Transboundary Air Pollution (CLRTAP)[16]

The CLRTAP is intended to prevent air pollution and protect the human environment. The parties to the Convention are determined to promote relations and cooperation in the field of trans-boundary air pollution. A high-level meeting within the framework of the ECE on the Protection of the Environment was held at a ministerial level in November 1979

[15] Convention for the Prevention of Marine Pollution by Dumping from Ships and Aircraft, entered into force, 7 April 1974, 932 UNTS 3.
[16] Geneva Convention on Long-range Transboundary Air Pollution, entered into force 16 March 1983, 1302 UNTS 217.

in Geneva. It resulted in the signature of the Convention on Long-range Transboundary Air Pollution by 34 governments and the European Community (EC). The Convention was the first international legally-binding instrument to deal with problems of air pollution on a broad regional basis. Besides laying down the general principles of international cooperation for the abatement of air pollution, the Convention set up an institutional framework combining research and policy.

SUSTAINABLE DEVELOPMENT

UN Conferences on Environment

The United Nations Conference on the Human Environment, held at Stockholm on 16 June 1972, brought into focus several alarming situations. It highlighted the immediate need to take steps to control the menace of pollution of the Mother Earth, air, and space, and cautioned mankind that the failure to do so could result in disastrous consequences.

The United Nations Conference on Environment and Development, held at Rio de Janeiro (Brazil) from 3 to 14 June 1992, reaffirmed the above decision with the goal of establishing a new and equitable global partnership through the creation of new levels of cooperation among states, key sectors of societies, and people. This summit is termed the 'Earth Summit' and has three main objects, that is, conservation of biological diversity, sustainable use of its components, and fair and equitable sharing of benefits arising from genetic resources.

One of the documents to arise from the meeting was Agenda 21. Chapter 1 intended for the protection of the environment and reads:

1.1. Humanity stands at a defining moment in history. We are confronted with a perpetuation of disparities between and within nations, a worsening of poverty, hunger, ill health and illiteracy, and the continuing deterioration of the ecosystems on which we depend for our well being. However, integration of environmental and developmental concerns and greater attention to them will lead to the fulfilment of basic needs, improved living standards for all, better protected and managed ecosystems, and a safer, more prosperous future. No nation can achieve this on its own; but together we can—in a global partnership for sustainable development.

1.2. This global partnership must build on the premises of General Assembly resolution 44/228 of 22 December 1989, which was adopted when the nations of the world called for the United Nations Conference on Environment and Development, and on the acceptance of the need to take a balanced and integrated approach to environment and development questions.

1.3. Agenda 21 addresses the pressing problems of today and also aims at preparing the world for the challenges of the next century. It reflects a global consensus and political commitment at the highest level to development and environment cooperation. Its successful implementation is first and foremost the responsibility of governments. National strategies, plans, policies, and processes are crucial in achieving this. International cooperation should support and supplement such national efforts. In this context, the United Nations system has a key role to play. Other international, regional, and sub-regional organizations are also called upon to contribute to this effort. The broadest public participation and the active involvement of NGOs and other groups should also be encouraged.

1.4. The developmental and environmental objectives of Agenda 21 will require a substantial flow of new and additional financial resources to developing countries, in order to cover the incremental costs for the actions they have to undertake to deal with global environmental problems and to accelerate sustainable development. Financial resources are also required for strengthening the capacity of international institutions for the implementation of Agenda 21. An indicative order of magnitude assessment of costs is included in each of the programme areas. This assessment will need to be examined and refined by the relevant implementing agencies and organizations.

1.5. In the implementation of the relevant programme areas identified in Agenda 21, special attention should be given to the particular circumstances facing the economies in transition. It must also be recognized that these countries are facing unprecedented challenges in transforming their economies, in some cases in the midst of considerable social and political tension.

1.6. The programme areas that constitute Agenda 21 are described in terms of the basis for action, objectives, activities, and means of implementation. Agenda 21 is a dynamic programme. It will be carried out by the various actors according to the different situations, capacities, and priorities of countries and in full respect of all the principles contained in the Rio Declaration on Environment and Development. It could evolve over time in the light of changing needs and circumstances. This process marks the beginning of a new global partnership for sustainable development.

1.7. Throughout Agenda 21, the term 'environmentally sound' means 'environmentally safe and sound', in particular when applied to the terms 'energy sources', 'energy supplies', 'energy systems', or 'technology/technologies'.

A note appended stated that when the term 'governments' is used, it will be deemed to include the European Economic Community within its areas of competence.

The UNEP is the designated authority of the United Nations system in relation to environmental issues at the global and regional level. Its mandate is to coordinate the development of environmental policy consensus by keeping the global environment under review and bring emerging issues to the attention of governments and the international community for action. The mandate and objectives of UNEP emanate from the United Nations General Assembly resolution 2997 (XXVII) of 15 December 1972 and subsequent amendments adopted at the UNCED in 1992, the Nairobi Declaration on the Role and Mandate of UNEP, adopted at the Nineteenth Session of the UNEP Governing Council, and the Malmö Ministerial Declaration of 31 May 2000.

The Indian Environmental (Protection) Act, 1986 was enacted to implement the decisions taken at the United Nations Conference on the Human Environment held at Stockholm in June 1972.

World Summit on Sustainable Development[17]

The World Summit on Sustainable Development was held in Johannesburg

[17] World Summit on Sustainable Development, 2002, at Johannesburg, South Africa, 4 September 2002, after review of ten years progress of UN Conference on Environment and Development (UNCED) held in Rio de Janeiro, 1992.

from 26 August to 4 September 2002, and acted as a ten-year review of the progress of the UNCED. The meet assessed the problems of environmental deterioration from Stockholm to Rio de Janeiro to Johannesburg. The world leaders declared that the 'deep fault line' between the rich and poor posed a major threat to global prosperity and stability. A broad plan was adopted to address this problem, containing specific global targets in poverty reduction, clean water and sanitation, and infant mortality. Adopting the Johannesburg Declaration on Sustainable Development, heads of state and government, reaffirming their commitment to Agenda 21, stated that globalization, the rapid integration of markets, mobility of capital, and increased investment flows had created new opportunities, but the benefits and costs were unevenly distributed. Further, they stated, the global environment continues to suffer from the loss of biodiversity, depletion of fish stocks, advancing desertification, worsening climate change, more frequent and devastating natural disasters, and increasingly vulnerable developing countries. They added:

We risk the entrenchment of these global disparities and unless we act in a manner that fundamentally changes their lives, the poor of the world may lose confidence in their representatives and the democratic systems to which we remain committed, seeing their representatives as nothing more than sounding brass or tinkling cymbals.

The wide-ranging implementation plan calls for halving the proportion of the world's population that lives on less than $1 a day; halving the number of people living without safe drinking water or basic sanitation; and reducing mortality rates for infants and children under five by two-thirds, and maternal mortality by three-quarters.

HAZARDOUS WASTE AND CHEMICALS

Basel Convention on the Control of Transboundary Movements of Hazardous Waste[18]

The Basel Convention conducted in 1989 had decided to regulate transboundary movement of hazardous wastes and their disposal The 170 parties who participated in the meet are obliged to ensure that such wastes are managed and disposed off in an environmentally sound manner from 1992.

India signed the Convention on 15 March 1990 and enacted the Hazarouds Wastes (Management and Handling) Rules, 1989 and the Manufacture, Storage, and Import of Hazardous Chemical Rules, 1989 for the purposes of minimizing the amount and toxicity of wastes generated, to ensure their environmentally sound management as closely as possible to the source of generation.

Thereafter in May 2008, the members of the Basel Convention met in Bali and reiterated to the world that it is too risky that some countries do not care about the dangerous impacts problems. A working group was also formed for the implementation.

In a case that came up for consideration before the Supreme Court of India, it was contended that the presence of PCBs contents at a detectable level in waste mineral oil was only marginal or minimal, and therefore fell inside the permissible limit of the Basel Convention. The prescription of more standards was challenged. The Supreme Court held that the provisions of the Basel Convention on the control of transboundary movement of hazardous wastes and their disposal are in the nature of guidelines only. It rejected the

proposed contention and held that individual countries can provide stricter conditions in their national law that would be applicable and will be the law of the country.[19]

Stockholm Convention on Persistent Organic Pollutants (POPs)[20]

The Stockholm Convention, held on 23 May 2001, is a global treaty to provide protection against pollutants that remain intact in the environment for long periods, become widely distributed geographically, accumulate in the fatty tissue of living organisms, and are toxic to humans and wildlife. POPs circulate globally and can cause damage wherever they travel. In implementing the Convention, governments are to take measures to eliminate or reduce the release of POPs into the environment.

The parties to this Convention, conscious of the need for global action on persistent organic pollutants, decided on 7 February 1997 to initiate international action to protect human health and the environment through measures that will reduce and/or eliminate emissions and discharges of POPs. India is a signatory to the Convention.

BIODIVERSTIY

Convention on International Trade in Endangered Species of Wild Fauna and Flora (CITES)[21]

CITES is an international agreement intended to ensure that international trade in specimens

---

[18] Basel Convention on the Control of Transboundary Movements of Hazardous Wastes and Their Disposal, entered into force 5 May 1992, 1673 UNTS 126.

[19] *Research Foundation for Science Technology National Resource Policy v. Union of India*, (2005) 13 SCC 186.
[20] Stockholm Convention on Persistent Organic Pollutants, 40 ILM 532 (2001); signed by The Union Ministry of Environment and Forests in May 2002.
[21] Convention on International Trade in Endangered Species of Wild Fauna and Flora, entered into force 1 July 1975, 993 UNTS 243.

of wild animals and plants does not threaten their survival. It was first formed in the year 1960. Because the trade in wild animals and plants crosses borders between countries, regulation requires international cooperation to safeguard certain species from over-exploitation. CITES was conceived in the spirit of such cooperation. Today, it accords varying degrees of protection to more than 30,000 species of animals and plants, whether they are traded as live specimens, fur coats, or dried herbs.

The text of the CITES was concluded on 3 March 1973 at Washington in the presence of the representatives of eighty countries. In Washington DC, India signed this agreement in July 1974 and deposited the instrument of ratification on 20 July 1976. Thus, India became a party to the CITES from 18 October 1976.

CITES was further amended at Bonn on 22 June 1979, and included avian migratory species throughout their range.

Indian law on wildlife protection is enacted on the basis of CITES. The Export and Exim Policy of the Government of India also provides for restrictions that are stricter than the Convention. Almost all wild species of fauna are protected under Indian law and virtually a complete ban on hunting and export of even non-CITES species is in existence in India.

Convention on Wetlands of International Importance especially as Waterfowl Habitat—Ramsar Convention[22]

The contracting parties of the Ramsar Convention came together:

1. Recognizing the interdependence of Man and his environment;
2. Considering the fundamental ecological functions of wetlands as regulators of water regimes and as habitats supporting a characteristic flora and fauna, especially waterfowl; [and]
3. Being convinced that wetlands constitute a resource of great economic, cultural, scientific, and recreational value, the loss of which would be irreparable, the convention agreed to protect wetlands and their flora and fauna by national policies with coordinated international action.[23]

Wetlands in their seasonal migrations may transcend frontiers and should be regarded as an international resource. For the purpose of this Convention, wetlands are areas of marsh, fen, peatland, or water, whether natural or artificial, permanent or temporary, with water that is static or flowing, fresh, brackish, or salt, including areas of marine water the depth of which at low tide does not exceed six metres.[24] Waterfowl are birds ecologically dependent on wetlands. The contracting parties are obligated to identify suitable wetlands within their territory for inclusion in the List of Wetlands of International Importance. Wetlands on this list attract certain protection and place various obligations on the state party. The convention agreement came into force with effect from 12 December 1975. India signed it on 1 August 1982, and twenty-five sites were identified totalling 677, 131 hectares.[25]

Convention on Biological Diversity[26]

On 29 January 2000, the Convention on Biological Diversity adopted a supplementary

[22] Convention on Wetlands of International Importance especially as Waterfowl Habitat, entered into force 27 December 1975, 996 UNTS 245.

[23] Convention on Wetlands of International Importance especially as Waterfowl Habitat, entered into force 27 December 1975, 996 UNTS 245.

[24] Ramsar, Convention, Article 1(1).

[25] http://www.ramsar.org (last visited 9 December 2007).

[26] Convention on Biological Diversity, entered into force 29 December 1993, 1760 UNTS 79.

agreement to the Convention known as the Cartagena Protocol on Bio-safety.[27] The Protocol seeks to protect biological diversity from the potential risks posed by living modified organisms resulting from modern biotechnology. It establishes an advance informed agreement (AIA) procedure for ensuring that countries are provided with the information necessary to make informed decisions before agreeing to the import of such organisms into their territory. The Protocol contains reference to a precautionary approach and reaffirms the precautionary language in Principle 15 of the Rio Declaration on Environment and Development. The Protocol also establishes a Bio-safety Clearing-House to facilitate the exchange of information on living modified organisms and assist countries in the implementation of the Protocol. India signed the protocol on bio-safety on 23 January 2001 and enacted the Bio-Diversity Act, 2002 to implement it.

Transboundary Cooperation

Convention on the Protection and Use of Transboundary Watercourses and International Lakes[28]

The meet was held at Helsinki on 17 March 1992. The Convention was conscious of a number of issues. Firstly, it had in mind the role of the United Nations Economic Commission for Europe in promoting international cooperation for the prevention, control, and reduction of trans-boundary water pollution and sustainable use of trans-boundary waters. It recalled the ECE Declaration of Policy on

Prevention and Control of Water Pollution, including Transboundary Pollution, the ECE Declaration of Policy on the Rational Use of Water; the ECE Principles Regarding Cooperation in the Field of Transboundary Waters, the ECE Charter on Groundwater Management, and the Code of Conduct on Accidental Pollution of Transboundary Inland Waters. On this basis, it decided to take a number of appropriate measures:

1. To prevent, control, and reduce pollution of waters causing or likely to cause trans-boundary impact.
2. To ensure that trans-boundary waters are used with the aim of ecologically sound and rational water management, conservation of water resources, and environmental protection.
3. To ensure that trans-boundary waters are used in a reasonable and equitable way, taking into particular account their trans-boundary character, in the case of activities which cause or are likely to cause trans-boundary impact.
4. To ensure conservation and, where necessary, restoration of ecosystems.

   (i) The precautionary principle, by virtue of which action to avoid the potential trans-boundary impact of the release of hazardous substances shall not be postponed on the ground that scientific research has not fully proved a causal link between those substances, on the one hand, and the potential trans-boundary impact, on the other hand;
   (ii) The polluter pays principle, by virtue of which costs of pollution prevention, control, and reduction measures shall be borne by the polluter;
   (iii) Water resources shall be managed so that the needs of the present generation are met without compromising the

[27] Cartagena Protocol on Biosafety to the Convention on Biological Diversity, entered into force 11 September 2003, UN Doc UNEP/CBD/ExCOP/1/3, at 42 (2000).
[28] Convention on the Protection and Use of Transboundary Watercourses and International Lakes, entered into force 6 October 1996, 1936 UNTS 269.

ability of future generations to meet their own needs.

THE ATMOSPHERE

Vienna Convention on the Ozone Layer[29]

The issue of ozone depletion was first discussed by the Governing Council of the UNEP in 1976. A meeting of experts on the ozone layer was convened in 1977, after which UNEP and the WMO set up the Coordinating Committee of the Ozone Layer (CCOL) to periodically assess ozone depletion. Intergovernmental negotiations for an international agreement to phase out ozone depleting substances started in 1981 and concluded with the adoption of the Vienna Convention for the Protection of the Ozone Layer in March 1985.

The Vienna Convention encourages intergovernmental cooperation on research, systematic observation of the ozone layer, monitoring of CFC production, and the exchange of information. India ratified the Convention on 18 March 1991.

Montreal Protocol on Substances that Deplete the Ozone Layer[30]

The Montreal Protocol on Substances that Deplete the Ozone Layer was adopted in September 1987. It was designed to phase out substances, mainly CFCs, which deplete the ozone layer. A number of schedules are devised and can be revised on the basis of periodic scientific and technological assessments. The Protocol was adjusted to accelerate the phase-out schedules. It has also been amended to introduce other kinds of control measures and to add new controlled substances to the list. Governments are not legally bound until they ratify the Protocol as well as the amendment. Unfortunately, while most governments have ratified the Protocol, ratification of the amendment and their stronger control measures lag behind. India ratified it on 19 June 1992 and the Montreal amendment on 3 March 2003.

Article II of the Montreal Protocol provides that the Meeting of the Parties (MOP) should be held at regular, unspecified intervals. MOP has been held annually and it has the powers to consider and approve procedures and institutional mechanisms for determining noncompliance. For effective implementation, MOP has powers for treatment of parties found to be non-compliant.[31]

London Amendment to the Montreal Protocol (1990)[32]

The amendment to the Montreal Protocol agreed by the Second MOPs in the meet held at London during 27–9 June 1990. The 6th preambular paragraph of the Protocol has been replaced by the following:

Determined to protect the ozone layer by taking precautionary measures to control equitably total global emissions of substances that deplete it, with the ultimate objective of their elimination on the basis of developments in scientific knowledge, taking into account technical and economic considerations and bearing in mind the developmental needs of developing countries,

The 7th preambular paragraph of the Protocol is amended to read:

---

[29] Convention for the Protection of the Ozone Layer, entered into force 22 September 1988, 1513 UNTS 323.

[30] Montreal Protocol on Substances that Deplete the Ozone Layer, entered into force 1 January 1989, 26 ILM 1550 (1987).

[31] *Improving Compliance with International Environmental Law*, James Cameron, Jacob Werksman, and Peter Roderick.

[32] Available at < http://ozone.unep.org/Treaties_and_Ratification/2Bi_1_London_amendment.shtml>

Acknowledging that a special provision is required to meet the needs of developing countries, including the provision of additional financial resources and access to relevant technologies, bearing in mind that the magnitude of funds necessary is predictable, and the funds can be expected to make a substantial difference in the world's ability to address the scientifically established problem of ozone depletion and its harmful effects.

The 9th paragraph of the Preamble of the Protocol is replaced by the following:

Considering the importance of promoting international cooperation in the research, development, and transfer of alternative technologies relating to the control and reduction of emissions of substances that deplete the ozone layer, bearing in mind in particular the needs of developing countries,

Several other amendments were also made to the Montreal Protocol. India ratified the said amendments on 19 June 1992. India also ratified the Beijing Amendment on 3 March 2003.

The United Nations Framework Convention on Climate Change[33]

The Convention set out an overall framework for intergovernmental efforts to tackle the challenge posed by climate change and was held in Heiligendamm, Germany on 8 June 2007. It called for a new global agreement under the UNFCCC by 2009 and was encouraged by the fact that this process was supported by the Group of five countries with emerging economies, that is, Brazil, China, India, Mexico, and South Africa. The Convention entered into force on 21 March 1994 and enjoys near universal membership, with 191 countries having ratified it.

Fundamental to the Convention is the recognition of the fact that the climate system

is a shared resource whose stability can be affected by industrial and other emissions of carbon dioxide and other GHGs. Under the Convention, governments carry out a number of obligations. They gather and share information on GHG emissions, national policies, and best practices. National strategies for addressing GHG emissions and adapting to expected impacts, including the provision of financial and technological support to developing countries, are launched. Furthermore, governments cooperate in preparing for adaptation to the impacts of climate change.

India signed the Convention on 10 June 1992, ratified it on 1 November 1993, and had it entered into force on 21 March 1994. In 2004, India made its initial communication[34] to the Convention in accordance with the requirements of Article 12. The communication emphasizes that it reflects the responsibilities prescribed for the group of Non-Annex-1 parties to which India belongs. It highlights the large climatic variability over the country, the wide variety of forest types, rainfall patterns, land-use patterns, and population trends. These factors are indicative of the capacity of the country to fulfil, the objects of the convention, the social, economic, and environmental areas that are most vulnerable to climate change and the types of measures that may be employed to adapt to and mitigate climate change. Notably, the executive summary points out that 'Notwithstanding the climate-friendly orientation of national policies, the development to meet the basic needs and aspirations of a vast and growing

---

[33] United Nations Framework Convention on Climate Change 1771 UNTS 107.

[34] Ministry Of Environment and Forests, Government of India, 'India's Initial Communication to the United Nations Framework Convention on Climate Change' (2004) available at <http//:www.unfccc.int/national_reports/non-annex_i_natcom/items/2979.php> (last visited 1 October 2007).

population will lead to increased GHG emissions in the future.'[35]

But the summary also recognizes that development conversely demands a reduction in GHGs, as climate change has the capacity to affect the Indian economy, which is often dependant on industries that rely on climate-sensitive ecosystems such as agriculture and forestry.[36] This perhaps demonstrates the plight of many Non-Annex-1 or developing country parties, as they aim to uphold the principle of sustainable development and meet the objectives of the Convention.

The Indian Government has framed the National Environmental Policy in 2006, detailing the country's GHG footprint. Both India and China have declared that they are not responsible for emissions in the past and have taken all steps to reduce emissions. As of November 2006, India had not made any further communications to the UNFCCC.[37]

The Kyoto Protocol—United Nations Framework Convention on Climate Change[38]

The United Nations Framework Convention on Climate Change has recognized the phenomenon of climate change and how it should be reduced. It prescribes quantified emmission limitations for each developed country party to the conference. Each party, in achieving its quantified emission limitation and reduction commitments specified therein, shall undertake to do the following in order to promote sustainable development:

(a) Implement and/or further elaborate policies and measures in accordance with its national circumstances, such as:

i) Enhancement of energy efficiency in relevant sectors of the national economy;

ii) Protection and enhancement of sinks and reservoirs of greenhouse gases not controlled by the Montreal Protocol, taking into account its commitments under relevant international environmental agreements; promotion of sustainable forest management practices, afforestation and reforestation;

iii) Promotion of sustainable forms of agriculture in light of climate change considerations;

iv) Promotion, research, development, and increased use of new and renewable forms of energy, of carbon dioxide sequestration technologies, and of advanced and innovative environmentally sound technologies;

v) Progressive reduction or phasing out of market imperfections, fiscal incentives, tax and duty exemptions and subsidies in all greenhouse gas emitting sectors that run counter to the objective of the Convention and apply market instruments;

vi) Encouragement of appropriate reforms in relevant sectors aimed at promoting policies and measures that limit or reduce emissions of greenhouse gases not controlled by the Montreal Protocol;

vii) Measures to limit and/or reduce emissions of greenhouse gases not controlled by the Montreal Protocol in the transport sector;

[35] Ministry Of Environment and Forests, Government of India 'India's Initial Communication to the United Nations Framework Convention on Climate Change' Executive Summary (2004), (ii)-(iii) available at <http//: www.unfccc.int/national_reports/non-annex_i_natcom/ items/2979.php> (last visited 1 October 2007).

[36] See ibid.

[37] United Nations Framework Convention on Climate Change, Submitted National Communications from Non-Annex I Parties <http://www.unfccc.int/national_ reports/non-annex_i_natcom/submitted_natcom/ items/653.php> (last visited 1 October 2007).

[38] Kyoto Protocol to the United Nations Framework Convention on Climate Change UN Doc FCCC/ CP/1997/7/Add. 1, 10 December 1997.

viii) Limitation and/or reduction of methane through recovery and use in waste management, as well as in the production, transport and distribution of energy;

India ratified the Kyoto Protocol on 26 August 2002, and the Convention entered into force on 15 February 2005. The country has been an active participant in the CDM that enables 'Annex I Parties to implement project activities that reduce emissions in non-Annex I Parties, in return for certified emission reductions (CERs).' To date, India has hosted 35.12 per cent of the registered project activities, which is more than any other non-Annex I party. (For more, see the chapter on Climate Change.) Despite this, India has not signed the Convention.[39]

DESERTIFICATION

The United Nations Convention to Combat Desertification (UNCCD)[40]

The UNCCD was adopted on 17 June 1994 by India. The Convention stresses the need for integrated efforts and long-term strategies on cross-sectoral issues such as environmental conservation, agricultural productivity, sustainable energy and fodder production and use, efficient management of land, water, and other natural resources, and developmental activities for local communities

to improve their living standards. Thus, the UNCCD provides a platform for addressing these issues not only in the national but also the global context.

India became a signatory to the UNCCD on 14 October 1994 and it came into effect on 17 March 1997. One of the obligations of all developing countries that are parties to the Convention, including India, is to prepare the National Action Programme to Combat Desertification and to mitigate the effects of drought. The Government of India (MoEF) initiated the process of preparation of a National Action Programme through the setting up of a High-Level Inter-Sectoral National Steering Committee (NSC) in July 1999. The NSC decided to constitute four working groups (WG) on various issues relevant to desertification: (1) Desertification Monitoring and Assessment, (2) Sustainable Land Use Practices for Combating Desertification, (3) Local Area Development Programme, and (4) Policy and Institutional Issues.[41]

To promote common protection of the environment through legal means, it can be said that we must 'think globally and act globally'. The same can be achieved only by the implementation of the said commitments in both letter and spirit across the world.

---

[39] United Nations Framework Convention on Climate Change Website, <http://www.maindb.unfccc.int/public/country.pl?country=IN> (last visited 1 October 2007).

[40] United Nations Convention to Combat Desertification in Countries Experiencing Serious Drought and/or Desertification, Particularly in Africa, entered into force 26 December 1996, 1954 UNTS 3.

[41] http://www.unccd.int//actionprogrammes/asia/national/2001/india-eng.pdf (last visited 16 August 2008).

II

Dealing with Different
Kinds of Pollution
Law and Policy

9 Pollutants in the Air

Air pollution is the presence of one or more pollutants or combinations of these pollutants in excess quantity, being injurious to health. In the Rigveda, *vayu* (air) is considered an agent for the welfare of the people and is treated as a god in Hindu mythology. Pure and clear air is the source of health and happiness and important for our life. The Bhagavad Gita[1] has observed that air has its origin in ether—it disappears in ether, springs from ether, remains in, and finally disappears into ether. Under no circumstances does air remain apart from ether, but never remains in it. Yet, ether has no connection whatsoever with the air, its movement, and other changes in it, and is always beyond it.

In the Hebrew Scriptures, air held a sacred meaning. The term *rûah* was used to describe the air in the atmosphere, the wind, and human breath.[2] It was often associated with God and given a divine character: even God has rûah

The recesses of the sea appeared,
The foundations of the earth were uncovered
At the roar of the Lord,

From the wind/breath of the wind/breath (ruah) of his *Nostrils* (2 Sam 22:16)[3].

In the above passage, the wind is described as God's breath, showing that God is connected with nature.[4] The use of the term rûah to describe both atmospheric air and breath symbolizes the interconnectedness of life, human beings, and the atmosphere.[5] We cannot survive without our atmosphere.

Air pollution is the contamination of the atmosphere. It is caused by the discharge of a wide range of toxic substances. The main air pollutant in India is the emissions from the motor vehicles. The greatest single cause of air pollution in the UK is motor vehicles, which are responsible for 85 per cent of the carbon monoxide and 45 per cent of the oxides of nitrogen present in the atmosphere.

There are four gases that have been globally declared primary air pollutants. They are: (1) oxides of sulphur, (2) oxides of nitrogen, (3) oxides of carbon, and (4) hydrocarbons. The suspended particulate matter (SPM), commonly known as dust and ash are also air pollutants. Secondary air pollutants are sulphurate, sulphuric acid, sulphurate

[1] Chapter 9, Verse 6.
[2] Theodore Hiebert, 'Air—The First Sacred Thing: The Conception of *rûah* in the Hebrew Scriptures.' *Harvard Seminar of Environmental Values*, 20 (Tuesday) April 1999.

[3] Ibid.
[4] Ibid.
[5] Ibid.

mixtures, cyton, aldehydride, acids proxy aisle nitrite (PAN), nitric acid, nitrogen pentoxide, nitrogen mixtures, and other mixtures.

The acidic deposition of acid rain is caused principally by sulphur dioxide (SO_2) and nitrogen oxide. These acids then return to earth as dew, drizzle, fog, rain, snow, and sleet. Acidic gases can travel over 500 kilometres or 300 miles per day; hence acid rain can be considered an example of transboundary pollution. Acid rain is linked with damage to and the death of forests and lake organisms in Scandinavia, Europe, and eastern North America. The main effect of acid rain is to damage the chemical balance of soil, which causes leaching of important minerals like magnesium and aluminium. Plants living in such soils, particularly conifers, suffer from the soil and pass into lakes and rivers, disturbing aquatic life, for instance, by damaging young fish. Lakes and rivers suffer damage as well because they become acidified by the rainfall draining directly from their drainage basin. The only visible solution to acid rain is the reduction of emissions of pollutant gases so as to attain an ambient air quality.[6]

INDIAN LEGISLATION

The Air (Prevention and Control of Pollution) Act was enacted in 1981 'to provide for the prevention, control, and abatement of air pollution'[7] and as stated by Section 1(2), it applies to the whole of India. The Act explicitly identifies itself as a means of implementing the Stockholm Declaration,[8] which was formulated at the Stockholm Conference, in

which India participated.[9] Principle 2 of the Declaration states that air is one of the earth's natural resources that 'must be safeguarded for the benefit of present and future generations through careful planning or management, as appropriate,' it being apparent that the Act aims to fulfil these objectives.

The term 'air pollutant' is defined by Section 2(a) as

any solid, liquid, or gaseous substance (including noise) present in the atmosphere in such concentration as may be or tend to be injurious to human beings or other living creatures or plants or property or environment.'[10]

It is questionable how slight or serious this level of injury must be, for the substance to be classified as an air pollutant. However, the Act prescribes the ambient air quality standards, which somewhat resolves this difficulty.

POLLUTION CONTROL AUTHORITIES

To ensure that the Act is administered correctly and its objectives achieved, it provides for the creation of State and Central bodies for the implementation of its provisions.

In any state that has a State Board for the Prevention and Control of Water Pollution, constituted under the Water (Prevention and Control of Pollution) Act, 1974, that Board will exercise the powers and functions of the State Board for the prevention and control of air pollution, as specified by Section 4 of the Act. Where the Act is not in force, or a State Board has not been constituted, Section 5 of the Act is to be followed to enable the creation of a State Board for the prevention and control of air pollution.

Section 5 outlines the constitution of the State Boards which bear a wide range of persons of varying expertise and capacities,

[6] Hutchinson Pocket Dictionary of the Environment—Indian Print 1996.

[7] Air (Prevention and Control of Pollution) Act, 1981(India), Preamble.

[8] Declaration of the United Nations Conference on the Human Environment (1972), 11 ILM 1416.

[9] Ibid.

[10] Ibid.

where members hold office for a term of three years according to Section 7(1). In particular, the Chairman must have practical knowledge or expertise in relation to environmental protection. There are also official representatives of state governments and state corporations, and other representatives of various industries such as agriculture, fisheries, and trade. Committees may be formed within the Board under Section 11. Such committees deal with particular matters of concern and the Board may enlist the expertise of outside persons to become members of these committees, despite the fact that they hold no membership with the Board. The Board has a wide range of expertise, both within itself and beyond, available to it, as Section 12 enables it to associate itself with outside persons for a particular purpose. Section 10 provides that the State Board is to meet at least once every three months and the committees are to meet at such time and place as prescribed, as per Section 11.

The powers and functions of the State Boards can be found under Section 17 of the Act. State Boards are charged with the power to create comprehensive programmes for the prevention, abatement, and control of air pollution in their jurisdiction. They hold the responsibility of collecting and disseminating information related to air pollution and are to advise the state government on matters of air pollution and in particular, provide advice on suitability of areas for the location of industries that may cause air pollution. With the guidance of the Central Board, the State Boards are to set air pollutant emission standards and organize training for personnel to be engaged in the furtherance of the objectives of the Act. The inspection of air pollution control areas, industrial plants, manufacturing processes, and equipment is also undertaken by the State Boards, where such steps or directions as necessary can be made to prevent, abate, or

control air pollution respectively. Finally, State Boards have a wide power to carry out any functions that they believe to be necessary to fulfil the purposes of the Act.

Each State Board is characterized as a corporate entity, as prescribed by Section 5(3).[11] Consequently, acts of its members can often be imputed to the Chairman or directors. Similarly, where an incorporated company has several manufacturing units beneath it, and one of these units commits an environmental offence, the managing director of the parent company can be held responsible. Although concerned with an offence under the Water (Prevention and Control of Pollution) Act, 1974, the ruling in *M.V. Arunachalam v. Tamil Nadu Pollution Control Board*[12] is easily applicable to offences involving air pollution. In this case, an incorporated company existed for the purposes of manufacturing and distributing cycles and parts and had several industrial units functioning underneath it. One of these manufacturing units was accused of dumping untreated cyanide waste into a canal, killing a number of buffaloes that drank the water, and endangering human health. These acts constituted an offence under Section 49 of the Water (Prevention and Control of Pollution) Act, 1974. The court held that since the industrial units were not legally recognized, the parent company could be held as the accused. Potential defences for the company included lack of knowledge of the acts and due diligence, these being matters to be raised at trial.[13] It should also be noted that if an individual of the company is to be charged for the conduct of the company, they must have been in charge of the business of the company[14] at the time

---

[11] Water (Prevention and Control of Pollution) Act, 1974.

[12] (Madras) 1992 Crl. LJ 188.

[13] *M.V. Arunachalam v. Tamil Nadu Pollution Control Board (Madras)*, 1992 Crl. LJ 188, Section 9.

[14] Supra note 10, Section 40.

the acts were committed, as per Section 40 of the Air Act. The High Court has quashed a prosecution against a Deputy Chairman of a company, citing the reason that such persons are not concerned with conduct of the affairs of the company.[15]

The Air Act does not provide a separate procedure for the constitution of the Central Board; instead, it endows the Central Board for the Prevention and Control of Water Pollution, constituted under the Water (Prevention and Control of Pollution) Act, 1974, with the powers and functions of the Central Board for Air Pollution, as per Section 3 of the Act.

The Central Board has a mandate to 'improve the quality of air and to prevent, control, or abate air pollution in the country', as dictated by Section 16(1). It has a number of powers outlined in Section 16(2), which are similar to those exercised by the State Boards, although they could be described as more systematic in nature, designed to facilitate widespread management of air pollution in India. These include advising the Central Government, devising a nationwide programme for the abatement, prevention, and control of air pollution, setting standards for air emissions, and collecting and disseminating information on air pollution.[16] The Central Board also acts as a resource and intermediary for the State Boards, resolving disputes among them, providing them with information, coordinating their activities, and providing them with funding for investigations and research. Finally, it is the function of the Central Board to educate and inform the public on matters of air pollution, employing the help of the mass media to carry out this task by implementing a comprehensive programme throughout India.

A hierarchy of accountability is established by Section 18 of the Act and can be used to resolve any conflicts between the various bodies.[17] The State Board is subject to directions of the State Government, the Central Board, and the Central Government. In the event that any of these directions conflict, the final decision rests with the Central Government. The Central Pollution Control Board (CPCB)[18] is subject to the directions of the Central Government. Despite this, government departments can still be held liable for contravention of the Act.[19]

INDIAN CASE LAW

The case of *Mystery Gas Spreads Panic* v. *The Director, A.P. Pollution Control Board, Hyderabad and Others*[20] is an excellent example of how the various bodies interact to combat air pollution. In this case a mischievous gas with a foul odour spread throughout a portion of the city and caused breathing problems for residents. Local newspapers reported the nuisance and the High Court of Andhra Pradesh instituted a suo motu writ petition. A preliminary investigation revealed that a number of industries in the area were overloading liquid incinerators and improperly discharging effluents. The State Board then investigated the matter and made detailed findings specifying the particulars of the pollution. A specialist committee consisting of the appropriate scientific bodies was created to further assess the pollution. It was found that the dumping of effluents into water bodies by tankers was taking place. Tankers used to carry public drinking water were even engaging in

---

[15] N.A. Palkhiwala v. M.P. Paradushan Nivaran Mandal, 1990 Crl LJ 1856.

[16] Water (Prevention and Control of Pollution) Act, 1974, Section 16.

[17] Ibid., Section 18.

[18] See <http://www.cpcb.nic.in/>

[19] Supra note 16, Section 41.

[20] Writ Petition No. 30006 of 1998 and 20435 of 1999.

such acts. In response, the State Government asked the Central Government to empower it to confiscate such tankers. The court reviewed the various measures taken by the bodies and concluded that a preventive approach was to be adopted. It directed the Board to carry out surprise checks on industries, directed the police to confiscate offending tankers, and even directed the officers of the motor vehicles department to carry out random checks on tankers to ensure compliance with the Motor Vehicles Act, 1988 (MVA).[21]

In *V.S. Damodaran Nair v. State of Kerala*,[22] the court was instrumental in facilitating cooperation between various bodies in the abatement of air pollution. In order to fully understand the extent of air pollution in Cochin, the court commissioned the expert opinion of NEERI. In addition to the evidence from the State Board, the court concluded that industries in the area were not complying with the conditions of consent orders. It also became apparent that the Cochin Corporation was not taking adequate steps to protect citizens from air pollution and it was subsequently ordered to prevent the dumping of waste into open sewage canals and construct underground sewage pipes. Each of the orders made by the court directly reflected the findings of NEERI, and the court even stated that the recommendations of NEERI and the State Board are binding on all parties.[23]

The main way by which the state can regulate air pollution under the Act is by declaring air pollution control areas by exercising its powers under Section 19.[24] This can be done via consultation with the State Board and public notification in the government gazette.[25] The state may give further effect to its declarations using Section 19(3) by prohibiting the use of a particular fuel in an air pollution control area, if the fuel is liable to cause air pollution. Similarly, the use of certain appliances or the burning of certain materials may be prohibited in air pollution control areas, if these activities are likely to cause air pollution, using Sections 19(4) and 19(5) respectively.

Section 21 provides that persons must obtain consent from the State Board to operate an industrial plant in an air pollution control area.[26] The industry must obtain consent in the form of site clearance before the establishment of the unit. After its establishment, consent to operate it is issued. It is always essential that the equipment installed for the suppression of air pollutants are calibrated and made functional before the issuance of such a certificate. Crooked industrialists sometimes bypass these environmental control measures to save money. The only solution is to create an online monitoring mechanism or to appoint a local independent committee.

Plants already in operation at the commencement of the declaration have three months from the date of the declaration in which to obtain the consent certificate.[27] Fresh consent may be required when an industrial plant changes its machinery. In Rajapalayam (Virudhungar District), Cotton Yarn Mills replaced diesel generator sets with furnace oil generators to increase efficiency and environmental sustainability. Although consent had already been received relating to their initial establishment, the Madras High Court applied Section 21(5)(ii) of the Air Act and

[21] Ibid.

[22] AIR 1996 Kerala 8.

[23] *V.S. Damodaran Nair v. State of Kerala*, AIR 1996 KERALA 8.

[24] See also Air (Prevention and Control of Pollution) Act, 1981.

[25] Ibid., Sections 19(1) and 54(k).

[26] Ibid., Section 21.

[27] Ibid.

concluded that 'the consent of the State Board for replacement is essential.'[28]

In *Rukhiya Beevi v. State of Kerala*,[29] action was brought against a woman who had failed to gain consent in respect of an industrial plant. She contended that she did not require consent as she was not causing any pollution to be emitted. The Kerala State Pollution Control Board conducted an inspection of her plant and categorized it as 'the most polluting red category' claiming that this in itself necessitates consent. Notably, the court stated that 'emission of air pollutant in quantities, assessed of such concentration as may be injurious to living organisms, etc., is a condition essential for categorizing it as an industry that requires consent for installation or operation.'[30] Not all industries fall within the ambit of the Act. No industry is presumed to be an 'industrial plant' for the purposes of the Act, as this must be established based on the character of the industry. The court held that the woman was not precluded from seeking consent just because the unit had already become functional and after finding that no evidence of pollution existed, she was allowed to carry on her business.

The Board may make an application to the court restraining plants from operation if air pollutants infringing Section 17 will be emitted.[31] However, if the Board wishes to cancel or withdraw its consent, it must give notice and give both parties the opportunity to fairly present their case.[32] Any remedial measures contemplated by the court must be adapted to the mitigation of air pollution and the court cannot simply order the closing of an industrial plant without such justification.[33]

The Act imposes a very strict regime for the regulation of an industry emitting air pollutants. An 'industrial plant' is widely defined by Section 2(k) as 'any plant used for any industrial or trade purposes and emitting any air pollutant into the atmosphere.'[34] The state is not authorized to excuse a certain type of industry from the application of the Act. In Gandhinagar (Kolar Town Municipality), the respondents operated a rice mill that caused air pollution by the emission of dust and husks adjacent to the appellant's home. The Deputy Commissioner had issued an exemption in respect of rice mill industries, excluding them from the operation of the Air Act. The Karnataka High Court held that since the rice mill is an industry within the meaning of the Act, consent on the part of the Pollution Control Board would be required for its operation and the state was not empowered to grant any exemptions to certain industrial plants.[35] The term 'plant' has not been defined in the Air Act. Adopting a dictionary meaning, it can be given a broadly defined. The Oxford Dictionary defines 'plant' as, 'a place where an industrial or manufacturing process takes place,'[36] where 'industrial' means, 'relating to or characterized by industry', and 'industry' is defined as 'economic activity concerned with the processing of raw materials and manufacture

---

[28] *Sudarsanam Spinning Mills and Others v. Tamil Nadu Pollution Control Board & Another*, WP Nos 21585, 21588, 21589, and 21613 of 2000 and WPMP Nos 31355, 31358, 31359, and 31396 of 2000, dated 16 November 2004.

[29] 2004 (2) KLT 938.

[30] *Rukhiya Beevi v. State of Kerala*, 2004 (2) KLT 938, Section 21.

[31] Ibid.

[32] *M/s DLF Power Ltd v. State of Jharkhand*, AIR 2004 JHARKHAND 85.

[33] *Chaitanya Pulvarising Industry v. Karnataka State Pollution Control Board*, AIR 1987 Kant 82.

[34] Ibid.

[35] *K. Muniswamy Gowda v. State of Karnataka*, AIR 1998 KARNATAKA 281.

[36] *Oxford Dictionary of English*, Oxford: Oxford University Press, 2nd edn, revised, (2005), p. 1346.

of goods in factories.'[37] So long as a process concerned with manufacture or industry occurs at the place, it may be characterized as a 'plant'.

DECLARATION OF AIR POLLUTION CONTROL AREA

In *Orissa State (Prevention and Control of Pollution) Board v. M/s Orient Paper Mills and Another*, the state failed to prescribe a procedure for the declaration of an air pollution control area as provided by Section 54(2)(k) of the Act, but exercised its powers under Section 19 in declaring an air pollution control area. The respondent, who was accused of violating the consent provisions for the control area, challenged the Section 19 declaration for want of procedure. The court held that 'the State would not be divested of its powers to notify in the Official Gazette any area declaring it to be an air pollution control area.'[38] The phrase 'in such manner as may be prescribed'[39] indicates that the prescription of procedural rules is not mandatory and the state has the liberty of discretion. In particular, the word 'as' was held to enable some degree of flexibility. In this sense, some members of industry may view the provisions as being arbitrary, where the prescription of a detailed procedure to be adhered to could promote a sense that justice is being done amongst the community.

In order to give practical effect to Sections 22 and 23, the State Board has the power to inspect industry.[40] The Act provides a procedure which the State Board must adopt if it wishes to take air or emission samples in the course of its inspections.[41] The occupier must be given notice, the sample must be taken in the occupier's presence and signed by them, and the sample must be sent to a laboratory of the State Board recognized under Section 17. Reports must then be furnished to the occupier, one kept for the court and one to the State Board.[42] If this procedure is not complied with, the samples may not be admitted as evidence in court. The Act is commendable in this respect, as the procedure ensures that the evidence is of a high quality and is procured in a fair manner.

The operation of the Air Act has given rise to claims regarding various constitutional rights. A number of merchants who carried on the business of used gunny bags in a densely populated area were causing air pollution and traffic congestion. The state government directed the merchants to move their business to a location where they would not cause an environmental hazard, pursuant to Section 5 of the Environment (Protection) Act, 1986. The merchants appealed, arguing that their right to carry on business or trade as guaranteed by the Constitution was infringed by the order. The court held that,

Article 19(1)(g) of the Constitution of India... is subject to any restriction that may be imposed by any law in force. The HMC Act, Air (Prevention and Control of Pollution) Act, 1981, and the Environment Act provide for such regulations. Therefore, the right of the petitioners to carry on business in old and used gunny bags cannot be said to be absolute.[43]

The constitutional right of individuals to carry on a business must be balanced against

[37] Ibid., p. 884.

[38] *Orissa State (Prevention and Control of Pollution) Board v. M/s Orient Paper Mills and Another*, AIR 2003 SC 1966 Criminal Appeal No. 331 of 2003 (Arising out of SLP (Crl) No. 3180 of 2001), dated 10 March 2003, Section 14.

[39] Ibid.

[40] Air (Prevention and Control of Pollution) Act, 1981, Section 19(1).

[41] Ibid.

[42] Ibid., Section 27.

[43] *A.P. Gunnies Merchants Association v. The Government of AP*, AIR 2001 AP 453.

the public right to enjoy an environment free from pollution.

In *Antony v. Commissioner, Corporation of Cochin*, the petitioner claimed that the operation of a cement godown in the midst of a shopping district infringed their right to life as guaranteed by the Indian Constitution. The court noted that the right to life is to be given an expanded meaning and includes, 'the right to pure drinking water, pollution-free air, and right to good roads, etc.'[44] and the 'finer graces of human civilization'.[45] The court did not hesitate in holding that the presence of the cement godowns posed a health threat to the residents in the area and that the respondents be refused a licence to carry on the conduct of the cement business in the shopping complex.

AIR POLLUTION AND NUISANCE

Issues of public nuisance can also become of relevance. In *P.C. Cherian v. State of Kerala*,[46] the defendant petitioner was engaged in the manufacture of rubber products. During manufacture, the mixing of carbon with rubber would occur in a building that was not fitted with the requisite devices to prevent the carbon black from escaping into the atmosphere. This ignited a number of complaints from residents in the surrounding area who were finding the carbon deposited on their clothes. Carbon even settled on various religious artefacts including the holy Eucharist at the local church and posed a general disturbance to the congregation. Proceedings were initiated under Section 133 of the Criminal Procedure Code (CrPC) and the magistrate directed the defendant to cease the mixing of carbon with

rubber. The petitioners appealed, stating that carbon is not toxic to the health of humans and their discharge of it was not a public nuisance. The court stated, 'to hold that the deposit of carbon black in the instant cases is a public nuisance, it need not necessarily be a hazard to the health of the people.'[47] The court's position expressly reflected Section 268 of the Indian Penal Code, 1860 (IPC), which defines a public nuisance as

a person is guilty of a public nuisance who does not act or is guilty of an illegal omission which causes any common injury, danger or annoyance to the public or to the people in general who dwell or occupy property in the vicinity, or which must necessarily cause injury, obstruction, danger or annoyance to persons who may have occasion to use any public right.[48]

Since the deposit of carbon poses an annoyance to the community and reduces its comfort, the petitioners were found liable for such acts. The court also employed a proportionality approach in rejecting the petitioners' final contention that the direction should be removed because it would deprive factory workers of their livelihood. It was certain that the nuisance caused to the public far outweighed the inconvenience to be caused to employees of the factory, noting that the nuisance adversely affects the employees themselves.

OFFENCES UNDER THE AIR ACT

Every person carrying on an industry, operation, or process requiring consent under the Air (Prevention and Control of Pollution) Act, 1984 must submit an environmental statement in the prescribed Form-V to the concerned State Pollution Control Board before 13 September 1993.[49] Unfortunately, no such

---

[44] *Antony v. Commissioner, Corporation of Cochin*, 1994 (1) KLT 169.

[45] Ibid.

[46] *P.C. Cherian v. State of Kerala*, 1981 KLT 113.

[47] Ibid.

[48] Ibid.

[49] Section 14, EPR.

statement is currently required for obtaining consent to establish a unit. As discussed earlier, Section 21 requires that a site clearance is acquired before consent to establish a plant is granted. However, this may not be as comprehensive as an environmental statement, leaving the fate of the environment somewhat uncertain at the establishment and operation phases. A requirement should be introduced that mandates an EIA for all industries seeking consent to establish.

Failure to comply with Section 21, 22, or an order under 31A attracts a term of imprisonment of at least one year and six months.[50] Defences for companies include due diligence and lack of knowledge[51] of the offending acts and the government may use the defence of good faith.[52] There is also a right of appeal for persons or bodies whom the State Board has issued orders against, the matter being subject to review by the appellate authority.[53]

There is scope for review of decisions made under the Air Act. When an appellate authority has been constituted for the purpose of hearing appeals under the Act, appeals cannot be made to a court of civil jurisdiction, as provided by Section 46.[54] Once the appellate authority has made its decision, it does not have the power to subsequently review it.[55] As stated by the Calcutta High Court, an appellate authority 'cannot clothe itself with said powers by virtue of Practice Direction framed by it, when statutory provisions are totally silent about it.'[56]

Air Pollution—Affecting Ancient Monuments and Archaeological Sites

Ancient monuments, archaeological sites, and heritage areas are also affected due to pollution generated by industries. The world famous Taj Mahal was under a threat of degradation due to the use of coke or coal by industries situated within the Taj Trapezium Zone (TTZ). The carbon particles emitting pollution have changed the colour of the marbles in the Taj Mahal Court. The offending industries were given the option of using gas instead of coal, or of shifting the industries from the area. When some of the industries refused to relocate, the Supreme Court directed their closure.[57]

Developments Abroad

Air pollution often has the potential for conflict between states as it often has transboundary effects. The Convention on Long-Range Transboundary Air Pollution minimizes the potential for such disputes as states that are parties pledge to reduce and prevent air pollution including long-range transboundary air pollution.[58] The Convention had 51 ratifications and 32 signatures as of 21 March 2007. India is not a party to this Convention.

Other countries have enacted legislation to address air pollution. For example, the USA has enacted the Federal Clean Air Act.[59] This Act empowers the EPA to make National Ambient Air Quality Standards to control air pollutants. 'Air pollutant' is widely defined by Section 7602(g) as 'any air pollution agent or combination of such agents, including any physical, chemical...

---

[50] Air (Prevention and Control of Pollution) Act, 1981.
[51] Ibid.
[52] Ibid.
[53] Ibid.
[54] *A.R. Ponnusamy v. Thoppalan @ Karuppa Gounder,* (2004) 16 ILD 230.
[55] *Manoj Kumar Roy v. Appellate Authority,* AIR 2002 Cal 216.
[56] Ibid.

[57] *M.C. Mehta v. Union of India,* AIR 1999 SC 3192, (1999) 6 SCC 611.
[58] Convention on Long-Range Transboundary Air Pollution, 1979.
[59] 42 USC 7401 et seq. (1970).

substance or matter which is emitted into or otherwise enters the ambient air....' This definition is wider than that in Indian legislation as it does not have the requirement that the substance is at a concentration that may be injurious to humans or the environment. This definition was recently called into question in *Massachusetts et. al v. Environmental Protection Agency et. al*[60] where the EPA refused to exercise its power under Section 202(a)(1), stating that four pollutants, including carbon dioxide, did not fit the definition of air pollutant. Section 202(a)(1) states that the EPA 'shall by regulation prescribe (and from time to time revise) in accordance with the provisions of this section, standards applicable to the emission of any air pollutant from any class or classes of new motor vehicles or new motor vehicle engines, which in his judgement cause, or contribute to, air pollution which may reasonably be anticipated to endanger public health or welfare.' The court held that repetition of the term 'any' throughout the definition gives it a wide scope so as to encompass 'all airborne compounds of whatever stripe'. It did not hesitate to hold that carbon dioxide, methane, nitrous oxide, and hydro fluorocarbons fall within this definition. Consequently, such emissions could prima facie be regulated using Section 202(a)(1).

The Supreme Court of Nepal also issued directions to the government to enforce essential measures to control air pollution to protect public health from vehicular pollution due to emission from vehicles running in Kathmandu Valley, like tempos, taxies, buses, mini-buses, trucks, tractors, and other vehicles, and to conduct essential studies or investigations with a view to prevent 'vehicular'

pollution outside the Valley.[61] As discussed earlier, Pollution Control Boards in India have similar powers.

BUCKET SAMPLING—MEASURING AIR POLLUTION IN THE USA

Many have asked, what is the best procedure to measure air pollution? Some have suggested the collection of air so that it may be analysed in a laboratory. An innovative way was invented in the USA with the help of a bucket. The sampler is a plastic bucket with a detachable bag inside it. To sample the air, the valve on the nozzle of the bucket is opened. This operates a pump that sucks in the air and fills up the bag. Once filled, the bag can be detached and couriered to the analytical laboratory. Data generated by the bucket provides information about the levels of several gases, some of them with known toxicological properties. The analytical data generated, combined with regularly maintained chemical odour incident records, provides a fair picture of air quality in an area. It would also alert us to the need, if any, for precautionary action to protect health. The bucket was co-developed as a community tool by the US EPA. Bucket samples that were analysed alongside samples taken simultaneously by well-established techniques yielded similar results. Quality assurance and quality control measures provide additional scientific information and increase the credibility of the bucket samples. Currently, Columbia Analytical Services, a US EPA-certified laboratory in California performs the sample analyses. The laboratory is placed among the top ten laboratories in the USA.[62]

---

[60] US Supreme Court, No. 05.1120, argued 29 November 2006; decided 2 April 2007.

[61] *Prakash Mani Sharma v. His Majesty's Government Cabinet Secretariat.* WP No. 3440 of 1996, dated 3 November 2003.

[62] http://www.gcmonitor.org/article.php?id=429

The simple procedure discussed above can be adopted in India for measuring the ambient air quality. The present machinery is very cumbersome, and requires the assistance of experts approved by the Pollution Control Board (PCB). In big cities, the PCB has put up electronic monitors showing the current air quality standards. But it is silent on what should be done if the reading exceeds the prescribed level. It would be more meaningful if an indicator was attached to the monitor, displaying the consequences if the air pollution exceeds the prescribed level. It is unfortunate that the services of private agencies are dependent on both the PCB as well as the public for measuring air quality standards.

NOISE POLLUTION

India is a secular country. Article 25(1) of the Constitution guarantees to every person the freedom of conscience and the right freely to profess, practise, and propagate any religion. The right is however, subject in every case to public order, health, morality, and other provisions of Part III.

In *Church of God (Full Gospel) in India v. KKR Majestic Colony Welfare Association*,[63] the court laid down certain rules relying on guidelines laid down in *Appa Rao's* case:[64]

1. No religion prescribes that prayers should be offered by disturbing the peace of others, nor does it preach that those who preach should use amplifiers or beat drums;
2. In a civilized society, activities that disturb old and infirm persons, students, and children getting their sleep in early hours, and other

persons carrying on other activities cannot be permitted in the name of religion;
3. Aged, sick people with psychic disturbance, and children up to six years are considered very sensitive to noise pollution and their rights are to be protected;
4. Under Rule 5 of the Environment Protection Act, 1986, and in the Noise Pollution (Regulation and Control) Rules, 2000, rules for control of noise pollution levels have been prescribed;
5. Noise pollution has become a serious problem;
6. The above problems affect not only human beings, but also the animal world.[65]

Courts have observed that noise pollution 'may cause interruption of sleep, affect communication, loss of efficiency, hearing loss or deafness, high blood pressure, depression, irritability, fatigue, gastro-intestinal problems, allergy, distraction, mental stress, and annoyance, and other problems.'[66]

As indicated in Section of 2(a) of the Air (Prevention and Control of Pollution) Act, noise is generally accepted as a form of air pollution and is subject to the statutory regime as described above. Noise is also subject to the Noise Pollution (Regulation and Control) Rules, 2000,[67] which were enacted by the Central Government pursuant to the Environment (Protection) Act, 1986[68] and the Environment (Protection) Rules, 1986.[69]

---

[63] AIR 2000 SC 2773; (2000) 7 SCC 282.

[64] *Appa Rao M.S. v. Government of Tamil Nadu*, (1995) 1 LW 319 (Mad); also see *Om Birangana Religious Society v. State*, (1995–6) 100 CWN 617 (Cal).

[65] (2000) 7 SCC 282, pp. 285–91.

[66] *Church of God (Full Gospel) in India v. KKR Majestic Colony Welfare Association*, AIR 2000 SC 2773, 2000 (3) KLT 651, 2000 (6) SCALE 163, Section 2.

[67] Noise Pollution (Regulation and Control) Rules, 2000 (India).

[68] Environment (Protection) Act, 1986 (29 of 1986), Sections 6(2)(b)(1), 3(2)(ii), 25.

[69] Environment (Protection) Rules, 1986 (EPR), Rule 5.

The Rules recognize that noise pollution in public places can 'have deleterious effects on human health and the psychological well being of the people, so it is considered necessary to regulate and control noise producing and generating sources with the objective of maintaining the ambient air quality standards in respect of noise'.[70] These rules can also be seen as a means of upholding Article 21 of the Constitution, as the act of healthy sleep is a necessary constituent of the right to life.[71]

Zoning of Areas—Limiting Noise

The Rules define four categories or 'zones', namely the industrial area, residential area, commercial area, and silent zone. A different ambient air quality standard is then prescribed for each zone.[72] The relevant authority is to ensure that noise does not exceed the prescribed limits in each of the zones.[73] Citizens are also granted the right to complain to the relevant authority if noise exceeds the limit for their zone.[74]

The power to prevent, prohibit, control, or regulate noise to ensure the comfort and safety of those in the vicinity, is given to the local authority.[75] Before this occurs, the authority must give the offender the opportunity to present their case and record reasons for the decision.[76]

Directions under Rule 8 restricting the use of loudspeakers and instrumental noise

have been challenged on the basis of the constitutional right to freedom of religion.[77] Often, religious congregations rely on amplifiers, loudspeakers, and music as part of their practice. Many a court has held that although Article 19 of the Constitution guarantees the right to freedom of speech, the right to use a loudspeaker is not a fundamental right in itself.[78] The Supreme Court has upheld noise regulation standards in the face of religious freedom and declared it integral that the comfort of all members of the community takes precedence. It has stated that the rules cannot be violated on the basis of religious freedom and that the enjoyment of one set of rights 'should not adversely affect the rights of others'.[79] Similarly, the KHC has held that noise pollution occurs 'when the effects of sound become undesirable'[80] and religious music or songs must take place within the constraints of the Noise Rules. Even if the song or music is of high quality, it should not be imposed on members of the public who do not subscribe to it.[81]

Religious Freedom—No Right to Create Noise

In Madras, the owner of a temple argued that freedom of expression as provided in Article 19 of the Constitution required that he be given consent to emit sounds from a loudspeaker at his temple. The court remarked that although such freedom exists, individual liberties must be subordinated

---

[70] Ministry of Environment and Forests Notification, New Delhi, 14 February 2000, SO 123(E).

[71] *Burrabazar Fire Works Dealers Association v. Commr of Police*, AIR 1998 Cal 121, 1997 (2) CWN 617.

[72] Schedule-1 Noise Pollution (Regulation and Control) Rules, 2000.

[73] Rule 4(2).

[74] Rule 7(1).

[75] Rule 8.

[76] Rule 8(2).

[77] Article 25, Constitution of India.

[78] For example, *Venu v. Director General of Police*, 1990(2) KLT 86, 1996 (2) KLT 153, ILR 1996 (3) Ker 501.

[79] Supra.

[80] *Anand Parthasarathy v. State of Kerala*, 2000 (1) KLT 566, ILR 2000 (2) Kerala 71.

[81] *Aravindakshan v. Superintendence*, 2002 (3) KLT 860.

to greater social interests[82] and 'to enforce freedom of speech in disregard of the rights of others would be harsh and arbitrary in itself.'[83] It can be observed that although the Constitution provides freedom of speech and religion, this freedom cannot be used to excuse noise that encroaches upon other rights of the community.

A limited degree of discretion lies at the hand of the State Government, which may allow loudspeakers to operate between the hours of 10 pm and midnight for a period not exceeding fifteen days, during a religious or cultural festival or occasion.[84] Such discretion enables a balance to be struck between the right to practise one's religion and the public interest in freedom from noise interference. The KHC erala has rejected the argument that on such occasions, the government may authorize the use of loudspeakers beyond midnight.[85] In ordinary circumstances, the rules prohibit the use of loudspeakers between 10 pm and 6 am.[86] However, Rule 5 specifies that loudspeakers may be used in 'closed premises' between 10 pm and 6 am if the institution exists or was created permanently for any religious, charitable, or other purposes like cultural, educational, and so on.' The KHC reinforced this rule when the government issued a press release to the effect that loudspeakers can be used within 'closed premises' between 10 pm and 6 am. It clarified that any such press release must be interpreted in the context of the Rules.[87]

States have placed restrictions or bans on various instruments or activities that produce a high level of noise. In Kerala, the High Court has held that users of fireworks are to carefully observe noise rules and the Supreme Court of India has stated that fireworks should not exceed the limit of 125Db.[88] The use of noisy fireworks is prohibited between the hours of 10:00 pm and 6:00 am.[89] The Calcutta High Court has issued directions to the state authorities to restrict the use of air and electronic horns due to their deleterious effect on human health.[90] Similarly, Rule 119 of the Central Motor Vehicles Rules prohibits the use of air horns. The court has issued a direction to the Central Motor Vehicles Authority to enforce this provision strictly.[91]

The Supreme Court of India has given a detailed account of noise pollution and the reasons as to why noise pollution is so prevalent in India. It deemed a lack of implementation on the part of the Executive, a lack of infrastructure for the enforcement of laws, and a lack of awareness of the effects of noise pollution amongst the people as

---

[82] M. Veerateswaran v. The Deputy Collector cum Sub-Divisional Executive Magistrate Revenue (Taluk Ofice) Karaikal, Union Territory of Pondicherry, 2003 (3) KLT SN. 13. P. 10.

[83] Ibid.

[84] Section 5(3) as amended by Noise Pollution (Regulation and Control) (Amendment) Rules, 2002.

[85] Pavithran v. District Superintendent of Police, 2005 (1) KLT 650.

[86] Supra Rule 5(3).

[87] Forum for the Prevention of Environmental and Sound Pollution v. State of Kerala and Others, CMP No. 55608/2001 IN OP No. 18197/2001-N.

[88] In re: Noise Pollution—Implementation of the Laws for Restricting Use of Loudspeakers and High Volume Producing Sound Systems, AIR 2005 SC 3136 (2005) 6 SCC 109, Section 158.

[89] In re: Noise Pollution—Implementation of the Laws for Restricting the Use of Loudspeakers and High Volume Producing Sound Systems v. Union of India and Others 2003 (8) SCALE 421; R.C. Lahoti and Ashok Bhan (JJ).

[90] Rabin Mukherjee v. State, AIR 1985 Cal 222; see also Malayath v. State of Kerala, 2005(3) KLT 190 and supra note 90.

[91] K.N. Neelakantan Namboodiri v. State of Kerala, ILR 2004 (1) Kerala 634 (2004).

contributing factors. Interestingly, it also stated that 'People generally accept noise pollution as a part of life, a necessary consequence of progress and prosperity.'[92] The Court thus issued directions that support a preventive approach[93] in relation to noise pollution, addressing the use of firecrackers, vehicular noise, and loudspeakers. It recommended that education regarding noise pollution be imposed upon children at a younger age.[94] It also stressed the need for legislation that is specifically tailored towards noise pollution and the development of infrastructure to enforce such laws.

Silence is a biological necessity. A citizen has certain rights being 'necessity of silence', 'necessity of sleep', 'process during sleep', and 'rest' which are biological necessities and essential for health. Silence is considered to be golden. It is considered to be one of the human rights as noise is injurious to human health which is required to be preserved at any cost, the Supreme Court observed.[95]

SMOKING IN PUBLIC PLACES

The 'Cigarettes and other Tobacco Products (Prohibition of Advertisement and Regulation of Trade and Commerce, Production, Supply, and Distribution) Act' was enacted in 2003 and effectively codified the general consensus that existed in case law in India relating to smoking in public places. It is also an explicit response to the resolution of the World Health Organization (WHO), which was passed in 1986 and reaffirmed in 1990,[96] and a reflection of Article 47 of the Indian Constitution.

Indian Law

The Parliament in India has been comprehensive in its approach towards discouraging and prohibiting smoking in public places. The purpose of the Act is clearly stated in the Preamble, 'to prohibit the advertisement of, and to provide for the regulation of trade and commerce in, and production, supply, and distribution of, cigarettes and other tobacco products and for matters connected therewith or incidental thereto.'[97]

Section 4 of the Act is explicit in stating that 'no person shall smoke in a public place' where the act of smoking 'means smoking of tobacco in any form whether in the form of cigarette, cigar, beedis, or otherwise with the aid of a pipe, wrapper, or any other instrument.'[98] A public place is defined as 'any place to which the public has access', not including any open space.[99] However, the court defined 'public place' as any place where people congregate, the definition of public place being slightly wider in the Act as it extends to a right of access and does not necessitate a congregation. It is clear that public vehicles like buses or taxis are considered public places, as the High Court held a bus driver who smoked throughout the journey guilty of contempt of court violating the ban.[100]

Indian Case Law

The KHC has ruled that smoking in public places infringes the rights under Article 21, and is therefore illegal. The Court went to great lengths to collate the scientific data that establishes the harms caused by passive smoking or Environmental Tobacco Smoke (ETS). It stressed that side-stream smoke is more harmful than the smoke inhaled

---

[92] Supra note 90.
[93] Ibid.
[94] Ibid.
[95] *Farhd. K.Wadia v. Union of India*, 2009 (2) SCC 442.
[96] Cigarettes and other Tobacco Products (Prohibition of Advertisement and Regulation of Trade and Commerce, Production, Supply, and Distribution) Act.

[97] Ibid., Preamble.
[98] Ibid., Section 4.
[99] Ibid., Section 3 (1).
[100] *Nebu John v. Babu*, 2000 (1) KLT 238.

by smokers as it contains 'three times more nicotine, three times more tar, and about 50 times more ammonia'.[101] In particular, it noted that ETS increases respiratory illness in children, increases asthma, and increases the incidence of a wide range of conditions including heart disease and lung cancer.

The Court emphasized that despite India's commitment to the WHO, implementation has been lagging behind. It refuted the arguments that the banning of smoking in public places would deprive the government of revenue generated from taxes and affect the livelihood of many farmers. The finance expended by the government in treating tobacco-related health problems far exceeds the money generated by taxes, and the premature death of tobacco users burdens their families, thus 'perpetuating the cycle of poverty'.[102] The Court regrettably refused to direct the legislature to ban smoking on grounds that it would infringe the separation of powers and intrude upon the functions of the Executive. But the Court did issue a writ of mandamus to the government and the authorities to enforce the existing law to protect citizens from ETS. It directed authorities to punish public smoking as a nuisance according to Section 268 of the IPC and prohibit smoking in public places using Section 133(a) of the CrPC The court's final remarks emphasized the nature of the rights under Article 21, stating that the right to life 'includes a right to a decent environment'[103] and 'maintenance of health and environment falls within the purview of Article 21 of the Constitution as it adversely affects the life of the citizens by slow and insidious poisoning thereby reducing the very life span itself.'[104]

Hence, it did not hesitate to conclude that the degradation of air by ETS infringes the right to life, and is unconstitutional.

Similarly, the Supreme Court of India has recognized the grave effects of cigarette smoke on health and deems it an absurdity that non-smokers be subjected to it for the mere reason that they grace public places. It considered this to be violative of Article 21 as it deprives individuals of the right to life without due process. In 2002, the Court directed a prohibition to be placed on smoking in public places, namely: auditoriums, hospital buildings, health institutions, educational institutions, libraries, court buildings, public offices, and public conveyances, including railways.[105]

The prohibition on smoking in public places should be read in the context of the Act's sweeping regime, intended to discourage smoking generally. Regulation of the trade, commerce, production, supply, and distribution of cigarettes and tobacco products is also imposed by the Act. The aforementioned activities are not to be carried out unless the packaging bears clear and distinctive labelling in accordance with the provisions of the Act.[106] Other measures taken by the legislature include the banning of advertisements encouraging the use of cigarettes or tobacco products where this includes direct and indirect suggestions or messages.[107] 'Advertisement' has a wide definition and includes verbal and oral material and announcements made by transmitting light, sound, smoke, or gas.[108] It is also an offence to receive sponsorship or scholarships from cigarette companies or to use cigarettes or tobacco products as prizes or gifts.[109]

---

[101] K. *Ramakrishnan v. State of Kerala*, 1999 (2) KLT 725.
[102] Ibid.
[103] Ibid.
[104] Ibid.

[105] *Murli S. Deora v. Union of India and Others*, 2002 (1) KLT 55.
[106] Supra note 96, Section 7.
[107] Ibid., Section 9.
[108] Ibid., Section 3(a).
[109] Ibid., Section 12.

Police officers have the right to inspect a place that engages in the trade, commerce, or creation of advertisements for cigarettes and tobacco products where a violation of the Act is suspected.[110] Courts too have recognized that enforcement is needed to decrease violations of smoking regulations. The KHC has noted a flagrant disregard for its directions and a lack of enforcement on the part of authorities.[111] It has responded by issuing a direction to shops that they should not provide lighter devices to the public as the wide availability of such devices encourages people to smoke in public places.[112] The Court also directed local authorities to make surprise inspections in places like cinemas, theatres, and restaurants, conditioning the licensing of such places on the enforcement of smoking bans.[113]

Foreign Case Law

India is not the first country to ban smoking in public places. Most countries now have legislation that prohibits or restricts smoking in public places. For example, in Australia, regulation of smoking in public places has been getting progressively stricter since the first state created such regulations in 1987.[114] As of 1 July 2007, it has become illegal to smoke in a public place in the United Kingdom.[115]

At the international level, there currently exists the WHO Framework Convention on Tobacco Control. This Convention entered into force on 27 February 2005, with 146

parties and 168 signatories. India signed the Convention in 2003 and ratified it on 5 February 2004. Article 8 of the Convention states that parties shall take the requisite measures to provide 'for the protection from exposure to tobacco smoke', in public places, including workplaces. Indian legislation is already in tune with this provision and it appears that greater measures are being taken in respect of enforcement.

MOTOR VEHICLES—EMISSIONS

Motor vehicles represent one of the biggest contributors to air pollution, ultimately contributing to global warming and visible smog. The Central Government has taken steps to combat the emission of gaseous substances like carbon monoxide, hydrocarbons, and nitrogen oxides in enacting the Motor Vehicles Rules, 1989 (MVR), which set specific standards for various emissions exerted by motor vehicles.

Rule 116 gives the police or inspector the power to inspect vehicles under suspicion of non-compliance with emission standards laid out by Rule 115 of the MVR. They may order the person to submit their vehicle to a check and give the certificate to the authority within seven days if the vehicle complies. In the event that the vehicle does not comply, the owner must rectify the defects, have the vehicle checked again and then forward the certificate. Despite the existence of this procedure, a Delhi court has held that a failure to carry a 'Pollution under Control Certificate is an offence in itself' and a person can be convicted under Section 190(2) of the MVA for a failure to do so.[116]

Bhure Lal Committee—More Conditions

The Bhure Lal Committee was established under Section 3 of the Environment

[110] Supra note 98, Section 12.
[111] 2000 (1) KLT 238.
[112] CMP No. 37139/99 IN OP No. 22492/99-C.
[113] *Institute of Social Welfare v. State of Kerala*, CMP No. 37139/99 IN OP No. 22492/99-C, Kerala High Court (unreported case).
[114] See for example, Public Health Act, 1997 (Tasmania).
[115] Smoke-free (Premises and Enforcement) Regulations, 2006 (UK).

[116] *State v. R.P. Sharama*, 1997(I) AD (Delhi) 113.

(Protection) Act, 1986 (EPA). This Committee, along with the EPA directed the phasing out of all non-CNG (compressed natural gas) buses in India. The court supported this move, but progress has been slow and the court has been forced to grant time extensions in this respect. In particular, the court issued directions in response to the Committee's finding to the effect that private (non-commercial) vehicles in Delhi conform to the Euro-I norm by 1 June 1999 and all private (non-commercial) vehicles conform to the Euro-II norm by 1 April 2000. Private (non-commercial) vehicles which conform to the Euro-II were permitted registration in the National Capital Region (NCR) without any restriction.[117]

Supreme Court Directions to Clear Air

Courts have been instrumental in regulating emissions from motor vehicles. Delhi, which was one of the most polluted cities in the world, has improved a lot only because of the intervention of the Supreme Court. The Supreme Court of India has issued a number of directions attempting to phase out certain vehicles that cause unacceptable levels of air pollution. In 1998, the Court issued a number of directions relating to commercial and transport vehicles. It stated that those that are over twenty years old shall be phased out and disallowed from plying in Delhi after October 1998. Those between the ages of seventeen and nineteen years old would be disallowed from plying in Delhi after 15 November 1998, and those which were between fifteen and sixteen years old would be disallowed from plying after 31 December 1998.[118]

In response to a direction issued by the Supreme Court of India, the governmental authorities lower[ed] the sulfur content in diesel to 0.50%, and then to 0.05%, ensured the supply of only lead-free petrol, required the fitting of catalytic converters, directed the supply of pre-mix 2T oil for lubrication of engines of two-wheelers and three-wheelers, directed the phasing out of grossly polluting old vehicles, directed the lowering of the benzene content in petrol, and ensured that new vehicles, petrol and diesel, meet Euro-II standards by September 2000.[119]

Despite the long-term existence of emission standards and the government's support for them, the government has done little beyond specifying such standards. It has excused itself on the claim that there is a shortage of CNG. In *M.C. Mehta* v. *Union of India*, the court stated that,

if there is a short supply of an essential commodity, then the priority must be of public health, as opposed to the health of the balance sheet of a private company. To enable industries to cut their losses, or make profit at the cost of public health, is not a sign of good governance, and this is contrary to the constitutional mandate of Articles 39(e), 47, and 48A.[120]

The court condemned the government for overcharging the transport industry for CNG and undercharging private industry. It also pointed out that there is no reason that CNG cannot be imported when crude oil is readily imported.[121] Hence, the court placed an obligation on the Union of India to ensure the supply of CNG and give priority to the transport sector. The court also ordered that the Director of Transport collect 'Rs 500 per bus per day increasing to Rs 1,000 per day after

---

[117] *M.C. Mehta* v. *Union of India*, (1999) 6 SCC 9, (1999) 6 SCC 12. also see (2003)10 SCC 570.
[118] *M.C. Mehta* v. *Union of India and Others*, AIR 1999 SC 291.

[119] *M.C. Mehta* v. *Union of India and Others*, AIR 2001 SC 1862.
[120] Ibid.
[121] Ibid.

30 days of operation of the diesel buses.'[122] The National Capital Territory (NCT) of Delhi was also ordered to phase out 800 diesel buses per month.

Action by State High Courts in India

In Karnataka, courts have directed the government to create a scheme for the phasing out of CNG vehicles.[123] The petitioner truck drivers opposed an order made by the government that all vehicles over fifteen years old be banned from the Outer Ring Road. They claimed that it infringed their rights as guaranteed by Article 19(1)(g) of the Constitution. The court affirmed the state government's power to issue such restrictions under Section 5 of the Environment Act and Section 20 of the Air Act. However, it reminded the government of its duties to the public at large and stressed the need for a more comprehensive scheme to combat vehicular pollution. It stated that the government 'should also give sufficient time to the vehicle owners for replacement of the old vehicles, in a phased manner, to make available the CNG fuel and to have the vehicles converted to it in a phased manner.'[124]

The KHC has also stressed the need for implementation of emission standards.[125] It stressed that four years after the coming into force of the MVR, the government had failed to take adequate steps for implementation. In particular, the government was urged to devise a manner by which to measure emissions in exercising its power under Section 116 of the Rules. Again, the court emphasized the importance of human life and the urgency of the matter of air pollution.

The vigilance of Indian courts in upholding the provisions of the Constitution in regards to human health and the environment is commendable. However, as stated by the High Court of Kerala, implementation requires further attention.

STONE CRUSHERS

Stone crushing is an important industry in India, required for developmental activities like the construction of roads, bridges, buildings, canals, and other construction works. The SPM[126] that emanates while crushing stones creates air pollution. Emissions are caused during mining, loading and unloading, crushing, material movement, transportation, stocking, and other related activities. A percentage of the fugitive dust emissions may settle down within the unit's premises itself, but a substantial percentage of airborne emissions are carried away to surrounding places.

For the operation of a crusher, consent must be obtained from the State Pollution Control Boards.[127] The SPM measured between 3 metres and 10 metres from any process equipment of a stone crushing unit shall not exceed 600 micrograms per cubic metre.[128] The SPM contribution value at a distance of 40 metres from a controlled isolated stone crusher as well as from a unit located in a cluster should be less than 600 mg/cu.Nm. This emission must be tested at least twice a month for all the twelve months in a year.[129] In addition, they have to provide suitable dust containment-

---

[122] Ibid.

[123] *Karnataka Lorry Malikara Okkuta (R) and Others v. The State of Karnataka and Others,* WP. No. 46850 of 2002 (GM-POL) and WP 46887-88/2002.

[124] Ibid., Section 18.

[125] *Murali Purushothaman v. Union of India,* 1993(1) KLT 595, ILR 1993(2) Kerala 728, AIR 1993 Ker 297; K.T. Thomas (J).

[126] Known as 'dust' in common parlance (already referred to on p. 182, para 2, line 3).

[127] Air (Prevention and Control of Pollution) Act, 1974, Section 21.

[128] Item No. 11, Schedule–I, EPR, 1986.

[129] Item No. 37, Schedule-I, EPR, 1986.

cum-suppression system for the equipment. To prevent the dust spreading in the areas, they have to provide wind-breaking walls and grow green belts throughout the periphery of the unit. The roads inside the premises must be tarred and the floors be cleaned.[130] Unfortunately, the said law is not effective in controlling the air pollution generated by the stone crushers.

The Supreme Court of India had the occasion to pass orders to stop illegal quarrying operations going around three hills that were declared as protected monuments. No stone crusher was allowed to be located within half a kilometre from the area of the protected monuments.[131]

In Mumbai, a stone crusher was carrying on operations without obtaining a licence. When the court issued a notice to him he gave an unconditional undertaking to take all measures to minimize dust pollution and install sprinklers system.[132] The Bombay High Court directed the authorities to ensure compliance of the undertaking and dismissed the writ petition.

As a measure for curbing air pollution in Delhi, the Supreme Court has issued directions to relocate the crushers. The Court has found that the Delhi Development Authority, Municipal Corporation of Delhi, CPCB, and Delhi Pollution Control Committee have failed in the performance of their statutory duties and have failed to protect the environment and control air pollution in the Union Territory of Delhi.[133]

Crushers Near Human Habitation

The installation of stone crushers near human habitats was a subject matter of litigation filed before the Orissa High Court. Installation of a crusher in the midst of human habitats and paddy fields would not only pose a health hazard, but would also cripple agriculture. The court directed the District Collector to conduct an enquiry and directed the government to consider the impact on the adjacent agricultural lands before permission for such a non-agricultural purpose could be given.[134]

The court has also held that guidelines prescribed by the government in respect of locating stone crushers should be followed strictly. It is the duty of the court to ensure closure of such industrial units that cause or have the possibility of causing imbalance to ecology or the environment. Government notifications and circulars were issued prescribing the guidelines to be observed while establishing a stone crusher unit. Such guidelines are mandatory in nature. While considering the application for establishing industrial units, the guidelines prescribed by the government are to be adhered to strictly. Units within 500 metres of a school were directed to be closed. The permission granted for a stone crusher that was working in gross violation of the said guidelines was quashed by the Court.[135]

The unplanned working of stone crushers in Karnataka was the subject matter of a PIL filed before the High Court. The court directed the state to formulate policy and identify 'safer zones'. Two safer zones shall not be located within a radius of 50 kilometres. Such safer zones shall not be located within the limit

[130] Ibid.

[131] *Surendra Kumar Singh v. State of Bihar*, AIR 1991 SC 1042, 1991 Supp 2 SCC 628.

[132] *M/s Susheel Traders v. Municipal Corporation for Greater Bombay*, AIR 2001 Bom 166.

[133] *M.C. Mehta v. Union of India*, 1992 (3) SCC 256, 1992 (4) JT 46.

[134] *Ramanath Das and Others v. Collector, Balasore*, AIR 2002 Orissa 132.

[135] *Nehru Paribhesha Suraskhya Committee v. State*, 94 (2002) CLT 34.

of two kilometres from national highways, habitats, temples, schools, and rivers; one-and-a-half kilometres from the state highway; five hundred metres from the link roads; eight kilometres from the boundary of Municipal Corporations; four kilometres from District Headquarters; two kilometres from the boundary limits of Taluk HQ (head quarters); one kilometre from an inhabited village or any land recorded as forest in government records or any private land which is shown as cultivable in revenue records. Each stone crusher unit shall be located in a minimum distance area of one acre owned by the stone crusher, State, or the Panchayat, stated the High Court when imposing the above conditions.[136]

In Punjab, the government has issued an order restraining the working of a stone crusher within five kilometres from the boundary of the metropolitan city. Several crushers were working in derogation of the parameters prescribed by the state. In a writ petition filed before the High Court, it was contended by the crusher operators that the distance is to be measured from the centre of the city and not the boundary. The Court, giving a broader view of the environmental principle, held that if such a contention is accepted, it would defeat the very purpose of the distance rule. The crushers were directed to be shifted and were made liable to pay compensation to citizens of the area who suffered because of pollution.[137]

Despite legislative restrictions, the lives of the people who reside near the operation area are in danger. There continues to be an adverse impact on the health of the workers engaged in stone crushing in its present form; some have experienced the onset of the condition of silicosis and others suffer from respiratory ailments. The laws concerning emissions must be strictly enforced and there should also be greater regulation on the types that can be crushed in the units. The matter which bears particles particularly injurious to human health and the environment should only be crushed in the most controlled environment and the health of the employees engaged in the work should be monitored regularly. By adopting this approach, the health of the workers, the surrounding community, and the environment can be protected. The operation of stone crushers demands regulation and cooperation between industrial relations law and environmental law.

Air pollution presents one of the most serious environmental problems of the present era. Under the guise of development, many activities are carried on that have resulted in the degradation of ambient air quality. Citizens, lawmakers, and policy-makers should be mindful of the fact that air cannot be manufactured like other commodities; we can only maintain what is available.

---

[136] *Obayya Pujari v. Member Secretary, KSPCB Banglore*, AIR 1999 Kant 157.
[137] *Iswar Singh v. State of Haryana*, AIR 1996 P. and H. 30.

10 Defilement of Fresh Water Bodies

In ancient times, the government assumed the responsibility of supplying water to the people. For this purpose, tanks were constructed for rainwater storage. Natural sources of drinking water, like rivers, ponds, lakes, and other water bodies, were protected by the state as duties of the son to the father.[1] The Manu Smriti[2] also prescribed the use of some herbs and plants to purify water.[3] Since water was considered an inexhaustible gift from God, under ancient water management, it was preserved carefully, used cautiously, and supplemented as and when necessary.[4]

Hindu tradition prescribes that a dip in the river Ganga is sacred—it will purify a person of his or her sins. In the Vedas, one finds prayers to give importance to water. Water shortages can be solved by performing *yajnas* that will bring water to the earth in great quantities.[5] Mother Earth is satisfied through rain and the sky is satisfied through fire.[6]

The ancient Indian text the Yajur Veda,[7] explains the importance of water as follows: 'Water is sacred for us. Water blesses us with good health, intellect and beauty. Just as mother makes her child drink milk similarly you are the life of people. May Water bless us with him and capacity to enjoy your sweet taste.'

The Koran gives water an eminent position as compared to other matter, and endows it with unique physical, chemical, and biological features. It mentions water over 50 times in the holy book, each time associating it with life; it becomes a source of income and purity, and one of the signs of His omnipotence for those who can understand and learn from the teachings. As per the Koran, everything was made from water.

'We made every (including man) living thing from water…'[8]

It is He Who sends down rain from the sky: from it ye drink, and out of it (grows) the vegetation on which ye feed your cattle. With it He produces for you corn, olives, date-palms, grapes, and every kind of fruit: verily in this is a Sign for those who give thought.[9]

The Bible also emphasizes the importance of water.

---

[1] Puthradharma as prescribed in the Dharmasasthra.

[2] Manava Dharmsastra is a treaty on dharma established in the fifth century, written by Manu. Manu is the authority.

[3] The Manusmriti (Sanskrit) is a work of Hindu law and ancient Indian society by Manu. It is also known as the Manava Dharma Sastra (6.4.46–48).

[4] Kautilaya, *Arthasasthra*.

[5] *Athara Veda*, 11/4–5.

[6] *Rig Veda*, 1/164–51.

[7] *Yajur Veda*, 11/50, 51, 52.

[8] 21.30.

[9] Bee, Sura XVI, verses 10 and 11.

In the beginning God created the heavens and the earth. The earth was without form and void, and darkness was upon the face of the deep; and the Spirit of God was moving over the face of the waters... And God said, 'Let the waters under the heavens be gathered together into one place, and let the dry land appear.' And it was so. God called the dry land Earth, and the waters that were gathered together he called Seas. And God saw that it was good.[10]

WATER POLLUTION

Water is important as it regularly maintains the ecological balance of an area. The natural environment of a place depends on the quality of water in the area. Water is polluted by the discharge of effluents from human activities. Water pollution also affects the ground water in adjacent areas. Further, any polluting activity on the land will ultimately pollute water bodies in the drainage basin.

The Water (Prevention and Control of Pollution) Act 1974

India has enacted the Water (Prevention and Control of Pollution) Act, 1974[11] for the prevention and control of water pollution, and for maintaining or restoring the wholesomeness of water. The powers of the Central Government under the Act are limited to Article 249 of the Indian Constitution.[12] For Parliament to legislate upon matters in the Act, the Council of States must declare by resolution 'supported by not less than two-thirds of the members present and voting that it is necessary or expedient in the national interest that Parliament should make laws with respect to any matter enumerated in the State

List specified in the resolution.'[13] The Act has since been adopted by all of the Indian states.

Under the Act, 'Water Pollution' is widely defined as,

contamination of water or such alteration of the physical, chemical or biological properties of water or such discharge of any sewage or trade effluent or of any other liquid, gaseous or solid substance into water (whether directly or indirectly) as may, or is likely to, create a nuisance or render such water harmful or injurious to public health or safety, or to domestic, commercial, industrial, agricultural or other legitimate uses, or to the life and health of animals or plants or of aquatic organisms.[14]

It is clear that the Act is intended to protect humans and the water environment itself. The CPCB is the statutory authority charged with the administration of the Act. There is also provision for State Pollution Control Boards. The Central Board has a general power 'to promote the cleanliness of streams and wells'[15] within the states. The term 'stream' encompasses most naturally occurring water bodies, namely, rivers, watercourses both flowing and dry, inland waters, subterranean waters, and seas or tidal waters to the extent that they are identified by the government.

Pollution Control Boards

The Water Act provides for the constitution of State and Central Boards to exercise the powers conferred under the Act.[16] The Board consists of a chairman, member-secretary, and other officials appointed by the state government. No specific qualification is required for becoming a member. The member-secretary, who is appointed by the state government, should

---

[10] Genesis 1:1–2, 9–10 RSV.

[11] Act 6 of 1974.

[12] Water (Prevention and Control of Pollution) Act 1974, Preamble.

[13] Constitution of India, Article 249.

[14] Water (Prevention and Control of Pollution) Act, 1974, Section 48A.

[15] Ibid., Section 16 (1).

[16] Ibid., Chapter II.

possess, however, qualifications, knowledge, and experience of scientific, engineering, or management aspects of pollution control and[17] the provisions that prescribe how the Boards are to be constituted seem quite straightforward, yet the constitution of these Boards has often been fraught with controversy and has led to much litigation.

The appointment of an Indian Administrative Service (IAS) officer[18] as member-secretary of the State Board by the Karnataka government was challenged before the Karnataka High Court. The said officer, the Chief Health Officer of the Bangalore Mahanagara Palika, was in charge of health and sanitation. The executive in charge of solid waste, segregation, transportation, discharge of solid waste was reporting to her. She was also involved with the solid waste management programme of the Bangalore Agenda Task Force. The court held that she had the requisite degree of experience in managing pollution and was doing so in her various capacities. Therefore, it could not be said that she lacked knowledge or experience as claimed by the petitioners. The Karnataka High Court has held that the government in its wisdom may appoint persons with engineering and/or scientific qualifications for the post of member secretary for the better performance of the role.[19] It is clear that expertise is very important to the proper functioning of the Board.

The Water (Prevention and Control of Pollution) Act, 1974 empowers the state government to supersede the Board if the latter persistently defaults in the performance of the duties imposed on it in the public interest. The cases of malfunctioning and misfeasance of the Board fall within the ambit of Sections 62 (1)(b) and 47 (1)(b) of the Act, the Punjab and Haryana High Court (HC) clarified. The preliminary report submitted by an enquiry officer demonstrated that the decision taken by the Chairman and the members of the Board was favourable to those industries which were guilty of water and air pollution and the Board acted against the public interest. Thus, the power of exercise of supervision is valid, the Punjab and Haryana HC held.[20]

In another case before the Punjab and Haryana HC, it was held that the State had superseded the Board without reason. On the basis of a complaint by the industries, the government decided that no consent would be required for the operation of a small-scale industrial unit. The Board objected to it and the State superseded the Board. The HC upheld the decision and held that government was justified in forming an opinion that circumstances existed that necessitated suppression of the Board.[21]

The State Pollution Control Boards have been entrusted with the task of exercising the power to implement the provisions of the Water (Prevention and Control of Pollution) Act, 1974. But the said agency has not been conferred with any responsibility to regulate water pollution under the Act. Section 58 provides that:

No civil court shall have jurisdiction to entertain any suit or proceeding in respect of any matter which an appellate authority constituted under this Act is empowered by or under this Act to determine, and no injunction shall be granted by any court or other authority in respect of any action

---

[17] Ibid., Section 4(2)(f).

[18] Indian Administrative Service Officer, as per Rule 9 of the Administrative Service (Pay) Rules, 1954, is one of the highly qualified executive officers in Indian Government Service.

[19] *Karnataka State Pollution Control Officers Association v. State of Karnataka*, WP No. 8460–8466 of 2004, dated 9 June 2004.

[20] *G.S. Oberoi v. State of Punjab*, AIR 1998 Punjab 67.

[21] *R.A. Goel v. Union of India*, AIR 2000 P&H 320.

taken or to be taken in pursuance of any power conferred by or under this Act.

The Supreme Court has had the occasion to note the casual disposal of a petition concerning water pollution by the Madras HC. The Madras HC disposed of the writ petition on the basis of a report by the PCB. The Supreme Court was of the view that the HC failed to appreciate the true significance of the matter regarding the need to arrest the unabated pollution, which had become a health hazard and environmental enemy because of the discharge of effluents from the distillery into Bhavani River and the adjoining areas. The HC fell into error when it disposed off the writ petition merely on the consent of the PCB. Further, the Supreme Court remanded the writ petition to the HC to consider the expert body report. In matters involving public interest requiring an in-depth examination by the HC, disposal is only warranted after an expert opinion has been given. The mere consent of the PCB is insufficient, the Supreme Court observed.[22]

In order to properly address the increase in water pollution, it is essential that such Boards are fixed with the onus of controlling pollution, as is the case with the EPA of the US. Officials must be held accountable for any water pollution. Accountability encourages better administration of the law and increases public confidence in the authorities.

Offences

Whoever contravenes or fails to comply with the provisions of the Water (Prevention and Control of Pollution) Act, 1974 commits an offence under the Act. The punishment prescribed is imprisonment, which may extend to three months, or a fine of up to

Rs 10,000.[23] As per Section 47 of the Act, if an offence is committed by a company, the person who is in charge of the conduct of the company is liable for punishment. In addition to the punishment if the offender commits an offence for the second time, then his name will be published in newspapers at the cost of the offender.[24]

What is the case, however, where the offence is committed by a government company? Can government servants be prosecuted, even without obtaining sanction from the government?[25] The question was considered by the Bombay High Court. The Court held that no sanction for their prosecution is necessary even if such companies fall within the meaning of 'State' under Article 12 of the Constitution of India. The plea that the offences are technical because the offenders had subsequently taken steps to comply with the directions of the Board is no ground for quashing the complaint, the Court added.[26]

If the offence is committed by a company, it is not necessary to expressly state in the complaint that the managing director was in charge of the affairs of the company. The Patna HC has held that the section does not mandate the incorporation of the allegation that the offence was committed with consent or connivance or was attributable to the neglect on the part of the chairman, director, or general manager of the company in the complaint itself. That is a matter that requires evidence.[27]

---

[22] *In Re Bhavani River*, AIR 1998 SC 2578, (1998) 6 SCC 335.

[23] Supra note 12, Section 48A.

[24] Water (Prevention and Control of Pollution Act), 1974, Section 46.

[25] Under Criminal Procedure Code, 1973 (Section197), sanction of the government is required to prosecute a government servant.

[26] *Pulgaon Cotton Mills Ltd v. Maharastra Pollution Control Board*, 2001 Crl LJ 610.

[27] *Madhumd Ali v. State*, AIR 1986 Pat 133.

Section 133 of the CPC, 1973, empowers the judicial magistrate to pass orders for the removal of nuisance. Can it be said that after the coming into force of the Water (Prevention and Control of Pollution) Act, 1974 the latter has been repealed? In Kerala, a magistrate passed an order restraining a company from discharging effluents. A contention was taken that the power enabling the magistrate to abate the nuisance had been impliedly repealed by the provisions of the new Act. The KHC rejected the contention that the Pollution Control Act and the CPC are 'special and general laws'. It stated that one deals with pollution and the other deals with maintenance of law and order. They are amenable to simultaneous obedience, and there is nothing irreconcilable between them.[28]

Pollution control laws are to be interpreted broadly so as to protect the environment. A person polluting the natural water body is committing a serious crime against the hundreds of persons who use the water. Destruction of the environment on such a massive scale should be viewed as more serious than manslaughter, and awarded maximum punishment.

The Granting of Consent for Industrial Units

Previous consent of the State Board is essential for the establishment of an industry near a water body. If a company proposes to establish any industry or carry out any process that is likely to discharge sewerage or effluent into a stream, well or sewer, or on land, it is bound to take prior consent of the State Board.[29] The State Board will grant consent subject to the above mentioned conditions.

Interpreting the said provisions, the Gujarat HC has held that a mere consent order issued by the State Board does not entitle an industry to discharge trade effluents into a stream. It is incumbent on the industry to comply with the conditions mentioned in the consent order, and put up the effluent treatment plant within the time prescribed in the order. The HC held that a failure in complying with the requirements of putting up an effluent treatment plant results in a lapse of consent.[30]

The State Board is also empowered to refuse or withdraw consent if the industry refuses to comply with the conditions imposed.[31] A person aggrieved by an order can file an appeal before the appellate authority constituted by Section 28 of the said Act. It is commendable that the courts have been stringent in upholding and enforcing consent orders and their attached conditions. The imposition of strict time limits is necessary for the proper protection of the environment. Where the environment is concerned, two days of failing to comply with the conditions of a consent order can mean the difference between environmental protection and environmental devastation.

Closure of Polluting Industries

The CPCB has categorized sixty-four types of polluting industries/industrial activities in a 'Red Category' on the basis of their emissions. Of these, seventeen[32] are heavily polluting industries. The State Pollution Control

---

[28] *Tata Tea Ltd v. State of Kerala*, 1984 KLT 645; *M. Krishna Panicker v. M. Appukuttan Nair*, 1993 (1) KLJ 725.

[29] Water Act, (1974), Section 25.

[30] *M/s Narula Dyeing and Printing Works v. Union of India*, AIR 1995 Guj 185.

[31] Water (Prevention and Control of Pollution) Act, 1974, Section 27.

[32] Distilleries, sugar, fertilizer, pulp and paper, chlor alkali, pharmaceuticals, dyes and dye intermediaries, pesticides, oil refineries, tanneries, petrochemicals, cement, thermal power plants, iron and steel, zinc smelter, copper smelter, and aluminum smelter.

Boards were asked to give special attention to these industries.[33]

Section 33A of the Water Act empowers the Board to issue directions to close, prohibit, or regulate any industry, operation, process, or storage. Directions can also be made to stop the supply of electricity, water, or any other service. The orders issued by the Boards on certain occasions have been challenged before the courts.

Where there are violations of various provisions of an Act and of conditions imposed for curtailing pollution, the order for closure of the industry will be valid. An industry was polluting the environment by discharging contaminated water. The Karnataka HC refused to interfere with the matter.[34]

The power to order closure of industry is to be used with caution. An industry commenced production after obtaining requisite licences and permissions from various statutory authorities, including consent from the Pollution Control Board. On the apprehension that there was likely to be a grave injury caused to the surrounding environment, the court ordered the establishment to be closed without hearing the industry. The order was passed not only in violation of the principles of natural justice, but also in contravention of the mandatory requirement of Rule 4(3b) of the Environment Protection Rules, observed the Karnataka HC, while interfering with the order.[35] It is important that all laws are enforced fairly, as this also generates respect for the law within the community and obeys the basic notions of justice available to mankind.

When the effluent treatment plant of a chemical industry was found to be in non-operation, an order was passed by the Pollution Control Board to close down the industry. The Andhra Pradesh High Court called for the records of the case and found that it was not possible to hold that the order passed by the Board directing the closure of industry was shockingly disproportionate, excessive, or severe.[36]

Certain industrialists feel that an investment for an effluent treatment plant is unnecessary. They adopt dishonest methods like discharging untreated sewage in nearby sewers or other water bodies. Sometimes they fail to operate the treatment plant at all. Since such unlawful practices jeopardize the lives of the people, it is essential that strict and stringent punishment be awarded to the violators.

Closure of the affecting source is the only way in which water pollution can be curtailed immediately. The damage done to the water body cannot be compensated for by money as too many people are adversely affected. Often, the only way to immediately alleviate the problem is to order immediate closure.

Civil Actions Under the Act

Most persons seeking directions for the abatement of pollution approach the writ courts. Only the HCs and the Supreme Court are empowered under the Constitution of India to deal with such matters. The remedies available under civil laws are seldom tapped. Pollution is a public nuisance and a suit for declaration and injunction or such other relief can be instituted in the appropriate circumstances by the Advocate General. Section 91 of the Code of Civil Procedure,

---

[33] Parviesh, *Polluting Industries*, Publication by CPCB, Delhi.

[34] *Stella Silks Ltd v. State of Karnataka*, AIR 2001 Kant 219.

[35] *Mandu Distilleries Pvt Ltd v. Madhya Pradesh Pradushan Niwaran Mandal*, AIR 1995 MP 57.

[36] *M/s Ambuga Petrochemicals Ltd v. A.P. Pollution Control Board and Others*, AIR 1997 AP 41.

1908 empowers the filing of such a suit by two persons with the leave of the court.

When a civil court was petitioned for an injunction to stop noxious fluids from flowing into a river, one contention was that the suit was not maintainable in view of the specific bar under Section 58 of the Water Act. Interpreting the said provision, the Andhra Pradesh HC held that the provision does not curtail the jurisdiction of a civil court to entertain any suit or proceedings restraining the defendant from causing pollution. The section is intended to preserve the statutory protection given to the Boards uninfluenced by interference of civil court actions. The court explained that the present action was only directed at preventing the defendant from polluting water and not aimed at the annulment of any orders passed by the authority constituted under the Act.[37]

Due to water contamination, several persons died in a beggar's home in Delhi. The Delhi HC intervened and the authorities have taken action against the culprits. The Court issued a direction to complete the proceedings and disburse compensation immediately.[38]

Ganga Pollution Case

The river Ganga is the longest river (2,510 kilometres) in India.[39] It is considered a sacred river by the followers of the Hindu religion. The discharge of substances by tanneries and other industries, including those involving cement, mining, and fertilizers, which are located on the banks of this river, has resulted in the river being polluted. M.C. Mehta, a noted environmentalist in India, filed a PIL against the said pollution.[40] Ordering the closure of the tanneries, the Supreme Court noted that the pollution of the Ganga is affecting the life, health, and ecology of the Indo-Gangetic plain.[41] In this case, the Supreme Court found that fundamental rights are violated by the alleged pollution, and that life, health, and ecology have greater importance compared to the unemployment and loss of revenue generated by the closure.

The Government of India has formulated a Ganga Action Plan for the establishment of 261 pollution-controlling projects, which includes the establishment of a common effluent treatment plant, sanitation projects, electric crematoriums, facilities at the water beds, diversion of waste waters, and such other projects.[42]

In the fifth M.C. Mehta case,[43] the Kanpur Municipality received severe criticism for its failure to discharge its statutory duties.[44] As such, several directions were issued to the municipality to improve the sewerage system and prevent the waters of the Ganga from being polluted.[45] The above directions were also extended mutatis mutandis to other mahapalikas and municipalities that have jurisdiction over the areas through which the river flows.[46] The ruling of the Supreme Court, in this case, is in line with the decision of the Court of Appeal in the Pride of Derby case.[47]

[37] M/s Sreenivasa Distilleries v. S.R. Thygarajan, AIR 1986 AP 328.

[38] M.S. Pattar v. Government of NCT of Delhi, AIR 2002 Del 133.

[39] Environmental Encyclopedia, Malayalam (vernacular), (Kerala State Institute of Encyclopedic Publications, Trivandrum, Kerala, 2000).

[40] M.C. Mehta v. Union of India, AIR 1987 SC 1037.

[41] Ibid.

[42] Ibid.

[43] M.C. Mehta v. Union of India, AIR 1988 SC 1115.

[44] They were: Uttar Pradesh Municipalities Act; the Uttar Pradesh Water Supply and Sewerage Act, 1975; Water (Prevention and Control of Pollution) Act, 1974.

[45] Ibid.

[46] Ibid.

[47] Pride of Derby v. British Celanese, (1953) All. ER 179; In this case, the Rivers Pollution Prevention Act, 1876,

The right to life includes the right to acquire water but in spite of its recognition by the Indian Constitution and the United Nations, it is a matter of great concern that water is not available to all citizens even for their basic drinking necessities, even after half a century of freedom. Ironically the situation is 'Water, water everywhere, but not a drop to drink'.[48] Courts have also raised concerns about falling ground water levels[49] and reminded governments and other local bodies of their duty to provide pure drinking water.[50]

Meanwhile, adorning the attire of a 'conservationist', the Supreme Court has reiterated the dire need to protect natural water sources.[51]

---

prohibited any solid or liquid sewerage flowing into any stream or river. There was a pollution to river Derwent, owing to the discharge untreated effluents, especially from The British Electricity Authority. The seweree works were maintained by Derby Corporation. An action was brought by Derbyshire Angling Association, against the defendants over pollution. In this case, Court of Appeal, through Raymond Evershed M.R., held that the statutory requirement obligating the corporation to pay compensation for damages sustained by reason of the exercise of its powers under Sec.113 of the Derby Corporation Act had no application because the pollution of the river was not due to the exercise of the powers under that section and so, the Corporation had no statutory defence. Also see supra note 35, p. 11–12.

[48] Poem quoted in *S.K. Garg v. State of Uttar Pradesh*, AIR 1999 All 41.

[49] *M.C. Mehta v. Union of India*, (1997) 11 SCC 312.

[50] *Attakoya Thangal v. Union of India*, 1990 (1) KLT 580; *Vishala Kochi Kudivella Samrakshana Samiti v. State of Kerala*, AIR 2006 NOC 744 (Kerala), 2006 (1) KLT 919; *Shajimon Joseph v. State of Kerala*, 2007 (1) KLT 368.

[51] *Andhra Pradesh Pollution Control Board v. M.V. Nayadu*, (1999) 2 SCC 718; also see *Susetha v. State of Tamil Nadu*, AIR 2006 SC 2893, (2006) 6 SCC 543.

Effluent Treatment Plant (ETP)

Discharge of effluents from industry is unavoidable in certain cases. In such cases, polluted water should be treated before being discharged into the public water body. The establishment of a treatment plant upholds the principle of sustainable development. The establishment and functioning of an ETP involves the expenditure of a substantial amount of money, which most industrialists consider unnecessary. The solution is the installation of a common ETP (CETP). Standards have been prescribed under the Environment (Protection) Rules, 1986[52] for CETPs, which lay down the quality of effluents for units, the total discharge of which is 25 KL/day. For each primary treatment plant and its constituent units, the State Board will prescribe standards as per local needs and conditions, but the same cannot be more than the above. For a cluster of units, the State Boards, with the concurrence of the CPCB, prescribe suitable limits. All efforts should be taken to remove colour and unpleasant odour as far as possible.

Discharge from tanneries causes water pollution in the state of West Bengal. The Supreme Court, with a view to control the pollution generated by tanneries, examined a proposal regarding the setting up of CETPs wherever tanneries were operating. In view of the categorical findings of NEERI and also several reports by the PCB, the Court found that there is no possibility of setting up CETPs at the existing locations. The tanneries would, instead, have to relocate. The tanneries, which declined to relocate, were not permitted to function at the present sites. A pollution fine of Rs 10,000 was imposed on each tannery. For further monitoring, the

[52] Item 58 of the Schedule to EP Rules, 1986.

matter has been sent to the 'Green Bench' of the Calcutta High Court.[53]

Reacting to pollution being created by factories carrying on the business of dyeing and printing cloth, which discharged toxic substances in water used for agriculture and drinking, the Rajasthan HC directed the industries, the state and its agencies to set up CETPs so that effluents would not be discharged into canals. The court has evolved six principles while interpreting the provisions of Articles 21, 48A and 51A(g). They are: (1) All human beings have the fundamental right to an unpolluted environment, pollution-free water and air; (2) the state is obliged to preserve and protect the environment; (3) it is mandatory for the state and its agencies to conceive, anticipate, prevent, and attack causes of environmental degradation; (4) industry cannot be permitted to continue as a matter of right in case it creates pollution; (5) the polluter must meet the cost of repairing environment and ecology and pay reparation to those who have suffered because of the pollution caused by him; and (6) considerations of economy cannot prevail over concerns for environment and ecology.[54]

A sugar factory was discharging effluents into the water body, creating pollution. The industry had undertaken before the court that ETP instruments would be fixed before it began operation the following season. The Supreme Court directed the State Pollution Control Board to ensure that the effluents were treated before the unit restarted and the boiler replaced within a designated time frame.[55]

A PIL alleged that a distillery had been discharging untreated effluents, chemical wastes and sewage beyond its premises, thereby contaminating the water resources and polluting the environment. The Patna HC permitted the said distillery company to restart its manufacturing with adequate safeguards in terms of a scheme framed by the HC on the basis of an Expert Committee's report. The HC directed that in case any further injuries, caused by the effluent discharged by the distillery, come to light, the company shall bear all expenses of their treatment and the question of compensation to the victim may also be considered.[56]

The Delhi HC had occasion to consider the discharge of trade effluents by a soft-drink manufacturing company. The HC found that the samples of water had not been taken in accordance with law[57] and it set aside the order of the magistrate passed against the industry that restrained it from discharging effluents.[58]

An ETP should be calibrated and be made functional. Only then will it be effective. The working of the ETP must be monitored by the PCB or some other locally available body. Online monitoring of its functioning can also be established for the effective control of water pollution.

GROUNDWATER

Groundwater is one of the essential sources of drinking water for many rural areas. Water is drawn with the help of wells from both traditional and tubewells. Unfortunately,

---

[53] *M.C. Mehta v. Union of India* (1997) 2 SCC 411, JT 1997 (1) Supreme Court 221.

[54] *Singh Punia v. Rajashtan State Board of Pollution Control of Water Pollution*, AIR 2003 Raj 286.

[55] *Satish Chandra Shukla v. State of UP*, 1992 Supp SCC 94.

[56] *Rajiv Ranjan Singh v. State of Bihar*, AIR 1992 Patna 86.

[57] Water (Prevention and Control of Pollution) Act, 1974, Section 21.

[58] *M/s Delhi Bottling Co. Pvt Ltd v. Central Board for Prevention and Control of Water Pollution*, AIR 1986 Delhi 152.

the unregulated and excess drawing of groundwater causes depletion of groundwater resources. It is a vulnerable resource because it is used extensively for drinking water needs, and once contaminated, is extremely costly to clean.

Legislation

There is no separate Central legislation to control groundwater usage. But the Environment (Protection) Act, 1986 is sufficient to protect groundwater resources.[59] For the protection of groundwater, there are several state legislations.[60] In invoking its powers to protect the environment of the country, the Central Government has constituted the Central Ground Water Board as an authority for the purpose of regulation and control of groundwater management and development.

Case Law

A news item titled 'Falling Groundwater Level Threatens City' resulted in the Supreme Court of India taking cognizance of a public interest case. After considering all the issues, the Supreme Court directed that a Central Groundwater Resource Management Authority[61] be constituted, with a mandate for coordination and implementation of all activities of planning, development, allocation, implementation, research, and monitoring of all water resources. The authority needs to be established to promote intra- and inter-generational equity, as also to operationalize the precautionary principle in sustainable water resource management, the Court noted.[62]

The Supreme Court sought the opinion of NEERI[63] before passing the above order. They have suggested for a holistic approach which is very much essential for water resource management.

Sustainable solutions to the water resource, land use, regulation on exploitation by education, implementations of environment laws, etc. are some of the approaches suggested by them. The recommendation includes the constitution of a Ground Water Management Authority (GRMA), both at the State and Central level for the coordination and implementation of all activities of planning, development, allocation, implementation, research and monitoring of all water resources need to be established to promote intra and inter-generational equity, as also to operationalize the precautionary principle in sustainable water resource management.

The Supreme Court has had the occasion to consider the question of ownership of groundwater while considering a question on mining. It has held that underground water belongs to the state on the basis of the Public Trust Doctrine. As a result, holders of land only have users' rights and cannot take any action or make deeds where the rights of others are affected. Even the right as user is confined to the purpose for which the land is held. A person who holds land for agricultural purposes may, therefore, subject to any reasonable restriction that may be made by the State, have the right to use water for irrigational purposes and for the said purpose he may also excavate tanks. But under no circumstances is he permitted to restrict the flow of water to neighbouring lands or to discharge effluents in such a manner as will affect the right of his neighbour to use

---

[59] Act 29 of 1986.

[60] Kerala Ground Water (Control and Regulation) Act, 2002.

[61] M.C. Mehta v. Union of India, 1997 (11) SCC 312.

[62] Supra.

[63] National Environmental Engineering Research Institute.

water for his own purposes. On the basis of this analogy, he does not have any right to contaminate the water or to cause damage to the holders of the neighbouring agricultural fields. Large-scale fouling of the quality of water that will make it unusable for others, the water becoming contaminated and un-potable, violates Article 21 of the Constitution.[64] The Supreme Court also referred to the judgement of the single judge in the above case, which was not brought to the notice of the Bench.

The Karnataka HC has had the occasion to consider the question of whether the digging of bore-wells to draw water can be restrained. The court held that the right to life enshrined in Article 21 of the Constitution means the right to live and includes all those aspects of life which go to make man's life meaningful, complete, and worth living. The word 'law' as used in Article 21 would not include mere executive or departmental instructions that have no statutory basis. Therefore, the right to dig bore-wells to draw underground water can be restricted or regulated only by an Act of the legislature, the court added.

The KHC had the occasion to say that mining should be stopped and all pits filled up when they reach groundwater level. If the licencees do not fill the land once mining has ceased, the geologist shall prepare estimates or cause to prepare estimates regarding the amount required for filling up the pits and recover it from the violator of the said condition.[65]

The Plight of the People at Plachimada[66]

The usage of groundwater by a multinational company in one of the small villages in Kerala

State has been the subject of judicial scrutiny by the KHC. When the local people complained about the use of excessive groundwater by the company, which was causing depletion of groundwater levels, the panchayat was forced to cancel the licence granted. The single judge of the KHC, taking a broader view of the public trust doctrine, held that groundwater belongs to the public. The state and its instrumentalities should act as trustees of this great wealth. The state has a duty to protect groundwater against excessive exploitation and the inaction of the state in this regard is tantamount to infringement of the right to life guaranteed under Article 21 of the Constitution. The company has no right to extract a substantial amount of national wealth and the extraction of groundwater is illegal.

The Court restrained the company from drawing groundwater for its use. It further directed that the panchayat shall, with the assistance of the Groundwater Department, calculate the quantity of water that a landowner with 34 acres of land can extract for domestic and agricultural purposes. A serious dispute was raised by the panchayat in regard to the direction of the government to conduct the study with the Groundwater Department and other official agencies. The complain was that the reports of such agencies lack credibility and people look upon these reports with suspicion. In dealing with the point, the Court observed that 'it is unfortunate that we have to make arrangements for "guarding the guards". I think the media can take that role.' The Groundwater Department was directed to hold the inspection with notice to the panchayat. The Court also directed them to publish the details of the instruments used and divulge to the parties the scientific principles based on which they work. The data collected was to be furnished to both sides and the media was permitted to watch the inspection.

[64] *State of West Bengal v. Kesoram Industries Ltd*, 2004 AIRSCW 5998, 2004 (10) SCC 201.
[65] *Soman v. Geologist*, 2004 (3) KLT 577.
[66] Rural area where the people were fighting against a multinational company that has attracted the attention of all.

Though their presence may be inconvenient or irritating to some, it would serve public interest. Transparency lends credence to the reports, the Court added. The company was permitted only to draw the quantity of water ascertained as above from open dug wells, in a transparent manner, subject to inspection and monitoring by the panchayat and Groundwater Department. The decision has given the people the opportunity to participate in the decision-making process and has given recognition to their voices.[67]

However, the company was not satisfied with the judgement and approached the Division Bench. The Bench took a different view and held that if a person has the right to extract water from his property, unless it is prohibited by a statute, extraction thereof cannot be illegal. It also declared that the panchayat had no ownership over such private water sources. The Court came to the conclusion that the panchayat was not justified in resorting to the steps that it took.[68]

The matter is now pending in the Supreme Court. Several questions of law arose in the said case. Is written legislation necessary for the Constitutional Court to declare that extraction of groundwater in excess is illegal, especially to protect the rights of the people? Did the judgement omit to take note of the general principles of the law of tort applicable to the facts? Could the Court extend the principle of strict liability laid down in *Rylands* v. *Fletcher* to apply to the facts of this case? If a person draws excessive water from his property causing damage to others, is he not answerable for the loss caused to others? The Supreme Court has a great task of interpreting the general

principles of common law so as to protect the environment. As stated in *Saunders Clark* v. *Grosvenor Mansion Company Ltd*:[69]

The court should have considered whether the owner of the land is using the property reasonably or not. If he is using it reasonably, there is nothing which at law can be generated a nuisance: but if he is not using it reasonably…then the plaintiff is entitled to relief.

The courts should have balanced the activity of the company in drawing groundwater against any difficulties experienced by the public.

While assessing India's legal framework, Thomas J. Schoenbaum and Ronald. H. Rosenberg in their book titled *Environmental Policy Law* stated that 'Indian Lawyers are court room advocates, unaccustomed to the searching investigation and fact development that a case like Bhopal demanded. India has an undeveloped tort law'.[70] The judicial framework requires more academic value, then will courts be able to render quality judgements.

Foreign Law—The European Union

The European Union (EU) has a very comprehensive strategy for the protection of groundwater within its member states. By popular demand from EU citizens, the European Commission put forward an integrated system of water management for European nations, which culminated in the adoption of the EU Water Framework Directive that was adopted in 2000. Article 174 of the treaty, which provides for the protection of the environment and sustainable use, is

---

[67] *Perumatty Grama Panchayat* v. *Hindustan Coca Cola,* 2004 (1) KLT 731.

[68] *Hindustan Coca Cola* v. *Perumatty Grama Panchayat,* 2005 (2) KLT 10.

[69] (1900) 2 Ch 373.

[70] Thomas J. Schoenbaum and Ronald H. Rosenberg , *Environmental Policy Law: Problems, Cases and Readings* (Second edition), University Case Book Series, 1991, USA.

one of the main principles of the Directive.[71] A particular point is the adoption of a single system of water management which is deemed 'river basin management.'[72] This is based on the premise that water is best regulated on the basis of its physical qualities and not so much on its political or administrative boundaries.[73] This is very interesting in terms of sovereignty, as water is not regulated with reference to state boundaries, but rather with reference to the various river basins. For states where the river basin stretches across territorial borders, a river basin management plan can be formulated pursuant to the Directive to ensure compliance.

The Directive 'ensures the progressive reduction of pollution of groundwater and prevents its further pollution.'[74] Much like the recommendations of the Supreme Court of India on the advice of NEERI, a holistic approach is taken and the directive emphasizes the interrelatedness of basins, groundwater, and surface water, calling for the coordination of measures in respect of each system. The convention identifies 'general protection of the aquatic ecology, specific protection of unique and valuable habitats, protection of drinking water resources, and protection of bathing water'[75] as key aims which must be synchronized in river basin management. Ultimately, parties are to aim to achieve 'good' water status and where it already exists, this should be maintained.[76]

The Directive is devised to progressively phase out and reduce hazardous substances and emissions in water[77] where the ultimate aim is to eliminate on priority hazardous substances and achieve near natural concentrations in the marine environment.[78] A very grassroots approach is taken as member states are urged to regulate the sources of pollution and adopt emission and environmental quality standards.[79]

A number of practical measures are adopted in pursuit of the aims of the Convention. Article 9 specifically endorses the polluter pays principle, proposing that states 'take account of the principle of recovery of the costs of water services, including environmental and resource costs.'[80] Annex III provides an economic analysis for the purposes of doing this, making it easier for states to internalize externalities.

The EU Directive is commendable in protecting groundwater, largely because of its holistic approach to water management. Central to the policy is the realization that water is a moving resource and that eventually each water body will connect with another water body, be it the marine environment, a drainage basin, or the groundwater table. Hence, the proper protection of water resources demands an integrated approach, aiming to keep all water bodies free from pollution. Although the recommendations of the Supreme Court propose a system of holistic water management, the Water Act in India is less explicit on this matter. For the protection of groundwater, it is best to look to individual state legislation and for the pollution of rivers and other water bodies, the Water Act is more applicable. The question is: Is this a difference in substance or in form? Maybe the Indian legislation could be more effective if framed

[71] Directive 2000/60/EC of the European Parliament and of the Council of 23 October 2000, Article 1(b).
[72] The European Commission, 'Introduction to the New EU Water Framework Directive.' < http://ec.europa.eu/environment/water/water-framework/info/intro_en.htm > (last visited 18 May 2007).
[73] Ibid.
[74] Ibid.
[75] Ibid.
[76] Ibid.

[77] Ibid.
[78] Ibid.
[79] Ibid.
[80] Ibid.

in a manner akin to the EU Directive. This would also be consistent with the approach of the Supreme Court.

WATER FOR IRRIGATION PURPOSES

When the release of water for irrigation purposes was questioned, the Andhra Pradesh HC held that it is for the state government to decide how the existing available water may be utilized and managed. It requires expertise and is a matter of choice and a policy decision by the state. This cannot be interfered with by the High Court merely due to the possibility of an alternative policy choice.

The validity of a scheme framed under the Water Parambikulam Aliyar Project (Regulation of Water Supply) Act, 1993 for supplying water for agricultural purposes was considered by the Supreme Court. The project was undertaken with a view to supply water for agricultural operations to some taluks of the Coimbatore District in Tamil Nadu. The project was intended to bring more of the dry lands in the drought-prone zones under cultivation. Under the new pattern, there will be continuous flow in all the canals throughout the year resulting in the increase in groundwater potential. All the wells in the Ayacut areas and adjacent areas will receive the indirect benefit of groundwater recharge, which will help the people to utilize the well water during the non-irrigation period for domestic and irrigation purposes. The present pattern is such that the flow of water in the canals is to their full length throughout the year. Thus, there was valid basis for the enactment of the impugned Act.[81]

RAINWATER HARVESTING AND CONSERVATION

Water is required for agriculture, industry, and human and cattle consumption, all of which are

increasing rapidly. Therefore, optimum use of water resources is absolutely essential and it can be done by adopting efficient management techniques. Better management of water resources is therefore the need of the hour.

The struggle for water started 6,000 years ago. People had to protect themselves against floods; on the other hand, they had to ensure safe water supply for domestic use and irrigation. As a result, it became essential to store water in cisterns in countries like Palestine and Greece. These cisterns were used to collect rainwater from roofs, from paved squares, and occasionally from water-bearing subsoil strata.

The ancient Hindu texts, written around 800–600 BC, reveal certain knowledge of hydrological relationships. The Vedic hymns, particularly those in the Rig Veda, contain many notes on irrigated agriculture, river courses, dykes, water reservoirs, wells and water-lifting structures. The *Chandogya*, one of the principal Upanishads (the philosophical reflections of the Vedas, numbering 108 in all) points out that: 'The rivers…all discharge their waters into the sea. They lead from sea to sea, the clouds raise them to the sky as vapour and release them in the form of rain…'[82]

Water shortage is rampant throughout the world. Countries like Slovakia and Israel use water about four to five times before disposing it of. Rainwater can be collected and stored for future use. Such an activity is termed 'Rain Water Harvesting and Conservation' and is intended to optimize the use of rainwater.

The Government of India issued a notification on 6 October 2000 directing proper modification of building laws in the country so as to ensure that all buildings that are erected provide for

---

[81] *Parambikulam APOA v. State of Tamil Nadu*, AIR 1999 SC 3092, (1999) 7 SCC 626.

[82] Extracted from 'Perennial Quest', in Anil Agarwal and Sunita Narain, *Dying Wisdom. State of India's Environment: A Citizens Report*, Centre for Science and Environment, 1997, New Delhi, India.

rainwater harvesting. All buildings that have a minimum discharge of 10,000 litres and above per day shall incorporate a wastewater recycling system. The recycled water should be used for agricultural purposes.[83] Storage of rainwater will keep the water table at optimum levels and will help the people obtain water throughout the year. Such a proactive response to water management is certainly commendable and it is likely that both the people and the government will reap the benefits from such a law. Water has the ability to collect human society's ills. A society is known by the water it keeps.

WATER BODIES OF INDIA

Rivers of India

The Government of India has been empowered to make laws for the regulation and development of interstate rivers and river valleys, to the extent to which such regulation and development under the control of the Union is declared by the laws of Parliament to be expedient in the public interest.[84]

Rivers are the main source of drinking water. They are polluted by the dumping of waste. Most rivers have turned into sewers due to such excessive dumping.

While considering the pollution of the river Gomati, the Supreme Court of India observed that courts cannot afford to deal lightly with cases involving pollution of air and water. The courts share the parliamentary concern on the escalating level of pollution to the environment. Those who discharge noxious polluting effluents into streams may be unconcerned about the enormity of the injury that it inflicts on the public health at large, the irreparable

impairment it causes to aquatic organisms, or the deleteriousness it imposes on the life and health of animals. Courts should not deal with prosecution in a causal or routine manner, added the Supreme Court when it refused to quash the prosecution proceedings initiated against discharging toxic effluents in the river.[85]

The Andhra Pradesh Government has banned the location of industries within a ten-kilometre radius of a reservoir from which water is used by the general public. Subsequently, certain industries were granted exemption. While interfering with the granting of exemption, the Supreme Court directed the state to identify the industries that are located within a ten-kilometre radius of lakes and to prevent pollution to the drinking water in these two reservoirs.[86]

Courts often monitor implementation of their orders so as to curtail water pollution. Noticing that the water quality of the river Yamuna had improved, the court granted an industry time to pay the pollution fine. Instead of giving notice to all the industries, the Supreme Court directed the Government of India to publish in newspapers a general notice requiring such industries to file their objections to the proposed action.

The Action Plan was framed by the CPCB for the improvement of the quality of twenty-seven grossly polluted river stretches of the country, on the basis of directions from the Supreme Court of India. The plan includes the prevention of pollution, construction of sewage treatment plants, electronic crematoria, river front development work, and the like, which are intended to protect the river ecology. The National River Conservation Directorate has been constituted by the Government of

---

[83] Notification No. 11011/9/98-DDVI/(Pt)/ DDIB, dated 28 July 2001, Ministry of Urban Development and Poverty Alleviation.

[84] Constitution of India, Seventh Schedule, List 1, Union List, Entry 56.

[85] *UP Pollution Control Board v. M/s Mohan Meakins Ltd*, AIR 2000 SC 1456.

[86] *AP Pollution Control Board—II v. M.V. Nayadu (Retd) and Others*, 2001 (2) SCC 62.

India for the purpose of implementing River Action Plans. These plans are monitored by the National River Conservation Authority (NRCA), which is chaired by the prime minister and has the union minister of environment and forests and other central ministers of concerned ministries, chief ministers, and members of parliament of the participating states as its members.

National River Conservation Plans were also formulated by the Government of India in 1995 for the improvement of the river ecology in the states.

Ponds, Tanks, Lakes, and Other Sources of Water in India

Natural ponds are important in maintaining the ecology of an area. The necessity to protect such lands has been highlighted by the courts in India on numerous occasions.

The Supreme Court of India in a landmark judgement clarified that natural water storage resources not only need to be protected but also measures are required to be taken for restoring them if they have fallen into disuse. The court observed:

The water bodies are required to be retained. Such requirement is envisaged not only in view of the fact that the right to water as also quality of life are envisaged under Article 21 of the Constitution of India, but also in view of the fact that the same has been recognized in Articles 47 and 48A of the Constitution of India. Article 51A of the Constitution furthermore makes it a fundamental duty of every citizen to protect and improve the natural environment including forest, lakes, rivers and, wildlife.[87]

Since time immemorial, it has been the duty of the state to take care of the water supply to the general public using several indigenous ways of storing rainwater in community tanks. But in Rajasthan, the government decided to acquire a pond for converting the land to build a hostel. The Rajasthan HC, intervened in the matter, and observed that it concerns the deprivation of a basic requirement and the right of villagers to have access to water by natural source. The court held that it will adversely affect the ecological balance of the area and also affect the rights of the villagers to have rainwater stored in a natural reservoir, affecting their right to life.[88]

Another case arose on account of a dispute pertaining to land, which was actually a public pond. It was pointed out that the pond, which is a public utility designated for public use, cannot be allotted in favour of any person. Accepting the argument, the Supreme Court of India held that material resources of the community like forests, tanks, ponds, hillocks, mountains, and other such resources are nature's bounty. They maintain the delicate ecological balance and they need to be protected for a proper and healthy environment which enables people to enjoy a quality of life that is the essence of the guaranteed right under Article 21 of the Constitution. The court directed the occupiers of the said land to vacate within six months and on failure, the court directed the state to demolish any constructions made and to acquire possession of the said land in accordance with law. The state was further directed to restore the pond and develop and maintain the same as a recreational spot in the best interests of the villagers. Further, these actions would help maintain the ecological balance and protect the environment, in regard to which this Court has repeatedly expressed its concern. Such measures must begin at the

[87] *Susetha v. State of Tamil Nadu*, 2006 (6) SCC 543.

[88] *Lakh Singh v. State of Rajasthan*, AIR 2003 NOC 363 (Raj), 2003 AIHC 1472.

grass-roots level if they are to become the nation's pride, the court added.[89]

In the state of Kerala, ponds form part of the temple. The law stated, 'The place of public worship and premises shall not be used for purposes not connected with or arising from the worship, usages and observations of such places of public worship.'[90] Thus, the pond cannot be divided and it is necessary for the use of the temple poojas. The KHC directed the authorities not to proceed with the agreement with regard to the portion of the pond which was to be divided.[91]

Temple tanks maintain the environment of the surrounding area. Such tanks are communal property and state authorities are its trustees to hold and manage such properties for the benefit of community. They cannot be allowed to commit any act or omission which will infringe upon the right of the community and alienate the property to any other person or body, the Supreme Court has held.[92] Explaining the principle of public trust, the court held as follows:

Public trust is more than an affirmation of state power to use public property for public purpose. It is an affirmation of the duty of the state to protect the people's common heritage of streams, lakes, marshland, and tidelands, surrendering the right only in those rare cases when the abandonment of the right is consistent with the purpose of trust.[93]

But the said principles cannot be applied in relation to artificial tanks. A temple tank had long lost its utility and was being used as a dumping yard. When the Panchayat used the tank for construction of a shopping complex and for the user thereof, the resettlement of those persons who were displaced due to the expansion of the highway project was approved by the court. Moreover, when the village in question is situated near the sea and has five water tanks therein, the conversion of the same into a building was not held to be at fault, the Supreme Court held.[94]

In the state of Gujarat, an opinion was given by the Chief Wildlife Warden (CWW) that a lake was a temporary habitat for migrating birds. The warden stated that the lake could not be declared as a sanctuary although the protection of birds was necessary. This was challenged before the Gujarat High Court. The court issued a direction to the state and CWW to convene a meeting of the Board for its decision. Landowners were allowed to continue their agricultural operations on the said land, but were restrained from changing the landscape so as to make it impossible for its retrieval and preservation of the lake.[95]

The villagers of Andhra Pradesh[96] have approached the HC against the proposal of the authorities to assign the land abutting or adjacent to an irrigation tank, which is the source of irrigation for about 400 acres of land. The HC directed the District Collector to look into their grievances based on the principles of sustainable development laid down by the Supreme Court and act accordingly.[97]

The immersion of Ganesha idols in religious festivals like Vinayaga Chathurthi has also come under the scrutiny of the Madras HC.

[89] *Hinch Lal Tiwari v. Kamla Devi*, 2001 AIRSCW 2865, 2001 (6) JT 88, 2001 (6) SCC 496.

[90] Kerala Hindu Places of Public Worship (Authorization of Entry) Rules, 1965.

[91] *K. Chandran v. Travancore Devaswom Board*, ILR 2003 (3) Ker 440: 2003 (2) KLJ 6 (NOC).

[92] *Intellectuals Forum, Tirupathy v. State of AP*, AIR 2006 SC 1350: (2006) 3 SCC 549.

[93] Ibid.

[94] *Susetha v. State of Tamil Nadu*, AIR 2006 SC 2893, 2006 AIRSCW 4026.

[95] *Sandeep Brahmbhatt v. State of Gujarat*, AIR 2002 NOC 71.

[96] The Water Users Association, Thimmayagari Pally.

[97] *Water Users Association v. State*, Writ Petition No. 20323 of 2000, dated 6 February 2002.

It is averred that the immersion of Ganesha idols, made of plaster of Paris and other material containing chemicals, in seas, rivers, and other water resources, causes pollution. The authorities thereafter took steps to prevent the water pollution caused by the immersion of such idols. The Court was satisfied with these steps and closed the case by observing that persons who are responsible for installing the idols and taking them in procession to the sea for the purpose of immersion shall remember the true religious significance of the procession and cooperate with the law enforcement agencies to maintain law and order.[98]

To curb water pollution in Nainital Lake, the Supreme Court issued directions restraining the construction of multistoried group housing and commercial complexes in the town area of Nainital. The building of small residential houses in flat areas was, however, permitted and the offence of illegal felling of trees was made cognizable. The Supreme Court also set up a monitoring committee.[99]

DRINKING WATER

The normal water available from natural sources has become unfit, resulting in people depending on bottled water for drinking. This has led to the rise of bottled water manufacturing industries. The legislature prescribed the standards for packaged drinking water by amending the Prevention of Food Adulteration Rules, 1955.[100] The term 'packaged drinking water' is defined thus:

Packaged Drinking Water means water derived from any source of potable water or sea water

or underground water or surface water, which may be subjected to the treatments, namely, decantation, filtration, combination of filtration, aeration, filtration with membrane filter, depth filter, cartridge filter, activated carbon filteration, demineralization, remineralization reverse osmosis, and packed. It may be disinfected to a level that will not lead to harmful contamination in the drinking water. It may be disinfected by means of chemical agents and/or physical methods to reduce the number of micro-organisms to a level that does not compromise food safety or suitability:

Provided that sea water, before being subjected to the above treatments, would be subjected to desalination and related processes.

After the introduction of the above enactment, all the sellers of manufactured drinking water maintain the standards prescribed by the said rules.

Supply of pure drinking water is the statutory duty of the Municipal Corporation and must be ensured to every citizen. In a PIL, the plight of some residents of Delhi who were not receiving sufficient water even for drinking was brought before the court by S.D. Sinha. The Supreme Court observed that where the interest of the community is involved, the individual interest must yield to the interest of the community or the general public.[101]

An inhabitant of Agra filed a writ petition, alleging therein that the supply of drinking water in the city was extremely polluted, the water being contaminated, filthy, and totally unhealthy for human consumption. It was also averred in the said petition that notwithstanding several laws, conferring power and duty on different agencies like Nagar Mahapalika, the State of Uttar Pradesh, the UP Pollution Control Board, those authorities have not exercised their

[98] *V. Elangovan v. Home Secretary, State of Tamil Nadu, and Others*, WP No. 25586 of 2004, WPMP Nos 31095 and 32504 of 2004, 17 September 2004.
[99] *Ajay Singh Rawat v. Union of India*, (1995) 3 SCC 266, JT 1995 (3) SC 39.
[100] Appendix B in Item A-333, introduced by amendment with effect from 4 August 2006.
[101] *D.K. Joshy v. Chief Secretary*, AIR 2000 SC 384, 1999 (9) SCC 578.

power and as a result the citizens of Agra were suffering. In the said writ petition, all the concerned authorities were added as respondents. The court considered the interests of the residents of the area, and also the interests of tourists, as Agra attracts a large number of tourists from various countries. The Supreme Court interfered with the issue and directed the appointment of a Monitoring Committee to be headed by the Commissioner of Agra. The Committee was to look into the effective functioning of several public authorities, who are made responsible for the supply of drinking water, providing adequate measures for disposal of solid waste.[102]

The Problem of Lakshadweep Islanders

The threat to drinking water sources in the Lakshadweep islands was brought to the notice of the KHC. To solve the issue, a technically viable scheme consistent with natural constraints must be evolved, the court observed. To decide on the modalities, the matter should receive a final look from the ministries of the government, according to the HC.[103]

The shortage of water supply in Lakshadweep again came to the notice of the KHC. The court found that there was large-scale withdrawal of water through electrical and mechanical pumps, depleting the water sources and causing seepage or intrusion of saline water from the Arabian Sea. The court observed that the executive government has the onerous responsibility in this matter of providing civic amenities. Over-exploitation of water sources must be contained. Environmentalists and scientists

in other disciplines have indicated the importance of water management in the present day and perhaps water management will be one of the biggest challenges in the opening decades of the next century. With changes in the way of life, even a basically conventional society may go in for modern means and make use of pumps to draw water from private wells, the court observed.[104]

Duty of the Municipal Authorities to Supply Water

In a municipal area, who has the duty to supply drinking water? In the state of Kerala, the government has constituted a separate authority (Kerala Water Authority) for supplying drinking water to the residents, but drinking water supply has not improved. The matter was brought to the notice of the HC. The court, relying on the provisions of the Kerala Municipalities Act, 1994, held that every municipality has a duty to supply clean drinking water to its people.[105]

The Andhra Pradesh HC directed the State Pollution Control Board to disallow the setting up of twenty highly polluting industries notified by the Central Government as falling within the purview of industrial licensing, to come up within the vicinity of, or catchment area of, Durgam Cheruvu lake. Such a direction was issued in the public interest so as to protect the water body.[106]

Despite the existence of two big rivers, Ganga and Yamuna, the people of Allahabad do not have enough water to drink. The Allahabad HC directed the formation of a committee consisting of a magistrate, senior

---

[102] *F.K. Hussain v. Union of India*, AIR 1990 Ker 321.
[103] *Attakoya Thangal v. Union of India*, 1990 (1) KLT 580, AIR 1991 Ker 321.

[104] *Shajimon v. State*, 2007 (1) KLT 368: 2006 (1) KLT 919, ILR 2006 (1) Ker 705.
[105] *T. Ramakrishna Rao v. Hyderabad Urban Development Authority*, 2002 (2) ALT 193.
[106] Ibid.

advocates, and bureaucrats, and others as members, to look into the matter of pollution seriously and immediately.[107]

Water Sharing Disputes between States

The Inter-State Water Disputes Act, 1956[108] provides for the constitution of tribunals for the adjudication of disputes relating to waters of interstate rivers and river valleys. A tribunal is constituted when a request is received from the concerned state government in respect of any water dispute where the settlement cannot be decided by negotiations.[109] The term 'water disputes' is defined as follows:

Water disputes mean any dispute or difference between two or more state governments with respect to—

1. the use, distribution, or control of the water of, or in, any interstate river or river valley; or
2. the interpretation of the terms of any agreement relating to the use, distribution, or control of such waters or the implementation of such agreement; or
3. the levy of any water rate in contravention of the prohibition of levy of seigniorage, etc.[110]

Water-sharing disputes between states is common in certain parts of the country. In a matter concerning the sharing of Kaveri water, the Supreme Court issued directions to the special tribunal to look into all the objections raised by the State of Andhra Pradesh.[111]

On another occasion, the Supreme Court considered an interim application filed by the state of Tamil Nadu and Pondicherry, seeking the release of water by the state of Karnataka, which was dismissed by the Cauvery Water Disputes Tribunal. A preliminary objection was raised, effectively claiming that the Supreme Court has no right to consider the validity of the order passed by the tribunal in view of the specific bar on the Supreme Court and other courts under Section 11 of the Inter-State Water Disputes Act, 1956. Repelling the contention, it has been held that the Supreme Court is the ultimate interpreter of the provisions of the said Act and has an authority to decide the limits, powers, and the jurisdiction of the tribunal constituted under the Act. The court not only has the power, but the obligation to decide whether the tribunal has any jurisdiction under the Act to entertain any interim application till it finally decides the dispute referred to it. Allowing the application, the Court held that under the constitutional set-up, it is one of the primary responsibilities of the Supreme Court to determine the jurisdictional power and limits of any tribunal or authority created under a statute.[112]

Disputes between states for sharing river water is common in India. A dam, commonly described as Mullapperiyar Dam, is being used by the state of Tamil Nadu for the needs of drinking water in the state. The state wanted to increase the height of the dam from 136 feet to 142 feet so that it may hold more water and therefore be available to more people. This was opposed by the neighbouring state of Kerala through which the river flows. The main contention was about the safety of the dam, and the damage to the ecology since the dam was constructed 100 years back. The Supreme Court, after considering rival claims, allowed

---

[107] Act 33 of 1956.

[108] Section 4 of the Act.

[109] Section 3 of the Act.

[110] *State of Karnataka v. State of Andhra Pradesh*, (2000) 9 SCC 572.

[111] *State of Tamil Nadu v. State of Karnataka*, 1991 Supp (1) SCC 240, 1991 (2) JT 3222.

[112] *Mullaperiyar Environmental Protection Forum v. Union of India*, AIR 2006 SC 1428, (2006) 3 SCC 643.

Tamil Nadu to raise the height by six feet after taking strengthening measures.[113]

The issue is still simmering, with the state of Kerala making a law so as to take measures for the protection of dams, which indirectly overcomes the judgement according to the state of Tamil Nadu.

Drinking Water—the Foreign Law

The United Nations

Access to drinking water has been described by the UN as a human right. Although water is not expressly defined as a human right in the primary human rights instruments, it has been read into such instruments due to its character as an essential ingredient for the existence of human life. The United Nations Committee on Economic, Social and Cultural Rights has commented that:

The human right to drinking water is fundamental for life and health. Sufficient and safe drinking water is a precondition for the realization of all human rights. Although the [Covenant for Social Cultural and Economic Rights] does not expressly refer to the word 'water', the right to drinking water is clearly essential for the rights contained in Articles 11 and 12, is supported by international legal standards, and has been a consistent feature of the Committee's practice.[114]

Article 11 states that everyone is to have the right 'to an adequate standard of living for himself and his family, including adequate food, clothing, and housing, and to the continuous improvement of living conditions.'[115] The Committee is confident that water falls within this class of provisions, as it is a basic human necessity. Furthermore, Article 12 recognizes 'the right of everyone to the enjoyment of the highest attainable standard of physical and mental health.'[116] This also demands a right to clean drinking water, as clean and potable water is vital to our very existence.[117]

The normative content of the right, as proposed by the Committee, is significantly wide. It 'entitles everyone to *safe, sufficient, affordable,* and *accessible* drinking water that is adequate for daily individual requirements (drinking, household sanitation, food preparation, and hygiene).'[118] States are to take steps toward the progressive realization of the right to drinking water, in a manner consistent with their maximum available resources, as defined by Article 2.1 of the Convention.[119] At the very least, states are to meet the minimum obligation of providing 'the minimum essential level of drinking water' so as to prevent disease and dehydration.[120] Failure to meet this minimum obligation is inexcusable under the Convention, the Committee has stressed. The obligation on States, as explained by this UN Committee, is consistent with the approach taken by some Indian courts and the interpretation of Article 21 of the Indian Constitution, which necessitates a right to water, as discussed above. The Indian Government and its states have taken various measures to increase the availability of drinking water in the country. The biggest hurdle is not in locating such water, but in ensuring that it is free from contamination and is, therefore, safe. With the presence of private companies

---

[113] Committee on Economic Social and Cultural Rights, General Comment No. 15 (2002) 'The right to water (Articles 11 and 12 of the International Covenant on Economic, Social and Cultural Rights)' E/C.12/2002/11, 29 July 2002, Section 1.

[114] International Covenant on Economic, Social and Cultural Rights 993 UNTS 3, Article 11 (1).

[115] Ibid., Article 12(1).

[116] Supra note 117, Section 2.

[117] Ibid., Section 7.

[118] Ibid., Section 9.

[119] Ibid., Section 29.

[120] *Sutradhar v. Natural Environment Research Council,* (2007) *Env. LR* 10 (Lord Hoffman), Section 2.

in many regions, who own water or have access to it in vast quantities, the issue of affordability is also relevant to India. The use of wells, storage tanks, and other initiatives for the catchment and storage of rainwater is welcomed and strongly encouraged as these have made water more accessible to the general public. Various measures taken by the courts in India have signified steps towards the country's fulfilment of the normative content of the right to drinking water, but further steps must be taken to properly fulfil these obligations.

United Kingdom

Suppliers of dangerous drinking water, in some circumstances, can be subject to tort actions in negligence. However, negligent actions are highly complicated and difficult to bring against scientists who publish reports on the potability of drinking water. The following case demonstrates the difficulty in establishing a duty of care on the part of scientists who publish such reports, particularly when the defendant is a foreign body or citizen.

In England, the House of Lords ruled a claim by a Bangladeshi person, who suffered arsenic poisoning from drinking water, against the National Environment and Research Council as 'hopeless'.[121] In 1983, the British Overseas Development Agency (ODA) began funding the Bangladesh Second Deep Tubewell Project, which aimed to provide 4,000 tubewells for irrigation purposes north of Dacca and ultimately provide greater opportunity for food production. For the purposes of testing their efficiency, the ODA commissioned the British Geological Society (BGS) to undertake hydrological tests. A geologist performed a number of tests at different intervals to identify any deterioration, one of which involved the taking of water and sediment samples. It was proposed that these samples would provide a better understanding of the functioning of the tubewells, but could also be used by a university to test for aluminium and iron, these being harmful to fish which the Bangladeshis were being encouraged to farm.[122] The geologist took samples from 150 sites, some of which were tubewells, but the majority of which were hand-pumped shallow wells, often used to provide drinking water.

A report was subsequently published, titled *Short term BGS Pilot Project to Assess the Hydrochemical Character of the Main Aquifer Units of Central and North-eastern Bangladesh and Possible Toxicity of Groundwater to Fish and Humans.* Around the time the report was released, there were a number of shallow hand-pumped tubewells created in Bangladesh by the United Nations Childrens Fund (UNICEF) and the World Bank for the purposes of providing drinking water. Arsenic was not among the chemicals tested for and the presence of arsenic in these wells went unnoticed by UNICEF and National Authorities until it was too late. In 2000, the WHO estimated that between 35 and 77 million Bangladeshi people were at risk of drinking the toxic water.

The applicant drank water from one of the wells and subsequently fell ill due to arsenic poisoning. He lived in a region where the BGS took some of its samples and claimed that BGS had been negligent in failing to test for arsenic and/or representing in the report that the water was safe for humans to drink.[123] He claimed that but for the defendant's acts and omissions, the public authorities would have taken steps to ensure the water was potable. If the report had specified that the water contained arsenic or alternatively if the

---

[121] Ibid., Section 12.

[122] Ibid., Section 24.
[123] Ibid., Section 25.

report did not represent that the water was potable, the Bangladeshi government would have taken steps to ensure the water was safe for its citizens, the applicant claimed.

The court considered whether BGS owed the claimant and other persons a duty of care to test for arsenic or a duty not to give the impression that the water was free of arsenic.[124] On the first question, the court affirmed that BGS owned no duty of care to the people of Bangladesh. In particular, it was not commissioned to test the potability of the water and the fact that the geologist tested for some elements did not impugn an obligation to test for arsenic.

In relation to the second question, the court stated that at most, BGS made an implied statement that it was unnecessary to test for arsenic and that this statement caused the government's failure to take protective measures. The court rejected this proposition on the basis of proximity and provided that even if BGS made an implied statement, the relationship between the publisher of the report and the people of Bangladesh was not sufficiently proximate so as to impose a duty of care upon BGS.[125] Nor did BGS have a proximate relationship with the supply of the drinking water, this being a matter for the Bangladeshi government. Finally, the report made it clear that arsenic was not tested for and since BGS was under no obligation to do so, it could not have been negligent in this case.[126]

This case demonstrates that although actions in negligence may be appropriate for addressing injuries from harmful drinking water, it may be difficult to establish a duty of care on the part of those who publish scientific information on water quality. Unless the publisher is an agent of one's own government and commissioned to investigate potability, the proximate link between the report and the injury may be left wanting. Citizens should be able to rely on their own governments for the provision of safe drinking water and should not have to look to foreign bodies for reassurance that their water is safe. Let this case be a lesson to many countries, including India, to take their duty to their citizens very seriously, test for water potability stringently, and not make any assumptions where citizens' lives are at risk.

INTERLINKING OF RIVERS

There are several rivers in India. But there is acute scarcity of water in most states. India has an average annual flow of 1,869 billion cubic metres (bcm) of water. By 2050, it is expected that the country's need for water will rise to 1,300 bcm. The president of India[127] made a speech saying that if all the rivers are connected together, then scarcity of water would be less. On the basis of a newspaper report about the President's speech, the Supreme Court entertained a PIL and issued various directions for the interlinking of rivers in Kerala. The court appointed an amicus curiae and brought to the notice of the court that in view of Entry 56, List I of the 7th Schedule to the Constitution of India, interlinking of interstate rivers can be done by the Central Government.[128]

The report prepared by the National Water Development Agency was placed before the Supreme Court. According to the Agency, which had carried out detailed studies and investigations for preparation of feasibility reports, thirty links were identified and the Agency prepared feasibility reports of six such

[124] Ibid., Section 36.

[125] Ibid., Section 40.

[126] *Sutradhar v. National Environmental Research Council*, (2007) Env. LR 10 (Lord Hoffman, Section 2).

[127] *In re Networking of Rivers*, 2002 (8) SCALE 194.

[128] *In re Networking of Rivers*, 2003 (1) SCALE 2.

links. The proposal has two main components, namely, the Himalayan Component and the Peninsular Component. The general idea is to transfer waters from 'surplus' eastern rivers to 'deficit' central, western, and southern regions. The supplementary idea is to partially diversify certain rivers flowing into the Arabian Sea eastwards to link with rivers flowing into the Bay of Bengal. This project is an answer to the problem of recurring flood and drought and it will generate large quantities of electricity. The project also provides employment to thousands of people, through a programme called 'Food for Thought'. The court also noticed that various basin states have expressed divergent views about the studies and feasibility reports prepared by the Agency. The report set a timetable for achieving the goal of interlinking of rivers by the end of 2016.[129]

Interlinking of rivers has been subject to severe criticism by experts. The cost of creating fourteen river links in the Himalayas and sixteen river links in the Peninsula is estimated to be Rs 5,60,000 crore. Environmentalists strongly oppose this project despite its economic benefits. Such projects should be preceded by the most detailed environmental impact statements and only undertaken with the utmost caution. Completion of the project in small stages would also help assess the environmental impact as the project progresses and construction could be halted if the environment is threatened in any way.

STATUTORY WATER MANAGEMENT IN OTHER COUNTRIES

Africa

The National Water Act of South Africa recognizes 'that the protection of the quality

of water resources is necessary to ensure sustainability of the nation's water resources in the interests of all water users.'[130] It implements the principle of Intergenerational Equity as it aims to meet the basic human needs of present and future generations.[131] Notably, other objects of the Act include 'redressing the results of past racial and gender discrimination,'[132] signifying the interrelatedness of water use and human rights. In this sense, the act is very much couched within the political history of South Africa and employs the principle of equity[133] in the apportionment of water resources, which is ideally void of political judgements.

The Act provides for the protection of water resources, which includes pollution prevention[134] where pollution attracts a similar meaning as under the Indian legislation.[135] Part Four is mainly concerned with pollution of water from land-based sources and states that

[t]he person who owns, controls, occupies or uses the land in question is responsible for taking measures to prevent pollution of water resources. If these measures are not taken, the catchment management agency concerned may itself do whatever is necessary to prevent the pollution or to remedy its effects, and to recover all reasonable costs from the persons responsible for the pollution.[136]

The act employs the Polluter Pays Principle in addressing water pollution. The onus is on the owner or person in control or occupation of the land to take reasonable measures for the prevention of water pollution.[137] The

---

[129] National Water Act, 1998 (Republic of South Africa), Preamble.

[130] Ibid., Section 2(a).
[131] Ibid., Section 2(c).
[132] Ibid., Ch. 1, interpretation and fundamental principles.
[133] Ibid., Part 4, Section 19.
[134] Ibid., Section 1(1)(xv).
[135] Ibid., Part 4.
[136] Ibid., Part 4, Section 19 (1).
[137] Ibid., Part 4 Section 19(3)–(8).

catchment management agency is akin to the State Pollution Control Board in India, and may direct the person to take steps to prevent, mitigate and remedy the pollution, bearing all of the costs associated with doing so.[138]

United States of America

The Federal Water Pollution Control Act Amendments of 1972 (Clean Water Act) Act[139] applies to the entirety of the US, but preserves the sovereignty of states in managing their own water resources. The Act expressly states that it is not to be construed so as to supersede, abrogate, or otherwise impair the function of the states to allocate water quantities within their jurisdiction.[140] Nor is it to be construed in a manner which supersedes or abrogates rights to quantities of water already guaranteed by the state.[141]

The EPA is deemed the administrator of the Act[142] and is granted standing under the Act to bring suit against those who offend its provisions.[143] A primary mechanism by which it controls pollution under the Act is by issuing permits under the National Pollution Discharge and Elimination System (NPDES) which is established by the Act.[144] The NPDES imposes effluent standards and limitations[145] and the permit system is a way of continually monitoring compliance with these standards, as holders are subject to various reporting procedures in relation to their activities.[146]

The amendments of 1972 have enabled citizens to bring suits under the Act to address water pollution.[147] In granting citizens standing, the Act enables citizens to bring actions against the state, the EPA, and other private individuals if they are able to show injury or the potential for injury. To invoke the jurisdiction of the court, citizens must 'allege violation of "an effluent standard or limitation under [the CWA]," or any order issued by EPA or a state in relation to such a standard or limitation.'[148] Citizen actions are also possible in India, as there are wide standing provisions in relation to the Water Act.

Section 1251 states that 'the objective of this chapter is to restore and maintain the chemical, physical, and biological integrity of the Nation's waters.'[149] A number of provisions are adopted to give effect to this goal. National goals of eliminating the discharge of pollutants into navigable waters by 1985[150] and attaining 'water quality which provides for the protection and propagation of fish, shellfish, and wildlife and provides for recreation in and on the water be achieved by 1 July 1983'[151] are adopted. A number of national policies are directed at mitigating and controlling and even eliminating water pollution. The discharge of toxic amounts of toxic pollutants is to be eliminated,[152] research and demonstration is to be directed toward the elimination of pollutants into various

---

[138] Federal Water Pollution Control Act, Amendments of 1972 (Clean Water Act) Act, 33 USCA.

[139] Ibid., Section 1251(g).

[140] Ibid., Section 1251(g).

[141] Ibid., Section 1251(d).

[142] Ibid., Section 1319(d).

[143] Ibid., Section 1342(a).

[144] Ibid., Section 1311(b).

[145] Ibid., Section 1318.

[146] Ibid., Section 1319.

[147] Ibid., Section 1365(a)(1) in Ann K. Wooster, 'Actions brought under Federal Water Pollution Control Act Amendments of 1972 (Clean Water Act) (33 USCA, Section 1251 et seq.)—Supreme Court cases' 163 ALR, Fed. 531 (Originally published in 2000).

[148] Section 1251(a).

[149] Section 1251(a)(1).

[150] Section 1251(a)(2).

[151] Section 1251(a)(3).

[152] Section 1251(a)(6).

water bodies,[153] and programmes are to be created to tackle non-point sources of water pollution.[154] Waste treatment also attracts a high priority, where the federal government is called upon to provide financial assistance for the construction of publicly owned waste treatment works[155] and states are to be subject to 'area-wide waste treatment management planning processes'.[156]

Numerous courts have had the opportunity to interpret the Act and permits have been at the root of much judicial activity. In *SD Warren Co. v. Maine Bd. of Environmental Protection*,[157] the court considered whether the operation of a hydroelectric dam resulted in a 'discharge' into navigable waters as defined by Section 401 of the Clean Water Act[158] and, consequently, whether it required state certification before a federal permit for operation could be issued. In order to gain a permit, the applicant must provide the agency with certification from the state, which details any effluents', standards or monitoring procedures which will require compliance.[159] The applicant operator of the dam claimed that there was, in fact, no discharge. It relied on a reading of the term 'discharge', which is largely undefined by the Act, as being restricted to the emission of one or more pollutants. It claimed that the water returned to the river did not add any pollutants or foreign substances to the water and that, consequently, there was no discharge. This argument was rejected by the court, which

noted that although 'discharge' was undefined by the Act, '[t]he term "discharge" when used without qualification includes a discharge of a pollutant, and a discharge of pollutants.'[160] Hence, the court said, the term 'discharge' is even wider and must be read 'in accordance with its ordinary or natural meaning.'[161] The meaning of the term is better read as 'flowing out' and is not limited by the presence of pollutants.

The court was adamant that the mere potential for discharge was enough to activate the Section 401 requirement. Despite Warren's arguments, it has been recognized that dams can, in fact, change the chemical composition of water due to the changes in flow and circulation. Water ecosystems are somewhat delicate and alterations in water flow can affect the oxygen content of water. Since Congress had enacted the Act to 'restore and maintain the chemical, physical, and biological integrity of the nation's waters,'[162] and pollution is defined as 'the man-made or man-induced alteration of the chemical, physical, biological, and radiological integrity of water',[163] the very potential for an alteration in water quality invites the attention of the state. The applicant's argument failed and the court held that state certification was required. The fears surrounding dams in the US are perhaps mimicked by their Indian environmentalist counterparts and such projects should not be taken lightly.

Particularly with the growing global climate crisis, the pressure on water resources is escalating. While much of the legislation discussed takes a holistic approach to water management, water management should also

---

[153] Section 1251(a)(7).

[154] Section 1251(a)(4).

[155] Section 1251(a)(5).

[156] *S.D. Warren Co. v. Maine Bd. of Environmental Protection*, 126 S. Ct. 1843.

[157] As codified by the supra note 142, Section 1341.

[158] Sec. 1311, Section 1312, Sec. 1316, Section 1317.

[159] 33 USC, Section 1362(16).

[160] *FDIC v. Meyer*, 510 U.S. 471, 476, 114 S.Ct. 996, 127 L.Ed.2d 308 (1994).

[161] Supra note 142, Section 1251(a).

[162] Ibid., Section 1362(19).

be viewed in terms of environmental protection as a whole. Central to the very existence of all ecosystems, the protection of water resources should be considered in all forms of environmental legislation, ensuring that it is afforded the highest priority as one of the earth's most valuable resources.

11 Marine Pollution

The sea (*sagar* in Sanskrit) is considered sacred in traditional culture and there are many stories connected to it. The resting place of the Hindu god Vishnu is supposed to be a bed that lies on the sea. Of the ten incarnations (*avatar*) of Lord Vishnu, two are marine species, namely the fish (*matsya*) and the tortoise (*koorma*). The state of Kerala is believed to be made up of land reclaimed from the sea by Parasurama, the sixth incarnation of Lord Vishnu. In another incarnation, when a demon named Hiranyaksa dragged the earth to the bottom of the sea, Vishnu reincarnated himself as a boar known as Varaha to save it. They fought for a thousand years until Varaha slayed the demon and raised the earth out of the water with his tusks.

In Hindu mythology the sea is personified as the diety Varuna. Before doing any activities affecting the sea, people pray to Varuna. Interestingly, many of the famous temples in India are located on the sea front.

The Bible also describes the divinity of the sea. The well-known story of Moses parting the waters of the Red Sea is explained in Exodus as follows:

And Moses stretched out his hand over the sea; and the Lord caused the sea to go back by a strong east wind all that night, and made the sea dry land, and the waters were divided. And the children of Israel went into the midst of the sea upon dry ground: the waters were a wall unto them on their right hand, and on their left.[1]

In modern times, the Government of India has taken steps to protect certain marine species. All cetaceans (whales, porpoises, and dolphins), ten species of elasmobranch (sharks and rays), holothurians, corals, nine species of molluscs, sea horses, and the giant grouper have been included in Schedule I of the Wildlife (Protection) Act, 1972 (WPA), thereby affording them the highest degree of protection. Hunting of these species is prohibited as per the provisions of the Act. With the amendments in the Act, the penalty for poaching species included in the Schedules of the Act and illegal trade in their parts and products has been enhanced.

India is a signatory to the International Whaling Commission (IWC), Convention on Migratory Species (CMS), and Convention on International Trade in Endangered Species of Wild Fauna and Flora (CITES) for conservation of marine species and their habitats, and for control of illegal trade in their parts and products.

MARINE POLLUTION

The disposal of low-level radioactive wastes, oil pollution from vessels, and pollution from land-based sources are some of the

---

[1] The Bible, Egyptians Drowned, The song of Mosses, Chapter XV–21.

main threats to maintaining a healthy marine environment in India.

The Convention on the Dumping of Wastes at Sea enacted in London, in November 1972[2] has a global character to regulate marine pollution and contributes to the international control and prevention of marine pollution. It prohibits the dumping of certain hazardous materials, and requires a prior special permit for the dumping of a number of other identified materials and a prior general permit for other wastes or matter.

'Dumping' has been defined as the deliberate disposal at sea of wastes or other matter from vessels, aircraft, platforms, or other man-made structures at sea, as well as the deliberate disposal at sea of vessels or aircrafts, platforms, or other man-made structures.[3]

Wastes derived from the exploration and exploitation of seabed mineral resources is, however, excluded from the definition. The provision of the Convention shall not apply when it is necessary to secure the safety of human life or of vessels in cases of force majeure.[4]

The Major Ports (Prevention and Control of Pollution) Rules, 1991[5] regulate pollution in port areas.[6] No vessel shall discharge, throw, allow to leak or flow, or allow to fall from a quay, jetty or pier, materials within the limits of a major port. The vessels are restrained from discharging ballast or oil mixtures within the port limits.[7] Where there is simultaneous loading of oils and deballasting, these are to be carried out by the master of the vessel only when he or she is satisfied that the loading pipeline has been efficiently separated, and the operation is conducted without polluting any waters.[8] Use of detergents to clear bilges or oil tanks is prohibited[9] and tank washings shall not be discharged overboard.[10] The discharge of hydrocarbons and escape of any oil is also restrained.[11] No vessel shall discharge, or allow the escape of, oil bilge water or any mixture of bilge water with chemicals or any noxious substance within the limits of a major port, without the written permission of the port authorities.[12]

The precautions prescribed in the Manual of Prevention of Oil Pollution and International Safety Guide should be strictly followed while loading, discharging, or transporting bunker ballast or deballast in port limits.[13] On arrival of a vessel, the port authorities shall verify whether a safety checklist of the above manual has been kept and the procedure prescribed in the checklist is followed.[14] If a vessel has any oil, water, or pollutant to be discharged at any major port, it shall give notice of at least twenty-four hours in the form annexed to the rules to the competent authority requesting him to arrange appropriate reception facilities.[15] The sea valves connected to oil cargo pipelines are to be tightly closed during the stay at the port.[16] No vessel shall bunker without permission in a major port by pipelines, barges, tanker lorries, or any

---

[2] London, Mexico City, Moscow, and Washington, dated 29 December 1972.

[3] Ibid., Article 3(a).

[4] Ibid., Article 3(b).

[5] Published in *the Gazette of India*, Ext, Part II Section 3(i) dated 1 May 1991.

[6] Major Ports (Prevention and Control of Pollution) Rules, 1991, Rule 3.

[7] Ibid., Rule 4.

[8] Ibid., Rule 5.

[9] Ibid., Rule 6.

[10] Ibid., Rule 7.

[11] Ibid., Rule 8.

[12] Ibid., Rule 9.

[13] Ibid., Rule 11.

[14] Ibid., Rule 17.

[15] Ibid., Rule 12.

[16] Ibid.

other means.[17] The master of a vessel and its terminal representative shall jointly ensure that the cargo and bunker house to be connected to the vessel are of approved type and quality, possessing a valid test certificate for use on the date, and the master shall be responsible for any pollution caused due to the bursting of a cargo bunker house.[18] The vessel must maintain a checklist on prevention of oil pollution.[19] If any oil or pollutant is found floating near or around a vessel, the onus of proving the same was not discharged from the said vessel is on the master of the ship.[20] The master must notify the competent authority immediately upon the occurrence of any oil spillage or contaminated water spillage from his own vessel or from any other vessel, if such spillage comes to his notice.[21]

LAWS FOR PROTECTING THE MARINE ENVIRONMENT

In the USA, major coastal and marine issues include the discharge of effluents, decline in fishery stocks, and development of off-shore oil platforms, coastal erosion, and natural coastal hazards, including storm surges. The Coastal Zone Management Act, 1972[22] lays down a framework for voluntary cooperation between the Federal Government and coastal States. The enactment identifies ten National Policy objectives, including the protection of natural resources, coastal development, and public access to information. Each state that possesses coastal areas imposes its own legislation, for example, the California Coastal Act, 1976, Connecticut Coastal Zone Management

Act, 1980, and Massachusetts Coastal Zone Management Programme.

In Canada, the Ocean Act, 1996[23] provides the framework for integrated management of the sea and protection of the marine environment from land-based activities that have an impact on estuaries and coastal waters.

In the UK, there are various laws for protecting marine resources. These laws are intended for fishery conservation, special economic zones, and other flora and fauna. The major coastal and marine issues are: pollution from industries and townships that damages the productive ecosystems, depletion of marine resources, and erosion of coastal areas.

The Convention on the Prevention of Marine Pollution by Dumping of Wastes and Other Matter[24] specifically regulates wastes loaded onto ships with the express intent of disposing them at sea, as opposed to discharge of wastes and other materials associated with ship operations. The Convention prohibits the dumping of certain substances including mercury, dichlorodiphenyltrichloroethane (DDT), Printed Circuit Boards, oil, and persistent plastics, and requires special sanctions for certain other wastes, such as low-level radioactive wastes, while allowing the dumping of other substances under a general permit.

Pollution from wastes associated with ship operations is regulated under the International Convention for the Prevention of Pollution from Ships, generally referred to as MARPOL, 73/78.[25] MARPOL contains five annexures, each directed at specific ship pollution issues, like pollution by oil, pollution by noxious liquid

---

[17] Ibid., Rule 13.
[18] Ibid., Rule 14.
[19] Ibid., Rule 17.
[20] Ibid., Rule 18.
[21] Ibid., Rule 19.
[22] Coastal Zone Management Act, 1972.

[23] Ocean Act, 1996.
[24] Convention on the Prevention of Marine Pollution by Dumping of Wastes and Other Matter, 1972, 1046 UNTS 120.
[25] 12 ILM1319 (1973) and 17 ILM 546 (1978). M.

substances carried in bulk, pollution by harmful substances carried in packages, pollution by ship sewage, and pollution by ship garbage.

Under the auspices of the Regional Seas Programme of the United Nations Environmental Program, countries around the world have developed coordinated action plans for addressing regional pollution problems.

Waste dumped into the ocean becomes a moving form of pollution, which raises interesting questions in terms of state and federal jurisdiction. In Canada,[26] a question arose before the court whether the dumping of waste in state waters could be regulated by federal statute where the said pollution was necessarily claimed to have a deleterious effect on federal waters. The respondent was charged on two counts under Section 4(1) of the Ocean Dumping Control Act,[27] each of which was the unlawful dumping of substances in the waters of Johnstone Strait near Beaver Cove in the province of British Columbia, without a permit. This section provides that 'no person shall dump except in accordance with the terms and conditions of a permit.'

The originating court held that the matter fell within the realm of provincial legislation and was not subject to the Federal Act, which purported to implement international conventions on dumping. The Crown further appealed these rulings and the question before the present court was whether Section 4(1) was ultra vires the power of the Canadian Parliament, and in particular was its application to the waters of Beaver Cove within the province of British Columbia ultra vires.[28]

The appellant successfully argued that the dumping of waste in provincial marine waters falls within the 'national concern doctrine…of the federal peace, order and good government power'[29] and was thus constitutional.[30] The court adopted the 'provincial inability' test that can be used to reach a 'finding that a particular matter is one of national concern falling within the peace, order and good government power [where a]…provincial failure to deal effectively with the intra-provincial aspects of the matter could have an adverse effect on extra-provincial interests.'[31] It stated that for a matter to fall within the doctrine, it must have a 'singleness or indivisibility' from national matters.[32]

The court stated that 'marine pollution, because of its predominantly extra-provincial as well as international character and implications, is clearly a matter of concern to Canada as a whole.'[33] In particular, it noted the nature of water pollution, finding favour with the appellant's argument that:

[T]he difficulty of ascertaining by visual observation the boundary between the territorial sea and the internal marine waters of a state creates an unacceptable degree of uncertainty for the application of regulatory and penal provisions. This, and not simply the possibility or likelihood of the movement of pollutants across that line, is what constitutes the essential indivisibility of the matter of marine pollution by the dumping of substances.[34]

In conclusion, the court did not hesitate to hold that Section 4(1) of the Ocean Dumping Control Act was constitutional and that the subject matter of the section fell within the National Concern Doctrine. Consequently, its

[26] R. v. Crown Zellerbach Canada Ltd, (1988) 1 SCR 401.

[27] Ocean Dumping Control Act, SC 1974–75–76, c. 55.

[28] Supra note 26, Section 15.

[29] See for example Attorney-General for Ontario v. Attorney-General for the Dominion, (1896) AC 348 at supra note 26, Section 24.

[30] Supra note 26, Section 23.

[31] Supra note 26, Section 35.

[32] Supra note 26, Section 35.

[33] Supra note 26, Section 37.

[34] Supra note 26, Section 38.

application to the provincial waters of British Columbia at Beaver Cove was valid.

Marine pollution in India is also an issue for the country as a whole, where states are often bound to create laws consistent with the overall law of the Central Government.

FISHERIES REGULATIONS

To maintain marine ecology, fishery activities must be controlled. The Indian Fisheries Act, 1897 is intended to protect freshwater fishes in private waters. This Act supplements other state enactments. It prohibits the use of dynamite[35] and poison in all waters.[36] The state government has been empowered to make rules regulating fishing activities, like the erection and use of fixed engines, construction of weirs, dimension, and kind of nets, and the like.[37]

State fisheries regulations and the WPA[38] protect sea turtles. The sea turtle's meat and eggs were available on the Orissa coast. The WPA[39] includes all sea turtles in the list of protected species of animals. The nesting beaches and offshore waters at Orissa, being the habitat of turtles, demand protection during the breeding and nesting season, by the Orissa Forest Department.

The studies conducted by the Tata Energy Research Institute (TERI) in 1996 concluded that the low-lying areas in Orissa, like Satabhya village, are vulnerable to sea level rise. The Satbhaya region, once a cluster of seven villages, is 25 kilometres from the Paradip Port at the confluence of the rivers Mahanadi and Brahmani, and close to the Bhitrkanika National Park. The road to Satbhaya has

prawn fisheries on both sides and the villagers have noticed that the sea water is rising every year.[40]

TRAWLING BAN

A common method of fishing is that of trawling. However, if fish stocks are continually trawled throughout the year, they can become significantly depleted.

The Bible contains several clear hints about the importance of non-working days. Resting for one day in seven was part of God's plan for human beings to be healthy. He also gave instructions about rest for the environment, especially for the land for growing crops on:

Plant and harvest your crops for six years, but let the land rest and lie fallow during the seventh year. Then let the poor among you harvest any volunteer crop that may come up. Leave the rest for the animals to eat. The same applies to your vineyards and olive groves.[41]

The same applies to fish stocks, which also need rest from human interference, so that they may recover healthily.

Trawling during the monsoon period can be particularly devastating for fish stocks because it is in this season that various species spawn. Particularly when bottom trawling occurs during the monsoon season, fish stocks are deprived of the opportunity to properly replenish themselves and conservation of marine resources is threatened.[42]

There is an abundance of fishery resources in the state of Kerala. However, this has been on the decline since 1980, which led to a

---

[35] Indian Fisheries Act, 1897, Section 4.

[36] Ibid., Section 5.

[37] Ibid., Section 6.

[38] Wildlife (Protection) Act, 1972.

[39] See separate head under Wildlife (Protection) Act.

[40] Sonu Jain, 'Sea Change', *The New Indian Express*, dated 10 July 2006.

[41] Bible, Exodus, Chapter 23, Verses 10–11.

[42] K.G. Kumar, 'Monsoon fishing woes', *The Hindu, Business Line* (6 June 2006) available at < http://www.blonnet.com/2006/06/06/stories/2006060601841900.htm> last accessed 6 June 2007.

demand for a scientific enquiry into the various causes, and institution of appropriate measures for stock enhancement. The state government decided to ban trawling in waters beyond a distance of 10 kilometres, night trawling, purse seining, ring seining, pelagic-trawling, mid-water-trawling, and monsoon trawling. The government appointed a Committee[43] to study the need for conservation of marine fishery resources. The opinion of the Committee was divided in regard to the specific need for adopting a closed season as a management measure for trawling boats. Consequently, the Government of Kerala appointed another Committee in 1984[44] to examine whether the existing area of restrictions under the Kerala Marine Fishing Regulation Act, 1980[45] on mechanized fishing requires alteration without adversely affecting the interests of traditional fishermen. The Kalawar Committee did not agree to ban monsoon trawling but suggested a series of measures for the conservation and management of resources, like a reduction in the number of boats. Unfortunately, the said recommendations could not be implemented, resulting in serious threats to the fishery sector. It is under the above circumstances that the Government of Kerala appointed another Committee[46] in 1989.

The Balakrishnan Nair Committee has recommended immediate measures like the following:

1. All bar mouths shall be declared protected zones devoid of any fishing activities.
2. With a view to minimizing very heavy fishing pressure on resources from the stake and Chinese nets, which have phenomenally increased during the past

five years, it is recommended that no fresh licence be given for new ones and all the existing unlicensed ones be promptly dismantled and removed. The large number of licensed nets already existing demands the need for the phasing out of at least 50 per cent of them. All the authorized (licensed) fixed engines (Chinese nets and Stake nets) existing at present are to be registered or re-registered before 31 August 1989 and an appropriate registration number allotted. The registration number must be compulsorily displayed on the fixed engines.

3. Fixed engines owned by persons other than fishermen and those existing with *benami* ownership are also to be removed. No organization, agency, board, or body except fishermen's cooperatives duly recognized by the Department of Fisheries shall be given licence to own and operate fixed engines.
4. Undesirable and destructive fishing practices such as the use of dynamite (*thotta*), poisoning, *madavala*, electric fishing, padal and torch fishing, and other such activities (to be identified by the Department of Fisheries) are to be banned.
5. Existing prohibition on fishing during high tide using fixed engines should be strictly enforced. Mesh size of the cod-end of state or Chinese nets should not be less than 25 mm.
6. A large-scale programme should be envisaged to convert all traditional prawn filtration fields into scientifically managed prawn or fish culture farms in due course.
7. Harvest by poisoning in prawn filtration fields is to be banned.
8. A large-scale welfare scheme shall be launched with a view to removing or

---

[43] Babu Paul Committee, 1981.

[44] A.G. Kalawar, 1984.

[45] Kerala Marine Fishing Regulation Act, 1980.

[46] Balakrishnan Nair Committee.

replacing all the hanging latrines built over or emptying into the backwaters.

9. The Fisheries Department and Pollution Control Board together should take up appropriate measures for preventing water pollution, which is deleterious to fish and other living resources.

10. Action shall be taken to declare backwaters and other identified areas adjacent to backwaters and the sea as aquaculture areas. Reclamation and use of these areas for non-fishery purposes shall be prohibited. Necessary laws to protect and use these areas have to be framed at the earliest.

11. An enforcement wing with necessary facilities and infrastructure should be set up separately for enforcing the regulations and law and order concerning the backwaters.

This report is now being used for curtailing activities in the fisheries sector. The imposition of trawling bans in some states has led to an undue advantage in favour of states that use their mechanized boats for trawling in the states where the bans exist. Such practices should be discouraged by the law and monitored by the authorities.

In 2006, the Supreme Court of India went beyond the measures adopted by the Kalawar Committee, and placed a uniform ban on fishing by mechanized boats and trawlers during the monsoon period on the west coast of India.[47] The Court considered the extent to which trawling depletes natural fish stocks when conducted throughout the monsoon period and was also mindful of the rights of traditional fisherman. The Court recounted that there was already a uniform ban imposed by the Government of India on deep sea fishing within

the exclusive economic zone and territorial waters of west coast states from 10 June to 15 August. Deep sea fishing is effectively banned on the west coast of India. On this basis, the Court imposed the ban on mechanized boats and trawlers in the coastal waters of Maharashtra, Gujarat, Goa, Karnataka, and Kerala from 10 June to 15 August. For the purposes of the ban, a mechanized boat or fishing vessel is defined as a vessel with mechanical means of propulsion and includes crafts that have an inboard or outboard motor above 10 BHP horse power. The Court further deemed the matter as subject to review before the monsoon period of 2008.

In the UK, the practice of pelagic pair trawling has come under scrutiny from environmental groups, due to its association with dolphin mortality.[48] Greenpeace contended that the Department for Environment Food and Rural Affairs (DEFRA) had failed to fulfil its obligations in respect of Article 12(4) of the European Union Habitats Directive when it made an order in respect of pair trawling for the purposes of minimizing dolphin bycatch mortality. The Directive[49]

requires Member States to establish a system to monitor the incidental killing of (among other animals) crustaceans, and in the light of the information gathered, to take further measures to ensure that incidental capture and killing do not have a significant negative impact on the species concerned.[50]

DEFRA agreed to impose a 12-nautical-mile ban on all sea bass pelagic pair trawling fisheries as this form of fishing had evidenced the greatest dolphin bycatch. It then proposed

---

[47] *Goa Environment Foundation v. Union of India and Others* (writ petition No. 33 of 2005).

[48] *The Queen on the Application of Greenpeace Limited v. The Secretary of State for the Environment, Food and Rural Affairs,* (2005) EWHC 2144 (Admin), Section 5.
[49] Habitats Directive (92/43EEC) of 21 May 1992 Article 12.4.
[50] Supra note 48.

to approach the European Commission to extend the ban to all bass pair trawling fisheries within the 12-mile zone. When the UK approached the Commission, it rejected their request to have the ban extended to vessels that pair trawl for bass, on the basis that it was arbitrary, and dolphin bycatch could also be attributed to other fisheries.[51]

Greenpeace and other organizations concerned with animal protection were confident that the twelve-mile ban would not mitigate dolphin loss; if anything, they feared that it would aggravate it. Data suggested that the greatest amount of dolphin loss due to the industry occurred beyond this twelve-mile limit and that some foreign fisheries were accountable for a greater percentage of the bycatch. The applicants sought the closure of the entirety of the bass fishing industry until proper means of reducing dolphin bycatch could be demonstrated.[52] In response to the ban, the UK Marine Conservation Society stated that the ban should apply to all UK vessels regardless of where they were fishing and to foreign vessels fishing in UK waters.[53]

In resolving the dispute, the court simply looked at the enabling statute to discern whether the Fisheries Minister had acted within the power. Under the Act, the minister was empowered to make restrictions 'for marine environment purposes', including the purpose of 'conserving fauna dependent on, or associated with, a marine or coastal environment'[54] and the order was such that it conformed to this power. Interestingly, the court noted the various claims as to the irrationality of the ban, but was quick to note

that administrative actions cannot be struck down lightly.

COASTAL ZONE MANAGEMENT—INDIA

India has a coastline of 6000 kilometres. For the protection of Indian coastal areas and compliance with the principles and requirements of environmental conservation, the Government of India (GOI) issued a notification dated 19 February 1991 under the Environment (Protection) Act, 1986, popularly called as the 'Coastal Regulation Zone (CRZ) Notification, 1991'.[55] The coastal stretches of the country, the land upto 500 metres on the landward side along the coast and the water area upto its territorial water limit, are declared as Coastal Regulation Zone (CRZ). In case of creek and other tidal influenced water bodies, the distance of regulation zone shall be only 100 metres or width of such water body, whichever is less. The water between low tide and high tide is also the CRZ.

The CRZ areas are classified into five different categories. The ecologically sensitive areas are classified as the CRZ-I areas. The developed areas close to the shoreline are the CRZ-II areas. The areas that are relatively undisturbed and those do not belong to other categories fall in the CRZ-III. The Andaman Nicobar and Lakshadweep islands are included in the CRZ-IV category.

More restrictions are imposed on constructions in the CRZ-I areas wherein no activities are permitted. In the CRZ-II areas constructions on the landward side of existing buildings or structures are permitted. In the CRZ-III areas up to 200 metres from the HTL is no development zone in case of seafront and 100 metres in case of backwaters.

[51] Supra note 48, Section 58.

[52] Supra note 48, Section 32.

[53] Supra note 48, Section 34.

[54] Sea Fish Conservation Act, 1967 (UK), Section 5A as amended by the Environment Act, 1995 (UK) in Supra note 48, Section 70.

[55] Notification No. S.O.114 (E), dated 19 February 1991; published in *the Gazette of India* (Extra) No. 105, dated 20 Feb 1997, Part II, Section 3(ii).

In the CRZ-IV category separate distance rules were imposed for Andaman and Nicobar and Lakshadweep Islands.

To identify the CRZ areas the states were required to prepare a Coastal Zone Management Plan (CZMP) classifying and identifying the said areas within their territory. The CRZ notification was amended on 29 December 1998 insisting for the demarcation of HTL uniformly in all parts of the country.

Though the notification came in 1991, it was not implemented, resulting in the Supreme Court of India interfering with a public interest litigation. The Court directed the states to prepare the CZMPs and implement the CRZ.[56] When the said PIL was pending, the GOI amended the notification in 1995[57] making six amendments to the 1991 notification. One of the amendments permitted and granted power to the GOI to relax the said notification on any part of the country. The Court struck down the said amendment which gave arbitrary, uncanalized, and unguided power, the exercise of which might result in serious ecological degradation and might make the CRZ ineffective.

The 1991 notification had led to a lot of ambiguity, and gave rise to a series of litigations. The construction of public toilets near the Gateway of India in Mumbai was opposed on the basis of an alleged violation of the CRZ. The Bombay High Court held that there was no violation as the said toilets were constructed on the footpath, that is, on the existing road,[58] and the area had already been completely developed. Rejecting the contention that as a historical area

it fell within the CRZ-I, the court held that the 'CRZ-I would not be applicable to an area which had a fully developed CRZ-II area, and was close to the shore line.

The construction of a bulk receiving station by an electric company in Mumbai was opposed as a violation of the CRZ laws. The Bombay High Court held that there was an utmost need for bulk receiving station in the locality and it is the larger public interest which will prevail, particularly in case of two competing public interests.[59]

It is alleged that the construction of a hotel complex in Goa altering the sand dunes on the beach is violation of the CRZ norms. The Supreme Court held that as the Central Government had taken due care in seeking reports and a spot inspection on the feasibility of the clearing up of the hotel project from the authorities, there was no violation of the CRZ.[60] The Court refused to accept the report of the National Institute of Oceanography on the pretext that the construction would have been carried out on the demolition of the sand dunes.

The laying of a petroleum pipeline through the Jamnagar Marine National Park and Sanctuary in the state of Gujarat was challenged before the Supreme Court. The Court held that the project was one of the exceptions to the general bar against any construction in the CRZ-I areas.[61] It could not be said that the invariable consequence of laying pipelines through ecologically sensitive areas was the destruction or removal of wildlife.

Cochin Marine Drive area was developed after 1991. A dispute arose before the Kerala

[56] *Indian Council For Enviro-Legal Action v. Union of India*, 1996 (5) SCC 281.
[57] Notification No. SO 595(E), dated 18 August 1994 issued by the Ministry of Environment and Forests.
[58] *Navin Kumar v. Bombay Municipal Corporation*, AIR 1997 Bom 342.

[59] *Sneha Mandal Co-operative Housing Society v. Union of India*. AIR 2000 SC 121.
[60] *Goa Foundation v. Diksha Holdings*, AIR 2001 SC 184: 2001 (2) SCC 97.
[61] *Essar Oil Limited v. Halar Ukarsh Samithi*, AIR 2004 SC 1834: 2004 (2) SCC 392.

High Court contending that the said lands fell within the CRZ area, and therefore construction was not possible. Repelling the contention, the court held that the area fell under the CRZ-II, wherein construction was possible on the landward side of the existing road. Though there was no road, the court held that the pathway which lay between land and the backwaters could be considered a road; and there was a proposal for the road on the said area, therefore construction could be permitted.[62]

The Bombay Municipal Corporation chose *Gorai* Creek as a dumping place in gross violation of the directives contained in the said CRZ notification, 1991. The Bombay High Court interfered with the matter and restrained them from dumping in the creek, which formed part of the CRZ.[63]

A building was constructed without securing permission from the competent authorities in a CRZ area. The Bombay High Court directed the demolition of the entire construction. The judgement was challenged before the Supreme Court. Upholding the demolition order, the Court stressed the need for protecting the environment and ecology in coastal areas.[64] Construction raised in violation of such regulations cannot be lightly condoned, the Court added. The judgement thus acts as a deterrent to others who seek to do the same.

The CZMP's were prepared by the State in 1996. Amendments were made to the CRZ notification thereafter. Certain agencies have prepared new CZMP's on the basis of the said new amendments including more areas. Supreme Court had held that the authorities cannot override the plan prepared and approved under paragraph 3 (3) (i) of the 1991 notification as the said paragraph leaves no manner of doubt that Plan prepared by State and duly approved by the MoEF is the relevant plan for identification and classification of CRZ areas.[65]

The series of judicial pronouncements, representations from stake holders, and recommendations of some committees led to the appointment of a committee headed by Dr M.S. Swaminathan, to review the reports of various experts on the field, international practices, and suggest the scientific principles for an integrated coastal zone management suited for the country.[66]

Taking note of the natural disasters and other development activities various recommendations were made. The committee was of the opinion that for addressing the coastal problems in a holistic manner, the water part, that is, the ocean, and tidal water bodies, should be included. The regulatory framework should aim at integrated and sustainable coastal zone management. Stakeholders' participation and decentralization of the decision making process and management are desirable objectives in their own right. The participation of local self government institutions is to be ensured. Provisions for a public review process should be made mandatory. The need for the raising of mangroves, plantations of casuarinas, saliconnia, leucaena, atriplex, palms, bamboo, and other trees species and hatophytes should be planted near the sea.

[62] *Institute of Social Welfare v. State.* 1997 (2) KLJ 153.

[63] *Vijay Mahadeo Daruwale v. Municipal Corporation of Greater Mumbai*, Writ Petition No. 489 Of 2004, dated 20 July 2005.

[64] *Piedade Filomena v. State of Goa*, 2004 (3) SCC 445: 2004 (3) SCALE 369.

[65] *M. Nizamudeen v. Chemplast.* AIR 2010 SC 1765 : 2010 (4) SCC 240

[66] Order No. 15 (8)/2004-IA-III, dated 19th July, 2004 of the Government of India, Ministry of Environment and Forests.

The ground water in coastal areas should be declared as social resource.[67]

Based on the said recommendations two separate notifications were issued. The one for the protection of Islands and the other is for the remaining coastal areas. Both the said Coastal Regulation Zone and the Island Coastal Regulation Zone notifications came into force with effect from 6 January 2011.[68]

Most of the provisions are almost similar. The 2011 notification gives a special status to certain areas of certain states like Kerala, Greater Mumbai, Sundarbans of West Bengal, and Goa. The new notifications are more transparent, which give local authorities a role in the preparation of the CZMP. The present law also contemplated the mapping of hazard line throughout the coast line by the Ministry of Environment and Forests. The guidelines for the preparation of these CZMPs insist on the demarcation of the High Tide Line. The common man will be able to identify and locate the HTL only if it is demarcated. For an effective implementation of the law it is essential that it should be understood by the people. The local level CZMPs can be used by the local bodies to facilitate effective implementation.

In addition to this, the 2011 notifications included the water and the bed area between low tide level to the territorial water limit (12 nautical miles) in case of sea and the water and the bed area between low water level on the bank to the low tide level on the opposite side of the bank, of tidal influenced water bodies. The water should have a salinity of 5 parts per thousand measured during the driest period of the year.[69]

Since the Island part of the 1991 notification has been included in the IRZ notification, 2011, the CRZ-IV has been used for including the water part, that is the area from Low Tide Line to twelve nautical miles on the seaward side. The backwater areas of Kerala including backwaters and backwater islands fall in this category. Critically vulnerable areas of the Sundarbans region of West Bengal and other ecologically sensitive areas also fall within this zone.[70]

In the CRZ-IV areas there are restrictions on discharge of untreated effluents, ballast water, ship washes, flay ash, and solid waste. There is no restriction on traditional fishing. The CRZ-V category gives special benefits to Greater Mumbai, backwaters of Kerla and Goa. For the construction of beach resorts or hotels in the designated areas of the CRZ-III and the CRZ-II for occupation of tourists or visitors certain constructions are allowed which require permission from the MoEF.[71]

One of the essential features of this notification is that it contemplates the preparation of demarcation of the said CRZ areas. Common man will not be able to understand the restrictive areas unless it is demarcated. The main failure of the CRZ, 1991 notification is that there is no clarity with regard to the scale at which demarcations have to be carried out.[72]

The CRZ, 2011 contemplates preparing a Coastal Zone Management Plan (CZMP) by the states and obtaining approval of the Central Government. The guidelines for the preparation of the CZMP gives public a hand in the preparation of the same. The suggestions and objections received from the local public

---

[67] Report of the Committee chaired by Professor M.S. Swaminathan, February 2005.

[68] Published in *the Gazettee of India*, Extraordinary, Part-II, Section 3, Sub-section (ii) dated 6 January 2011.

[69] Clause 1 (i) to (iii) of the CRZ notification dated 6ᵗ January 2011.

[70] Clause 7 of the CRZ Notification, 2011.

[71] Annexure-II of the CRZ Notification, 2011.

[72] See paragraph 3.4.24 of the report of the M.S. Swamninathan, February 2005.

on the draft maps have to be considered before the preparation of the final CZMP.[73]

It is taking note of the need of the traditional coastal communities including fishermen and incorporating the necessary disaster management provisions. Sanitation and certain activities are permitted in the no-development zone in the CRZ-III areas. The said activities include agriculture, horticulture, gardens, pastures, parks, play fields, and forestry. The construction of dispensaries, schools, public rain shelter, community toilets, bridges, roads, provision of facilities for water supply, drainage, sewarge, crematoria, cemeteries, and electric sub-stations which are required for the local inhabitants may be permitted on case to case basis by the CZMA. Green field airport in Greater Mumbai is also permitted. In coastal areas between 200 metres to 500 metres construction of hotels or beach resorts for tourists or visitors subject to certain conditions is permitted. The re-construction of existing authorized structures is also permitted.[74]

After the said notification, the GOI issued an office memorandum permitting removal of sand bar by traditional coastal communities by manual method in various coastal states subject to certain conditions.[75]

The islands of Andaman Nicobar and Lakshadweep are governed by the Island Coastal Regulations Zone Notification, 2011 which also contains similar provisions as in the CRZ. The islands are classified into four categories. Certain activities like destruction of corals, mining of sand, hard constructions for shore protection, disposal of untreated sewage or effluents, disposal of solid wastes including fly ash, industrial waste, medical waste, non-biodegradable waste, and the like.[76]

The damages caused by the Tsunami in Japan in March 2011, stress the need for protecting the coastal areas. The destruction of Fukushima Nuclear power plant in Japan has stressed the need to keep the coast free from constructions. The distance rule imposed by law is also intended for the safety of the public at large.

COAST GUARD—SECURITY OF MARITIME ZONES

India has the Coast Guard Act, 1978 for the constitution and regulation of the Armed Forces for the Union to ensure the security of the maritime zones of India, and protect maritime and other national interests in such zones and matters ancillary to this. The duties and functions of the Coast Guard include the protection, by measures it deems fit, of the maritime and other national interests of India in the maritime zones of India. Such measures include taking necessary preventive to preserve and protect the maritime environment, and prevent and control marine pollution.[77] They also have a duty to protect the artificial islands, off-shore terminals, installations, and other structures and devices in any maritime zone. The Coast Guard works in liaison with Union agencies, institutions, and authorities so as to avoid duplication of effort.

COASTAL RESTRICTIONS—DEVELOPMENTS ABROAD

India is not the only country to have coastal restrictions. The coastal restrictions imposed on developed countries and developing countries differ. Most of the developed countries such

---

[73] Annexure–I of the CRZ Notification, 2011.

[74] Clause 8–III of the CRZ notification, 2011.

[75] Office Memorandum No. 11-83/2005-IA-III (Vol–III) dated 8 November 2011.

[76] Island Coastal Regualation Zone Notification, 2011.

[77] Coast Guard Act, 1978, Section 14(c).

as the USA, UK, and New Zealand have prepared vulnerability maps of their coastal areas. Different countries have adopted different setback zones based on developed activities, geomorphology, ecosystems, and other such parameters. Ecuador has a setback distance of 8 metres, and New Zealand has a distance of 20 metres. The set up distance for the USSR-Coast of the Black Sea is 3,000 metres. Countries like Oregon and the Philippines have set up permanent vegetation lines as the setback distance.

In the USA, the Coastal Zone Management Act, 1972 lays down a framework for voluntary cooperation between the Federal Government and coastal states as in India, the states have a duty to implement the coastal management systems. The states determine the boundaries of the coastal zone, the main problems in coastal areas, and the policies and the laws that address them. Local governments, including cities, countries, and sub-state regional entities are the implanting agencies of the state coastal policies and programmes. Under the Coastal Zone Management Authority, all three levels of government—federal, state, and central—are given important roles to play and considerable flexibility in defining these roles.

In Canada, there are various enactments, which include the Fraser River Estuary Management Programme, 1985, the Great Lakes Water Quality Programme, 1987, Atlantic Coastal Action Plan, 1986 and the Canada Ocean Act, 1996.

In the UK, there are thirty pieces of legislation for the protection of marine resources. Most of them are sectoral, applying either to the land or the sea. In the absence of an integrated policy for protection of the coastal environment, the coastal zone management is not being implemented properly. Shoreline management plans based on the sediment cell concept have been prepared on a priority-basis and are being implemented.

The main problems faced by the Australian coast are habitat destruction, resource depletion, stakeholder conflicts, and Government fragmentation due to sectoral approaches, offshore development programmes, and excessive coastal fisheries. The following are examples of regulations available: Western Australia State Coastal Review of 1994 and 1995, Queensland Coastal Management Bill, 1995, Victoria Coastal and Bay Management Act, 1995, New South Wales Revised Coastal Policy, 1996, Tasmanian Draft State Coastal Policy, the Commonwealth Coastal Policy, 1997, and the National Ocean Policy,1996.

New South Wales has the Coastal Protection Act, 1979, which is similar to the Indian legislation (CRZ Notification). The Act requires public authorities to prepare the Coastal Zone Management Plans in certain circumstances, in accordance with the Coastline Management Manual, 1990.

For the protection of the coastal environment, the Netherlands has the North Sea Harmonisation Policy, 1984; Dynamic Preservation Strategy, 1991; and the Coastal Defence Act, 1995. The main problems faced are habitat destruction, resource depletion, and stakeholder conflicts due to offshore development programmes, excessive fishing operations, and Government fragmentation due to a segmental approach.

The Shore Act, 1988 and Regional Guidelines for Coastal Zone, 1992 have been legislated to protect the coastal areas of Spain.

Developing countries like Brazil have enacted Ocean Planning, 1994; Environmental Laws, 1980, and Coastal Programme, 1983 for coastal management.

The Jamaican Beach Control Act, 1956 provides that no person shall be deemed to have any rights in or over the foreshore of the island or the floor of the sea save such as are derived from or acquired or preserved under or by virtue of this Act. It prevents encroachments and licence for using the beach front.

In Thailand, various national initiatives have been taken up, including the National Coral Reef Management Strategy, 1991, and an Integrated Coastal Zone Management Plan in Ban Doon Bay and Phangaga Bay. Coastal zone management has been moderately effective and some initiatives have been taken up for integrated management of coastal areas.

Initiatives taken in Malaysia include the National and Coastal Resource Management Policy, 1992 and South Johore Coastal Plan, 1992. These regulate the prevention of coastal erosion and conservation of mangrove forests.

Sri Lanka has enacted the Coast Conservation Act, 1983, Coast Permit System, 1988, Coastal Zone Management Plan, 1980, Marine Pollution Prevention Authority, 1990, and the Special Area Management Plan, 1996. The setback line is 300 metres from the sea based on a coastal erosion rate, cyclones, geomorphological characteristics, vulnerability to coastal habitats, cultural sites, and other conditions. Coastal zone management plans are prepared for each state, identifying restrictive areas.

It can be concluded that India is apace with many other nations in its Coastal Management Strategies.

COASTAL RESTRICTIONS—FOREIGN CASE LAW

United States of America

The *Mountain Rhythms*[78] case demonstrates the cooperation required between State and Federal

Agencies under the Coastal Zone Management Act. In this case, the petitioners wanted to build a hydroelectric dam in Washington, in an area that was designated as part of the Coastal Management Zone pursuant to the Act. The Coastal Zone under the Act is described as

the coastal waters…and the adjacent shorelands… and includes islands, transitional and intertidal areas, salt marshes, wetlands, and beaches…. The zone extends inland from the shorelines only to the extent necessary to control shorelands, the uses of which have a direct and significant impact on the coastal waters.[79]

In order to undertake their project, the petitioners were required to acquire a licence from the Federal Energy Regulatory Commission. However, since the area fell within the Coastal Management Zone, this licence was in many respects contingent on the approval of the State Department of Ecology that the project would not stifle the objectives of the Coastal Zone Management Plan, as formulated under the Act. In order for the state to grant approval, they needed a permit from the particular county.

The petitioners thought it fanciful that an area so far from the coastline be designated as part of the zone. Hence, they did not seek a permit and were consequently denied a permit by the FERC to build the dam. They argued that the coastal zone was too widely defined by the map formulated by the state of Washington and that such a wide zone violates the Act, being unnecessary to control shorelands:[80]

Mountain Rhythm Companies argue that the project sites are located so far from the coastline, some 45 miles as the fish swims up river, some 30 miles as the bald eagle flies (when it is flying

---

[78] *Mountain Rhythm Resources v. Federal Energy Regulatory Commission. Mountain Water Resources; Watersong Resources v. Federal Energy Regulatory Commission*, 302 F. 3d 958, 964.

[79] Coastal Zone Mangement Act 16 USC, Section 1453(1).

[80] Supra note 78.

straight), that they should not be considered within Washington's coastal zone.[81]

In considering the matter, the court took an ecosystem-based approach, which is often the case with Indian courts, noting the existence of mountain streams in the area and the fact that water runs downstream for 45 miles before hitting the coastline. Sediments expelled by the dam could ultimately affect the marine environment. The definition of the coastal zone was left intact and the court stressed that Mountain Rhythms had failed to access the correct administrative channels[82] and hence, there was no improper action on the part of the state or federal authorities.

Chile

In Chile, a mining company deposited its copper tailing wastes directly onto the beaches of Chanaral, destroying all traces of marine life in the area. A survey conducted in 1983 by the UNEP listed Chanaral as one of the Pacific Ocean's most serious cases of marine pollution from industrial waste. To halt further environmental degradation, a number of Chanaral residents and various organizations approached the Supreme Court. The Court of Appeals of Copiapo made a personal survey and report of the pollution at Chanaral. Through aerial and terrestrial inspections, this report concluded that the Chanaral coastline has been devastated by pollution from mining activities. The company has a one-year period, from the date of the decision, to put a definitive end to its dumping of mineral tailings into the Pacific Ocean. The company was directed to build a dam to dispose off its wastes.[83]

---

[81] Ibid.
[82] Supra note 79.
[83] *Pedro Flores Y Otros v. Corporacion Del Cobre, Codelco, Division Salvador*, Recurso De Proteccion.Copiapo Rol. 12.753. Fs. 641 (1988).

Hawaii

In India, many disputes regarding coastal management arise when a development is proposed in a defined coastal zone and the same can be said for other jurisdictions. In the Hawaiian case, *Larry T. Topliss, dba Pacific Land Company v. The Planning Commission and the Planning Department of the County of Hawaii*,[84] the petitioner was denied the permission to construct an apartment building within the Special Management Area (SMA) as declared under the Coastal Zone Management Act. The petitioner argued that his property should be excluded from the SMA and pleaded for review of the denial of the permit.

The court reiterated the legislature's intent in enacting the authorizing statute, affirming that

[S]pecial controls on developments within an area along the shoreline are necessary to avoid permanent losses of valuable resources and the foreclosure of management options, and to ensure that adequate access, by dedication or other means, to public owned or used beaches, recreation areas, and natural reserves is provided.[85]

Much like the *Mountain Rhythms* case, the petitioner argued that the said area should not form part of the SMA as it posed 'no potential for direct or substantial impact upon either the coastal water or the coastal resources to be protected.'[86] The court noted that amongst the objectives of the Act is the protection of the public right to enjoy views of the shoreline. There is mention of 'coastal scenic resources',[87] which is interesting as it appears

---

[84] *Larry T. Topliss, dba Pacific Land Company v. The Planning Commission and The Planning Department of the County of Hawaii*, 9 Haw. App. 377.
[85] Hawaii Revised Statutes, Section 205A-21 (1985) cited in 385.
[86] Supra note 83.
[87] Ibid.

that the zoning may be used to protect the environment in its aesthetic beauty as it exists for the enjoyment of present and future generations, this being similar to the Indian view of the environment. The court did not hesitate to hold that the petitioner's property fell within the SMA in conformity with the Act, noting that protection of the environment and ecology is only one of the objectives of the Act. However, the appeal against the denial of the permit found favour with the court and it is worth noting in brief, the reasons for this. The Commission had found that construction would have an adverse impact on the adjacent highway system and on this basis it denied the permit. The court was adamant that the Commission had failed to point at a 'substantial adverse environmental or ecological effect on the coastal zone'[88] and that consequently, it was bound to exercise its discretion in favour of the petitioner. In order to deny the permit, the Commission would have had to ground its reasons in the objectives of Coastal Zone Management Act and if no such reasons existed, the development was to proceed.

South Africa

In South Africa, an associated group of anglers sought a declaration that government regulations prohibiting the use of vehicles on the beach was ultra vires the authorizing Act. This case demonstrates the various interests that must be balanced in managing coastal areas. The applicants sought to prove that the regulations made by the Minister of Environmental Affairs and Tourism under Section 44 of the NEMA (107 of 1998) were ultra vires and unconstitutional. The regulations restricted the recreational use of certain vehicles within the coastal zone except for in limited

circumstances, upon the successful granting of a permit by the minister.

In arguing that the regulations were ultra vires, the applicants contended that the minister of Environmental Affairs and Tourism intruded upon the powers of the Minister for Transport to make regulations under the Seashore Act (21 of 1935). Under Section 10 of the Act, the Minister for Transport may make regulations 'concerning the use of the seashore' whereas the NEMA empowers the minister to make regulations 'generally, to carry out the purposes and the provisions of this Act.'[89] The applicants forwarded that the powers of the Minister for Environmental Affairs and Tourism are subordinate to those of the Minister for Transport in respect of the seashore, and that the Minister for Transport has the power to regulate the said area. In particular, Regulation 23 is ultra vires as it goes beyond the powers of the enabling Act, that is, NEMA.

The court acknowledged that the powers of the ministers do overlap and that this may pose the potential for conflict. However, this does not detract or nullify their respective powers under the Acts as they possess different objectives,[90] and although they may overlap, they are not inconsistent.[91]

The applicants argued that the Act was unconstitutional. In attempting to activate the court's power of judicial review over the administrative matter, it is argued that these regulations unreasonably interfered with their activities, that in some places it would be impossible to conduct competition fishing,

---

[88] Ibid.

[89] *South African Shore Angling Association and Die Oesterbaai Se Balasting-Betalersvereniging v. The Minister of Environmental Affairs and Tourism,* (High Court of South Africa) No. 63/02, 3.

[90] Supra note 83.

[91] Ibid.

as the only means of access is by vehicle. It was also contended that the regulations discriminate against elderly and disabled persons who have difficulty in otherwise accessing the beach area, which was about six kilometres away from the village, if it were not for the use of vehicles. The enjoyment of the beach in hard-to-reach areas would be unreasonably interfered with. A decrease in property values was also foreshadowed as sections of the shoreline would be inaccessible to residents by vehicle. Overall, this would negatively impact the tourism industry, the applicants concluded.

The court analysed the scheme imposed by the regulations and was satisfied that it effectively imposed a ban on the use of off-road vehicles but was fair in allowing exceptions and licensing for activities that would not harm the coastal environment. Section 24 of the Constitution, which is effectively the right to a healthy environment, was identified as the basis for NEMA. Section 2(r) of NEMA gives effect to this constitutional provision.[92]

The regulations reflected both the Act and the Constitution. The arguments presented by the applicants in relation to the economic disadvantages of the regulations were credible; however, in view of the objectives of NEMA, the court held that economic development and environmental protection must be properly balanced. Since the regulations provided procedures for exemption from the ban and licensing, this balance could be fairly met in any given case.

As in India, the South African Court was faced with the task of balancing competing interests. The balance between coastal protection, public enjoyment, and economic development can be struck with the use of creative schemes.

INTERNATIONAL LAW ON COASTAL PROTECTION

International agencies have recommended various measures for the protection of coastal zone management. The United Nations Conference on Environment and Development (UNCED) (Agenda 21), chapter 17 deals with protection of the oceans, seas, and coastal areas. It recommends integrated management and sustainable development, with an emphasis on marine environment protection, sustainable use, and conservation of living resources and climate change.

UNEP guidelines state that 'integrated management of coastal areas is required to lay the foundation for sustainable development.'[93] UNEP does not recommend specific boundaries. However, the first step of the planning stage is the prescriptive definition of coastal area boundaries. The goals are to provide guidelines for legal and institutional strategy in area management and planning, forming of committees for dispute resolution, and combine land use control and economic tools for pollution control and conservation. These guidelines include the use of National Coastal Management Acts and other legislation for ensuring enforcement of various sectoral laws.

The OECD stresses the need for ecologically sustainable development of the coastal zone. The guidelines suggest legislation to create institutional bodies or a management council (legal agency) and to allow for coordination. Recommendations are given for the structure and process for Integrated Coastal Zone Management Plans, including the creation of institutional bodies, generation of information, assessment of current policies, preparation of alternative plans, selection of a final plan, and monitoring and evaluation.

---

[92] Ibid.

[93] Conference and in view of 1982 Convention on the Law of the Sea.

The International Union for Conservation of Nature (IUCN) guidelines are provided for the development of a coastal area plan that can be applied at a national level, through a review of coastal problems and the need for Integrated Cross-Sectoral Management (ICSM).[94] However, these guidelines provide no specific recommendations or suggestions for the setting up of those legal and institutional arrangements. They only emphasize the need for integration among the legal, administrative, socio-economic, and bio-geophysical components amongst the public, scientists, managers, and users, including a provision for dispute resolution mechanisms.

Guidelines are designed by the World Bank to 'ensure that development and management plans for coastal zones are integrated with environmental (including social) goals and are made with the participation of those affected.' These include sections on institutional roles and responsibilities, and on triggering the need for Integrated Coastal Zone Management (ICZM). There should be legislation setting boundaries and zoning of coastal areas. These guidelines also suggest giving the value of natural coastal resources and the fact that the coastal zone is a 'dynamic area with frequently changing biological, chemical, and geological attributes'.

The World Coast Conference Report guidelines also stress an urgent need for coastal authorities to strengthen their capabilities for ICZM and the need to develop strategies and programmes by the 2000. ICZM functions are to anticipate and respond to long-term concerns while addressing present day challenges and opportunities, stimulate sustainable development of coastal areas, and promote increased economic development and benefits.

The protection of the Great Barrier Reef in Australia presents an example of how various international laws can overlap to provide various types of protection for specific marine ecosystems. Like most marine environments, coral reefs are extremely vulnerable to global environmental problems such as transboundary pollution from land and marine-based sources and mass coral bleaching episodes attributable to climate change. The protection of coral reefs demands international cooperation. The United Nations Convention Concerning the Protection of the World Cultural and Natural Heritage[95] has been signed by Australia, and the Great Barrier Reef is a listed site under the Convention. Due to their rich biological diversity, coral reefs are also appropriate for protection under the Convention on Biological Diversity.[96] Since coral reefs are under stress due to the trade of coral and reef species, the Convention on International Trade in Endangered Species of Wild Fauna and Flora[97] is also applicable. Under this convention, approximately 230 species of coral are protected, with strict restrictions imposed on their trade. Coral reefs are also vulnerable to the effects of climate change. The United Nations Framework Convention on Climate Change[98] has been signed by Australia and the government has taken steps to address climate change. Other international conventions

---

[94] Extracted from the report of the M.S. Swaminathan Committee on CRZ, 1991.

[95] United Nations Convention Concerning the Protection of the World Cultural and Natural Heritage ratified 22 August 1974, 1037 UNTS 151 (hereinafter World Heritage Convention).

[96] Convention on Biological Diversity, ratified 18 June 1993, 1760 UNTS 79 (hereinafter CBD).

[97] Convention on International Trade in Endangered Species of Wild Fauna and Flora, ratified 29 July 1976, 993 UNTS 243.

[98] United Nations Framework Convention on Climate Change, ratified December 1992, 1771 UNTS 107.

such as the MARPOL 73/78[99] and United Nations Convention on The Law of the Sea[100] are also applicable. The Great Barrier Reef Marine Park Authority identifies these various international laws as applicable to the protection, preservation, and use of the Great Barrier Reef.[101]

OFFSHORE AREAS—REGULATION OF ACTIVITIES

The Government of India has framed the Offshore Areas Mineral (Development and Regulation) Act, 2002[102] to provide for the development and regulation of mineral resources in the territorial waters, continental shelf, exclusive economic zone, and other maritime zones of India, and to provide for matters connected therewith or incidental thereto. The Act restrains persons from undertaking any reconnaissance, exploration, or production operations in the offshore areas without a permit.[103] Such permits shall be given only to Indian nationals or companies. The Central Government is empowered to reserve areas that have not been operated so far and they may close any areas of operation in public interest. The administrative authority is empowered to grant a reconnaissance permit, production lease, and exploration licence to eligible persons. The Central Government is authorized to survey, research, and conduct scientific investigations in areas covered under the operating rights. The government must prescribe measures for the prevention and control of pollution and protection of the marine environment due to activities in the area. Any person who violates the provisions of this Act can be imprisoned for a term which may extend to five years and/or a fine which may extend to fifty thousand rupees. In addition, the violator has a civil liability to pay an amount which shall not be less than one lakh rupees and which may extend to ten lakh rupees.[104]

COASTAL SHRIMP AQUACULTURE

Coastal shrimp aquaculture is an old practice in West Bengal and Kerala. The method followed is known as 'trap and culture', by which shrimps enter the farms at high tide. By closing the shutter, the shrimps that enter the farms are unable to go out at low tide.

The Supreme Court has held that the shrimp culture industry is covered by the prohibition contained in paragraph 2(1) of the CRZ notification. The intention of the judgement is to develop shrimp aquaculture in a sustainable and eco-friendly manner. The judgement also permitted farmers practising traditional and improved traditional systems of shrimp farming to adopt improved technology for increased production, productivity, and returns with the prior approval of the Aquaculture Authority. The judgement has jeopardized many aqua farms and the case (S. Jagannath v. Union of India)[105] has now reopened and is pending consideration.

[99] International Convention for the Prevention of Pollution from Ships, came into force on 2 October 1983, 340 UNTS 184, amended by Protocol of 1978 relating to the International Convention for the Prevention of Pollution from Ships, 2 October 1983, 1340 UNTS 61 (hereinafter, MARPOL 73/78).

[100] United Nations Convention on the Law of the Sea, came into force on 16 November 1994, 1833 UNTS 3 (hereinafter UNCLOS).

[101] The Great Barrier Reef Marine Park Authority http://www.gbrmpa.gov.au/corp_site/about_us/legislation_regulations#conventions (last visited 30 May 2007).

[102] Act 17 of 2003 came into force with effect from 31 January 2003.

[103] Section 5 of the Offshore Areas Mineral Development and Regulation Act, 2002.

[104] Section 23. Ibid.

[105] S. Jagannath v. Union of India, 1996 (9) SCALE 167, 1997(1) JT 160.

The judgement was rendered mainly on the acceptance of the Alagarswami Report, which permitted the traditional system of culture. This system is fully tide-fed, has salinity variations according to the monsoon regime, and has seed resources of mixed species from the adjoining creeks and canals by auto-stocking. It also depends on natural food, water intake, and drainage managed through sluice gates depending on local tidal effect, no feeding, period harvesting during full and new moon periods, collection at sluice gates by traps and bag nets, and seasonal fields alternating paddy crop (monsoon) with shrimp or fish crop (inter-monsoon). The improved traditional system is different from the traditional system, only in stock entry control and supplementary stocking with desired species of shrimp seed (*penaeus monodon and p. indicus*). The court while permitting the traditional and improved traditional systems, also permitted improved technology for these systems to increase production, productivity, and returns.

This judgement, based on the principle of sustainable development, has been subjected to severe criticism. It is not a viable proposition to draw sea water to a long distance and start an aqua farm. The fact that fishes will have to go to the farms through the natural flow has been ignored by the court. Several review petitions are still pending consideration.

In the meanwhile, for regulating activities connected with coastal aquaculture in the coastal areas and for matters connected therewith, the Government of India has enacted the Coastal Aquaculture Authority Act, 2005.[106] The area of land within a distance of two kilometres from the HTL of seas, rivers, creeks, and backwaters are declared as coastal areas for the purposes of the enactment.[107]

These restrictions are essential for the adoption of sustainable and eco-friendly farming.

WETLAND CONSERVATION

Wetlands are transitional zones that occupy an intermediate position between dry land and open water. Wetlands play an important part in the proper maintenance of the environmental equilibrium. For maintaining groundwater, the wetlands are important. The International Biological Programme (IBP) with its project Aqua, and IUCN provided the initial impetus. A series of conferences and technical meetings were held mainly under the auspices of the International Waterfowl and Wetland Research Bureau (IWRB), UK, and culminated in the Convention on Wetlands of International Importance.[108] It is better known as the Ramsar Convention (1971), a treaty which provides the framework for international cooperation for the conservation of wetland habitats. There is a general obligation on the parties to formulate and implement plans to promote the wise use of wetlands in their territories, thereby ensuring the preservation of the ecological character of these habitats. Wetlands of international importance are identified in terms of ecology, botany, zoology, limnology, or hydrology. The contracting parties are obliged to promote the conservation of wetlands in their territory through the establishment of nature reserves.

Initially, 325 wetland sites, totalling 20 million hectares, were identified globally by the IUCN. In 1991, it was increased to 32 million hectares identifying 527 sites. India acceded to the Ramsar Convention in October 1981 and has declared protected sites at

---

[106] Came into force with effect from 20 January 2006.
[107] SO 72 (E), dated 20 January 2006.

[108] Convention on Wetlands of International Importance especially as Waterfowl Habitat came into force on 21 December 1975, 996 UNTS 245, TIAS 11084.

Chilika Lake, Keoladeo National Park, Wular Lake, Harike Lake, Loktak Lake, Sambhar Lake, Kanjli, Ropar, Ashtamudi Wetland, Bhitarkanika Mangroves, Bhoj Wetland, Deepor Beel, East Calcutta Wetlands, Kolleru Lake, Point Calimere Wildlife and Bird Sanctuary, Pong Dam Lake, Sasthamkotta Lake, Tsomoriri, Vembanad-Kol Wetland, Chandertal Wetland, Hokera Wetland, Renuka Wetland, Rudrasagar Lake, Surinsar-Mansar Lakes, and Upper Ganga River (Brijghat to Narora Stretch).

The most valuable function of wetlands is the cleansing and detoxification of polluted waters. In a highly populated country like India, where epidemics may be attributed to polluted waters and poor sanitation, and where industrialization has resulted in heavy metal build-up in the lakes and rivers, the functioning of wetlands assumes particular significance. The wetland plants control pollution by absorbing nutrients with greater efficiency, at a lower cost than conventional water treatment facilities. In addition, suspended sediments are eliminated and clarity is restored to the water that flows through a wetland.

The necessity to preserve the said wetlands has been very elaborately dealt with by the Calcutta HC. From 20,000 acres, the Kolkata wetlands gradually shrunk to 10,000 acres out of private initiative. Substantial areas have been reclaimed and the sprawling metropolis of Salt Lake City, a satellite township has been developed. The wetlands have also been used for pisiculture, agriculture, garbage, dumping of solid wastes, and horticulture on garbage dumps. In view of the importance of the wetlands, the Calcutta HC has granted an injunction against the proposed reclamation of wetlands situated near Calcutta. The court also restrained the change of user of the land, from agriculture to residential or commercial in a wetland area. All encroachments are to be stopped, and maintenance of the ecology of the area is to be pursued, the court directed.[109]

There are no laws on common land use in India. In Kerala, under the Essential Commodities Order, the government issued a notification restraining the conversion of paddy lands for other uses. Deep underground water belongs to the State in the sense that the Public Trust Doctrine extends thereto.

Conversion of agricultural land into shrimp culture farms and the digging of bore wells also creates problems in the nearby agricultural lands. A person who holds land for agricultural purposes may, subject to reasonable restrictions that may be made by the State, have the right to use water for irrigational purposes and excavate a tank for the said purpose. But under no circumstances can he be permitted to restrict the flow of water to the neighbouring lands or discharge of effluents in such a manner so as to affect the right of his neighbour to use water for his own purposes.[110]

The wetlands of the country are vanishing. Some of them are converted into agricultural land and others are used for construction of buildings. The conservation value of several of the country's wetlands has decreased greatly on account of habitat degradation and loss of biodiversity. While pollution and wetland destruction have been one of the major causes of faunal decline, a more direct threat is the hunting and poaching of waterfowl and other animals prevalent in many parts of the country.[111] Unfortunately, there is no separate enactment for the protection of wetlands in India.

[109] *People United for Better Living in Calcutta-Public v. State of West Bengal*, AIR 1993 Cal 215.
[110] *M.P. Rambabu v. DFO*, AIR 2002 AP 256.
[111] India's Wetlands Mangroves and Coral Reefs, Report by WWF India, October, 1992.

MANGROVE PROTECTION

Mangroves are salt-tolerant forest ecosystems, found mainly in tropical and sub-tropical intertidal regions in the world. Mangroves have been under threat of extinction for the past several years. Considering their important role in coastal ecosystems, particularly fisheries, they deserve utmost care, preservation, and development.

Mangrove cover in India has been estimated at approximately 3,15,000 ha confined mainly along the east (Orissa and West Bengal) coast and the Andaman and Nicobar islands. Sunderbans in West Bengal has one of the largest mangrove forests in the world. The mangrove flora of India comprises of fifty exclusive species belonging to twenty genera. Approximately one million people in 3,651 villages of India situated along the coast are employed in marine capture fisheries. Indian fisheries also support several ancillary activities such as boat building, processing plants, and other similar activities. All of these features make this an important sector from an economic and social viewpoint.[112]

For the protection of the mangroves, there is no separate legislation other than the 'CRZ Notification, 1991', which classifies the mangrove areas as ecologically sensitive areas. Mangrove areas come under the umbrella of areas of rich genetic diversity and are likely to be inundated due to rises in sea level. Thereafter, the notification was amended in 2001 permitting constructions relating to the Department of Atomic Energy. These CRZ restrictions were again amended in 2002,[113] permitting the construction of dispensaries, schools, public rain shelters, community toilets, bridges, roads, jetties, water supply, drainage, and sewerage which is required for traditional inhabitants of the Sundarbans bio-sphere reserve area of West Bengal, on a case-by-case basis by the State Coastal Zone Management Authority. Similarly, the restrictions do not apply to the construction of salt harvesting by solar evaporation of sea water, desalination plants, and storage of non-hazardous cargo such as edible oil and fertilizers and food grain within notified ports.

In Mumbai, a mangrove area had been used for the dumping of wastes from a nearby bus station. In a PIL filed before it, the Bombay High Court considered the need to maintain a healthy and clean environment, the needs of the travelling public, and also the protection of mangrove areas, which adjoin the bus stand. It stated that any scheme prepared should necessarily result in the provision of easy access for commuters and a clean environment in which the mangrove areas were protected. The Court also stressed that the protection of the mangrove areas was necessary as they also exist as breeding grounds for various types of fish and other aquatic flora and fauna.[114]

Gorai Creek was being used as a dumping ground in Mumbai. The Bombay HC passed an order to prevent the further destruction of mangroves in the said area. The dumping of garbage in the coastal area is extremely dangerous for the health of the people living in close proximity. By reason of this illegal act on the part of the Municipal Corporation, a great amount of pollution was caused, the coastal and environmental ecological balance was greatly disturbed, and mangroves were destroyed. Consequently, the Court stopped the dumping.[115]

---

[112] *Marine Environment*, chapter 11, New Delhi, MoEF, http://envfor.nic.in/divisions/ic/wssd/doc2/ch11.pdf
[113] Substituted by SO 100 (E), dated 19 October 2002.

[114] *Shri Yeshwant Palekar v. The Managing Director, Kadamba Transport Corporation and Others*, Writ Petition No. 107 of 2003, dated 13 August 2003. Calcutta High Court (unreported).
[115] *Vijay Mahadeo Daruwale v. Municipal Corporation of Greater Mumbai*, Writ Petition No. 489 of 2004, dated 20 July 2005. Bombay High Court.

When the Tourism Department of the Kerala Government proposed the construction of a boat jetty at Kollam District in Kerala, the same was challenged before the HC. On the basis of the inspection being conducted by the Expert Commission, the Court directed the authorities to take all the necessary measures required for the preservation of the mangroves in the compound.[116]

The KHC had the occasion to consider the issue of destruction of mangroves at Kumarkom in the Kottayam District in Kerala. The Court constituted a committee for the monitoring of the same and this committee has been asked to submit a report every six months.[117]

The mangroves act as a protective barrier against the high tides, floods, and tsunamis. Apart from this, they are a natural holding pond for rainwater, and allow water to drain into the sea. Our mangroves and salt pans must be protected at any cost.

The Supreme Court refused to convert a mangrove forest area for the purpose of using it as salt pans by using solar energy.[118]

The Kerala Law Reforms Commission headed by V.R. Krishna Iyer has recommended a separate legislation to provide for the conservation and wise use of mangroves in the state of Kerala. The Bill recommends vesting ownership of all mangroves in the state and its duty to protect it. It imposes a restriction that no person shall alter or prune, or cause to be altered or pruned, any mangrove within the landward extent of wetlands and other surface waters in the state of Kerala without the written consent of the authority.[119]

The protection of marine ecology requires both domestic and international cooperation. As recognized by the Canadian court in *R. v. Crown Zellerbach Canada Ltd*, the line between internal state waters and territorial waters is not visually obvious. The coastal zone may be affected by pollution that occurs significantly inland, as rivers and streams can carry substances for many miles until they eventually hit the shoreline. It is on this basis that regulation should proceed, acknowledging the sensitivity of marine ecology to various land and marine-based sources, from whichever jurisdiction they originate.

---

[116] *N. Ravi v. Government of Kerala and Others*, O.P. No. 3794/89, dated 7 August 1998. Kerala High Court (unreported).

[117] *A.K. Sadasivan v. State of Kerala*, O.P. No. 6398 of 1997, dated 3 March 2000. Kerala High Court (unreported).

[118] *Krishadevi v. Bombay Environmental Action Group*, AIR 2011 SC 1140: 2011 (3) SCC 363.

[119] http://keralalawcommission.nic.in/ <accessed on 6 December 2008>

12 Degradation of Land and Forests

LAND POLLUTION

The increased need for resources always results in the degradation of the physical and biological environment. There has been a considerable growth in population, which has increased the demand for basic resources. The high population has resulted in deterioration of the economic base of society. People started exploiting natural resources by engaging in activities like excessive mining. However, it is also essential that there are proper town planning and building rules for a better living environment. Man's harmonious interaction with the environment can be achieved by land-use practices in the region.

MINING

Mining is another environmental problem faced by India. Mining from forest areas adversely affects the flora and fauna of the area. Mining from rivers disturbs the river ecology. Mining from other places causes hardship to the nearby residents and adversely affects the environment of the area. At the same time, mining is essential for development. The question is: should mining be 'dollar-friendly' or 'eco-friendly'? Let us examine the law on the subject.

Mining Laws in India

There are several pieces of legislation on mining: the Mines and Minerals (Development and Regulation) Act, 1957, Coal-Bearing Areas (Acquisition and Development) Act, 1957, Cooking Coal Mines (Nationalization) Act, 1972, Atomic Energy Act, 1962, and other such Acts. Most of these enactments contain provisions for the protection of various elements of the environment and human health.

The Mines and Minerals (Development and Regulation) Act, 1957, empowers the state government to regulate the grant of quarry leases, mining leases, and other mineral concessions in respect of minor minerals. Section 15(1-A)(i) empowers the state government to make rules for the manner in which the flora and other vegetation such as trees, shrubs, and the like are destroyed by quarrying or mining operations in designated areas or in any other area selected by the state government.

The mine holder must take all possible precautions for the protection of the environment and control of pollution while conducting or prospecting mining beneficiation or metallurgical operations in the mining area, as per Rule 34 of the Mineral Conservation

Development Rules, 1988. Steps for the storage of overburden, waste rock, rejects, and fines created during mining shall be stored in separate dumps. The lands affected by mining are to be reclaimed and rehabilitated, and all precautions are to be taken against vibration. Air pollution due to fires, dust, smoke, or gaseous emissions during prospecting, mining, beneficiation, or metallurgical operations, and related activities shall be controlled and kept within permissible limits prescribed under the Air (Prevention and Control of Pollution) Act, 1981 and the Environment (Protection) Act, 1986 by the holder of the mining lease or licence.[1]

The Granite Conservation and Development Rules, 1999 cast an obligation on the holder of a prospecting licence or lease to take all possible precautions for the protection of the environment and control of pollution while conducting prospecting, mining, or processing of granite in the area for which such licence or lease is granted.[2] The overburden, waste rock, and non-saleable granite generated during prospecting or mining operations for granite shall be stored separately in properly formed dumps on earmarked ground. The mine shall be reclaimed and rehabilitated. Air pollution due to dust, exhaust emissions, or fumes during prospecting, mining, or processing operations for granite and related activities shall be controlled and kept within permissible limits specified under any environmental laws for the time being in force.[3]

The granite mine-holder is obligated to take all precautions to prevent, or reduce to a minimum, the discharge of toxic and objectionable liquid effluents from granite

quarries, workshops, or processing plants into surface or groundwater bodies and usable lands. These effluents must conform to the standards prescribed by law. The noise generated from these activities is also to be curtailed. The holder of the mine shall take immediate measures for planting in the area, such number of trees sufficient to improve the environment and to minimize the effects of land degradation during the entire period of the lease.[4]

The Metalliferous Mines Regulations, 1961 apply to every mine other than a coal or oil mine. The holder of the mine is to take all steps necessary for the minimizing and suppression of the emission of dust that enters the air at any workplace below the ground or on the surface. Holders are also bound to ensure that the exposure of workers to respirable dust is limited to the extent that is reasonably practicable, but in any case should not exceed the limits that are harmful to the health of a person.

Similarly, the Coal Mines Regulations, 1957 are intended to regulate coal mines, and for matters connected therewith. The owner and employees must take such steps as are necessary to minimize emissions of dust and for the suppression of dust that enters the air at any workspace below ground or on the surface. The owner and employees are also bound to ensure that the exposure of workers to respirable dust is limited to the extent that is reasonable practicable, but in any case does not exceed the limit that is harmful to the health of persons.[5] All machineries for the suppression of dust are to be employed. There shall be constant checks on measures for dust control and precautions have to be taken by providing stone dust barriers to prevent ignition or

---

[1] Mineral Conservation Development Rules, 1988, Rules 34, 35, and 37.

[2] Granite Conservation and Development Rules, 1999, Rule 29.

[3] Ibid., Rules 31, 32, and 33.

[4] Ibid., Rules 34, 35, and 37.

[5] Coal Mines Regulations, 1957, Rule 123.

explosion from extending from one part of the mine to the other.[6] These regulations are complementary to the Air Act, as they help ensure an ambient air quality.

The Atomic Energy (Working of the Mines Minerals and Handling of Prescribed Substance) Rules, 1984 cast a duty on the Safety Officer of the mine to carry out surveys relating to noise level, illumination, air-borne toxic substances, and any other survey relating to industrial hygiene, while ensuring that the employees work in a safe atmosphere. The officer must also conduct a periodic ventilation survey in the installation to ensure that the ventilation is satisfactory.

The Oil Mines Regulations, 1984 protect against gases and fires. No person shall enter any cellar, sump, pit, or any confined space or zone 'O' hazardous area or the area where a flare has been accidentally extinguished, unless a test by a competent person indicates that the confirmed space is gas-free. No smoking is permitted within 30 metres from any well or storage place. The emission of toxic dust, gases, fumes, and ionizing radiation shall be prevented or controlled at the source. Any oil discharged from a well during its completion, testing, and repairs shall be collected and placed in adequately fenced disposal pits. Formation of water, oil, drilling fluid waste, chemical substances, or refuse from a well, tank, or other production installation shall not be permitted to create any hazard to public health and safety.[7] Several other safety measures are also prescribed under the said regulations.

The National Mineral Policy, 1993 for non-fuel and non-atomic minerals also emphasizes the protection of the forests, environment, and ecology from the adverse effects of mining. The basic objective of the mineral policy in respect of minerals is to minimize the adverse effects of mineral development on forests and the environment and ecology through appropriate protective measures, while also ensuring that the conduct of mining operations is carried out with due regard to the safety and health of all concerned.

The Central legislative scheme is quite comprehensive in providing a general framework for addressing most environmental and health issues involved in mining. Besides the above Central laws, there exist several state enactments to protect ecology from the adverse effects of mining.

Mining in Hilly Areas

Mining authorities are only concerned with the granting of permits to them. The statutes do not prescribe that the carrying out of mining is contingent on the prerequisite that no harm will be inflicted upon the environment. However, it must be remembered that it is the social obligation and duty of every Indian enshrined in Article 51A(g) of the Constitution to protect the environment of the country.

A mining operation in the Musoorie Hill range of the Himalayas was the subject matter of a PIL filed before the Supreme Court of India. Several interim orders were passed to protect the environment. The Court found that immediate closure of mining would cause hardship to the owners, but emphasized that this is the inevitable price to be paid for protecting the right of the people to live in a healthy environment.[8]

Environmental disturbances caused by limestone mining must be balanced and weighed against the need for limestone quarrying for industrial purposes. The Court

---

[6] Ibid., Reg 123C.
[7] Oil Mines Regulations, 1984, Reg. 96.

[8] *Rural Litigation and Entitlement Kendra v. State of UP*, (1985) 2 SCC 431, AIR 1985 SC 652.

was conscious of the fact that as a result of closure of the mines, workmen employed in the mines would be out of work. It thus directed that immediate steps be taken for reclamation of the areas forming part of such quarries and that where possible, affected workmen be equitably and expediently provided employment in the reforestation and soil conservation programmes proposed for the area.[9] This case demonstrates how the court can tailor specific directions to help produce a result that is both environment-friendly and dollar friendly.

Mining in Forest Areas

All non-forest activities in forest areas have been prohibited by law. Since mining is a non-forest activity, it is thus prohibited in forest areas. Several cases have come before courts challenging mining activities conducted near forest areas.

The Forest (Conservation) Act, 1980 came into force with effect from 25 October 1980, making it mandatory to obtain sanction from the Central Government for (1) de-reservation of reserved forest and (2) for use of forest land for non-forest purposes. In the state of Gujarat, quarry leases have been granted prior to 1980, but the state refused to renew them after the said date, because that would be contrary to the Forest Act, 1980. The state government rejected the application for renewal of mining in a forest area on the basis that it was not in conformity with the new Forest (Conservation) Act. Upholding the rejection, the court held that the Forest Act, 1980 recognized the fact that deforestation and ecological imbalance have become a social menace and should be prevented.[10]

The legal position has been clarified by the Jharkhand HC wherein the court held that all mining activities within forest areas require 'prior permission' of the Central Government on the coming into force of the Forest (Conservation) Act, 1980, with effect from 25 October 1980.[11]

Uncontrolled mining is always an environmental problem. Courts have dealt with the issue on several occasions. The question as to whether mining can be done inside a protected area, namely the Sariska Tiger Park in Rajasthan, came under the consideration of the Supreme Court. The Court held that wherever admittedly or indisputably mines are situated within a protected area, mining activities must be stopped. But if upon demarcation of the boundary line, any mining area is shown to fall clearly outside the protected area, the ban order will not operate.[12]

The Supreme Court laid down the law that once an area is declared as a protected forest, it becomes forestland. As per Section 2 of the Forest (Conservation) Act, 1980, a grant of mining leases or licences within a protected forest is contingent on clearance from the Central Government. If the condition imposed is not satisfied, mines situated within the protected forest must be closed forthwith, and mines situated partly within and partly outside the protected forest should also be closed forthwith insofar as they fall within the protected forest, the grant of leases or licences being illegal. The Court also directed that the state government request the Central Government (MoEF) for permission to delete from the list of protected forests, an area of about five square kilometres in which mines

[9] Ibid.

[10] *Ambica Quarry Works v. State of Gujarat*, AIR 1987 SC 1073, 1987(1) SCC 213.

[11] *Naresh Kumar v. Dy. Commissioner, Hazaribagh*, AIR 2006 Jhar 96.

[12] *Tarun Bharath Sangh v. Union of India*, AIR 1992 SC 514 1993 Supp (3) SCC 115.

were located from the protected forests. This is to be done after due examination by the MoEF.[13]

Mining operations in Badkal Lake and Surajkund in the state of Haryana came into contention in the Supreme Court. NEERI, an expert body, reported that mining activities in the vicinity of tourist resorts may disturb the rain water drains, adversely affecting the water level as well as the water quality of these water bodies. Mining can also cause fractures and cracks in the sub-surface rock layer, causing disturbance to the aquifers, which are the source of groundwater. This may also disturb the hydrology of the area, the complaint stated. On the basis of the report, the Court directed that all development schemes and the plans for all types of constructions relating to all types of buildings in the area from one kilometre to a five-kilometre radius of the Badkal Lake and Surajkund (excluding areas in Delhi) shall require the prior approval of the CPCB and the Haryana Pollution Control Board. No construction of any type is currently permitted within the green belt (as shown in the report). The environment and ecology of the area shall be protected and preserved by all concerned. A very small area may be permitted for the use, if it is of utmost necessity, for recreational and tourism purposes. Construction within one kilometre of the green belt shall be prohibited.[14]

Mining activities within an area up to five kilometres from the Delhi-Haryana border on the Haryana side of the ridge, and also in the Aravalli Hills, caused environmental degradation, and directions were sought from the Supreme Court. The Court held that mining cannot be permitted in forest areas.

The grant of leases for mining operations over such an area would be wholly arbitrary, unreasonable, and illogical. Mining activities result in disturbance of the land surface, altering drainage patterns and land use. They also cause pollution in the air and water, noise pollution, and solid waste pollution. The obligation to society must predominate over the obligation to individuals. The Court also held that without conducting an EIA, no permit for mining can be renewed.[15]

The Andhra Pradesh HC held that even for the renewal of mining operations, sanction from the Central Government is essential. The lessee has no vested right for grant of renewal. It is at the discretion of the state government to grant a renewal, by operation of Section 2 of the Forest (Conservation) Act, 1960. If the mines are situated within the reserve forest area, no forest land or any portion thereof may be used except with the prior approval of the Central Government. It is mandatory that the state government obtain prior approval of the Central Government, the HC held.[16]

Mining by Digging Plain Land

In the absence of an agreement, the presumption of law is that the owner of the freehold land has a right to the minerals underneath. Often, a person is entitled to both the mines and the land above.

Under Indian law,[17] if a person is an owner of immovable property, it does not include the ownership of standing timber, growing crops, or grass. But he is the owner of property attached to the earth, as is the case with walls or buildings. A 'benefit to arise out of land' is

[13] Ibid.

[14] M.C. Mehta v. Union of India, Writ Petition (Civil) No. 4677 of 1985, dated 11 October 1996.

[15] M.C. Mehta v. Union of India, AIR 2004 SC 4016, 2004 AIRSCW 4033.

[16] B.V. Joshy v. State of Andhra Pradesh, AIR 1989 AP 122.

[17] Transfer of Property Act, 1882, Section 3.

an interest in land and therefore immovable property. The first Indian Law Commissioners, in their report of 1879 said that they had 'abstained from the almost impracticable task of defining the various kinds of interests in immovable things which are considered immovable property'. Can a person dig the land as he likes and acquire the minerals beneath it? Digging of the land and mining are two different activities. Digging is simply the physical process of removing or relocating earth or soil, for the purpose of planting trees or installing a well, for instance. If the land is dug to extract minerals beneath it, it is called mining. If the digging is for acquiring minerals, mining restrictions apply. Mining beyond a permissible limit is always a threat to others and affects the ecology of the area.

In the state of Kerala, one of the district authorities for granting a licence for mining has imposed a condition that 'no dewatering the mine pit using pump is permissible and mining has to be ceased once this becomes necessary, and mining should be done manually.' This was challenged before the KHC by some licencees on the grounds that the Kerala Minor Mineral Concession Rules, 1967 do not permit the imposition of any additional condition at the whim of the licensor. The authority contended that the prohibition against the use of pumps was imposed to avoid the possibility of a lateral collapse in the sand mining pit. It ensures that the mining operation is stopped at the level of occurrence of groundwater. If the mine pit is dewatered and the mining continues, it can result in the collapse of boundaries, adversely affecting the safety of adjacent lands and structures. Draining of potable groundwater from the mine pit has a deleterious effect on the level and quality of groundwater, which will lead to a scarcity of groundwater. If more pumps are used, the availability of drinking water to neighbouring landowners will be affected. Therefore, the condition was imposed to safeguard the interests of the public and the environment.

Accepting the principle of sustainable development, the KHC has held that the above condition is imposed to protect the environment, 'If every land owner, driven by profit motive, is to dig his land to win sand, no land except pits will be left for the future generations.' Therefore licencees are to stop mining when it reaches the groundwater level and immediately fill up all pits, as provided in the condition. If the licencees fail to fill the land once mining has ceased, the geologist shall prepare estimates, or cause estimates to be prepared, regarding the amount required for filling up the pits, as laid down by the Court.[18]

The common law is that an owner of property can use the land in accordance with law. There is no law that restricts the removal of normal earth. But to what extent is such removal permissible? Can a person who has got a right over the property dig the same so as to sell the mud from it? The KHC, in extending the principle of sustainable development, has held that no person can claim absolute right to indulge in activities resulting in environmental degradation of even his own land.[19]

Mining in Sanctuaries: Forest Areas

Mining of the sea for the extraction of quarrying shell lime under water will affect the zooplankton and phytoplankton, which form part of the diet for fish and prawns, the Madras HC held. When the food chain system in the Pulicut Birds Sanctuary area is affected, it will naturally affect the arrival of migratory birds. A major portion of the lake is a shallow

[18] *Soman v. Geologist*, 2004 (3) KLT 577.
[19] *Thilakan v. Circle Inspector of Police*, 2007 (4) KLT 536.

water area that is covered with plenty of birds migrating from various places, making it fit for the feeding and breeding purposes of a bird sanctuary. If mining is allowed in such shallow water, the depth increases day by day and causes a reduction of food for migratory birds. In due course they will stop coming to the sanctuary area. It was further held that if such a mining lease is granted, damages can only be assessed by experts in the field and not by the court.[20]

The correctness of the order of sanction granted for mining in Kudrekukh National Park came under the consideration of the Supreme Court in another case. The Centrally Empowered Committee constituted by the Court was of the view that the mining company be propelled to wind up its operations within a period of five years, or on the exhaustion of the oxidized weathered secondary ore, whichever is earlier, in the already broken-up area. The state and the Central Government were not very consistent in their approach on the period for which the activities could be permitted. Reasons have been highlighted to justify the somersault. Whatever be the justification, it was but imperative that due application of mind be made before taking a particular stand. The Court observed that it was not wise of the authorities to change their colours like a chameleon. It needs to be highlighted that the Convention on Biological Diversity has been acceded to by India and therefore, it must implement the same. It is necessary for the government to keep in view international obligations while exercising discretionary powers under the Forest Act, unless there are compelling reasons to diverge, the Court

observed. No mining operations can commence without an EIA. Mere approval of a mining plan by the Government of India (Ministry of Mines), does not absolve the lease holder from complying with other provisions.[21]

Mining in Himachal Pradesh

A case was filed by a group of residents before the Himachal Pradesh HC in 1987, challenging the excavation of limestone from Khasra, situated in the village Sangrah, Tehsil Renuka, of the Sirmaur district. The Court directed the state government to constitute a committee to determine whether a proper balance was being kept between the tapping of mineral resources for development and industrial growth, and the ecology and the environment while making the grant. It also directed an investigation into whether the mines were being scientifically operated, or worked in an erratic and uncontrolled manner posing a present and potential danger to various elements of the environment. In particular, attention was paid to the soil, agriculture, forests, water resources and water supply schemes, rivers, streams, flora and fauna, ecology, the environment, and life and living conditions of the people and their property. All operations of limestone mining are to be reviewed by the said committee.[22]

The people of Saproon Valley in Himachal Pradesh have approached the HC alleging that the mining of limestone causes great damage to the fields below and the environment, having led to an ecological imbalance due to pollution of water and soil erosion of the surrounding land. The reports made to the court by the authorities were found to be differing from one another and a committee was constituted to conduct an in-depth

---

[20] *Development Society v. State of Tamil Nadu and Others*, WP Nos 4491 of 1995 and 8043 of 2001; dated 1 July 2003.

[21] *M.C. Mehta v. Union of India*, AIR 2004 SC 4033.

[22] *Kinkiri Devi v. State of HP*, AIR 1988 HP 4.

study of the problem. The committee's report classified mines into two categories and suggested the closure of one set of mines and the adoption of curative steps. The report was accepted and the court appointed a monitoring committee to inspect the areas and monitor the curative steps.[23]

Mining from Rivers

Rivers are one of the most important life support systems of nature and are used on a large scale by the people of the country. The rapid growth of population and the sheer need to generate resources for developmental activities imposes immense pressure on these ecosystems. Excessive mining from freshwater rivers adversely affects the river ecology. The adverse effects of excessive sand mining are as follows:

1. The river bed goes down resulting in the intrusion of saline water from the nearby sea. This causes scarcity of the fresh water necessary to sustain life.
2. Foundations of bridges are weakened, leading to their collapse.
3. Threats are posed to river banks where the risk of a landslide can lead to the destruction of houses.
4. Clay bed scouring contaminates water as there is an increase in particulate level, turbidity, and other pollutants like oils, grease, chemicals, and other contaminants.
5. There is a threat to bath takers, who are vulnerable to falling into the pits created by sand miners.
6. The increase in biological oxygen demand (BOD) and decrease in dissolved oxygen (DO) levels in areas close to mining sites.

River sand is a non-renewable natural resource in terms of human life. Whatever replenishment occurs in the lowland part of rivers is derived mainly from the reworking of older flood plain deposits evolved through a process that took thousands of years. River sand is used for building and construction purposes, and the demand for sand has increased as a result of such activities. Excessive mining has adversely affected the general public, which depends on rivers as a basic necessity. When the authorities fail to discharge their duties, the people have often turned to the courts of law for assistance.

In a PIL, the Supreme Court appointed a committee and recommended the confinement of the area of exploitation to maintain a proper balance between the unhampered flow of the river and preservation of its bed and the local needs for the sand.[24]

In order to protect rivers, the KHC directed the authorities to clearly demarcate the river boundaries with permanent marks. This involved earmarking the prohibited area on either side of bridges, dams, and other structures so as to implement the 300-metre ban. Normal sand-bed levels were to be specified in respect of the rivers by clear demarcation of the river bank. Areas where the sand deposited was less were to be declared prohibited before the resumption of extraction for the relevant year. The authorities were also directed to construct retaining walls along the river banks where there exists the possibility of landslides, to the extent practicable, to protect the forty-four rivers of the state.[25]

Sand mining has always been a problem in states where the rivers depended upon for drinking water are situated near the coast.

---

[23] *General Public of Saproon Valley v. State of HP*, AIR 1993 HP 52.

[24] *Mukthi Sangharsh Movement v. State of Maharashtra*, 1990 Supp SCC 37.

[25] *Chandrasekharan Pillai v. State of Kerala*, 1998 (2) KLT 648.

The KHC had the occasion to consider the question of river sand mining in a batch of cases. In addition to government orders restraining mining, the court has ordered that no sand mining shall be allowed, unless the conditions incorporated therein are followed, including the obtaining of a report from the experts so as to determine the quantity of sand. Collection of sand within one kilometre of bridges and irrigation projects is prohibited. Illegally mined sand shall be returned to the river. As pointed out by the experts, constructions within rivers that are reported to cause an adverse effect on river ecology shall be demolished immediately by the local authority, and the expenses incurred on this account shall be recovered from the offenders. Steps shall be taken to demarcate the river boundaries and protect them. The state government shall also consider the feasibility of alternatives to river sand in developmental activities. It shall be the duty of the state government, through its administrative and police officers at sufficiently high levels, to ensure that these directions are strictly complied with and there is no cause for grievance. The court added that sand mining is clandestinely and illegally carried out despite these directions.[26]

In the state of Tamil Nadu, river bridges and railway tracks were severely damaged by sand mining in violation of rules and lease deeds. The court found that flooding of agricultural lands was due to a break in linkage between discharge or channels and river basins. This led to destruction of agricultural and mangrove ecosystems. Houses and buildings collapsed due to erosion and the groundwater table had reduced in all the river basins, affecting agriculture severely. The sand mining permitted in private lands adjacent to river beds enabled private owners to encroach

upon the river bed illegally. Public roads were seriously damaged, drinking water turned saline, and accidents occurred due to heavy lorry traffic. The noise and dust thrown up by the lorries carrying quarried sand affected the health of the people. The Madras HC directed that there should be a special river protection force mobilized for patrolling and policing the river areas, and apprehending the culprits indulging in illicit quarrying. Such a force should be composed of high calibre personnel and should not fall prey to enticements, the court added.[27]

The state of Orissa has also battled with the problem of excessive river sand mining. When the issue was brought to the notice of the Orissa HC, it issued a direction to the authorities to ascertain whether the removal of sand would damage the embankment. Protection of people's interests in preserving the river and the environment in order to allow the river to recoup was demanded. The court concluded that the embankment was not to be used for any other purpose other than that of reaching the public road.[28]

The mining problems in the state of Andhra Pradesh were considered by the HC. The court issued a set of directions. The District Level Committee shall notify any river, stream, or other place where sand is in deposit for auction only after obtaining the report and opinion from the concerned head of the water agency in the district. It shall also invite objections from the people of the locality and consider these recommendations before issuing a notification. The District Collector of each district is bound to review the groundwater situation at least once every quarter, ending with March, June,

---

[26] *Association for Environment Protection v. Union of India*, 2001 (2) KLT 703.

[27] *M.K. Janardanan v. District Collector*, Contempt Application No. 561 of 2001 in WP No. 985 of 2000, dated 26 July 2002.

[28] *Binayak Behra v. State*, 94 (2002) Cuttack Law Times 257.

September, and December, in consultation with the authorities of the groundwater department and Panchayat Raj Department. In the eventuality that it emerges in any of the reviews that it is no longer permissible to permit the grant of continuance to a mining lease in any particular area, quarrying shall be terminated forthwith. Since the extraction of sand through the process of filter beds or similar activities has not been permitted by any law and shall be treated as prohibited, it shall be the duty of the Revenue Divisional Officer and the Sub-Divisional Police Officer concerned, to ensure that no such activity takes place. The court further directed that it shall be open to members of any public or voluntary organization to bring to the notice of the District Collector or District Legal Authority, constituted under the Legal Services Authorities Act, any violations of this provision. For effective implementation of the said conditions, the court held that matters so brought to the notice of the said agencies shall be treated as a dereliction in duty per se on the part of the concerned official, which in turn shall be forwarded to their respective appointing authorities for further action.[29]

Sand is a minor mineral as defined in the Mines and Minerals (Regulations and Development) Act, 1957. The Andhra Pradesh HC has held that quarry permits for the lifting of sand which is a minor mineral cannot be granted if it is a violation of the fundamental right enshrined under Article 21 of the Constitution of India, under which a citizen has a right to water for drinking and agriculture. Quarrying and lifting of sand from river beds and streams in panchayat areas resulted in reduced percolation of water and depletion of groundwater levels in the nearby lands, affecting agriculture. Directions were issued

to the state government to take preventive measures to arrest the illegal operations being carried out. The district authorities must see that an exemption from ban orders is made on a rational basis, taking into account expert reports from the Government Water Department.[30]

The state of Kerala has an enactment, Kerala Protection of River Banks and Regulation of Removal of Sand Act, 2001. Interpreting the provisions of the said enactment the Kerala High Court held:

Though the word 'lake' is absent in the preamble to the Act, it will not exclude the lakes from the domain of the Act. 'Lakes' form part of the environment; and apparently it is for the protection of the water body system which covers not only rivers, but also lakes. As according to the value judgment of the legislature, presence of sand in these water bodies has been found sufficiently dangerous to require protection by the enactment of the law, the said Act is enacted.[31]

River Protection Authority

Only the sand that accrues can be legally mined. The requirement of sand for construction purposes should be determined, and the quantity of sand mined should be fixed. Proper restrictions are to be imposed to avoid all illegal mining. A River Protection Authority with ample powers and responsibilities should be constituted with proper persons. The Authority must be entrusted with the control of rivers in the states, including pollution, usage of country boats, construction of river banks, irrigation projects, mining, and all other steps required for the protection of rivers.

Alternatives to sand like crushed sand, quarry dust, sea sand (washed), glass powder, and the like are used in many constructions, which also indirectly protect the river ecology.

---

[29] *V. Bhaskar v. State of AP and Others*, Writ Petition No. 18359 of 2002, dated 16 February 2004.

[30] *Bheemagari v. RDO*, AIR 2001 AP 492.
[31] *Manju v. State of Kerala*, 2011 (3) KLT 150.

Stringent legislation is required to provide justice to rivers and the surrounding ecology from mining. As an activity, mining is particularly suited to regulation and the law is an extremely useful tool in this respect. India has a vast array of laws adapted to mitigating the effects of mining on the environment, and with the cooperation of the authorities and directions of the courts, this objective has been achieved to some extent. Mining should most definitely be eco-friendly, yet the dollar hungry need not fret, for the preservation of natural mineral sites and the surrounding ecology ensures that operations are environmentally and economically sustainable, thus benefitting society at large.

FOREST CONSERVATION

Aranya in Sanskrit means 'forest' and is a manifestation of Vishnu, the Hindu god, who is considered the preserver in Hindu mythology. Preservation and conservation of trees in particular, and nature in general, have been an integral part of Hindu religion. The Atharva Veda (*aranya to preethivi sayo namastu*) goes on to pray that the forests and plants on Earth may have a pleasing effect on people. Buddha was born under a sal tree in full bloom; he attained enlightenment under a Bodhi tree, and his death took place in a grove of sal trees in full bloom. This suggests that even extraordinary events take place in a natural setting. Furthermore, Lord Buddha had once said:

A tree is unique. It has unlimited tolerance, patience, and generosity. It provides a congenial atmosphere for many living organisms to survive. It also keeps on providing shade (as long as it stands) even to the man who attempts to destroy the tree with his axe.[32]

[32] Extracted from the article 'Moral Education for Environmental Protection, the Sarvodaya Model, H.M.D.R. Herath. http://ignca.nic.in/cd_0701.htm

The necessity to maintain fruit-bearing trees was emphasized in the Bible also: 'When you are besieging a town and the war drags on, do not destroy the trees. Eat the fruit but do not cut down the trees. They are not enemies that need to be attacked!'[33]

One of the major religions in the world, Hinduism, begins with Vedic scriptures called Aranyakas, or forest books, which are written by sages living in the forest. 'The culture of the forest has fuelled the culture of India,' modern poet Rabindranath Tagore wrote. 'The unifying principle of life in diversity, of democratic pluralism, thus became the principle of Indian civilization.'[34]

INDIAN LEGISLATION

Indian forests are protected by laws and judicial activism. Though there are several central and state laws, there is a continuous monitoring of forest conservation activities by the Supreme Court.

Indian Forest Act, 1927

The first National Forest Policy for the protection of forests in India was declared by the British, who were ruling India, in 1894. The Indian Forest Act, 1878 classified various forests as industrial forests, fragile forests, small forests, and grazing fields. The intention was to derive income from industrial forests.[35]

The said law was modified by the Indian Forest Act, 1927,[36] consolidating the law

[33] Book of Deuteronomy, Chapter 20, Verse 19.
[34] Environmental History Timeline: Ancient Civilizations. http://www.runet.edu/~wkovarik/envhist/1ancient.html
[35] Environmental Encyclopaedia, Kerala State Encyclopaedia Institute, 2000, p. 286.
[36] Act 16 of 1927, with effect from 21 September 1927.
[36] Indian Forest Act, 1927, Section 2(1).

relating to forests, the transit of forest produce, and the duty leviable on timber and other forest produce. This Act contains a very broad definition of the word 'cattle', which includes elephants, camels, buffaloes, horse, mares, geldings, ponies, colts, fillies, mules, asses, pigs, rams, ewes, sheep, lambs goats, and kids.[37] But this Act is now not applicable in states that have their own enactments for forest protection.

The Madhya Pradesh HC has held that land that was declared a reserve forest or village forest by the erstwhile rulers will be treated as forests and the Forest Act, 1927 is applicable to such areas. Consequently, no non-forestry activities can be permitted in such areas.[38]

After 1952, a new Forest Policy was declared. The main purpose was to maintain one-third of the land as forest. It was also intended to protect the wildlife, prevent exploitation of forest resources, increase protection for present forests, promote afforestation, and promote programmes for the protection of forests in the country.[39]

Forest Conservation Act, 1980

Deforestation causes an ecological imbalance and leads to environmental deterioration. With a view to check deforestation, the Forest (Conservation) Ordinance, 1980 was promulgated, which was later replaced by the Forest Conservation Act, 1980 (FCA).[40]

The term 'forest land' mentioned in Section 2 of the FCA refers to reserved forest, protected forest, or any recorded forest in government records. Lands that are notified under Section 4 of the FCA would also come within the purview of the Act. All proposals for diversions of such areas to any non-forest purpose, even if the area is privately owned, require the prior approval of the Central Government.

Does the term 'forest' mean only 'reserved forest', and are such activities only restrained in reserved places? The Supreme Court of India, in widening the scope of the Act, has held the word 'forest' must be understood according to its dictionary meaning. It includes all statutorily recognized forests, whether designated as reserved, protected or otherwise. The prior approval of the Central Government is required for any non-forest activity within the area of any 'forest'.[41] In accordance with Section 2 of the Act, all ongoing activity within any forest in any state throughout the country, without the prior approval of the Central Government, must be stopped. The court held that the running of saw mills of any kind including veneer or plywood mills, and mining of any mineral are non-forest purposes and are therefore not permissible without prior approval of the Central Government.[42] The normal rule of interpretation of law is that the Court cannot supplement a meaning to an enactment which the legislature has not intended. But in order to protect the forests, the Court has gone a step ahead and given a new rule of interpretation extending the meaning to a word which the statute has not intended, resulting in judicial activism.

The United Nations Convention on Combating Desertification defines forest as a '[d]ense canopy with multilayered structure including large trees in the upper storey.'[43]

---

[38] *Kamal Kishore v. State of MP*, AIR 2006 MP 167.

[39] Indian Forest Act, 1927.

[40] Statement of Objects and Reasons of the Bill, leading to the Forest (Conservation) Act, 1980.

[41] Section 2 of the Forestry (Conservation) Act, 1980.

[42] *T.N. Godavarman Thirumulpad v. Union of India*, AIR 1997 SC 1228, (1997) 3 JT 338; reiterated in AIR 1997 SC 3381.

[43] United Nations Convention to Combat Desertification in Countries Experiencing Serious Drought and/or Desertification, Particularly in Africa; came into force on 26 December 1996, 1954 UNTS 3.

The United Nations Framework Convention on Climate Change defines a forest as:

Young natural stands and all plantations which have yet to reach a crown density of 10–30 per cent or tree height of 2–5 meters are included under forest, as are areas normally forming part of forest area which are temporarily unstocked as a result of human intervention such as harvesting or natural causes but which are expected to revert to forest.[44]

It is very difficult for the law to give a definition of the term 'forest'. It perhaps suffices to say that forests are everything other than non-forests.

Duty of the States to Protect Forests

The Constitution of India casts an obligation on the state government to protect and improve the environment and safeguard the forests and wildlife of the country.[45]

There are several state laws relating to forest lands. The Kerala Private Forests (Vesting and Assignment) Act, 1971[46] was enacted to provide for the vesting of private forests in the state government, and for assignment thereof to agriculturists and agricultural labourers for cultivation, as in the opinion of the state legislature, that all the private forests in the state of Kerala were agricultural lands. The lands that are used principally for the cultivation of tea, coffee, cocoa, rubber, cardamom, or cinnamon and for any purpose ancillary to cultivation is private forest, as per the said state legislation.

An application was filed by a person claiming exemption from the Kerala Act on the ground that he had planted 100.05 acres which were already planted with cardamom. The Commissioner appointed by the Forest Tribunal found that the cardamom plants were in existence at least twenty-five years prior to the date of his visit. The Supreme Court held that such part of land cannot be taken as forest land for the purposes of the Kerala Act.[47]

The Andhra Pradesh Forest Act, 1967, Assam Forest Regulation Act, 1891, Jammu and Kashmir Forest Act, 1987, Karnataka Forest Act, 1963, Mizoram (Forest) Act, 1953, Nagaland Forest Act, 1968, Orissa Forest Act, 1972, Rajasthan Forest Act, 1953, and Tamil Nadu Forest Act, 1882 are some of the state enactments.

In Himachal Pradesh, the state government has banned the setting up of *katha* industry, which requires the cutting of *khair* trees. The industries challenged the said order, contending that there is no statute empowering the state to issue such ban orders. Industry is a Central subject as per the Constitution of India and the state government is not empowered to legislate on the subject and cannot pass any ban orders. The Himachal Pradesh HC while accepting the arguments allowed the contention. The Supreme Court of India, while reversing the judgement, held that the Himachal Pradesh Land Preservation Act, 1978 confers extensive powers to regulate, restrict, and prohibit the cutting of trees and their removal. The Himachal Pradesh Private Forests Act, 1955 contains elaborate provisions empowering the State Government to prohibit the cutting and felling of trees in specified forests. These enactments have a crucial bearing on the establishment and running of forest-based industries, the Supreme Court added.[48]

---

[44] United Nations Framework Convention on Climate Change; came into force on 21 March 1994, 1771 UNTS 107, http://www.fao.org/docrep/009/j9345e/j9345e05.htm

[45] Article 48A, Constitution of India.

[46] Extends to the state of Kerala.

[47] *Kumari Varma v. State of Kerala*, AIR 2006 SC 1622.

[48] *State of Himachal Pradesh v. Ganesh Wood Products*, AIR 1996 SC 149, (1995) 6 SCC 363.

Clearance from the Ministry of Forests for Non-Forestry Activities

Deforestation had been taking place on a large scale in the country and it had caused widespread concern. With a view to checking further deforestation, the Government of India enacted the Forest (Conservation) Act, 1980.[49] For the conservation of forests, the de-reservation of reserved forests, and the use of forest land for non-forest purposes, prior approval of the Central Government is necessary.

Any activity which requires the diversion of forest land for non-forest use must first be cleared by the MoEF. This process also stipulates a role for the Forest Advisory Committee (FAC) before the grant of clearance. The MoEF refers every proposal with complete documentation to the FAC, which then takes a view based on the following parameters:

1. Whether the forest land to be converted is part of a nature reserve, national park, wildlife sanctuary, biosphere reserve, or forms part of the habitat of any endangered or threatened species of flora and fauna or of an area lying in severely eroded catchment?
2. Whether the use of any forest land is for agricultural purposes or for the rehabilitation of persons displaced from their residence by reason of any river valley or hydro-electric project?
3. Whether all feasible alternatives have been considered by the State Government or the other authority and that the required area is the minimum needed for the purpose?
4. Whether the state government or the other authority undertakes to provide at its cost for the acquisition of land of an equivalent area and afforestation?[50]

Following this scrutiny, the FAC advises the MoEF on whether the forest land should be allowed to be diverted, and if permitted, then under what conditions and restrictions.

The state government has the power to specify the limits of forest land within their state and declare it as 'reserved forests'.[51] The state government is also empowered to declare any forest land or waste land, which is the property of government as 'protected forests'.[52] Once land is declared as a reserved or protected forest, or noted as forest land in the revenue records, the state government must obtain the prior approval of the Central Government to use the land for any non-forest purpose. If the state government proposes to assign any forest land by way of lease or otherwise to any person or clear any trees or alter the character of reservation as forest they must obtain the sanction of the Central Government.[53]

The term 'non-forest purpose' means the breaking up or clearing of any forest land or portion thereof for the cultivation of any tea, coffee, spices, rubber palms, oil bearing plants, horticulture crops, or medicinal plants. But the term does not include any work relating or ancillary to conservation, development, and management of forests and wildlife, namely: the establishment of checkposts, fire lines, wireless communications, and construction of fencing, bridges, culverts and dams, waterholes, trench marks, boundary marks, pipelines, or other like purposes. Harvesting of fodder grass, legumes, and other such crops, which grow naturally in forest areas, without removal of the tree growth, will not require prior approval of the Central Government.

Insofar as Union Territories are concerned, the Bombay HC has taken a view that as the

---

[49] Came into force with effect from 25 October 1980.
[50] Rule 7 of the Forest (Conservation) Rules, 2003.
[51] Supra note 5, Section 3.
[52] Supra note 5, Section 29.
[53] Forest (Conservation) Act, 1980, Section 2.

District Collector is a Central Government employee, no separate sanction from the Central Government is required under Section 2 of the FCA. The Supreme Court of India, reversing the said view, has held that the matter must be looked into by the FCA and the MoEF. The District Collector of the Union Territory is not an officer of the Central Government so as to grant sanction under the Act or take prior approval of the Central Government.[54]

Centrally Empowered Committee

The Supreme Court of India has constituted a Centrally Empowered Committee (CEC) to oversee the strict and faithful implementation of its orders in the north-east region. The Committee must oversee the preparation of an inventory of timber in all forms lying in the forest and mill premises. The CEC may, if it considers appropriate, permit the use or sale of any part of the timber or timber products. The Central Government has been asked to provide suitable office space, and provide other secretarial facilities in Delhi, including travel expenses. The state governments are directed to provide accommodation when the members of the CEC visit the concerned states.[55]

Accepting the recommendations of the CEC, the Supreme Court has passed an order permitting removal of weeds, clearing and burning of vegetation for fire lines, maintenance of fair weather roads, habitat improvement, digging temporary waterholes, construction of anti-poaching camps, chowkies, checkposts, entry barriers, water towers, small civil works, research and monitoring activities. These activities are necessary for the day-to-day management of the protected areas and do not involve any type of commercial exploitation.[56]

The CEC thereafter examined the issue of encroachments in forests and forest lands in the country. It recommended to the Supreme Court that only the First Offence Report issued under the relevant Forest Act be the basis to decide whether the encroachment has taken place or not.

The CEC nominated six independent persons to be included in the FCA, in December 2007. The MoEF has objected on the basis that the guidelines[57] relating to the appointment of non-official experts to various decision-making bodies require the possession of a formal qualification and relevant professional experience, and the six persons nominated do not have the qualification. The MoEF seems to have forgotten the fact that the six persons have served on MoEF's own committees in the past, including expert committees for environment clearances of projects, or others related to hazardous wastes. The court has asked the ministry to submit a list of all committees that have the 'rejected names' as members and is also seeking clarity on whether the FAC is a 'decision-making body' or just an 'advisory' body.

Distinction Between Forest Activity and Non-Forest Activity

The Supreme Court, interpreting the provisions of the FCA, has held that once a notification declaring a land as reserve forest is published under Section 20 of the Act, then all the rights in the said land claimed by any person come to an end and are no longer available.[58]

---

[54] *Union of India v. Kamath Holiday Resorts Pvt Ltd*, AIR 1996 SC 1040, 1996 (1) SCC 774.

[55] *T.N. Godavarman Thirumulpad v. Union of India*, WP(C) No. 202/95, dated 4 March 1997.

[56] *T.N. Godavarman Thirumulpad v. Union of India*, WP(C) No. 202/95, dated 25 November 2005.

[57] http://envfor.nic.in/rti/order-guidelines.pdf

[58] *State of UP v. Dy. Director of Consolidation*, AIR 1996 SC 2432, 1996 (5) SCC 194.

The KHC has held that construction of a forest lodge at Parambikkulam Wild Sanctury was a non-forest activity and therefore, previous permission of the Central government was mandatory.[59]

Afforestation and Conservation

Trees in forests are being cut for developmental activities in the country. Consequently, they are replanted in an effort to maintain the ecology. Reforestation is necessary to replace the vanishing forests and is a continuous integrated process. The word 'conservation' in the FCA is not limited to preservation but also includes afforestation, the Andhra Pradesh HC held.[60]

To compensate the de-reservation or diversion of forest land for non-forest purposes, a comprehensive afforestation scheme has been stipulated. Such afforestation is done over an equivalent area of non-forest land contiguous or in the proximity of a reserved or protected forest to enable the Forest Department to effectively manage the newly planted area. For proposals like the extraction of minor minerals from the river bed, construction of a link road, small water works, minor irrigation works, school building dispensaries, hospitals, tiny rural industrial sheds of the government, laying of transmission lines, mulberry plantation, and other such works, compensatory afforestation may be raised over the degraded forest land and shall be twice the extent of forest area being diverted or de-reserved. Such land should be transferred to the Forest Department.

When forest land is used for non-forest purposes, damage is caused. This raises the question as to what steps may be taken to compensate the loss that has been caused

to ecology. The issue is, whether prior to the diversion of forest land for non-forest purposes and consequential loss of benefits accruing from the forests, should not the user agency of such land be required to compensate for the diversion? If so, should not the user agency be required to make payment of the Net Present Value (NPV) of such diverted land so as to utilize the amounts received for returning in the long run, the benefits that are lost by such diversion? What guidelines should be issued to determine the NPV? Should guidelines apply uniformly to all? How should the NPV be calculated? Should some projects be exempted from payment of the NPV?

The CEC submitted a report recommending that a 'Compensatory Afforestation Fund' be created, in which all the monies received from the user-agencies towards compensatory afforestation, additional compensatory afforestation, penal compensatory afforestation, net present value of forest land, Catchment Area Treatment Plan funds, and others, shall be deposited. The recommendations also explain how the amount should be utilized and steps for monitoring its utilization. It also suggested that a part of the fund should be used for assisted natural regeneration wherein the natural forests are allowed to regenerate and grow by undertaking silvicultural and cultural operations such as fire tracing, signalling of seedlings, protection, and other methods. These activities help in regenerating the rootstock which may exist in the degraded forests and help to restore natural forests, which is not possible through plantations. It also noted that to compensate for the loss of tangible as well as intangible benefits flowing from the forest lands which have been diverted for non-forest use, the NPV of such land is being recovered from the user agency in the states of Madhya Pradesh, Chhattisgarh, and Bihar.

---

[59] Jair Raj. A.P. v. The Chief Conservator of Forests and Others, ILR 1996 (2) Ker 270.
[60] M/s Anupama Minerals v. Union of India, AIR 1986 AP 225.

Thereafter, the Central Government constituted the Compensatory Afforestation Fund Management and Planning Authority (CAMPA) to carry out a variety of functions.[61] It is charged with managing the funds for compensatory afforestation, NPV, and any other money recoverable in pursuance of the Supreme Court's order and in compliance with the conditions stipulated by the Central Government, while according approval under the FCA for non-forest uses of forest land. For government projects like hospitals, dispensaries, schools, and the like, all other projects shall be required to pay NPV till the matter is reconsidered by the court.[62] The Court also made it clear that the CAMPA must be used for regeneration of ecosystems and the same cannot be handed over to any state government on the premise that ecology is not the property of any state, but belongs to all beings as a gift of nature for the entire nation. The payment of the NPV is for protection of the environment and not in relation to any propriety rights.

The Andhra Pradesh HC has also held that the conservation of forests includes both preservation and reforestation, as forests must be cut on a regular basis to meet the needs of the country. At the same time, reforestation should go on to replace the vanishing forest.[63]

Establishment of Saw Mills Near Forest Area Prohibited

Establishment of saw mills adjacent to forest areas better enables poachers to convert the same into timber. To avoid this, the Orissa Saw Mills and Saw Pits (Control) Act, 1991 was enacted, imposing a total ban on the saw mill businesses within a distance of ten kilometres from reserved forest. The validity of the said enactment was challenged, stating that it infringes the fundamental right to carry on trade. The Supreme Court has held that the legislation is in public interest, intended to preserve forest wealth and environment, and to stop the illicit felling of forest growth. Thus, it is not violative of Article 14, and is not arbitrary, unreasonable, or discriminatory.[64]

The Supreme Court of India, in the interest of protecting the forests of the country has issued sweeping directions in the case of *T.N. Godavaraman Thirumulkpad v. Union of India*,[65] completely banning the movement of cut trees and timber from any of the seven north-eastern states to any other states. All state governments were directed to constitute an Expert Committee to identify the forest lands in their state. The court declared that the running of saw mills of any kind including veneer or plywood mills, and the mining of any mineral are non-forest activities. In addition, the court has ordered the closure of all saw mills within 100 metres from the border in Assam and Arunachal Pradesh. In the state of Jammu and Kashmir, the court has banned all saw mills at a distance of eight kilometres from the boundary of forests.

In Mumbai, a minister in the state government granted a sanction for the establishment of a saw mill in gross violation of the ban order imposed by the Supreme Court. The matter came to the notice of the Supreme Court, and it initiated *suo moto* contempt proceedings. The minister finally tendered an unconditional apology. But the Court refused

---

[61] Notification dated 23 April 2004 issued by MoEF in exercise of the powers conferred by sub-section (3) of Section 3 of the EP Act.

[62] *T.N. Godavarman Thirumulpad v. Union of India*, 2006 (1) SCC 1.

[63] Supra note 60.

[64] *Sushila Saw Mills v. State of Orissa*, (1995) SCC 615, AIR 1995 SC 2484.

[65] Reported in AIR 1997 SC 1228.

to accept it, observing that an 'apology shall not be paper apology and expression of sorrow should come from the heart and not from the pen. For it is one thing to "say" sorry—it is another to "feel" sorry.'[66]

Judicial Activism for Protection of Forests

The Supreme Court of India has always been in the forefront for the protection of forests in the country. There are several instances in which the Supreme Court interfered to protect the trees in forests.

In Madhya Pradesh, under the garb of removing infected sal trees, trees that do not have any disease had also been cut. When the Supreme Court noticed this, it restrained the state government and its functionaries from cutting any trees, even if the opinion of the state government was that they were diseased.[67]

When railway wagons containing illegal timber were detained at a railway station, the Supreme Court authorized the MoEF to take steps that it deemed proper for the necessary investigation, storage, disposal, and other steps, of the detained timber. The Court also directed that detainment of trucks will be permitted only on the issuance of certificates by the respective Collectors themselves to the effect that the said trucks are only transiting through the state of Madhya Pradesh with legal timber and that no part of the timber contained in the trucks is of Madhya Pradesh origin.[68]

The Supreme Court has put restrictions on the export of timber. The quantity of the timber and firewood to be exported from the state shall be determined on the basis of availability of forest produce after catering to the needs and requirements of the local people of the state, which has power to regulate the transit of timber and other forest produce.[69]

A scheme was framed under the Capital of Punjab (Development and Regulation) Act, 1952 for the allotment of industrial plots, ignoring the notification declaring the said land as reserved forest. When the allotments were cancelled, the industrial owners approached the court. It was contended by them that they were entitled to the allotment as they had paid the entire amount. The Supreme Court held that the doctrines of 'estoppel' and 'legitimate expectation' cannot be applied against the administration to compel it to allot the original plots because that would permit violation of statutes intended to conserve forest and restrictions imposed in the interests of the general public and the security of the nation under the Aircrafts Act. The Supreme Court cannot direct the administration to commit a breach of statutory provisions and thus harm general public interests.[70]

A road was proposed through a national park. The Supreme Court interfered with the matter and directed the realignment through a place that did not pass through the park.[71]

The Madhya Pradesh HC has issued directions to the state to constitute a task force of a permanent nature to protect the forests. The aim is to see that there is no encroachment of the forests involved in the present case. No person should be allowed to carry on any activity which is alien to the basic concept of afforestation. If any land is allowed in favour of any landless person out of the

[66] T.N.Godavaraman Thirumulpad v. Union of India, (2006) 5 SCC, p. 1.

[67] T.N. Godavaraman Thirumulpad v. Union of India, AIR 1999 SC 43, 1998 (9) SCC 660.

[68] T.N. Godavarman Thirumulpad v. Union of India, AIR 2000 SC 1636.

[69] State of Tripura v. Sudhir Rajan Nath, AIR 1997 SC 1168, (1997) 3 SCC 665.

[70] Hira Tikkoo v. Union Territory Chandigarh and Others, 2004 AIRSCW 3569.

[71] Navin. M. Raheja v. Union of India, 2003 AIRSCW 3013, 2002 (2) SCALE 319.

forest area, immediate steps should be taken to dispossess him. Any encroachment under continuance shall be removed within a period of three months. Encroachments that have been removed and those that are to be removed shall be converted into forest areas by planting trees which are likely to grow on the aforesaid soil as per the opinion of experts. Any person who has felled the trees and has come to the notice of the authorities shall be subject to criminal prosecution as per law, and efforts should be made to bring the case to its logical conclusion as expeditiously as possible. No approach road to any village should be encroached upon and the police and revenue authorities should make a concerted effort in enforcement of this provision. A High Power Committee consisting of the Secretary, Forests, Government of Madhya Pradesh, Chief Conservator of Forests, and the concerned Divisional Forest Officer should be constituted to oversee all the steps as directed above, the court held.[72]

The Supreme Court of India has played an active role in protecting the forests of the country. On several occasions, it has acted beyond the scope of its power of judicial review. The Court was compelled to initiate contempt proceedings against many officials, including ministers. Though the directive principles enshrined in the Constitution cast an obligation to protect the forests and wildlife, they are being ignored when executing the provisions of law.

Right of Indigenous People to Occupy Forest Land

Indigenous people living in the forests in India were termed 'Adivasis'. They are the repositories of medical wisdom and know how to live in complete harmony with nature. They do not exploit nature or its resources, and are often referred to as the 'best friends of nature'.[73] They raise huts for their shelter and use jungles by raising crops for their needs. The non-forest activities of the forest officials used to interfere with their living. Do tribals who live in forests have any right to live therein?

The Indian Constitution does not define what a tribe is or who tribal people are. However, under Article 342 of the Constitution, the President of India can specify tribes or tribal communities, by issuance of a public notification. They are to be treated as tribes under the Fifth Schedule with respect to a state, and be deemed as a 'scheduled tribe'. The role of indigenous population in environmental management and development has been recognized by the international legal regime.[74]

Adivasis living in Duhi and Robertganj Tehsils in the district of Mirzapur in Uttar Pradesh were threatened when the government took steps for the acquisition of their land for the establishment of a thermal plant. The court, accepting the rights of the adivasis, directed the constitution of a Forest Settlement Officer and directed him to consider the claims of the adivasis for regularization. The court

---

[72] *Patiram Chandel v. State of Madhya Pradesh*, (2004) 15 ILD 589.

[73] Satish C. Shastri, 'Law Relating to Preservation and Protection of the Rights of Tribal People in India' in Satish C. Shastri (ed.) *Human Rights, Development and Environmental Law—An Anthology*, New Delhi: Bharat Law Publications, 2006), pp. 304–5.

[74] *The Report of the World Commission on Environment and Development, 1987; Rio Declaration, 1992*, Principle 22, 'Indigenous population and their community and local communities have a vital role in environmental management and development because of their knowledge and traditional practices. State should recognize and duly support their identity, culture and interests and enable their effective participation in the achievement of sustainable development'; *The Convention on Biological Diversity, 1992; Year 1990, celebrated by UNO as International Year for the World's Indigenous People* etc.

also made it clear that under the cover of this order, no adivasis should be permitted to cut any trees.[75]

The order of the Madhya Pradesh state government permitting the villagers living in or around the proposed parks and sanctuaries to enter such places and collect *tendu* leaves has been questioned before the Supreme Court. One of the reasons for the shrinkage of forests being the entry of villagers and tribals living in and around sanctuaries and the national parks, there can be no doubt that urgent steps must be taken to prevent any destruction or damage to the environment, the flora and fauna, and wildlife in those areas. The Court made clear, the duty to protect forests despite the need to respect the traditions of indigenous people.[76]

When tribals were granted fishing rights in the Pench National Park in the state of Madhya Pradesh, it was questioned in public interest before the Supreme Court. Directing the proper implementation of the licensing conditions and monitoring of fishing activity, the Supreme Court held that every effort should be made to ensure that the tribals, when resettled, are in a position to earn their livelihood.[77]

Protecting the interest of indigenous people, the Madras HC has held that mere payment of compensation for the land acquired in tribal areas without taking into consideration their prevailing situation where they are living was not enough to avoid social disorganization and economic destitution of the affected people, creating conditions of discontent and unrest in the scheduled areas. The flora and fauna in tribal areas maintains the tribal economy

and should not be disturbed. Clearance of the Tribal Welfare Department of the state shall be taken before taking up any schemes in the tribal areas of the state. No new irrigation schemes should be taken up in areas where there will be a submergence of tribal land. In such cases, construction of major and medium irrigation projects shall be avoided to the extent possible and small check dams, lift-irrigation schemes, and other such projects, should be taken up, the Court added.[78]

The tribal population is very vulnerable. In order to protect Scheduled Tribes, there has been a constitutional and legal scheme in place. The scheme of the Constitution (Schedule V) is to realize the constitutional objective of removing social and economic inequality and to work towards equality of status. The primary responsibility of the state is to create conditions favourable to the realization of the Right to Development which is a part of Right to Life enshrined in Article 21 of the Constitution.[79]

The Government of India has enacted the Scheduled Tribes and other Traditional Forest Dwellers (Recognition of Forest Rights) Act, 2006 to recognize and vest forest rights in such forest dwelling scheduled tribes on forest land and their habitat, where they are scheduled and have been living for generations. They have been given the right to take the forest produce.

Protecting Cardamom Hills

An extent of 334 square miles in the *taluks* of Devicolam, Peermade, and Udumbanchola in the Kottayam district in Kerala, have been declared a Cardamom Hill Reserve (CHR)

[75] *Banwasi Seva Asram v. State of UP,* (1987) 3 SCC 304, AIR 1987 SC 374; also *Pradip. D. Prabhu v. State of Maharastra,* 1995 Supp (3) SCC 450.

[76] *Krishnen v. Union of India,* 1996 (8) SCC 599, AIR 1996 SC 2040.

[77] *Animal and Environmental Legal Defence Fund v. Union of India,* AIR 1997 SC 1071.

[78] *Sarapu Chinna Potharaju Dora v. The District Collector, East Godavari,* Writ Petition No. 8476 of 2001, dated 12 February 2002.

[79] *Samatha v. State of Andhra Pradesh,* AIR 1997 SC 3297 p. 3329–44; also *P. Rami Reddy v. State of Andhra Pradesh,* AIR 1988 SC 1626; also supra note 189, p. 319–21.

area and was not notified as reserved forest in 1897 by the then Maharaja of Travancore. Later on, when the state of Kerala was formed in 1956, it was found that those lands were in the possession of certain encroachers. The state government has found a novel way of protecting the said lands which have been encroached upon by cardamom cultivators for about twenty years, by framing the Rules for Lease of Government Lands for Cardamom Cultivation, 1961.[80] The government has leased such lands to the encroachers on the condition that the assignee shall not change the use of the land to that other than for cardamom cultivation.

The Cardamom hills area falls in a vital area adjacent to fragile forests in a place called Munnar, and is part of the Periyar Tiger Reserve. Encroachment on a massive scale took place in Munnar area as per the report of the Additional Director General of Police (Intelligence) Idukki, Rajan K. Madhekar:

There is formation that large scale encroachment of revenue/forest land an issue of forged pattayams[81] are going on in Idukki District especially in Munnar, Devikulam, Kannan Devan Hills Village, etc. with the active support of the concerned revenue official. It is known that about 3,000 forged pattayams were issued in the Idukki district. Political parties/ religious organizations/government employees/ traders/businessmen are also included among these illegal occupants. Some of these illegal occupants obtained huge amounts from banks/financial establishments as loans, by producing these forged pattayams. Though cases are being registered in this regard, the action is not being continued allegedly due to political influence.

The Centrally Empowered Committee of the Supreme Court referred the said matter to the Supreme Court of India and the Court has taken up the issue very seriously.[82]

This above enactment is clearly an example of sustainable development. The usage of land as cardamom plantations will help to keep the area fragile while also being productive. But enactment of the law alone will not help to make the area green unless it is implemented in its letter and spirit.

Mining in Forests[83]

Mining in forest areas adversely affects flora and fauna. Mining from rivers disturbs the river ecology. In forests, non-forest activities are prohibited. To carry out such activities, sanction from MoEF is required.

The Kudremukh National Park, a notified natural park in the state of Karnataka, is rich in wildlife and comprises of evergreen forests. The correctness of the order of sanction granted for mining in Kudremukh National Park was considered by the Supreme Court. The committee constituted by the Court filed a report to wind up all mining operations within a period of five years. The Central Government and the state were inconsistent in their approach towards the justified period for which the activities could be permitted. Reasons have been highlighted to justify the somersault, the Court observed. However, it was imperative that due application of mind be made before taking a particular stand, this being preferred to the chameleon-like behaviour that ensued. It was reiterated by the Court that a duty is cast upon the government under Article 21 of the Constitution of India to protect the environment and the two salutary principles

---

[80] Rules framed in exercise of the powers under Section 7 of the Kerala Government Land Assignment Act, 1960.

[81] Pattayams are title deeds issued by the Government.

[82] *T.N. Godavarman Thirumulpad v. Union of India*, IA No. 1408, dated 7 October 2005.

[83] For a detailed discussion on Mining in Forests, see 'Mining in Forest Areas' in the section on 'Land Pollution'.

which govern the law of environment are: (i) the principle of sustainable development and (ii) the precautionary principle. It needs to be highlighted that the Convention on Biological Diversity has been acceded to by our country and therefore, its implementation is essential. It is necessary for the government to keep in view its international obligations while exercising discretionary powers under the Conservation Act unless there are compelling reasons to depart there from, the Court observed.[84]

A company applied for the renewal of a mining lease, but suppressed the fact that it was a reserved forest area. As per law, it should have obtained prior sanction from the Central Government. The HC rejected the application, citing the reason that the company had defrauded the court.[85]

Forest Produce

The term 'forest produce' as in the Indian Forest Act, 1927. It reads as follows:

Forest produce includes:

(a) the following whether found in, or brought from, a forest or not, that is to say:
   timber, charcoal, caoutchouc, catechu, wood-oil, resin, natural varnish, bark, lac, mahua flowers, mahua seeds, kuth and myraboloams, and

(b) the following when found in, or brought from, a forest, that is to say:
   i.   trees and leaves, flowers and fruits, and all other parts or produce, not herein-before mentioned, of trees,
   ii. plants not being trees (including grass, creepers, reeds, and moss), and all parts or produce of such plants,

   iii. wild animals and skins, tusks, horns, bones, silk cocoons, honey, and wax, and all other parts or produce of animals, and
   iv. peat, surface oil, rock, and minerals (including limestone, laterite, mineral oil and all products of mines or quarries).

The above definition has been subjected to judicial interpretation several times. The Madhya Pradesh HC stated that dung dropping from cattle grazing in the forest area is not produce.[86] A question has arisen about whether the 'daruni'[87] tree is forest produce. From the definition of forest produce, it would become crystal clear that trees, leaves, flowers, fruits, and all other parts or produce would be forest produce, and since the daruni tree fits this definition it cannot be cut down.[88]

Handicraft items such as mats, which are made of bamboo chips are common in India. The Supreme Court has held that bamboo carpet is not forest produce in the eyes of the law. The Court held that though bamboo as a whole is forest produce, 'if a product, commercially new and distinct, known to the business community as totally different is brought into existence by human labour, such an article and product would cease to be a forest produce.'[89] It held that the expression 'forest produce' does not take within its meaning an article or thing which is totally different from forest produce, having a distinct character. Bamboo is a tree that falls within the definition of 'forest produce'; however items[90] made of bamboo chips would not fall within the definition of forest

---

[84] K.M. Chinnappa, T.N. Godavarman Thirumalpad (2002) 10 SCC 606, AIR 2003 SC 724.

[85] *Reliance Granite v. Government of Andhra Pradesh*, AIR 2006 AP 292.

[86] *Barkat and Others v. State of MP*, AIR 1987 MP 162.

[87] A kind of tree, the wood of which is used as firewood.

[88] *Range Officer v. Balkrishnan*, AIR 2002 J&K 42; also *Sanjay Lodha v. State of Jharkhand*, AIR 2003 Jhar 64.

[89] *Suresh Lohiya v. State of Maharastra*, (1996)10 SCC 397, 1996 AIRSCW 4111.

[90] Toplas, supdas, and palas made of bamboo chips.

produce.[91] But 'katha or catechu,'[92] is a forest produce, according to the Allahabad HC.[93]

The Allahabad HC has gone to the extent of declaring that 'even mines and minerals which remained beneath the surface of earth with stones and other products locked up in the land' are 'forest produce'. If such products are taken through a forest area, a transit fee is liable to be paid. The court held that stones, boulders, and other such materials, will be treated as 'brought from forest' and thus liable to certain fees, if they pass through forest area.[94]

DEVELOPMENTS ABROAD

United Kingdom

The Forestry Act, 1967 mandates that for felling trees, a licence is required from the Forestry Commission. Under Section 9 (2), the felling of trees over 8 centimetres in diameter measured from 1.3 metres from the ground, sanction must be obtained. But no such sanction is required for fruit trees, trees in gardens, orchards, churchyards, or open public spaces, topping or lopping of trees, operations under the forestry dedication scheme, or where less than 30 cubic centimetres of timber per quarter is harvested. It is the duty of the Commission to endeavour to achieve a balance between the management of forests and the conservation of landscape and nature. It has a duty to consult the local planning authority. If the sanction is granted, there is an obligation to restock the land, unless the Commission waives it.[95] The scheme is thus

similar to the Indian legislation that provides for afforestation also.

Germany

The Federal Nature Conservation Act of 25 March 2002 is directed at nature conservation and landscape management, and lays out a comprehensive scheme which can be used to protect forests. The ecosystem at its delimited spatial scales shall be secured and protected in such a way that the biological functions, material and energy flows of the site in question, as well as the characteristic features of the landscape are conserved, developed, or restored. The non-regenerating natural resources shall be used in a rational and sustainable manner. The use of regenerating natural resources deserves particular attention as they must only be used in a way that ensures their sustained availability for the future. Adverse environmental impacts shall be minimized also by measures of nature conservation and landscape management, while vulnerable components of the ecosystem must not be allowed to suffer any lasting damage.

The soil shall be preserved in a way that allows it to function properly in the ecosystem, and erosion shall be prevented. The natural, closed, and littoral vegetation shall be secured and protected. In the case of land not used for agricultural, silvicultural, or horticultural purposes, the vegetation cover of which has been removed, the development of appropriately adjusted site-specific vegetation shall be allowed.

The exploration and extraction of mineral resources, excavation, and tipping shall be performed in such a way that any lasting damage to the ecosystem or the destruction of valuable parts and components of landscapes is prevented. Any unavoidable impairment of nature and landscape shall be compensated for or mitigated, in particular by encouraging the natural succession, as well as through restoration

---

[91] M/s Indian Wood Products Co. Ltd v. State of UP, AIR 1999 All 222.

[92] Catechu is an extract of Acasia.

[93] Supra note 91.

[94] Ashok Kumar v. State of Maharastra, AIR 1978 Bom 119 (FB).

[95] Simon Bell and Stuart Bell, Environmental Law, 2nd edn, New Delhi: Universal Law Publishing Co. Pvt Ltd.

to a more natural state ('re-naturing'), semi-natural landscaping, rehabilitation, land reclamation, or re-cultivation.

To safeguard the functioning of the ecosystem and its services, the biological diversity shall be preserved and developed. Biological diversity includes the diversity of habitats and biocoenoses, the diversity of species and genetic diversity at the species-scale. Wild species of fauna and flora, including their biocoenoses, as an integral part of the ecosystem, shall be preserved in their natural and historically evolved diversity. Within the areas of human settlement too, existing natural stocks such as forest stands, hedgerows, baulks and other eco-tones, brooks and streamlets, ponds, and other ecologically significant smaller landscape structures shall be preserved and developed. In view of their relevance to the ecosystem and for recreation, non-built up areas shall be preserved, the individual and overall expanse and the properties and functions of which enable them to fulfil their purpose in this context. Sealed surfaces that are not required any longer shall be restored to a more natural state ('re-natured') or, where de-sealing is not possible or is excessively expensive, they shall be left to natural development or succession.

Other activities such as water engineering and development measures, which must be geared to preserve natural conditions to the extent possible, are also restricted. The development of a sustainable energy supply, particularly through the increasing use of renewable energy resources, is of particular importance. Forest and other areas with favourable climatic effects as well as local air-exchange pathways shall be preserved, developed, or restored.

A general awareness and understanding of the tasks and objectives of nature conservation and landscape management shall be promoted by appropriate means. In the case of measures planned for nature conservation and landscape management, the early exchange of information with parties concerned and interested segments of the general public shall be safeguarded.[96] By a comprehensive scheme of general nature conservation, Germany is able to protect its forests just as effectively as India, which has taken a different approach in making a number of forest-specific enactments.

Bangladesh

The Forest Act, 1927 is enacted to protect forests, the transit of forest produce, and the duty leviable on timber and other forest produce. The government is empowered to reserve any forest land or waste land or any other land suitable for afforestation in the prescribed manner.[97] Such lands are declared as protected forests.[98] Sanction of the government is necessary for land clearing, use of pesticides, harvest on steep slopes, or other forest management activities on private land.[99] For the purpose of trying offences under the Act, a Forest Magistrate has been specially constituted.[100]

Forests are important for ecological, economic, and aesthetic reasons. The state and Central legislatures of India have attempted to balance the various interests that exist in relation to forests. Essentially incorporating the concept of sustainable development, forests may be used by humans under the watchful eye of the authorities, which facilitate various mechanisms to replace forests that have been removed. The judiciary has also played a vital role in protecting forests and consequently, India is quite fortunate to have a comprehensive framework in the sphere of environmental protection and conservation.

[96] Principles of Nature Conservation and Landscape Management, Article 2.
[97] The Forest Act, 1927, Section 5.
[98] Ibid., Section 29.
[99] Ibid., Section 29A.
[100] Ibid., Section 67A.

TOWN PLANNING

Town planning regulations are land use laws intended to better the environment in which we live. The exploration of built and social environments falls within the ambit of this law. For a sustainable city, proper town planning is essential.

Indian Laws

There are several town planning laws in India, which are administered by the states and intended to regulate the development of towns. They are meant to give present and future inhabitants well-planned cities with proper sanitary conditions, amenities, and conveniences. The laws tackle the allotment of land for streets, open spaces, gardens, houses, buildings for religious and charitable purposes, recreation grounds, schools, markets, shops, factories, hospitals, dispensaries, government and municipal buildings, and other public amenities. Such laws also provide for the imposition of conditions and restrictions on the character, number, architectural features and dimensions of buildings allowed in specified areas. They may also regulate the purpose for which buildings or specified areas may be appropriated, and the provision and maintenance of sufficient open space around buildings. The law provides for the preparation of a town planning scheme, determining the lines on which the improvement and development of the areas are included in the scheme. For a healthy environment, it is essential that development be carried out as per the town planning laws of the concerned state.

Chandigarh, Ahmedabad, Bhubaneshwar, and New Raipur are some of the well-planned cities in India. The violation of the Delhi town planning scheme has resulted in the establishment of industries in residential areas, the removal of which is often directed by the courts. Green Benches of the courts are now monitoring development closely.

Case Law

Can it be said that the conversion of an open space reserved for a public park into a privately owned and managed hospital for private gain is not an alteration or improvement of the scheme? Protection of the environment, open spaces for recreation and fresh air, playgrounds for children, promenades for residents, and other conveniences or amenities are matters of great public concern and must be included in a development scheme. The public has an interest in the preservation of open space for parks and playgrounds and this cannot be sacrificed by leasing or selling such sites to private persons for conversion to other uses. Any such act is contrary to legislative intent and inconsistent with statutory requirements. Reservation of open spaces for public parks and playgrounds is universally recognized as a legitimate exercise of the statutory power for the protection of residents from the ill-effects of urbanization.

Open lands are often vested in the municipality and are meant to maintain the ecology, and for use as recreation parks and playgrounds, and for access to fresh air. A direction for the construction of buildings on such land affects health, environment, and sanitation in the locality. Where land is taken from the citizens for a public purpose, the municipality is required to use the land for the protection or preservation of hygienic conditions for the local residents in particular, and the people in general, and not for any other purpose.[101]

There have been many rulings by the courts in India that protect the public right to have access to open spaces. The Supreme Court has

[101] *Virender Gaur v. State of Haryana*, 1995 (2) SCC 577.

held null and void and ultra vires a resolution of the Bangalore Development Authority approving a government order to convert a site designated as a public park and civic amenity into a private nursing home by the Bangalore Medical Trust.[102] But the Supreme Court has subsequently diluted the above dictum. It considered whether the government can deprive a person of the use of his land without acquiring the land. Answering the question in the negative, the Court held that the mere fact that the development plan was prepared and the area had been earmarked for a definite purpose could not deprive a person of his own use of his land.[103] This illustrates that the court must carefully balance public rights against individual rights.

The Delhi High Court has held that the conversion of a residential area into a commercial area cannot be justified.[104] Delhi has often been made miserable for living due to the establishment of several industries. The second Master Plan of Delhi[105] in 1990 stipulated that industries may be set up only in industrial areas earmarked for the purpose. A large number of industries have come up in residential areas. Despite the lapse of three years since the preparation of the Master Plan, nothing significant in respect of infrastructure or other conditions had been done by the government. The Supreme Court interfered and issued directions stipulating a time limit.[106]

In 2001, the Delhi Development Authority identified an area for urban use and planned to develop the area for construction of hotels and convention centres. The Expert Committee reported violation of environmental norms and the Supreme Court directed the Central Government to decide what remedial measures, including the imposition of fines, could be taken.[107]

Questioning industrial activity in a residential area, a writ petition was filed before the Karnataka HC. The development plan of the city earmarked the area for a residential purpose. Consequently, the industrialists who were establishing industries in the area in violation of the provisions of various Acts were directed to stop such activities.[108]

The Madras HC has also interfered with the conversion of an open land reserved for a public park into house sites and restrained the construction of buildings.[109]

A town planning scheme was framed under Section 192(2) of the Punjab Municipal Act,[110] preserving a particular place as an open space for developing a park, which would provide lung space for the inhabitants of the locality. As the area was earmarked as an open space, the owners of the space could not successfully assert ownership over the area.[111]

The KHC found that the very object of the town planning scheme would be vulnerable to defeat if the scheme was not implemented within a reasonable period. It found that there was no time limit for initiating land acquisition proceedings for

[102] Bangalore Medical Trust v. Mudappa, AIR 1991 SC 1902, 1991 SCC (4) 54.

[103] Raju S. Jethmalani and others v. State of Maharashtra and Others, Civil 2005(4) SCC 235, CDJ 2005 SC 471.

[104] B-Block Residents Welfare Association v. DDA, AIR 2003 Delhi 169.

[105] Enforced wef 1 August 1990.

[106] M.C. Mehta v. Union of India, 2004 AIRSCW 4173.

[107] T.N. Godavarman Thirumulpad v. Union of India, 2006 AIRSCW 5660.

[108] V. Lakshmipathy v. State, AIR 1992 Kant 57.

[109] Rama Doss v. Secy Municipal Administration, (2000) 3 MLJ 317.

[110] Punjab Municipal Act, 1911 Section 192 (2).

[111] Municipal Corporation v. Balinder Bachan Singh, (2004) 5 SCC 182.

the implementation of the scheme framed under the Town Planning Act.[112]

It has been considered whether exemption can be granted from the town planning regulations. The Supreme Court has held that the authorities have the power to grant exemption. While exercising such power, the authority must keep in mind the purpose and the policy of the Act and the relief must equate the resultant effect of such exemption on both the public and the individual. So long as it does not materially affect the public cause, the exemption would try to eliminate individual hardship, which would be within the permissible limit of the exercise of the power. But where it erodes public safety, convenience, health, and the like, the exercise of the power does not further the purpose of the Act. Minor abrasions here and there to eliminate greater hardship may be appropriate and justified in a given case, but not where the public at large is affected, the Supreme Court clarified.[113]

The KHC also held that the granting of individual exemptions for constructions is not permitted by the local legislation and is arbitrary.[114]

The open space in a residential area or a busy township is treated as lung space for residents of that area. The same cannot be bartered for the financial gain of the local authority. The local authority was restrained by a judgement of the KHC from selling any portion of the land set apart as an open space for the establishment of parks and a nursery school.[115]

When an open space for the construction of a public park is preserved and earmarked in the town plan, the Development Authority is bound to develop that open space into a public park within a reasonable time, the Allahabad HC clarified. The expansive layout of good parks is not only for aesthetic appreciation, but also a necessity in fast-developing towns, which are often just a conglomeration of buildings. In crowded towns where residents are burdened by an atmosphere polluted by smoke and fumes emitted by endless vehicular traffic and factories, the efficacy of beautifully laid-out parks can be likened to the lungs of a human being. It is the verdant cover provided by public parks and green belts in a town that renders considerable relief to the restless public. Hence, the importance of public parks or private lawns cannot be under-estimated nor can they be considered a luxury. A public park is a gift of modern civilization and is a significant factor for the improvement of the quality of life. The provision of open space for a public park is an essential feature of modern planning and development, as it greatly contributes to the improvement of social ecology. Amendment of the town plan by the Development Authority or state government is not permitted if it destroys such basic features in allowing the conversion of open spaces designated for public parks, the court held.[116]

Directions were sought for the preservation and maintenance of Cubbon Park, an important park in Bangalore, 'the Garden City'. In particular, directions were sought to give effect to the full extent of the notification of 1983, which designated the area as a park. The Supreme Court issued directions prohibiting any further construction in the park.[117]

---

[112] Town Planning Act 1108; *Francis v. Chalakudy Municipality*, 1999 (3) KLT 560.

[113] *Consumer Action Group v. State of Tamil Nadu*, AIR 2000 SC 3060.

[114] *Sayeesh Kumar and Others v. The State of Kerala represented by the Secretary and Others*, 2005 (4) KLT 1027.

[115] *Shasthri Nagar Colony Welfare Commiteee v. Calicut Development Authority*, 2006 (1) KLT 294, AIR 2006 Ker 46.

[116] *D.D. Vyas v. Ghaziabad Development Authority*, AIR 1993 ALL 57.

[117] *Shri Bimal. N. Desai v. State of Karnataka*, AIR 2003 SC 2246, 2003 (5) SCC 395.

Ponds in temples in India are considered sacred and also help to maintain the surrounding environment. They are fundamental to the prayers of devotees and for positioning of the idol. The Rule provides that: 'the place of public worship and premises shall not be used for purposes not connected with or arising from the worship, usages and observations of such places of public worship.'

In applying the said rule, a pond cannot be divided as it is necessary that it remain whole for the performance of pooja, or ritual, in the temple. On the basis of the above view, the KHC directed the Travancore Devaswom Board not to proceed with an agreement that proposed the division of a portion of a pond.[118]

The Supreme Court has held that in future, before lands are acquired for development, the consequence and adverse impact of development on the environment must be properly comprehended and the acquisition may take place only if it will not gravely impair ecology and the environment.[119]

The granting of a sanction allowing a public meeting to be held in a sports stadium was the subject of litigation. The Supreme Court of India noted that crores of taxpayers' money had been spent to erect the stadium. Taxpayers have a right to see that the stadium is maintained for its specified purpose and not treated as a regular public place to be hired at the convenience of anyone. The court condemned the practice of hiring out the stadium and was not persuaded by the justification that the wealth of the state would be benefited by the Rs 2 lakh gained from daily rental.[120]

The Supreme Court has declared that there exists a stark distinction between the interpretation of planning and zoning statutes that enforce ecological balance and regulate industrial effluents and hazardous industries, and those that relate to efforts that rehabilitate industry. Whether a legislation would be declared ultra vires, or what would be the effect and purport of legislation upon interpretation thereof, will depend upon the legislation in question vis-à-vis the constitutional provisions and other relevant factors. In one batch of cases, the Supreme Court was considering the validity of regulations framed by the Maharashtra Regional and Town Planning Act, 1996, to deal with a situation arising out of the closure or non-viability of various cotton textile mills. The regulations provided for the development of the surplus land made available because of the closure of such mills. The court, in public interest, held that a balance should be struck between various interests like ecology, rights of owners, the interest of workers and sick industries that are closed and the scheme framed by the Board of Industrial and Financial Reconstruction for revival of those units.[121]

Foreign Laws

Similar town planning regulations are found across the globe. In the UK, the Town and Country Planning (Transitional Arrangements) (England) Regulations, 2004 were framed in exercise of the powers conferred by paragraphs 17(1), (2), and 18 of Schedule 8 of the Planning and Compulsory Purchase Act, 2004.

In the UK, an application was made before the court to cancel permission for a football club to rebuild part of its stadium on the banks

---

[118] K. Chandran v. Travancore Devaswom Board , ILR 2003 (3) Ker 440.

[119] Karnataka Industrial Areas Development Board v. C. Kenchappa, 2006 AIRSCW 2547.

[120] J. Jayalalitha v. Government of Tamil Nadu, AIR 1999 SC 2330, 1999 (1) SCC 53.

[121] Bombay Dyeing and Mfg Co. Ltd v. Bombay Environmental Action Group, (2006) 3 SCC 434.

of the river Thames. The proposal involved the creation of a riverside walkway which would encroach slightly upon the river and involve the remodelling of a retaining wall, which would affect the river's habitat. The House of Lords held that the Town and Country Planning (Assessment of Environmental Effects) Regulations, 1982 require that projects that are likely to have a significant effect on the environment be made subject to an assessment of those effects. Planning permission is not to be granted in respect of an application, unless account has been taken of information provided by the developer by way of an environmental statement prepared in accordance with law. As no EIA was conducted, the permission granted was cancelled by the House of Lords.[122]

ILLEGAL CONSTRUCTIONS

India

In order to construct a building one must obtain sanctions from the concerned self-government institution such as the municipality, Maharpalika, or Grama Panchayat. Building rules are in force in all states and the Building Code prescribes certain restrictions. Municipal authorities are public bodies constituted for the principal statutory duty of ensuring sanitation and health and are, therefore, obliged to properly maintain roads, streets, canals, and other facilities. Constructions contrary to the said rules are deemed illegal, being hazardous to people and posing a threat to life. Despite this, such illegal constructions are common in India.

The Municipal Corporation is the custodian of the rights of the people and has been given by law the right to enforce its by-laws by refusing sanction, preventing constructions, and demolishing buildings that may violate any law and/or by-law.

Complaints of unauthorized constructions are taken very seriously by the Supreme Court of India. In one landmark case, a municipality permitted a private builder to construct a new underground shopping complex in a park of historical importance, which went against the Master Plan for the area. The court held that a few crores spent on construction cannot be of great importance when the construction is in clear violation of local law and Article 21 of the Constitution. Unauthorized and illegal construction cannot be compounded and demands demolition. The court outlined the nature of its duty and explained that judicial discretion cannot be guided by expediency and courts are not free from statutory fetters. Judges are not entitled to exercise discretion wearing the robes of judicial discretion and pass orders based solely on their personal predilections and peculiar dispositions. The exercise of judicial discretion must be in accordance with the law and set legal principles. Any commercial activity places an additional burden on the locality.

The primary concern of the court was to eliminate the negative impact of underground shopping complexes on environmental conditions in the area, including increased congestion or roads on account of increased traffic and people visiting the complex. There was no reasonable alternative to the dismantlement of the whole structure and restoration of the park to its original condition while leaving a portion constructed for parking. The court was fully aware that it may not be possible to restore the park fully to its original condition for some time, as many trees had been damaged or removed, but was confident that beginning the task was necessary.[123] This case demonstrates

---

[122] *Berkeley v. Secretary of the State for Environment* (citation), dated 4 June 2003. http://www.elaw.org/resources/text.asp?ID=1771

[123] *M.I. Builders v. Radhey Shyam*, AIR 1999 SC 2468, (1999) 6 SCC 464.

just how vigilant the courts are in ensuring compliance with town planning regulations and how each case acts to deter others from breaking the law.

A person was granted sanction to construct a cinema theatre in a locality where he had only been granted a licence to construct a *Kalyan Mantap*-cum-lecture hall. In a writ petition, the Madras HC held that the cinema theatre could only be constructed at a specified locality with proper sanction, but since the defendant had spent a large sum of money on the construction, the court did not quash the said order granting sanction. The matter was taken up before the Supreme Court. If a scheme is nullified by arbitrary acts in excess and derogation of the powers of the municipality, the court will quash orders passed by the municipality. The court enforces the performance of statutory duties performed by public bodies as an obligation to rate payers who have a legal right to demand compliance by a local authority, with its duty to observe statutory rights alone. The special and substantial interest of the residents in the area was injured by the illegal construction and the Supreme Court quashed the order, contrary to the decision of the HC.[124] Again, developers cannot simply be excused from the law on the basis that they have engaged in personal expenditure.

In another case from Madhya Pradesh, the Cantonment Board granted construction of a building, which was later cancelled. The HC allowed the petition on the grounds that the cancellation was made without giving notice to the developer and the construction had already commenced. The Supreme Court found that the land in question was in a cantonment area, the title of which vests in the Cantonment

Board. The competent officer to grant a sanction was the 'Defence Estates Officer' and therefore sanction should have been obtained from him, which had not been done by the earlier order. The Supreme Court directed the matter to be reconsidered. The court made it clear that construction made in contravention of the law would not be a premium to extend equity so as to facilitate violation of the mandatory requirements of the law.[125]

A housing society in Mumbai made a construction in violation of the Floor Space Index ratio prescribed by the statute. The Municipal Corporation issued a show cause notice and the HC upheld it. Challenging the same, the society approached the Supreme Court. Rejecting the petition, the Supreme Court observed that the case should be a signal to all builders that the making of unauthorized constructions never pays and is against the interests of society at large. The rules, regulations, and by-laws are made by the corporations or development authorities taking into account the larger public interest; it being the bounden duty of citizens to obey and follow such rules which are made for their own benefit, the court added.[126]

A petition was filed before the Delhi High Court by a group of residents of Sarita Vihar colony, which was developed by the Delhi Development Authority (DDA). It was contended that the DDA permitted the construction and establishment of a nursery school contrary to the provisions of The Delhi Development Act, 1957. The Delhi High Court dismissed their petition, but after considering the provisions of the Act and the

---

[124] *K. Ramadas Shenoy v. The Chief Officers, Town Municipal Council, Udipi et al.*, AIR 1974 SC 2177, (1974) 2 SCC 506.

[125] *Cantonment Board, Jabalpur et al. v. S.N. Avasthi et al.*, 1995 Supp (4) SCC 595.

[126] *Pratibha Cooperative Housing Society Ltd and Another v. State of Maharashtra et al.*, AIR 1991 SC 1453, (1991 (3) SCC 341.

Master and Zonal Development Plans, the Supreme Court found that the site at which the school was permitted to operate was meant for a park. The Supreme Court stated that it was not open to the DDA to carve out a space for the construction of a nursery school in a place which was reserved for a park. Using the allotment to open a nursery school equated to a misuse of power and the allotment was cancelled. The Supreme Court observed that the construction put up by the allottee, even though permanent, was of no relevance as it had been carried out on a plot of land allotted to it in contravention of the law. As to the submission that dislocation from the present site would cause difficulty for the young children, the Supreme Court was not persuaded and noted that this argument had only been made to provoke sympathy from the court. It was open for the children to be placed in nursery schools in adjoining areas, whether these be set up by the allottee or by some other person. A six-month period was also granted to the allottee in which to make alternative arrangements to shift the school so that the children were not put in a disadvantageous position. Strong warnings were given by the Supreme Court against such illegal constructions.[127]

A building was constructed in gross violation of local law and the court ordered that the flats on the top four floors be demolished. The demolition was challenged in the high court, which considered the plight of those who had already purchased flats in the said building. The high court directed the return of any payments made, in addition to the escalation charges. The Supreme Court, finding that the escalated price as on the date was around Rs 1.5 crore per flat and taking into consideration the totality of the circumstances, directed

the builder to pay Rs 60 lakh, including the amount paid by the allottees.[128]

An unauthorized construction in the city of Kolkata was earmarked for demolition by the Corporation of Kolkata. The Supreme Court found that the builder had taken undue advantage of the interim order obtained, suppressing material facts and taken legal process to delay the process and solicit tenants. The court dismissed the case and imposed exemplary costs while dismissing the writ petition.[129]

A hotel was constructed in a hilly area of Kodaikanal in the state of Tamil Nadu in blatant violation of Building Rules. The Supreme Court directed the demolition of the illegal building and directed the launch of appropriate prosecution steps.[130]

An application was submitted for repair of the ground and upper floors of a building. The application was granted even though no such upper floors existed. The builder took advantage of the approved application and constructed six floors. Subsequently, the municipal authority regularized the construction. The Supreme Court held that there is no statutory power to regularize such illegal construction under the Maharashtra Regional and Town Planning Act, 1966, and the construction was declared illegal.[131]

Adopting a very serious view of the rampant unauthorized constructions in Cuttack, the Supreme Court directed that the high court could suo motu register a PIL in certain circumstances. This power can be

---

[127] *G.N. Khajuria et. al v. Delhi Development Authority et. al*, AIR 1996 SC 253, 1995 (5) SCC 762.

[128] *Manju Bhatia and Another v. New Delhi Municipal Committee et. al*, AIR 1998 SC 223, (1997) 6 SCC 370.
[129] *Ram Awatar Agarwal et. al, v. Corporation of Calcutta*, (1996) 6 SCC 531.
[130] *Pleasant Stay Hotel and Another v. Palani Hills Conservation Council et. al*, (1995) 6 SCC 127.
[131] *Mahendra Baburao Mahadik v. Subhash Krishna Kantikar*, 2005 AIRSCW 1579.

used where the high court feels that illegal and unauthorized building activities in Cuttack are so rampant that they necessitate judicial attention, where the monitoring of the same by issuing directions can be used to curb such activities and fix liability and accountability.[132]

It is common practice in certain parts of India to construct temples on public land, which is illegal. However, the authorities are afraid to take action against such persons due to the religious sentiments of the people. The Supreme Court of India, taking a very serious view of the matter, held that the said constructions are illegal and if constructed on public land, must be removed forthwith.[133]

Development can be carried out only with the approval or sanction of the authority concerned and the erection of a building must be as per the building by-laws and the Building Code of India. Any violation is always open to action by the competent authority. The Delhi High Court, taking a serious view of the matter, directed the Chief Fire Officer to take immediate action to see that fire safety measures are provided in high-rise buildings, business buildings, or mercantile buildings in accordance with building by-laws and the National Building Code of India. In the event of any contravention, the Chief Fire Officer was directed to take action as indicated in the provisions contained in the Fire Safety Act.[134]

The continuation of rampant illegal constructions has been taken cognizance of by the Supreme Court despite all the above directions. A suggestion was mooted that whenever an illegal construction comes to notice, at first an opportunity should be granted to the wrong-doer to carry out the rectification and demolition. In the event of his failure to do so, the illegal construction should automatically and by operation of law, vest in the state, free from all encumbrances, with no obligation on the state to pay any compensation in respect thereof. The issue of how to address the increasing trend of illegal constructions is still open to debate.[135]

The state of Kerala framed a unique legislation to regularize all illegal constructions on payment of a prescribed fee. The KHC interfered with the matter and held that there shall be no compromise of public safety, health, and convenience while considering such applications.[136] The Madras HC also recently interfered with such an amendment, which had the effect of bypassing the existing laws on constructions.[137]

The Supreme Court of India had the occasion to observe that in many parts of the country common village land has been grabbed by the unscrupulous persons using muscle power, money power, or political clout, and in many states now there is not an inch of such land left for the common use of the people of the village. The Court has issued directions to all the state governments to prepare a scheme to evict all the illegal or unauthorized occupants of the land. The Court made it clear that regularization should be done only in case where lease has been granted to landless

---

[132] *Friends Colony Development Committee v. State of Orissa*, AIR 2005 SC 1, (2004) 8 SCC 733.

[133] *Mahesh Prasad Gupta v. Rg. High Court*, (Rg High Court) (2003)10 SCC 691.

[134] *B.L. Wadheera v. Union of India*, CMP No. 6904/2004 in WP(C) No. 2710/1998, August 2004.

[135a] *Supreme Court Monitoring Committee v. Mussoorie Deharaum Dev*, AIR 2002 SC 2876: (2003) 10 SCC 445.

[136] *Institute of Social Welfare v. State*, 2006 (2) KLT 871.

[137] *Consumer Action Group v. State*, WP Nos 18898 of 2000 and other cases, 23 August 2006.

labourers or members of Scheduled Caste/ Scheduled Tribes or where there is already a school, dispensary, or other public utility on the land.[138]

In order to provide a safe and healthy environment, it is necessary to recognize that our environment has both natural and man-made elements. Town Planning legislation seeks to regulate the impact of a man-made environment on the natural environment and on the health of the people. Proper implementation and enforcement of these laws ensures that we may have the facilities necessary for a functional life while preserving the natural environment that is integral to a comfortable and happy one.

[138] *Jaspal Singh v. State of Punjab*, 2011 AIR SCW 990.

13 Endangered Wildlife

Wildlife forms part of the cultural heritage of India in the same manner as other archaeological monuments, paintings, literature, and the like. All animals play a vital role in maintaining the ecological balance. In the third century BC, King Asoka, emperor of India, 273–232 BC issued an order that has a particularly contemporary ring in the matter of preservation of wildlife and the environment. Towards the end of his reign he wrote:

Twenty six years after my coronation I declared that the following animals were not to be killed: parrots (mynas), the aruna, ruddy geese, Wild geese the andimukha cranes, bats, queen ants, terrapins, boneless fish, tortoises, porcupines, squirrels, twelve-antler deer, household animals and vermit, rhinoceroses, white pigeons, domestic pigeons, and quadrupeds which are not useful or edible... Forests must not be burned.[1]

Asoka practised Buddhism, which holds that animals should not be eaten and that an aged or disabled cow or work animal should be retired and well-treated. Interrupting a hunt upon arrival in Sri Lanka in 247 BC, 'Arahat Mahinda[2] stopped King Devanampiyatissa from killing the deer and told the king that every living creature has an equal right to live,' according to Sri Lankan elephant conservationist Jawantha Jayewardene.[3] Persuaded, the king became a Buddhist and 'decreed that no one should kill or harm any living being.' The King, Jayewardene continued. 'He set apart a large area around his palace as a sanctuary that gave protection to all fauna and flora. This was called Mahamevuna Uyana, and is believed to be the first sanctuary in the world.' Arahat Mahinda and the other Asokan emissaries also introduced animal sheltering as a central function of monasteries wherever they went. Buddhist monasteries in Thailand and Sri Lanka to this day often double as animal shelters, though at some point the custom was distorted and just a lone chained temple elephant is kept.[4]

In the Bible it was especially emphasized that animals should be cared for and it is stated that 'The Godly are concerned for the welfare of their animals.'[5]

India is home to 411 mammals, 1,232 birds, 456 reptiles, 2,546 fishes, 83,436 invertebrates, and over 50,000 plant species. The tiger, one-horned rhinoceros, and Asian elephant are among the rarest species in the country. Indian wildlife also contains twenty-five of the world's hotspots, sixteen of the world's most important wetlands, and five natural world heritage sites

[1] *Fundamentals of Conservation Biology* by Malcolm L. Hunter and Andrea Sulzer. Blackwell Publishing, 2002.
[2] Son of Asoka, sent to propagate Buddhism.
[3] Sri Lankan ruler.
[4] M. Clifton 2007.
[5] Book of Proverbs, Chapter 12, Verse 10.

as defined by UNESCO. Home to ten bio-geographic regions, the country is the last refuge for a number of highly endangered and threatened species.

CONVENTION ON INTERNATIONAL TRADE IN ENDANGERED SPECIES OF WILD FAUNA AND FLORA (CITES)[6]

On 3 March 1973, a significant international convention, popularly known as the Convention on International Trade in Endangered Species of Wild Fauna and Flora (CITES), took place in Washington. India signed this agreement in July 1974 and submitted the instrument for ratification on 20 July 1976. Thus, India became a party to the CITES from 18 October 1976. The CITES was amended at Bonn, on 22 June 1979.

Appendix I of the instrument includes all species threatened with extinction or that are or may be affected by trade, where hunting of the same is prohibited. Trade in specimens of these species is made subject to strict restrictions in order to not further endanger their survival. The animals in Appendix III do not attract the same treatment as those in Appendix I, and can be killed and hunted. The African elephant is included in Appendix III. The net effect of this was that while hunting of the Asian elephant was banned, and international trade in Asian ivory was virtually prohibited, the African elephant could still be hunted. In October 1989 at Lausanne, the parties to CITES again met and included the African elephant in Appendix I, thus removing the anomaly. The meet, held in June 2007 at Hague, has added a new species, the European eel, and the pau brasil tree of Brazil.

[6] Convention on International Trade in Endangered Species of Wild Fauna and Flora, came into force on 1 July 1975, 993 UNTS 243.

Indian law on wildlife protection is much more powerful in protecting wildlife than CITES, which is an international instrument. The Exim Policy of the Government of India also provides restrictions that are stricter than those in the convention. Almost all wild species of fauna are protected under Indian law and virtually a complete ban on hunting and export of even non-CITES species is in existence in India.

LAW OF ANIMALS IN INDIA

Wild Life Protection Act, 1972

The first legislation for the protection of birds was the Wild Birds Protection Act, 1887. However, the purpose of the Act was limited as it prohibited the possession or sale of only certain kinds of wild birds during the breeding season. As a consequence of the wanton killing of birds and animals, more comprehensive legislation was needed, the result being the Wild Birds and Animals (Protection) Act, 1912. The Act empowered the government to declare for any period, what was deemed a 'close time', during which specified kinds of wild birds or animals would not be killed and it was made unlawful to capture, kill, sell, buy, or possess any such bird or animal. In 1935, the Act was again amended, empowering the government to declare any area a sanctuary for birds or animals and their killing was made unlawful. Though the concept of 'sanctuary' was framed for the first time, the legislation could not effectively protect the birds. The rapid decline of India's wild animals and birds has been a matter of great concern. Existing laws are found often to work ineffectively or are not implemented zealously. After thirty-five years, the Wildlife Protection Act, 1972 (WPA) was enacted, which came into force with effect from 1 February 1973. The enactment mainly relates to control of hunting and does not emphasize the other factors that also attribute to the decline of India's wildlife, namely, taxidermy and trade in wildlife. The Preamble of the Act 'provides for the protection of wild animals and birds and for matters connected therewith or ancillary thereto.'

Animals are classified as mammals, amphibians and reptiles, fishes, birds, crustacean and insects, coelenterates, and mollusca in the schedule to the WPA. Animals that are captured, kept, or bred in captivity are called captive animals.[7]

According to the WPA, trade or commerce in wild animals, animal articles, and trophies within the country is permissible. However, as these things have a good market abroad, most of the items are smuggled out. This clandestine trade is abetted by the illegal practice of poaching, which has taken a heavy toll on the wild animals and birds in the country. Traders who declared their stocks at the commencement of the 1972 enactment misused the declaration to acquire more of these items. Therefore, the government decided to amend the 1972 legislation to prohibit trade in certain specified wild animals or their derivatives.

In 1982, the Act was amended and the exemption granted to ivory dealers was removed, imposing a total ban on dealing in Indian ivory. The amendment also provided some regulations over the manufacture and trade of articles made out of imported ivory.

The situation had not improved, and in 1986 the Act was again amended on the basis of recommendations of the Standing Committee of the Indian Board for Wildlife and various ministries of government. Prior to the coming into force of the Act, certain persons used to hold animals, especially elephants, and other animal articles such as

the trophy, derived from the animal. As per Section 40 of the WPA, every person having an elephant in custody or possession, had to make a declaration to the concerned Chief Wildlife Warden (CWW) before 31 June 1973.[8] The person will be given an ownership certificate. From 2003 onwards, the transfer of such ownership is prohibited.[9] If any person inherits the said animal, he has to intimate the Warden of such inheritance.[10] But these restrictions are not applicable to live elephants and recognized zoos.[11]

Though the WPA protects animals, it does not protect victims of these animals and there is no provision for providing damages to the victims of animal attacks. The mere fact that the killing of such animal is prohibited under the law and protection is provided to them does not make the state the owner of such wild animals.[12]

Chief Wildlife Warden

The authority to enforce the WPA is given to the CWW.[13] He is subject to directions from the state government. Once an area has been declared a sanctuary, entry into the area is restricted and regulated, and subject to permission being granted by the CWW.[14]

Right to entry in the sanctuary is not absolute and must be sanctioned by the CWW. The authority of the CWW was questioned when he prescribed entry fees for a sanctuary. The Rajasthan HC, upholding the action of the CWW, held that conditions

---

[7] WPA, Section 2 (5).

[8] Ibid., Section 40.

[9] WPA, Section 40 (2A), amended by Act 16 of 2003.

[10] Ibid., Section 40(2B).

[11] WPA , Section 40 (3).

[12] *State of HP v. Halli Devi*, AIR 2000 HP 113.

[13] Supra note 6, Section 4.

[14] *Essar Oil Ltd v. HU Samithi*, AIR 2004 SC 1834.

imposed by him, like a roster system[15] are in accordance with law.[16]

It has been questioned whether the CWW can delegate its powers to file a complaint for prosecuting the violators of the WPA against the normal principle of delegation that a delegate cannot delegate his powers unless he is empowered by law. The Patna HC has held that as the Bihar Wildlife Protection Rules, 1973 empower the Divisional Forest Officer (DFO) or Deputy Conservator of Forests to file complaints in addition to the CWW, the complaint filed on behalf of the DFO after obtaining sanction is valid.[17]

Wildlife Wardens

People's participation and support is essential for the conservation of wildlife. Section 4 of the Act also empowered the state government to appoint honorary Wildlife Wardens and payment of rewards to persons who help apprehend offenders. Wardens are public servants within the meaning of Section 21 of the IPC 1860. They can also detect and prosecute offences under the WPA. The Wildlife Advisory Board or the CWW of the state can entrust them with any other matter for the protection of wildlife in the country.

Immunization of Wild Animals

To curb large-scale mortality in wild animals due to communicable diseases, the enactment provides for compulsory immunization of livestock in and around national parks and sanctuaries. Realizing the need to protect offshore marine flora and fauna, the

provisions on national parks and sanctuaries are extended to territorial waters. It is also provided that while declaring any part of territorial waters a sanctuary, due precaution shall be taken to safeguard the occupational interests of local fishermen.

While making the provisions of the Act more effective and stringent, due regard has also been given to the rights of the local people, particularly indigenous people. Except for areas under reserve forests (where the rights of the people have already been settled) and the territorial waters, no area can be declared a sanctuary unless the rights of the people have been settled. State Wildlife Advisory Boards are also made responsible for suggesting ways and means to harmonize the needs of tribal people with the protection of wildlife.

Captive Animals

Animals that are captured and kept or bred in captivity are called 'captive animals'.[18] A captive animal is different from livestock and domestic animals.

Zoos are establishments, whether stationary or mobile, where captive animals are kept for exhibition to the public, and include circuses and rescue centres but do not include an establishment of a licensed dealer in captive animals. Zoos, if managed properly, serve a useful role in the preservation of wild animals. The growing awareness for nature and wildlife conservation has made zoos a popular institution. There are about 350 animal collections in India, which are visited by more than 50 million people annually.[19]

Section 38A of the WPA requires the constitution of a Central Zoo Authority (CZA). Standards have been prescribed for recognition by the Recognition of Zoo Rules,

---

[15] Identifying seven routes for plying of vehicles and types of vehicles.

[16] *Forest Friendly Camps Pvt Ltd v. State of Rajasthan*, AIR 2002 Raj 214.

[17] *Jagdish Singh v. State of Bihar*, 1983 Crl LJ 1314. (Patna High Court).

[18] Section 2 (5) WPA.

[19] National Zoo Policy, 1998.

1992.[20] CZA is responsible for overseeing the functioning and development of zoos in the country.

The Authority shall grant recognition with due regard to the interests of protection and conservation of wildlife, and such standards, norms, and other matters including the enclosures in which animals are to be kept, hygiene, feeding, upkeep, animal care, veterinary facilities, breeding of animals, and such other measures.[21] Zoos are classified into large, medium, small, and mini depending on the area they occupy.[22] Only recognized zoos are allowed to operate and the maintenance of animals must be in accordance with the norms and standards prescribed by the Authority.

The duties and responsibilities of zoo authorities have been reiterated by the Delhi HC. These authorities have to keep the animals in such a manner that under no circumstances are they able to cause any damage or injury to any visitors.[23]

The definition of a zoo is a broad one, and includes circuses and rescue centres. Looking at the pathetic conditions in which animals are kept, the Supreme Court of India, in public interest, has held that no new zoos can be set up without obtaining clearances from the CZA as well as specific orders from the court.[24]

The law presumes that where a person is in possession, custody, or control of any captive animal or animal article (meat, trophy, uncured, specified plant or part or derivative thereof), the said person is keeping it knowingly and has committed an offence. The said possessor must prove that he has not committed any offence.[25] The burden of proving lawful possession is on the accused.[26]

The threats faced by captive animals were considered by the Supreme Court in the case of skinning a live tigress in a zoo in Hyderabad (Andhra Pradesh), and a large number of deaths of white tigers in Bhubaneshwar (Orissa). In the case of *Navin M. Raheja* v. *Union of India*, the court issued directions to take steps to prevent the killing and poaching of tigers, and to focus attention on the status of tigers and other animals in captivity, particularly in zoos.[27]

The use of tetra packs inside the stalls in zoos was banned and subsequently challenged before the Orissa HC. The Court held that the ban was proper. It also held that the policy adopted of refusing the issue or renewal of a licence or lease, and establishment of such counters inside a zoo was not unreasonable as it ensures the health and welfare of animals.[28]

An application for recognition of a mobile zoo was rejected. While challenging the said order, the respondent also asked for compensation for the reason that he had surrendered the animals to the state. The Delhi HC, rejecting the plea, held that no compensation for animals that were illegally held in possession could be ordered.[29]

Over-exploitation has endangered the survival of certain plant species. Provisions have been made in the WPA to prohibit collection and exploitation of wild plants that are threatened with extinction. Cultivation

---

[20] Enacted under the WPA, Section 63.

[21] Recognition of Zoo Rules, 1992, Rule 10.

[22] Ibid., Rule 9.

[23] *Nitia Walia* v. *Union of India*, AIR 2001 Del 140.

[24] *Navin Raheja* v. *Union of India*, WP (C) No. 47 of 1998, dated 20 November 2000.

[25] WPA, Section 57.

[26] *Babu Lal* v. *State*, (1981) 20 *Delhi Law Times* 354.

[27] Supra note 23, also further orders in (2001)1 SCC 962: (2001) 9 SCC 505.

[28] *Narasingh Podhiary* v. *State of Orissa*, AIR 2001 Oris 176.

[29] *All India Mobile Zoo Owners* v. *Animal Welfare Association*, AIR 2000 Delhi 449.

and trade of such plants would, however, be permitted under licence. The provisions however, would not affect the collection of traditionally used plants for the bona fide personal use of tribal people.

Wildlife Sanctuaries and National Parks

Wildlife conservation also includes good management of parks and sanctuaries. Realizing the need to protect offshore marine flora and fauna, the same legal provisions have been extended to territorial waters.

Section 18 of the WPA empowers the state government to notify its intention to define sanctuaries. A sanctuary can be constituted of any area other than an area within any reserve forest or the territorial waters if it is considered that such an area is of adequate ecological, faunal, floral, geo-morphological, natural, or zoological significance, for the purpose of protecting, propagating, or developing wildlife or its environment. The District Collector has been empowered to entertain and determine claims in respect of or over the notified area under Sections 21 to 24. After considering all claims, the state government is required under Section 26A to issue a notification specifying the limits of the areas to fall within the sanctuary, after which the area shall be a sanctuary on and from such date as may be specified in the notification. Under subsection (3) of Section 26A, 'no alteration of the boundaries of a sanctuary shall be made except on a resolution passed by the Legislature of a State.' Once an area has been declared a sanctuary, entry into the area is restricted and regulated under Sections 27 and 28 and subject to permission being granted by the CWW who, under Section 33, is empowered to control, manage, and maintain all sanctuaries. The CWW is appointed under Section 4 of the Act, and sub-section (2) of Section 4 provides that in the performance of his duties

and exercise of his powers by or under this Act, the CWW shall be subject to such general or special directions as the state government may, from time to time, give.

The procedure for declaring an area a national park is substantially similar to the procedure relating to sanctuaries, and the power is vested in the state government.[30] In 1973, when the Kerala State Electricity Board proposed to construct a hydroelectric project by putting up a dam across Kunthipuzha, flowing through a place called the 'Silent Valley', it was met by opposition from the people. This was the first historical campaign which quickly symbolized the quest for the new paradigm termed 'development without destruction'. Later on, the government accepted the people's voice and declared the area a national park.[31]

If the procedure prescribed for declaration of an area as sanctuary is not followed, then the declaration itself becomes illegal.[32]

When the laying of pipelines was permitted through the Jamnagar Marine National Park and Sanctuary, it was questioned before the Supreme Court. It was contended that the state government can accord permission under Section 29 of the WPA only if it is necessary for the improvement and better management of wildlife. Since the laying of a pipeline through the sanctuary was not for the improvement and better management of the wildlife, no permit could be granted under Section 29. The court, after examining the law, held that the laying of pipelines does not fall under any of the prohibitions. The legislative intent is that the state government should apply its mind and achieve the requisite satisfaction.

[30] WPA, Section 35.

[31] SRO. No. 1462/1985, dated 23 November 1984.

[32] *Jakdhar Chakma v. Dy Commissioner, Aizwal*, AIR 1983 Gau 180.

Once the state government has exercised this power, it is not open to the CWW to decide to the contrary.[33] But the Court instructed the state that grant of the permit in any case does not result in destruction of the wildlife, while also stating that the habitat of wildlife is at least sustained.

Section 33A of the Act casts a duty on the CWW to take appropriate measures for the immunization against communicable diseases of livestock within five kilometres of a sanctuary. The immediate vicinity of each national park or sanctuary must possess a veterinary centre of the Animal Husbandry Department, which undertakes the immediate immunization of livestock that are being taken to the national park or sanctuary. When no such steps are taken, the Supreme Court of India must issue a direction in public, for the establishment of such centres in the immediate vicinity of the national park or sanctuary within their territory within two months.[34]

When a notification was issued reducing the area of the Narayan Sarovar Chinkara Sanctuary in the Gujarat district, it was challenged. The HC, after scrutinizing the documents, was of the view that the state legislature was quite aware about the wildlife. Here, without in any way diluting the commitment to protect wildlife and to improve the habitat, positive steps were taken so neither the wildlife nor the improvement was affected.[35]

The HC held that for about 1,200 chinkaras, the area of 444.23 square kilometres was quite sufficient. It further held that economic development of the area was likely to benefit the people of the Kutch district at large, and help in the protection, preservation, and development of flora and fauna of that area. In regard to the setting up of a cement plant near that area and mining of the de-notified area, the court held that proper conditions had been imposed for the prevention of pollution and satisfaction of other environmental requirements.[36] The issue went to the Supreme Court of India on appeal. Instead of quashing the notification, the Supreme Court permitted the restricted and controlled exploitation of mineral wealth, on the provision that the effects of the project were monitored for five years and a comprehensive environmental study was conducted. The state was directed to constitute a committee to monitor the work and was restrained from giving permission to others to carry on any mining operation or set up a cement plant within an area of ten kilometres from the periphery of the old sanctuary area, without prior permission from the Supreme Court.[37]

Assignment of private land situated inside a national park for running the business of boarding, lodging, and a restaurant has been challenged before the Karnataka HC. Interpreting the provisions of the Forest (Conservation) Act, 1980 and the WPA, the court held that there is an absolute prohibition on the grant of rights in respect of the part of the 'national park' and 'reserve forest' in favour of a company without the prior approval of the Central Government. Without the fulfilment of this requirement, the grant is void and cannot be acted upon.[38]

The restriction on the entry of vehicles into wildlife sanctuaries between 6 PM and 6 AM has been challenged before the Madras HC. The

---

[33] *Essar Oil Ltd v. Halar Utkarsh Samiti et. al*, AIR 2004 SC 1834.

[34] *Centre for Environmental Law WWF-I v. Union of India*, AIR 1999 SC 354.

[35] Ibid.

[36] *Consumer Education and Research Society v. Union of India*, AIR 1995 Guj 140.

[37] *Consumer Education and Research Society, Ahmedabad v. Union of India*, AIR 2000 SC 975.

[38] *Nagarhole Budakattu Hakku Sthapana Samithi v. State of Karnataka*, AIR 1997 Kant 288.

court held that once a particular area is declared and notified as a wildlife sanctuary, any private right of a person should be subject to the objectives of the Act. The right to use roads in the sanctuary is subject to any conditions imposed by the CWW or officers authorized by him. Such authorities are empowered to impose reasonable restrictions and conditions in the matter of entry and use of roads in the sanctuary area, taking into consideration the security, preservation, interests, habits, and movements of the wild animals in the sanctuary and general preservation of the area. The court held that the restriction imposed on the entry of vehicles at a certain time of the day in order to achieve the above object, cannot be complained as arbitrary and unreasonable or innocuous.[39]

Similarly, the introduction of a roster system[40] for tourist vehicles was challenged before the Rajasthan HC. The Court held that it is an environment-friendly concept and is not arbitrary.[41]

The state government is empowered to acquire more lands for the purpose of national parks.[42] The Supreme Court of India has clarified that acquisition of land for sanctuaries is not challengeable. Once the state government finds that such an area is of adequate ecological, faunal, floral, geomorphological, natural, or zoological significance for the purpose of protecting, propagating, or developing wildlife or its environment, the grievance of a person having right over any such property is limited to the determination.[43] Once an area is declared as a Wild Life Sanctuary, District Collectors concerned have to enquire into and determine the existence, nature, and extent of the rights of any person in or over the land comprised within the limits of the sanctuary. Till a final notification[44] is issued declaring the said area a national park, the state government does not have any power to bar the entry of villagers living in and around the sanctuaries and national parks.[45]

In a forest area, fishing operations were being carried out. The authorities initiated the process to declare the area a wildlife sanctuary, and restrained the fishing operations. The Andhra Pradesh HC, interfering with the matter, held that no authority is entitled to interfere with fishing operations in the area until the final notification is issued under the WPA.[46]

All commercial activities inside the sanctuary are prohibited. Even the formation of fish tanks for aquaculture, which has got the effect of restraining the flow of water into or outside the sanctuary, has to be stopped.[47]

But at the same time, construction of roads, bridges, buildings, fences, barrier gates, or other works necessary for the purpose of a sanctuary may be permitted. The KHC has held that for roads, only a small portion of the sanctuary is utilized and it is essential for the upkeep of the biological park and in a case where a few trees are cut from the area, one cannot jump to the conclusion that as a result of the project, the forest has been plundered.[48]

[39] *Bombay Burma Trading Corporation v. Field Director,* reported in AIR 2000 Mad 163.

[40] Time schedule.

[41] *Forest Friendly Camps Pvt Ltd v. State of Rajasthan,* AIR 2002 Raj 214.

[42] WPA, Section 18.

[43] *Nagar Palika Parishad v. State of UP,* AIR 1998 All 232.

[44] WPA, Section 26A or 35.

[45] *Pradeep Krishnan v. Union of India,* AIR 1996 SC 2040: (1996) 8 SCC 599.

[46] *Kumapuraju Rangaraju v. Government of AP,* AIR 1998 AP 273.

[47] *T.N. Godavaraman v. Union of India,* IA No. 1486–87 in WP(C) No. 202 of 1995, decided on 10 April 2006.

[48] *Niyamavedi v. State of Kerala,* 1993 (3) KLT 10. (Kerala).

Section 34A of the WPA empowers the officers of forests, not below the rank of Assistant Conservator of Forests, to evict any person from a sanctuary or national park who occupies the area without authorization.

Refugees from Pakistan were allotted certain land in 1978 under a scheme for rehabilitation. Later on, the area was declared a wildlife sanctuary in 2001. The said decision was challenged before the court on the ground that the refugees had a prior right. The Gujarat HC held that no one has a right to enter or possess a land in a sanctuary except under a permit granted by the CWW as per the scheme provided under Sections 27 and 28 of the WPA.[49]

When can an area be deemed to be a sanctuary? Rajasthan HC had the occasion to consider the question when it held that when the area does not fall in the forest landing according to Government records, it should not be treated as forest land.[50]

The Government of India launched a programme called Project Tiger[51] in 1972 to ensure a viable population of tigers in India for scientific, economic, aesthetic, cultural, and ecological values and to preserve for all time, areas of biological importance as a natural heritage for the benefit, education, and enjoyment of the people. The main objectives under the scheme include wildlife management, protection measures, and site specific eco-development to reduce the dependency of local communities on tiger reserve resources. The project is intended for conservation in specially constituted tiger reserves representative of various bio-geographical regions throughout India. It strives to maintain a viable tiger population in their natural environment. In 2007, there were 28 Project Tiger wildlife reserves covering an area of 37,761 square kilometres. Project Tiger helped increase the population of these tigers from 1,200 in the 1970s to 3,500 in the 1990s.[52]

HUNTING OF ANIMALS

The poaching of wild animals and illegal trade of products derived from them, together with the degradation and depletion of their habitat, has seriously affected the wildlife population. In order to address this trend, the new law prohibited the hunting of all wild animals (other than vermin). However, hunting of wild animals in exceptional circumstances, particularly for the purpose of protection of life and property and for education, research, scientific management, and captive breeding continues. It is becoming mandatory for every transporter to gain proper permission before engaging in the transportation of any wildlife product.

Section 9(1) of the WPA provides that no person shall 'hunt' any wild animal. The expression 'wild animal' is defined in Section 2(36) as any 'animal found wild in nature and includes any animal specified in Schedule 1, etc.' The expression 'hunting' is defined in Section 2(16) in a comprehensive manner, with its grammatical variations and cognate expressions as:

a. capturing, killing, poisoning, snaring, and trapping of any wild animal and every attempt to do so.

b. driving any wild animal for any of the purposes specified in sub-clause (a).

c. injuring or destroying or taking any part of the body of any such animal or, in the case of wild birds or reptiles, damaging the eggs of such birds or reptiles or, disturbing the eggs or nests of such birds or reptiles.

---

[49] *Mukesh Ali v. State of Assam*, (2006) 5 SCC 485.
[50] *Uma Palliwal v. Union of India*, AIR 2002 Raj 348.
[51] Implemented from 1 April 1973.

[52] www.projecttiger.nic.in

Can a person be granted a licence for dealing in birds in captivity? Hunting of birds specified in the schedule to the WPA is prohibited. No person can be granted a licence to deal in birds in captivity that are procured by hunting, which would also include trapping.[53]

Hunting of animals is prohibited, but the CWW may, if he is satisfied that any wild animal has become dangerous to human life or is disabled or diseased beyond recovery, grant permission to hunt such animal.[54] Such an order can be made only if he is satisfied that the animal cannot be captured, tranquilized, or relocated. The captured animal cannot be kept in captivity unless the CWW is satisfied that such animal cannot be rehabilitated in the wild and the reasons for the same are recorded in writing. The trauma caused to the animal while bring caught or relocated must be minimized.[55]

But in self-defence, one can kill or wound an animal.[56] An animal killed or wounded in self-defence shall be the property of the government.[57]

In a PIL, the Supreme Court passed an order to effectively control poaching in forests. The administration was directed to ensure that forest guards in sanctuaries and national parks are provided modern arms, communication facilities, that is, wireless sets and other necessary equipment, so as to effectively oppose poachers who possess modern weapons.[58]

Section 34 of the WPA mandates that within three months from the declaration of any area as a sanctuary, every person residing in or within ten kilometres of any such sanctuary and holding a licence[59] should register with the CWW. The issuance of new licences in such areas is prohibited.

Wild Animals, Animal Articles, Trophies—Property of Government

Every wild animal (other than a vermin), animal article, trophy, or meat derived from any wild animal, and ivory imported to India and articles made from such ivory, shall be the property of the Central Government. The vehicle, vessel, weapon, trap, or tool used for committing an offence under the WPA also belongs to the government.[60] Any person who obtained any such property shall report it to the nearest police station within forty-eight hours. No person shall, without the previous permission in writing of the CWW, acquire or keep in his possession, custody, or control or transfer to any person, whether by way of gift, sale, or otherwise or destroy or damage such government property.[61]

Vehicles used for committing offences under the WPA can be seized and confiscated.[62] The Supreme Court of India has made it clear that in so far as seizures of vehicles involved in forest offences are concerned, a liberal approach should be avoided as it will tempt forest officials to repeat the offences.[63]

The import of ivory is no longer possible in view of Section 49(B), which was introduced by the Amending Act 28 of 1986, by which dealings in trophies, animal articles, and other items, are banned. If the ivory trade is allowed to continue, it will lead to

---

[53] *Chief Forest Conservator v. Nisar Khan*, AIR 2003 SC 1867: (2003) 4 SCC 595.
[54] WPA, Section 11.
[55] Ibid.
[56] WPA, Section 12.
[57] WPA, Sections 11 (2) and (3).
[58] *Centre for Environmental Law, WWF-I v. Union of India*, AIR 1999 SC 354.

[59] Arms Act, 1959.
[60] WPA, Section 39.
[61] WPA, Section 39 (3).
[62] Supra note 59.
[63] *State of Karnataka v. K. Krishnan*, AIR 2000 SC 2729: 2000 (7) SCC 80.

large-scale poaching of Indian elephants. International trade in ivory was also banned. The amendment by which the ivory trade was banned was challenged by the Ivory Traders and Manufacturing Association in the Delhi HC.[64] While upholding the validity of the amendment, the court found that the elephant is an endangered species requiring not only protection from being hunted but also a chance to recoup its depleting numbers.[65] The amendment was held valid and the Supreme Court of India made it clear that no compensation will be given to the traders in the trade of prohibited items.[66]

The prohibition of trade in ivory has raised many issues. It is contended in one of the cases that the term 'ivory' in the Act was limited only to elephant ivory. Rejecting the contention, the Supreme Court has held that the Act not only bans trade in imported elephant ivory but ivory of every description, so that poaching of elephants can be effectively restricted. Ivory, as per its dictionary meaning, is not confined to elephant ivory.[67]

A defamation suit was filed for the publishing of an article with the caption 'theft of elephant tusk'. The defendant claimed that the elephant was shot dead while it was on the estate of the plaintiff, and therefore the removal of tusk in such a situation does not constitute removal of property from the possession of another without his consent. The ownership of the tusk in such circumstances came up for consideration by the court. Interpreting the provision of the WPA, the KHC held that the elephant is a wild animal and tusks are the property of the state government in such circumstances.[68]

There are a lot of snake charmers in India. They extract venom from the snake. After the introduction of the WPA, it has become difficult for them to work in public, since this has become an offence. Snake venom is a precious item in medical science and is used for preparation of medicines including the lifesaving vaccines against snakebites. Snake venom can be extracted for medicinal purposes after obtaining a permit from the CWW. The law empowers the CWW to grant permission to hunt animals for education, scientific research, and scientific management.[69]

The WPA was again amended in 1986; after the amendment, permission for the export of snakeskin was stopped. The manufacturers and traders of tanned, cured, and finished skins of animals approached the Delhi HC challenging the banning of the trade and business in animal skins and articles made from them. According to the manufacturers, certain animals are harmful to human lives or properties and serve no useful purpose. The court, rejecting the contention of the traders, held that it cannot be said that certain animals have no role to play in nature or are detrimental to human life. The mortality rate in the country due to snake bites is less than 0.0005 per cent, which is very low compared to deaths and fatalities caused by other diseases and animal bites. Snakes are the natural killers of rats, which cause loss of nearly 33 million tons of stored cereals, aside from dreaded diseases like the plague. Russel's Vipers and rat snakes are known to have a fascination for eating rats. Therefore, the court, rejecting the writ petitions and upholding the validity of the

---

[64] *M/s Ivory Traders and Manufacturing Association v. Union of India*, AIR 1997 Del 267.

[65] Ibid.

[66] *Indian Handicraft Emporium v. Union of India*, (2003) 7 SCC 589; AIR 2003 SC 3240.

[67] *Balram Kumawat v. Union of India*, (2003) 7 SCC 628; AIR 2003 SC 3268.

[68] *Nellikka Achuthan v. The Desabhimani Printing and Publishing House*, AIR 1986 Ker 41.

[69] Supra note 55.

enactment, stated that the provisions are valid and sustainable.[70]

A shop-owner was found in possession of trophies of chinkara[71] skins meant for sale. When prosecuted, he pleaded that those trophies were made out of goat skin, after being painted, and that the skins were not of wild animals prohibited by the WPA. But the court declined to accept the plea of the shop-owner, especially when the specially trained officer gave evidence to the effect that it is a chinkara skin.[72]

Offences under the Wild Life (Protection) Act

The policy and object of wildlife laws have a long history and are the result of an increasing awareness of the compelling need to restore the serious ecological imbalance introduced by the depredations inflicted on nature by man. The preservation of flora and fauna, some species of which are becoming extinct at an alarming rate, has been an urgent necessity for the survival of humanity and these laws reflect a last-ditch battle for the survival, in part at least, from the grave situation emerging from a long history of callous insensitivity towards the enormity of the risks to mankind that go with the deterioration of the environment.

In his foreword to *International Wildlife Law*, Prince Philip, The Duke of Edinburgh said:

Many people seem to think that the conservation of nature is simply a matter of being kind to animals and enjoying walks in the countryside. Sadly, perhaps, it is a great deal more complicated than that...

...As usual with all legal systems, the crucial requirement is for the terms of the conventions to be widely accepted and rapidly implemented. Regretfully progress in this direction is proving disastrously slow.[73]

Section 51 of the Act provides for penalties. Violation of Section 9(1) is an offence under Section 51(1). Section 55 deals with cognizance of offences, which restrains the courts from taking cognizance except on the complaint of the CWW or such other officer as the state government may authorize on their behalf.

The power to take action against offences is conferred on the Director of Wildlife Preservation, CWW, Honorary Wildlife Warden, any forest officer, and other officers authorized by the CWW. The new amendment to the WPA has broadened the definition of a forest officer to include any forest officer as defined under the Forest Act, 1927 and also in any other law.

In a very interesting case that came up for consideration by the Supreme Court, an elephant was shot and killed for the removal of its ivory tusk. It was a scheduled animal. The police registered a case under Sections 447, 429, and 379 of the IPC read with Sections 34 and 39 of the WPA. The fact that the police, after due investigation, had filed a final report that no offence was made out under Section 429 of the IPC, would not bar the initiation of fresh proceedings under Section 9(1) read with Section 51 of the WPA, the court clarified. The court also explained the inherent powers of the HC,[74] that where it is alleged in the written complaint filed by the

---

[70] *G.R. Simon et al v. Union of India*, AIR 1997 Delhi 301.

[71] It is a species of gazelle found in South Asia; found in grasslands and desert areas in India.

[72] *Rajendra Kumar v. Union of India*, AIR 1995 SC 1159.

[73] See Simon Lyster (ed.), *International Wildlife Law*, Cambridge: Grotius Publications Limited, 1985.

[74] Criminal Procedure Code, Section 482—grants inherent powers to the High Court to make orders as it deems necessary to prevent abuse of process of court.

Range Forest Officer that the accused persons shot and killed an elephant in a particular range forest and removed ivory tusks of the elephant, will tantamount to an offence.[75] The offence envisaged by Section 9(1) of the WPA in its ingredients and content, is not the same or substantially the same as Section 429 of the IPC, which reads,

429. *Mischief by killing or maiming cattle, etc., of any value or any animal of the value of fifty rupees* - Whoever commits mischief by killing, poisoning, maiming, or rendering useless, any elephant, camel, horse, mule, buffalo, bull, cow, or ox, whatever may be the value thereof, or any other animal of the value of fifty rupees or upwards, shall be punished with imprisonment of either description for a term which may extend to five years, or with fine, or with both (emphasis in original).

The offence of hunting any wild animal as defined in Section 9 (1) read with Section 2 (16) of the WPA is much wider. Section 56 of the Act provides that:

Nothing in this Act shall be deemed to prevent any person from being prosecuted under any other law for the time being in force, for any act or omission which constitutes an offence against this Act or from being liable under such other law to any higher punishment or penalty than that provided by this Act, provided that no person shall be punished twice for the same offence.

Where an act or omission constitutes an offence under two or more enactments, the offender shall be liable to be prosecuted and punished under either or any of those enactments, but shall not be liable to be punished twice for the same offence.[76] Taking a wider angle, protection against a second offence or multiple punishment for the same offence, technical complexities aside, includes

a protection against re-prosecution after acquittal, a protection against re-prosecution after conviction, and a protection against double or multiple punishment for the same offence. These protections have since received constitutional guarantee under Article 20(2) of the Constitution of India which bars double jeopardy. But there are difficulties in the application of the principle in the context of what is meant by 'same offence'.

A statement made before a forest officer has more credibility than a statement before a police officer. Therefore, a statement made before a forest officer stands on a different footing and is admissible in evidence.[77] The Bombay HC, by its judgement in the *E.C. Richard* case, made it clear that a statement made before a Forest Range Officer is admissible in evidence and it has its own solemnity.[78]

Distinct statutory provisions will be treated as involving separate offences for double jeopardy purposes only if each provision requires proof of an additional fact that the other does not.[79] Where the same evidence suffices to prove both crimes, they are the same for purposes of double jeopardy and the clause forbids successive trials and cumulative punishment for the two crimes. The offences must be joined in one indictment and tried together unless the defendant requests that they be tried separately.[80]

It has been considered whether the CBI is authorized to investigate an offence which is punishable under the WPA. The Central Government has issued a notification dated 21 March 2000 under Sections 5 and 6 of the Delhi Special Police Establishment Act, 1946 empowering the CBI to carry out

---

[75] *State of Bihar v. Murad Ali Khan*, AIR 1989 SC 1: (1988) 4 SCC 655.
[76] General Clauses Act, 1897, Section 26.

[77] Sections 23, 41, 52, and 63.
[78] *Ayyub v. State of Rajasthan*, 2003 Crl LJ 2954.
[79] *Blockburger v. United States*, 284 US 299, 304 1932.
[80] *Jeffers v. United States*, 432 US 137 1977.

investigations for the purposes of prosecution under the WPA. The court made it clear that a police officer is also empowered to investigate the offences, and search and seize the offending articles under the WPA. Section 50(8) confers on the Assistant Director of Wildlife Preservation or Wildlife Warden to issue search warrant, summon witnesses and documents and record evidence for the purpose of investigation.[81] Technical pleas are always rejected when general principles of interpretation of law are undertaken. Courts, fully knowing the handicap of officers who are engaged in protecting the forests, always interpret the law in favour of the environment for whose benefit the laws are made. Animals cannot speak, but for them the court always speaks for their protection.

The Criminal Procedure Code, 1973 empowers the court to release on probation, on account of good conduct or after admonition, any person above the age of twenty-one years, if it appears to the court that based on the antecedents of the offender and the circumstances in which the offence was committed , it is expedient that the offender should be released on probation. A separate procedure is also prescribed. But the Allahabad HC, taking a broad view of the provisions of the WPA, has held that the said benefit cannot be extended to a person engaged in the profession and who kills innocent animals for the purpose of his business.[82]

Prevention of Cruelty to Animals Act, 1960

Cruelty inflicted on animals cannot be evaluated and measured in quantitative terms. The objective of a particular activity has often signified an important yardstick, for example,

research for medical purposes and animal husbandry, which benefits the society at large and needs to be continued even if it involves some cruelty. However, activities that are not essential to the progress and welfare of society but are merely to subserve as entertainment or exhibiting spectacles, can easily be curtailed. The (unnatural) tricks or performances, against the basic nature of animals and which lead to abnormal behaviour, need to be discontinued.[83]

By invoking the powers conferred under sub-clause (ii) of Section 22 of the Prevention of Cruelty to Animals Act, 1960, the government issued a notification dated 2 March 1991 banning the training and exhibition of five animals, that is, bears, monkeys, tigers, panthers, and dogs. Subsequently, by a corrigendum dated 7 August 1991, the ban on the training and exhibition of dogs was withdrawn.

The validity of the notification was challenged before the Delhi HC by the Indian Circus Federation (ICF) and the KHC. The Delhi HC, by interfering with the order, directed the government to reconsider the issue as to whether the banning of animals for a circus is essential.[84] The Government of India then appointed a committee to determine whether circuses contribute to the conservation of endangered species. The said committee found that breeding in circuses is only accidental or incidental, and in no way fosters a national conservation programme. The inbred stocks lose their heterogeneity and vigour. Adequate running and exercise yards are necessary for keeping the animals fit

---

[81] *Moti Lal v. Central Bureau of Investigation*, AIR 2002 SC 1691.

[82] *Mumtaj v. State of UP*, 2000 Crl LJ 4497.

[83] Extract from the committee constituted to consider the banning of animals, constituted in the case of Indian Circus Federation, by the Delhi High Court, WP (C) No. 890 of 1991, dated 21 August 1997.

[84] WP (C) No. 890 of 1991, dated 21 August 1997, Delhi High Court case filed by Indian Circus Federation.

and to avoid behavioural anomalies amongst the animals. No such exercise is given to animals in circuses. The history of human evolution reveals that tigers, panthers, and bears are different from animals that were domesticated by mankind. These animals are not only unpredictable, but also quite shy and tend to shy away from human beings. Bears love climbing trees and probing into the soil, and develop stereotypical behaviour when they are kept in small and dingy cases. The committee felt that it is not possible to provide such facilities in circuses. Monkeys are social animals, and there is no justification for keeping them isolated in captivity. But what will happen if its number increases and becomes a public nuisance. The monkey menace of Delhi has drawn the attention of the judiciary. The Delhi HC has declared that no person shall feed monkeys in public places where they are present in large numbers. The Municipal authorities are empowered to fine the violators. Feed for the monkeys may be handed over at the collection centres set up by the civil authorities.[85]

The ICF relied mainly on the fact that many European countries allow the display of animals in circuses. Even if this contention is accepted, the ethos and perception of the people of India differs greatly from its western counterparts. In India, people see the same soul being represented in all living beings on this planet. It is because of this ideology that a provision has been made in the Constitution of India to have love and compassion for all living beings. The committee found that it may not be appropriate to be guided by, or blindly follow, what is being practised in other parts of the world.

The Government of India has decided to close zoos that are not congenial to the health of animals, and a number of ill-planned zoos (at least 25 per cent) have been de-recognized as their cages are dingy and lack enough space for movement of animals to meet their biological requirements. It was also noted that mobile zoos have been refused permission keeping in mind the stress that animals were subjected to during transportation, and the size of enclosures to which the animals have to be confined. The said committee observed:

There have been no significant improvements in the captive environments of other species of animals, many of which continue to live within the small confines of the 'beast wagon', with only limited access to small, barren exercise areas. Travelling circuses are inherently restricted in the amount of space they can provide for animals. All the structures in which animals are housed or exercised have to be easily transportable, and fit within the confines of a standard lorry unit. In many cases, particularly with animals such as the big cats and bears which are a potential danger to the public, the transport cage or 'beast wagon' is their permanent home, where a space of less than 2.5 metres square per animal is normally provided Static circuses (of which there is currently only one in the UK) are equally restricted by the space available in their permanent facilities. The society believes the use of animals for any form of entertainment cannot be justified where distress or suffering is likely to be caused.[86]

The court came to the conclusion that circus animals are being forced to perform unnatural tricks and face undignified ways of life. They are housed in cramped cages, subjected to fear, hunger, and pain with no respite. The impugned notification has been issued in conformity with the changing scenario, values of human life, philosophy of the Constitution, prevailing conditions, and surrounding circumstances to prevent the infliction of unnecessary pain or suffering on

---

[85] *New Friends Colony v. Union of India*, WP (C) No. 2600/2001, dated 14 March 2007 (unreported).

[86] Supra note 83.

animals. The lives of humans and animals are equally valuable and their interests should be weighed accordingly. The contribution to the health of humans that animals provide is invaluable, especially considering that nearly every advance in health care and combating human diseases has been based on animal research. Animals provide models for the study of human diseases as new drugs are tested on animals to help determine their potentials for causing cancer or another disease or for holding embryos and foetuses in the womb. Therefore, it is not only our fundamental duty to show compassion to our animal friends, but also to recognize and protect their rights. If humans are entitled to fundamental rights, then why are not animals?[87]

Transportation of Animals Using Vehicles

The Transport of Animals Rules, 1978 demand that a valid health certificate by a qualified veterinary surgeon to the effect that dogs or cats are in a fit condition to travel by rail, road, inland waterway, sea, or air and are free of infectious or contagious diseases including rabies, shall accompany each consignment. This rule was amended in 2001 to extend to poultries also, where the term 'poultry' includes day old chicks and turkey poults, chickens, quails, guinea fowls, ducks, geese, and turkeys.[88]

In cities like Mumbai, there is a lucrative market for birds brought from forests. They are transported in a inhumane and cruel manner. There is not sufficient space for these birds to move in the cages or containers in which they are transported. The Bombay HC, while dealing with the issue of non-

implementation of the rules, has ordered the constitution of a committee. The committee is directed to supervise implementation of the provisions of Acts, Rules, and directions given by the Supreme Court from time to time. The committee must identify the cruelties to birds or animals, particularly as to the method and manner of carrying them, space for movement, food, and other provisions. The committee shall verify whether the birds are being dealt with illegally or illicitly for trade, in contravention of the provisions of the WPA.[89]

Transporting Animals on Foot

The Prevention of Cruelty to Animals (Transport of Animals on Foot) Rules, 2001 were enacted to ensure that every animal being transported on foot is healthy and in good condition for such transport. As per Section 2(a), the rules apply to cattle horses, donkeys; goats and pigs. These rules shall apply to the transport of animals on foot when the distance from the boundary of the village or town or city of the origin of such transport to the last destination is five or more kilometres. Transportation of animals during night time is prohibited. No animal shall be made to walk on foot under conditions of heavy rain, thunderstorms, or extremely dry or sultry conditions during its transport. No animal shall be transported on foot beyond the distance, time, rest interval, and temperature specified for such animal in the enactment. Different time limits are prescribed for different animals.

A certificate of a veterinary doctor in respect of each animal to be transported to the effect that such animal is in a fit condition for such transportation, and is not suffering from any infectious, contagious, or parasitic

[87] *Jumbo Circus v. Union of India*, 2000 (2) KLT 625: AIR 2000 Ker 340.
[88] Section76 incorporated by Transport of Animals (Amendment) Rules, 2001.
[89] *Viniyog Parivar Trust v. Union of India*, AIR 1998 Bom 71.

diseases and that it has been vaccinated against any such diseases shall accompany such animal. Likewise, newborn animals of which the navel has not completely healed or an animal that is diseased, blind, emaciated, lame, fatigued, or having given birth during the preceding seventy-two hours or likely to give birth during transport shall not be transported on foot. Animals shall also be transported in their own farm social groups that are to be established at least one week prior to journey.

The owner of the animals shall provide veterinary first aid equipment to be carried with such animals while transported on foot. The owner must also make water arrangements en route during transport of such animals on foot. Sufficient feed and fodder, with adequate reserve of such feed and fodder, for the animals shall be made available by their owner during their transport on foot. No person shall use a whip or a stick in order to force the animal to walk or to hasten the pace of their walk, nor shall they apply chillies or any other substance to any part of the body of the animal for this purpose during their transportation on foot. If any animal needs to be tied during transport on foot, it shall be tied by a rope covered with suitable cushioning such as cloth, and such animal shall not be tied by its nose, legs, or any other part of the body except by its neck.

For transporting elephants in the state of Kerala, the Kerala Captive Elephants (Management and Maintenance) Rules, 2003 prescribe certain conditions. If the elephants are transported by rail, the wagon shall not contain more than three elephants. If the transportation is by truck or rail, care shall be taken to maintain constant speed, avoiding jerks and sudden stops, and reducing effects of shocks and jolts to the minimum. Each truck or wagon should have at least two attendants.[90]

The transporting of elephants continuously for twelve hours at a stretch, without providing adequate facilities for fodder and drinking water, and without proper pads, is held tantamount to cruelty.[91]

Protection of Dogs

Stray dogs are always a threat to people, as they can become ferocious and attack people. According to the WHO, India has about 80 per cent of the world's rabies fatalities and the largest reservoir for the disease is dogs. The Government of India has enacted Animal Birth Control (Dogs) Rules, 2001[92] to protect dogs. Dogs are classified into the categories of pet dogs and street dogs. The owner of pet dogs is responsible for the controlled breeding, immunization, and sterilization of the dogs and must possess a local licence. Street dogs shall be sterilized and immunized, which is made possible by the participation of animal welfare organizations, private individuals, and the local authorities.

The Rules create an obligation on the local authority to establish a sufficient number of dog pounds including animal kennels or shelters, dog vans for transportation, ambulances and incinerators for the disposal of carcasses, and other measures. Captured dogs shall be brought to dog kennels or dog pounds managed by animal welfare organizations. Once brought to such places, the dogs must be given proper treatment and thereafter sterilized and immunized. Incurably ill and mortally wounded dogs as diagnosed by a qualified veterinarian shall be euthanized. To monitor the implementation of the rules, a monitoring committee has been constituted.

---

[90] Rule 8 of the said Rules.

[91] Rule 12 of the said Rules.

[92] Published in *Gazzette of India*, No. 929, dated 24 December 2001.

Unfortunately, the Animal Birth Control (ABC) Programme is not being implemented in many parts of the country. The result is that stray dogs are wandering at large on the streets, and are being killed by the local municipal personnel in any manner they like. On this basis, the KHC observed that the rule is concerned more with stray dogs than with lives of the people. The Court concluded that the right to life as enshrined under Article 21 is a fundamental right and would take precedence over dog rules.[93] Consequently, the court refused to issue directions to preserve stray dogs even though they have become unwanted because of the fatal and dangerous diseases with which they are afflicted. The Prevention of Cruelty to Animals Act, 2001 provides for the destruction of unwanted animals by the local authorities. Moreover, the present rules make provisions for the preservation and immunization of stray dogs, but are not applicable to dogs afflicted with fatal diseases or suffering from rabies. Such infected animals cannot be protected at the cost of invaluable human lives.[94]

Protection of Elephants

The Indian elephant (*elephas maximus*) is used in festivals, for carrying persons, and for pulling logs extensively in the country. Thus, it is categorized as a captive animal.[95] The hunting of an elephant is prohibited.[96] But it is still being used in many states like Kerala, Orissa, Bihar, and Tamil Nadu.

In the state of Kerala, it is extensively used for parading in festivals. As the elephants are being exhibited in public places, a mahout is always necessary. The Government of Kerala, for the effective management and maintenance of the said captive elephants, has framed the Kerala Captive Elephants (Management and Maintenance) Rules, 2003.[97] These rules also prescribe necessary requisites of a place where the elephant is to be kept.[98] A person using elephants in programmes has to obtain a fitness certificate.[99] The rules prescribe the minimum feed to be given to elephants, the work load of elephants, norms for transportation, cutting of tusks, and retirement of elephants. The owner of the elephant is bound to keep a record of the vaccination given, disease treatment records, movement register, feeding register, and work register.[100]

Certain acts are declared as tantamount to cruelty to elephants, like beating, kicking, overdriving, overloading, torturing, or treating any elephant so as to subject it to unnecessary pain or suffering. Apart from these, employing the elephant for any hard work which it cannot do, due to old age, disease, or any other infirmity also amounts to cruelty. Administering any injurious drug or intoxicant is also an offence. Conveying or carrying an elephant in a manner or position that causes pain or accident is prohibited. Keeping of elephants in small sheds is prohibited. Elephants are chained when they are displayed in public. But the rules prohibit keeping an elephant chained using spiked chains for an unreasonable time. If the elephant is not fed properly, it is an offence. Abandoning the elephant, causing suffering to the animal, and offering for sale an elephant suffering from

---

[93] *Animal Welfare Board of India v. Ombudsman*, AIR 2006 Ker 201: 2006 (2) KLT 91.

[94] Indian Law Institute, *Annual Survey of Indian Law—2006*, New Delhi.

[95] Wild Life (Protection) Act, 1972, Section 2(5).

[96] WPA, Section 9.

[97] Framed in exercise of the powers under the WPA, Section 64 (2).

[98] Kerala Captive Elephants (Management and Maintenance) Rules, 2003, Rule 4.

[99] Ibid., Rule 5 (5) the Kerala Captive Elephants (Management and Maintenance) Rules, 2003.

[100] Ibid., Rule 10.

any pain is also prohibited. Forcefully weaning away an elephant calf below two years of age from its mother is not permitted. Marching a sick, injured, or pregnant elephant or a young calf over a very long duration at a stretch and on tarred road is an offence.[101]

The Government of India sponsored a scheme titled 'Project Elephant' to provide financial and technical support to major elephant-bearing states in the country for the protection of elephants, their habitats, and corridors. It also seeks to address the issues of human–elephant conflict and welfare of domesticated elephants. The project is being implemented in thirteen states. The main activities of the project are as follows:

1. Ecological restoration of existing natural habitats and migratory routes of elephants;
2. Development of scientific and planned management for conservation of elephant habitats and viable population of wild Asiatic elephants in India;
3. Promotion of measures for the mitigation of human-elephant conflict in crucial habitats and moderating pressures of human and domestic stock activities in crucial elephant habitats;
4. Strengthening of measures for protection of wild elephants from poachers and unnatural causes of death;
5. Research on elephant management related issues;
6. Public education and awareness programmes;
7. Eco-development;
8. Veterinary care.

The project also initiated a programme for registration of domesticated elephants by using microchips.

[101] Available at http://moef.nic.in/pe/pe.html (last accessed 13 May 2012).

Protection of Cattle

The Bombay Animal Preservation Act, 1954 was amended in 1994, putting a ban on the slaughter of cows, calves, and other milch and draught animals. This was challenged on the ground that it restricts the freedom enjoyed by all. The Supreme Court of India, while upholding the said amendment, held that there is no complete ban on slaughter, but it put a restriction on cows, calves, and other milch and draught animals only. Such a ban will amount to a reasonable restriction, which is permitted by law. Cattle, which has served human beings for a long time, is also entitled to compassion when it grows old and ceases to be milch or draught cattle.[102]

The Mysore Prevention of Cow Slaughter and Cattle Preservation Act, 1964 prohibits the slaughtering of cows. The Supreme Court clarified that the protection available under Articles 48A and 51A(g) applies only to cows and calves, and to those animals that are at present capable of yielding milk or doing work as draught cattle. Thus, slaughtering of a cow that has ceased to be used for milch or draught purposes is permitted.[103]

Ox or bullock cart races are common in south India. In order to make the animals run fast, injuries are inflicted on them, like twisting of their tails, causing injuries with sharp weapons, putting chilly powder in the anus, and other means of ill-treatment. This treatment of the animal will amount to cruelty as per Section 11(1) of the Prevention of Cruelty to Animals Act, 1960. But the said type of cruelty continues, with religious festivals being cited as an excuse. When the same was questioned, the Madras HC held that persons cannot be permitted to cause violence and cruelty to

[102] *State of Gujarat v. Mirzapur, Moti Kureshi Kassab Jamat,* AIR 2006 SC 212.

[103] *Umesh v. State of Karnataka,* (2006) 4 SCC 162.

animals during religious festivals. Such an act of cruelty is a form of violation of the right to life and habitat. The court made it clear that in the absence of a statutory right, the human species has a corresponding duty towards other species to forbear from inflicting injuries and pain under the garb of an ox or bullock cart race. Such races cannot be permitted to be conducted just because they are customary, hereditary, or have been conducted for more than seventy-five years.[104]

Experiments on Animals

The Government of India has brought into effect the Breeding of and Experiments on Animals (Control and Supervision) Rules, 1998.[105] These Rules decentralized the clearance procedure to the institutional committees, with representation from the Committee for the Purpose of Control and Supervision of Experiments on Animals (CPCSEA). The rules allow transfers only among laboratories already registered with the Indian government, in effect limiting the pool to domestic facilities. These rules envisage that no animal experimentation is to be carried out without the explicit written approval of the CPCSEA. The Rules still provide that all biomedical institutions must register with the CPCSEA and possess ethical committees. All contract and collaborative research that many of the Indian laboratories carried out on behalf of overseas agencies was banned. Consequently, animal experimentation only occurs in limited circumstances in India.

European Union: Animals for Experiments

The use of laboratory animals is a matter of great public concern. In the EU, there is a general need and commitment to reduce the number of animals used in laboratories for experimental and other scientific purposes to the minimum level scientifically necessary. Recent statistics that provide information on how and where animals are currently used for experimental purposes are now available in the EU.

Key findings show that the total number of animals used for experiments in the European Community in 1996 was 11.6 million. By comparison, the first report for 1991–2 showed a total of 11.8 million animals used but these figures covered only ten member states instead of fifteen today.[106] This demonstrates that member states are making substantial efforts to reduce the number of animals used for experimental purposes.

By far, the biggest share of animals used in the Community is of rodents and rabbits, which amount to 81 per cent of the total. Fish and other cold-blooded animals account for 13 per cent, followed by birds at 4 per cent. The use of non-human primates in experiments is of special public concern and their use equates to 0.09 per cent of all animals used.[107]

Marine Fishes

The WPA included fishes like the whale shark (*rhincodon typus*) and shark and ray.[108] Sea turtles are also on the list of protected species of animals. The Act declared the consumption, trade, hunting, and inquiry of turtles as prohibited and the enforcement of the Act eventually led to the decline of turtle trade in Orissa. Significantly, the Act does not make a clear distinction between incidental and accidental capture of turtles in fishing nets and

---

[104] *K. Muniasamy Thevar v. Deputy Superintendent of Police*, AIR 2006 Mad 255.

[105] SO 134 (E), dated 15 February 2001.

[106] http://ec.europa.eu/environment/docum/99191_en.htm

[107] Ibid.

[108] Schedule I, Part IIA 'Fishes'.

poaching. Therefore, fisherfolk found with sea turtles in their fishing nets can be penalized in the same manner as poachers, irrespective of whether the catch takes place within or outside a protected area.

When the Central Government issued a notification including Sea Fans a 'coral' within the definition of the wildlife the same was challenged before the Madras HC. The exporters contended that they were using a hard, white calcareous substance called 'coral'. This coral is a lifeless substance which is secreted by marine polyps (also called coral). When the marine polyps die due to various reasons, the secreted calcareous lifeless substance breaks from the coral and falls on the sea floor, and is carried away by sea currents and washed ashore. Fisher folk collect this coral and sell it for the manufacture of lime. The same cannot be termed as 'wildlife'. The court has held that it is not necessary to give a wider definition to the word 'coral' (so as to include both the meanings of the word 'coral') to subserve the purposes of the Act. But the court made it clear that as long as the writ petitioners do not catch and kill live animals by severing their external skeleton, but only purchase the coral reef being the outer skeleton of the dead sea animal which is washed ashore after the death of the reef building coral, the authorities have no right to interfere with the activities as they do not violate the provision of the Act.[109]

DEVELOPMENTS ABROAD

United States of America

To conserve to the extent practicable the various species of fish or wildlife and plants

facing extinction, the legislature of the USA has enacted the Endangered Species Act, 1973 (ESA). The Secretary has been empowered to determine the endangered species solely on the basis of the best scientific and commercial data available. He or she may do so after conducting a review of the status of the species and after taking into account efforts, if any, being made by any state or foreign nation, to protect such species whether by predator control, protection of habitat and food supply, or other conservation practices, within any area under its jurisdiction, or on the high seas. A detailed procedure has been prescribed for determination purposes. To conserve such threatened species, the Secretary has been empowered to issue such regulations as deemed necessary and advisable to provide for the conservation. An inherent power has been given to the Secretary to treat any species, which is not listed, if they find that such species resembles in appearance, a species which is listed as an endangered species. The Endangered Species Committee has been granted the power to grant exemptions, after obtaining report of the Secretary, for national security reasons or in a declared disaster area. It is unlawful for any person to engage in any trade in any specimens contrary to CITES or possess any specimens traded contrary to the provisions of the Act. Violators of the enactment must pay a heavy civil penalty of US $ 500–$ 25,000. In addition, such persons can be fined not more than US $ 50,000 or imprisonment of not more than one year.

Jamaica

The Endangered Species (Protection, Conservation and Regulation of Trade) Act, 2000 was created to regulate the trading of endangered species. The first schedule contains a list of endangered species and fauna threatened with extinction. It provides

---

[109] *State of Tamil Nadu v. M/s Kaypee Industrial Chemicals (P) Ltd et. al*, Writ Appeal Nos 723 to 725 of 2004 and WAMP Nos 3026, 3027, 4393 to 4395 and 1351 to 1353 of 2004, dated 29 March 2005.

for the constitution of the Natural Resources Conservation Authority to oversee that the Act is properly administered.

Kenya

The High Court of Kenya has considered a case attempting to restrain the Kenya Government Agency, operating under an Act of Parliament, from removing or dislocating a rare and endangered species named the 'hirola' from its natural habitat.[110] Applying the principle of common law, the Court observed that according to the customary law of the people, those entitled to use of the land are also entitled to the fruits thereof, which include the flora and fauna, unless this has been changed by law. According to the Wildlife Conservation Act, the defendant is required to conserve wild animals in their natural state. The Court held that the respondent would be acting outside its powers if it were to remove any animals or flora from their natural habitat.

The treatment of wildlife, and in particular animals, poses many moral and ethical questions. The way in which we view animals in comparison to ourselves is likely to influence such considerations and society's view on this matter as a whole should be reflected in the law. At this point, we should ask ourselves: does the law present wildlife and animals as inferior to human beings? Or does it provide a level of protection to them which represents the unique position they occupy in nature, equal to that of human beings? If an affirmative answer is given to the former, we should definitely question both the validity of our own perceptions and those of the law.

BIOLOGICAL DIVERSITY

Biological diversity, commonly termed 'biodiversity,' is the term given to the variety of life on Earth and the natural patterns it forms. It is the creation of nature during the billions of years of evolution. Biodiversity also includes genetic differences within each species, like between varieties of crops and breeds of livestock. Chromosomes, genes, and deoxyribonucleic acid (DNA) are the building blocks of life, and determine the uniqueness of each individual and each species. Looking from another angle, biodiversity is the variety of ecosystems such as those that occur in deserts, forests, wetlands, mountains, lakes, rivers, and agricultural landscapes. In each ecosystem, living creatures, including humans, form a community, interacting with one another and with the natural environment around them.

Indian Law

India is rich in biological diversity, and associated traditional and contemporary knowledge systems relating thereto. The United Nations Convention on Biological Diversity,[111] at Rio de Janeiro on 5 June 1992, affirmed the sovereign rights of states over biological resources. The Convention has the main objective of conservation of biological diversity, sustainable use of its components, and fair and equitable sharing of the benefits arising out of utilization of genetic resources. The Government of India, finding that it is necessary to provide for the conservation, sustainable utilization, and equitable sharing of the benefits arising out of utilization of genetic resources and also to give effect to the said Convention, has enacted the law.

---

[110] *Abdikadir Sheika Hassan v. Kenya Wildlife Service*, Civil Case No. 2059 of 1996.

[111] Convention on Biological Diversity, came into force on 29 December 1993, 1760 UNTS 79.

The Biological Diversity Act, 2002 is intended to provide for conservation of biological diversity, sustainable use of its components, and fair and equitable sharing of the benefits arising out of the use of biological resources, knowledge and for matters connected therewith or incidental thereto. Section 2(d) of the Act defines biological resources as follows:

(b) 'biological diversity' means the variability among living organisms from all sources and the ecological complexes of which they are part, and includes diversity within species or between species and of eco systems.

The Act provides for the constitution of a National Biodiversity Authority[112] (NBA) and its prior approval is necessary to obtain any biological resource occurring in India or knowledge associated thereto, for research or for commercial utilization or for bio-survey and bio-utilization.[113] This restriction applies to foreigners, bodies corporate, associations, and organizations. No person shall, without the approval of the NBA, transfer the results of any research relating to any biological resources occurring in, or obtained from India to any person. These restrictions also apply to collaborative research projects.[114] Section 6 restrains any person from making an application for intellectual property rights without the approval of the NBA. The law also restrains the obtaining of a biological resource for commercial utilization or bio-survey and bio-utilization for commercial utilization except after giving prior intimation to the State Biodiversity Board (SBA) concerned. A person who contravenes the provisions of this enactment is liable for imprisonment which may extend to five years or a fine which may extend to ten lakhs or whatever is commensurate to the damage caused.[115] Penalties are also prescribed for those who fail to obey the directions issued by the government, the NBA, and the SBA.

The Government of India also framed the Biological Diversity Rules, 2004 which prescribe the procedure for access to biological resources and associated traditional knowledge, procedure for seeking approval of transferring results of research, procedure for seeking prior approval before applying for intellectual property protection, third party transfer, criteria for equitable benefit sharing, and application of national biodiversity fund.[116] The Rules prescribe the manner in which the Biodiversity Management Committees is to be formed by the local bodies.[117]

Foreign Laws

Bangladesh has also enacted Biodiversity and Community Knowledge Protection Act, 1998 largely mirroring the Indian legislation. The Act aims to 'ensure the conservation and sustainable use of biological and genetic resources.' However, the emphasis is very much on preservation of the knowledge that relates to these resources. According to Article 2, the general objectives of the Act are to:

...[P]rotect the sovereign rights of the Communities that have knowledge of biodiversity, and have managed, maintained, conserved, reproduced, and enhanced biodiversity, genetic resources and traditional knowledge, culture, and various forms of practice related to these resources, and which are always held in common [and to] strengthen the informal knowledge system and the collective innovation of the Communities that prohibit claim

---

[112] National Biodiversity Authority <http://www.nbaindia.org> (last visited 21 July 2007).
[113] Biological Diversity Act, Section 3.
[114] Ibid., Section 5.

[115] Ibid., Section 55.
[116] Biological Rules, 2004, Rule 14 to 18.
[117] Ibid., Rule 22.

for private ownership, private intellectual property rights or privileges that do not exist now, and that are against the moral, intellectual and cultural values of the Communities.

The Act thus recognizes that traditional community and indigenous systems of preserving such knowledge may not be compatible with private notions of ownership and it respects this division. In order to articulate primary ownership that indigenous people may have over biological and genetic resources, the Act uses the term 'residual title'. This is because the state has sovereign rights over all biological and genetic resources in Bangladesh, and holds them on trust for the benefit of the people. The state respects this residual title, insofar that prior informed consent must be obtained from the community concerned in order for it to deal with or interfere with these residual rights. Had this been 'free' prior informed consent, the Act would be consistent with the international law relating to indigenous people and their contemporary claims.[118]

Biological diversity is largely regulated within the EU by two directives, the Habitats Directive[119] and the Birds Directive.[120] The Habitats Directive aims 'to contribute towards ensuring biodiversity through the conservation of natural habitats and of wild fauna and flora in the European territory of the Member States to which the Treaty applies.' It sets up Natura 2000, a network in which habitats and species may be listed for conservation. 'Natural habitat types in danger of disappearance'

are listed as 'priority habitats' in Annex I,[121] as are areas which possess characteristics of the biogeographical regions: Alpine, Atlantic, Continental, Macaronesian, and Mediterranean. Species that are rare, vulnerable, endangered, or endemic may be listed in Annex II and/or Annex IV or V.[122] The monitoring and conservation of listed habitats and species is then to take place. In addition to this, a number of acts that harm species listed in Annex IV(a) are to be prohibited[123] as are acts that harm plant species listed in Annex IV(b).[124] There is a general obligation on all member states to 'bring into force the laws, regulations, and administrative provisions necessary to comply with this Directive within two years of its notification.'[125]

The Birds Directive recognizes that the decline in species of wild birds within the European Community calls for specific action 'particularly because of biological balances.'[126] Since many birds are migratory species, their conservation is quite obviously a community task. The Directive applies to all species of birds within the European Community and their eggs, nests, and habitats. Parties are to adopt measures to maintain such species, including the creation of protected areas, upkeep and management of habitats, re-establishment of destroyed biotypes, and creation of biotypes.[127] Article 4 provides that special conservation measures be prescribed for some species which are listed in Annex 1. There are varying degrees of protection for species listed in Annex II and III according to their vulnerability, where prohibited acts are also prescribed in relation

---

[118] For example, see Draft Declaration on the Rights of Indigenous Peoples, UN Doc. E/CN.4/Sub.2/1994/56 (1994), Article 11.
[119] Council Directive 92/43/EEC of 21 May 1992 on the conservation of natural habitats and of wild fauna and flora.
[120] Council Directive 79/409/EEC of 2 April 1979 on the conservation of wild birds.

[121] Ibid., Article 1(d).
[122] Ibid., Article 1(g).
[123] Ibid., Article 12.
[124] Ibid., Article 13.
[125] Ibid., Article 23(1).
[126] Supra note 118.
[127] Ibid., Article 3.

to the hunting and capture of such birds in a manner reflective of their status. States are to impose a general ban on the destruction or taking of nests and eggs of all species of birds naturally occurring in the member states. There is also a general prohibition on the killing of such birds.[128]

Members of the European Community are also permitted to enact their own legislation to preserve biodiversity, as long as it is consistent with the Directives. Scotland has enacted the Nature Conservation (Scotland) Act, 2004, which provides for a National Biodiversity Strategy. Bodies or office holders charged with various powers under the Act must carry out their functions with regard to the Biodiversity Convention.[129] The listing technique is again used and Scottish ministers are to publish a list of habitat and species of flora and fauna which are of importance to the conservation of biological diversity. There is a toolkit of powers given to Scottish ministers, including the designation of specific scientific interest, the making of nature conservation orders, and land management orders. Under Section 51, Scottish Natural Heritage is also to publish a code termed the Scottish Marine Wildlife Watching Code, which specifies guidelines and recommendations for the carrying out of commercial and leisure activities that involve watching marine wildlife so that such wildlife is not disturbed.

Similarly, the UK has enacted the Countryside and Rights of Way Act, 2000 where the various authorities charged with functions under the Act are to have proper regard to the purpose of conserving biodiversity.[130]

The term 'biodiversity' is accorded the same meaning as given by the Convention on Biological Diversity. Again, a listing procedure is provided where the appropriate listing authority is to list living organisms or habitat of specific importance in terms of biological diversity.[131] The practice of hunting has also raised questions of species conservation and consequently, the Hunting Act, 2004 prohibits the hunting of wild animals with the aid of a dog unless the hunting is exempt. According to Schedule 1, stalking or flushing out a wild animal from its cover is exempt hunting if

[U]ndertaken for the purpose... of preventing or reducing serious damage which the wild mammal would otherwise cause... to the biological diversity of an area (within the meaning of the United Nations Environmental Programme Convention on Biological Diversity of 1992).[132]

CITES is also highly adapted to the preservation of biological diversity as it enables specific species to be protected and conserved. The Convention recognizes that

[W]ild fauna and flora in their many beautiful and varied forms are an irreplaceable part of the natural systems of the earth which must be protected for this and the generations to come; [and] international cooperation is essential for the protection of certain species of wild fauna and flora against over-exploitation through international trade.[133]

It employs a listing procedure in which member states are to list species if they are already vulnerable to extinction, and those that are or may be threatened by trade; species will be vulnerable to extinction if trade in them is not properly regulated and those that are vulnerable to exploitation if the trade of them

---

[128] Ibid., Article 5.
[129] Nature Conservation (Scotland) Act, 2004, Section 1(2).
[130] Countryside and Rights of Way Act, 2000, Chapter 37, Section 74(1).

[131] Ibid., Section 74.
[132] Hunting Act, 2004, Chapter 37, Schedule 1.
[133] Convention on International Trade in Endangered Species of Wild Fauna and Flora, came into force on 1 July 1975, 993 UNTS 243.

is not properly regulated.[134] Each of the three categories is listed in its respective schedule and attracts varying degrees of regulation reflective of its status, such as the requirement of export permits that meet certain criteria. Although not appropriate as an overall strategy for biodiversity, the Convention can be used to buttress existing frameworks, working to conserve individual species.

The Unites States Congress has enacted the ESA[135] in order to implement the CITES amongst other bilateral and multilateral agreements, and conserve endangered and threatened species. Section 1533 empowers the Secretary of the Interior or the Secretary of Commerce to list threatened and endangered species and their 'critical habitat'. The Secretary is then to implement a programme to conserve the listed species and habitats via a land acquisition scheme as provided by Section 1534. In exercising these powers, the Secretary is to act with the cooperation of the states and other federal agencies (Section 1536). A number of prohibited acts are also specified by Section 1538, including the import, export, transportation, selling, and receiving of any endangered species, unless in specific circumstances. 'Takes' of such species or destruction of their environment is also prohibited, subject to some exceptions. It is also explicitly unlawful to violate the provision of the CITES according to this section. Violation of the provisions of the Act can attract civil and criminal penalties, and the latter can extend to a $50,000 fine or one year imprisonment or both (Section 1540(b)).

Despite the fact that the EU is not a party to the CITES, EC Council Regulation 338/97[136] on the protection of species of wild fauna and flora by regulating trade therein (the Basic Regulation) and Commission Regulation (EC) No. 865/2006 (the Implementing Regulation), implement the CITES within the European Community. Member states are at liberty to enact additional legislation to implement it at a regional level; however this may not impair freedom of trade within the community, so members may not be able to go too far beyond the restraints imposed by the Convention. This is perhaps why the Convention has not been signed by the EU, for the freedom of trade between member states and lack of strict border controls is a fundamental feature of the system.[137]

Biodiversity is essential to humans for a number of reasons. It has economic significance, cultural value, and is a measure of sustainable development.[138] Biodiversity can be used to measure the successful implementation of the principle of intergenerational equity, as we ask ourselves: will this beautiful and bountiful nature be available for our grandchildren to enjoy? Despite the value of biodiversity to humans, it is important to remember that nature has its own intrinsic value. The complex web of life can only continue to function if biological diversity is conserved. Through proper legislation and management, humans can sustain their own complex lives while according due respect to the natural world.

---

[136] EUROPA 'How does the European Union Implement CITES?'

[137] http://ec.europa.eu/environment/cites/legislation_en.htm (last visited 27 July 2007).

[138] Biodiversity Scotland, 'Why is biodiversity important?' <http://www.biodiversityscotland.gov.uk/pageType2.php?id=2&type=2&navID=24> (last visited 27 July 2007).

---

[134] Ibid., Article 2.

[135] 16 USCA, Sections 1531–1544.

14 Safe Disposal of Waste

Though there are several cities in India, only a few have a systematic sewage mechanism. Many cities dispose off their domestic and industrial waste in nearby water bodies. With the country's population at over one billion and the occurrence of unplanned development and rapid urbanization, the generation of waste has also increased phenomenally. A proper, efficient, and sustainable waste management system is still uncommon in India.

BIO-MEDICAL WASTES

For the purposes of managing medical wastes the Central Government has enacted the Bio-Medical Waste (Management and Handling) Rules,[1] (BMW Rules). The enactment is a piece of subordinate legislation under the Environment (Protection) Act.[2]

The BMW Rules were framed in exercise of the powers conferred by Sections 6, 8, and 25 of the Environment (Protection) Act. The rules specify that it is the duty of the occupier of an institution generating bio-medical waste (which includes a hospital, nursing home, clinic, dispensary, veterinary institution, animal house, pathological laboratory, blood bank, and other organizations) to take all steps to ensure that such waste is handled

[1] Bio-Medical Waste (Management and Handling) Rules, 1998.
[2] Environment (Protection) Act, 1986.

without any adverse effect on human health and the environment. In compliance with the standards prescribed by Schedule V of the Rules, such waste is to be disposed of in accordance with Schedule I. Waste is categorized and treatment and disposal is expected to be carried out in the manner prescribed. Human anatomical waste is to be disposed of by incineration or deep burial (below five metres). Microbiology and biotechnology wastes are to be disposed of by local autoclaving, microwaving, or incineration. Waste sharps like needles, syringes, scalpels, blades, glass, must be disinfected and shredded or mutilated. Discarded medicines, solid waste, and liquid waste are to be appropriately treated as prescribed by the Schedule. As can be observed in Schedule VI, a time schedule has also been prescribed, requiring that hospitals and nursing homes in towns with a population of thirty lakhs and above complete the process by 31 December 1999. In respect of other institutions, the deadline varies from 31 December 1999 to 31 December 2002. State Pollution Control Boards have been empowered to implement the same.

The BMW Rules were amended and guidelines were framed for a common biomedical waste treatment facility and the design and construction of a biomedical waste incinerator. The Rules have not been implemented to their full effect in India. The KHC had the occasion to issue a direction to implement the said rules.[3]

Can it be said that the incineration of wastes as suggested by the rules is environmentally friendly? The burning of wastes is not a healthy technology and is banned in developed countries. The process of incineration involves the burning of wastes in two chambers. The primary chamber burns the waste and the secondary chamber aims at destroying the toxic gases that are formed during the burning process in the primary chamber. The required temperature in the primary chamber is +800 degrees Celsius and the secondary chamber requires +1000 degrees Celsius. But the required temperatures are rarely achieved during the operation, which results in the emission of toxic gases, particularly when medical waste is burned. People residing near the said incinerators are the worst affected because they inhale the toxic gases.

Incineration is responsible for the release of Persistent Organic Pollutants (POPs) that are carried over long distances by wind, experiencing various chemical and physical transformations, from air to soil, vegetation, and water. Such polluting substances are consumed by innocent victims. The ash disposed off from incinerators contains contaminants like heavy metals, such as mercury, lead, and other pollutants. These are carried by the wind and deposited on land, vegetation, and in water bodies. Animals during foraging consume the toxic ash, which is then indirectly carried out by animal products such as meat, milk. This is commonly known as bio-magnification and has been identified by the US National Research Council's 'Waste Incineration and Public Health,

2000'.[4] A plume of smoke from an incinerator adversely affects many people who consume the toxic gas emissions. Incinerators emit greenhouse gases that ultimately affect the ozone layer. Every kilogram of waste arising from incineration generates 1.2 kilograms of carbon dioxide, which contributes to global warming activities. Incineration also pollutes sub-soil water resources and soil because the ash contains heavy chemicals. Incinerators cause more pollution problems than they solve as they generate and emit toxic gases like dioxin and furan, which are injurious to human health.

India is a signatory to 'the Stockholm Convention'[5] for phasing out incinerators. The Convention identified twelve of the most dangerous POPs', commonly known as the 'dirty dozen', including dioxins and furans that are generated on incineration, and focuses on reducing and eliminating their use.[6] India has also signed and ratified the Kyoto Protocol,[7] and is thus committed to phasing out already installed incinerators. Installing new incinerators anywhere in the country is contrary to the Stockholm Declaration. Installing incinerators is against the accepted policy of the Central Government and is therefore unconstitutional. But in India, the authorities are forcing the installation of costly and outdated incinerators for the disposal of bio-medical wastes as the Rules in force permit

---

[3] *Environment Monitoring Forum v. State*, 2003 (3) KLT SN.130.P.102: ILR 2004 (1) Kerala 476.

[4] National Research Council, Committee on Health Effects of Waste Incineration, Board on Environmental Studies, and Toxicology Staff *Waste Incineration and Public Health*, Washington DC: National Academy Press, 2000.

[5] Stockholm Convention on Persistent Organic Pollutants, 40 ILM 532 (2001).

[6] United Nations Environment Programme.

[7] Kyoto Protocol to the United Nations Framework Convention on Climate Change, 37 ILM 22 (1998).

this option, even though the environmental dangers are well recognized.

The controversial RM 1.5 billion incinerator project in Broga, Semenyih, Selangor has been finally terminated by the Malaysian Government. Instead of constructing an incinerator, the government will be focusing on waste reduction. The project was designed to reduce Kuala Lumpur's dependence on landfills for waste management. The residents first filed a lawsuit against it in 2005, and obtained a temporary injunction to prevent further work from continuing. However, when the injunction expired, work resumed and the residents filed a second lawsuit. The residents complained that they were not consulted about the project and that it failed to undergo EIA. They expressed fears for their health and the environmental effects it would generate if built in their town. Had the project materialized, the 1,500-tonne thermal incinerator would have been the biggest in the country.[8]

Developments Abroad

The Philippines Clean Air Act[9] bans the incineration of wastes. In 1985, Sweden implemented a two-year moratorium on the construction of all new incinerators.[10] The United States Environment Protection Agency has released a set of new operating parameters that will have the effect of shutting down 70 per cent of incinerators and cause the expenditure of millions of dollars in state-of-the-art pollution control devices. Since 1985, about 280 incinerator proposals in the

US have been refused or abandoned due to public opposition.[11]

The Japanese Government has announced that it will not allow new garbage incinerators to be built in areas where dioxin concentrations exceed the prescribed limit. However, the government has not imposed restrictions on small-sized incinerators which burn waste at a rate less than 200 kilograms per hour.

The President of Costa Rica banned incineration from July 1999. Australia has no national hazardous waste incinerator or any other incinerator that is licensed to burn hazardous waste.

In countries like the UK, Germany, Spain, and the US, there is public support for phasing out incinerators already in operation. Demonstrations and petitions calling for a ban on incineration have been organized on many occasions.

In an Irish case, *Hanrahan* v. *Merck*,[12] an Irish dairy farmer was awarded damages against a transnational corporation, Merck, Sharp and Dohme, when 220 of his prized cows died of health problems caused by incinerator emissions. The scientists found dioxins and polychlorinated biphenyls (PCBs) in the soil and vegetation of the farm from which the crows were grazing.

In April 1992, following three years of local opposition, the federal environmental authorities cancelled incineration proposals in Mexico.[13]

Although India is not the only country to allow the operation of incinerators for various purposes, it can be observed that it is generally lagging behind the rest of the world in terms of the volume of incinerators in operation and the phasing out of the practice. The Supreme

---

[8] Bernama Online, Malaysian National News Agency, Website www.bernama.com (accessed on 6 July 2007). Broga Incinerator Project Off.

[9] Clean Air Act, 1999 (Philippines).

[10] 'Non-Incineration Medical Waste Treatment Technologies', August 2001, www.noharm.org.

[11] Ibid.

[12] *Hanrahan* v. *Merck*, [1988] ILRM 629 (5 July 1988).

[13] Supra note 10.

Court of India admitted a PIL challenging the installation of incinerators for the disposal of bio-medical waste and any other waste by way of burning technology based on the above aspects and the case is pending consideration.[14] This case thus has the potential to be a step in the right direction.

MUNICIPAL WASTES

Domestic garbage and sewage are large contributors of solid waste in India. A large number of inhabitants live in unauthorized colonies, with no proper means of dealing with the domestic effluents, or in slums with no care for hygiene, which adds further complexity to the problem.

The duties of the municipalities to the community in constructing sanitation facilities at a cost and on a time-bound basis has been highlighted by the Supreme Court of India, as early as in 1980. The Supreme Court directed the Ratlam Municipality to take immediate action to stop effluents from flowing into the street and to stop pollution. A direction was also issued to construct a sufficient number of latrines and special instructions to stop mosquito breeding, fill up cesspools and other pits of filth, and use its sanitary staff to keep the place free from accumulations of filth.[15] The waste management problem still subsists in India. The words of V.R. Krishna Iyer, while rendering the judgement, stand as golden pillars of the Indian judicial system:

Why drive common people to public interest action? Where directive principles have found statutory expression in do's and don't's the court will not sit idly by and allow municipal government to become a statutory mockery. The law will

relentlessly be enforced and the plea of poor finance will be a poor alibi when people in misery cry for justice. The dynamics of the judicial process have a new 'enforcement' dimension not merely through some of the provisions of the criminal procedure code (as here), but also through activated tort consciousness. The officers in charge and even the elected representatives will have to face the penalty of the law if what the Constitution and follow up legislation direct them to do are defied or denied wrongfully. The wages of violation is punishment, corporate and personal.

But the state of waste management in India has not improved. In 1996, the Supreme Court of India[16] recounted the management of wastes in the country as follows:

[The] historic city of Delhi—the capital of India—is one of the most polluted cities in the world. The authorities, responsible for pollution control and environment protection, have not been able to provide clean and healthy environment to the residents of Delhi. The ambient air is so much polluted that it is difficult to breathe. More and more residents of Delhi are suffering from respiratory diseases and throat infections. [The] river Yamuna—the main source of drinking water supply—is the free dumping place for untreated sewage and industrial waste. Apart from air and water pollution, the city is virtually an open dustbin. Garbage strewn all over Delhi is a common sight. The Municipal Corporation of Delhi (the MCD) constituted under the Delhi Municipal Corporation Act, 1957 (Delhi Act) and the New Delhi Municipal Council (the NDMC) constituted under the New Delhi Municipal Council Act, 1994 (New Delhi Act) are wholly remiss in the discharge of their duties under law. It is undoubtedly correct that rapid industrial developments and a regular flow of persons from rural to urban areas have made major contribution towards environmental degradation, but at the same time the authorities—entrusted with the

---

[14] *Common Cause v. Union of India*, Writ Petition (C) No. 160 of 2005.

[15] *Municipal Council, Ratlam v. Vadhichand*, AIR 1980 SC 1622: (1980) 2 SCC162.

[16] *B.L. Wadhera v. Union of India and Others*, 1996 (2) SCC 594 at 595.

work of pollution control—cannot be permitted to sit back with folded hands on the pretext that they have no financial or other means to control pollution and protect the environment.

The Court then proceeded to issue certain directions in an effort to see that the capital of the biggest democracy in the world is not branded as one of the most polluted cities in the world.

The Supreme Court has also held that there is a statutory obligation to scavenge and clean the city. It is mandatory for authorities to collect and dispose of garbage and waste generated from various sources in the city. Non-availability of funds, inadequacy or inefficiency of staff, or insufficient machinery, cannot be pleaded as grounds for non-performance of their statutory obligations.[17]

Surat, a city in the state of Gujarat, had for time immemorial been known as one of the dirtiest cities in the country. The plague there in 1995 was the result of the filth that had accumulated therein. Nevertheless, the dedication of the Municipal Commissioner, who worked in the field and in the office, resulted in not only eradicating the plague and cleaning up Surat, but gave the city of Surat the distinction of being the second cleanest city in the whole of India. The people of Surat who threw garbage all around were so affected by the tireless efforts of one person that they themselves have now become zealous guardians of their new found clean city. This shows what one man as the head of an organization like the Municipal Corporation, with selfless zeal, initiative, and dedication, can achieve by motivating his employees to clean up the city while acting fairly, justly, and efficiently within the fold of the law.

Municipal Solid Waste (Management and Handling) Rules 1999

No one wants to live in the vicinity of a waste treatment facility, and local residents generally come together to oppose the use of nearby land for waste disposal. The widespread phenomenon of opposing waste disposal and treatment facilities is known as NIMBY (not in my background).[18] The NIMBY syndrome can be overcome if waste is managed in an environmentally friendly manner. Following the suspected plague outbreak in India during 1994, the Planning Commission constituted a high power committee to discuss an urban solid waste management plan. The new Municipal Solid Waste (Management and Handling) Rules, 1999 were framed for the purpose of proper management of such wastes, bearing in mind the principles enunciated in the said judgement of the Supreme Court and the recommendations of the said committee.

As per these rules, every municipal authority is responsible for implementation of the provisions for any infrastructure development and for the collection, storage, segregation, transportation, processing, and disposal of municipal solid wastes. The municipalities must obtain authorization to set up waste processing and disposal facilities including landfills, from the State Board or the Committee in order to comply with the implementation programme laid down in the rules.

For implementation of the said law, the Supreme Court has directed the Government of the NCT of Delhi to appoint magistrates under Section 20 and/or 21 of the Code of Criminal Procedure for each Board/Circle/Ward for ensuring compliance of the provisions of the MCD and NDMC Acts and to try offences

---

[17] *Virenda Gaur and Others v. State of Haryana and Others,* (1995) 2 SCC 577.

[18] Available at http://en.wikipedia.org/wiki/NIMBY (last accessed 13 May 2012).

SAFE DISPOSAL OF WASTE

specified in the Code relating to littering, nuisance, sanitation, and public health.[19]

Case Law

The Vishakhapatnam Municipal Corporation was restrained by the Andhra Pradesh HC from dumping garbage in the park in question or in any other park. The Corporation was required to restore the lost glory of the Green Park, and maintain it properly, the court held. The Andhra Pradesh Pollution Control Board is obligated to monitor the maintenance of the Green Park on a regular basis, and in the event that it comes to its notice that the Corporation is not maintaining the park and is violating provisions of the Municipal Wastes (Management and Handling) Rules, it may initiate criminal proceedings against the Corporation. Amongst a number of sweeping orders which the court made, the Board was also directed to issue a circular to all the municipal bodies in the state directing compliance of the aforementioned Rules.[20]

The KHC also issued directions to inspect a site where vermin composting was constructed by the municipality and to take appropriate action to ensure effective functioning of the plant. The Pollution Control Board was also directed to conduct inspections within the municipal area for carrying out the duties entrusted to them by the Act and the Rules aforesaid.[21]

It is the primary duty of the Municipal Council to remove filth, rubbish, night-soil, odour, or any other noxious or offensive matter. It is for the municipality to ensure the performance of the primary duties and to raise funds for this purpose, the Rajasthan HC has held.[22]

The Jammu and Kashmir HC reiterated the duties of the municipalities. Providing drainage and road systems, which are not pompous and attractive, but in working condition and sufficient to meet the needs of the people, cannot be evaded if the concerned authorities are to justify their existence. Basic amenity of access to potable water is not a luxury but a prerequisite to sustain life. Any plea of financial inability or discriminatory treatment raised by any concerned authority is of no significance because human rights granted under the Constitution must be respected by the state regardless of budgetary constraints. Otherwise, a pachydermic governmental agency may legally defy duties under the law, by representing in self-defence, a self-created bankruptcy or perverted expenditure budget, the court added.[23]

The construction of high-rise buildings was often coupled with the practice of discharging waste generated from construction into public sewers. The Andhra Pradesh HC has reminded that there is an absolute liability on the part of those who are engaged in construction work, particularly of multistoried structures, not to create a nuisance by discharging effluent from their drainage system.[24]

In the city of Kolkota, a refuse-liquid from a shellac factory was discharged into a municipal drain. When it was questioned, the company denied that it was noxious or that it had injuriously affected the plaintiff. The court interfered with the same and granted an injunction and damages. The statutes did not sanction the company's conduct, nor

---

[19] *Almitra H. Patel v. Union of India*, 2000 AIRSCW 924.

[20] *C. Uma Devi v. Government of AP*, AIR 2000 AP 260.

[21] *Sumit T.P. v. State of Kerala*, 2004 (1) KLT 438.

[22] *L.K. Koolwal v. State of Rajasthan*, AIR 1988 Raj 2.

[23] *Masood Ahmad v. State of J and K*, AIR 1997 J and K 75.

[24] *M/s Ajay Constructions v. Kkateeya Nagar*, AIR 1991 AP 294.

did they give the company any right to create a nuisance.[25]

The Calcutta HC has reiterated that the Municipal Corporation has a statutory obligation to clean and/or collect the garbage to keep the city clean. The Corporation was also directed to see that any plan submitted for the construction of a house or place within the city be denied permission if the designated land was originally part of a pond and the character of the land was otherwise filled up by surreptitious means.[26]

M.C. Mehta[27] filed a PIL before the Orissa HC complaining about the discharge of a storm water drain from the Medical College campus. A report by the Pollution Control Board was not taken into account by the state government. The court directed the authorities to take immediate action to prevent and control water pollution.[28]

A PIL was lodged before the Orissa HC challenging a decision of the Municipal Corporation to open a college. It was contended that the Municipal Corporation should not run a college while in total bankruptcy and failing to provide minimum basic amenities to its taxpayers. Accepting the argument, the court held that the Municipal Corporation was failing to discharge its constitutional or statutory obligations and duties towards the general public and taxpayers of the city in regard to maintenance of roads, drainage systems, and other amenities. In attempting to open a college in the face of its carelessness, it had started functioning in a manner that is not expected of a civil body.[29]

The Municipal Board is under a statutory obligation to construct sewers and drains for the discharge of domestic and rain water, which is likely to cause a public nuisance if left for a lengthy time, the Rajasthan HC held.[30]

The Rajasthan HC has issued a direction to the municipality to construct toilets for public use. People who do not have dwelling places use roads and footpaths for easing themselves under compulsion. It presents an ugly sight and creates unhygienic conditions in the city while also compromising human dignity. On this basis, the HC directed the municipality to construct toilets.[31]

For the purposes of addressing the dumping and disposal of garbage in Goa, the HC directed the government to frame a scheme and form special committees. The court also directed the appointment of an officer to specially be in charge of garbage management. A number of directions were issued to the municipal councils, including the provision of continuous public awareness programmes regarding the existence of garbage collection schemes and the official coordination of ragpicker associations and NGOs in the collection and disposal of non-biodegradable waste. Biodegradable waste is to be collected in a container of suitable dimensions, which is green in colour, and non-biodegradable in a black container, where both containers are to be kept in a proper place within an establishment.[32]

The grievance of pollution created by the daily burning of plastic scraps was taken cognizance by the Andhra Pradesh HC on receipt of a telegram. The court directed the

---

[25] C. Galistaun v. Dunia Lal Seal, (1905) 9 CWN 612.
[26] Arun Sanyal v. State of West Bengal, AIR 1998 Cal 331.
[27] Noted environmentalist who has filed numerous petitions before the Supreme Court of India.
[28] M.C. Mehta v. State, AIR 1992 Orissa 225.
[29] Shri Sidheswar v. State, 2002 (1) Orissa Law Reporter 121.

[30] Rampal v. State of Rajasthan, AIR 1981 Raj 12€.
[31] Vimal Chowdary v. Nagar Nigam, AIR 2004 Raj 17.
[32] Claudio Fernandes and Others v. Margao Municipal Council and Others, Writ Petitions No. 417 of 2002 and 28 of 2003, dated 30 July 2003.

authorities to ensure that no garbage is burnt in any thickly populated residential area without clearance from the Andhra Pradesh Pollution Control Board. The Board was directed to depute a qualified person for making surprise inspections as to how garbage collected from the railways is disposed of. The Commissioner of the Municipal Corporation of Hyderabad and all other authorities were also requested to see that no pollution is caused by reason of the burning of garbage, and in this regard they must render their full cooperation to the authorities of the Andhra Pradesh Pollution Control Board.[33]

The Supreme Court had the occasion to constitute a committee to examine issues of sewerage management in detail and submit a report to the Court. The report proposed an action plan and identified authorities responsible for implementation. The Court issued directions to the committee to ensure that various works mentioned in the action plan were undertaken in accordance with the schedule.[34]

Solid Waste Management— Slaughterhouses

There are about 2,702 registered slaughterhouses in India. Amongst the solid wastes generated by slaughterhouses are carcasses and various types of offal that are by-products of its operations. By-products can be divided into two groups, edible and inedible. The components left uncovered form solid wastes. The quantity of waste varies from place to place. It has been observed by the CPCB that there is no organized system for the disposal of solid wastes in the majority of slaughterhouses in India.[35]

Most solid waste generated by slaughterhouses is collected and disposed of as landfill. In certain slaughterhouses, dung and *rumer digesta* are collected separately for composing. The slaughterhouse waste contains mostly biodegradable matter. Every by-product of the slaughterhouse can be utilized, although various circumstances do not always permit by-product recovery. This may be due to an inadequacy in the quantity of materials, lack of markets, or the cost of processing. In such circumstances, they simply form part of waste oil, for which different methods of processing and disposal must be considered. Landfilling, when carried out poorly, contaminates groundwater, which once contaminated, is very difficult to purify.

All methods of waste management, except incineration, facilitate recovery of secondary by-products such as manure, biogas, fat, bone, and meat meal, and others while disposing of the wastes in an environmentally sound manner.

In a country as populated as India, waste management is always going to be a challenge. It can now be said, however, that the country is slowly developing the statutory framework that is pertinent for the disposal of waste in a sustainable fashion. While taking notice of international standards and encouraging pride and cooperation on the part of local authorities, the future of waste management in India seems more optimistic.

ELECTRONIC WASTE IN INDIA

The contemporary world is 'techno-savvy'. In fact, electronics have become an integral part of twenty-first century lifestyle. The world has

[33] *Akhil v. Secretary, State Pollution Control Board*, Writ Petition No. 15490 of 2001, dated 3 October 2001.
[34] *Sector 14 Residents Association v. Delhi Municipal Corporation*, AIR 1999 SC 308: 1999 (1) SCC 161.
[35] Parivesh, *Solid Waste Management in Slaughter House*, New Delhi, Central Pollution Control Board, September 2004.

witnessed an astounding change from transistor and Black and White Television to the high-tech world of computers (desktops, laptops, notebooks, and palmtops), 3G mobile phones, and the new sensation, that is, the iPhone. All this pomp and luxury has come at a terrible cost. With each electronic product produced or bought, subsequent waste is generated. Electronic consumer goods that have reached their end-life or have become obsolete are tossed on the waste pile only to be replaced by supposedly more sophisticated goods that will later join their predecessors. Such discards are popularly known as electronic waste or e-waste. The common agents of e-waste are personal computers (PCs), mobile phones, televisions, and other electronic items. Electronic waste produces a number of toxic substances like lead, cadmium, mercury, plastics, and more such toxics.[36] These highly toxic substances and chemicals have an adverse effect not only on the environment, but also on human beings and other living organisms, if not properly handled.[37]

The Crux of the Problem

Developing countries like China and India are not only hubs for big information technology (IT) and mobile firms, but also the preferred destinations for developed countries like the USA for the dumping of electronic wastes.[38] This is in addition to the domestic heaving of about 1,050 tonnes of electronic scrap generated by India alone. What is luring these developed countries into packing their scrap into Asian continents is, not surprisingly, monetary consideration together with the relatively cheap labour and lax standards to regulate the problem. It is estimated that it is about ten times cheaper to ship cathode ray tubes (CRTs) to countries like China and India than to domestically recycle it, according to a study conducted by the World Watch Institute in 2004. In addition to this, the sprawling domestic industry of e-waste recycling has only come as a 'shot in the arm' to developed countries. This will have an overwhelmingly negative effect on human health and the environment.

The Legal Implication

The menace of electronic waste is spiralling out of control more than ever before. The legal mechanism to deal with the problem is the pale, impotent Hazardous Waste (Management and Handling) Rules, 1989. The 'Magna Carta' that provided the foundation for the Rules is the Basel Convention[39] and the EPA 1989.[40]

---

[36] Lead and cadmium are found in printed circuit boards (PCB); lead oxide in cathode ray tubes; mercury in flat screen monitors; cadmium in computer batteries; PCB in capacitors and transformers; brominated flame retardant in PCB and plastic cable casings; PVC in cable insulation, coating, etc.

[37] Lead can cause brain damage, retardation, impairment of cognitive and behavioural development, silicosis; cadmium can cause renal damage; mercury can lead to inhibition of enzyme activity and cell damage; plastic which constitutes the bulk of ewaste disposed of through landfills or burning can cause severe ecological damage and atmospheric pollution<>http://earthtrends.wri.org/features/view_feature.php?theme=3&fid=66 (accessed on 11 July 2007).

[38] It is estimated that about 50 to 80 per cent of electronic waste that the US produces is being sent to Asian countries like India, China, etc.

[39] Basel Convention on the Control of Transboundary Movement of Hazardous Waste, 1989, as amended and came into force on 8 October, 2005.

[40] In pursuance of powers conferred by Sections 6, 8, 25 of Environment (Protection) Act, 1986; Section 6, which states 'Rules to regulate environmental pollution' sub-section 2 (c) deals with rule making power to provide for the procedures and safeguards for the handling of hazardous substances; Section 8.

Although the Basel Convention (to which India is a signatory) inspired the rules, in reality they are a species of the EPA. The Rules apply to the handling of hazardous wastes as specified in Schedule 1 and the management, including the export and import, of such hazardous wastes. Entry 31 of Schedule 1 includes the hazardous wastes of the electronic industry, which includes its residues also. Schedule 2 prescribes the concentration limits for waste effluents.[41] Schedule 3, which is included in concomitance with the Annexure VIII of the Basel Convention, enlists wastes that are applicable for export and import (EXIM). This includes electronic waste also.[42]

The rules provide a procedural framework for the handling and management of hazardous waste, like: the granting of authorization for occupiers of a facility; suspension or cancellation of authorization; packaging, labelling, and transportation of such wastes; identification of disposal sites; import and export of waste for recycle and reuse. However, a careful look at the rules exposes their flaws. Firstly, there is no enforcement agency. Although the State Pollution Control Board is responsible for policing hazardous waste, its activities are generally supervisory. Secondly, the onus of proper collection, reception, treatment, storage, disposal, and transportation and identification of disposal sites, vests with the occupier of the facility. There is little duty on the part of the enforcing authority,

except in granting authorization and general supervision. Finally, when it comes to enforcing liability upon the occupier of a facility for any damages caused to the environment, the rules state in a dreary manner that such occupier of the facility shall be liable to reinstate or replace the damaged elements. But the rules remain hushed on how this should be achieved. Moreover, in the case of a violation, the rules prescribe that the violator shall be liable to pay a fine levied by the State Pollution Control Board. However, the want of stringent penal provisions makes the rules a travesty.

The Way Out

As long as consumerism shows no signs of abatement, the problem of e-waste will be further aggravated. So, India must be on guard to see through this quagmire. The idea of a comprehensive definition of e-waste within a proposed E-Waste (Management, Handling and Recycling) Act and Rules seems to be a pertinent one. This is all the more pressing because the current legal regime is 'beating in the bush' for want of a comprehensive definition of 'electronic waste'. Therefore, the first task of this incumbent Act is to define 'electronic waste'. Currently, there are a number of rules scattered here and there that directly or indirectly deal with electronic waste.[43] In addition to this, there are sections of the Indian Penal Code, 1860 that can be utilized.[44] All this can be codified to make a compendium that can go a long way in dealing with the issue of e-waste.

---

[41] This list is based on BAGA (Netherlands Environment Protection Agency), and deals with persons handling hazardous substances to comply with procedural safeguards; Section 25 deals with rule making powers of Central Government.

[42] Waste Electrical and electronic assemblies or scrap containing, compounds and as accumulators and other batteries, mercury switches, glass from cathode-ray tubes and other activated glass and PCB capacitors, Electrical and electronic assemblies, etc.

[43] The Manufacture, Storage and Import of Hazardous Chemical Rules, 1989; the Recycled Plastics Manufacture and Usage Rules, 1999; the Batteries (Management and Handling) Rules, 2001 etc.

[44] Chapter XIV, Of Offences Affecting the Public Health, Safety, Convenience, Decency and Morals; Section 278 specifically deals with making atmosphere noxious to health.

There must be an enforcement agency to supervise the management, handling, recycling, export, import, and other aspects, of hazardous waste. It must be given more teeth, in that its domain should not be restrained to mere supervision alone. In the event of disputes or adjudication, the matter must be sent for consideration to National or State Environment Tribunals.

Mere provision of penal sanctions will not suffice. Stress should also be placed on 'recycling' domestically. One option is for the state to set up its own recycling system. Perhaps, one should look at the example set by California in this respect. In 2003, the American state of California enacted what has been called a landmark statute in the field of electronic waste management, the Electronic Waste Recycling Act, 2003. This Act is aimed at reducing hazardous substances used in electronic substances sold in the state of California, by recycling them and collecting some sort of 'electronic waste recycling fee' at the point of purchase of an electronic product from consumers. It also prescribes a 'directive' suggesting environmentally preferred criteria for state agencies to adopt in purchasing electronic equipments. This was implemented by the California Integrated Waste Management Board (CIWMB) on 12 July 2007. Following California's example, at least half of the American states have passed laws dealing with electronic waste recycling.[45] Another method of curbing the effects of consumerism is to specify that manufactures hold the responsibility of recycling their products after use. The principle of 'extended producer responsibility' can be employed, placing an obligation on producers or manufacturers to take responsibility for the entire life of their products, up until their ultimate fate. They cannot hide behind the acts of third parties like distributors and are thus forced to manufacture products which are environmentally sustainable in the first place. The Japanese legislation is a good example,[46] although its success in Japan is unlikely to be mirrored in India. This legislation will no doubt provide a framework for any future legislation on the subject.

In addition to strengthening the internal regulatory mechanism for e-waste, care must also be taken to prevent the import of hazardous substances. Bans, like those in the European Union (EU), must be put on any substance if it is found to have a far-reaching impact on human health and the environment. Perhaps India needs to make the EU its role model in framing a comprehensive policy on the 'management and disposal of electronic waste'.

The foundation of this directive is the precautionary principle. This directive aims at approximating the laws made by member states in the field of restriction of hazardous electrical and electronic substances, and to contribute to the protection of human health and the environmentally sound recovery and disposal of used electrical and electronic equipment. The dominating concern behind these directives seems to be the overwhelming concern for human health and the environment; finding out technically and economically feasible ways to reduce the risks posed by these substances, including substitution of hazardous substances with environment friendly alternatives to ensure protection to consumers. The EU member countries were obliged to transpose the WEEE Directive waste Electrical and Electronic Equipments into their domestic laws by 13 August 2004.

---

[45] Sankar Radhakrishnan, 'Smart Way to Tackle E-Waste', *The Hindu Business Line*, 29 January 2007.

[46] Specified Home Appliances Recycling Law, 2001 (Japan).

Non-compliance by member states would invite penalties.[47]

The notions of environmental protection and prudent utilization of natural resources are the prime objectives of European environmental policy.[48] This policy is anchored on the *grund norms* of the following principles: precautionary, polluter pays, and sustainable development. Sustainable development calls for a paradigm shift in the current patterns of development, and advocates, in the reduction of wasteful reduction of consumption of natural resources and prevention of pollution through re-use, recycling and recovery for its energy. It identifies WEEE as one of the targeted areas to be regulated. This directive introduces the 'principle of producer's responsibility'. It also calls for companies to set up infrastructure for collecting WEEE, so as to encourage the consumers to return them 'free of charge'. The producers or third parties are also required to use such WEEE in an 'eco-friendly manner', either through refurbishment or reuse. The compliance of most of the EU member states to the deadline set by the directive is testimony of its effectiveness.

Technology has propelled human civilization beyond light years. Electronics is the progeny of this human prodigy. The evolution of electronics, from crude handmade devices to high-tech gadgets, is a part of human history. It is the past, present, and future of mankind and is here to stay. But techno savvy humans should not jeopardize the environment. It must be remembered that the survival of a pristine and serene environment is a basic human right. In the meantime, technology is increasingly being relied upon for environmental conservation. There must be a fine balance between these disciplines. The quandary posed by electronic waste can be overcome by prudent legislation, dexterous management, and perfect coordination.

Hazardous Substances

Hazardous wastes are highly toxic in nature. Industrialization has had the effect of generating huge quantities of hazardous wastes. They require adequate and proper control and handling, and sound efforts to minimize their occurrence. In developing nations, there are additional problems including the dumping of hazardous waste from foreign nations that view this as more affordable than destroying waste within their own borders.

An example of this is when the Supreme Court Monitoring Committee (SCMC) found that a Danish ship carrying hazardous waste was beached at the Alang ship-breaking yard in Gujarat. The carrying of the toxic waste was noticed by the Government of Denmark and they ordered the ship to remain there till its decontamination was complete. But the ship changed its name and went to India. The SCMC ordered it to return to its country of origin.[49] Unfortunately, not all culprits are detected as they were in this case.

Hazardous Substances Management and Handling Rules

The perils of hazardous waste and other allied problems gave birth to the Basel Convention.[50] The key objectives of the Basel Convention are:

---

[47] RoHS (Restriction of the use of certain hazardous substances in electrical and electronic equipments) (Directive 2002/95/EC) (alternatively, Directive on the Restriction of Hazardous Substances in Electrical and Electronical Equipment, 2002/95/EC).

[48] Directive on Waste Electrical and Electronic Equipments (WEEE) (Directive 2002/96/ EC).

[49] *Down to Earth*, 30 June 2005 (Magazine published by Society for Environmental Publications, New Delhi).

[50] Basel Convention on the Control of Transboundary Movement of Hazardous Wastes and their disposal.

1. Minimize the generation of hazardous wastes in terms of quantity and hazardousness.
2. To dispose of them as close to the source of generation as possible.
3. To reduce the trans-boundary movement of hazardous wastes.

India signed the Basel Convention on 15 March 1990 and ratified it on 24 June 1992. Based on the Basel Convention, the Hazardous Wastes (Management and Handling) Rules[51] are framed with the intention of regulating the management and handling of hazardous waste. It is also actively involved in the work relating to the preparation of technical guidelines for environmentally sound management of ship-breaking along with Norway and the Netherlands under this Convention. It is on the said principles that the Hazardous Wastes (Management and Handling) Rules, 1989[52] were founded. The law is intended for the environmentally sound management of hazardous wastes in a manner that will protect health and the environment against the adverse effects which may result from such wastes. Any waste which by reason of its physical, chemical, reactive, toxic flammable, explosive, or corrosive characteristics causes danger or is likely to cause danger to health or the environment on its own accord or in culmination with other substances, is deemed hazardous waste.[53] A list of such wastes is provided in the schedule annexed to the enactment. Hazardous wastes shall be collected, treated, stored, and disposed of only in such facilities as may be authorized. Every occupier who handles hazardous

waste, or a recycler of hazardous wastes, must obtain an authorization from the authorities concerned. The law also permits the establishment of a common treatment, storage, and disposal facility.

The occupier or operator is obligated to ensure that hazardous wastes are packaged based on their composition, in a manner suitable for handling, storage, and transport. A general label has to be provided to identify the substance, and labelling on the packaging should be easily visible and be able to withstand physical conditions and climatic factors. The design and set-up of the disposal facility must be as per the guidelines of the Central Government and monitored by the state government. The occupier or operator is responsible for the safe and environmentally sound operation of the facility. Rule 11 prohibits the import and export of hazardous wastes for dumping, disposal, recycling, and reuse from any country to and from India. The transboundary movement of hazardous wastes is routinely monitored by the MoEF.

By an order dated 5 May 1997, the Supreme Court of India, inter alia, directed that no authorization or permission would be given by any authority for the import of hazardous waste items that have already been banned by the Central Government or by any order made by any court or any other authority. It further directed that no import would be made or permitted by any authority or any person, of any hazardous waste that is already banned under the Basel Convention or to be banned hereafter with effect from the dates specified therein. In view of the magnitude of the problem and its impact, state governments were directed to show cause, as to why an order should not be made directing closure of units utilizing the hazardous waste, where provision has not already been made for requisite safe disposal

---

[51] Hazardous Wastes (Management and Handling) Rules, 1989.

[52] Subordinate laws under the EPA; came into force with effect from 28 July 1989.

[53] Hazardous Wastes (Management and Handling) Rules, 1989, Rule 3(14).

sites. It was further ordered that cause be shown as to why an immediate order should not be issued for closure of all unauthorized hazardous waste handling units.

Based on the report of the expert committees, directions were issued to the MoEF to monitor the implementation of the said rules and recommendations. For monitoring the implementation, the High Powered Committee was set-up to oversee that the directions of the Supreme Court are implemented in a timely fashion.[54] The said Committee has issued various directions, including for the closure of industries. Unfortunately, after some time there was no action taken by courts, and certain HCs also started interfering with the said directions.

Even before the coming into force of the said rules, the Supreme Court had the occasion to consider the principles and norms for determining liability of large enterprises engaged in the manufacture and sale of hazardous products. It examined the basis on which damages in the case of such liability enterprises should be allowed to continue to function in thickly populated areas and if they are permitted to continue, what measures must be taken for the purpose of reducing to a minimum the hazard to the workmen and the community living in the neighbourhood. These matters arose in connection with the leakage of methyl isocyanate (MIC) gas from the Union Carbide Plant in Bhopal. The court has held that chlorine gas is dangerous to the life and health of the community and if it escapes from the storage tanks, filled cylinders, or another point in the course of production, it is likely to affect the health and well-being of the workmen and the people living in the vicinity. There can be

no doubt, particularly having regard to the opinion of various committees, that the possibility of hazard or risk to the community is considerably minimized and there is no appreciable risk of danger to the community if the chlorine plant is allowed to be restarted, the Court added in public interest.[55]

Manufacture, Storage, and Import of Hazardous Chemical Rules, 1989

The Bhopal Tragedy[56] awakened the legislature to the necessity to make laws to prevent a recurrence in future. The Manufacture, Storage, and Import of Hazardous Chemical Rules[57] will apply to chemical industries scheduled to the enactment and any industry must obtain prior approval before the commencement of operations.

If an industrial activity involves the handling of hazardous chemicals, and includes on-site transport which is associated with the operation of process, isolated storage, and pipelines, then it has a general responsibility to ensure that it has identified major accidental hazards, and taken adequate steps to prevent such accidents.[58] The authorities must inspect the industrial activity and undertake a full analysis of major accidents.

These rules also control the import of hazardous chemicals. If the authority is satisfied that the chemical being imported is likely to cause major accidents, it may direct the importer to take such safety measures as the concerned authority of the state may deem

---

[54] *Research Foundation for Science Technology National Resource Policy v. Union of India*, 2003 (8) SCALE 258.

[55] *M.C. Mehta v. Union of India*, AIR 1987 SC 965: (1986) 2 SCC 176.

[56] See for more details under the chapter on Disaster Management.

[57] Published in *the Gazette of India* No. 787, dated 27 November 1989.

[58] Manufacture, Storage, and Import of Hazardous Chemical Rules, 1989, Rule 4.

appropriate. If the authority is of the opinion that a person has contravened the provisions of these rules, that person can be asked to remedy the contravention.[59]

Recycled Plastics (Manufacture and Usage) Rules, 1999

The use of plastic bags for the convenience of consumerism has had a deleterious effect on the environment. In particular, marine wildlife has suffered the most as birds and animals are suffocated by the bags that are washed into their habitat. Plastic bags also represent an unsightly type of pollution, their weight and texture making them incredibly mobile as they show up in the most unlikely of places. In Australia, a farmer in 'New South Wales carried out an autopsy on a dead calf and found eight plastic bags in its stomach'.[60] Therefore, legislation is needed to curb the use of plastic bags and provide for their phasing out.

The Government of India has framed the Recycled Plastics (Manufacture and Usage) Rules, 1999[61] for the purpose of regulating the manufacture and use of recycled plastics, carry bags, and containers. Carry bags are defined as bags which have a self-carrying feature commonly known as vest type bags or any other feature used to carry commodities, such as 'D' punched bags.[62] The Rules prohibit the use of carry bags or containers made of recycled plastics for storing, carrying, dispensing, or packaging foodstuff. The minimum thickness

of carry bags made of virgin plastics or recycled plastics shall not be less than 20 microns. Rule 4 restrains the manufacture, sale, distribution, and use of virgin and recycled plastic carry bags and recycled plastic containers that are less than 8 x 12 inches (20 x 30 centimetres) in size and do not conform to the minimum thickness of 20 microns. Recycling of plastics shall be undertaken strictly in accordance with the standards prescribed by the Bureau of Indian Standards specification: IS 14534: 1998, entitled 'The Guidelines for Recycling of Plastics'.

But it was brought to the notice of the Supreme Court that the thickness prescribed is not sufficient. The Supreme Court directed amicus curiae to sit with the MoEF to raise the ban on plastic carry bags from 20 to 40 microns. Such increased ban is in force in West Bengal and Goa.[63]

Taking *suo moto* action on the basis of a telegram raising the grievances of pollution created by the daily burning of plastic scraps at Nampally station, the Andhra Pradesh HC directed the authorities to see to it that no garbage is burnt in any thickly populated residential area without clearance from the AP PCB. They were also directed to depute a qualified person to make surprise inspections as to how and in what manner garbage collected from the railways is disposed off. The Commissioner of the Municipal Corporation of Hyderabad and all other authorities are also requested to see that no pollution is caused by the burning of garbage and in this regard, they must render their full cooperation to the authorities of the AP PCB.[64]

In Delhi, the use of degradable plastic bags shall be compulsory for all restaurants and eating places with seating capacity of

---

[59] Rule 19. Manufacture, Storage, and Import of Hazardous Chemical Rules, 1989.

[60] Planet Ark, 'Why are Plastic Bags a Problem?' http://www.planetark.com/campaignspage.cfm/newsid/52/newsDate/7/story.htm (last visited 24 July 2007)

[61] EPA, Section3 , published in *the Gazette of India*, Part II, Section 3(ii), dated 2 September 1999.

[62] Plastic Manufacture, Sale and Usage Rules, 1999, Rule 3(b).

[63] 2004 (8) SCALE 548.

[64] *Akhil v. SPCB*, Writ Petition No. 15490 of 2001; dated 3 October 2001.

more than fifty seats, all fruit and vegetable outlets of Mother Dairy, liquors, vends, and all shopping malls.[65]

Ireland has often been hailed for its success in reducing the use of plastic bags, by implementing stringent legislation. In 2001, the Waste Management (Environmental Levy) (Plastic Bag) Regulations were created.[66] The levy aims at deterring consumers from requesting plastic bags, so that alternative and more environment-friendly means of carrying goods are sought. Consumers are charged a levy of 15 cents for each plastic bag that they obtain from a retailer. There are, however, a number of exemptions in relation to unpackaged foodstuff such as fresh fish, meat and poultry, fruit, vegetables, dairy, ice, and confectionery. Where such bags are 'not greater in dimension than 225 mm in width (exclusive of any gussets), by 345mm in depth (inclusive of any gussets), by 450mm in length, (inclusive of any handles)'[67] and used to carry specified goods, they will not fall within the definition of a plastic bag.

In Australia, the state of Victoria proposed to restrict the provision of plastic bags by retailers when it amended the Environment Protection Act in 2006. The amendment, which is to come into force in 2009, inserts the definition of a plastic bag into the principal Act reading: '"plastic bag" means a carry bag, the body [of] which comprises polymers in whole or part, provided by a retailer for the carrying or transporting of goods, but does not include a carry bag which complies with prescribed design criteria.'[68]

The Australian definition is wider than the Indian definition, as it is not restricted to recycled plastics. However, the restrictions are less stringent in that the amendment only provides that retailers are not to supply a plastic bag to a consumer upon a transaction, unless an amount is charged for the bag, being not less than the prescribed amount.[69] In this sense, Australian legislation is largely reflective of the Irish position. It is also unlikely that the ban will apply to small businesses or biodegradable bags.[70]

Batteries Management Rules

The lead acid battery, which is a source of electrical energy, contains lead metal. The usage of old batteries after recycling, if not carried out properly, damages the environment. To control the damage that may be caused to the environment, the Government of India has enacted the Batteries (Management and Handling) Rules, 2000. Rule 4 casts a responsibility on the manufacturer, importer, assembler, and re-conditioner:

1. To ensure that the used batteries are collected as prescribed against new batteries sold excluding those sold to the original equipment manufacturer and bulk consumer.
2. To set up collection centres for the used batteries and sent the same to approved recyclers only.
3. To ensure that no damage to the environment occurs during transportation and file annual return

---

[65] Notification No. SO450(E), dated 25 May 2006 issued by the MoEF.

[66] Waste Management (Environmental Levy) (Plastic Bag) Regulations, 2001 (Ireland) S.I. No. 605/2001.

[67] Ibid., reg. 5.

[68] Environment Protection Act, 1970 (Vic), Section 4(1) as amended by Environment Protection (Amendment) Act, 2006, (Vic) Clause 46.

[69] Environment Protection Act 1970 (Vic), Section 71(kb) as amended by Environment Protection (Amendment) Act 2006 (Vic) Clause 45.

[70] Rick Wallace, 'Giveaway Plastic Bags Banned' The Australian (18 July 2006) available at <http://www.austlii.edu.au/au/legis/vic/bill/epb2006374/> (last visited 24 July 2006).

4. To create awareness of hazards of lead, responsibility of consumers to return their used batteries only to dealers, address of dealers and collection centres, use of international recycling sign on batteries, and bring to the notice of the government any violations.

Responsibilities are imposed on the dealer and recycler to obtain registration and manage the used batteries as prescribed. It is the duty of the consumer to ensure that used batteries are not disposed off in any manner other than depositing the same with the dealer, manufacturer, importer, assembler, registered recycler, re-conditioner, or at a designated collection centre.

Pesticides

Chemicals other than food, air, and water have always been part of man's environment in some measure. The mechanization and modernization of agricultural operations has led to the use of fertilizers and spraying pesticides to achieve self sufficiency in food grains, commercial corps, and other products. The main hurdle in agriculture boosting is the loss and destruction of crops and plants from the harm caused by pests and insects. To meet the said problem, farmers have started using insecticides and pesticides to protect crops and plants from these menaces. The excessive use of chemicals and pesticides for optimizing agricultural production has created an alarming danger to the health and safety of living beings in general, and agricultural workers in particular. Pesticides 'affect man's' ecosystem, and their residues have the potential to enter the food chain which can result in the process of bio-magnification and eventual harm to the ultimate consumer.

To regulate the import, manufacture, sale, transport, distribution, and use of insecticides and with a view to prevent risk to human beings or animals, and for matters connected therewith, the Government of India has enacted the Insecticides Act, 1968. A person dealing in insecticides must obtain registration under the Act. It also prohibits the sale of certain insecticides.

The Supreme Court has brought health hazards due to pollution and the use of harmful drugs within the ambit of right to life conferred under Article 21 of the Constitution of India.[71] A healthy body is the very foundation of all human activities and in a welfare state, it is the obligation of the state to ensure the creation and the sustenance of conditions congenial to good health.

On another occasion the Supreme Court has converted a letter into a PIL. The letter stated that several insecticides, colour additives, and food additives, which have already been banned in several advanced countries because they are carcinogens, are in widespread use in India.[72] The Supreme Court found that once a substance is specified in the schedule under the Insecticides Act, 1968, there is no provision for cancelling the registration certificate issued in respect of the same substance, even if on scientific study it appears that the substance in question is grossly detrimental to human health. The Supreme Court has held that steps should be taken to fill up this lacuna.

India is the largest producer of Endosulfan, an organochlorine pesticide. Endosulfan is said to have been banned in ten countries and its use is restricted in twenty-two countries. But the Plantation Corporation of Kerala has been spraying the substance through helicopters on cashew plantations in the state. The blood, milk, vegetables, and cashews samples of the

---

[71] *Vincent Panikulangara v. Union of India*, (1987) 2 SCC (2) 165.

[72] *Ashok v. Union of India*, AIR 1997 SC 2298: (1997) 5 SCC 10.

Padre Village of Kasaragod District contained perilously high levels of Endosulfan. Cases of cerebral palsy, cancer of the liver, retardation of mental and/or physical growth, epilepsy, and other medical problems, were found among the people of the area. Considering all the relevant issues, the KHC has directed the Central Government to take a decision and pending the same, the use of Endosulfan is prohibited.[73]

The Basel Convention is not the only international convention that aims at protecting human health and the environment from the use of hazardous chemicals. The Rotterdam Convention[74] is intended to cover pesticides and industrial chemicals that have been banned or severely restricted for health or environmental reasons by the parties and which have been notified by parties for inclusion in the Prior Informed Consent (PIC) procedure. Severely hazardous pesticide formulations that present a hazard under conditions of use in developing countries or countries with economies in transition may also be nominated for inclusion. The Stockholm Convention, on Persistent Organic Pollutants (POPs Treaty) aims to phase out the 'dirty dozen' persistent organic pollutants, where most pesticides fall within this class. These specific substances were identified because of their capacity to travel long distances and bio-accumulate in the fatty tissue of animals.[75] POPs in particular are heavily regulated by the international regime, as they are covered by the abovementioned Convention, the Basel Convention and the Rotterdam Convention. India signed the Stockholm Convention on POPs in May 2002. The Convention seeks to eliminate the production, use, import, and export of twelve identified POPs namely Adrin, Endrin, Dieldrin, Chlordane, DDT, Heptachlor, Toxaphene, Mirex, Hexachlorobenzene, Polychlorinated Biphenyls, Dioxins, and Furans.

Fly Ash from Thermal Stations

Fly ash from thermal power stations causes pollution. To protect the environment, conserve top soil, and prevent the dumping and disposal of fly ash discharged from coal or lignite based thermal power plants on land, the Government of India issued a notification on 14 September 1999. The law makes the following restrictions:

1. No person shall, within a radius of fifty kilometres from coal or lignite based thermal power plants, manufacture clay bricks or tiles or blocks for use in construction activities without mixing at least 25 per cent of ash (fly ash, bottom ash, or pond ash) with soil on a weight to weight basis.

2. The authority for ensuring the use of specified quantity of ash as per para (1) above shall be the concerned Regional Officer of the State Pollution Control Board or the Pollution Control Committee as the case may be. In case of non-compliance, the said authority, in addition to cancellation of the consent order issued to establish the brick kiln, shall move the district administration for cancellation of the mining lease. The cancellation of a mining lease shall be decided after due hearing. To enable the said authority to verify the

[73] *Thiruvankulam Natural Lovers Movement v. Union of India*, OP Nos 20716/2002, 17026/2002, 16300/2002 and 29371 of 2001, dated 8 December 2002 of Kerala High Court.

[74] Convention on the Prior Informed Consent Procedure for Certain Hazardous Chemicals and Pesticides in International Trade, came into force on 24 February 2004, 38 ILM 1 (1999).

[75] Stockholm Convention on Persistent Organic Pollutants <http://www.pops.int/default.htm> (last visited 25 July 2007).

actual use of ash, the thermal power plant shall maintain month-wise records of ash made available to each brick kiln.

3. In case of non-availability of ash from the thermal power plant in sufficient quantities as certified by the said power plant, the stipulation under paragraph (1) shall be suitably modified (waived or relaxed) by the concerned State or Union Territory Government.

4. Each coal or lignite based thermal power plant shall constitute a dispute settlement committee, which shall include the General Manager of the thermal power plant and a representative of the All India Brick and Tile Manufacturers' Federation (AIBTMF). Such a committee shall ensure unhindered loading and transport of ash without any undue loss of time. Any unresolved dispute shall be dealt with by a committee set up by the state or Union Territory comprising of Member Secretary of the State Pollution Control Board or Pollution Control Committee, representatives of Ministry of Power in the State or Union Territory Government and a representative of the AIBTMF.

Conditions have been prescribed for the coal or lignite based thermal power plants to utilize the fly ash. All such plants shall make available ash, without any payment or other consideration, for the purpose of manufacturing ash-based products such as cement, concrete blocks, bricks, panels, or any other material or for construction of roads, embankments, dams, dykes, or for any other construction activity. Every existing coal or lignite based thermal power plant shall phase out the dumping and disposal of fly ash on land. Such an action plan shall provide for 30 per cent of the fly ash utilization, within three years from the publication of this notification with further increase in utilization by at least

10 per cent every year progressively for the next six years to enable utilization of the entire fly ash generated in the power plant at least by the end of the ninth year.[76]

Central and state government agencies, State Electricity Boards, the National Thermal Power Corporation, and the management of the thermal power plants shall facilitate the availability of land, electricity, and water for manufacturing activities and provide access to the ash-lifting area for promoting and setting up of ash-based production units in the proximity of the area where ash is generated by the power plant. These Rules also prescribed specifications for use of ash-based products.[77]

Hazardous Substances in the United States of America

The USA has a large legislative framework for dealing with hazardous substances. The Emergency Planning and Community Right to Know Act[78] was largely a response to the Bhopal tragedy, and required owners of facilities that hold hazardous substances beyond the specified threshold[79] to comply with certain reporting obligations[80] regarding precautionary and proposed emergency response measures to be utilized in case of an accident. Under the Act, citizens can also compel holders of such substances to release information, hence the appropriate title. In order to track, monitor, and regulate toxic substances, Congress has also enacted the Toxic Substances Control Act.[81] The Act is based on the finding that

[76] Fly Ash Notification, 1999, Rule 2.

[77] Ibid., Rule 3.

[78] Emergency Planning and Community Right to Know Act, 42 USC, Section 11001 et seq. (1986).

[79] Ibid., Section 11002(a) et seq. (1986).

[80] Ibid., Section 11021, 11022, et seq. (1986) 11023.

[81] Toxic Substances Control Act, 15 U.S.C. s/s 2601 et seq. (1976).

1. human beings and the environment are being exposed each year to a large number of chemical substances and mixtures; [and]
2. among the many chemical substances and mixtures which are constantly being developed and produced, there are some whose manufacture, processing, and distribution in commerce, use, or disposal may present an unreasonable risk of injury to health or the environment.[82]

Consequently, the Act aims at increasing the knowledge available in relation to the effects of such substances so that they may be properly regulated. The burden of developing this knowledge through research or otherwise is firmly placed on those who manufacture and process the substances. Having said this however, the Act employs a proportionality approach and is explicit that the operation of the Act shall not

impede unduly or create unnecessary economic barriers to technological innovation while fulfilling the primary purpose of this chapter to assure that such innovation and commerce in such chemical substances and mixtures do not present an unreasonable risk of injury to health or the environment.[83]

An appropriate balance between development and the environment is thus envisaged by the legislation.

The Comprehensive Environmental Response, Compensation, and Liability Act, 1980 (CERCLA)[84] is directed at those who operate or own facilities that hold or manufacture hazardous chemicals and those who are in charge of treating, disposing off,

or transporting such hazardous chemicals.[85] The Act imposes a tax on operators of hazardous waste and petroleum facilities, in order to establish a 'trust fund for cleaning up abandoned or uncontrolled hazardous waste sites'.[86] The fund is to be used in instances where the culprit responsible for the expulsion of hazardous substances cannot be identified; otherwise, such person is held liable. The Superfund Amendments and Reauthorization Act (SARA)[87] amended the principal legislation in 1986. This 'increased the focus on human health problems posed by hazardous waste sites'[88] largely by reassessing the Hazard Ranking System used to classify types of hazardous waste and allocate appropriate obligations. In doing so, the amendment aimed at making the system more reflective of the potential harm to human health caused by various substances. The legislation thus encourages the proper handling of hazardous substances, as those who cause such substances to be misused are to be held responsible.

The Resource Conservation and Recovery Act[89] (RCRA) is the first comprehensive, 'cradle to grave' programme for controlling hazardous waste, to be administered by the EPA. The RCRA requires the EPA to create a comprehensive regulatory scheme for the treatment, storage, and disposal of hazardous waste. These regulations establish standards for: identifying and listing hazardous wastes, generators of hazardous waste, transporters, hazardous waste managers

[82] Ibid., s 2601(a) et seq. (1976).

[83] Ibid., s 2601(b)(1)(3) et seq. (1976).

[84] Compensation, and Liability Act, 42 U.S.C. s/s 9601 et seq. (1980).

[85] Ibid., Section 9607 et seq. (1980).

[86] US Environmental Protection Agency, 'CERCLA Overview' http://www.epa.gov/superfund/policy/cercla. htm (last visited 24 July 2007).

[87] Superfund Amendments and Reauthorization Act 42 USC 9601 et seq. (1986).

[88] US Environmental Protection Agency, 'SARA Overview' http://www.epa.gov/superfund/policy/sara. htm (last visited 25 July 2007).

[89] 42 USC s/s 6901 et seq., (1976).

awaiting administrative disposition of their permits, and managers with permits. In order to protect groundwater, the Hazardous and Solid Waste Amendments, 1984 introduced the following requirements:

1. New technological standards for land disposal facilities (double liners, leachate collection systems, groundwater monitoring);
2. New requirements for the management and treatment of small quantities of hazardous waste, such as those generated by auto repair shops or dry cleaners;
3. New regulations for underground tanks that store liquid petroleum and chemical products;
4. Restrictions on the future land disposal of many treated hazardous wastes.

Land disposal has been a dominant hazardous waste disposal alternative, in part because it has been less expensive than incineration, neutralization, stabilization, and other non-land based options. To address the public health and environmental problems posed by the landfill of hazardous waste, the 1984 law provides a strict schedule for determining whether to phase out land disposal of untreated hazardous wastes between 1986 and 1990. It also creates new and more stringent requirements for land disposal facilities that now exist and for those that will be created to deal with the residue of wastes requiring land disposal.[90]

Chemicals are a double-edged sword of the modern world. They enable us to conquer the limitations of nature in its pure form as we overcome diseases and manufacture new products to make our lives easier. However, the mixing of chemicals can also have disastrous effects. Not only do chemicals react with one another, but also with the environment and human beings. A controlled creation within a factory or laboratory can reap desired rewards, but when leaked into the environment, it can be hazardous. Hazardous wastes are chemical substances that are in search of a final destination. No longer required for the creating process, they are destined to react with the environment in a devastating way if not properly treated. The complexities of modern day society unfortunately encourage the continued generation of hazardous wastes. Legislation provides a contemporary solution: with the proper storage, handling, and treatment of hazardous wastes, we can minimize the effects they have on human health and the environment. The long-term solution: a simpler way of life. Perhaps the phasing out of dangerous substances such as POPs is one small step in this direction.

---

[90] Thomas J. Schoenbaum and Ronald H. Rosenberg. *Environmental Policy Law: Problems, Cases, and Readings,* 2nd edition, University Casebook Series, Foundation Press, 1991.

15 Relevance of the Law on Public Nuisance

The common law of tort provided a legal mechanism for controlling environmental pollution. Industrial activities are now controlled through statutes. However, tort law still serves sufferers of pollution, as it is often the only means of recovery for personal injury.

The emanation of pollution attracts liability under various theories. Consider, for example, a person who fills his land with hazardous waste. This landfill will adversely affect the nearby groundwater source. It is a nuisance because it interferes with the use and enjoyment of another's land. It is a trespass, as it involves physical intrusion into the property of another. The conduct of landfilling without taking precautions tantamounts to negligence. The common principle of strict liability, as laid down in *Rylands* v. *Fletcher*,[1] has imposed tort liability on the parties without regard to whether they were negligent or otherwise at fault.

As per Section 268 of the IPC, 1860, a person is guilty of a public nuisance if he or she commits an illegal act or omission, which causes any common injury, danger, or annoyance to the public or to the people in general who dwell or occupy property in the vicinity, or which must necessarily cause injury, obstruction, danger, or annoyance to persons who may have occasion to use any public right.

REMOVAL OF PUBLIC NUISANCE—SECTION 133 CrPC

District Magistrates have been empowered by the CPC, 1973 to remove public nuisances. Any unlawful obstruction or nuisance should be removed from any public place or from any way, river, or channel that is or may be lawfully used by the public.[2] Magistrates are empowered to pass orders that compel the person causing the obstruction or nuisance to remove it. Before passing such final orders, the magistrate has to make a conditional order requiring the person causing such obstruction or nuisance to remove such obstruction or nuisance. For example, the person may be required to alter the way they conduct their trade or business, dispose off nuisance-causing goods, or merchandise or remove such obstructions. The power conferred on the magistrate is very wide. The magistrate is empowered to make orders, including any conditional orders using the prescribed

---

[1] *Rylands* v. *Fletcher*, (1868) LR 3 HL 330.

[2] Criminal Procedure Code, 1973, Section 113.

procedure. Civil courts are barred from questioning the validity of such orders.

The above mentioned provision is intended to provide a speedy remedy in the interest of the public. The magistrate should guard against any tendency to use it as a substitute for litigation in civil courts for the settlement of private disputes.[3] This provision does not apply to private nuisance.[4]

The Supreme Court of India had the occasion to interpret the above provisions in a landmark case, popularly known as the *Ratlam Municipality* case.[5] According to the Court, Section 133 becomes active whenever there is a public nuisance.

The public power of the magistrate under the Code is a public duty to the members of the public who are victims of the nuisance, where the exercise of this power is activated by the presence of jurisdictional facts. All power is a trust—that we are accountable for its exercise—that, from the people, and for the people, all springs, and all must exist. Discretion becomes a duty when the beneficiary brings home the circumstances for its benign exercise,

the Supreme Court explained.

India Case Law

Residents of a rural area approached the Sub-Divisional Magistrate complaining that a[6] godown that stored large quantity of chillies was causing nuisance to them. The magistrate exercised his power and directed the owner not to keep, store, and transport chillies in the godown. The court came to the following conclusions:

i) People in general in the locality in sufficient number are suffering from the loading and unloading of dry chillies and its storage in the godown;

ii) It has resulted not only in their adverse health and discomfort but a few are permanently suffering in the sense that some of them are suffering from sickness and ailment;

iii) Even the witnesses of the non-applicant admitted that due to this business, there is discomfort and injury to physical health.

The power of the magistrate is a duty to the members of the public who are victims of the nuisance. The conduct of the trade must be injurious in *presenti* to the health or physical comfort of the community. There must be an imminent danger to the health or physical comfort of the community in the locality where the trade or occupation is conducted. In upholding the orders of a magistrate, the Supreme Court has held that it is the function of the magistrate to conduct an enquiry and decide whether there is sufficient evidence to necessitate action under Section 133.[7]

Nuisance is an inconvenience that materially interferes with the ordinary physical comfort of human existence. It is not capable of precise definition. The object and purpose underlying Section 133 of the Code is to prevent public nuisance and involves a sense of urgency, failure by the Magistrate to take recourse immediately could pose irreparable danger to the public. It applies to a condition of the nuisance at the time when the order is passed and is not intended to apply to future likelihood or what may happen at some later point in time. It does not deal with all potential

---

[3] 1973 Crl LJ 359, ILR 1991 Ker 987, AIR 1958 Pat 210.

[4] AIR 1962 SC 1794.

[5] *Municipal Council, Ratlam v. Vardhichand*, AIR 1980 SC 1622, (1980) 4 SCC 162.

[6] A warehouse or store room.

[7] *Kachrulal Bhagirath Agrawal and Others v. State of Maharashtra and Others*, Criminal Appeal No. 1350 of 2003, dated 22 September 2004.

nuisances and only applies when the nuisance is in existence.[8]

CONFLICT BETWEEN THE POWER OF THE MAGISTRATE AND THE POLLUTION CONTROL BOARD

A question has arisen as to whether Section 113 of the CrPC has been impliedly repealed by the coming into force of Section 30 of the Water (Prevention and Control of Pollution) Act, 1974 and Section 18 of the Air (Prevention and Control of Pollution) Act, 1981. The Supreme Court has held that the area of operation of the Code and the pollution laws in question are different with wholly different aims and objects: although they both alleviate nuisance, they are not of an identical nature. They operate in their respective fields and there is no impediment to their co-existence.[9] There is no implied repeal of Section 133 of the CrPC and therefore, it continues to hold its position empowering the magistrate to remove nuisance, even though it is pollution.

EXERCISE OF POWER BY THE MAGISTRATES

If the Magistrate, on receipt of information, considers that any unlawful obstruction or nuisance should be removed from any public place or from any way, river, or channel that may be used by the public, he has to make a conditional order requiring the person causing such nuisance to remove it within a fixed time. If the said person objects, he has to appear before the magistrate and cite reasons.[10]

Several cases have arisen questioning the powers of the magistrate. In one such case, the magistrate issued an order prohibiting the lighting of an oven in a bakery, which was emitting smoke from the chimney. The magistrate found that people living or working in the proximity of the bakery were adversely affected.[11] The oven was directed to be demolished because it caused nuisance to the general public.

In the state of Rajasthan, a magistrate found that the 'fodder tals' in a residential colony were causing nuisance. The following are instances of public nuisance: carrying on trade, causing intolerable noise, and spreading sand-laden wind containing particles of fodder over rooftops and inside houses of residents. Once noise and dust wind has met the requisite degree of nuisance, it is not a defence to contend that it is was the consequence of a lawful business. The Rajasthan HC affirmed the magistrate's ruling that an inadvertent dropping of a lit matchstick can engulf the locality in a disastrous fire, which may cause loss to persons and property of those who are living in the neighbouring colony.[12]

In Mumbai, a complaint was made against a tea stall that interfered with the free flow of traffic because of the space taken up by its miscellaneous articles and its clients. The Supreme Court held that the tea stall was a nuisance on the road as well as a source of nuisance to the plaintiff, who owned the building to which the tea stall was annexed. It was also found that a kerosene pressure stove being used for the preparation of tea and coffee in the stall was a fire hazard. The structure was found to be causing nuisance for the occupants of the building as well as a hindrance to the free flow of traffic and movement of pedestrians. The structure was not permissible as it

---

[8] *Vasant Manga Nikumba v. Baburao Bhikanna Naidu*, 1995 Supp (4) SCC 54.

[9] *State of MP v. Kedia Leather and Liquor Ltd and Others*, AIR 2003 SC 3235, (2003) 7 SCC 389.

[10] Supra note 2, Section 133.

[11] *Gobind Singh v. Santhi Swarup*, AIR 1979 SC 149: 1979 (2) SCC 267.

[12] *Himmat Singh v. Bhagawana Ram*, 1988 Crl LJ 614.

prejudicially affected the rights of the appellant qua enjoyment of his property, and the Court ordered it be removed.[13]

In the case of *Krishna Gopal v. State of MP*, a boiler was installed in a residential area for the purposes of manufacturing glucose saline. Discovering a violation of Section 133 of the CrPC, the magistrate ordered the closing of a factory that contained a boiler which emitted smoke and ash while also depriving residents of a good night's sleep. The defendant appealed, and the HC upheld the finding of the magistrate, stating 'the nuisance to the community at large is not by mere installation of the boiler but also by the factory itself.'[14] It was particularly scathing in its condemnation of environmental polluters and showed disgust that the facility was given permission to operate in a residential area in the first place.

EVIDENCE IN PUBLIC NUISANCE CASES

The KHC has given a broader interpretation to Section 133, taking into consideration the precautionary principle and polluter pays principle. Taking notice of the new principles, the court has held that it is the duty of the party against whom a complaint is lodged to prove that nuisance has abated. In the said case, a tyre reconditioning unit was functioning day and night, causing nuisance in a residential area. Petrol, sulphur, rubber, and other chemicals were used without any precautionary measures, causing serious health hazards. Based on reports of the Pollution Control Board and Revenue Inspector, the magistrate took action.[15]

PUBLIC NUISANCE—CIVIL REMEDY

Public nuisance can be abated by approaching a civil court. Section 90 of the Code of Civil Procedure, 1908 (Indian) permits the filing of a suit for declaration and injunction in the case of public nuisances and other wrongful acts affecting or likely to affect the public as may be appropriate in the circumstances of the case. Such suit may be instituted by the Advocate General or by two or more persons, even though no special damages have been caused to such persons by reason of such public nuisance or other wrongful act.

DEVELOPMENTS ABROAD

In both the UK and the USA, the tort of nuisance also exists and can be used to alleviate environmental pollution. A private nuisance action is only available to a person whose property rights have been infringed.[16] A public nuisance action is only available to the Attorney General or public authority charged with the guarding of public rights.[17] In many countries, fierce statutory regimes exist that classify public environmental nuisances as criminal offences,[18] and so the state is propelled to act to remedy the problem. As in India, where an individual seeks to bring an action

---

[13] *A.L. Ranjane v. Ravindra Ishwardas Sethna and Others*, 2003 (1) SCC 379, AIR 2003 SC 300.

[14] *Krishna Gopal v. State of MP*, 1986 Crl LJ 397.

[15] *Sujatha v. Prema*, 2005 (3) KLT 458, ILR 2005 (3) Ker 258.

[16] Halsbury's Laws of England/Nuisance (Vol. 34 (Reissue))/1. Scope of Nuisance/(1) Description and Classification/(i) Public, Private, and Statutory Nuisances/1. Meaning of 'nuisance'.

[17] Attorney General ex rel. Emmons v. City of Grand Rapids, 175 Mich. 503, 141 N.W. 890; State ex rel. *Board of Health of Saddle Brook Tp. v. Sommers Rendering Co.*, 66 N.J. Super. 334, 169 A.2d 165 (App. Div. 1961) American Jurisprudence, 2nd edn, (updated January 2007).

[18] Environmental Protection Act, 1990 (UK), Sections 79-82 (as amended). Australia also imposes criminal liability for environmental nuisance, see Environmental Protection Act 1993 (SA), Section 82.

in public nuisance, they must show that their injury is above and beyond that of an ordinary member of the public.[19]

The Australian case of *Whyalla Red Dust Action Group Inc v. Onesteel Manufacturing Pty Ltd*[20] illustrates that in some common law countries, even public interest non-profit incorporated associations, formed for the purposes of protecting the environment and public health, must show that they have a special or peculiar interest in the public nuisance to have standing. In this case, a group of residents brought a civil enforcement action against a steel works, alleging statutory[21] public nuisance on the basis that dust was affecting the quality of air in the region. Fortunately, the association was granted standing as the subject matter of the litigation had a direct bearing upon its rights: its members were residents living in the area and formed the group for the sole purpose of defeating the very nuisance that was alleged. Other environmental associations in Australia who have sought standing in relation to enforce public rights have not been so fortunate.[22]

Rights to the enjoyment of property that exist in regional human rights instruments have also been used to bring actions that reflect the elements of common law nuisance. In *Fadeyeva v. Russia,*[23] the applicant brought an action against the government for its failure to protect her from the nuisance of a local steel plant that polluted the air with gas and fumes to the extent that it damaged her health. The applicant, who was living in government provided housing, claimed a violation of her right to respect for her private and family life under Article 8 of the European Convention for the Protection of Human Rights and Fundamental Freedoms,[24] on the basis that the government failed to resettle her in an area that was safe from pollution and failed to properly regulate and enforce environmental regulations in relation to the plant. The court held that there had been a violation of her right under Article 8, but declined to direct the state as to the means of remedying the violation.

Every person has a right to use the public highway. If, while he is using it, something happens to him that causes an obstruction to the highway, but is no way referable to his fault, it is wrong to suppose that ipso facto and immediately a nuisance is created. Whether or not a nuisance is created depends on the facts of each case.[25]

Despite its increasing codification by statute, the common law of nuisance still represents one of the tools that individuals can use to protect the environment from pollution. Individuals still have the right to enjoy property rights free of interference and in many countries, the state is charged with the responsibility of protecting common public rights from nuisance.

BANDHS AND HARTALS—INDIAN FORMS OF PUBLIC NUISANCE

Bandhs and hartals (B&H) are another form of public nuisance in India. B&H

[19] *Wade v. Campbell*, 200 Cal. App. 2d 54, 19 Cal. Rptr. 173, 92 A.L.R.2d 966 (5th Dist. 1962) in American Jurisprudence 2nd edn (updated January 2007); *The Wagon Mound (No. 2) Overseas Tankship (UK) Ltd v. The Miller Steamship Co Pty Ltd and Another,* (1966) 2 All ER 709.

[20] *Whyalla Red Dust Action Group Inc v. Onesteel Manufacturing Pty Ltd,* (2005) SAERDC 102.

[21] Environment Protection Act, 1993 (South Australia), Section 82.

[22] See *Australian Conservation Foundation Inc v. Commonwealth*, (1980) 146 CLR 49.

[23] *Fadeyeva v. Russia*, (ECHR) Application no. 55723/00.

[24] European Convention for the Protection of Human Rights and Fundamental Freedoms.

[25] *Maitland v. Raisbeck*, (1944) 2 All ER 272, (1944) 1 KB 689.

were recognized as a weapon during the independence struggle in India by Mahatma Gandhi. After independence, B&H were used as a weapon by political parties. Calling for a bandh entails resorting to violence and physically restraining the movement of others. By the calling of the bandh and the holding of it, people are prevented from attending to their avocations and traders are prevented from keeping open their shops or from carrying on their business activities. With a view to purvey terror, the organizers of the bandh also indulge in wanton acts of vandalism like destruction of public property and transport vehicles. Members of the public who oppose such bandh or hartal calls are sometimes manhandled, causing severe injuries. This type of vandalism has attracted the attention of the judiciary in India.

It was the KHC that made the first attempt to define a 'bandh'. It is a Hindi word meaning 'closed' or 'locked'. The expression therefore conveys an idea that everything is to be blocked or closed. The intention of callers of a bandh, that is, to ensure that no activity, either public or private, is carried on that day, is also clear from their statements to the effect that sometimes, newspapers, hospitals, and the milk supply is excluded from the bandh. This implies that otherwise, the intention is that those services are also affected. It is no doubt true that while calling for a bandh, it is also not announced that any citizen not participating in the bandh will be physically prevented or attacked. The leaders of the political parties who call for a bandh cannot escape by saying that they are not compelling the people to participate and not directing its members to use force. The court, after defining the bandh, has held that calling of a bandh and the enforcement of that call is illegal and unconstitutional. Political parties and the organizers that call for bandhs and enforce them are liable to compensate the

government and the public and private citizen for the losses suffered by them.[26]

The distinction made between B&H by the KHC has been upheld by the Supreme Court of India,[27] which clarified that a hartal without a compulsion is not a bandh.

The Patna HC[28] has also followed the above judgement, and held that supporters of a bandh forcing closure of the courts interfered with its working and prevented unlawfully, the lawyers from attending their cases. It was held that they committed contempt of court. Government, being duty-bound to protect people, has to prevent unlawful activities like bandhs, rallies, and other such activities that invade or threaten to invade their life, liberty, and property. It is not open to any person, organization, or political party to hold people to ransom, nor is it permissible for the government to allow such unlawful activities. Such activities have to be nipped in the bud, else it may not be possible for the government to stop such unlawful activities.

Despite these judgements, bandhs have started reappearing as hartals. The effect of a hartal call is also the same. The KHC was again approached for a consideration of what a hartal is.[29] The Court held that mere calling of a hartal or the advocating of it as understood in the strict sense, cannot be held to be objectionable. But the moment it comes out of the concept of a so-called hartal and seeks to impinge on the rights of others, it ceases to be a hartal in the real sense of the term

[26] Bharat Kumar v. State, 1997 (2) KLT 287, AIR 1997 Ker 291.

[27] Communist Party of India (Marxist) v. Bharat Kumar and Others, AIR (1998) SC 184.

[28] Ranchi Bar Association v. State of Bihar, AIR 1999 Patna 169.

[29] Kerala Vyapari Vyavasayi Ekopana Samithi v. State of Kerala, 2000 (2) KLT 430.

and becomes a violent demonstration affecting the rights of others. This facet of it has to be curtailed because it infringes the constitutional rights of others who have equal constitutional rights. The court found that what is called and enforced as a hartal is not what is strictly meant by that term but is a form of bandh involving intimidation and coercion of those who do not want to respond to the call or to participate in it. Therefore, the Court declared that the enforcement of a hartal call by force, intimidation, or physical or mental coercion would amount to an unconstitutional act and a party, association, or organization that calls for a hartal has no right to enforce it by resorting to force or intimidation.

But the problem continued. In certain places, the normal picketing started adversely affecting the court premises. The KHC, considering the gravity of the situation, added that the state government shall ensure that the court premises are kept separate from the government officers both in the district headquarters and in other places. The presiding officer of the court should inform the HC of any attempt made by anyone to interfere within the ingress to and egress from court premises of judges. No slogan shouting with or without the use of loudspeakers shall be permitted within the vicinity of the court premises that would have the effect of disrupting or disturbing the working of court premises. The District Collector and the Superintendent of Police shall be responsible to forthwith remove the cause of such disturbance, the Supreme Court added.

Yet, the political virus continued. The KHC was forced to re-consider the issue. The court directed the government to take adequate measures to see that normal life of the citizens is not paralysed. That is to be done not by declaring holidays or postponing examinations, but by giving effective protection to those who are not participating in such hartals or strikes. Government should be able to deal with the situation with strong hands. Considering the past experience, if the government feels that it is unable to give adequate protection, it should request the Centre to depute the Army or para-military forces so that there should not be any constitutional breakdown and violation of fundamental rights of the citizens. In cases of damage to public property, action should be taken to recover the damages from the persons who actually cause damages and also from the political parties, organizers, and persons who actually call for such hartals or general strikes. In view of the happenings in the past, they cannot say that they did not visualize such a situation that was created by anti-social elements and directions issued earlier. Effective action should be taken under the Prevention of Damages to Public Property Act, 1984 and those who call for hartals or strikes by whatever reason should make it clear in their call that nobody will be compelled to participate in the hartals or strikes, that traffic will not be obstructed, and those who are willing to can go for work and that fundamental rights of others to move about will not be affected., They should also instruct their supporters to see that no coercion or force is used for compelling others to participate in the strike or hartal. With regard to the injuries and damages caused to private persons and their properties, government should adequately compensate them immediately since it has failed to fulfil its constitutional obligation to protect lives and properties of the citizens. The government should take steps to recover the same from the persons who caused such damages or injuries and also from the persons and political parties or organizations who called for such hartals or general strikes. Criminal cases should be registered against the offenders as well as the abettors to the offence. Such criminal cases should be pursued with enthusiasm and should not be withdrawn merely due to political pressure. The investigation should be conducted fairly, and not with a purpose of filing a subsequent refer report closing the case as undetected. The government should ensure that an atmosphere is created where citizens can move about freely on the roads without fear, and vehicular traffic is not obstructed and public transport can ply without any hindrance. Damages caused to public or private properties and recovery steps initiated should be published by the Government. Government should also take appropriate action against the district administration and police authorities if effective steps are not taken by them against persons who use force or who are trying to impose their will on others to deprive the majority of the citizens of their fundamental rights in the guise of hartals and general strikes.

When the Kodungallur Merchants Union approached the High Court seeking compensation for the reason that their shop was damaged by the hartal callers, the Court was not hesitant in awarding damages.[30]

On the day of a bandh, a person was running his bread factory and flour mill. The callers made demands to close down the mill. An altercation took place. The activists persisted for the closure of the mill and locked the gate. The accused went to his house, took his gun, and fired at the bandh activists. The trial court convicted him and the KHC upheld it. But the Supreme Court set aside the conviction and the sentence was imposed.[31] The Court observed that in the name of B&H, no person has any right to cause inconvenience to any other person or to cause in any manner

a threat or apprehension of risk to life, liberty, or property of any citizen or destruction of life and property, including that of any government or public property. Unless such acts are controlled with iron hands, innocent citizens are bound to suffer and they shall be the victims of the high-handed acts of some fanatics with queer notions of democracy and freedom of speech or association.

The Bombay HC ordered the Bharatiya Janta Party (BJP) and Shiv Sena to pay Rs 20 lakh each as financial compensation for having held Mumbai to ransom on 30 July 2003. The court also issued certain guidelines on how to deal with such issues. The Shiv Sena and BJP, two political parties, challenged the same in the Supreme Court. But the court refused to accept the appeal and passed an interim order to the effect that unless the entire amount is not deposited, their appeals shall not be listed.[32]

The question whether the calling for bandh is an offence under any law has been left open in the above cases and it is being considered by the KHC.

There are enough mechanisms to solve disputes in a democratic manner. A bandh should only be used as a last resort when all else has failed, and then too, it should be within the limits of civilized conduct. Governments of the day do not even bother to contest such actions and the efforts of the courts have been fitful. Many bandhs are now called by 'action committees' that are difficult to identify so as to penalize. A country that stands on the threshold of greatness is being engulfed in a maelstrom of violence all under the name of upholding the right of each citizen to make his demands heard.

---

[30] *Kodungallur Merchants Association v. State*, ILR 2006 (1) Kerala 503.

[31] *James Martin v. State*, 2004 (1) KLT 513.

[32] *G. Deshmukh and Others v. State of Maharashtra and Others*, CDJ 2006 BHC 267.

III

The Environment and the Task Ahead

16 The Challenge of Climate Change

A part of the radiation from the sun that falls on the earth is absorbed by the earth and some of it is reflected back into the atmosphere. This enables people, animals, and plants to live safely. Carbon dioxide is one of the gases responsible for this effect. Naturally occurring gases known as greenhouse gases help capture the sun's energy, keeping the earth warm enough to sustain life. Deforestation, burning of fossil, emissions, and the like result in an increase in the average temperature of the atmosphere. As the earth's aveerage temperature gradually increases over time, it causes climatic changes. This phenomenon is referred to as climate change.

Terminology

Climate change refers to the fluctuation in temperature, precipitation, wind, and other elements of the earth's climate system over time. The phenomenon has also been labelled 'global warming', as one of the main aspects of climate change is the heating up of the earth. The phrase 'climate change' has been given slightly different meanings by different agencies.

The glossary of terms provided by the Intergovernmental Panel on Climate Change (IPCC) explains that 'a narrow definition of the term 'climate' yields to a 'statistical description in terms of the mean and variability of relevant

quantities over a period of time ranging from months to thousands or millions of years' or commonly to 'average weather'. The classical period is thirty years, as defined by the World Meteorological Organization (WMO). These quantities are most often surface variables such as temperature, precipitation, and wind. Climate in a wider sense is the state, including a statistical description, of the climate system.'[1]

A narrow definition of the term climate, however, does not deprive the phrase 'climate change' of a broad scope. The IPCC defines climate change as

a statistically significant variation in either the mean state of the climate or in its variability, persisting for an extended period (typically decades or longer). Climate change may be due to natural internal processes or external forcings, or to persistent anthropogenic changes in the composition of the atmosphere or in land use.[2]

It thus identifies what qualifies as climate change and what causes climate change.

[1] Contribution of Working Group I to the Third Assessment Report of the Intergovernmental Panel on Climate Change, *Climate Change 2001: The Scientific Basis*, Appendix and glossary, Cambridge University Press, 2001, available at <http://www.grida.no/climate/ipcc_tar/wg1/518.htm>

[2] Contribution of Working Group I to the Third Assessment Report of the Intergovernmental Panel on Climate Change, *Climate Change 2001: The Scientific Basis*, Cambridge University Press, 2001.

Interestingly, Article 1 of the United Nations Framework Convention on Climate Change presents a different definition: 'a change of climate which is attributed directly or indirectly to human activity that alters the composition of the global atmosphere and which is in addition to natural climate variability observed over comparable time periods.'[3]

The IPCC notes that this definition distinguishes between the change in atmospheric composition due to human activity and the natural occurrence of 'climate variability'.[4] Throughout this chapter, the phrase 'climate change' will be used in its wider sense as espoused by the IPCC, encompassing both a change in climate due to natural forces and human activity.

THE INTERGOVERNMENTAL PANEL ON CLIMATE CHANGE (IPCC)

The IPCC, established jointly in 1988 by the WMO and the UNEP, has been mandated to 'assess on a comprehensive, objective, open, and transparent basis the scientific, technical, and socio-economic information relevant to understanding the scientific basis of risk of human-induced climate change, its potential impact, and options for adaptation and mitigation.'[5] The IPCC meets in plenary sessions approximately once a year and is constituted of three working groups and a taskforce of National Greenhouse Gas Inventories. The first Working Group is responsible for reporting on the scientific basis for climate change, the second reports on the vulnerability of social, economic, and ecological systems to climate change, the

positive and negative aspects of climate change, and how to assess it, and the third Working Group investigates ways to reduce greenhouse gases and mitigate climate change.[6] There is also a taskforce on National Greenhouse Gas Inventories called the IPCC National GHG Inventory Programme. The work of the IPCC is a valuable resource for governments, policy makers, and the public alike, providing the most up-to-date and reliable information regarding climate change.

THE CAUSES OF CLIMATE CHANGE

As can be observed from the recent contribution of Working Group I to the Fourth Assessment Report of the IPCC, the scientific foundations on which climate change information rests have significantly stabilized. As stated in the report: 'Warming of the climate system is unequivocal, as is now evident from observations of increases in global average air and ocean temperatures, widespread melting of snow and ice, and rising global average sea level.'[7]

Furthermore, the report makes it evident that such changes are due to increased emissions,

Most of the observed increase in globally averaged temperatures since the mid-20th century is *very likely* due to the observed increase in anthropogenic greenhouse gas concentrations. This is an advance since the Third Assessment Report's conclusion that 'most of the observed warming over the last 50 years is *likely* to have been due to the increase in greenhouse gas concentrations.'[8]

---

[3] United Nations Framework Convention on Climate Change, 1771 UNTS 107, Article 2 (hereinafter UNFCCC).

[4] Supra note 2.

[5] IPCC website, <http://www.ipcc-wg2.org/> (last visited 20 April 2007).

[6] Ibid.

[7] Contribution of Working Group II to the Fourth Assessment Report of the Intergovernmental Panel on Climate Change, *Climate Change 200: Climate Change Impacts, Adaptation and Vulnerability*. Summary for Policymakers, 5 (hereinafter, Working Group II Contribution).

[8] Working Group II Contribution, 10, see ibid.

The terms 'likely' and 'very likely' are quantified by the report, where likely can be deemed as a 66–90 per cent probability of occurrence, and 'very likely' a 90–9 per cent probability of occurrence.[9]

The argument over who or what is to blame for global warming has become one of the most urgent—and hotly debated—environmental issues of the twenty-first century. It is difficult to claim that such an increase in GHG emissions is simply a natural phenomenon. However, because other factors affect the Eearth's temperature and because the science of global warming is not exact, some groups, who disagree with efforts to reduce emissions, have discounted not only the phenomenon itself, but also its effects on the environment.

Most scientists do agree, however, that global warming is occurring and that along with other factors including natural changes in the climate, human activity is accelerating it. 'Greenhouse gases are accumulating in earth's atmosphere as a result of human activities, causing surface air temperatures and subsurface ocean temperatures to rise', a 2001 report commissioned by the National Research Council stated.

Temperatures are, in fact, rising. The changes observed over the last several decades are likely mostly due to human activities, but we cannot rule out that some significant part of these changes is also a reflection of natural variability. Human-induced warming and associated sea level rises are expected to continue through the 21st century.

THE EFFECTS OF CLIMATE CHANGE

Many scientists and policy-makers see this trend, commonly referred to as 'global warming', as a threat to the environment and its inhabitants.

[9] Working Group II Contribution, 21, see ibid.

Most natural ecosystems are somewhat climate-dependent and have exhibited many changes. The Working Group II Contribution to the IPCC Fourth Assessment Report, 2007 has noted that 'Observational evidence from all continents and most oceans shows that many natural systems are being affected by regional climate changes, particularly temperature increases.'[10]

Evidence that the earth is warming can be found in the melting of Arctic and other glaciers, changes in weather patterns such as the increase of hurricanes and droughts, and in rising sea levels—globally, the sea level has risen four inches to eight inches in the past century, according to the EPA. The IPCC states:

At continental, regional, and ocean basin scales, numerous long-term changes in climate have been observed. These include changes in Arctic temperatures and ice, widespread changes in precipitation amounts, ocean salinity, wind patterns and aspects of extreme weather including droughts, heavy precipitation, heat waves and the intensity of tropical cyclones.[11]

Advocacy groups have based their arguments on such research. Natural disasters like the 2004 tsunami that hit South Asia and Hurricane Katrina, which destroyed major parts of the US Gulf Coast in 2005, have been attributed in part to global warming. The nonprofit organization called Stop Globalwarming.org predicts that, 'We will experience extreme temperatures, rises in sea levels, and storms of unimaginable destructive fury.'[12] The group also emphasizes that, 'Recently, alarming events that are consistent with scientific predictions about the effects of climate change have become more and more commonplace.'[13]

[10] Working Group II Contribution, 2, see ibid.
[11] Working Group II Contribution, 8, see ibid.
[12] <http://www. stop globalwarming.org>
[13] Ibid.

Warming of water has affected changes in marine and freshwater ecosystems. In high-latitude oceans, there have been 'shifts in ranges and changes in algal, plankton, and fish abundance.' In high-latitude lakes, there have been increases in algal and zooplankton abundance.'[14] Spring occurs noticeably earlier and this results in the occurrence of events such as a leaf unfolding and bird migration and egg-laying at an earlier date.[15] The report also discusses other events or occurrences caused by a change of climate, although it is reluctant to deem these as trends. Examples include reductions in growing seasons in parts of Africa due to drier climate, coastal flooding, and loss of coastal wetlands and mangroves.[16]

Predictions for the future are equally dire. The predicted reduction of freshwater resources is of great significance for human population. It is very likely that there will be an increased incidence of heat waves in most land areas that can cause algal blooms in water resources and endanger the quality of water. Heavy precipitation events are likely to threaten the quality of groundwater supplies and it is likely that drought will continue in many areas, placing further stress on water resources.[17]

Climate change also poses a great risk to biological diversity. A number of plant and animal species are likely to be at risk of extinction. The IPCC Report predicts that 20–30 per cent of plant and animal species assessed by it so far are likely to be at 'increased risk of extinction, if increase in global average temperatures exceed 1.5–2.5 degrees Celsius.'[18] Coral reefs, often termed the 'rainforests of the sea'[19] due to their rich biological diversity, are also likely to suffer as increase in ocean temperature will cause coral bleaching.[20]

Low elevation coastal zones (those that are less than ten metres above sea level) are at greater risk from climate change. This poses a large risk to human population as these areas account for 10 per cent of the world's population.[21] This also places poor and developing countries at greater risk from the effects of climate change as '11 of the 15 coastal mega-cities listed by UN-Habitat in 2005 are in low-medium income countries.'[22]

There is some opposition to the general consensus that climate change does significant harm to the environment and its inhabitants. Some, including advocates for large industry, say the danger is overstated. Jerry Taylor, director of natural resource studies at the Cato Institute, wrote in a 2004 commentary,

While the planet is indeed warming—probably due in no small part to industrial greenhouse gas emissions—the warming has been modest, benign, and largely confined to northern latitudes during winter nights. There are good reasons to expect that

[14] Working Group II Contribution, 3.

[15] Ibid.

[16] Working Group II Contribution to the Inter-governmental Panel on Climate Change Fourth Assessment Report, 'Climate Change 200: Climate Change Impacts, Adaptation and Vulnerability', Summary for Policymakers, p. 4.

[17] Working Group II Contribution , 8.

[18] Working Group II Contribution, Table SPM-2, 16.

[19] Hawaii Coral Reef Initiative Project, *Rainforests of the Sea*, http://www.hawaii.edu/ssri/hcri/cta/rainforests_of_the_sea.htm (last updated 26 August 2005).

[20] Working Group II Contribution , 8.

[21] Srabani Roy, 'Climate Change: Coastal Mega-Cities in for a Bumpy Ride', Wednesday, 28 March 2007, *Inter Press Service*.

[22] 'In conjunction with the findings of the Centre for International Earth Sciences Information Network-International Institute Environmental and Development study, 11 of the 15 coastal mega-cities listed by UN-Habitat in 2005 are in low-medium income countries' as discussed in Srabani Roy, 'Climate Change: Coastal Mega-Cities in for a Bumpy Ride', Wednesday, 28 March 2007, *Inter Press Service*.

warming pattern to continue. And that warming pattern does not threaten to usher in the convulsive climatic events we are warned about in the press or in the movie theaters. In fact, some scientists and economists can make a pretty good case that global warming will prove a net plus to both the economy and the global environment.

Interestingly, the recent report by the IPCC predicts that crop yields in Asia and Southeast Asia could increase by up to 20 per cent.[23] Similarly, northern Europe may experience increased crop yields and increased forest growth, although the report is quick to note that the perceived negative impact of climate change is likely to outweigh the benefits.[24]

INTERNATIONAL AGREEMENTS

Because climate change is a global environmental problem to which a myriad of nations contribute, there is a lot of activity in the international arena on the subject, providing the foundations for domestic action.

The principal international agreement to address climate change is the United Nations Framework Convention on Climate Change (UNFCCC), which frames its objective as the:

stabilization of greenhouse gas concentrations in the atmosphere at a level that would prevent dangerous anthropogenic interference with the climate system. Such a level should be achieved within a time frame sufficient to allow ecosystems to adapt naturally to climate change, to ensure that food production is not threatened and to enable economic development to proceed in a sustainable manner.[25]

In pursuing this aim, parties are to undertake a number of commitments that are specified in Article 4(1) of the UNFCCC. These can be generally summarized as follows:

[23] Working Group II Contribution, 11.
[24] Working Group II Contribution, 12.
[25] Supra note 3.

1. To create and make available an up-to-date inventory of anthropogenic emissions by sources and removals by sinks of all greenhouse gases';[26]

2. To create 'regional programmes containing measures to mitigate climate change by addressing anthropogenic emissions',[27] including measures to adapt to climate change;

3. To promote and participate in the sharing of technologies and information over a range of industries 'that control, reduce, or prevent anthropogenic emissions of greenhouse gases';[28]

4. To promote the sustainability'of sinks and reservoirs of all greenhouse gases'[29] within various ecosystems;

5. To create plans that address the impacts of climate change and promote adaptation to climatic events such as floods and desertification;[30]

6. To incorporate climate change considerations within social, economic, and environmental policies and actions[31] minimizing the potential for adverse affects;

7. Promote and contribute to programmes that increase the certainty with which climate change is understood in various disciplines and increase the understanding of the consequences that are likely to result from various response strategies;[32]

8. To contribute to the exchange of information in various fields, which address the economic and social implications of various climate change response strategies;[33]

[26] Ibid., Article 4(1)(a).
[27] Ibid., Article 4(1)(b).
[28] Ibid., Article 4(1)(c).
[29] Ibid., Article 4(1)(d).
[30] Ibid., Article 4(1)(e).
[31] Ibid., Article 4(1)(f).
[32] Ibid., Article 4(1)(g).
[33] Ibid., Article 4(1)(h).

9. To facilitate education, training, awareness, and participation of the public and NGO's in matters dealing with climate change;[34]

10. Communicate to the Conference of the Parties, information related to implementation, in accordance with Article 12[35] that defines the scope, method, and timing of the communication.

Article 3 of the UNFCCC presents the principles to be adhered to in implementing these various commitments. These principles are commonly identified as general principles of international environmental law and include: Intergenerational Equity,[36] Common but Differentiated Responsibility,[37] the Precautionary Principle,[38] and Sustainable Development.[39]

The principle of Common but Differentiated Responsibility is well expressed in the UNFCCC. It immediately distinguishes between developing and developed countries, noting that developed countries have been the highest contributors of GHG emissions. Parties in Annexure I are referred to as the 'Developed Country Parties,'[40] with India being absent from this list.

The Kyoto Protocol was created in 1997 to better meet the objectives of the UNFCCC in a better manner. By 2005, 140 countries had ratified the Protocol,[41] an international agreement that forces developed nations to reduce their emission of GHGs to pre-1990 levels by 2012. It is a practical instrument and facilitates reduction of GHG emissions by the contracting parties. The Protocol places an obligation on parties to reduce their gas emissions by at least 5 per cent below 1990 emissions during 2008–12. It applies to the following GHGs: carbon dioxide, methane, nitrous oxide, hydrofluorocarbons, perfluorocarbons, and sulphur hexafluoride. Like the UNFCCC, it does not regulate the gases already covered by the Montreal Protocol, some of which are recognized contributors to climate change. In order to ensure overall efficacy of the system, parties are to devise 'a national system for the estimation of anthropogenic emissions by sources and removals by sinks of all greenhouse gases not controlled by the Montreal Protocol'.[42]

The Protocol is guided by the Article 3 principles of the UNFCCC, and in some instances it gives greater content to them in their application. A key functional feature of the Protocol is the implementation of the principle of Common but Differentiated Responsibility. The developed country parties are bound to meet their quantified emission limitation, whereas the parties not listed in Annex I of the UNFCCC are expected to contribute to the ultimate objective of the UNFCCC and the Protocol.[43] Common but Differentiated Responsibility gives effect to sustainable development as it recognizes that the costs of meeting the commitments in Article 4(1) of the UNFCCC may not be properly met by developing countries. Article 11 of the Protocol provides that Annex 1 parties shall

provide new and additional financial resources to meet the agreed full costs incurred by developing

---

[34] Ibid., Article 4(1)(i).

[35] Ibid., Article 4(1)(j).

[36] Ibid., Article 3(1).

[37] Ibid., Article 3(2), Article 4.

[38] Ibid., Article 3(3).

[39] Ibid., Article 3(4).

[40] See for example, Kyoto Protocol, Preamble, Article 3(1).

[41] Kyoto Protocol to the United Nations Framework Convention on Climate Change, UN Doc FCCC/CP/1997/7/Add. 1, 10 December 1997 (hereinafter, Kyoto Protocol).

[42] Ibid., Article 5(1).

[43] Ibid., Article 12.

country parties in advancing the implementation' of the requirement to create national inventories of anthropogenic emissions.'[44]

This also includes the transfer of technology where required and developed country parties are to share the burden of doing this.[45]

The Clean Development Mechanism defined by Article 12 of the Protocol also reflects Common but Differentiated Responsibility and expressly aims to help developing country parties achieve sustainable development. The mechanism enables developing country parties to benefit from certified emission reductions by using them to meet the objectives of the Convention. These reductions may often be obtained using a scheme or project that removes carbon dioxide from the atmosphere, a wind farm, for example. To be used as a means of complying with the quantified emissions limitation, the project must be certified by the conference of the parties that will consider whether the scheme operates by voluntary participation, whether there were real long-term benefits to the mitigation of climate change, and whether the reduction in emissions would have occurred in the absence of the specified project.[46] This final consideration is aimed at ensuring that the Clean Development Mechanism (CDM) actually removes additional emissions from the atmosphere and is not used to brand projects that operate independently of this. An Executive Board operates under the Protocol to administer the Clean Development Mechanism and provide guidance for its implementation. The Board is fully accountable to the Conference of the Parties or Meeting of the Parties.[47] Parties seeking to utilize the CDM submit

their project for validation by a third party, where the findings are then presented to the Board that may register the project, if it fulfills the relevant UNFCCC criteria. The project is then verified after a certain period to ascertain whether it met the proposed reduction in anthropogenic emissions.[48]

India has recently registered a number of projects that implement the CDM. On 8 June 2007, Chithradurga, Karnataka registered a bundled wind power project with the Board, with the proposed reduction of 20,523 metric tonnes of CO_2 equivalent per annum.[49] The upgradation of pre-heater in cement manufacturing was also registered on 8 June 2007. The upgrade effectively results in the reduction of the energy consumed by the pre-heater and utilization of waste heat. The Third Party validation report states that the upgrade 'increases the energy efficiency and reduces the fossil fuel use, that is, CO_2 emissions and...claims to contribute to sustainable development at the local, regional, and global levels.'[50]

On 5 June 2007, a project by Rajaram Maize Products, which captures methane for

---

[44] Ibid., Article 10; United Nations Framework Convention on Climate Change 1992, Article 4 (1)(a).
[45] Ibid., Article 11(b).
[46] Ibid., Article 5.

[47] UN Framework Convention on Climate Change, 'Clean Development Mechanism: Background' <http://cdm.unfccc.int/EB/background.html> (last visited 8 June 2007).
[48] UN Framework Convention on Climate Change, 'CDM Project Activity Cycle' http://cdm.unfccc.int/Projects/pac/index.html (last visited 10 June 2007).
[49] UN Framework Convention on Climate Change, 'Clean Development Mechanism: Registered Projects' http://cdm.unfccc.int/Projects/registered.html (last visited 10 June 2007).
[50] SGS Climate Change Programme, Validation Report, 'Vikram Cement (VC) Energy Efficiency Improvement by Upgradation of Preheater in Cement Manufacturing', CDM.Val0958, 31 March 2007, p. 5, available at http://cdm.unfccc.int/UserManagement/FileStorage/8F3ECB6TYG48VHP141X0CSQVFV3LY3

the use of fuel, was registered. The project utilizes biogas from effluents at the maize processing plant, and uses it as a source of fuel for the drying of maize products.

This will reduce direct on-site methane emissions in addition to the CO_2 emissions due to the combustion of furnace oil for drying products in the flash dryer... [and]... The average anticipated emission reduction due to the project activity is expected to be around 4,609 tonnes of CO_2 equivalent per year.[51]

Annexure I parties are given some degree of flexibility in the way they choose to meet their emission reduction targets. They may transfer emission reduction units under Article 3(10) of the Protocol, where this amount will be subtracted from the assigned amount for the transferor.[52] This is useful for parties whose emissions are less than their assigned amount, as they may transfer units to a party that is having difficulty in satisfying its target. Parties may also agree to fulfill their Article 3 commitments together, specifying a total combined level of emission reductions. However, in the event that they fail to meet this target, each party will be individually responsible for its own level of emissions as specified in the agreement.[53]

As of early 2006, the USA had not signed the agreement. The Bush administration said that placing mandatory restrictions on emissions could hurt large industry and damage the US economy by making it less competitive compared to a country like China, which is exempt from emission reductions

targets because of its status as a developing nation. The USA has for some time been the biggest emitter of GHGs, although a report in June 2007 suggests that China has recently assumed this position.[54]

Similarly, despite its participation in negotiations, Australia has refused to sign the Kyoto Protocol, largely on the basis that developing country parties are not bound by Article 3. Alliances have been formed between Australia, the USA, and Asia-Pacific nations such as China and Japan. The US-led coalition 'focuses on technology to make fossil fuels cleaner rather than cutting industry emissions'[55] and this approach has come under criticism from those who feel that its failure is guaranteed by a lack of concrete emissions targets. Despite this, the Australian government is insistent that Kyoto will fail, as the USA is not a party and developing nations have too much freedom under the agreement.[56]

INDIAN LEGISLATION AND CLIMATE CHANGE

International Agreements

India has experienced a dramatic growth in fossil fuel CO_2 emissions, and the data compiled by various agencies shows an increase of nearly 5.9 per cent since 1950. India is rated as the sixth largest contributor of CO_2 emissions, and in 2003 contributed to 4.43 per

---

[51] Det Norske Veritas, Validation Report, 'Methane Capture and Use as Fuel at Rajaram Maize Products in India', Report No. 2005-9007, Revision No. 3, pp. 1–2, available at http://cdm.unfccc.int/UserManagement/FileStorage/JGOC49GEY95525XUOYLKXM53BO6HRR
[52] Supra note 42, Article 3(11).
[53] Ibid., Article 4(5).

[54] Reuters, ABC News 'China Overtakes US as top CO2 emitter' available at <http://www.abc.net.au/news/stories/2007/06/21/1957322.htm> (last visited 28 June 2007).
[55] Jewel Topsfield, 'Downer Adds Fuel to Kyoto Criticism', *The Age*, 1 August 2005, (Australian Newspaper).
[56] Joint Media Release Minister for the Environment and Heritage Dr David Kemp and Alexander Downer, Minister for Foreign Affairs, 'Global Greenhouse Challenge: The Way Ahead for Australia', 15 August 2002.

cent of the world's GHG emissions.[57] In India, the main contributor to the emissions is coal burning.[58] India ratified[59] the Kyoto Protocol on 26 August 2002, and is thus committed to the furtherance of the objectives of the Convention, which came into force on 16 February 2005. Not signing does not detract from India's obligations under the Protocol and this procedural aspect is missing because the agreement was only open for signature between 16 March 1998 and 15 March 1999 as per Article 24 of the Protocol. India decided to join after this window and hence deposited the instrument for ratification.

However, due to its status as a developing nation, India is not designated as an Annexure 1 party by the UNFCCC and is, thus, not bound by the Kyoto Protocol to reduce its emissions to pre-1990 levels. Despite this, it may engage in emissions trading under the CDM and cooperate in mitigating global climate change.

The *Gazette of India*, on 19 July 2000, notified rules for regulation of ODS phase-out called the Ozone Depleting Substances (Regulation and Control) Rules, 2000.[60] (ODS) They were notified under the Environment (Protection) Act, 1986. No person shall produce or cause to produce any ozone-depleting substances, as notified in the schedule to the enactment after the specified date unless he is registered with the authority.

Import of ODS and export of the same to certain countries is totally prohibited. A person who, having received financial assistance from multilateral funds in accordance with Article 10 and 10A of the Montreal Protocol to which the Central Government is a party, for gradual reduction of production of ODS specified in the enactment, shall limits the production of these substances in each year from August 2000 to January 2010 to the quantities specified therein as per the agreement approved, by the Executive Committee of the Multilateral Fund.[61] The rules regulate the selling and purchase of ODS and also prohibit new investments with them.[62] The rules implement the Montreal Protocol on Substances that Deplete the Ozone Layer, which was adopted on 16 September 1987.[63] Although the Convention is 'conscious of the potential climatic effect of emissions', it does not include CO_2 emissions in its list of regulated substances and these fall within the purview of Kyoto. Bearing in mind India's lack of responsibility under the Kyoto Protocol, it can be concluded that India is not bound to reduce its CO_2 emissions by any international instrument.

Consumption under the ODS Rules is defined as 'the amount of that substance produced in India in addition to the amount imported, less the amount exported.'[64] This is identical to the definition in the Kyoto Protocol and is aimed at eliminating double counting of emissions between parties to the Convention. It does, however, excuse countries from the responsibility of ODS that they export to

[57] Climate Analysis Indicators Tool (CAIT) Version 4.0, Washington, DC: World Resources Institute, 2007.

[58] Sixth compilation and synthesis of initial national communications from parties not included in Annex I to the Convention. Note by the secretariat. Addendum. Inventories of anthropogenic emissions by sources and removal by sinks of greenhouse gases.

[59] UNFCCC website, India Ratification Status, http://maindb.unfccc.int/public/country.pl?country=IN (last visited 22 October 2007).

[60] Published in *the Gazette of India (Extraordinary)*, Part III, Eec. 3 dated 26 January 2000.

[61] Rule 3(3) of the Ozone Depleting Substances (Regulation and Control) Rules, 2000.

[62] Rule 5, ibid.

[63] Montreal Protocol on Substances that Deplete the Ozone Layer, 26 ILM 1550 (1987).

[64] Ozone Depleting Substances (Regulation and Control) Rules (India), 2000, Rule 2(d).

countries that are not party to the Protocol or does not uphold its obligations. Where India exports ODS to a country that is not a party to the Protocol, these remain unaccounted for. There seems to be no general international law on equality.

Indian Legislation

There is an array of waste management legislation in India that is not very climate friendly. Some recommended waste management practices create more environmental harm than they alleviate and inevitably contribute to climate change.

Bio-Medical Waste (Management and Handling) Rules, 1988

The Bio-Medical Waste (Management and Handling) Rules, 1998, as they now stand, do not advance the objectives of the Framework Convention on Climate Change. Incineration as a means of dealing with waste is recommended by a number of statutes and is not adapted to address climate change.

Under these rules, incineration[65] is suggested for various biomedical waste products,[66] which include human anatomical waste, animal waste, microbiology and biotechnology waste, discarded medicines, and cytotoxic drugs and solid waste.[67] The Act prescribes emission standards[68] for incinerators and provides that they must have a combustion efficiency of at least 99 per cent and use only low sulphur fuel like L.D.0dLS.H.S.1Diesel.

The Bio-Medical Waste Rules are not the only rules that prescribe incineration. The Municipal Solid Wastes (Management and Handling) Rules, 2000 prescribe incineration of municipal solid wastes for specific cases.[69] Municipal solid waste 'includes commercial and residential wastes generated in municipal or notified areas in either solid or semi-solid form excluding industrial hazardous wastes but including treated bio-medical wastes'.[70] Standards provided for incineration mimic those of the Bio-Medical Waste (Management and Handling) Rules.[71] The Environment (Protection) Third Amendment Rules, 2005 deem incineration an environmentally acceptable method of disposing drill waste, providing that a proposal is submitted to the Pollution Control Board for approval.[72]

The authorization and even suggestion of incineration is in conflict with the requirement that 'waste is handled without any adverse effect to human health and the environment'[73] as it is widely recognized that incineration is deleterious to human health and the environment. According to the Global Alliance for Incinerator Alternatives (GAIA),

incinerators are an unsustainable and obsolete method for dealing with waste. As global opposition to incineration continues to grow, innovative philosophies and practices for sustainable management of discards are being developed and adopted around the world.[74]

---

[65] Bio-Medical Waste (Management and Handling) Rules, 1998, Section 5(2).

[66] Ibid., Schedule 1.

[67] Solids include 'items contaminated with blood, and body fluids including cotton, dressings, soiled plaster casts, lines, beddings, other material contaminated with blood', as per Schedule 1 of the Act.

[68] Supra note 65, Schedule V(B).

[69] Municipal Solid Wastes (Management and Handling) Rules, 2000, Schedule 2, Serial No. 5.

[70] Ibid., Section 3(xv).

[71] Ibid., Schedule IV(A).

[72] Environment (Protection) Rules, 1986, Schedule I(C) serial No. 72 as amended by the Environment (Protection) Third Amendment Rules, 2005, Section 2(iii).

[73] Supra note 65, Section 4.

[74] Neil Tangri, Essential Action for Global Alternatives for Incinerator A, Global Anti-Incinerator Alliance/

Incineration releases a large amount of dioxins into the atmosphere. Such pollutants bio-magnify as they accumulate along the food chain, and can cause a number of health problems such as cancer and reproductive and immune system damage in humans. Incinerators also release mercury into the atmosphere and 'other (non-dioxin) halogenated hydrocarbons; acid gases that are precursors of acid rain; particulates, which impair lung function; and GHGs.'[75] Incinerators are thought to produce 'approximately one ton of CO_2 for each ton of municipal waste incinerated'.[76] GAIA also notes that incinerators use a large amount of energy, despite being billed as energy producers due to their capacity to produce electricity. Notably, the Municipal Solid Wastes (Management and Handling) Rules provide for incineration with or without energy recovery and, thus, have a limited energy producing or saving capacity.

The complete destruction of products by incineration also obscures opportunities for recycling and the re-manufacture of goods consumes even more energy.[77] Overt energy consumption is yet another way in which incinerators contribute to global warming. In short, incineration is a band-aid for consumerism.

Incineration is severely restricted under the provisions of the Stockholm Persistent Organic

Pollutants (POPs) treaty, to which India is a party.[78] This treaty aims to phase out a number of POPs, in particular 'the dirty dozen', many of which emanate from incinerators. Despite the obvious connection between incinerators and POPs, it should also be noted that the practice of incineration runs contrary to the objectives of the Convention and the Kyoto Protocol. The banning of incineration should hold a place in climate change discourse.

Initially, the KHC supported the implementation of the Bio-Medical Waste (Management and Handling) Rules, 1998 'in letter and in spirit,'[79] stating that

It is the duty of the occupier of an institution generating bio-medical waste (which includes a hospital, nursing, home, clinic, dispensary, veterinary institution, animal house, pathological laboratory, blood bank etc.) to take all steps to ensure that such waste is handled without any adverse effect to human health and environment.[80]

It was thought that incineration did not pose an adverse effect to human health and the environment. However, since then, the Ombudsman for local self-government has had the opportunity to consider the matter again *in extensor* and has ruled that the practice of incineration by the Rules is inappropriate. The Ombudsman cites the Stockholm Convention on Persistent Organic Pollutants,[81] to which India is a party, and rightly states that incineration is a pollutant and that 'Developed countries therefore are shunning incineration as a treatment and

---

Global Alliance for Incinerator Alternatives, *Waste Incineration: A Dying Technology* 2003, p. 1. http://Inoorn.live.radicaldesigns.org

[75] Ibid.

[76] USEPA, 'Greenhouse Gas Emissions from Management of Selected Materials in Municipal Solid Waste', EPA530-R-98-013, September 1998a, p. ES-15 in supra note 73, p. 18.

[77] Jeffrey Morris and Diana Canzoneri, *Recycling Versus Incineration: An Energy Conservation Analysis*, Sound Resource Management Group (SRMG) Seattle, Washington, September, 1992 in supra note 73, p. 17.

[78] Stockholm Convention on Persistent Organic Pollutants, 40 ILM 532 (2001); signed by the Union Ministry of Environment and Forests in May 2002.

[79] *Environment Monitoring Forum v. State of Kerala*, 2004 (1) KLJ (NOC) 10, Section 7.

[80] Ibid., Section 4.

[81] Stockholm Convention on Persistent Organic Pollutants, 40 ILM 532 (2001).

disposal system.'[82] The Rules thus produce an *excuses legem*, 'there is a necessary or invincible disability to perform the mandatory part of the law or to forbear the prohibitory.'[83]

This ruling signifies the need for amendment. Reasonable alternatives for the disposal of biomedical waste by hospitals are discussed by the Ombudsman, drawing upon recent studies by Cochin University of Science and Technology (CUSAT), which were sponsored by the Qualified Medical Practitioners and the Hospital Association of Kerala. CUSAT researched and developed two new technologies for the collection, treatment, and disposal of biomedical waste from hospitals, that is, the 'Placents Anaerobic Bio-Reactor' and the 'Body Parts Anaerobic Bio Reactor.'[84] The Ombudsman for the local self government institution hence directed hospitals and health care institutions within the area to install the named reactors within six months of the direction.[85]

The Bio-Medical Waste (Management and Handling) Rules, 1998 should thus be amended to reflect the newer and more environment-friendly technologies available, and India's international obligations under the Kyoto Protocol and the POPs treaty.

Municipal Solid Wastes (Management and Handling) Rules, 2000

Schedule 2 of the Rules specify that biodegradable waste is to be 'processed by composting, vermicomposting, anaerobic digestion, or any other appropriate biological processing for stabilization of wastes.'[86] Compost can be an environmentally sustainable way of disposing organic matter. However, this is entirely dependent on proper sorting of wastes, as mixed waste is not suitable for compost. The rules permit landfilling of mixed waste where it is not suitable for waste processing.[87]

The courts have upheld these rules and have had the occasion to issue directions for their implementation. In the case of *Almitra H. Patel and Another v. Union of India*,[88] the court directed the Union of India via its agents to identify landfill sites[89] in New Delhi and develop appropriate sites for compost plants[90] for the purposes of managing municipal waste.

When properly segregated, some waste can be suitable for landfill. However, a landfill of municipal solid waste may also contribute to climate change, as methane is released by the anaerobic decomposition of organic matter. Methane is a recognized contributor to global warming. Methane generated at landfill sites is not to exceed 25 per cent of the lower explosive limit[91] and landfill gas control systems and gas collection systems are to be installed at landfill sites to prevent the gas from escaping the area.[92] However, this is highly dependent on the technology available to implement the rules, and enforcement on the part of the authorities for non-compliance.

In New Delhi, organic matter accounts for 79–84 per cent of municipal waste in high-income areas and approximately 65–71

---

[82] *A.K. Sabhapathy v. Corporation of Cochin*, O.P. No. 397 of 2004, order of Ombudsman for Local Self Government for the State of Kerala.

[83] *CIT v. Tej Singh*, AIR 1999 SC 352 at 356, cited in ibid.

[84] 'Bio-Medical Waste (Management and Handling) Rules, 1998: Its Inappropriateness in the Present Context and New Appropriate Management Options Developed by CUSAT'—a discussion note.

[85] Supra note 82.

[86] Municipal Solid Wastes Rules, 2000, Schedule 2, Item No. 5(i).

[87] Ibid., Schedule 2, Serial No. 6.

[88] AIR 2000 SCW 924.

[89] *Almitra H. Patel and Another v. Union of India*, AIR 2000 SCW 924.

[90] Ibid.

[91] Supra note 86, Rule 26.

[92] Ibid., Schedule 3, Rule 26.

per cent of waste in low-income areas.[93] Due to failure in waste segregation and implementation of the rules, it is probable that a significant amount of organic matter finds its way into a landfill that is ordinarily 'restricted to non-biodegradable, inert waste and other waste that are not suitable either for recycling or for biological processing'.[94] There have been many instances of dumping of untreated and unsegregated waste at so-called dumping sites. In some instances, burning of such waste also takes place,[95] which emits toxic substances into the atmosphere and ultimately contributes to global warming.[96] Fortunately, in some cases courts have directed that the burning of rubbish is prohibited[97] particularly in thickly populated residential areas.[98] A blanket ban on the burning of rubbish, however, is recommended to properly conform with international obligations under the POPs treaty and the objectives of the Convention.

THE ROLE OF JUDICIAL INSTITUTIONS IN ADDRESSING GLOBAL WARMING

A lot of focus has been on the dialogue that exists at the international level regarding global warming. This is not surprising, considering the magnitude of the global environmental dilemma; however it should also be remembered that there is some role for adjudicators in the

matter. It is often said that the courts respond to the tide of public opinion, applying the law as a living instrument. The next four cases show how individuals have attempted to use the court system to address global warming, trying to find an answer to the problem in the law as it exists today.

Gray v. *The Minister for Planning and Others* (New South Wales, Australia)

Although the outcome in the *Gray* case may be insignificant for the applicant, the legal ramifications for climate change are enormous. In this case, the applicant, Peter Gray, sought review of a decision by the Director General of the Department of Planning, made under Pt3A of the Environmental Planning and Assessment Act, 1979[99] (EP&A Act). The applicant challenged the approval of an Environmental Assessment (EA) made in relation to the building of a large open coal cut mine in Anvil Hill, New South Wales which would be mined for twenty-one years. The land has a deposit of approximately 150 million tonnes of thermal coal, which would be burnt in New South Wales and overseas, releasing monstrous amounts of GHGs into the atmosphere. The Director General had declared that the EA met the environment requirements for public exhibition, and the applicant wanted this decision to be held void and without effect because the assessment failed to address the effect of the development on global warming. This case is important because it tests the bounds of state responsibility on the issue of global warming.

Under Pt3A of the EP&A Act, major infrastructure and other projects are required to submit an EA for approval.[100] Section 75H

[93] Manoj Dutta (ed.), *Waste Disposal in Engineered Landfills*, New Delhi: Narosa Publishing House, 1997 in supra note 73, p. 47.

[94] Supra note 86, Schedule 2, Item No. 6.

[95] *Claudio Fernandes and Others v. Margao Municipal Council and Others*, Writ Petitions No. 417 of 2002 and 28 of 2003, 30 July 2003.

[96] This also releases persistent organic pollutants (POPs).

[97] Supra note 89.

[98] *Akhil v. Secretary, AP Pollution Control Board and Others*, Writ Petition No. 15490 of 2001, dated 3 October 2001.

[99] Environmental Planning and Assessment Act, 1979 (NSW, Australia).

[100] Ibid., Div 2, Pt3A, Section 75F.

provides that once the EA has been accepted by the Director General, it must be made publicly available for at least thirty days.[101] During this period, the public are invited to make submissions and the Director General may ask the developer to respond to the issues raised. The Director General is then to furnish a copy of the report to the Minister for the Environment which includes the EA,[102] so that the Minister can decide whether to approve the project.

The assessment may address the environmental impact of the proposed project or any issue of public interest that may be relevant and the suitability of the site for the project.[103] The Director General also specified Environmental Assessment Regulations as authorized by Section 75F(2) of the Act, which demanded an assessment of 'air quality—including a detailed greenhouse gas assessment' effectuated by the mine.

The applicant submitted a detailed GHG assessment,[104] which only addressed certain emissions. Three types of emissions are defined by the World Resources Institute Green House Gas Protocol, 2004.[105] Scope 1 emissions are those that are direct GHG emissions from sources owned or controlled by the company. GHG emissions not covered by the Kyoto Protocol (CFCs, NOx) are not to be included in Scope 1, but reported separately. Scope 2 emissions are those that occur due to the generation of purchased electricity consumed by the company. Scope 3 emissions are all other indirect emissions that occur from sources not owned or controlled by the company. This includes the burning of coal by third parties and GHG emissions arising in this context. Scope 3 emissions are highly contentious as they require consideration of coal that is exported. There are fears that this may give rise to double counting as the recipient of the coal may regulate the emissions produced by it in its own jurisdiction.

The EA submitted by the applicant did not include Scope 3 emissions. Under ministerial terms of reference, it was stated that 'while it is recognized that the burning of coal extracted from coal mines produces significant amounts of greenhouse gases, and that increasing greenhouse gas levels in the atmosphere has implications for global warming and climate change, the Department does not believe it is either necessary or appropriate for the panel of experts to examine the implications of the project on climate change.'[106] The applicant's case was that the placing of this information before the public would have led to rejection of the EA and the exclusion of Scope 3 emissions should invalidate its approval.

The court considered whether the impact of the GHG emissions on global warming and climate change should be considered by the EA before it is produced before the public. The court stated that there must be 'a real and sufficient link'[107] between the operation of the mine and global warming for causation to be established. If the causal link exists, the consequences of burning coal from the mine may be included in the EA. In analysing the question of causation, the court noted that actions by third parties can form part of the causal link and the burning of coal by third parties does not break the chain of causation

---

[101] Ibid., Section 75H(3).

[102] Ibid., Section 75I.

[103] Ibid., Section 8B.

[104] *Gray v. Minister for Planning and Others*, [2006] NSWLEC 720, Section 18.

[105] World Resources Institute Green House Gas Protocol, 2004, (available at http://www.wri.org/business/pubs_description.cfm?pid=3872).

[106] Supra note 103, Section 24.

[107] Ibid., Section 84.

between the operation of the mine and global warming. Furthermore, the EA is to be broader than site-specific impacts[108] and must include a 'wide consideration of the consequences'.[109] The court was satisfied that the burning of thermal coal from the mine would release a significant amount of GHGs into the atmosphere and contribute to climate change, having an impact on Australia in general, and NSW in particular. The test of causation was met[110] and the GHG contribution of the coal when burnt was required in Pt 3A assessment.

The applicant also argued that there was a failure to take into account the principles of Ecologically Sustainable Development as required by Section 5(a)(vii) of the EP&A Act and Section 6(2) of the Protection of the Environment Administration Act, 1991.[112] In particular, failure to take into account the effect of mines on climate change neglected the Precautionary Principle and the principle of Intergenerational Equity.

Due to the doctrine of Separation of Powers, the judiciary is not at liberty to interfere with executive action. The court could, thus, only decide whether the principles of Ecologically Sustainable Development were taken into account, and could not rule as to whether the final project should be approved. The court held that there was a failure to take into account the Precautionary Principle and the principle of Intergenerational Equity. A failure to take into account downstream Scope 3 emissions equated to a failure to consider the cumulative impact of the burning of coal from the proposed mine and placed future generations at risk. Although it was unclear

the extent to which the Precautionary Principle applied at this stage, the court was adamant that there should be enough information before the minister to assess the scientific certainty and potential risks of the project before he made his decision. The court finally ruled that the decision that the EA effectively addressed the Director General's requirements was void and without effect.

Interestingly, according to the respondent, 'no international or national instrument referred to in these proceedings requires that Scope 3 emissions be calculated because of methodological issues related to, inter alia, double counting'.[112] Here perhaps, lies one of the flaws in the allocation of responsibility for climate change. As earlier noted, even consumption as defined in the Montreal Protocol does not extend to export. States are often freed of the responsibility for the products that they manufacture, once these products leave their shores. Clearly, the court in this case took a very progressive approach, signifying the impact of global environmental problems in the local sphere. Although decided in the narrow context of an EA, this case possibly illustrates a tendency toward extended producer responsibility. It may no longer be acceptable for manufacturers to use third parties as a shield when their products ultimately contribute to global warming, for global dilemmas also have local effects.

Friends of the Earth Inc et al v. Robert Mosbacher JR et. al

A proposed EA was also brought before the courts in the USA. Friends of the Earth Inc and others bought a suit against the President and Chief Executive Officer of the Overseas Private Investment Corporation ('OPIC') and

---

[108] Supra note 104.

[109] Ibid.

[110] Ibid.

[111] Protection of the Environment Administration Act, 1991 (New South Wales, Australia).

[112] Supra note 104.

the President and Chairman of the Export-Import Bank ('Ex-Im').

The plaintiffs claimed that the defendants' funded international fossil fuel projects that emit significant amounts of GHGs affecting the domestic environment and that they are, therefore, required to conduct an environmental review pursuant to the NEPA before initiating funding of any specified project. Seven 'illustrative' projects, each of which involved oil or coal extraction, were identified by the plaintiffs who urged the court to impose an injunction propelling the defendants to EAs in respect of each project, which included both direct and indirect emissions. They also sought a declaration that the financing of such projects falls within the ambit of the NEPA, and that the defendants had violated the NEPA in failing to prepare an EA, amongst other claims.

The plaintiffs successfully established standing and the matter came before the United States District Court for the Northern District of California, which addressed the merits of the claim for summary judgement.

Both OPIC and Ex-Im established environmental procedures that propel the conduct of an EA prior to funding. The defendants claimed that their own environmental procedures displace the operation of the NEPA. The Court rejected this argument, affirming that

The standard for determining whether the implementation of a proposal would significantly affect the human environment, and thereby trigger the need to prepare an EIS, is whether the plaintiff has alleged facts which, if true, show that the proposed project may significantly degrade some human environmental factor.[113]

On this basis, the court held that OPIC and Ex-Im were subject to the NEPA.

Furthermore, the court rejected the defendants' argument that the application of NEPA to foreign operations involves extra-territorial application of the legislation that is impermissible. It was recognized that climate change has *domestic effects* and that the defendants' actions affect 'the quality of the human environment'.[114] the extra-territorial application of the act not being required.

Although this was a significant victory, NEPA only applies to major federal actions. A project may be a major federal action even if the actors are non-federal, if the nature of the federal funds used and the extent of federal involvement is significant.[115] The court could not come to a conclusion on these matters due to the multiple stakeholders in the projects. Although the defendants did exert some influence on the projects, it was not possible to say if a withdrawal of their funds would signify the termination of the project as third parties were also responsible for funding. Both parties' motions were denied in this respect.

This case is significant as it recognizes that climate change has domestic effects. Such an acknowledgement may help overcome barriers such as standing requirements and jurisdictional issues. Climate change is very much a transboundary environmental problem that affects all people and nations. With this in mind, judicial redress becomes more accessible.

---

[113] *Foundation for North American Wild Sheep* v. *USDA*, 681 F.2d 1172, 1177-78 (9th Circuit 1982).

[114] Public Citizen, 541 U.S. at 763; see also *Sierra Club* v. *Watkins*, 808 F. Supp 852, 859 (DDC1991) in *Friends of the Earth Inc and et. al* v. *Robert Mosbacher JR et. al*, Case 3:02-cv-04106-JSW Document 172, filed 30 March 2007, 27.

[115] *Friends of the Earth Inc et. al. v Robert Mosbacher JR et. al.*, Case 3:02-cv-04106-JSW Document 172 filed 30 March 2007, 32.

Massachusetts et al v. Environmental Protection Agency et. al[116] (Massachusetts, United States)

Administrative agencies are often charged with the power to enforce environmental standards under statute. When these agencies fail to act, the courts may be called upon to rule on the legitimacy of their inaction. This case tests the very limits of administrative action and the contention surrounding global warming as an environmental and political issue. Essentially, the ruling signifies that climate change is a real environmental concern and that it no longer exists only in the political arena.

In 1999, nineteen private environmental organizations petitioned for the EPA to regulate GHG emissions from new motor vehicles under Section 202 of the Clean Air Act.[117] The EPA refused to regulate the emissions, claiming that it did not have the power to issue mandatory regulations regarding climate change, and even if it did have the power, it would not be 'wise' to exercise it.[118]

Its main concerns were that it would encroach upon the power of Congress, as climate change is such a politically charged issue.[119] It stated that Congress had already addressed climate change in other legislation and, thus, it was not its intent to charge the EPA with the power to act in this respect. Relating these arguments back to the statute, the EPA concluded that GHGs were not air pollutants within the meaning of the Act.

The EPA also supported NRC reports[120] that causal links between GHG emissions and climate change 'cannot be unequivocally established.'

Courts are often reluctant to rule on the validity of executive or administrative action, and are careful not to tread on the Separation of Powers doctrine. When the petitioners appealed to the United States Court of Appeals for the District of Columbia Circuit, they were met with failure as the Court held that the EPA had properly exercised its discretion in refusing to regulate GHGs.

They then appealed to the US Supreme Court, which heard their case and decided in their favour. Instead of construing the question of regulation of GHGs as political, the Court posed it as a question of statutory interpretation: could GHGs be regulated by the EPA under the Act?

Massachusetts was able to show that it had standing under Section 7607(b)(1) as the court was confident that the effects of climate change, in particular the likelihood of rising sea levels and increased frequency of natural disasters,[121] posed a risk of actual and imminent harm to the state of Massachusetts.[122] This was thought to meet the requisite degree of particularization.

The test of causation was met, and the court rejected the EPA's argument that the GHG emissions it has failed to regulate contribute so insignificantly to Massachusetts' injuries that it cannot be called into court to answer for them.[123] A step-by-step approach to addressing climate change was suggested by the Court. The failure of countries such as India and China to reduce GHG emissions could not shadow the need for domestic regulation, especially considering that the USA is the third largest GHG contributor. Even if the remedy sought (the regulation of GHGs

---

[116] *Massachusetts et. al v. Environmental Protection Agency et. al*, 549 US_(2007).

[117] Clean Air Act 42 USC s/s 7401 et seq. (1970).

[118] Ibid.

[119] Ibid.

[120] Ibid.

[121] Ibid.

[122] Ibid.

[123] Ibid.

under the Clean Air Act) could not alleviate climate change in its entirety, the court stated that 'a reduction in domestic emissions would slow the pace of global emissions increases, no matter what happens elsewhere'[124] and therefore the remedy was sufficiently adapted to the harm. It was also noted that the EPA had agreed with the President to address the issue of climate change.[125] In concluding that Massachusetts had standing, the court noted that rising sea levels due to global climate change has, and will continue to, harm the state and that this risk will be reduced if the court granted the relief sought.[126]

As also noted in the *Gray* case, judicial review of administrative action is narrow because administrative agencies have wide discretion. This discretion peaks when an agency decides not to enforce.[127] However, the Court distinguished between rule-making and enforcement, stating that rule-making is more dependent on law, not facts, and requires a public explanation.[128] According to Section 7607(d)(9) of the Clean Air Act, a court may 'reverse any such action found to be ... arbitrary, capricious, an abuse of discretion, or otherwise not in accordance with law'.

The court reversed the decision of the EPA on this very basis. It examined the nature of the EPA's power and stated that the EPA has wide powers to regulate any air pollutant that endangers public welfare. Section 202(a)(1) uses the term 'any', which is significantly wide and thus, Congress could not intend to deprive the EPA of the power to regulate climate change.[129] The limits on the discretion

of the EPA were examined and the court was confident that this discretion was fettered by statutory requirements. When the EPA made its judgement under Section 7521(a)(1), it could only refuse to regulate GHGs if the statutory requirements for regulation were not made out. It was to ask itself the question: do GHGs cause or contribute to air pollution that may be reasonably anticipated to endanger public health or welfare? Instead of answering this question, the EPA gave a number of policy arguments that were insufficient and unconnected to the statutory requirements.[130] The court stated that the EPA had failed to ground its reasons for action or inaction in the statute, and thus its reasoning was 'arbitrary, capricious or otherwise not in accordance with the law.'[131]

Is the EPA now required to regulate GHGs arising from new motor vehicles under the Clean Air Act? It may appear so. As an administrative agency, the EPA is charged with the responsibility of protecting public welfare and the environment. Climate change endangers both of these. The consideration of GHGs as a threat to the local environment is being compelled by various jurisdictions around the world. Climate change is both real and imminent, and action is required on the part of all three arms of government.

Petition to the Inter-American Commission[132]

According to Mary Simon, President of Inuit Tapiriit Kanatami: 'the Arctic is the barometer

---

[124] Ibid., 23.
[125] Ibid., 23.
[126] Ibid., 24.
[127] Ibid.
[128] Ibid., 25.
[129] Supra note 116.

[130] Ibid., 32.
[131] Ibid.
[132] Petition to the Inter-American Commission on Human Rights seeking relief from violations resulting from Global Warming caused by Acts and Omissions of the United States. Submitted by Sheila Watt-Cloutier with the support of the Inuit Circumpolar Conference,

of global environmental health.'[133] It would be difficult to come across any other place in the world where climate change has had an effect as profound as in the Arctic. The Arctic suffers disproportionately from the effects of global warming. 'In fact, annual arctic temperatures have increased at almost twice the rate as that of the rest of the world over the past few decades.'[134] Indigenous people of the Arctic have attempted to utilize the regional inter-American human rights system as a way of drawing attention to these changes and compelling the USA to address global warming.

In 2005, Sheila Watt-Cloutier petitioned the Inter-American Commission on Human Rights on behalf of the Inuit people of the Arctic and with the support of the Inuit Circumpolar Conference.[135] They sought relief from human rights violations caused by the acts and or omissions of the USA in failing to address climate change.

The 2007 report of the IPCC remarks with medium confidence that the effect of increased temperatures in the Arctic has affected human activities such as travelling and hunting.[136] Inuit communities would undoubtedly take this further, and the petition notes that

radical changes have transformed the Arctic environment and the Inuit way of life. Sea ice is melting and thinning—it no longer extends as far as it used to. Ice sheets are melting, and often fail to present the thickness that was once safe enough for the Inuit to confidently travel upon. Movement for animals is also difficult and many of them are driven to change their migration patterns. For example, the caribou, which form an integral part of the Inuit diet, are also declining in number as they can no longer safely travel across the thinning ice at certain times of the year. Inuit have noticed an alteration of species and their habitat in general; breeding times are shifting and development is changing.

The Inuit know their world by 'Inuit Qaujimajatuqangit' or 'IQ', which can be equated with a world view of a system of ecological knowledge that enables the Inuit to survive the harsh Arctic climate. Historically, it is reliable and is passed from one generation to the next,[137] forming a distinct part of Inuit culture and identity. 'Changes [in ice and snow conditions] have damaged their subsistence harvest, the animals they harvest to survive, and their cultural practices.'[138] IQ is threatened as the Inuit can no longer reliably predict when to safely travel and where the hunt is located. They also say that they are forced to change traditional harvest methods. They can no longer build the igloos for which they are renowned as the snow has changed its consistency and is no longer good for these purposes. These are just a few of the changes that form the basis for the alleged interference with human rights. The Inuit hold the USA responsible as (a) the US has a duty to uphold and respect their rights under the petition and (b) 'the US is the world's largest contributor to global warming and its damaging effects on the

on behalf of all Inuit of the Arctic regions of the United States and Canada, 7 December 2005 (hereinafter Petition to the Inter-American Commission).

[133] See Inuit Circumpolar Conference, Canada, Press Release: 'Inuit Leader Congratulate Sheila Watt-Cloutier for Nobel Peace Prize Nomination' (1 February 2007).

[134] 'Petition to the Inter-American Commission on Human Rights Seeking Relief from Violations Resulting From Global Warming Caused By Act and Omissions of the United States', submitted by Sheila Watt-Cloutier with the support of the Inuit Circumpolar Conference, on behalf of all Inuit of the Arctic regions of the United States and Canada, 7 December 2005 (hereinafter Petition to the Inter-American Commission).

[135] Petition to the Inter-American Commission, 9.

[136] Working Group II Contribution, 4.

[137] Supra note 133.

[138] Ibid., 39.

Inuit'. In particular, the US has allegedly failed to honour its commitments to the objective of the United Nations Framework Convention on Climate Change.[139] The Inuit claim that this also constitutes a violation of the Precautionary Principle and the Principle of Transboundary Harm and Sustainable Development.

In constructing their argument, the petitioners note that the application of the American Declaration to indigenous people must occur within 'the unique context of indigenous culture and history'.[140] As indigenous people are so intrinsically linked with their environment, the petition states that protection of their human rights also necessitates protection of their environment.[141]

Against this backdrop, the violation of a number of rights is alleged;

1. The right to enjoy the benefits of their culture[142]
2. The right to use and enjoy the lands they have traditionally occupied[143]
3. The right to use and enjoy their personal, intangible, and intellectual property[144]
4. The right to preservation of health[145]
5. The right to life, physical integrity, and security[146]
6. The right to subsist[147]

7. The right to residence, movement, and inviolability of the home.[148]

Some of these rights exist in international instruments specifically for indigenous people and are not yet binding international law. However, they have been used in the past to interpret or give content to established rights by the Commission,[149] where some may even be approaching crystallization as customary norms.

The petition attempts to bypass the requirement that domestic remedies are exhausted on the basis that no suitable remedy exists.[150] The Inuit seek a declaration by the Commission that the US is responsible for violations of the American Declaration of the Rights and Duties of Man and the other relevant instruments and will 'adopt mandatory measures to limit its emissions of greenhouse gases'. They also want the US to protect the Inuit and their environment, mitigate any harm caused by climate change, and if it is too late, create plans that facilitate adaptation to the effects of climate change.[151]

Since the filing of the petition, Sheila Watt-Cloutier was nominated for a Nobel Peace Prize for her advocacy in bringing international attention to climate change and its effect on the peoples of the Arctic, along with the then US Vice-President, Al Gore. On 1 March 2007, the Commission heard the petition, despite having dismissed it in 2005. The persistence of Sheila Watt-Cloutier paid off and she was granted the opportunity to speak to the Commission.

---

[139] Ibid., 133.

[140] Ibid.

[141] Ibid.

[142] American Declaration of the Rights and Duties of Man, 43 AJIL Supp. 133 (1949), Article XXVII (hereinafter American Declaration).

[143] American Declaration, Article XXIII.

[144] Caso de la Comunidad Mayagna (Sumo) Awas Tingni, Inter-Am. Ct. H.R. Ser. C, No. 79, Section 144; Proposed American Declaration on the Rights of Indigenous Peoples, OEA/Ser/L/V/.II.95 (1997).

[145] Ibid., 142.

[146] Ibid., Article I.

[147] Ibid.; International Convenant on Civil and Political Rights, 6 ILM 368 (1967) Art 1(2).

[148] Supra note 142, Article VIII.

[149] Case of Mary and Carrie Dann, Report No. 75/02, Case 11.140 (United States), Inter-Am. C.H.R., 2002, Section 129.

[150] Ibid.

[151] Ibid., 118.

Dimmock v. Secretary of State for Education and Skills (United Kingdom)

Public awareness and education in relation to climate change is supported by Articles 4 and 6 of the UNFCCC[152] and Article 10 of the Kyoto Protocol.[153] The film *An Inconvenient Truth*, created by the former US Vice-President Al Gore, has shocked and even horrified many and was awarded an Oscar in 2007 for the Best Documentary Film. It presents the science surrounding the climate change phenomena and the various events around the world that can be attributed to global warming. It is very provoking, very informative, and often very political.

In the UK, the Secretary of State for Education and Skills sent a copy of the film to every state secondary school within its jurisdiction, in an effort to educate pupils on climate change and to provoke discussion on the subject. It was to be shown in the context of science, geography, or citizenship classes. Along with each film was an information pack that contained reference to the website 'Teachernet', an aid for teachers, which hosted guidance notes for stimulating conversation, explaining the film, and structuring lessons around the materials.

The case of *Dimmock v. Secretary of State for Education and Skills*[154] arose when the Secretary's actions came under attack by a Dimmock who was the father of two sons attending school and also the school governor. He alleged that distributing and showing the film in schools amounts to a promotion of partisan political views, and thus contravenes Sections 406 and 407 of the Education Act.[155]

Section 406 states that '[t]he local education authority, governing body and head teachers shall forbid...the promotion of partisan political views in the teaching of any subject in the school'.[156] Section 407 provides that where political issues are brought to the attention of students, the teacher must be careful that students 'are offered a balanced presentation of opposing views'.[157]

Burton acknowledged that the film is, in fact, political in nature, despite the fact that it is not affiliated with any party in particular.[158] However, the court refuted the argument that the distribution of the film in schools amounts to political indoctrination, as this in itself did not promote partisan political views. This, however, depended largely on the context in which the film was shown and the guidance note provided with it. The court felt that mere reference to the website 'Teachernet', containing the guidance note, was insufficient to ensure compliance with Section 407 and supported the defendant's willingness to distribute the guidance note in hard copy.

It was also alleged by the claimant that the guidance note must make available the counter views to the ideas contained in the film, in order to comply with Section 407. The court interpreted the term 'balanced' in a looser fashion, describing it as 'nothing more than fair and dispassionate'.[159] Burton then turned to the film and, importantly, acknowledged that 'Al Gore's presentation of the causes and

---

[152] Article 4(1)(i).

[153] Article 10(e).

[154] *Dimmock v. Secretary of State for Education and Skills*, [2007] EWHC 2288 (Admin) (10 October 2007) available at http://www.bailii.org/ew/cases/EWHC/Admin/2007/2288.html (last visited 22 October 2007).

[155] Education Act, 1996 (United Kingdom).

[156] Ibid., Section 406(1)(b).

[157] Ibid., Section 407(1).

[158] The term 'political' is not limited to party political; see *McGovern v. AG*, [1982] Ch 321 at 340 in *Dimmock v. Secretary of State for Education and Skills*, [2007] EWHC 2288 (Admin) (10 October 2007) at Section 4.

[159] Ibid.

likely effects of climate change in the film was broadly accurate.'[160] The court deemed the Fourth Assessment report of the IPCC as representing mainstream scientific opinion, stating that the film does in some instances deviate from this and exhibits errors of fact. Such facts are theoretically designed to advance Gore's political thesis and the court thought it necessary that the defendant make clear that 'some or all of those matters are not supported or promoted by the Defendant' and 'there is a view to the contrary, that is, (at least) the mainstream view' to ensure compliance with Sections 406 and 407 respectively.[161]

Nine errors where the film deviates from fact and/or the consensus of the IPCC are identified by the court. Al Gore cites climate change as the direct culprit of a number of extreme climatic events such as Hurricane Katrina, the disappearance of snow on Mount Kilimanjaro, the drying up of lake Chad, and coral bleaching. In these cases, the court found that there was not enough evidence to substantiate such claims and that the causes of these events were often numerous, it being difficult to attribute the event to any one cause.

The court supported an amended version of the guidance note that expressly acknowledges that the film contains partisan political views and warns teachers against urging children to adopt one political view over another. Identification of the nine errors, or departures from consensus, is included in the amended version, where these issues are often juxtaposed against what the IPCC report says. The proposition that teachers ask students, 'what can be done to put pressure on politicians to respond to climate change?' was also removed. As amended, the guidance note served the purpose of 'setting the film into a context in which it can be shown by teachers, and not so that the Defendant itself or the schools are *promoting partisan views* contained in the film, and is putting it into a context in which a balanced presentation of opposing views can and will be offered.'[162]

The above case has great symbolic significance as well as practical ramifications. It signals that climate change is firmly within the realm of public discourse. Amidst the political haze, there is the acknowledgement that climate change is supported by science and the findings of the IPCC are gathering momentum as the judiciary has been willing to rule the Fourth Report as representing the general consensus. Consequently, it is accepted that climate change is real and that it is more than likely caused by humans. The issue has become so mainstream and so important that it is finding its way into school curricula. In accordance with the UNFCCC and the Kyoto Protocol, education can be used as a tool for informing citizens and catalysing action.

THE WAY FORWARD

How to address climate change is a highly contentious issue. Many groups propose and advocate a wide range of political and scientific solutions.

Sustainable Development

The IPCC Report advocates sustainable development as a way of reducing vulnerability to climate change. 'Sustainable development can reduce vulnerability to climate change by enhancing adaptive capacity and increasing resilience. At present, however, few plans for promoting sustainability have explicitly included either adapting to climate change impacts, or promoting adaptive capacity.'[163]

[160] Supra note 155, Section 22.
[161] Ibid., Section 19.
[162] Ibid., Section 44.
[163] Working Group II Contribution, 20.

Perhaps the ruling in the *Gray* case presents one way in which sustainable development can take climate change into account. If EAs are to include an assessment of all GHGs, then precaution can be exercised, where due, to give effect to sustainable development. However,

Even the most stringent mitigation efforts cannot avoid further impacts of climate change in the next few decades, which makes adaptation essential, particularly in addressing near-term impacts. Unmitigated climate change would, in the long term, be likely to exceed the capacity of natural, managed and human systems to adapt.

Realistically, countries are thus compelled to take steps to mitigate climate change and respond to it. The remedies sought by the Inuit before the Inter-American Commission identify a number of responses that can be used to address the impact of climate change in the present and in the future. Countries should devise plans to adapt to the effects of climate change that are inevitable.

One other suggestion is to encourage investment in cleaner energy and enforce the Polluter Pays Principle by putting a price on CO_2 emissions. A carbon tax would be preferable because companies would then be able to build a fixed price into their investments.[164]

Extended Producer Responsibility

The principle of Extended Producer Responsibility[165] can be employed to make producers more accountable for the products they manufacture, where their responsibility continues beyond the point of sale. Thus, manufacturers may be motivated to create goods that are recyclable or reuseable, internalizing the costs which would otherwise be borne by consumers or the environment.

Extended producer responsibility should incorporate materials management in favour of waste management, as suggested by GAIA. A careful line must be drawn between materials that are discards and can be reused in some way, and materials that are true waste.[166] Materials management begins at the manufacture end and is traced through consumption, where each stage is viewed as a part of a continuous cycle. This can be applied to energy production, car manufacture, and the manufacture of basic products that we use in everyday life. The aim is to reduce emissions at source and create products that are not so expendable. If this process is employed, a proactive instead of reactive approach may be taken to address GHGs, and proper precautions may be taken.

Carbon Offsetting

Some argue that carbon offsetting can be used to reduce the amount of carbon emissions released into the atmosphere. Carbon offsetting operates by calculating the emissions from a given activity such as driving, and then working out the cots of removing these emissions using some other activity or scheme. For example, a carbon surcharge may be imposed on a person taking a flight, and this surcharge used to fund a wind farm or tree-planting scheme that removes carbon from the atmosphere.[167] It is essentially the practice used in the CDM in the Kyoto Protocol.

Some groups are opposed to carbon offsetting as they believe that it is an inadequate substitution for legislation and does not effect the systematic change in consumption habits which is required for long-term mitigation of climate change. The environmental organization, Friends of the Earth Inc.

---

164 *The Economist*, 2 July 2007.
165 See p. 258 also.

166 Ibid.
167 Friends of the Earth, Briefing Note: Carbon Offsetting, (2007).

advocates a shift to a low-carbon economy and is not in support of carbon offsetting. One of its fears is that 'offsetting looks like a way to carry on the polluting activity because you can buy your way out of the problem'.[168] Also, if offsetting schemes are directed toward projects that would exist even if the offsetting funds were not provided, we are not actually better off, as CO_2 emissions are not being reduced.[169] Consequently, Friends of the Earth Inc. advocates the adoption of a government policy that promotes and mandates a low-carbon economy.[170] Again, this supports a proactive approach that decreases emissions at their source, instead of reacting to them with schemes such as offsetting.

Action by the Government of India

The Government of India has a high-power National Council on Climate Change headed by the prime minister, to coordinate national action plans for assessment, adaptation, and mitigation of climate change. It will advise the government on proactive measures that can be taken by India to deal with the challenge of climate change. It will also facilitate inter-ministerial coordination and guide policies in relevant areas. It launched the Green India campaign on 15 August 2007 with the major focus being on afforestation. The Council also decided to fund the research on melting of Himalayan glaciers, and its effect on agriculture and rivers.[171] Such councils and regional bodies are integral for thinking globally and acting locally.

Climate change is a provocative issue in many ways. It raises questions on our own definitions of responsibility and accountability to the rest of the human race. The issue is moral, philosophical, and political on many levels.

The atmosphere knows no boundaries, and emissions produced by one state will affect the planet as a whole. Global climate change must be addressed on a local scale, but we cannot confine our minds only to local impact. In deciding what action to take, we should be guided by the answers to these questions: What does inter-generational equity mean? What is my responsibility? And so should our governments. These considerations go to the heart of policy *and* humanity.

---

[168] Ibid.
[169] Ibid.
[170] Ibid.

[171] Press Release on 14 July 2007 at Delhi.

17 The Need for Environmental Courts

In what type of courts should environmental cases be adjudicated? It is questionable whether ordinary courts are equipped for dealing with the highly technological or scientific data that may come forth in an environmental dispute. Lord Woolf, in his Garner lecture to the United Kingdom Environmental Law Association (UKELA) on the theme, 'Are the Judiciary Environmentally Myopic?'[1] commented upon the problem of increased specialization in environmental law and on the difficulty of the courts, in their present form, in moving beyond their traditional role of detached 'Wednesbury' review. He pointed out the need for a specialized court or courts with wider discretion, so that they may determine their own procedure and bring to bear specialist experience on environmental issues in the most effective way. Lord Woolf pointed out the need for

a multi-faceted, multi-skilled body that would combine the services provided by existing courts, tribunals and inspectors in the environmental field. It would be a 'one-stop shop', which should lead to faster, cheaper and more effective resolution of disputes in the environmental area. It would avoid increasing the load on already over-burdened lay institutions by trying to compel them to resolve issues with which they are not designed to deal. It could be a forum in which the judges could play a different role; a role that enables them not to examine environmental problems with limited vision. It would, however, be based on our existing experience, combining the skills of the existing inspectorate, the land tribunal and other administrative bodies. It could be an exciting project.[2]

According to Lord Woolf, 'While environmental law is now clearly a permanent feature of the legal scene, it still lacks clear boundaries.' It might be 'preferable that the boundaries are left to be established by judicial decision as the law developed. After all, the great strength of the English law has been its pragmatic approach.'[3] Further, where urgent decisions are required, there are often no easy options for preserving the status quo pending the resolution of the dispute. If a project is allowed to go ahead, there may be irreparable damage to the environment, and if it is stopped, there may be irreparable damage to an important economic interest.[4]

[1] Lord Woolf, 'Are the Judiciary Environmentally Myopic?', *Journal of Environmental Law*, 1992, vol. 4, no. 1, p. 1.

[2] Ibid.
[3] Ibid.
[4] See Robert Carnwath, 'Environment Enforcement : The Need for a Specialised Court', *Journal of Planning and Environment Law*, 1992, p. 798 at 806.

Robert Carnwath advocates the constitution of a unified tribunal with a simple
procedure that looks at the needs of parties,
taking the form of a court or an expert panel.
The allocation of a procedure should be
adapted to the needs of each case and the court
should operate at two levels: the first tier by a
single judge or technical person, and second, a
review by a panel of experts presided over by
a high court judge. Such a court would not be
limited to 'Wednesbury' grounds.

Scientists may refine, modify, or discard
certain variables; however, agencies and courts
must make choices based on existing scientific
knowledge. In addition, decision-making
evidence for an agency is generally presented
in a scientific form that cannot be easily tested.
Therefore, inadequacies in the record due to
uncertainty or insufficient knowledge may not
be properly considered.[5] The inadequacies of
science result from, firstly, the identification of
adverse effects of a hazard and then working
backwards to find the cause. Secondly, clinical
tests are performed, particularly where toxins
are involved, on animals and not on humans,
that is, they are based on animal studies or
short-term cell testing. Thirdly, conclusions
based on epidemiological studies are flawed
by the scientist's inability to control, or even
accurately assess, past exposure of the subjects.
These studies do not permit the scientist to
isolate the effects of the substance of concern.
The latency period of many carcinogens and
other toxins exacerbates problems of later
interpretation. The timing between exposure
and observable effect creates intolerable delays

before regulation occurs.[6] The very nature of
science and the uncertainties involved make
environmental disputes particularly hard to
adjudicate.

In India, the high courts often deal with
environmental matters in large public interest.
The special benches dealing with such cases
are popularly termed 'Green Benches.' On one
occasion, the Supreme Court of India felt the
necessity to pass an order requesting the Chief
Justice of the Madras HC to constitute a Special
Bench or 'Green Bench' to deal with the case
and other environmental matters. Such Green
Benches now function in Kolkata, Madhya
Pradesh, and some other high courts.[7]

NATIONAL GREEN TRIBUNAL

An environmental court had been envisaged
by the Supreme Court of India as far back as
1986. Bhagwati, CJ in M.C. Mehta v. Union of
India and Shriram Foods and Fertilizers Case,[8]
observed:

We would also suggest to the Government of India
that since cases involving issues of environmental
pollution, ecological destructions and conflicts over
national resources are increasingly coming up for
adjudication and these cases involve assessment
and evolution of scientific and technical data,
it might be desirable to set up environmental
courts on the regional basis with one professional
judge and two experts drawn from the Ecological
Sciences Research Group keeping in view the
nature of the case and the expertise required for
its adjudication. There would of course be a right
of appeal to this Court from the decision of the
Environment Court.

Likewise in another case on pollution, the
Supreme Court criticized the action of the

[5] Charmian Barton, 'The Status of the Precautionary
Principle in Australia', Harvard Environmental Law
Review, 1998, vol. 22, pp. 509, 510–11; See Alyson
C. Flournay, 'Scientific Uncertainty in Protective
Environmental Decision-Making', Harvard Environmental
Law Review, 1991, vol. 15, pp. 327, 333–5.

[6] See Flournay (Ibid.).
[7] Vellore Citizens Forum v. Union of India, AIR 1996 SC
2715: (1996) 5 SCC 647.
[8] 1986(2) SCC 175 (at page 202).

Government of India in the appointment of an authority under Section 3(3) of the Environment (Protection) Act, 1996 on the basis of a lack of expertise. Kuldip Singh, J. observed that the Central Government should constitute an authority under Section 3(3), 'headed by a retired judge of the High Court and it may have other members—preferably with expertise in the field of pollution control and environmental protection—to be appointed by the Central Government.[9]

The Indian legislature has enacted the National Green Tribunal Act, 2011[10] to implement the judicial decisions referred to above and recognize the right to healthy environment as a part of the right to life under Article 21 of the Constitution of India. The Tribunal is having jurisdiction over all civil cases where a substantial question relating to environment (including enforcement of any legal right relating to environment) is involved and such question as arises out of this implementation of any of the provisions of any of the enactments intended for the protection of environment.[11] The Tribunal has power to grant relief and compensation to the victims of pollution and other environmental damage arising out of the said enactments including accidents occurring while handling hazardous substances. It can also order restitution of any property damaged and for restitution of the environment for such area or areas.[12] Where death of, or injury to, any person (other than a workman) or damage to any property or environment has resulted from an accident or the adverse impact of an activity or operation or process, under any enactment specified, the person shall be responsible to pay such relief or compensation for such death, injury, or damage, under all or any of the heads specified to the schedule-II[13] of the enactment. The civil courts are barred from entertaining any appeal in respect of any matter, which the Tribunal is empowered to determine under its appellate jurisdiction.[14]

The Green Tribunal is headed by a chairperson who has been empowered to invite any one or more persons having specialized knowledge and experience in a particular case before the Tribunal to assist the Tribunal in that case.[15] The post of the chairperson is reserved for former judges of the Supreme Court and chief justices of high courts.[16] A retired judge of a high court is qualified for appointment as a judicial member of the Tribunal.

Monitoring and Implementation

For the implementation of environmental laws, proper monitoring is essential. The Supreme Court of India has constituted several committees for the purpose of effectively implementing environmental laws. The implementation of the Hazardous Waste (Management and Handling) Rules, 1989 is monitored under a repetition committee constituted by the Supreme Court, which has wide powers including the power to issue closure orders.[17]

Several high courts have also formed Citizen Committees to deal with the problems

---

[9] *Vellore Citizens Welfare Forum v. Union of India and Others.* AIR 1996 SC 2715: (1996) 5 SCC 647.

[10] Gazette of India, Extraordinary, No. 25, dated 2 June 2010.

[11] Section 14 of the Green Tribunal Act, 2010.

[12] Section 16 of the Green Tribunal Act, 2010.

[13] Compensation can be claimed on death, permanent or temporary, disability, or other injury or sickness, loss of wages, medical expenses, damages to private property, etc. (for more see the Schedule-II of the enactment).

[14] Section 29 of the Green Tribunal Act, 2000.

[15] Section 4 of the Green Tribunal Act, 2000.

[16] Section 5 of the Green Tribunal Act, 2010.

[17] Supreme Court Monitoring Committee on Hazardous Waste, <http://www.scmc.info/> (last visited 20 July 2007).

of lack of civil amenities and infrastructure. When the Allahabad Municipal Council could not solve the issue of waterlogging in the city, the high court formed a committee in a PIL.[18] When the high court issues such directions for the formation of committees consisting of citizens, is it not an encroachment on the functions of the department concerned? M. Katju, a Supreme Court judge, made some observations and suggestions while forming the committee by judicial orders:

1. The committees comprise of citizens (lawyers, doctors, teachers, businessmen, journalists, technical experts, and others) and bureaucrats (the District Magistrate, officials of water works, electricity, and telephone departments, and other government departments). However, the chairman was always a non-bureaucrat, and we usually appoint a reputed senior lawyer of the Allahabad High Court.

2. Technical experts were always kept in the committee, because the problem usually requires technical expertise to solve.

3. The chairman of the committee was authorized to nominate more persons of the committee.

4. The committee was authorized to issue directives to officials and others, and the state government was directed to give all help, technical, financial, or otherwise, to the committee.

5. The committee was empowered to call for accounts of government grants and expenditures pertaining to the matter they were dealing with.

6. The initial members of the committee were carefully chosen by the court. Since they were nominated, not elected members, we had to see that no neta type of person was

appointed; otherwise he would be more interested in serving his own ends rather than serving the citizens.[19]

The said committees are empowered to issue directions. Of course, it is a form of outsourcing of the legal powers of the court, but even the judges have admitted that they are not technical experts and it would be a mistake for them to attempt to resolve the problem themselves. They should inform the committee of its task, empower it to issue directives, and then monitor its functioning by listing the case every month or two and requesting progress reports from the committee. It has been acknowledged that this is only a judicial experiment and that there will potentially be failures, followed by re-assessment and correction in the future.

Human minds have creative power. Once people become aware of an opportunity, they will often solve their own problems using their own mental capacities. The committee acts as a watchdog on behalf of the citizens and holds accountable the corrupt bureaucrats. The constitution of the committee is not illegal and does not amount to a transgression upon the jurisdiction of executive power. Katju explained as follows:

To this, the reply is that citizens' lives are more important than legal technicalities. In an era of crises, we have to innovate, not always follow the conventional path. Had the municipal corporations been discharging their functions properly, the problems of the cities would not have arisen, but everyone knows that they are centres of corruption. Should the citizens keep 'Waiting for Godot'? I think not, and the way out, to my mind, is to

---

[18] *J.N. Chaturvedi v. Commr*, AIR 2001, Allahabad 148.

[19] Speech delivered by M. Katju as Allahabad High Court judge at a seminar held in Delhi on 2 March 2002, organized by the International Law Association. Published in the Journal Section of (2002) 3 SCC (J) at page 3.

create Citizen Committees in the above manner to deal with the problems of civic amenities and infrastructure in the cities of India. That is the democratic approach too.[20]

DEVELOPMENTS ABROAD

Australia

The Land and Environment Court of New South Wales in Australia, established in 1980, could possibly be hailed as the model judicial body for dealing with environmental disputes, the one-stop shop envisaged by Lord Woolf if you like. Its enabling act is the Land and Environment Court Act 1979 (NSW), which 'vests power in the court to determine environmental, development, building and planning disputes.'[21] It is a superior court of record with six permanent judges and nine permanent commissioners who have expertise in one or more of the following areas: administration and local government, environmental or town planning, science or EIAs, law, architecture or building, or natural resource management. Since the court also resolves matters under the Aboriginal Land Rights Act, 1983, there are also aboriginal commissioners to assist the court.

Its jurisdiction combines appeal, judicial review, and enforcement functions, and can be divided into seven types of matters:

1. Environmental planning and protection appeals, which are generally appeals under the Environmental Planning and Assessment Act 1979 (NSW), and can extend to merits-based review.
2. Local government appeals and other appeals or applications that are often in respect of decisions made under the Local Government Act 1993 (NSW) and various other acts.
3. Land tenure, valuation, rating, and compensation matters including those which arise under the Aboriginal Land Rights Act 1983 (NSW).
4. Civil enforcement in relation to environmental matters arising under various environmental laws.
5. Criminal prosecution and enforcement in relation to environmental offences.
6. Appeals in relation to criminal environmental offences.
7. Other appeals in respect of criminal environmental offences.

Some cases are heard by commissioners, some by judges, and others by a combination of the two. The court adopts a flexible approach towards procedural matters and, interestingly, it is not bound by the rules of evidence[22] that significantly complicate most hearings in Australian courts. Such a composition is necessary and ideal in environmental matters, as it integrates the necessary areas of specialization within a judicial framework, enabling disputes to be resolved as expeditiously as possible.

United States of America

Concern over the adjudication of environmental disputes led to the Carnegie Commission of Science and Technology (1993) and to the government undertaking a study of the challenges of science and technology in judicial decision-making. In the introduction to its final report, the Commission concluded that:

---

[20] Ibid.

[21] Land and Environment Court, 'Court Jurisdiction' http://www.lawlink.nsw.gov.au/lawlink/lec/ll_lec.nsf/pages/LEC_jurisdictionfull (last visited 20 July 2007).

[22] Land and Environment Court Act, 1979 Section 38, in Land and Environment Court, 'Court Jurisdiction' http://www.lawlink.nsw.gov.au/lawlink/lec/ll_lec.nsf/pages/LEC_jurisdictionfull (last visited 20 July 2007).

The courts' ability to handle complex science-rich cases has recently been called into question, with widespread allegations that the judicial system is increasingly unable to manage and adjudicate science and technology (SandT) issues. Critics have objected that judges cannot make appropriate decisions because they lack technical training, that the jurors do not comprehend the complexity of the evidence they are supposed to analyse, and that the expert witnesses on whom the system relies are mercenaries whose biased testimony frequently affects the decisions. If these claims go unanswered, or are not dealt with, confidence in the judiciary will be undermined as the public becomes convinced that the courts as now constituted are incapable of correctly resolving some of the more pressing legal issues of our day.

In the environmental field, the uncertainty of scientific opinions has created serious problems for judges to deal with. Being mindful of this handicap, in regard to the different goals of science and the law in the ascertainment of truth, the US Supreme Court observed in *Daubert v. Merrel Dow Pharmaceuticals Inc* that[23]

...there are important differences between the quest for truth in the courtroom and the quest for truth in the laboratory. Scientific conclusions are subject to perpetual revision. Law, on the other hand, must resolve disputes finally and quickly.

It has also been stated by Brian Wynne in *Uncertainty and Environment Learning: Reconceiving Science and Policy in the Preventive Paradigm,*'[24] that 'Uncertainty, resulting from inadequate data, ignorance, and indeterminacy, is an inherent part of science'. Adjudicatory bodies for environmental matters need to be conscious of such limitations in reconciling law and science.

New Zealand

The Environment Court[25] was constituted by the Resource Management Amendment Act, 1996. It is a court of record consisting of environment judges (who are also District Court Judges) and environment commissioners. The commissioners come from a variety of backgrounds including architecture, resource management, forestry, building, and civil engineering. In most sittings, matters are heard by one environment judge and two environment commissioners.

The court has jurisdiction to adjudicate a wide range of matters that arise under the Resource Management Act. The court also has jurisdiction to adjudicate some matters arising under the following Acts: Public Works Act,[26] Historic Places Act,[27] Forests Act,[28] Local Government Act,[29] Transit NZ Act.[30] Similar to the Land and Environment Court of NSW, the court sometimes adjudicates disputes that relate to its indigenous people, the Maori, and their relationship, rights, and interests in the land.

The New Zealand Environment Court, like the NSW Court, does not adopt a technical manner and is not bound by the rules of evidence. This, perhaps, reflects the fact that many of the matters that it hears deal with public interest. It also encourages mediation where possible as an alternative form of dispute resolution, and is empowered by Section 238 of the Resource Management Act[31] to compel mediation.

---

[23] (1993) 113 S.Ct 2786.

[24] 2 Global Environmental Change 111, (1992).

[25] New Zealand Government, Ministry of Justice, 'Environment Court' <http://www.justice.govt.nz/environment/#jurisdiction> (accessed on 18 November 2007).

[26] Public Works Act, 1981 (New Zealand).

[27] Historic Places Act, 1993 (New Zealand).

[28] Forests Act, 1949 (New Zealand).

[29] Local Government Act, 2002 (New Zealand).

[30] Transit NZ Act, 1989 (New Zealand).

[31] Resource Management Act, 1991 (New Zealand).

Pakistan

The Pakistan Environment Protection Act, 1997 contemplates the establishment of an Environment Tribunal and Environmental Magistrates Court to deal with offences under the Act. An appeal can be filed in the High Court against the decision of the Environment Tribunal.[32]

Bangladesh

The Forest Act, 1927 empowers the government to appoint Forest Magistrates to try offences exclusively under the said Act.[33]

INTERNATIONAL COURT OF JUSTICE

The International Court of Justice (ICJ) has established a seven-member Chamber for Environmental Matters. This decision followed a previous consideration by the court on the possible formation of such a chamber, and was taken in view of the developments in the field of environmental law that have taken place in the last few years and the need to be prepared to the fullest possible extent to deal with any environmental case falling within its jurisdiction.[34]

The ICJ has never fully dealt with major international environmental disputes. But it has had the opportunity with natural resource issues to consider matters concerning the environment and conservation, or to give judgements that establish important general principles. In situations involving damage to the environment, or consequential damage to people or property or other economic loss, a state will probably not find it difficult to claim

that it is an 'injured state' and that it may bring an international claim.[35]

Cases before the ICJ that have particularly influenced the development of international environmental law include: (i) the *Corfu Channel* case, where the Court affirmed 'every state's obligation not to knowingly allow its territory to be used for acts contrary to the rights of other states,'[36] (ii) the *Fisheries Jurisdiction* case, where the ICJ set forth basic principles governing consultations and other arrangements concerning the conservation of shared natural resources.[37]

Another case raising environmental issues concerning certain phosphate lands in Nauru was settled between the parties in August 1993 (*Nauru v. Australia*). It concerned the obligation, of any of the trustee states for, inter alia, the physical destruction of the island as a unit of self-determination accompanied by a failure to rehabilitate the land; as well as the nature and extent of obligations relating to permanent sovereignty over natural resources and entitlement to the costs of rehabilitation.[38] The settlement of the case, three years after it had been filed by Nauru and after the court had rejected the Australian claim that the case should be struck out on the ground that it was inadmissible, illustrates the potential role of the court as a forum for settling violations of international law.[39]

The ICJ has the power to pass interim orders for the protection and preservation

---

[32] Sections 22, 23, and 24 of the said Act.

[33] Forest Act, 1927, Section 67A.

[34] 1963, Vienna Convention, Optional Protocol Concerning the Compulsory Settlement of Disputes , Article 1 (not in force).

[35] James Cameron, Jacob Werkman, and Peter Roderick, *Improving Compliance with International Environmental Law*, Law and Sustainable Development Series.

[36] *Corfu Channel (Merits)* Case, ICJ Report (1959), page 4.

[37] *United Kingdom v. Iceland*, (1974) ICJ Reports 3. (Fisheries Jurisdiction case).

[38] Charter of the United Nations, Article 96 (1).

[39] Supra note 33.

of the rights of the parties to disputes, if required by circumstances. The irreparability of environmental damage will make interim measures particularly important in cases concerning environmental protection. During the preliminary phase of the *Nuclear Tests* cases, the court indicated interim measures of protection, asking\the parties to ensure that no action is taken that might aggravate or extend the dispute or prejudice the rights of another party, and called on France to 'avoid nuclear tests causing the deposit of radioactive fall-out on Australian territory'.[40]

The ICJ also has advisory jurisdiction. The Charter of the UN allows the General Assembly or the Security Council to request the ICJ to give an advisory opinion on any legal question[41] and allows other organs of the UN and specialized agencies authorized by the General Assembly to request advisory opinions of the court on legal questions arising within the scope of their activities.[42]

EUROPEAN COURT OF JUSTICE

The European Court of Justice (ECJ) is intended to ensure that in the interpretation and application of the EEC Treaty, 'the law is observed'.[43] Most environmental cases reach the ECJ under Article 169 of the EEC Treaty, and since 1980, the EC Commission has brought more than forty cases to the ECJ, alleging failure of member states to comply with its EEC environmental obligations, in which it is usually successful. Its judgements

have been useful to determine, inter alia, that member states may not plead provisions, practices, or circumstances existing in their internal legal system to justify a failure to comply with an environmental obligation,[44] that mere administrative practices that may be altered at the whim of the administration do not constitute the proper fulfilment of an environmental obligation under a directive, and that legal obligations imposed on a member state by an environmental directive are limited to those dangerous substances specifically listed in the directive and not to other unlisted dangerous substances as well.[45]

Article 173 of the EC Treaty empowers the ECJ to review the legality of certain acts of the EC Council and Commission on the grounds of lack of competence, infringement of an essential procedural requirement, infringement of the EEC Treaty, or any rule relating to the application or misuse of powers. Action may be brought by a member state, the Council, or the Commission, as well as by any legal or natural person, provided that the act concerned is a decision addressed to that person or body, or is of direct or individual concern to the person or body.[46]

It is not just a 'Green Bench' but a view, to understand the environment, the science and the law that is required to deal with environmental cases. 'The cynicism about "equal justice under the law" sours into "show

---

[40] *United Kingdom v. Ireland,* Order re Interim measures, ICJ Reports (1972), p. 12; *Federal Republic of Germany v. Iceland,* ICJ Report (1972), p. 30.

[41] Article 96(2) ECOSOC, the Trustship Council and 15 of the specialized agencies have been authorized by the General Assembly.

[42] Statute ICJ, Article 41.

[43] *EC Commission v. Italian Republic,* (1981) ECR 3379.

[44] *Commission of the European Communities v. Netherlands,* (1989) CMLR 479.

[45] Case 182/89, Ibid.

[46] Case C-300/89, *EC Commission v. Council,* (dated 11 June 1991), declaring void Council directive for harmonizing the programmes for the reduction and eventual elimination of pollution caused by waste from titanium dioxide industry, on the grounds that the Council adopted the Directive on the basis of the wrong treaty provision; but see more cases. C-155/91 *EC Commission v. Council,* ECJ, 17 March 1993.

me the man and I will show you the law".[47] The democratic system must ensure that the environment is given priority over business power, which is confident that the dollar can be used to solve any problem. Proper judicial systems for the resolution of environmental disputes provide an appropriate avenue to vindicate the importance of the environment, as they can be better equipped to apply the green view, with experts in science and law at their disposal.

---

[47] *In re* Special Courts Bill, AIR 1979 SC 478. V.R. Krishna Iyer (separate judgement).

18 Enforcing the 'Polluter Pays' Principle
Environmental Taxes

Natural resources like rivers, springs, lakes, reservoirs, and wells have been tapped for extracting water from ancient times. In waterless regions, wells and waterworks were constructed by the states. Canals were constructed to divert the water stored in dams. A water cess (*udakubhgam*) over and above the normal land revenue was levied by the state on all users of irrigation facilities. Even those who were using their own waterworks had to pay the said amount.[1]

One of the core principles of sustainable development is that of 'Polluter Pays', which recognizes that the polluter should pay for any environmental damage created. This principle was first discussed in the United Nations Conference on Environment and Development, held in Rio de Janeiro, Brazil in June 1992.

National authorities should promote the internalization of environmental costs and the use of economic instruments, taking into account the approach that the polluter should, in principle, bear the cost of pollution. (Rio Declaration, Principle 16.)

[1] Arthashastra, a treatise on government and economics in ancient India, ascribed to Kautilya, the chief adviser to India's first emperor Chandragupta Maurya.

A polluter is someone who directly or indirectly damages the environment. Pollution is the imposition of harmful waste product or emission on the person or property of another without that person's consent, which amounts to 'trespass' under the principles of common law. If the damages caused on account of the said trespass can be tolerated and compensated in terms of money, a tax can be imposed on it.

'Green Taxes' are a recognized and effective means for discouraging the consumption of natural things. The best way to a cleaner environment is to make the polluter pay by putting a price on the emission. The Kyoto Protocol lists specific mechanisms to tackle emission reductions. These include an international 'emissions trading' regime that enables developed countries to buy and sell emission credits and cooperate in projects under a system of joint implementation, where one country can finance emission reductions in another. These taxes are intended to promote ecologically sustainable activities through economic incentives.

According to the IPCC, the body set up under the auspices of the United Nations to establish a consensus on global warming, a price of somewhere between $20 and $50 per tonne of CO_2 by 2020 or 2030 should start to stabilize CO_2' concentrations at around 550 parts per million (widely reckoned to be a safe level) by the end of this century. A $50 price tag would raise petrol prices in America by around 15 per cent and electricity prices by around 35 per cent—hardly draconian when set alongside recent fluctuations. The IPCC reckons that stabilizing of 550 ppm would knock approximately 0.1 per cent off global economic growth annually.

A carbon price can be established either through a tax or through a cap-and-trade system, such as the one Europe adopted after signing the Kyoto Protocol. A carbon tax would be preferable, because companies would then be able to build a fixed price into their investment plans, but business people and politicians are both strangely averse to the word 'tax'. A cap-and-trade system can be made to work, but the price has to settle at a level that affects commercial decisions.

Europe has tightened its system up, and the carbon price has risen to a level that could start to make a difference. But Europe, by itself, will not save the planet. It is America that matters, not just because it is the world's biggest polluter, but also because without its participation, the biggest polluters of the future, that is, China and India, will not do anything.

The best news in the fight against climate change is that business is starting to invest in clear energy seriously. But these investments will flourish only if governments are prepared to put a price on carbon. The costs of doing that are not huge.[2]

INDIAN LAWS

Industrialization affects the pollution in rivers. With a view to control the pollution of rivers and streams, which has assumed considerable importance and urgency, the Government of India has enacted the Water (Prevention and Control of Pollution) Cess Act, 1977. The enactment is intended to ensure that domestic and industrial effluents are not allowed to be discharged into water courses without adequate treatment. The income generated from these sources is also used for the working of Pollution Control Boards. Persons carrying on any industrial activity have to pay the cess calculated on the basis of water being consumed by them.[3]

Industrialization has led to growing risks from accidents. Such accidents lead to a lot of death, injury, and damages. Most of the affected persons are economically weaker. Though the affected workers in such industries are protected by labour welfare laws, there is not enough protection to the outsiders. Taking legal steps to obtain compensation from them through legal processes takes substantial time. For the purpose of providing immediate relief to the persons affected by accidents occurring while handling any hazardous substances, the Public Liability Insurance Act, 1991[4] has been enacted. When death or injury to any person (other than a workman) or damage to any property has been caused due to any accident, the owner has to give relief as specified in the enactment.[5] It provides for reimbursement of medical expenses up to a maximum of Rs 12, 500 in each case. For fatal accidents, permanent disability, loss of wages, and damage

[2] 'How business is starting to tackle climate change, and how governments need to help', *The Economist*, 2–8 July 2007.

[3] Section 3 of the Act by amendment in 2003 included all the industries, which were previously specified industries.

[4] Act 6 of 1991, with effect from 22 January 1991.

[5] Public Liability Insurance Act, 1991, Section 3.

to property, separate damages are provided in the enactment. While making the claim, it is not necessary to plead and establish that the death, injury, or damage in respect of which the claim has been made was due to any wrongful act, neglect, or default of any person. The industrialist has to take out insurance policies if he is dealing in hazardous substances. The application for a claim has to be made before the concerned District Collector, who is duty bound to award relief to the victims.

COMPENSATORY AFFORESTATION FUND

The Central Government has constituted the Compensatory Afforestation Fund Management and Planning Authority (CAMPA) to manage the funds for compensatory afforestation, Net Prevent Value (NPV), and any other money recoverable in pursuance of the Supreme Court's order and in compliance of the conditions stipulated by the Central Government while according approval under the FCA for non-forest uses of the forest land.[6] For grant of approval under Section 2 of the FCA besides payment of NPV as being presently calculated by MoEF, the user agencies are propelled to give undertakings to pay the remaining amount, if any, pending finalization of determination by the experts. The payment of NPV is for protection of the environment and not in relation to any propriety rights. For government projects like hospitals, dispensaries, and schools referred to in the body of the judgement, all other projects shall be required to pay NPV though the final decision on this matter is taken after receipt of the Expert Committee Report by the Supreme Court.[7]

[6] Notification dated 23 April 2004 issued by MoEF in exercise of the powers conferred by sub-section (3) of Section 3 of the EP Act.

[7] *T.N. Godavarman Thirumulpad v. Union of India*, 2006 (1) SCC 1.

FOREIGN LAWS

In the USA, corporations that have a taxable income over $2,000,000 must pay a general environmental tax of 0.12 per cent ($12 per $10,000) of the excess of the 'modified alternative minimum taxable income.'[8]

Property tax exemptions are an important aspect of state and local tax policy. By the 1960s, about twenty states had granted real and personal property tax exemptions to pollution control facilities.[9]

An operator of a commercial hazardous waste facility challenged the constitutionality of a statute of the state of Alabama, imposing additional fees on all hazardous waste generated outside the state but disposed in Alabama. The US Supreme Court held that additional disposal fees imposed by Alabama on hazardous waste generated outside of Alabama discriminated against interstate commerce in violation of the commerce clause of the US Constitution.[10]

In Wisconsin, there is a sales and use tax exemption for motor vehicles that are not required to be licensed for highway use and are exclusively used in conjunction with waste reduction or recycling activities that reduce the amount of solid waste generated, reuse solid waste, recycle waste, compact solid waste, or recover energy from solid waste.[11]

The state of Arkansas enacted credits for corporate and individual taxpayers to promote the use of surface water. They encourage the construction of facilities to use available surface

[8] 26 USC Section 59A(e); Section 59A of the United States Federal Tax Code.

[9] See McNulty, 'State Tax Incentives to Fight Pollution', 56, *American Bar Association Journal* at pages 747, 748, and no. 8 (August 1970), Id., at 344.

[10] *Chemical Waste Management, Inc. v. Hunt*, 504 US 334 (1992).

[11] Margaret A. Suprak, 14 Journal of Taxation 35 (1995) (citing Wis. Stat. Section 77.54).

water, the conversion from groundwater use to surface water use, and the levelling of land to reduce agricultural irrigation use. Any taxpayer qualifying for the credits is also entitled to a tax deduction in an amount equal to the project cost, less the total amount the taxpayer is entitled to. In this way, the groundwater resources of the state of Arkansas are conserved.[12]

In the UK, any action by the EEC relating to the environment shall be based on the principles that preventive action should be taken, that environmental damage should as a priority be rectified at source, and that the polluter should pay.[13] These principles have been implemented by a number of European states, using a variety of tax measures, charges, and liability provisions of national law. The UK, for instance, has imposed pollution charges for watercourse discharges and higher taxes for leaded petrol.

The British Government announced credits for pensioners who insulate their dwellings up to $7,875 and increased grants to people who install home wind turbines or solar panels. In the US, users of energy saving insulation, skylights, exterior doors, and windows can earn credits upto $500.

Sweden enacted a carbon tax on the use of oil, coal, natural gas, liquefied petroleum gas, petrol, and aviation fuel used in domestic travel.[14] Industrial users paid half the rate (between 1993 and 1997, 25 per cent of the rate), and certain high-energy industries such as commercial horticulture, mining, manufacturing, and the pulp and paper industry were fully exempted from these new

taxes. Finland, the Netherlands, and Norway have also introduced a similar tax on carbon emissions.

Germany has introduced a tax on electricity and petroleum at variable rates based on environmental considerations. At the same time, renewable sources of electricity are not taxed. Tax concessions are also given to efficient conventional power plants. They also increased the tax on petroleum. The Netherlands and Portugal have inserted differentiations into their car registration taxes to encourage car buyers to opt for the cleanest car models.

The CO_2 Energy Tax

European Community (EC) Ministers decided on 15 December 1993 to ratify the Climate Change Convention in the absence of the CO_2 energy tax despite the fact that the tax was originally seen as a key instrument for cutting back greenhouse gas emissions. The tax as currently proposed would be split fifty-fifty between the carbon and energy content of fossil fuels and other energy sources (except renewables). Energy based on the burning of fossil fuels, such as oil, gas, and coal would be taxed both on the carbon emissions and on the energy content. The tax would be levied on all solid, viscose, or gaseous fossil fuels, either in their crude state where they are used as motor or heating fuel, or in their final form where the motor or heating fuel is obtained by processing the crude product. Thus, raw materials are not taxed, but nuclear energy and hydroelectric power, though emitting no carbon dioxide, are taxed on the basis of the energy they use. In the case of electricity and heat generated as secondary sources of energy where the carbon dioxide emissions component of the tax, the heat and electricity produced from primary possible sources of

---

[12] Ark. Stat. sec. 26.51 and Ark. Tax Rep. Sections 13–250.

[13] Single European Act,1986, Article 25.

[14] A tax of 0.25 SEK/kg ($100 per ton). The rate was raised to 0.365 SEK/kg ($150 per ton) of CO_2 released.

energy are not taxed as such, but on the basis of fossil inputs used.[15]

The debate surrounding the EC carbon or energy tax contributes to the development of issues in the trade or environment context, such as the use of unilateral measures in tackling global environmental problems, the use of economic instruments to achieve environmental objectives, green subsidies, the internationalization of external environmental costs, green product discrimination, the eligibility of taxes to be adjusted at the border, like products, and technology transfer.[16]

Natural resources are assets of a country to be enjoyed by all. Tax is to be imposed not only for revenue purposes, but also as a punitive measure for discouraging the damages caused to the environment. No one shall be allowed to pay green tax as a consideration for destructing nature. Environmental tax shall not be taken as a licence to destroy the natural resources, but shall be preventive in nature.

---

[15] James Cameron, Jacob Werksman, and Peter Roderick, *Improving Compliance with International Environmental Law*, Law and Sustainable Development Series.

[16] Ibid.

19 Disaster Management and Rehabilitation

A disaster is the result of a natural or man-made hazard that affects people and the environment. Natural disasters like volcanic eruptions, earthquakes, landslides, tsunamis, hurricanes, and others, adversely affect a lot of people who are not prepared to meet the calamity.

There are a variety of disasters and crises that jeopardize the health and stability of the environment. Perhaps, due to the phenomenon of climate change, natural disasters are becoming more frequent across the globe and some even view this as the retaliation of the environment against the disrespect accorded to it by humans over the past few decades. James Lovelock explains,

if we continue to fool around with the atmosphere, and continue to increase global warming by the unreasonable burning of fossil fuels, then Gaia will react, and storms and other catastrophic climatic events with consequences somewhat comparable to those of the recent tsunami…will result and will occur more and more frequently as time passes.[1]

The tsunami in the Indian Ocean is an example of a natural environmental disaster that caused insurmountable devastation to the environment and human settlements. There are also human-induced disasters that affect the environment, such as the Exxon Valdez oil spill and the Bhopal gas disaster in India. Other disasters or crises, which at the surface do not pose a direct threat to the environment, should also be noted as certain environmental protection may be suspended or compromised in favour of other objectives.

THE ROLE OF THE LAW

The law, and legislation in particular, has some role to play in the preparation, prevention, and mitigation of disasters. In the case of a natural disaster, the role of law has traditionally been more reactive than proactive. However, it has been acknowledged that even in the case of such events, the law does have a role to play in the minimization of risk, guaranteeing the mitigation of events to come. The risk of cyclones, hurricanes, and earthquakes has been a long-standing concern of a lot of building legislation that often reflects the possibility of such events occurring, as structures are built to withstand certain conditions.

It has been argued that the law does not take the possibility of great natural disasters seriously enough. Posner stresses that in the face of climate change, there is the potential

[1] Official site of Professor James Lovelock, 'About Tsunamis, GAIA and Ecology' http://www.ecolo.org/lovelock/gaia_tsunamis-article-01_05.htm, last visited on 22 June 2007.

for absolute catastrophe that is not yet reflected in the law. Measures such as the imposition of taxes on CO_2 should be further employed to decrease the acceleration of climate change and contribute to the overall reduction of risk.[2] The upholding of state environmental legislation may also demand that states have adequate legislation to address disasters to the extent that it implements the principle of sustainable development. It has long been recognized that sustainable development has a role to play in the mitigation of natural disasters and that the very occurrence of natural disasters can conversely threaten sustainability.

Since the tsunami in the Indian Ocean, there has been an emphasis on the need for disaster preparation. There is a 'need not only to respond effectively to disasters but also to prepare for, and protect communities from, disasters that occur'.[3] This has signalled an inclination towards a 'front end' disaster policy, which is largely directed at disaster preparation, prevention, and mitigation[4] as opposed to the purely responsive brands of policies.

Quite evidently, however, the mere occurrence of disasters means that there is still an active role for the law to play in responding to disasters. Just how comprehensive disaster response regimes need to be is debatable. They need to be complex enough to address all aspects of disaster management and provide an adequate response, but liberal enough to permit workability in the face of a crisis.[5] Due to the unique nature of any one disaster and the characteristics of the area it affects, some degree of discretion is usually permitted by disaster management authorities who are responsible for coordinating the response. Furthermore, disaster legislation should constantly be reviewed to take into account new risks and developments in geographical regions. Building codes may now be out of date or ill suited to particular areas. For example, houses may have been built to withstand only a certain type of a natural disaster, that is, an earthquake or hurricane. The safety that was once guaranteed by compliance with these codes may be rendered illusory if the area is now at a higher risk of stronger disasters. Risk analysis should therefore be a constant process so that new and existing laws can reflect the real probability of the occurrence of natural disasters.

In India, the lack of a scientific disaster management plan hampers the rescue in many cases. Two major environmental disasters that India has responded to are the Bhopal gas tragedy and the Indian Ocean tsunami. Each of these events outlines the need for both proactive and reactive lawmaking in relation to holistic disaster management.

THE BHOPAL GAS TRAGEDY

On 13 December 1984, forty tonnes of highly toxic methyl isocynate (MIC) escaped from the plant of Union Carbide India (UCIL) at Bhopal. The number of people and animals killed were 3,828, and 2,544 respectively and as many as 30,000 people were injured. The Government of Madhya Pradesh set up the 'Bhopal Poisonous Gas Leakage Commission', presided by a sitting judge of the HC. Several claims were lodged before the American

---

[2] 'Book Note: The Days After Tomorrow', a review of Richard A. Posner, *Catastrophe: Risk and Response* (New York: Oxford University Press) (2004), 118 Harv. L. Rev. 1342 2004–5, p. 1342.

[3] David P. Fidler, 'Disaster Relief and Governance After the Indian Ocean Tsunami: What Role for International Law?' (2005), *Melbourne Journal of International Law*, vol. 16, available at < http://www.austlii.edu.au//cgi-bin/disp.pl/au/journals/MelbJIL/2005/16.html?query=disaster%20and%20law> (inserted from En 18).

[4] Ibid.

[5] Beverley Adam and Alison Smith, 'Coping with a crisis,' *New Law Journal* (2002), 152 (7054).

courts. To ensure payment of claims, the Government of India enacted the Bhopal Gas Leak Disaster (Processing of Claims) Act, 1985. It conferred an exclusive right to the government to represent all claimants both within and outside India. The Government of India sued the UCIL in the USA in Keenan's court. The American court rejected the claim on the basis of *forum non conveniens*, declaring that the proper forum is the Indian court.[6] This order was upheld by the Court of Appeals and subsequently, the American Supreme Court refused to interfere with the order.[7]

In the meanwhile, the Government of India and several individuals filed suits claiming compensation before the District Court (DC). The DC awarded interim damages that were reduced by the Madhya Pradesh High Court to Rs 250 crores (US $192 million). Challenging the same, the UCIL has approached Supreme Court of India. While the matter was pending, the Bhopal Gas Peedit Mahila Udyog Sangathan has moved the Supreme Court for interim relief. The Supreme Court directed the Principal Secretary, Gas Relief Department of the Government of Madhya Pradesh to implement the scheme framed by him to speed up verifications, selection of eligible beneficiaries, and other relief measures.

UCIL officials challenged the validity of the criminal cases filed against them before the Supreme Court. Thereafter, on the basis of settlement, the Supreme Court quashed the entire criminal proceedings and settled the compensation at US $470 million.

Meanwhile, the Supreme Court has upheld the validity of the Bhopal Gas Leak Disaster (Processing of Claims) Act, 1985, and held that it is valid and not violative of Article 14 of the Constitution of India, which guarantees equality before the law.

This settlement of the claim and the quashing of criminal proceedings has been criticized by many. The Supreme Court reviewed the judgement, and the criminal proceedings were revived.[8] The Magistrate Court declared the two company officials as proclaimed offenders and decided to attach the share of UCIL. The company formed a trust and diverted its funds. But the magistrate refused to accept the said trust and attached 1,65,84,750 shares that had originally been endowed upon the said trust by UCIL. UCIL simultaneously deposited an amount of US $420 million along with a demand draft of Rs 68.99 crores in the Supreme Court. Thereafter, an application was moved before the Supreme Court by Ian Percival, the sole trustee, for the modification of the above interim order. The Supreme Court modified it and directed the trust to deliver the said shareholdings, comprising 1,65,84,750 shares of UCIL originally held by the UCC and now endowed to the 'Bhopal Gas Hospital Trust', for sale in the international share market. The said sale proceeds, after deducting the reasonable expenses incurred for such sale such as commission, stamp duty, and other incidental costs, a sum of Rs 46.2 cores, along with Rs 7.5 crores to be contributed by the UCIL for purposes of the hospital project, and certain directions were issued about how the remaining amount was to be utilized.

For the disbursement of the amount, the Madhya Pradesh Government identified the victims, took steps, and filed a report. Thereafter, orders were passed by the Supreme Court transferring the fund in the name of

---

[6] *Sajida Bano v. Union Carbide Corporation*, 99 Civ 11329 (JFK).
[7] Ibid.

[8] *Union Carbide Corporation v. Union of India*, 1995 (4) SCC Supp 59: 1994 SCALE (1) 811.

the Welfare Commissioner, after keeping the amount for three-and-a-half years. The Supreme Court cautioned that no part of this fund shall be withdrawn or utilized to meet any administrative expenses or diverted for any other purpose, other than payment to or applied in satisfaction of the claims of the victims towards compensation determined according to law. Directions were also issued to release funds for the completion of construction by the state government.

As the time has lapsed, several claim applications remained unrepresented. It was dismissed for default. But the Supreme Court, taking into consideration the peculiar circumstances of the case, allowed the restoration of such applications.

In 1992, the Government of India announced a scheme of interim relief of Rs 200 per month to the victims, subject to a maximum of Rs 5 lakhs per month beginning from 1 April 1990. At the instance of the Bhopal Gas Peedith Mahila Udyog Sanghathan, the Supreme Court appointed a Monitoring Committee of five members and a seven-member Advisory Committee for the medical rehabilitation of victims. For providing medical relief to the victims, more equipment is necessary. To purchase the same, orders have been issued by the Supreme Court from time to time.

The victims of the Bhopal crisis are still awaiting justice and with the present judicial system, the court has not been able to disburse even the compensation to them.

The Bhopal Gas Tragedy has opened the eyes of the Central Government and prompted the creation of the Chemical Accidents (Emergency Planning, Preparedness and

Response) Rules, 1996,[9] which were framed by invoking the powers under Sections 6, 8, and 25 of the Environment (Protection) Act, 1986. These Rules give a list of hazardous chemicals that are the main cause of chemical accidents. The Central Government must constitute a Central Crisis Group and Crisis Alert System for the management of chemical accidents. The state governments are also empowered to constitute similar State Crisis Groups and District and Local Crisis Groups. The Major Accident Hazard installations in the industrial pockets in the district shall aid, assist, and facilitate the functioning of the District Crisis Group. It is the duty of the Central Crisis Group to provide information on request regarding chemical accident prevention, preparedness, and mitigation in the country.

Only upon the effective coordination and functioning of these groups will the public benefit from the legislation in the event of a chemical crisis.

The Indian Ocean Tsunami

There is an old saying about the Pacific Islands: 'You must be unlucky to die without tsunami; you must be even more unlucky to die seeing one'.

On 26 December 2004, enormous tidal waves, propagated by the world's most powerful earthquake, struck India at 7.00 AM Indian Standard Time (IST). The Richter scale recorded a magnitude of nine, which was the most powerful in forty years. The tsunami, which had its origin near the Sumatra Island of Indonesia, reached the north-east maritime state of India, that is, Tamil Nadu. The sea level rise ended at the west coast (Kerala) at 2.00 PM. The lack of proper crisis management and warning system aggravated the calamity, resulting in the loss of 10,749 lives in India. The shock of the tsunami has adversely affected many, both physically and

[9] Chemical Accidents (Emergency Planning, Preparedness and Response) Rules, 1996 (came into force with effect from 2 August 1996).

psychologically. They cannot sleep peacefully at night. The sound of waves has now become a nightmare.

A number of rehabilitation measures were taken. Relief camps were set up in many places where the waves hit, and ex-gratia money was sanctioned and distributed amongst the affected immediately. The Kerala Legal Services Authority had organized a Lok Adalat (a legal aid camp) to provide legal help in securing ration cards, degree certificates, title deeds of properties, and other important documents lost in the tsunami. The government decided to set up a disaster management and warning system. NGOs offered substantial monetary help in rebuilding houses in the adversely affected areas. To overcome the trauma of the affected and the aversion on fish products, the important personalities of the area have conducted gatherings and made people believe that a tsunami like the one that happened is an isolated instance.

Catastrophic events like tsunamis cannot be avoided. But the strict implementation of the laws intended to protect the coastal ecology could have saved the lives of many. The coastal area regulations in India prohibit construction within 500 metres, but in thickly populated states, it is very difficult to implement such harsh laws. The people living at the seashore are traditional people who depend on marine resources for subsistence. They do not have the infrastructure to live a safe distance from the coast and transport their boat in a trailer to the sea as required. The result is that they were constrained to live within the prohibited distance and their lives and investments were taken away by the tsunami.

A number of steps for disaster management should be adopted to be better prepared for future tsunamis. Creating awareness among the people for the implementation of environmental laws like coastal protection regulations, which are intended not only to protect the environment but also to protect their life, is necessary. The maintenance and planting of mangroves and other suitable species of plants can maintain the coastal ecology and protect the coast in the natural way, providing some mitigation for the impact of large waves if they arise.

When the tsunami struck, the authorities had to search for safer places in the region to which they could relocate hundreds of families. An action plan was missing. The authorities were slow in assigning responsibilities to agencies at different levels. Disaster management continues to be a problem for the administrators, despite the National Informatics Centre (NIC) including all major places in the country for the implementation of the Geographical Information System (GIS) based emergency planning and responsive system. Even the support of the coast guard was sought for, only after hours.

The advanced technology available has made it possible to make warnings and predictions. The International Tsunami Warning System[10] collects data from all stations all round the Pacific basin. They will be able to pinpoint the epicentre and volcanic eruptions if tsunamis are generated, and predict their arrival times and amplitude at various shores by measuring the length and speed. If an earthquake measuring seven or more on the Richter scale occurs, it is likely to cause a tsunami.

Upon the sounding of a warning signal, it is advisable to put out to sea if your ship is docked, or head for a high place if you are on land. Experts also suggest that if a big quake hits, it is wise to wait for the ground to stop shaking and then run. The tsunami warning signs, 'Tsunami Hazard Zone—In case of

[10] Established at Ewa Beach, near Honolulu, Hawaii.

earthquake, go to high ground or inland'. The amount of time it takes to strike the coast depends on the distance from the fault. If the quake is very near to coast, it is likely to strike the coast even before the sounding of the siren.

The Public Liability Insurance Act, 1991

The increase in hazardous industries and the Bhopal Gas Tragedy has opened the eyes of the legislature. Such accidents lead to death and injury to human beings and damage properties. The worst affected are the persons living below the poverty line. Very often, the majority of the people suffer due to delayed disbursal of relief and compensation. Though the persons working in the industry are protected by labour welfare laws, the public are not assured of any relief except through local legal processes. Some such industrial unit may not have the financial resources to provide even the minimum relief.

In order to provide for mandatory public liability insurance for such installations handling hazardous substances to provide minimum relief to the victims, the Indian legislature has enacted the Public Liability Insurance Act, 1991.[11]

As per this Act, the industrialists handling hazardous substances are to pay specified amounts to the victims as interim relief based on the no fault liability principle.[12] It is mandatory for every industry handling hazardous substances to take out insurance policies under this law.[13]

But the government finds it difficult to implement the same due to the disagreement of the insurance companies. Therefore, the Act was amended in 1992 by which the liability of the insurance company was limited to the amount of the insurance policy, though the owner's liability shall continue to be unlimited under the Act. It is also proposed that a Environmental Relief Fund be created with the additional funds collected from the industries, and the same will be used to meet the requirement of immediate relief to the victims.[14]

The amended Act also prevents the transfer of property by the owner in case he intended to do so for evading his liability to pay compensation. The victim has to make an application for claim or relief to the Collector of the district where the accident has occurred.[15] On receipt of the said application, and after hearing both the parties and conducting an enquiry the collector will make an award determining the relief that appears to be just and the persons entitled to get it. The said award has to be passed within three months from the date of receipt of the application.[16]

The intention of the legislature seems to be very honest. But practical problems arise in Indian conditions. Even after two decades, the compensation to the Bhopal victims has not be given. Though the PLI Act contemplates the passing of an award within three months, the law does not cast any obligation on the said authority to pass award thereby creating a lack of accountability.

Crisis Management—the Law

The Bhopal Gas Tragedy has also opened the eyes of the Central Government and the result is the Chemical Accidents (Emergency Planning, Preparedness and Response) Rules, 1996,[17] which were framed by invoking the

---

[11] Act No. 6 of 1991, dated 22 January 1991.
[12] Public Liability Insurance Act, 1991, Section 3.
[13] Ibid., Section 4.
[14] Amendment Act 11 of 1992, Section 7A.
[15] Supra note 12, Section 6.
[16] Ibid., Section 7 (7).
[17] Came into force with effect from 2 August 1996.

powers under Sections 6, 8, and 25 of the Environment (Protection) Act, 1986. These Rules gives a list of hazardous chemicals that are the main cause of chemical accidents. The Central Government has to constitute a Central Crisis Group and Crisis Alert System for the management of chemical accidents. The state governments are also empowered to constitute similar State Crisis Group, District and Local Crisis Group. The Major Accident Hazard installations in the industrial pockets in the district shall aid, assist, and facilitate functioning of the District Crisis Group. It is the duty of the Central Crisis Group to provide information on request regarding chemical accident prevention, preparedness, and mitigation in the country.

Only on the effective functioning of these groups will the public benefit. The law should not only be enacted but also be made functional.

INTERNATIONAL JURISDICTION

In the international sphere, there are a number of actors, both state and non-state, which have given assistance in the event of disasters. Natural disasters, in particular, symbolize our vulnerability as the human race. Emmerich de Vattel has written that

To give assistance in such extreme necessity…is so essentially conformable to humanity, that the duty is seldom neglected by any nation that has received the slightest polish of civilization.[18]

Consequently, where a large disaster or crisis takes place, the dispatch of assistance is rarely confined to the capacities of the state in which it has occurred.

Historically, international law has provided a small degree of assistance in disaster relief. In 1927, a convention and statute establishing an International Relief Union ('IRU Treaty') created an intergovernmental organization that was mandated to provide both proactive and reactive assistance in disaster management.[19] It also gave significant powers to the league of Red Cross societies to participate in the giving of aid. The IRU was dissolved in 1968, its demise partly due to a lack of financial means to pursue its objectives.[20] The Red Cross is still an active provider of humanitarian and disaster relief assistance.

International law is active in providing guidelines for ships that aim to prevent and mitigate marine disasters. There are various conventions that address compensation and liability in the event of an oil spill, for example, the International Convention on Civil Liability for Oil Pollution Damage, 1969 (CLC 1969)[21] and its Protocols[22] and the International Convention on the Establishment of an International Fund for Compensation for Oil Pollution Damage, 1971 (FUND 1971)[23] and its protocols.[24]

---

[18] Emmerich de Vattel, *The Law of Nations; or, Principles of the Law of Nature, Applied to the Conduct and Affairs of Nations and Sovereigns*, (Charles G. Fenwick trans, 1916 ed.) bk II, ch I, Section 5 [trans of: Emmerich de Vattel, *Le Droit des Gens, ou Principes de la loi Naturelle, Appliqués à la Conduite et aux Affaires des Nations et des Souverains*, Adamant Media Corporation, first published 1758; in supra note 3.

[19] Supra note 3.

[20] Ibid.

[21] Entered into force 19 June 1975, 973 UNTS 3.

[22] Protocol (of 1976) to the International Convention on Civil Liability for Oil Pollution Damage, 1969 (CLC PROT 1976), entered into force 8 April 1981,1225 UNTS 356; Protocol of 1984 to amend the International Convention on Civil Liability for Oil Pollution Damage, 1969 (CLC PROT 1984), adopted 25 May 1984, 23 ILM 177; Protocol of 1992 to amend the International Convention on Civil Liability for Oil Pollution Damage, 1969 (CLC PROT 1992), entered into force 30 May 1996, UKTS 86 (1996).

[23] Entered into force 16 October 1978, 1110 UNTS 57.

[24] Eg., Protocol to the International Convention on the Establishment of an International Fund for

The UNCLOS[25] encompasses both proactive and reactive disaster management. Articles 194(3)(b) and 211(1) mandate that measures be taken by ships to reduce the possibility of accidents. Article 199 provides for joint action or cooperation between states in the event of a marine emergency. Article 221 permits states to take action beyond their territorial waters in the event of a maritime casualty. This recognizes the nature of marine pollution, as such action is preventive and aims to limit the movement of the pollution into the territorial waters of the state. UNCLOS is generally accepted as customary international law.

The International Convention Relating to Intervention on the High Seas in Cases of Oil Pollution Casualties provides that states may take

such measures on the high seas as may be necessary to prevent, mitigate, or eliminate grave and imminent danger to their coastline or related interests from pollution or threat of pollution of the sea by oil, following upon a maritime casualty ... which may reasonably be expected to result in major harmful consequences.[26]

Since 1973, the adoption of a Protocol has signified a wider application of the provision, as it not only applies to oil but to other substances also.[27]

Wars or conflicts are crises in themselves, yet they provide further opportunities for environmental crises. In times of international or non-international armed conflict, international humanitarian law and the Geneva Convention attempt to provide some form of environmental protection. For example, in the case of international conflicts, Additional Protocol One provides that

Care shall be taken in warfare to protect the natural environment against widespread, long-term and severe damage. This protection includes a prohibition of the use of methods or means of warfare which are intended or may be expected to cause such damage to the natural environment and thereby to prejudice the health or survival of the population.[28]

Furthermore, as an object indispensable to human survival, water and food sources can also attract a high level of protection under Article 54 of the Protocol.

Although there are some international laws in relation to environmental disasters, some claim that 'international policy on natural disasters has not depended on international legal instruments'.[29] When the volume of humanitarian law applicable to wartime disaster is juxtaposed against the amount of attention given to peacetime disasters, the latter appears in neglect according to Fidler, who cites the International Federation of Red Cross and Red Crescent Societies.[30] Hence, there is a scarcity in international legal protections

---

Compensation for Oil Pollution Damage, 1971 (FUND PROT 1976), entered into force 22 November 1994, UKTS 28 (1996); for additional protocols see IMO website, 'Liability and compensation conventions', <http://www.imo.org/InfoResource/mainframe.asp?topic_id=831#01>

[25] United Nations Law of the Sea Convention, entered into force 16 November 1994, 1833 UNTS 3.

[26] International Convention for the Prevention of Pollution of the Sea by Oil, 1954, as amended (OILPOL) 1954, entered into force 26 July 1958, 327 UNTS 3 (E/F) Art 1.

[27] Protocol relating to Intervention on the High Seas in

Cases of Pollution by Substances other than Oil, 1973, as amended ([PROT (amended) 1973] entered into force 30 March 1983, 1313 UNTS 3 (E/F/R/S).

[28] Protocol Additional to the Geneva Conventions of 12 August 1949, and relating to the Protection of Victims of International Armed Conflicts (Protocol I), 8 June 1977, Article 55.

[29] Supra note 3.

[30] International Federation, World Disasters Report 2000 (2000) 157, 14–149 in Supra note 3.

in the event of a natural environmental disaster. Such disasters can be contrasted to wars, epidemics, and accidents which have frequently been addressed using international law. Fidler attributes this skew to the fact that the aforementioned events are readily perceived as having a significant impact on the material interests of the state in international relations. Perhaps the randomness of natural disasters places them in a different stead, their episodic character being more likely to attract some kind of humanitarian assistance.[31]

Despite the lack of international law in the field, NGOs and INGOs have been extremely active in responding to natural disasters. Notably, the Australian government website for emergency management identifies the active role played by NGOs such as the Red Cross in disaster mitigation and recovery.[32] The United States Disaster Mitigation Act, 2000[33] grants the Red Cross membership amongst federal agencies and state and local government organizations in the taskforce for disaster management.[34] The launch of the International Disaster Response Law (IDRL) Project in November 2001[35] is likely to increase the clout that the Red Cross has in this field as a leading organization in disaster response.

UNEP is also active in promoting disaster mitigation strategies. In particular, the International Environmental Technology Centre positions disaster management as one of its focal areas. Its approach is founded on the disaster cycle: prevention, mitigation, preparedness, response, and recovery or rehabilitation. Disaster prevention is at the forefront and environmental management is employed to reduce the potential for natural disasters and mitigate their impact.[36]

Fidler is confident that the response generated from NGOs and INGOs in the wake of the tsunami in the Indian Ocean demonstrates that these actors have not been handicapped by the scarcity of international law in the field. However, he does not propose that international law would be of no use, and outlines a number of benefits in placing disaster management within an international legal framework. The International Federation is adamant that international law is required to better assist victims of natural disasters.[37] According to Fidler, if this is to occur, states need to change the way they perceive natural disasters. Instead of viewing disasters as

short-lived crises that are handled as humanitarian matters, part of the 'low politics' of international relations they must adopt a policy in which natural disasters connect directly to more serious political interests that states possess.[38]

In order to make this transition, natural disasters must be taken more seriously and the effect they have on the concrete interests of the state, life, and the environment must

[31] Ibid.

[32] Australian Government, Attorney General's Department: Emergency Management Australia, http://www.ema.gov.au/ema/emaInternet.nsf/AllDocs/RWP8068B438E9360F4FCA256C8700361BAF?OpenDocument, (last visited 22 June 2007).

[33] (DMA 2000) (PL 106-390).

[34] Robert T. Stafford Disaster Relief and Emergency Assistance Act (42 USC 5141 et seq.), Section 204(c), as amended by the Disaster Mitigation Act of 2000 (DMA 2000) (PL 106–390), Section 104.

[35] See International Federation of Red Cross and Red Crescent Societies, 'International Disaster Response Laws, Rules and Principles programme (IDRL)', http://www.ifrc.org/what/disasters/IDRL/index.asp (last visited 22 June 2007).

[36] United Nations Environment Programme: Division of Technology, Industry and Economics, 'Disaster Management', <http://www.unep.or.jp/ietc/dm/index.asp> (last visited 22 June 2007).

[37] International Federation, World Disasters Report 2000 (2000) 157 in supra note 3.

[38] Ibid.

be recognized. One need only peruse the figures regarding economic loss from recent environmental catastrophes to realize that disaster management is in the state's best interests. Natural disasters, in fact, have long-term effects on infrastructure, health, and the environment.

Questions of sovereignty add another dimension to the argument over whether the volume and scope of international law on disaster response should be increased. The receipt of help often represents an encroachment on state sovereignty. Furthermore, the state offering the aid may harbour ulterior motives, using their position as a form of political leverage.[39] However, on an ethical basis one should consider whether states should be able to refuse aid in the face of natural disasters where humans and/or the environment are suffering?[40] This raises further questions regarding human rights, that is, do disaster victims have a human right to assistance?[41] Although debatable, it is difficult to deny that international law could clarify the roles of both state and non-state actors in the event of natural disasters, and provide some certainty as to the rights of human beings and the environment.

Australia

Australia experiences a variety of natural disasters and extreme environmental events. The Ash Wednesday bushfires of 1983 are forever etched in the minds of many, as one of the worst fires the nation has experienced. Bushfires and heat waves are common, as Australian summers reach very high temperatures and the land is characteristically dry. Typically, the tropical north experiences a vast array of natural disasters such as cyclones, storms, and floods. However, the increase in type and occurrence of natural disasters has emerged in other parts of Australia. In the beginning of June 2007, regions of the state of New South Wales on the east coast of Australia experienced a series of storms of a severity that was quite unusual for the area. Australian insurance group Suncorp expected the damage from the disaster, which killed nine people,[42] to reach a staggering $160 million AU$ in claims.[43]

The responsibility of disaster management primarily rests with the state or territory governments, as guaranteed by the Constitution, which grants the states with jurisdiction over the protection of life and property. States may, however, call on the Federal government for funding in the event of a natural disaster that exceeds their own resources and capabilities. Each state or territory has its own legislation in relation to natural disasters. South Australia has the State Disaster Act, 1980 (amended 1995),[44] New South Wales has the State Emergency and Rescue Management Act, 1989,[45] and Tasmania has the Emergency Services Act, 1976.[46] Essentially, each of the Acts provide for a state disaster committee, management plan, and emergency service.

---

39 Ibid.
40 Ibid.
41 Ibid.

42 Count as of 19 June 2007 in ABC News, 'Rain, winds batter NSW coast' 19 June 2007, <http://abc.net.au/news/stories/2007/06/19/1956142.htm>, (last visited 2 June 2007).
43 ABC News '$160m storm damage bill hits Suncorp', 20 June 2007, http://www.abc.net.au/news/stories/2007/06/20/1957046.htm (last visited 22 June 2007).
44 State Disaster Act, 1980 (amended 1995) (South Australia).
45 State Emergency and Rescue Management Act, 1989 (New South Wales).
46 Emergency Services Act, 1976 (Tasmania).

The Queensland Disaster Management Act, 2003[47] is a useful example of state disaster legislation in Australia. This Act replaced the State Counter-Disaster Organization Act,[48] and one of its main features is the replacement of the term 'state of disaster' with 'disaster situation', widening the scope of disaster legislation as it may be applied to part of the state without necessitating a total state of disaster. 'Disaster' is defined as a 'serious disruption in a community, caused by the impact of an event that requires a significant coordinated response by the state and other entities'[49] in order to achieve recovery. Both damage to the environment and environmental hazards or natural disasters fall within the definition of disaster. The term 'serious disruption' expressly includes 'widespread or severe damage to the environment'.[50] The Act applies to a wide variety of environmental events, where 'event' includes 'a cyclone, earthquake, flood, storm, storm tide, tornado, tsunami, volcanic eruption, or other natural happening'.[51] Human-induced or non-natural events that may harm the environment or human life such as 'an explosion or fire, a chemical, fuel, or oil spill, or a gas leak' are also covered.[52]

The main objectives of the Act are to help communities mitigate the potential adverse effects of an event, prepare for the management of such effects, and respond to and recover from a disaster or emergency situation.[53] It also aims to

...(b) provide for effective disaster management for the state, (c) [and] to establish a framework for the management of the state Emergency service and service units to ensure the effective performance of their functions.[54]

The District Disaster Coordinator has the power to declare a disaster situation where a disaster has happened or is likely to happen and it is necessary for the officer to exercise their powers to prevent or minimize loss to human life or damage to the environment.[55] The Act establishes a hierarchy of executive bodies that exercise the various functions and powers in pursuit of the objectives of the Act.

The occurrence of bushfires in Australia is a natural phenomenon, although they are often catalysed by humans, particularly by the dropping of cigarette buts. In March 2006, Australian Standards released a recommendation on fire-safe cigarettes, which differ from ordinary cigarettes due to their self-extinguishing properties.[56] Legislation has already been adopted by many of the states of the USA, including New York, which require cigarettes that are manufactured or sold to be fire-safe. The Australian Standards are thought to be a positive step towards the adoption of legislation that mandates all cigarettes in Australia to be self-extinguishing. It has been proposed that the requirement be incorporated into existing trade practices legislation, which is applicable to the whole of Australia.[57]

European Union

The EU has a regional agreement that addresses natural disasters. The governing

---

[47] Disaster Management Act, 2003 (Queensland).

[48] State Counter-Disaster Organisation Act 1975 (Queensland).

[49] Supra note 47, Section 13(1).

[50] Ibid., Section 13(2)(c).

[51] Ibid., Section 16(1)(a).

[52] Ibid., Section 16(1)(b).

[53] Ibid., Section 3(a).

[54] Ibid., Section 3(b)-(c).

[55] Ibid., Section 64.

[56] Standard for Reduced Fire Risk Cigarettes (RFR) AS4830–2007, titled 'Determination of the extinction propensity of cigarettes' (released 9 March 2007).

[57] Trade Practices Act, 1975 (Cth).

legislation is the Community Mechanism for Civil Protection, which was established by the Council Decision 23 October 2001.[58] Twenty-seven EU states and three other states are parties to the Mechanism, which 'supports and facilitates the mobilization of vital civil protection assistance for the immediate needs of disaster-stricken countries'.[59] It can be utilized in response to disasters that occur within member states or non-member states. The assistance derived from the Mechanism differs from humanitarian assistance as it is usually for a shorter duration and is directed at the immediate aftermath of the event.

Subsidiarity is an essential principle of the Mechanism, as participating states pool their resources, and these can be drawn upon by an affected state in the event of an emergency. The sharing of resources ensures that an adequate and adapted response may follow in the event of a disaster. There is the Monitoring and Information Centre (MIC), which gives practical efficacy to the principle of subsidiarity. The MIC has been described as 'one-stop-shop' for civil protection.[60] It coordinates assistance, acts as an information clearing house, and facilitates communication between the various bodies that may be involved in aid. The MIC provides the practical basis for the functioning of the Mechanism. It is the source of information and calling point for the activation of resources in the event of a disaster.

Training also forms part of the tool kit utilized by the Mechanism. There are three elements to the training programme, which include training courses, simulation exercises which act as field tests for the operation of the mechanism in a disaster situation, and an exchange of experts that involves the placement of an expert from one state under the administration of another participating state in order to better understand different approaches.

In April 2005, the Commission to the Council, the European Parliament, The European Economic and Social Committee and the Committee of the Regions, at the direction of the Council and Parliament, reassessed civil protection laws directed at disaster response and management, partly due to the tsunami in the Indian Ocean that made apparent a number of deficiencies in the current scheme. After the tsunami, the European Parliament identified the need for:

the creation of a pool of specialised civilian civil protection units, with appropriate material, which should undertake joint training and be available in the event of natural, humanitarian or environmental disasters, or those associated with industrial risks, within the Union or in the rest of the world.[61]

---

[58] EUROPA, 'Council decision of 23 October 2001: establishing a Community mechanism to facilitate reinforced cooperation in civil protection assistance interventions', (2001/792/EC, Euratom), available at <http://eur-lex.europa.eu/pri/en/oj/dat/2001/l_297/l_29720011115en00070011.pdf >

[59] Commission of the European Communities, 'Communication from the Commission to the Council, the European Parliament, the European Economic and Social Committee and the Committee of the Regions: Improving the Community Civil Protection Mechanism', COM (2005) 137, p. 2 available at http://ec.europa.eu/environment/civil/pdfdocs/com_2005_137_en.pdf (hereinafter Improving the Community Civil Protection Mechanism).

[60] EUROPA, 'The Community Mechanism for Civil Protection' <http://ec.europa.eu/environment/civil/prote/mechanism.htm>

[61] European Parliament Resolution on the recent tsunami disaster in the Indian Ocean, 13 January 2005; in Improving the Community Civil Protection Mechanism, 3. (this is a sub-topic of a document, available at http://ec.europa.eu/environment/civil/pdfdocs/com_2005_137_en.pdf).

The Communication[62] identifies a number of improvements to be made to the mechanism and proposes the adoption of a Rapid Response and Preparedness Instrument for major emergencies, but suggests changes and additions to the current mechanism as opposed to the creation of a new mechanism altogether.

A follow-up from the communication was the recasting of Council Decision in January 2006, which recasts the text of the 2001 decision, in order to renew the objectives of the mechanism. The recast technique enables the desired provisions of the original instrument to be merged with the new amendments. The changes were intended to strengthen the mechanism and enable additional community interventions while bettering the implementation of the subsidiarity principle. It proposed increased financial and technical community support for the transport of civil protection assistance, which is to be achieved by the sharing of transport resources and availability of community funding where national transport within a particular state is inadequate to mobilize resources.[63] This was to be contrasted to the original mechanism, which relied on states to effectively utilize their own national transport systems, despite their respective capacities. Another feature is increased rapid reaction capability by member states. This is to be achieved by state identification of military resources available in responding to a disaster, and the development of civil protection modules that are like pre-arranged bundles of civil protection

assistance, designed to identify resources made available by each member state in the event of an emergency. The recast also calls on the community to create logistical units for the purposes of complementing national intervention teams. These units are to act as a safety net[64] in the event that states are unable to effectively respond.

Another field in which the mechanism needed improvement was the issuance of early warnings. Consequently, the recast foresees the upgradation of existing early warning systems and better coordination between the mechanisms that exist. Finally, the coordination of interventions in third countries is given consideration by the recast. Better awareness of the various roles and functions of bodies providing humanitarian assistance and community protection measures is reflected in the recast. It also tightens the relationship between the Presidency and the Commission, enabling the Presidency to call on the Commission to coordinate political measures. The Commission can thus be utilized as a neutral actor, overcoming political boundaries that may exist between various states.

In the future, civil protection may also feature in the proposed European Constitution. The Constitution will clarify that civil protection falls within the jurisdiction of the Union, Article I-17 providing that 'the Union shall have competence to carry out supporting, coordinating, or complementary action'[65] with respect to the subject. It will also reflect the current objective of civil protection laws, providing that 'the Union shall encourage cooperation between Member States in order to improve the effectiveness of systems for

[62] Communication from the Commission to the Council, The European Parliament, The European Economic and Social Committee of the Regions. Available at http://eur-lex.europa.eu/LexUriServ/LexUriServ.do?uri=CELEX:52005DCO137:EN:NOT (accessed on 26 August 2008).

[63] Recast of Council Decision (2001/792/EC) 27 January 2006, p. 8.

[64] Ibid., p. 10.

[65] The Future for European Civil Protection, <http://ec.europa.eu/environment/civil/prote/perspectives_en.htm>

preventing and protecting against natural or man-made disasters' in Article III-284.

The Civil Protection Mechanism has been utilized in a number of environmental emergencies.

In August 2006, extreme forest fires swept across Galicia in Spain, affecting some 80,000 hectares. Spain utilized the Civil Protection Mechanism, and via the MIC, it received assistance from Italy and France, who provided aircrafts, and Portugal, who provided a relief task force consisting of vehicles and forestfire fighters. With the help of these measures and changing weather conditions, the fire was eventually tamed two weeks after it had ignited.[66]

Bolivia also received assistance from the EU in 2007, when it experienced severe flooding, attributable to El Nino. Colder weather and water-borne diseases exacerbated the effects of the flooding, and Bolivia requested assistance from the MIC on 27 February 2007, approximately one month after the flooding began. An expert team was created to address mainly sanitation issues and water management, and it worked in conjunction with UNICEF on the matter.[67]

Indonesia

In Indonesia, the National Coordination Board for Disaster Management (BAKORNAS PB) manages planning and response to natural disasters.[68]

On 27 May 2006, Indonesia experienced an environmental catastrophe when a well in a gas exploration venture leaked, which then disgorged a river of hot toxic mud that engulfed more than twelve square kilometres and displaced more than 10,000 people. The leak was also believed to be responsible for an explosion in a gas pipeline that killed thirteen people.[69] The blame was largely placed on the Australian company Santos, which held an 18 per cent interest in the venture, and on an Indonesian company, Lapindo Brantas, which is indirectly controlled by PT Energi Mega Persada Tbk. Investigations revealed that a metal casing that would have prevented the leak was not properly fitted.

One year on from the disaster, mud was still flowing at a rate of 148,000 cubic metres per day, despite the government's efforts to block the outlet crater using a giant concrete ball.[70] The devastation caused to the environment and people was huge. Many villages were more than one metre deep in mud and people experienced health problems such as breathing difficulties, sore throats, diarrhoea, nausea, and even burns to the legs. Water sources have been contaminated and paddy fields and vegetation have been suffocated and destroyed. Environmental groups such as Greenpeace also fear that the mud represents a significant risk to the marine and water ecosystems as it finds its way into rivers and water outlets both naturally and by human intervention.[71]

[66] Civil Protection, 'Spain: Forest Fires', http://ec.europa.eu/environment/civil/forestfires_es_2006.htm

[67] Bolivia Floods 2007, http://ec.europa.eu/environment/civil/bolivia2007.htm

[68] Bakornas PB, http://www.bakornaspbp.go.id/new/, last visited 22 June 2007.

[69] Reuters Foundation, 'Indonesia Energi wants partners to share mud flow costs' 1 February 2007, http://www.reliefweb.int/rw/rwb.nsf/db900SID/KHII-6XZ9SA?OpenDocument

[70] Reuters Foundation, 'Indonesian Mudflow victims pray for relief', 29 May 2007, http://www.reliefweb.int/rw/RWB.NSF/db900SID/JBRN-73NDH8?OpenDocument&rc=3&emid=AC-2006-000170-IDN

[71] Greenpeace South East Asia, 'Mudflow slipping Beyond Control', http://www.greenpeace.org/seasia/en/press/releases/mudflow-slipping-beyond-contro, last visited 22 June 2007.

Not much has been effectual in containing the disaster. The Indonesian President has ordered Lapindo Brantas to pay $434.8 million in costs to the victims and recovery associated with the disaster.[72] A negligence suit was brought against Lapindo Brantas in America by another partner in the venture, but it did not reach court as the plaintiff's interest in the project was subsequently bought by another company.[73] Other measures to dispose of the mud have been implemented, such as diverting the mudflow into the river Porong, which eventually flows into the sea. This poses even further risk to the environment as experts fear that mud sediment may eventually choke the river mouth, ultimately posing a risk of flooding to adjacent settlements.[74] Despite police investigations over the incident, no one had been prosecuted as of May 2007.

Disasters such as this and the Bhopal tragedy in India display the difficulty experienced in prosecuting foreign defendants who cause environmental disasters. A greater body of international law could possibly address this dilemma, while access to information by the public can enable firms to be accountable to citizens and shareholders while operating abroad.

United States of America

There is a substantial body of American legislation directed at non-natural and natural disasters. Rehabilitation of the environment is a feature of much legislation that deals with disaster management.

The principal legislation to address disaster management in the USA is the Disaster Mitigation Act, 2000[75] amending

the Robert T. Stafford Disaster Relief and Emergency Assistance Act (The Act)…[emphasizing]…the need for state, tribal, and local entities to closely coordinate mitigation planning and implementation efforts.[76]

The Act clearly applies to natural disasters and acknowledges that 'natural disasters, including earthquakes, tsunamis, tornadoes, hurricanes, flooding, and wildfires, pose great danger to human life and to property throughout the United States.'[77] The Act provides for states to apply for federal grants under the National Pre-Disaster Mitigation Fund for the purposes of implementing 'pre-disaster hazard mitigation measures that are cost-effective'[78] and are directed at the creation of disaster mitigation partnerships, assessing the community's vulnerability to natural hazards and creating hazard mitigation plans and priorities.[79] Some of the measures proposed by the Act in relation to pre-disaster management include the formulation of multi-hazard advisory maps that show areas of potential disaster overlap for states that are often affected by natural disasters.[80]

[72] Reuters Foundation, 'Indonesian Mudflow victims pray for relief', 29 May 2007, supra note 69.

[73] Mark Forbes, The Age 'Mud Volcano Threatens Endless Ruin as Magical Solutions Fail', http://www.theage.com.au/news/world/mud-volcano-threatens-ruin/2007/05/25/1179601669797.html?page=3 (last visited 26 May 2007).

[74] Ibid.

[75] Supra note 33.

[76] US Department of Homeland Security, 'The Disaster Mitigation Act of 2000' <http://www.fema.gov/plan/mitplanning/DMA.shtm> last visited 22 June 2007. (site did not open)

[77] Supra note 33, Section 101(a)(1).

[78] Robert T. Stafford Disaster Relief and Emergency Assistance Act (42 USC 5141 et seq.), Section 203(e)(1)(A) as amended by the Disaster Mitigation Act of 2000 (DMA 2000) (PL 106-390), Section 102.

[79] Robert T. Stafford Disaster Relief and Emergency Assistance Act (42 USC 5141 et seq.), Section 203(e)(1)(B) as amended by the Disaster Mitigation Act of 2000 (DMA 2000) (PL 106–390), Section 102.

[80] Robert T. Stafford Disaster Relief and Emergency

To address disaster mitigation, the Act foresees the establishment of an Interagency Task Force 'for the purpose of coordinating the implementation of pre-disaster hazard mitigation programs administered by the Federal Government.'[81] Mitigation plans are to be devised that identify potential hazards and delineate ways to address them, including the practical mobilization of resources where appropriate.[82] In amending the original Act, there is also an attempt to streamline disaster management and reduce costs.[83]

In 1990, the Oil Pollution Act[84] was enacted to minimize the risk of oil spills and to provide for reactionary measures in the event of their occurrence. The Act established the Oil Spill Liability Trust Fund, which essentially derived a tax from the sale of oil to act as insurance in the event of an oil spill or disaster.[85] An Oil Pollution Research and Development Program was also established and membership was granted to various government departments that engaged in a collaborative effort to address oil pollution.[86] There are both proactive and reactive aspects to the research that develops

oil pollution technologies, ways to prevent oil pollution, and mechanisms to effectively clean up oil spills if they occur.

Section 2702 imposes liability on 'each responsible party for a vessel or a facility from which oil is discharged, or which poses the substantial threat of a discharge of oil, into or upon the navigable waters or adjoining shorelines or the exclusive economic zone.'[87] Such liability extends to removal costs incurred by those who clean up the spill and also to a number of heads of damage. Damages for injury and destruction or loss of natural resources are recoverable by the state as trustee of natural resources. The state may also recover damages for additional public services such as fire prevention, which it may be forced to provide in response to the spill. Notably, Indian tribes may also have rights to damages where they can act as the trustee for natural resources[88] or prove that subsistence use has been impaired by the spill.

The Emergency Planning and Community Right to Know Act[89] 'was designated to help local communities protect public health, safety, and the environment from chemical hazards.' It has also been hypothesized that the Act was a response to the Bhopal tragedy in India,[90] as it ensures that the public and various agencies have the information necessary to anticipate chemical accidents and provide an immediate response to them in the event that they occur. The Act imposes various reporting obligations[91] and emergency planning requirements on facilities

---

Assistance Act (42 USC 5141 et seq.), Section 203(k) as amended by the Disaster Mitigation Act of 2000 (DMA 2000) (PL 106–390), Section 102.

[81] Robert T. Stafford Disaster Relief and Emergency Assistance Act (42 USC 5141 et seq.) Section 204(a). as amended by The Disaster Mitigation Act of 2000 (DMA 2000) (PL 106–390) Section 103.

[82] Robert T. Stafford Disaster Relief and Emergency Assistance Act (42 USC 5141 et seq.), Section 322, as amended by the Disaster Mitigation Act of 2000 (DMA 2000) (PL 106–390), Section 103.

[83] Supra note 33, Title 2.

[84] 33 USC.

[85] United States EPA, 'Oil Pollution Act'. <http://www.epa.gov/Region5/defs/html/opa.htm> (last visited 22 Jun 2007).

[86] Oil Pollution Act, 1990, 33 USC 2702, 2761, Section 2761.

[87] Ibid., Section 2702(a).

[88] Ibid., Section 2706.

[89] Emergency Planning and Community Right-to-Know-Act, 1986, 42 USC 11001 et seq.

[90] Michael B. Gerrard, 'Emergency Exemptions from Environmental Laws after Disasters' *Natural Resources and Environment* (2006), volume 20, p. 10.

[91] Supra note 88, Sections 11021, 11022, 11023.

that hold hazardous substances in excess of the threshold amount as specified pursuant to Section 11002(a) of the Act. The public is empowered under the Act to compel such industries to provide information on hazardous substances under their control and default in reporting obligations are actionable by an ordinary citizen.[92] State Emergency Response Commissions are to be created under the Act and they are mandated to establish procedures for receiving and processing requests for information by the public. The Commissions then appoint local State Emergency Planning Committees, which consist of various government bodies, experts, and community groups, for each designated Emergency Planning District.[93] These committees are to formulate comprehensive emergency response plans that provide a wide range of mechanisms to address accidents involving hazardous substances.

Much attention has been drawn to exemptions from environmental laws in the USA, which are triggered off in times of emergency. This highlights that it is not only natural disasters that threaten the environment; other forms of public crises or disasters may also pose some risk. Davis et. al identify that in the aftermath of a natural disaster, certain environmental protections may be suspended.[94] For example, Section 7410(f) of the Clean Air Act[95] provides that upon the declaration of a national emergency by the President, emission restrictions on stationary fuel burning sources

can be excused. The aftermath of acts of God or war attract exemption under the Clean Water Act,[96] Section 1321(f)(1) and the Endangered Species Act[97] allows prohibited 'takes' after specified major disasters.[98] Davis et. al argue that the harm to the environment is exacerbated by these exemptions, particularly when combined with the lack of mandatory obligations on statutory environmental agencies in addressing environmental concerns after a disaster. They pose that a lot of environmental and even emergency legislation focuses too much on functions and discretionary powers, failing to propel concrete action when it is required.

As the incidence of natural disasters increases, legislative regimes that provide a holistic approach to disaster management need to be implemented. Environmental management should be a consideration in the preparation and response to non-natural disasters and existing environmental protection should only be suspended in extreme circumstances. Perhaps a greater emphasis on international law is needed to encourage appropriate state and local policies in this area, or maybe a bottom-up approach, which creates grassroot efforts to address disaster management, should be further encouraged. Whichever approach is taken, diaster management and environmental rehabilitation need to be taken seriously by the law, and we cannot afford to sit back and wait till a natural disaster strikes.

---

[92] Ibid., Section 11046.

[93] Ibid., Section 11001.

[94] Michael Davis et. al, 'Environmental Protection After a Disaster: A Right or a Privilege?', Natural Resources and Environment (2006), vol. 20, p. 15.

[95] 42 USC, Section 7410(f) in Davis et. al, above n. 84, 16.

[96] 33 USC, Section 1321(f)(1) in Davis et. al, above n. 84, 16.

[97] 16 USC, Section 1536(p) in Davis et. al, above n. 84, 17.

[98] Davis et. al, above n. 84, 17.

Bibliography

Adams, William Mark, 1992, *Environment and Sustainability in the Third World*, New York: Routledge, p. 146.

Agarwal, Anil and Sunitha Narain, 1997, *Dying Wisdom: State of India's Environment, A Citizen's Report*, India: Centre for Science and Environment.

Applegate, John S., 2005, 'The Story of Reserve Mining: Managing Scientific Uncertain in Environmental Regulation', in Richard Lazarus and Oliver Houck (eds), *Environmental Laws Stories*, US: Thomson and West.

al-Munemi, Fayd al-Qadir, 2002, iii, 30, extracted from the Doctoral Research Paper, *An Islamic Approach to the Environment* by Ibrahim Ozdemir.

Barton, Charmian, 1998, 'Precautionary Principle in Australia', *Harv. Env. L. Rev.*, vol. 22 (509), p. 549.

Batta, R.N. and J.P. Bhatti, 2004, 'Environmental Policy Challenges of the New Millennium', in S. Radha and Amar Singh Sankhyan, (eds), *Environmental Challenges of the 21st Century*, New Delhi: Deep & Deep Publications, p. 4.

Beder, Sharon, 1995, 'Strategic Law Suits Against Public Participation: Coming to a Controversy Near You', *Current Affairs Bulletin*, 72(3), 22 October/November.

Bell, Simon and Stuart Bell, 2003, *Environmental Law*, 2nd edn, New Delhi: Universal Law Publishing Co. Pvt Ltd.

Beverley, Adam and Alison Smith, 2002, 'Coping with a Crisis', *The New Law Journal*, 152 (7054).

Bianchi, Andrea, 1996, 'Harm to the Environment in Italian Practice: The Interaction of International Law and Domestic Law', in Peter Wetterstein (ed), *Harm to the Environment: The Right to Compensation and the Assessment of Damages*, Oxford: Clarendon Press, ch 7.

Bio-Medical Waste (Management and Handling) Rules, 1998: Its Inappropriateness in the Present Context and New Appropriate Management Options Developed by Cochin University of Science and Technology: India, Kerala. An unpublished discussion note.

Cameron, James, Jacob Werksman, and Peter Roderick, 1995, *Improving Compliance with International Environmental Law*, Law and Sustainable Development Series, London: Earthscan Ltd.

Cassar, Angela Z. and Carl E. Bruch, 2003, 'Transboundary Environmental Impact Assessment in International Watercourse Management', *NYUELJ*, 12 (169), p. 175.

Chandran, Sarath U., 2002, 'Human Rights and Environment Protection', India: *Cochin University Law Review*, p. 175.

Citron, Danielle Keats, 2008, 'Reservoirs of Danger: The Evolution of Public and Private Law at Dawn of the Information Age', *Southern California Law Review*, *University of Maryland Legal Studies Research*, 80 (S), p. 24.

Climate Analysis Indicators Tool (CAIT) Version 4.0, 2007, Washington, DC: World Resources Institute.

Constable, A., 1991, 'The Role of Science in Environment Protection', *Australian Journal of*

Marine and Freshwater Research, in Hewison G., 'The Precautionary Principle and Application to the Management of Straddling Stocks and Highly Migratory Fish (Hewison)', a Paper presented to the Greenpeace symposium on high seas fishing on 2 July 1993, at Wellington, New Zealand.

Contribution of Working Group I to the Third Assessment Report of the Intergovernmental Panel on Climate Change, 'Climate Change 2001: The Scientific Basis,' England: Cambridge University Press.

Cranwath, Robert, 1992, *Environment Enforcement: The Need for a Specialised Court*, UK: Oxford University Press.

CRZ, 1991, *The Law Relating to Protection of Coastal Areas*, 6th edn, Cochin, Kerala: Swamy Publishers.

Davis, Michael, Ethan Strell, and Judith Wallace, 2005–6, 'Environmental Protection After a Disaster: A Right or a Privilege?', *Natural Resources and Environment*, 20 (4, Spring), American Bar Association.

de Sadeleer, Nicholas, 2005, *Environmental Principles—from Political Slogans to Legal Rules*, India: Oxford University Press, p. 14.

Dharmadhikari, D.M., 2004, 'Environment—Problems and Solutions, *All India Reporter Journal Section*, Nagpur, p. 161.

Divan, Shyam and Armin Rosencranz, 2005, *Environment Law and Policy in India* (2nd edn, 7th Impression), New Delhi, India: Oxford India Paperbacks.

Doabia, T.S., 2004, *Environmental and Pollution Laws in India*, vol. 1, Nagpur: Wadhwa Publications, p. 460.

——, 2005, *Environmental & Pollution Laws in India*, Nagpur, India: Wadhwa Publications.

Down to Earth, Delhi: Magazine published by the Society for Environment Protection.

Dutta, Manoj (ed.), 1997, *Waste Disposal in Engineered Landfills*, New Delhi: Narosa Publishing House.

Emmerich de Vattek, 1758, Charles G. Fenwick, (ed. and trans.), *The Law of Nations, or the Principles of Natural Law, Applied to the Conduct and to the Affairs of Nations and of Sovereigns*, USA, Adamad Media Corporation.

Environmental Encyclopaedia (*Paristhithi Vijnanakoshan*), 2006, Thiruvananthapuram (Kerala): Kerala State Encyclopedia Institute.

Fidler, David P., 2005, 'Disaster Relief and Governance After the Indian Ocean Tsunami: What Role for International Law?', *Journal of International Law*, Melbourne, p. 16.

Founex Meeting of Experts, 1971, 'The Conference on Environment & Development', Switzerland: United Nations General Assembly, no. 2849 (XXVI).

Friends of the Earth, 2007, 'Carbon Off setting', Briefing Note.

Gage, Andrew, 2006, 'Public Rights and the Lost Principle of Statutory Interpretation', *Journal of Environmental Law and Practice*, Canada, 15 April, p. 107.

Gerrard, Michael B., 2005–6, 'Emergency Exemptions from Environmental Laws after Disasters', *Natural Resources and Environment*, 20 (10), p. 10.

Goel, Aruna, 2003, *Environment and Ancient Sanskrit Literature*, New Delhi: Deep and Deep Publications Pvt Ltd.

Gupta, V., 1987, 'Kautilyan Jurisprudence', in Shyam Divan and Rosencranz Armin, *Environment Law and Policy in India, 2005*, India: Oxford University Press.

Halsbury's Laws of England, Fourth Edition, 1990 (reissue), vol. 6, p. 1, vol. 8, p. 1, vol. 34, p. 1, vol. 38, p. 66, London: Butterworths.

Hassan, Parvez and Azim Azfar, 2003, 'Securing Environmental Rights Through Public Interest Litigation in South Asia', *Va. Envl LJ*, 22 (4, 215), p. 217.

Heibert, Theodore, 1999, 'Air—The First Sacred Thing: The Conception of *rûah* in the Hebrew Scriptures', Harvard Seminar on Environmental Values, April.

Huffman, James L., 1989, 'Fish Out of Water: The Public Trust Doctrine in Constitutional Democracy', 19 *Envtl L. Rev.* 527.

Hunter, Malcolm L. and James Gibbs, 2002, *Fundamentals of Conservation Biology*, New York: Blackwell Publishing.

——, 2007, *Fundamentals of Conservation Biology*, New York: Blackwell Publishing.

Hutchinson, 1996, *Hutchinson Pocket Dictionary of the Environment*, UK: Helicon Publishing Ltd.

International Federation, 2000, 'World Disasters Report', vol. 157, pp. 14–149.

Inuit Circumpolar Conference, 2007, 'Inuit Leader Congratulate Sheila Watt-Cloutier for Nobel Peace Prize Nomination', Press Release, Canada, 1 February.

Jaffrey, Morris and Diana Canzoneri, 1992, *Recycling vs. Incineration: An Energy Conservation Analysis*, Washington: Sound Resource Group.

Kamala Priya P.T., 2002, 'Environment and Sustainable Development', *Madras Law Journal*, vol. 8, part III, p. 9.

Karkara, G.S., 2006, 'Environment—Development as Human Rights Imperative', in Satish C. Shastri (ed.), *Human Rights, Development and Environmental Law—An Anthology*, Delhi: Bharat Law Publications.

Kashyap, Subhash C., 2006, *Constitution of India—Review and Reassessment*, Delhi: Universal Law Publishing, pp. 166–7.

Kelson, Hans, 1999, *General Theory of Law and State*, NJ: The Lawbook Exchange Limited.

Kemp, David and Minister for Foreign Affairs Alexander Downer, 15 August 2002, 'Global Greenhouse Challenge: The Way Ahead for Australia', Joint Media Release, Minister for the Environment and Heritage.

Kenyon, Andrew T., 2001, 'Defamation and Critique: Political Speech and New York, *Times v. Sullivan*', in Australia and England, *Melb. U. L. Rev.*, 25 (522, 530).

Koe, Adriana, 1998, 'Damming the Dambe: The International Court of Justice and the Gabcikovo-Nagmeros Project (*Hungary v. Slovakia Sydney Law Review*.

Kumar S., Shantha, 2001, *Environmental Law—An Introduction*, Chennai, India: Surya Publications.

Lakshmi V., Rajya ,1999, *Sustainable Development—What it Means?, A Few Reflections*, 23 (1 and 2), India: The Academy Law Review, p.107.

Leelakrishnan, P., 2005, *Environmental Law in India* (2nd edn), Delhi: LexisNexis Butterworths, p. 195.

Markandeya, Katju, 2002, *Supreme Court Cases-Journal Section*, vol. 3, p. 3.

Marr, Simon, 2003, *The Precautionary Principle in the Law of the Sea: Modern Decision Making in International Law*, Leiden: Martinus Nijhoff Publishers.

Muir, Ramsay, 1979, 'The Interdependent World and its Problems', in David W. Orr and Marvin S. Soroos (eds), *The Global Predicament; Ecological Perspectives on World Order*, Chapel Hill: The University of North Caroline Press, p. 284.

National Commission to Review of Working of Constitution (NCRWC) Report, 2000, US National Research Council, 'Waste Incineration and Public Health', Washington: The National Academics Press.

Olivelle, Patrick (trans.), 2004, *Manu's Code of Law*, (translated from *Manava Dharmasastra*), India: Oxford University Press.

Olson, James M., 1990, 'Shifting the Burden of Proof', *Envtl Law*, vol. 20, p. 891, 898.

Oxford Dictionary of English, 2005, 2nd edn, revised, p. 1346.

Parviesh, *Polluting Industries*, Delhi: CPCB.

Pemmaraju, Sreenivasa Rao, 1998, 'Special Reporter', *International Law Commission*, 2 April, para 61.

Pigou, A.C., 1924, *The Economics of Welfare* (2nd edn), London: Macmillan.

Pillai, P.S.A., 2004, *Law of Tort*, 9th edn, Delhi: Eastern Book Company.

Posner, Richard A., 2004, *Book Note: Review of 'The Days After Tomorrow: Catastrophe: Risk and Response'*, New York: Oxford University Press.

Preiss, Erika L., 1999, 'The International Obligation to Conduct Environmental Impact Assessment: The ICJ Case Concerning Gabcikovo-Nagymoros Project', *NYUELJ*, vol. 7, p. 307.

Rangarajan, L.N., 1997, (trans of *Manusmriti*, VII: 14: Kautilya's *Arthasasthra*), Delhi: Penguin Books, pp. 180–1.

Sadler, B. and R. Verheem, 1996, *Strategic Environment Assessment Status, Challenges and Future Directions*, The Netherlands: Ministry of Housing.

Saldanha, Leo, Abhayraj Naik, Arpita Joshi, Subramanya Sastry, 2006, *Green Tapism, 'A Review of the Environmental Impact Assessment Notification—2006'*, Bangalore: Environmental Support Group, p. 105.

Sands, Philippe, 1995, 'Principles of International Environmental Law', *Frameworks, Standards and Implementation*, vol. 1, UK: Manchester University Press, p. 198, 576.

Sax, Joseph. L., 1970, 'Public Trust Doctrine in Natural Resource Law: Effective Judicial Intervention', *Michigan Law Review*, vol. 68, part 1, pp. 473.

Schoenbaum, Thomas J. and Ronald H. Rosenberg, 1991, *Environmental Policy Law Problems, Cases and Readings* (2nd edn), USA: University Case Book Series.

Seervai, H.M., 2005, *Constitutional Law of India*, vol. II (4th edn, reprint), Delhi: Universal Law Publishing Pvt Ltd, p. 2019.

Sen, Amartya, 1999, *Development as Freedom*, Oxford: Oxford University Press.

Shastri, Satish C., January–March 2000, 'The Polluters Pays Principle & the Supreme Court of India', *JILI*, 42 (1), p. 108.

—— (ed.), 2006, *Human Rights, Development and Environmental Law—An Anthology*, Rajasthan, India: Bharat Law Publications.

Tangri, Neil, 2003, 'Waste Incineration: A Dying Technology', *Essential Action for GAIA, Global Anti-Incinerator Alliance/ Global Alliance for Incinerator Alternatives*, p. 1.

Thapar, Romila, 1973, *Asoka and the Decline of Maurya* (2nd edn), India: Oxford University Press.

Topsfield, Jewel, 2005, 'Downer Adds Fuel to Kyoto Criticism', *The Age*, 1 August, Australia.

UNEP, 'The Manual in Perspective', *EIA Training Resource Manual*, 2002.

WBGU Report, 1988, *World in Transition Strategies for Managing Global Environmental Risks*.

Wetterstein, Peter (ed.), 1995, *Harm to the Environment: The Right to Compensation and the Assessment of Damages*, Oxford: Clarendon Press.

Woolf, Lord, 1992, 'Are the Judiciary Environmentally Myopic', *Journal of Environmental Law*, vol. 4, p. 1.

Wooster, Ann K., 1972, 'Actions brought under Federal Water Pollution Control Act Amendments of 1972 (Clean Water Act) (33 USCA §§ 1251 et seq.)—Supreme Court cases', *ALR Fed.*, 163 (531).

World Commission on Dams, *Dams and Development—A New Framework for Decision-making*, 2000, the report of the World Commission on Dams, London and Sterling, VA: Earthscan Publications.

Wynne, 1992, 'Global Environmental Change', *Uncertainty and Environmental Learning*, vol. III, p. 123.

Statute Index

Case Index

Subject Index